MW00617367

Between Truth and Power

The Legal Constructions of Informational Capitalism

JULIE E. COHEN

OXFORD
UNIVERSITY PRESS

OXFORD

UNIVERSITY PRESS

Oxford University Press is a department of the University of Oxford. It furthers
the University's objective of excellence in research, scholarship, and education
by publishing worldwide. Oxford is a registered trade mark of Oxford University
Press in the UK and certain other countries.

Published in the United States of America by Oxford University Press
198 Madison Avenue, New York, NY 10016, United States of America.

© Julie E. Cohen 2019

All rights reserved. No part of this publication may be reproduced, stored in
a retrieval system, or transmitted, in any form or by any means, without the
prior permission in writing of Oxford University Press, or as expressly permitted
by law, by license, or under terms agreed with the appropriate reproduction
rights organization. Inquiries concerning reproduction outside the scope of the
above should be sent to the Rights Department, Oxford University Press, at the
address above.

You must not circulate this work in any other form
and you must impose this same condition on any acquirer.

Library of Congress Cataloging-in-Publication Data
Names: Cohen, Julie E., author.
Title: Between truth and power : the legal constructions of informational
capitalism / Julie E. Cohen.
Description: New York, NY : Oxford University Press, 2019. |
Includes bibliographical references.
Identifiers: LCCN 2019002684 | ISBN 9780190246693 (hardcover)
Subjects: LCSH: Internet industry—Law and legislation—United States. |
Trade regulation—United States.
Classification: LCC KF1617.C65 C64 2019 | DDC 343.7309/944—dc23
LC record available at https://lccn.loc.gov/2019002684

3 5 7 9 8 6 4 2

Printed by Sheridan Books, Inc., United States of America

For Natalie and Donald Cohen
parents, teachers, contrarians

CONTENTS

Between Truth and Power

Introduction

Transforming Institutions

This book is a meditation on the future of law and legal institutions in the networked information age. Its central claims are that as our political economy transforms, our legal institutions too are undergoing transformation, and the two sets of processes are inextricably related.

Encounters between networked information technologies and law tend to be framed as examples of what happens when an irresistible force meets an immovable object. So, for example, some argue that networked information and communication technologies are technologies of freedom, able to help human civilizations solve all of our most pressing problems—if only the law, which cannot move at the speed of human thought, will stop undermining technology's potential and either get with the program or get out of the way. Others assert that it is information technology that fatally undermines the rule of law—that unbreakable encryption and untraceable alternative currencies will plunge society into chaos, or that unaccountable and fundamentally nonhuman artificial intelligences spell the end for slower and more humane traditions of governance.

Whether any of those inspiring or doom-laden predictions will come to pass is beyond my ability to know, but their premises are wrong. To begin with, technology is not a monolithic, irresistible force. Networked information technologies inevitably will alter, and are already altering, the future of law, but not because there is any single, inevitable arc of technological progress. The reason, rather, is very nearly the opposite: Information technologies are highly configurable, and their configurability offers multiple points of entry for interested and well-resourced parties to shape their development. To understand what technology signifies for the future of law, we must understand how the design of networked information technologies within business models reflects and reproduces economic and political power.

For similar reasons, law is not an immovable object. Legal scholars who work on information policy have been intensely concerned with questions about how existing doctrinal and regulatory frameworks should apply to information, algorithms, technical protocols, and online behavior, perhaps undergoing some changes in coverage or emphasis along the way. They have asked, in other words, *how law should respond* to the changes occurring all around it. For the most part, they have not asked the broader, reflexive questions about how core legal institutions *are already evolving* in response to the ongoing transformation in our political economy—questions, in other words, not about how law should apply to information-economy disputes, but rather about how both information-economy disputes and new informational capabilities are reshaping the enterprise of law at the institutional level. That is a mistake. Law is one of the moving parts, and it is already responding.

Legal institutions too offer multiple points of entry for economic and political power, and as they are enlisted to help produce the profound economic and sociotechnical transformations that we see all around us, they too are being changed. Struggles to shape the patterns of information flow are seeking out new modes of recognition and accommodation within the legal system. Slowly but surely, that process is restructuring the legal system itself, altering the substance and interpretation of fundamental legal guarantees, the fora within which legal rights and obligations are defined, and the ways that they are enforced.

None of this should surprise us, because our current legal system is to a great extent the product of an earlier period of sociotechnical and economic transformation. From the late eighteenth century through the mid-twentieth century, as accountability for industrial-age harms became a pervasive source of conflict, legal systems in the industrializing world underwent profound, tectonic shifts. In the United States, important doctrinal, procedural, and institutional changes included the emergence and gradual refinement of the modern corporate form, standardized commercial laws, newly expansive conceptions of tort liability, new rules for exercising personal jurisdiction over faraway parties to civil disputes, liberalized pleading standards, the structure of the modern regulatory state, and new paradigms for understanding constitutional rights and their limits.

Today, ownership of information-age resources and accountability for information-age harms have become pervasive sources of conflict, and different kinds of change are emerging: new claims about entitlement and accountability; new procedural devices for vindicating (or declining to vindicate) those claims in litigation; new mechanisms for extrajudicial definition and enforcement of claimed legal rights; new obligations relating to financial stability, data protection, and network management; new regulatory mechanisms for defining and policing compliance with those obligations; and new transnational institutions for economic and network governance. In many cases, those changes are hotly contested. We are witnessing the emergence of legal institutions adapted to the information age, but their form and their substance remain undetermined.

This book interrogates the possible futures of a legal system that we have come to take for granted. Its premise is that when attempting to find one's way through the jungle, it is useful to consider paths of least resistance, but it is also essential to understand the overall topography, lest one inadvertently stumble into quicksand or wander over a cliff. Rather than offering specific prescriptions for legal reform, it simply seeks to help the reader understand and parse the profound, systemic changes that are already underway.

The balance of this introductory chapter lays some essential groundwork. It begins by situating networked information technologies and law in relation to economic and political power. It then briefly sketches the ongoing and interrelated transformations in political economy and political ideology (or governmentality) that are now underway. Finally, it returns to law, situating legal institutions within processes of economic and ideological transformation.

Negotiations: Code and Law between Truth and Power

This book derives its title from that of a deceptively small pamphlet, titled "Speak Truth to Power" and circulated by intellectual leaders of the Quaker faith in 1955 as the Cold War military buildup gathered momentum.[1] The pamphlet opposed the buildup and advocated a peaceful resolution. Critically, it focused not only on the moral costs of militarization but also on the opportunity costs. Resources devoted to the production and strategic deployment of expensive weapons were resources that could not be devoted to improving standards of living for the world's neediest people. For the writers of the pamphlet, speaking truth to power meant confronting power with a fundamental choice between military domination and human well-being, a choice played out not only at the level of policy but also and more fundamentally at the level of political economy.

In the decades since the Cold War, the notion of speaking truth to power has become a familiar protest trope, deployed in a wide variety to contexts to signal both the power of the moral high ground and the necessity of resistance. Those themes reverberate through contemporary discussions of the nature and social impact of networked information and communications technologies. They are extraordinarily important but their expression is often extraordinarily naïve.

At its inception, the internet was conceived as the inevitable servant of truth—as a "technology of freedom" that would enable both political and economic self-determination.[2] We have known for some time now that this rather deterministic view is too simple. Scholarship in science and technology studies has shown that new technologies do not have predetermined, neutral trajectories, but rather evolve in ways that reflect the particular, situated values and priorities of both their developers and their users. The various technological layers and protocols that comprise the internet and the diverse array of devices that connect to it are no different.

As already noted, networked information and communication technologies are highly configurable, and that characteristic inevitably draws attention to the behavioral changes that different configurations might produce. The plasticity of digital "code" affords points of regulatory leverage to both state and private actors.[3]

Contemporary legal and policy discussions about the internet and digital technologies, however, nonetheless have retained more than a little of their original idealism. Informed by characterizations of code as regulatory, deterministic claims about the way that code "is" have evolved into normative claims about the way that it should be. For the last two decades, a loose coalition of social movements, nongovernmental organizations (NGOs), and academics, joined at one time or another by various other actors, has promoted a vision of networked information and communication technologies as tools for advancing the goal of freedom from political oppression. In those efforts, a different kind of technological essentialism has persisted, which resides in the formulation of claims about the nature of fundamental rights to internet access and use. Such claims seem to presume that tools for censorship and surveillance of information flows are afterthoughts or hostile add-ons, and that market forces will route around them, incentivizing technological development that is connective and egalitarian.[4] As we will see throughout this book, that view is mistaken on a number of levels. Even the technologies in use in democratic societies increasingly incorporate, at their core, capabilities for differentiation, modulation, and interdiction of information flows.

Accounts of the political and cultural functions of law can be similarly idealistic. The law school where I teach takes as its motto the statement that "Law is but the means; justice is the end," and many law schools would describe their mission similarly. Lawyers understand themselves to be stewards of the principles and institutions that hold a society accountable to its citizens and take that mission seriously. But lawyers at work play many different roles in relationship to both state and private power. They serve as activists for legal modernization and as agents for the powerful interests that seek to alter existing principles and institutions to their own advantage. As we will see throughout this book, moreover, those two roles often converge; initiatives for legal modernization have a way of aligning with the efficiencies that powerful interests have identified and the rationalizations they advance to frame particular kinds of change as desirable.

By the same token, legal institutions are not fixed, Archimedean points around which modes of economic development shift and cohere. They are arenas in which interested parties struggle to define what constitutes "normal" economic or government activity and what qualifies as actual or potential harm, and they are also artifacts whose form and function are not preordained. We should not be surprised to see the tensions between these competing functions become particularly acute during periods of rapid sociotechnical and economic change. And we should not be surprised if, as a result, the institutions themselves begin to change, as well.

In short, networked digital media technologies and infrastructures are not—and never could be—simply instrumentalities of liberation, and law is not—and never could be—simply an instrumentality for the promotion of just outcomes, a neutral arbiter of disputes, or a disinterested agent of modernization. In their different ways, both networked media infrastructures and legal institutions sit between truth and power. They can be means for resisting domination or vehicles for embedding it, but even that formulation is too simple. Through their capacities to authorize, channel, and modulate information flows and behavior patterns, code and law *mediate* between truth and power. The terms of the dialogue are shaped by the technological and institutional settlements that emerge as struggles to shape the emerging networked world wind their way toward resolution.

According to the conventions of many academic disciplines, at this point it would be appropriate to offer a theory of power in which to ground the inquiry we are about to undertake. The study of law and legal institutions, however, teaches both appreciation for power's resourcefulness and skepticism about the quest for a perfect theoretical construction capable of describing it. The essence of power lies precisely in its ability to shape-shift—to elude the perfect, crystalline characterizations with which scholars have attempted to both capture and cabin its methods of operation. Power in operation is pragmatic, seeking and finding paths of least resistance and mobilizing the practical and conceptual resources that appear ready to hand. The subject of this inquiry will not be power in the abstract, but rather power in legal-institutional context. That project calls for a different kind of table setting.

Transformations: Political Economy as/and Governmentality

For some time now, political economies in the developed world have been undergoing a transformation from industrial to informational capitalism. That transformation in turn has begun to elicit new ways of framing and understanding the roles of government, and of systems for social ordering more broadly, in relation to private economic activity.

Following the sociologist and theorist of the information society Manuel Castells, I use "informational capitalism" to refer to the alignment of capitalism as a mode of production with informationalism as a mode of development. Capitalism "is oriented toward profit-maximizing, that is, toward increasing the amount of surplus appropriated by capital on the basis of the private control over the means of production and circulation," while informationalism "is oriented . . . toward the

accumulation of knowledge and towards higher levels of complexity in information processing."[5] In a regime of informational capitalism, market actors use knowledge, culture, and networked information technologies as means of extracting and
appropriating surplus value, including consumer surplus.

My intent in adopting that framing is not to suggest that regulation of industrial-era processes and markets is no longer important or that the corresponding
regulatory constructs are necessarily obsolete. Institutional changes are slow and
piecemeal, and shifts in political economy can span decades or even centuries. More
generally, the relationship between industrialism and informationalism is not se-
quential, but rather cumulative. The emergence of informationalism as a mode of
economic development also is powerfully shaped by its articulation within capitalist modes of production, with all of the economic, sociotechnical, organizational,
and ideological baggage that that history entails.[6]

In referring to the shift from industrialism to informationalism, then, I do not
mean to make rapturous (or apocalyptic) pronouncements about the end of industry but rather to indicate two kinds of fundamental transformation. First is a
movement away from an economy oriented principally toward manufacturing and
related activities toward one oriented principally toward the production, accumulation, and processing of information. In an information economy, the mass model of
production that emerged in the industrial era is itself increasingly redirected toward
development of intellectual and informational goods and services, production and
distribution of consumer information technologies, and ownership of service-de-
livery enterprises.[7] Second is a transformation in the conduct of even traditional
industrial activity. In an information economy, information technology assumes an
increasingly prominent role in the control of industrial production and in the management of all kinds of enterprises.[8]

Some academics and lay commentators who study the emerging networked information society identify additional, distinct phases of political economic transformation. Some of those phases—such as consumer capitalism, managerial capitalism,
financial capitalism, and surveillance capitalism—involve changes in the means
of surplus extraction.[9] Although there is much to learn from the details of such
developments, in my view focusing first and foremost on such divisions threatens
to diminish the underlying transformative importance of the sociotechnical shift
to informationalism as a mode of development. Other formulations—including
notably the "Fourth Industrial Revolution" framing popularized by the World
Economic Forum—foreground the technological at the expense of the social.[10]
It is important not to lose sight of the sociotechnical, and of the contingency and
constructedness of the changes that powerful, self-interested actors have set in
motion.

The continuing orientation toward capitalist production, surplus extraction,
and accumulation points toward a second, related transformation, which concerns

the ideological framework that serves to legitimate and facilitate economic activity and, therefore and relatedly, to underwrite processes of governmental and social reorganization. Following the tradition of critical social theory, I will refer to that framework together with its organizational and practical entailments as governmentality.[11]

The dominant forms of governmentality associated with industrial political economy were liberal, broadly speaking; the dominant forms of governmentality associated with informational capitalism are neoliberal. Relative to liberal governmentality, neoliberal governmentality represents both continuity and change. Liberal political philosophy radically decentered the sovereign state, positioning the sovereign individual as the ultimate source of political authority; liberal governmentality undertook a parallel decentering, positioning enlightened, self-interested rationality as the origin point for social ordering.[12] Neoliberal governmentality similarly emphasizes the primacy of private ordering, but both the scope that neoliberalism claims for private ordering and the role that it envisions for government are different.

In one frequently cited formulation, the political philosophy of neoliberalism "propos[es] that human well-being can best be advanced by the maximization of entrepreneurial freedoms within an institutional framework characterized by private property rights, individual liberty, unencumbered markets, and free trade."[13] Notably, however, the neoliberal political orientation emphasizes not only market liberties but also a market-based approach to structuring political and social participation. Viewed through the prism of neoliberal governmentality, the most virtuous and effective forms of social ordering are mimetic, incorporating and responding to marketized feedback about efficacy and value.[14]

Neoliberal governmentality does not simply elevate processes of private economic ordering; it also works to reshape government processes in their image. As many have remarked, liberal governmentality contained an embedded contradiction. Markets are not self-sustaining; left entirely to their own devices, they tend toward monopoly, destructive extraction, and rent-seeking. Therefore, they require vigilant stewardship precisely to ensure they remain sufficiently marketlike. Neoliberal governmentality resolves that embedded contradiction by bringing market dynamics and associated managerial techniques into government, infusing processes of legal and regulatory oversight with a competitive and capitalist ethos.[15] Transforming government in the image of markets is not an abstract exercise. It requires changes in the nature and operation of the institutions and practices that comprise government, including not only the faceless bureaucracies typically demonized within contemporary morality tales about the primacy of markets but also legislatures, courts, and legal doctrines. The story of neoliberalization, in other words, is also and unavoidably a story about the institutional transformation of law.

Institutions: Mapping the Interplay between Power and Constraint

Law's *facilitative* role in these processes of economic and ideological transformation is foundational and generally unremarked. Scholars who study the relationship between law and political economy have begun to argue that law is not simply superstructure but rather the means through which expressions of economic rationality and governmentality become specific, detailed, and actionable.[16] This book brings that perspective to bear on the intertwined processes of informationalization and neoliberalization. Both processes have mobilized the institutional resources afforded by legal systems worldwide. At the same time, however, those processes also are transforming legal institutions, gradually optimizing them for the new roles they are called upon to play.

Consider first two examples from earlier moments in Anglo-American legal history. In his influential account of the "great transformation" in British political economy, Karl Polanyi interrogated Britain's centuries-long transition from an agrarian system of political economy to an industrial and capitalist system, identifying the mismatches between the demands of the emerging market system and those of human well-being and tracing the gradual emergence of a protective countermovement that included distinctively legal components.[17] The initial movement to industrial capitalism, however, also entailed both reliance on and restructuring of legal institutions. Processes of enclosure of common lands, appropriation of other natural resources, displacement of populations from farms to cities, construction of factories for extraction of the value of commodity inputs (including wage labor), and trade in the resulting products all required enabling legal constructs in order to work. A series of gradual, ineluctable changes in the British legal system worked to facilitate each of those developments, providing the frameworks within with enclosure, appropriation, extraction, and accumulation could proceed.

A century later, the American political economic landscape underwent a parallel transformation. The part of that story with which contemporary lawyers and legal scholars are most familiar involves the American version of the protective countermovement—the creation of the modern administrative state during the first half of the twentieth century and the bitter disputes about constitutional law that accompanied it. As legal historian Morton Horwitz has shown, however, those disputes were themselves shaped by earlier doctrinal and conceptual realignments that privileged rising industrial and commercial interests. The development of private and commercial law during both the antebellum period and the post–Civil War years, and critically the emergence of an instrumental, rationalist view of the common law's purpose, established the distributive backdrop for the disputes about public law that unfolded later.[18]

Today, as accountability for information-age harms has become a pervasive source of conflict, different kinds of change are on the table. Once again, powerful interests have a stake in the outcome, and once again, they are enlisting law to produce new institutional settlements that alter the horizon of possibility for protective countermovements. And once again, critics of law's neoliberalization have focused principally on a set of burgeoning crises for public law but have largely neglected to ask a set of more fundamental questions about implicit distributional and institutional predicates.[19] Law for the information economy is emerging not via discrete, purposive changes, but rather via the ordinary, uncoordinated but self-interested efforts of information-economy participants and the lawyers and lobbyists they employ. Slowly but surely, those efforts are rearranging the legal landscape, producing results that reflect intertwined processes of conceptual and practical neoliberalization at work.

At the same time, however, the story of the complex and richly productive relationships among political economy, neoliberal governmentality, and legal institutions is a story about power both asserted and constrained. Legal institutions are the mechanisms through which changes in governmentality assume concrete forms that shape the options available to social and economic participants, and those forms also impose limitations. Some limitations reflect historical and sociotechnical contingency; the previous era's institutional settlements become the residue with which the next era's institutional entrepreneurs must contend. Other limitations are more durable and demanding. In societies with stable rule-of-law traditions, power confronts principles and commitments that must be honored. Legal institutions therefore are much more than simply substrates to be made and remade according to perceived economic and political imperatives; they are also the sites at which the project of mediation between truth and power unfolds.

The focus on institutions dictates a certain amount of geographic and cultural specificity. This project focuses principally on the legal-institutional trajectories that have emerged in the United States. That focus, I think, is also defensible for another reason: the United States is where many (though not all) of the major global information businesses now reshaping the political economic landscape are headquartered. The institutional settlements now emerging within the U.S. legal system are therefore relevant both domestically and globally. My hope is that scholars more familiar with other legal systems will undertake similar projects.

Plan of the Book

The chapters that follow map processes of legal-institutional transformation on two complementary and mutually reinforcing levels.

The first level on which legal-institutional transformation is occurring involves baseline understandings of legal entitlement and disentitlement. In the emerging information economy, the understandings that characterized the industrial economy are shifting in ways that extend across preexisting doctrinal boundaries and that challenge the distinctions such boundaries attempt to impose. Chapter 1 describes the increasing virtualization and datafication of important economic resources and traces the emergence of the platform as the core organizational logic of the informational economy. Chapter 2 identifies the enabling legal construct that underwrites new techniques of personal data harvesting and processing and explores its doctrinal, architectural, and policy entailments. Chapters 3 and 4 move beyond appropriation of resources to consider other patterns of entitlement and disentitlement that involve accountability, immunity, authority, and obligation. Chapter 3 explores the affordances of contemporary, platform-based, massively intermediated information environments and traces the emergence of a constellation of powerful de jure and de facto legal immunities that insulate their architects and operators from accountability for a wide and growing variety of harms. Chapter 4 interrogates the evolving debates about interdiction of information flows, framing those debates as three-way struggles among nation-states, global entertainment businesses, and information platforms and identifying several more durable changes that those struggles are producing.

The second level on which legal-institutional transformation is occurring involves the structure and operation of regulatory and governance institutions. Chapter 5 considers patterns of change in legal processes for dispute resolution, including both the evolution of conceptions of justiciable injury and the emergence of new, explicitly managerial conventions for routing different kinds of disputes for different kinds of processing. Chapter 6 shifts the focus to the regulatory state, exploring the ways that informationalization of economic activity has both disrupted long-established regulatory constructs and elicited new, neoliberalized mechanisms for regulatory oversight. Chapters 7 and 8 adopt a more explicitly transnational and experimental focus. Chapter 7 investigates the emergence of network-and-standard-based legal-institutional arrangements for transnational governance, parsing the mechanisms through which neoliberalized agendas for the management of economic and network processes have begun to "route around" the disruptions imposed by older, less adaptable legal forms. Chapter 8 explores the widening mismatch between information-economy threats to fundamental human rights and institutions dedicated to protecting and preserving those rights.

In interrogating the relationships between political economy and the structure of legal entitlements and institutions, I hope also to prompt reflection on the ways that transformations in political economy shape the horizons of possibility for protective countermovements. The book therefore concludes with a brief meditation on that question.

PART I

PATTERNS OF ENTITLEMENT
AND DISENTITLEMENT

The chapters in this part of the book are about the ways that law and legal institutions have facilitated the emergence of informational capitalism by defining patterns of entitlement and disentitlement in new informational resources. Some parts of that story are well understood. Legal scholars are keenly aware of the central importance of intellectual property rights in the emerging information economy, and of the corresponding pressures to define those rights ever more broadly. Legal scholarship also has helped policymakers and judges understand the ways that control of code can confer control over information flows.[1] Legal scholars of the information economy, however, have tended to focus a bit too narrowly on the themes of propertization and control and not enough on others that are equally important.

As we will see throughout Part I, the ways that law shapes processes of entitlement definition are complex. A useful starting point from which to begin thinking through the issues is the classic taxonomy of jural "primitives" developed by Wesley Hohfeld over a century ago.[2] Hohfeld's central insight was that entitlements are relational and that the rights-duties relationship—the relationship that arises when one person has a right that others have a duty to respect—is only one of the possibilities. Entitlements also may take the form of privileges, powers, or immunities, each of which affects others in different kinds of ways. In choosing that particular starting point, I do not mean to invoke the taxonomy as a substantive legal (or moral) theory about the ways that information-economy entitlements should be defined or allocated. Rather, my purpose is the one described by Pierre Schlag: the taxonomy is an analytical method for identifying "mistakes of ambiguity, slippage, and blending" in descriptions of legal relations.[3] So understood, Hohfeldian analysis takes aim at a particular kind of analytical sloppiness that, as a practical matter, tends to unspool in ways that benefit and entrench political and economic power.

But the accounts of information-economy entitlements and disentitlements developed in Part I also introduce significant complications. At bottom, Hohfeldian analysis is an exercise in intellectual purism. For example, if one finds that party A enjoys a privilege to engage in certain conduct, one should find that party B is under a correlative disentitlement to require A to act differently, and if one finds that A's privilege has been misdescribed as a right in order to justify imposing legal duties on B, then one is justified both in concluding that sloppy thinking has occurred and in thinking that, once the sloppy thinking has been identified, the relevant decision-makers, typically judges, will realize the error of their ways. And yet the landscape of entitlements and disentitlements that we are about to explore is in motion in ways that the Hohfeldian account did not contemplate. A descriptive thesis that emerges powerfully from the chapters in Part I is that, during periods of rapid transformation in the mode of political economy, decomposition and recomposition of entitlements and disentitlements is the rule rather than the exception.

In particular, the chapters in this part of the book highlight two factors that have facilitated the remixing of entitlements in ways that benefit powerful information-economy actors. First, networked information and communication and technologies can be configured to tilt the playing field this way or that. So, for example, we will see in chapters 1 and 2 that the networked information environment has been systematically configured to facilitate the extraction and enclosure of data flows of various types, and we will see in chapters 3 and 4 that platform-based, algorithmic processes for intermediating and filtering information flows have facilitated the emergence of new legal relations revolving around legal immunity, legal power, and the interplay between them.

Second and relatedly, processes of decomposition and recomposition are fundamentally performative. Online interactions between information businesses and users of their services play outsize roles in stabilizing and reifying emerging patterns of entitlement and disentitlement. Additionally, in an age in which communication is cheap and nearly instantaneous, and in which information overload has replaced information scarcity as the defining characteristic of the contemporary media landscape, it is essential to understand the ways that participants in information-economy legal debates use discursive strategies—including especially narratives about innovation and markets that are rooted in the dominant ideology of neo-liberal governmentality—to shape prevailing perceptions about both the existing legal landscape and possible pathways for legal change. Those narrative unfold within an institutional landscape that offers many more points of entry for legal and normative entrepreneurship than the one that Hohfeld's illustrations and explanations described.

1

Everything Old Is New Again—Or Is It?

We've changed our internal motto from "Move fast and break things" to
"Move fast with stable infrastructure."
—Mark Zuckerberg, Remarks at F8 Developer Conference, April 2014

To understand the emergence of the informational economy and the role of legal
entitlements in facilitating it, it is instructive to begin by looking backward. Among
economic historians, a useful frame for understanding the emergence of industrial
capitalism is Karl Polanyi's analysis of a "great transformation" in the system of political economy that involved appropriation of newly important resources but that
also moved on conceptual and organizational levels. The basic factors of industrial
production—labor, land, and money—were reconceptualized as commodities,
while at the same time patterns of barter and exchange became detached from local
communities and re-embedded in the constructed mechanism of "the market." Both
developments lent momentum and legitimacy to the resource-directed activities
about which so much has been written—large-scale enclosures of land, displacement of populations, extraction of natural resources, and construction of factories.
Together, those appropriative, conceptual, and organizational shifts produced a de-
cisive movement toward a capitalist political economy. Then, when the resulting
dislocations become too extreme, they prompted a protective countermovement
aimed at ameliorating their effects.[1]

Extending the analytical frame and the metaphor of the double movement,
this chapter frames the emergence of informational capitalism in terms of three
large-scale shifts that together constitute the movement toward informational
capitalism: the propertization (or enclosure) of intangible resources, the dematerialization and datafication of the basic factors of industrial production, and the
embedding (and rematerialization) of patterns of barter and exchange within information platforms. Whether the effects of those changes will elicit a meaningful
countermovement is yet to be seen.

This chapter sketches the ongoing processes of propertization, datafication, and
platformization, with particular attention to the shifting, emergent relationships

between control of intangible intellectual resources and political economy. First, it traces the evolution of modern regimes of intellectual property protection, identifying a series of profound changes that relate to both imagined justifications and patterns of exploitation and use. Second, it explores some of the ways that the basic factors of industrial production identified by Polanyi—labor, land, and money—are becoming dematerialized and datafied to facilitate their more efficient exploitation. Finally, it interrogates the ongoing shift from a market-based economy to a platform-based economy, identifying ways in which that shift has begun to reshape both the nature of informationalized production and understandings of information ownership. Laying bare the key structural elements of the movement to an informational economy underscores both the facilitative role of law and the extent to which the landscape of legal entitlements in information is in motion.

Capital without Industry?

At the most general level, an informational economy is one oriented principally toward the production, accumulation, and processing of information, but that description leaves substantial room for debate over the rules governing control of informational resources. Scholars of the information society have waged heated debates about intellectual property's optimal contours and essential characteristics. My concern here is with historical and material contingencies rather than metaphysical essentials. This section describes important trends in the evolution of formal legal entitlements in intellectual property from the mid-twentieth century through the present. As we will see, the movement to an informational political economy has both relied on and reshaped the legal rules governing propertization of intangible intellectual goods. Information-era intellectual property rights, both old and new, have evolved in ways that reproduce and deepen existing patterns of control over and concentration of capital. The changes have entailed corresponding shifts in prevailing narratives about both ownership of intangible production and the kinds of rights that ownership confers.

Production Values

In the pantheon of intellectual property rights, the grandest rights are patents and copyrights, which are designed—or so the story goes—to motivate and reward individual inventors and creators. From the beginning of the modern era, however, debates about patent and copyright policy have concerned the relationships between individual creators and production intermediaries—industrial firms on the patent side and publishers, motion picture producers, and record labels on the copyright side. As the movement to an informational economy has gathered speed, new strands of justification have begun to emerge that emphasize the claims of intermediaries more directly. The ever-increasing primacy of production intermediaries also has produced deeper shifts in the ways that rightholders describe, understand, and exploit patents and copyrights, which relate to appropriation strategies, methods of valuation, and mechanisms for ensuring access to certain types of persistently individualized inputs.

Some of the reasons for the primacy of production intermediaries within the industrial-era patent and copyright systems were technological and some were organizational. Industrial firms with access to capital assembled the research teams and the material resources needed to solve large-scale technical problems and built the production and transit facilities needed to manufacture and distribute the resulting industrial and consumer products. Similarly, before the advent of powerful desktop computing platforms put professional-quality editing capabilities within easy reach, access to specialized equipment was necessary to produce cultural goods in forms suitable for the mass market. Dissemination of creative outputs required access to printing presses, newsstands and bookstores, movie theaters, or broadcast airwaves. Terminology in the creative industries came to reflect the reality of intermediated creative production; so, for example, in some circles it became customary to describe cultural goods in terms of production values. Even today, production intermediaries can perform well some tasks—such as marketing and promotion—that most creators themselves perform very poorly.

Unsurprisingly, the patent and copyright regimes that evolved in the United States beginning in the late nineteenth century were increasingly optimized for facilitating industrial processes of intangible production. One important set of developments concerned corporate ownership of intellectual creations. Although neither the Patent Act nor, initially, the Copyright Act gave employers rights to their employees' creations, judge-made rules developed to validate corporate practices of asserting ownership over employee-created inventions and creative works. Strands of state tort and contract law coalesced into trade secrecy doctrines providing that those who employed people for "inventive" duties owned the resulting inventions; that default rule, in turn, made subsequent assignment of any issued patents to one's employer ordinary and expected.[2] Courts in copyright cases involving employers reasoned that authorship of commissioned works should flow to the party that had assumed the economic risk. The 1909 revision of the Copyright Act codified copyright's emergent work-made-for-hire conventions, and the 1976 revision added a series of detailed provisions covering works commissioned from certain types of freelancers.[3]

Other developments altered the scope of patents and copyrights in ways that favored powerful new industries. Courts rejected a long-standing rule allowing competitors to exploit "unworked" patents in exchange for a reasonable royalty, clearing the way for corporate patent owners to amass portfolios of patents and make unilateral decisions about their use or nonuse. The 1952 revision of the Patent Act rejected various judicially developed limitations on patentability; eliminated uncertainties about the patentability of improvements to existing inventions and of methods combining well-known materials and steps; and defined patent rights in a way that ratified the use of blocking patents as bargaining chips.[4] On the copyright side, a series of statutory amendments extending over the course of the century vastly extended the duration of both future and already-subsisting copyrights and expanded the scope of copyright protection to cover the byproducts of new recording and broadcast technologies. The 1976 revision of the Copyright Act contained broad, general rights and narrow, specific limitations, eliminating the latitude that formerly had existed for many nonprofit and downstream uses of copyrighted works. It also codified for the first time a broad right to control preparation of so-called derivative works based on or adapted from other works.[5]

The increasingly pronounced statutory and doctrinal orientation toward industrial production and distribution of intangible intellectual goods accounts for the strange dual quality of the rhetoric in debates about intellectual property policy. Legal scholars have disagreed about whether romantic creatorship or economic instrumentalism is the dominant strand in that narrative, and about the goodness of fit between both justifications and the actual practices of individual creators and creative communities. Those disagreements, however, often overlook the way that desert-based and instrumentalist narratives began to work together to bolster a particular regime of legal protection for intangibles that relied on and reinforced the role of capital in underwriting intellectual production.[6]

Twentieth-century debates about intellectual property policy also reveal a gradual shift in the tenor of the instrumentalist justification for granting patents and copyrights. Whereas nineteenth-century rhetoric had emphasized the public and democratic benefits to be gained from underwriting progress in science and learning, the distinctive flavor of instrumentalism that developed beginning in the mid-twentieth century focused more narrowly on incentives to production. The emergence and rapid ascendancy of Chicago-School neoclassical economic analysis, which emphasized the role of individual choice, accelerated the turn to incentive-based reasoning. It also provided a point of entry for express consideration of the incentives of the production intermediaries without which, as the argument went, many intangible intellectual goods would not be produced and distributed at all.[7] Most recently, in disputes raising questions about harmonization with international intellectual property developments, some courts and commentators have evinced a willingness to abandon creator-centric rhetoric altogether, focusing instead on concerns about the balance of power in international trade. Industry associations that used to bring individual authors to testify before Congress now send their own officials, who make arguments about distribution incentives, trade balances, and gross national product.[8] The Supreme Court has cited both the argument from intermediary incentives and the argument from trade as ineluctable realities.[9]

As intellectual property rhetoric has evolved to emphasize the primacy of corporate claims, deeper conceptual and structural changes in the patent and copyright systems have been underway. Although individual patents and copyrights remain the theoretical basic units of protection, intellectual property law's formal atomism belies some of the ways that the foundations for the industrial organization of cultural and technical production have shifted to facilitate amassing intangible capital at scale. Because many intangible assets are most valuable when exploited in combination, large rightholders now routinely and deliberately amass strategic portfolios of intangible assets.[10] Portfolio-based intellectual property strategies in turn exert ripple effects on both judge-made doctrines and customary practice. So, for example, courts initially were reluctant to recognize copyrights in any but the most central literary characters, worrying that such copyrights would work to the detriment of authors who had assigned their copyrights to publishers. Today, however, character copyrights are cornerstones of merchandising campaigns that extend across movie and television franchises, and the test for character copyrightability has evolved to facilitate the coordinated exploitation of entertainment properties that extend over multiple works.[11] A patent grant requires disclosure sufficient to enable a person ordinarily skilled in the art to practice the claimed invention. Courts interpreting the enablement requirement have framed the conceptualization of the person ordinarily skilled in the art in a way that permits drafters in certain industries to practice systematic vagueness, and firms also have learned to practice selective, patent-preempting disclosure in ways that both strengthen their own portfolio positions and disadvantage their competitors.[12]

Meanwhile, the perceived need for comprehensive and consistent methods of defining and valuing legal entitlements in intangible intellectual goods has begun to reshape entire areas of business-related law: What is the best way to express the effects of patents and research programs on stock prices—and what disclosures should securities regulators therefore require? Are there alternative avenues for capitalization that do not require comparable levels of disclosure about intellectual property-in-the-making? What is the appropriate basis for taxation of intangible intellectual assets, and where geographically should those assets be deemed to reside for tax purposes? How can intangible intellectual assets and portfolios of those assets be collateralized, and how should such assets be valued in bankruptcy proceedings? How should the risk of infringement liability affect insurance availability and pricing?[13] Each of those legal fields, moreover, values certainty and predictability in asset definition, and that overarching need shapes the way firms assert intellectual property claims, disfavoring doctrines perceived as vague and uncertain. The repeated, self-interested assertion of positions aimed at minimizing uncertainties has begun to produce doctrinal shifts. So, for example, many fair use disputes have become disputes about the weight to be given to norms and practices favoring licensing. Courts in patent obviousness disputes have developed ancillary tests that emphasize commercial success and diminish the likelihood of an "obvious to try" finding, and the doctrine of equivalents plays a much less significant role in the patent infringement litigation landscape.[14]

Last and importantly, secondary intermediaries that perform market-clearing functions have become increasingly crucial to information-economy activities. Many uses of intangible intellectual goods are cumulative or fractional (or both). Despite the increasing efficacy of techniques for asserting corporate authorship or ownership of intellectual goods, some types of creative production—in particular, photography, sculpture, and musical composition—remain persistently individualized. Others inevitably aggregate content from multiple corporate sources. For example, clips from news programs and popular audiovisual works appear as featured or background material in documentary and feature films; public performance rights in popular songs are licensed for synchronization with films, television programs, and advertisements; and photographs and other visual artworks may appear in advertisements or in the promotional materials for corporations and other organizations. On the technical side, some types of production inevitably rely on the contributions of many firms and research labs. Operating systems for personal computers and mobile devices implicate thousands upon thousands of patents. Correspondingly, collective rights management institutions such as patent pools, technical standards bodies, performing rights organizations, and organizations that grant reproduction "clearances" play central roles in mediating access to and use of intangible resources.[15]

Brand Values

Within the traditional hierarchy of intellectual property rights that emerged over the nineteenth and early twentieth centuries, trademarks were inferior rights. Nineteenth century courts and commentators understood trademark law as providing a narrow, limited form of protection for existing commercial goodwill.[16] The enactment of federal trademark legislation in the United States in 1905, followed by the more comprehensive and modern Lanham Trade-Mark Act of 1946, responded to the emergence of a nationwide manufacturing economy within which the meaning of marks of origin as signifiers of corporate reputation was no longer only local.[17] Even as Congress was moving to federalize limited statutory protection for trademarks as signals of commercial goodwill, however, brands and branding had begun to assume a very different, overtly persuasive function. As the movement to an informational economy has gathered speed, the expressive power of corporate brands has continued to grow in importance, and legal protection for trademarks and brands has grown increasingly broad.

The growing prominence of brands and branding during the first half of the twentieth century reflected both the proliferation of mass-manufactured, prepackaged goods and the efforts of the nascent marketing industry. Early in the twentieth century, marketers' influence already had begun to shape both print media content and the structure of print media markets, producing content and accompanying advertisements that were self-consciously designed to appeal to a particular readership.[18] Information about tastes was rudimentary and incomplete, however, and in any case marketers sought not only to understand tastes but also to shape them. Attention to branding was a logical extension of the drive to reach and retain desired consumers. As nationwide mass media markets and technologies evolved and consumption boomed in the prosperous postwar decades, however, class-based models of expected consumer behavior began to give way to lifestyle-based and motivational approaches, and marketers sought more overtly not only to inform but also to persuade.[19]

In more recent decades, persuasive branding strategies have evolved in ways that both reflect and offset the increasingly informationalized nature of consumer goods and services. Tension between persuasion and informational opacity is an endemic feature of many information-economy markets—think, for example, of the lengthy lists of artificial ingredients on processed food packages and the turgid-yet-alarming disclaimers that accompany over-the-counter pharmaceutical products. Effective branding can convey, for example, low-fat or non-drowsy or eco-friendly properties—and can obfuscate other, more complex considerations bearing on consumption decisions. In developed economies, many consumer electronic devices and associated services have begun to approach commodity status, and branding strategies have become important vehicles for differentiating functionally identical offerings and crafting appeals to different market segments. (Dell Computer's pink-themed "Della" website, supposedly geared toward the unique computing needs of women, is a memorable reminder that the latter strategy can backfire hilariously.)[20]

For consumers on the receiving end of these strategies, brands and branding have come to function both as tools for self-articulation and as heuristics for social sorting. Brands and branding underwrite complex systems of performative and fundamentally social consumption, enabling consumers to signify class allegiance and to draw conclusions about others' allegiances and social status.[21] Those systems reflect the deliberate efforts of marketers who seem to have internalized the core tenets of post-structuralist thought about the cultural construction of identity and meaning. Contemporary marketers devise endlessly inventive ways of reaching eyeballs and attention, and understand their own mission as a type of applied anthropology.[22]

Modern trademark policy's engagement with the evolving purposes and practices of branding has been uneven. Mid-century commentators on trademarks and trademark law were keenly aware of the increasing power of commercial persuasion, but seemed unsure what, if anything, trademark law ought to do about it.[23] At the same time, the mid-century emergence of Chicago-School economic reasoning worked to bolster the emerging "search costs" justification for trademark protection. According to that justification, trademarks facilitate signaling about product quality. Consumers looking to distinguish among the goods and services offered by different providers can learn to recognize their trademarks, and over time (or so the account goes) can rely on those marks as indicia of consistency. Legal protection for trademarks therefore facilitates efficient markets.[24]

The result, as many contemporary scholars have noted, is a fairly significant disconnect between what marks do and what leading doctrinal and instrumental accounts of trademark law say they do. As Barton Beebe puts it, modern trademark law fulfills many of the functions of a sumptuary code, effectively regulating performances of status.[25] Trademark law's official narratives are different and far less attentive to branding's cultural purposes and effects. The statutory structure of trademark law also militates against direct acknowledgment of the purposes and practices of branding. As is the case with patent law and copyright law, trademark and unfair competition law is formally atomistic. Within the legal framework established by the Lanham Act, the basic unit of protection for brand reputation nominally remains the individual mark. Federal registration is available only for specific marks, and causes of action for infringement must be pleaded on a mark-specific basis.

At the same time, though, case law interpreting the Lanham Act's "likelihood of confusion" standard has given trademarks' presumptive claims on consumer thought processes broader and broader scope. So, for example, although courts and commentators initially thought that trademarks reproduced on logo merchandise served purely aesthetic and hence nontrademark purposes, mark owners eventually convinced courts that most such reproductions signified sponsorship and therefore required authorization. That result effectively sheltered an increasingly broad web of licensing designed to encourage performative consumption and bolster brand atmospherics.[26] Although courts and commentators initially characterized infringement lawsuits against down-market counterfeits as doctrinally and economically baseless, mark owners eventually convinced courts to find infringement based on a novel theory of "post-sale confusion," or cognitive dissonance resulting from the mismatch between luxury signifier and down-market context.[27]

In parallel with these judicially driven developments, business communities have developed robust conventions for valuing both marks and brands.[28] And, as for patents and copyrights, new approaches to valuation have engendered doctrinal ripples. Strict rules barring so-called naked licensing— licensing without oversight for quality control—and prohibiting transfers of marks without the accompanying goodwill have been relaxed, allowing complex webs of franchising, merchandising, and co-branding to flourish.[29] In disputes about the use of trademarks as search terms, corporate interests lost some battles but won the war; search has been pervasively monetized in ways that reward brand owners with revenue rather than with exclusivity.[30]

Meanwhile, supplementary entitlements in brands have proliferated in ways that tacitly acknowledge and reinforce the expressive power of capital. The general cause of action for unfair competition, originally intended to provide much narrower protection, now functions as a catch-all that is routinely recruited to cover a wide variety of situations implicating brands rather than particular marks. In particular, legal protection for trade dress—originally understood to mean specific elements of packaging associated with a product or service—has continued to expand and now provides broad protection for the "look and feel" of products, services, and even business establishments.[31] As we will see next, that expansion is part of a broader shift toward a more diverse and differentiated landscape of intangible intellectual property entitlements.

New (and Old) Legal Hybrids

The story of trademark law's evolution hints at a third essential strand in the story of intellectual property's evolution in the era of informational capitalism. As intangible intellectual goods have become more varied, more important, and potentially more profitable, the carefully delineated intellectual property taxonomies that originated in an earlier era have come to seem increasingly inadequate. New types of entitlements—some legislatively decreed and others judicially invented—have mushroomed around the edges of existing entitlement schemes, blurring their borders and extending their reach. With them have come heated legal battles about whether the traditional taxonomies represent sacred canons or outmoded constraints. For the most part, the new legal hybrids are winning those battles.[32]

One important constellation of new rights works to protect the cognitive and affective capital that brand owners have developed. Congress has supplemented the traditional trademark and unfair competition prohibitions against deceptive or confusing conduct in commerce with additional protections against dilution, tarnishment, and cybersquatting. Only owners of "famous" marks can invoke the anti-dilution and anti-tarnishment provisions, a rule that sets up a rich-get-richer dynamic benefiting the most well-known marks.[33] The anti-cybersquatting statute, which provides remedies that are theoretically accessible to all mark-holders, represents a concerted attempt to realign ownership of internet domains with ownership of brands.[34]

Firms seeking broader protection for the design of their products than modern copyright or trademark law can provide have rediscovered a type of intellectual property right that is very old. Copyright protects product design only to the extent that expressive aspects can be separately identified, but design patent protection applies much more broadly. Formerly an obscure backwater of the patent system, the office that handles design patent applications has seen its business surge to record levels, nearly doubling as a percentage of utility patent applications and more than doubling as a percentage of utility patent grants.[35] The courts have responded to the upsurge of interest by defining the standard for infringement downward. Together, copyright law, trademark law, and design patent law regimes are coalescing to produce a powerful new "law of look and feel" for the outputs of industrial designers.[36]

Meanwhile, new federal legislation has both reinforced and expanded trade secrecy protections formerly available only under state law. The Economic Espionage Act of 1996 authorized federal criminal prosecution for certain knowing misappropriations of valuable information. The Defend Trade Secrets Act of 2016 completed the federalization of trade secrecy law by conferring private rights of action on those harmed and authorizing civil seizures of items embodying misappropriated knowledge.[37] The federal Computer Fraud and Abuse Act also has been deputized as a tool for protecting corporate entities' interests in controlling access to their systems and networks. Lawsuits over data scraping from publicly available websites have proliferated, and prosecutions and civil suits against defecting employees for using their credentials to gain "unauthorized access" to system resources also have become principal uses of the statute.[38]

Still other new statutory entitlements supplement the patent and copyright regimes in circumstances involving publicly distributed products that trade secrecy cannot protect. The regulatory disclosures required to bring certain types of biomedical and biotechnology innovations to market work at cross purposes to strategies based on secrecy. Instead, a small cluster of new entitlements has begun to emerge in the domains of biotechnology and biomedicine that expand the window of exclusivity for patented products facing competition from generics.[39] In the domain of copyright, new statutory protections against "circumvention" of copy-protection technologies provide digital works with an extra layer of protection against copying and also work to shield proprietary media platforms against unauthorized access.[40]

Efforts by intellectual property scholars and activists to stem the expansion and proliferation of intangible intellectual entitlements have been notably ineffective. In amicus briefs, position papers, and law review articles, opponents of expansion and proliferation have offered two very different types of arguments. Some defend the existing boundaries by reference to tradition and originalist understanding, while others argue that continued expansion and proliferation of intangible intellectual entitlements will undermine both competition and continued innovation.[41] Those in the latter group, however, have been unable to marshal substantial empirical evidence to support claims that sound fundamentally in empiricism. History supplies many examples of intellectual property granted or expanded and fewer of protection withheld or narrowed, and assertions resting on counterfactual premises can be difficult to prove.[42] Equally important, the two types of arguments are difficult to synthesize into a coherent narrative. Arguments from tradition seem willfully blind to the realities of the contemporary networked information economy, while normative claims that prioritize innovation work at cross purposes with arguments from tradition. It is unsurprising, then, that opponents of intangible entitlements' expansion and proliferation have been unable to disrupt the powerful syllogism linking propertization with increased progress.

Labor, Land, and Money Reimagined

Two seeming exceptions to the narrative of intellectual property expansion and reconceptualization are data and algorithms—perhaps the paradigmatic information-era resources. Despite repeated efforts over the course of the twentieth century, both data and algorithms have proved powerfully resistant to formal propertization.[43] Appearances can be deceptive, however. As the movement to informational capitalism has gathered momentum, the three inputs that Polanyi identified as the basic factors of production in a capitalist political economy are undergoing a new process of transformation. The movement to an industrial economy reconstructed labor, land, and money as commodities; the movement to an informational economy is reconstructing labor, land, and money as datafied inputs to new algorithmic modes of profit extraction. At the same time, data and algorithms have become the subjects of active appropriation strategies—strategies that represent both economic and legal entrepreneurship.

New business models based on old resources often are labeled disruptors because of their effects on the economic, social, and legal arrangements that had coalesced around the older models. Notably for my purposes in this book, many of the legal arrangements now under threat trace their origins to Polanyi's protective countermovement. Disruptive business models route around the modern versions of the regulatory constraints put in place to mitigate the harshest consequences of commodification for human societies. Contemporary processes of datafication therefore have ramifications for human well-being as profound as those Polanyi chronicled in an earlier era. The regulatory mechanisms may have become obsolete, but the regulatory goals of the earlier countermovement remain profoundly relevant today, and I return to them in Part II.

This chapter, however, is concerned with emergent dynamics of propertization, and as we will begin to see in this section, law is not just something that bites on new business models after the fact. While debates about the legal status of data and algorithms as property have been frozen in stalemate, the landscape of de facto appropriation and enclosure is in rapid and productive motion. Processes of datafication supply inputs for new processes of intellectual property entrepreneurship, and participants in those processes are mobilizing law and legal institutions to help them reconfigure labor, land, and money in the formats they require.

Money without Investment

In financial markets, processes of dematerialization and informationalization have been underway since early in the twentieth century. Money—a medium of exchange that is valuable only for what it represents—is an inherently abstract construct. As the movement to informational capitalism has gained velocity, however, the idea of money has grown increasingly notional and has become increasingly detached from the real-world activities that it was designed to enable. A set of interrelated sociotechnical, institutional, and business changes—the advent of networked digital information and communication technologies, exponential growth in computing and processing power, the breakdown of regulatory barriers that separated "banking" and "investing" and slowed the flow of capital across state borders, and the development of new platforms for specialized intermediation of financial activities—has fundamentally restructured both the way that money behaves and the prevailing understanding of what finance is for. Within the political economy of informational capitalism, the financial sector has become an independent site of surplus extraction. As that sector has grown in size and economic power, many other, ostensibly more tangible activities have come to be understood as sites of financialization—as inputs to the extractive activities of finance capital.[44]

One story that is commonly told about financial markets links the rise of financialization to the advent of networked digital information and communications technologies. By itself, that story is too simple. Both the turn toward informationalized abstraction and the drive to trade on information about the future have older, deeper roots. In the United States, trading in commodity futures originated in the nineteenth century with practices of "forward trading" intended to help finance shipments of grain, lumber, and the like. The first known precursor of the modern mutual fund was a scheme for risk diversification created by a Dutch merchant in 1774, and currency trading has been an essential function of merchant banks for hundreds of years.[45] The early twentieth century witnessed the creation of new market institutions for both speculative trading and risk diversification across the financial sector. New commodity exchanges opened, margin trading migrated from commodity markets to securities and currency markets, and investment companies emerged and ballooned as a proportion of overall investment.[46]

A constellation of late twentieth-century developments, however, both engendered quantum leaps in financial complexity and undermined the premises on which regulatory oversight had rested. One factor was rapid acceleration in technological capability. New digital information and communications networks enabled trades to be made and recorded instantaneously in both national and global markets. Aided by rapid increases in processing power, investment bankers began using complex computational models to devise more complex trades and automated trading algorithms capable of responding instantaneously to market fluctuations. As interest in complex trading intensified, market participants begin to define new, ever more exotic instruments for "securitizing" a wide variety of activities. Trading in such instruments, including derivatives, credit default swaps, and the like, now dwarfs trading in more conventional securities markets. A vast and largely unregulated shadow banking sector undergirds these activities.[47]

Another factor was rising demand for new vehicles for capital formation—and for new permutations of existing vehicles designed to avoid the accountability obligations that corporate law and securities law imposed. Aided by a growing theoretical and ideological orientation toward understanding the legal rules governing economic activities as defaults, corporate lawyers and their clients experimented with dual-class ownership structures designed to give privileged groups of shareholders greater voting power and control. An emerging class of venture capitalists developed information-gathering networks designed to identify promising start-up enterprises and contractual devices that enabled them to bankroll such enterprises in exchange for either large payouts at the time of their initial public offerings or continuing control using dual-class ownership arrangements. Hedge funds controlled by secretive, wealthy investors—including venture capitalists and other private equity investors—created new secondary markets in early-stage capital formation and other private extractive activities.[48]

Meanwhile, new forms of intermediation were disrupting and restructuring financial markets. In the heady early days of the commercial internet, pundits prophesied that informed amateurs would break the financial services industry's stranglehold on brokerage and investment advising. They were both right and wrong. Disintermediated "day trading" is yesterday's news; today's internet-based platforms for online trading are more likely to be subsidiaries of large financial conglomerates, which can more readily exploit the potential returns to scale that come with access to new streams of information about financial markets and participants. Such entities have pursued a variety of information-based strategies for positioning themselves as the new intermediaries of choice. At the same time, the rise of hedge funds and proprietary exchanges for exotic derivative instruments, as well as the emergence of opportunities for "flash trading" in brief, technologically mediated windows of market advantage, has partially disintermediated conventional trading exchanges, affording new opportunities to existing, well-resourced players.[49] As a practical matter, financial markets today are comprised of a heterogeneous assortment of trading platforms serving varying constituencies, interconnected by flows of data about trades and investments but with different relationships to those flows.

Albeit with less fanfare, consumer banking has undergone a parallel and equally dramatic transformation. As banks pursued the vast profits that new financial instruments and deregulation offered, they began to reconceptualize the more humdrum activities associated with consumer banking as strategies for extracting surplus via account fees. As consumer-facing banks learned to deal in volume rather than in relationships, consumer finance offerings were redesigned to trigger charges that effectively escalated as consumers' resources declined: overdraft fees, fees for failing to meet minimum balance requirements, ATM transaction fees that landed most heavily on those who made repeated, small-volume withdrawals, and so on. Those changes, implemented over the second half of the twentieth century and continuing into the present, helped set in motion a process that Lisa Servon has christened the "unbanking of America." Increasingly large numbers of ordinary people—the poor, the young, the very old, and the barely making it—cannot afford to maintain bank accounts, while others rely on revolving credit to make ends meet. The unbanked, for their part, rely on check cashing services, payday lenders, and other "fringe finance" businesses that charge high fees for access to ready cash.[50]

The next horizon in consumer finance, and the next competitive battleground for old and new financial intermediaries, is demonetization. Over the past two decades, volumes of credit and debit card transactions have grown steadily, in part because increasing amounts of commerce are conducted online but in part because banks and payment providers have made concerted efforts to extend fee-generating credit and debit card networks throughout sites of commerce in real space. Major information platform businesses such as Apple and Facebook have rolled out competing payment systems of their own, and alternative payment processors and fringe finance providers also compete vigorously for cashless payment business. Because many cashless payment systems operate outside the traditional banking system and its associated overlay of insurance and fraud-protection rules, however, they expose consumers who now take those protections for granted to a variety of hidden risks.[51] Meanwhile, in the developing world, partnerships among governments, private foundations, and for-profit companies have framed new cashless payment platforms as tools for financial inclusion. Cashless payment systems, however, also undermine the flexibility, anonymity, and capacity for informality that are hallmarks of cash economies, and abrupt demonetization in such economies can disrupt markets and essential public services.[52]

Perhaps the ultimate examples of financial dematerialization and datafication are new blockchain-based technologies for authenticating digital transactions. Like peer-to-peer trading platforms, blockchain technologies have been widely hailed for their disintermediating, democratizing potential—with the difference that the impact some have envisaged for blockchain technologies is even more radical. According to some digital-economy pundits (and a number of self-styled crypto-anarchists), blockchain technologies promise the end of state monopolies over currency, with a wide and disorienting set of implications for everything from income tax reporting systems to state-centered governance.[53] Yet the development of blockchain is beginning to follow a less apocalyptic and more predictable path: attracted to blockchain for its built-in security, finance capitalists are underwriting major new efforts to develop and leverage blockchain-based trading platforms. Understood simply as a new and more efficient way to authenticate transactions and move money across borders, blockchain also seems more likely to reinforce the dominance of finance capital than to disrupt it.[54]

Well-known narratives link the ongoing processes of dis- and reintermediation in finance to the disintermediation and dissolution of traditional regulatory institutions. Under the influence of ascendant neoliberal ideologies about the centrality of market processes and market-based innovation, policymakers and financial regulators came to see the financial sector as an important source of innovation in its own right. They gradually dismantled regulatory barriers to bank speculation and to the movement of capital across borders, and began to understand their own function as primarily that of facilitating capital formation and industry self-governance. Many commentators have chronicled both the rapid upsurge in financialization that followed the major deregulatory movements of the 1980s and 1990s and the subsequent, spectacular failures of secondary, ostensibly self-regulatory measures intended to guard against systemic risk.[55]

This chapter, however, is not a lament for the demise of either the particular forms of financial activity that dominated in the heyday of the industrial economy or the characteristic forms of early-to-mid-twentieth century financial regulation. Rather, I want to underscore two very different points:

The first important point simply is that, as both banking and investment have changed beyond recognition, the various structural and institutional barriers that comprised the industrial era's Polanyian countermovement—the safety nets insulating ordinary people against ruinous consequences—disappeared, to be replaced with an apparent consensus that no such barriers were desirable or even feasible. Legislative and policy reforms instituted following the global financial crisis of 2008 were piecemeal and have remained continually under threat. As we will see in Part II, the existing regulatory toolkit also is poorly adapted to information-era realities. Meanwhile, internet-based disruption and disintermediation have proved double-edged swords. The emergence of the internet and the rise of alternative trading platforms and technologies, all heralded as inevitably democratizing developments, have both disrupted the visible structure of the finance industry and consolidated the increasing dominance of finance capital as an extractive enterprise.

The second important point is that narratives about regulatory absence are too simple to describe the roles that law and legal institutions have played and continue to play in the construction of the new realities. Participants in processes of datafication and dis- and reintermediation have mobilized legal resources, most notably contracts law, corporate law, and securities law, to help create and appropriate new derivative instruments, new capital ownership structures, and new intermediation arrangements. As new derivative strategies have become regularized, they have taken on reified form as financial instruments with distinct names and parameters and have engendered distinct sets of trading conventions. Venture capital arrangements and the changes in corporate governance that they have engendered have undergone parallel processes of normalization. New intermediation ventures rely on contracts and also implicate other, highly entrepreneurial appropriation strategies. In particular, an important theme running through the new language of financialization, and a common denominator driving all of the intermediation strategies discussed previously, is privileged access to flows of data about trades and transactions. As we will see in the remainder of this section, privileged access to data is a common denominator in the ongoing reconstructions of labor and land as well.

Labor without Employment

Over the last half century, the movement to informational capitalism also has produced similarly dramatic changes in the conditions of labor. A series of interrelated and mutually reinforcing shifts, including the informationalization of production, the emergence of networked digital information and communications technologies useful for coordinating production across space and time, and the growing financialization of industrial activity, has comprehensively reconfigured patterns of work in the manufacturing and service economies. More recently, new platform-based ventures for intermediating various kinds of information and service work have thrown arrangements in a number of industries into disarray. In parallel with these changes, creative economies too are being reconfigured around new types of extractive practices that emphasize temporary employment and freelance production.

Like the informationalization of finance, the reconfiguration of labor markets has roots in the late nineteenth and early twentieth centuries. The Second Industrial Revolution ushered in not only the rapid mechanization and electrification of production and distribution, but also new theories about efficient ways of adapting labor practices to the mechanized rhythms of the factory floor, including most famously the time-and-motion-based approach to standardization developed by Frederick Winslow Taylor. Taylorist production methods transferred control over workflow from laborers to managers, speeding production and also facilitating efforts to extract the surplus value of labor. Notably, the Taylorist reconfiguration of the factory floor necessitated a parallel reconfiguration and informationalization of management, according to which "every activity in production [must] have its several parallel activities in the management center: each must be devised, precalculated, tested, laid out, assigned and ordered, checked and inspected, and recorded throughout its duration and upon completion."[56] In due course, managerial theories produced comparable reorganizations of other types of work, including management itself. Over the course of the mid-twentieth century, new management subdivisions—marketing, finance, human resources, and so on—emerged and became defined through sets of formalized administrative practices.[57] Developments in information processing and communication that enabled more precise control of production, distribution, and administration lent the iteration and refinement of managerial theories and approaches additional momentum.[58]

Over the last several decades of the twentieth century, the growing pace of informationalization has profoundly altered the relationship between capital and labor. Digital communications networks have enabled just-in-time extraction of raw materials; automated, on-demand manufacturing of goods; and delivery of goods and services at the times and in the quantities needed. The combined impact of changing production practices and increasing financialization has engendered new types of worker hiring and retention practices. Workforce needs are more variable but also amenable to data-driven forecasting, and the communication challenges that formerly would have prevented on-demand labor scheduling have been all but eliminated. In many industries, the expenses of maintaining a permanent work-force are perceived as undercutting the level of return that investors and secured creditors require. The result has been a rise in scheduling practices that are flex-ible from the employer's perspective and unpredictable from the worker's, changing season by season and sometimes day by day. In the terminology used by scholars of information-era labor practices, the proletariat has given way to the precariat, an in-termittently employed workforce that is retained and compensated on an as-needed basis.[59]

The newest developments in efficient workforce management purport to elim-inate centralized management altogether. New platform-based services in the so-called "gig economy" match workers directly with jobs: TaskRabbit and Mechanical Turk for temporary office work, Uber and Lyft for transportation, Airbnb for lodging, and so on. These entities call themselves information businesses rather than, for example, temporary employment agencies or transportation businesses, and insist that, except for the people they hire to write their code and conduct their government relations operations, they do not actually employ anyone. Their true business, they argue, is disintermediation; they are simply facilitating the emer-gence of a new, freelancer-driven economy that is nimbler, more cost-effective, and less impersonal.[60]

The newfound precarity of wage labor in the informationalized economy is, in reality, quite old, and like the labor practices in newly-constituted industrial-era factories, it has a way of placing extreme and often unsustainable burdens on "the human individual who happens to be the bearer of this peculiar commodity."[61] Arrangements in the era of precarity externalize the costs of work—the Starbuck's barista's mobile phone bills, the Uber driver's fuel and auto insurance payments, and so on—and internalize the benefits. Lacking the ability to forecast income or the timing of work obligations from week to week or month to month with any confidence, precarious workers often must struggle to pay basic expenses and ful-fill child- and elder-care responsibilities. More ambitious goals—pursuing higher education or technical training, saving for retirement, and so on—are beyond their reach, and life's ordinary minor disruptions—a blown tire or an emergency room visit—can have catastrophic effects.[62]

Narratives about the disintermediation of work and the virtualization of produc-tion also work to erase (and, sometimes, to de-race) the physical labor that the in-formational economy requires. The energy and labor inputs to online shopping are nearly invisible to consumers. Packages from Amazon.com and other online retailers appear as if by magic, and used packing materials are speedily carted away to equally invisible landfills. The Amazon warehouse worker's outlays for back braces and physical therapy represent yet another kind of externalized cost that rarely figures in policy discussions about the benefits of e-commerce. To scan the books that form the corpus of its Google Book Search service, Google hired temporary, low-wage workers; restricted them to a separate building on Google's lush Mountain View campus; and forbade them to interact with members of its permanent workforce. Soon after, the corpus simply appeared online, representing yet another example of the seemingly magical ability of networked digital technologies' ability to transcend space, time, and matter. The repetitive manual labor of the precarious workforce that called it into being can be glimpsed only as an occasional, latex-gloved, (brown or black) finger fragment hovering at the edge of a page.[63] (Physical labor is not the only resource rendered invisible. According to a 2013 report, the global network of information and communication technologies and associated personal devices accounted for about 10 percent of the world's total energy consumption, and that number has surely grown.[64])

Some of the most celebratory justifications for the freelance economy emphasize the freedom that a "world without work" creates to engage in creative pursuits and nonmarket production, while other, more skeptical narratives emphasize the reorganization of economic activity for the benefit of the Silicon Valley technorati.[65] To focus only on the dematerialization of industrial and service work, however, would be to miss important parallel developments affecting the structure of work in the creative industries. As the movement to informational capitalism gains in velocity, creative work is also in the process of being reconfigured for optimal human capital extraction.

As we saw earlier in this chapter, the complex doctrines that have evolved to mediate relationships between corporate intellectual production intermediaries and creative employees systematically favor the former with respect to intellectual property ownership. Similar asymmetries appear in other aspects of the employment relationship. As Orly Lobel has shown, production intermediaries in the creative and technical industries increasingly deploy a range of contract-based techniques, including restrictive lock-in agreements, noncompete provisions, and clauses extending control of innovative output into both pre- and post-employment periods.[66] Like other firms, moreover, information-economy firms often opt to proceed without conventional employment relationships; consequently, freelance creative and technical workers can (and do) experience precarity, too. Contracting practices in the copyright industries also shape the substance of creative production, locking creative workers into arrangements that attempt to freeze their future outputs into predictably lucrative patterns.[67] All of these techniques have as their goal and effect a pervasive enclosure of the inputs to creative production. Put differently, they are ways of dematerializing, standardizing, and appropriating the creative capital that makes the informational economy work.

Here again, there is nothing sacred about the categories of "employer" and "employee," categories that themselves originated as ad hoc adaptations intended as fulcrum points from which to mitigate the excesses of the industrial economy. As before, my purpose here is to underscore the same two basic points:

The first point relates to the dismantling of those components of the Polanyian countermovement that related to the protection of labor. People have needs for stability and support that the system of wage labor for employers and its associated regulatory overlay addressed—never fully or perfectly, but at least deliberately and systematically. The freelancer-driven economy is indeed lighter, nimbler, and more efficient; those descriptions, however, apply most aptly to the processes of surplus extraction that it is designed to enable, which derive their power in part from their ability to avoid burdensome protective obligations that had coalesced around the old categories. Newer protective arrangements tailored to the growing freelance economy have yet to be put in place. More basically—and something that protracted litigation over who is "really" an employer does not address—the categories that would support such arrangements have yet to be determined.[68] Additionally, the new precarity is globalized in ways that the earlier era's labor-related dislocations were not. The extension of gig-economy ventures into developing countries has begun to exert extreme downward pressure on the earnings of user-workers located in developed countries. Efforts to achieve universal internet access rely in complex and unacknowledged ways on the labor required to extract the rare earth metals that today's smart devices require, manufacture the microprocessors that cause them to function, and assemble those devices in factories half a world away.[69]

The second point, once again, concerns the productive role of law. In the search for a regulator of first resort, it is important not to pass too quickly over the entrepreneurial legal arrangements that underlie the data-driven reconfiguration of labor. Both temporary-employment arrangements and the details of user-workers' relationships with platform companies must be specified. Over time, ad hoc contracting practices requiring workers to disclaim the indicia of employment relationships have coalesced into regularized, standard-form agreements.[70] Writing about gig-economy instruments that take the form of licenses to use the matching services of entities such as Uber and TaskRabbit, Martin Kenney and John Zysman analogize the resulting model to the "putting out" of prefabricated pieces for assembly that occurred early in the industrial era.[71] As anyone who has ever assembled a piece of prefabricated furniture or a modular closet system knows, piecework makes certain types of goods more widely accessible, but it is also tyrannical as to form; its component parts are intended to be assembled only in particular, predetermined ways. Boilerplate access-for-labor instruments work similarly, configuring labor as a modular input to the profit models of employers and intermediaries (and, as we will see in Chapter 5, keeping disputes about the terms and conditions of work out of court and out of the limelight). As in the case of finance, the same arrangements also iterate and reiterate appropriation strategies. Gig-economy businesses such as Uber and TaskRabbit are disintermediators but also reintermediators, converting the labor of user-workers (and user-customers) into flows of monetizable data to which they enjoy privileged access.

Land without Presence

Of the three Polanyian factors of industrial production, land might seem the most difficult to dematerialize. Yet land too has come to play an important role in the ongoing datafication of industrial-era resources. In the United States in the decades following World War II, policymakers seeking to foster more widespread distribution of homeownership crafted a series of federal initiatives designed to expand access to mortgage financing. One strategy involved the resale of mortgage obligations and was conceived as a device for connecting individual borrowers with the deeper pockets and more diverse risk portfolios of participants in nationwide capital markets.[72] Ultimately, however, that strategy did much more than simply increase access; it fundamentally transformed the way that ownership of real property is understood and valued. It thereby opened the way for a set of processes with ultimate effects that were the opposite of democratic and that proved powerful enough to destabilize the global economy.

As in the cases of money and labor, one vector of change was technological: The information technology explosion of the 1980s and 1990s enabled a fundamental shift in practices of bundling and reselling local mortgage loans. Initially, mortgage obligations with the same general profiles were simply bundled and resold. Consistent with the pattern of informationalized "innovation" in financial markets generally, new digital information and communication technologies enabled the creation of new and increasingly complex derivative instruments based on the payment streams from mortgage lending. Rather than simply bundling loans together, investment bankers used flows of data and algorithmic modeling to construct elaborate arrangements for converting portfolios of loans into synthetic investment "tranches"—for which, in the best Ponzi-scheme tradition, they projected high revenues and low risks.[73]

As is now well known, during the 1990s and 2000s, secondary market demand came to dominate the mortgage lending landscape. As new investment vehicles based on securitized mortgage loans become more and more specialized and complex, they were touted and eagerly received as surefire recipes for reaping large profits. To satisfy the secondary market demand, the nominal owners of the underlying real properties were encouraged to assume more and more debt—debt that was purely notional or imaginary to the investors but that threatened real, concrete consequences for its subjects if the bottom fell out, as it eventually did. Unsavory lending practices and deeply rooted cultural romanticism about the promise of home ownership also played roles in leading many first-time home buyers to assume debts that they could not possibly repay. At the same time, conventions for structuring mortgage-backed securities that supposedly guaranteed broad and rock-solid risk distribution instead guaranteed the absence of oversight.[74]

So far, the role of law is in this story is unremarkable. Self-evidently, mortgage lending requires the preparation and execution of legal instruments. One might

assume, then that the ordinary rules of contract and real property law simply provided the neutral background against which individual mortgage loan instruments
were drafted, signed, and enforced.

That story, though, overlooks the extent to which mortgage securitization both
relied upon fundamental conceptual and institutional shifts in the legal landscape
and precipitated others. To begin with, practices of mortgage resale and securitization that today are regarded as routine would not have been possible without prior
acceptance of the idea of owning debt obligations as assets. The idea of negotiability
has roots in the earlier practice of assigning debts to third parties for collection,
but with an important difference: the purchaser of a negotiable instrument can lay
claim to the payment stream without regard to the nature of the underlying agreement that generated the debt. The point of negotiability is to detach the obligation
to pay from the circumstances that define (and may limit) it. Beginning in the late
nineteenth century, this act of conceptual jujitsu elicited and then naturalized new
legal tools, most notably the provisions of the Uniform Negotiable Instruments
Law of 1897, which preceded the negotiable instruments provisions of the Uniform
Commercial Code and stands as an important conceptual precursor for the securitization of mortgage debt. Notably, although the justifications advanced for drafting
uniform negotiability rules emphasized a need to facilitate business-to-business
transactions, the new rules were used principally to facilitate trade in consumer
obligations.[75]

The next step in the legal project of detaching interests in real property from the
material world was both less considered and more venal. As the fever for mortgage
securitization took hold, desire for regulatory avoidance took aim at real property
law's recordation formalities. Under state real property recordation laws, when a
mortgage loan changes hands, timely recordation of the transfer is important to preserve the chain of title and protect the mortgage holder in case of default. Mortgages
subjected to securitization changed hands rapidly—often multiple times in the
course of a single deal—and the underwriters who concocted the securities came to
view the transaction costs imposed by local real property recording offices as a drag
on financial innovation. Some of the largest players turned to their lawyers to craft
an institutional workaround. The result was the Mortgage Electronic Recordation
System (MERS), an organized, bank-funded scheme for disintermediation of local
property recordation requirements and fees. Under the MERS system, when a
member bank purchased a mortgage loan (or a large number of them), it would
enter MERS in the local property register as the "nominee of record" and pay the
required fee just once. It would then separate the promissory note (the document
creating the borrower's legal obligation to repay the loan) from the mortgage instrument (the document creating an interest in real property as security for the
loan) and convey the latter to MERS to hold while the note was traded amongst the
member banks. No rerecordation need be made (or so the argument went) as long
as the loan remained within the MERS system.[76]

In fact, the MERS system and its participants did not maintain good internal records of member bank trades. The continuing fallout from that decision plays out now-familiar themes about the burdens of economic dislocation, the horizons of possibility for protective countermovements, and the productive nature of the relationship between law and economic power. MERS' failures of recordkeeping have made it nearly impossible to reconstruct chains of title for many securitized loans and the underlying real properties. Across the country, a crucial component of record title has simply vanished into the ether. The inability of foreclosure claimants to trace title undeniably worsened the foreclosure crisis that contributed to the 2008 market crash.[77] It also theoretically compromises all future transfers of many properties, a state of affairs that has slowed recovery in some local markets and that likely will require new processes of legal innovation to overcome.

Here the story of land's dematerialization differs to some extent from those of money and labor: Perhaps because home ownership is woven into the fabric of the "American dream" in ways that sound labor policy is not—or perhaps because the consequences of the foreclosure crisis came to rest on the middle class, and so received media coverage that made them more visible and visceral than the constant, grinding woes of the working poor—both federal and state governments moved quickly to craft protective measures designed to blunt financialization's bite. The results of those efforts, however, speak volumes about the ability of the political process to mount an effective response. Measures that would have aided homeowners already facing foreclosure or unable to sell their homes were implemented only partially and halfheartedly.[78] The most visible reforms were prospective, raising standards for future mortgage lending—and thereby improving inputs to future financialization.[79]

Where lawyers are concerned, some accounts of the foreclosure crisis have assigned responsibility principally to bad actors rather than to the underlying institutions. On some retellings, the lending and contracting practices that led to gaps in the chain of title, and that in turn gave rise to the phenomenon of robosigning legal documents in foreclosure proceedings, were failures of professional discipline at the bottom of the legal profession's food chain.[80] But sloppiness and venality at the bottom of the food chain took their cues from sloppiness and venality at the top, on the part of those who created MERS while either ignoring or deliberately disregarding the systemic destabilization it threatened. Those who concocted MERS, moreover, seemed either to have overlooked other weedy but essential details of 50 separate state property systems—for example, the rules that determined whether mortgage and note could be held separately and whether MERS could claim dual status as both agent and "nominee"—or brushed the details aside in the supreme confidence that courts too would see them as obstacles to progress.

As before, there is nothing sacred about local recordation per se. Arguably, in a nationwide economy, operating thousands of small local sites for recordation of land ownership is inefficient; undeniably, systems comprised of paper record books and/or incompatible legacy databases are error-prone and difficult to search. There is also nothing sacred about the paper-based formalities that MERS ignored and that continue to underlie negotiable instruments law more generally. In the pages of law journals, a debate is now underway about whether the negotiability requirements that traditionally have applied to mortgage loan instruments should be reformed or scrapped entirely in favor of some more efficient information-age alternative.[81] But MERS did not open its platform to the public, and it did not collect the information necessary to preserve chain of title in any form. Rather, it was optimized for redistributing as much as possible of the economic surplus flowing from mortgage lending to secondary investors. When all is said and done, self-interested, privatized institutional innovation in the form of the MERS system catalyzed both a massive redistribution of land-based wealth to financial institutions and their well-heeled clients and a massive privatization of resources that formerly had flowed to the public sector to pay for maintenance of roads and other common infrastructure. In operation, it reconstituted the system of record title as tabula rasa for the new appropriation strategies.

From Markets to Platforms

The processes of datafication and reintermediation described in the previous section point to a third dimension of the ongoing movement to informational capitalism, which is structural and organizational. In the industrial-era economy, the locus for activities of barter and exchange was the market, an idealized site of encounter between buyers and sellers within which the characteristics, quantities, and prices of goods and services were regulated autonomically by the laws of supply and demand. In the emerging informational economy, the locus for those activities is the platform, a site of encounter where interactions are materially and algorithmically intermediated. As we have just seen, the emergence of platform-based business models has reshaped patterns of financial activity, workforce management, and land ownership. Platforms have also reshaped information transmission, entertainment, social interaction, and consumption of goods and services, and have destabilized the locally embedded systems that previously mediated those activities in many different types of communities.

Vibrant and fast-growing literatures explore the power that platforms exert over economic life, social interaction, and public discourse. I will return to each of those topics in later chapters, but my goal in this section is the more modest one of teasing out the connections between platform logics and the emergent design of informational property institutions. As the perceived imperatives of access to data and to data processing capacity have sharpened, the platform has emerged as a key site of appropriation, and platform-driven cycles of dis- and reintermediation of data and attention have emerged as key motifs in information-economy narratives about resource ownership and access. Along the way, the particular data flows of greatest interest to competing platforms—data extracted from people as they invest, work, operate businesses, socialize, and engage in innumerable other activities—have emerged as a vitally important fourth dematerialized factor of production.

Prologue: Access and Legibility

No form of economic or social organization is ever wholly new. Preexisting modes of organization impose their own logics, and path-dependencies matter. It is important to begin by recognizing two important ways in which platforms represent continuity as well as change. The intertwined functions that platforms provide—intermediation that provides would-be counterparties with *access* to one another and techniques for rendering users *legible* to those seeking to market goods and services to them—have evolved to become the core organizational logic of contemporary informational capitalism. Those functions, however, have important antecedents in twentieth-century direct marketing and advertising practices.

To appreciate both the continuity and the change that platforms represent, it is instructive to consider two early precursors: the Sears, Roebuck catalog and the Nielsen ratings system. Over two decades at the turn of the twentieth century, entrepreneurs Richard Sears and Alvah Curtis Roebuck parlayed a mail-order watch and jewelry business into a wildly successful mail-order empire selling everything from jewelry to farm equipment. Inclusion of a product in the Sears, Roebuck catalog gave its manufacturer access to a marketing juggernaut with the ability to reach consumers nationwide, the range to offer concert grand pianos and engraved shotguns, and the power to undercut the prices charged by local "five-and-ten-cent stores" for everyday essentials.[82] Three decades later, Arthur Nielsen, a pioneer in the field of statistical market research, began to develop a system designed to give subscribing advertisers and their clients a different kind of access to consumers, based on aggregate measurements rather than solely on one-way communication. The system originated as a simple "audimeter" that recorded when household radios were on and the stations to which they were tuned; over time, the company expanded to television and developed techniques for correlating the recorded information with demographic information and individual viewing information collected from participating households via paper "diaries."[83] In this manner, it gradually began to develop more granular profiles of the viewing population.

Both the Sears, Roebuck catalog and the Nielsen ratings system provided access to vast pools of consumers, but they ways they provided access and the relationships they envisioned between and among manufacturers, intermediaries, and consumers were different. To use Dan Bouk's periodization, the catalog represents the era of the ideal customer as social imaginary. Sears, Roebuck & Co. lacked and likely could not imagine collecting precise, granular information about customer desires and resources, so it sold products it envisioned customers as wanting.[84] To the extent that measurements factored into those determinations, they did so as proxies for the ideal customer rather than as empirical representations of any particular customer. The Nielsen system represents the era of the mass audience, constructed on the basis of numerical aggregates that purported to represent the audience itself.[85] The era of the mass audience also represents a critical inflection point, in which the legibility rubric supplied by an intermediary became both an object of regularized economic exchange and an increasingly powerful, institutionalized arbiter of the knowledge upon which market participants relied. The Nielsen ratings did not simply describe the mass audience but also encoded both a way of understanding it and strategies for managing it.[86]

Information platforms echo some aspects of these early precursors, but also re-work the basic themes of access and legibility in ways that neither Richard Sears nor Arthur Nielsen could have envisioned. Selection of one's product for inclusion in the Sears, Roebuck catalog might have offered a ticket to marketplace success, but it wasn't essential for economic survival in an era in which much commerce remained local. Many manufacturers refused the opportunity because of the production quantities demanded or because they feared that local retailers who opposed the spread of mail-order businesses would boycott their wares.[87] Access to basic media infrastructures—the postal system and print advertising distributed via newspapers and magazines—was becoming more nearly essential for survival, but the relevant infrastructures were available to (almost) anyone willing and able to pay the re-quired fees. As media infrastructures—now digital and networked—have evolved into platforms, both the conditions of access and the need for access have changed. Access to the facilities offered by Amazon or Google or Visa/Mastercard or the iOS operating system requires assent to complex sets of legal and technical protocols. And access to platforms—whether online marketplaces or search engines or pay-ment systems or computing environments—is increasingly essential to reaching any customers at all.

The story of legibility is more complicated still. In the late 1980s, proprietary infrastructures for radio and television broadcast began to give way to a far more complex ecosystem that included proprietary infrastructures for cable television and internet access and open protocols for internet publishing. The proliferation of cable channels and home video recording technologies initially caused an exis-tential crisis for advertisers, whose aggregate measures of the mass audience and its tastes began to dissolve into seemingly unmanageable fragments.[88] That frag-mentation, however, also lent momentum to practices of targeted marketing that had originated in the early twentieth century, and that were premised on the im-portance of reaching specialized pools of desirable consumers.[89] At the same time, new technologies for networked digital communication were emerging. Efforts to adapt those technologies for commercial exploitation ultimately produced new, highly granular ways of measuring audiences and predicting audience appeal. As mass media technologies evolved in ways that facilitated specialization and differentiation, the mass consumer gave way to the individual consumer, and the aggregate measure to the data double (a construct that we will consider more carefully in Chapter 2).[90]

At the same time, and reflecting the increasing normative force of legibility as an overarching frame for commercial endeavor, the legibility function began to burrow into the core of the infrastructure itself. The emergence of the commercial internet, with its enormous number and variety of information sources, accelerated the centripetal movement. A world with a vast diversity of information sources required intermediation for those sources to be meaningfully accessible, and legibility became the essential function for an intermediary to provide to advertisers seeking access to users.

A Platform Is Not (Just) a Network

Reorganization around intermediation and legibility has engendered profound structural changes in the architecture of contemporary networked communication. In discussions of the information economy, the terms "network," "infrastructure," and "platform" are often used interchangeably, but platforms are not the same as networks, nor are they simply infrastructures. Platforms represent infrastructure-based strategies for introducing friction into networks. Those strategies both rely on and reinforce the centrality of a particular way of (re)configuring networked digital communications infrastructures for data-based surplus extraction.

Over the past several decades, scholars in a wide variety of fields have identified networks and infrastructures as important organizing concepts for studying the information economy. A *network* is a mode of organization in which hubs and nodes structure the flows of transactions and interactions. Network organization is not a unique property of digital information and communications networks; rather, as network scientists have shown, such networks simply make visible a latent characteristic of the many human activities that rely on communication and interconnection.[91] Digital information and communications networks do, however, reduce many of the costs and lag times formerly associated with such activities. In addition, participants in networks reap generalized benefits (network externalities) as those networks grow in size and scale, and the relatively low costs of digital interconnection have enabled digital networks to become very large.[92]

Infrastructures are shared resources that facilitate downstream production of other goods. Roads and electric power grids, for example, play essential roles as inputs into a variety of downstream goods, as do less tangible resources such as linguistic and scientific conventions. Notably, infrastructures may be managed as commons but need not be: some infrastructures, such as the interbank wire transfer system, are club goods financed and controlled by their members; others, such as local electric power suppliers, are managed as utilities and financed based on metered consumption charges; and still others, including facilities for internet access in most countries, are privately provided but subject to various regulatory obligations.[93]

Digital information and communications technologies function both as infrastructures and as networks. As scholars in fields ranging from industrial organization to geography to media and communications studies have shown, the forms of connectivity they provide have reshaped seemingly every area of human activity.[94] In theory, the networked information infrastructure still known as the internet is "open," and for some purposes, that characterization is accurate. For most practical purposes, however, the "network of networks" is becoming a network of platforms; for most users, internet access and use are intermediated from beginning to end.

As we will see in more detail in Chapter 2, the platform business model emerged at a point of fortuitous technological and economic convergence. New techniques for customer tracking, immersive social design, and data analysis all promised new possibilities for profiting from targeted marketing in an increasingly fragmented media system. At the same time, legibility became a service most effectively and profitably provided at the infrastructural level. Venture capital investors whose support offered a path to wider capital markets demanded a revenue model, and the demands of that model in turn began to drive platform design. One important result of those shifts was a pervasive financialization of platform firm structure along the lines described earlier in this chapter. In particular, dual-class ownership arrangements that vest continuing control in founding "innovators" and early-stage venture capital investors have become ordinary and expected.[95] Another result was the emergence of a fourth dematerialized and informationalized factor of production: the data flows extracted from people. Today, such flows underwrite a wide and growing variety of profit-making activities. Additionally, the commercial and extractive logics that drove emergence of the platform business model now impose more sweeping design imperatives for datafication and intermediation of the networked information environment. As a result, networked media infrastructures have become pervasively platformized.

Platforms exploit the affordances of digital information and communications networks and supply infrastructures that facilitate particular types of interactions, but they also represent strategies for bounding networks and privatizing and disciplining infrastructures. They operate with the goal of making clusters of transactions and relationships stickier—sticky enough to adhere to the platform despite participants' theoretical ability to exit and look elsewhere for other intermediation options. To accomplish that goal, platforms must provide services that participants view as desirable and empowering, thereby generating and enabling participants to leverage network externalities. But they also must thwart certain other kinds of networking that might facilitate defection to rival platforms.

Platforms use technical protocols and centralized control to define networked spaces in which users can conduct a heterogeneous array of activities and to structure that space for ease of use. The vehicle for managing the tensions between heterogeneity and ease of use is modularity; platform protocols impose a modular structure that enables certain types of flexibility but at the same time forecloses others. Protocol-based control also enables intermediation and facilitates legibility, allowing the platform to serve its own priorities.[96] In Tarleton Gillespie's formulation, the term "platform" appears to offer users a "raised, level surface" on which to present themselves, but at the same time it elides the necessary work of policing the platform's edges.[97] The latter power is one that the fictionalized construct of the market lacked, and it comprehensively reshapes the conditions of economic exchange.

How Platforms Shape Economic Exchange

Economically speaking, platforms represent both horizontal and vertical strategies for extracting the surplus value of user data. Because that project requires large numbers of users generating large amounts of data, the platform provider's goal is to become and remain the indispensable point of intermediation for parties in its target markets. Commentators have begun to puzzle over the implications of the dominance and the staggering market capitalization of the largest platform firms.[98] The characteristic "rich-get-richer" pattern of network organization, however, militates in favor of the emergence of dominant platforms, and platform firms also have devised a variety of other strategies for attaining and maintaining dominance, each targeting multiple user groups.[99]

To begin with, platforms both enable and benefit from competitive dynamics of economic exchange that differ in profoundly important ways from those of traditional, one-sided markets. A core tenet of microeconomic theory is that, ordinarily, markets have porous boundaries and therefore are open to entry and potentially to disruption by transformative offerings that reshape market boundaries altogether. Even dominant incumbents remain vulnerable unless some factor—either anticompetitive behavior or a natural or regulatory monopoly—enables those incumbents, or incumbent business models more generally, to become entrenched. The most reliable sign of such entrenchment is supracompetitive pricing, although antitrust lawyers and competition regulators also employ various secondary heuristics.

The platform economy rewrites all parts of that story, reshaping the conditions of entry, the scope for disruption, and the sources and manifestations of economic power. Platforms do not simply enter markets, they replace (and rematerialize) them. And platforms, unlike markets, have taken shape as discrete legal entities with their own aims and agendas.

The exchanges constituted by platforms are two- or multi-sided: they serve buyers, the sellers seeking to reach them, and often advertisers seeking the buyers' attention. Because the platform forms relationships with members of each group separately, it can define the terms of each relationship differently. So, for example, it can charge little or nothing to participants on one side of a target market and make its profit on another side. A dominant platform can reduce prices to one group—for example, book buyers or consumers of professional networking services—below marginal cost and still maintain its dominance by charging fees to some other group, and a provider of free services to consumers can attain and maintain dominance by controlling access to the "market for eyeballs." Because the economics of platforms permit so many different arrangements, pricing ceases to be a reliable sign of market power, and courts and regulators lose a previously reliable metric for determining whether power has been abused.[100]

Another set of strategies for leveraging economies of scale into more durable patterns of competitive advantage involves preferential placement, and exploits a conundrum that confronts platform users as platform economies of scale become more and more overpowering. Platform users—whether buyers and sellers or social network members seeking their counterparts—seek access to platforms in order to be found. They soon discover, though, that while access to platforms is a necessity, access alone is insufficient; competitive or reputational success in a platform environment requires information-based strategies for being visible to other users. In theory, the platform's legibility function should provide effective matching in ways that take account of "long tail" patterns of supply and demand; in reality, the results of algorithmic matching often seem to prioritize the most popular results. Platforms have developed various techniques for offering and monetizing preferential placement, such as "sponsored search results" (e.g., Google's AdWords and AdSense programs) and "enhanced listing placement" (e.g., Amazon's Featured Merchant program).[101] Because of the platform environment's operational secrecy, however, purchasers of these services cannot easily monitor the quality of what they have purchased. More generally, platform users cannot easily determine whether platform firms are engaging in other, undisclosed varieties of preferential placement.[102]

A third set of strategies for leveraging economies of scale into more durable patterns of competitive advantage involves interplatform affiliation. Smaller and more specialized platforms may contract with more dominant platforms to provide particular services—for example, payment processing, streaming video, games for social network users, and so on. Such arrangements benefit both dominant and niche platforms, giving niche platforms access to a larger pool of users and dominant platforms access to a larger and deeper pool of information about users' online activities. It is unsurprising, then, that the interrelationships among platforms have become increasingly dense and complex. Such agreements, though, also create risks for both parties. A dominant platform must consider the possibility that what had been envisioned as a niche or add-on service will become a new species of dominant intermediary in its own right, as internet browsers, search engines, social networks, and mobile operating systems all have done. Niche platforms, meanwhile, are no better placed than platform users to monitor the behavior of dominant platforms. They may find themselves receiving fewer or different benefits than expected or competing with the dominant platform's own offerings under conditions that seem to place them at a disadvantage.[103]

From the perspective of users, advertisers, and niche platforms, dominant platforms function in a manner analogous to utilities, supplying basic information services now deemed essential to a wide variety of economic and social activities. The tools for effecting legibility constructed by giant information businesses such as Google, Apple, and Facebook have become global platform-based "superstructures," subsuming and rematerializing not only markets but also and more broadly information-gathering and social interaction.[104] At the same time, however, modeling and understanding the economic, social, and informational dynamics of the platform environment has become extraordinarily difficult. As we will see next, platforms also use legal strategies to maintain and deepen the informational asymmetries on which their competitive strategies rely.

Points of Access, Points of Control

Platform-based competitive strategies revolve fundamentally around control of access in two different and complementary senses. Platform users seek access to the essential social, commercial, and cultural connectivity that platforms provide, while platform providers seek access to the data necessary to create and sustain a competitive advantage in their chosen field(s) of intermediation. The result is a bargain that appears relatively straightforward—access for data—but that in reality is complex and importantly generative. In subsequent chapters, I will consider some of the implications of that bargain for patterns of information flow to and about platform users and for society more generally; here, I focus more narrowly on implications for the landscape of intellectual property law. One important byproduct of the access-for-data arrangement is a quiet revolution in the legal status of data and algorithms as (de facto if not de jure) proprietary information property.

A principal worry for any platform is disintermediation by a would-be competitor, and so platform providers work to define both collected data and algorithmic logics as zones of exclusivity. Platforms use contracts systematically to facilitate and protect their own legibility function, extracting transparency from users but shielding basic operational knowledge from third-party vendors, users, and advertisers alike.

The particular form of the access-for-data contract extended to users—a boilerplate terms-of-use agreement not open to negotiation—asserts a nonnegotiable authority over the conditions of access that operates in the background of even the most generative information-economy service. The terms-of-use agreement represents an example par excellence of the turn to boilerplate that now characterizes so much routine commercial interaction. Boilerplate agreements are contractual in form but mandatory in operation, and so are a powerful tool both for private ordering of behavior and for private reordering of even the most bedrock legal rights and obligations.[105]

From an intellectual property perspective, the contractual arrangements employed by platform firms function as points of entry for institutional entrepreneurship targeting the form and substance of legal entitlements in information. In a process that is fundamentally performative, the terms-of-use agreement steps in where the map of formal legal entitlements ends. Scholars of property law have begun to pay attention to the constructed "thingness" of certain types of interests that today are understood as property-like but that are contractual in origin.[106] Trade secrecy law, a shifting and uncertain hybrid between property and contract, traditionally has presented fertile ground for opportunistic propertization via contract, but negotiated trade secrecy agreements generally are ad hoc and context-dependent just as the underlying secrets are. Platform contracts work in tandem with platform protocols to leverage trade secrecy entitlements into de facto property arrangements that affect large numbers of people with no direct relationship with the platform owner. The terms themselves are, of course, "only words"—and, for that matter, words that most users do not read—but they gain powerful normative force from both their continual assertion and reassertion and their propagation within algorithmically intermediated environments that use technical protocols to define the parameters of permitted behavior.[107] The combination of scale, asserted contractual control, and technical control enacts enclosure of both data and algorithmic logics as an inexorable reality of twenty-first century networked commercial life.

The *logic of performative enclosure* that infuses the access-for-data bargain carries over into platform dealings with app developers, advertisers, and other commercial counterparties, where it is paired with subsidiary strategies of performative openness. Even as they jealously guard access to both data collected from users and the algorithms used to process the data, platforms entice developers and advertisers with promises of access. So, for example, Facebook offers advertisers placement precisely targeted to the inferred needs and desires of its billions of users but never direct access to the data or algorithms themselves. Application developers receive access to carefully curated data sets, data structures, and programming interfaces. Google's vaunted commitments to open data and open code do not extend to its algorithms or to the data it collects about its users, and it imposes other restrictive conditions on developers seeking to offer Android devices or Android-compatible applications. Amazon releases programming interfaces to developers but simultaneously maintains tight, cryptographically enforced control over other operational aspects of its system.[108]

For the most part, traditional intellectual property rights play helpful but only secondary roles in the process of de facto propertization, functioning as sources of leverage that can be invoked to channel would-be users toward entering the access-for-data bargain on the platform's terms and/or to prevent would-be competitors from gaining access to information stored on the platform by other means. Access to a branded exchange as an Amazon reseller, a Google AdSense partner, or an iPhone- or Facebook-authorized app enables third-party vendors to position their products and services as more desirable to consumers. When access to a platform requires technical interoperability—as is the case, for example, with apps for desktop and mobile operating systems—patents and copyrights can supply important points of leverage against unauthorized access by third-party vendors and would-be platform competitors. As the example of Alphabet (Google) shows, however, not all platforms consider copyrights a necessary tool for limiting access. At least from Google's perspective, exclusive control of data and algorithms is a more reliable guarantor of dominance than copyrights might be.[109]

The roles of patents in the platform economy are more varied. Because the communal founding ethos of the internet retains strong normative force in technical communities, holders of information technology patents must contend with norms favoring licensing on a fair, reasonable, and nondiscriminatory basis. Pooling arrangements for standard-essential patents have thrived, but interests in patenting protocols and in holding out for preferential treatment in pooling also have persisted. What is standard-essential also is open to some debate. Although there has been broad agreement that basic internet protocols are too important to monopolize, patents and patent portfolio strategies play significant roles in many information technology markets.[110] Platformization also has begun to shape biotechnology research and development, with a number of new start-up firms organized around diagnostic or therapeutic protocols with multiple downstream applications.[111]

In sum, the access-for-data arrangement is both a concrete bargain and a complex act of institutional entrepreneurship, with a number of interrelated implications for the intellectual property system that are still playing out. In addition to their other roles, platforms are in an important sense intellectual property entrepreneurs, working to refine and propagate appropriation strategies that serve their economic interests. As we are about to see in the next chapter, platforms are not the only information-economy actors using performative strategies to appropriate new data flows. Platforms' organizational centrality within the information economy, however, lends their strategies powerful resonance.

Law and the Construction of Information Property: Conclusions and Questions

This chapter has advanced three primary arguments: First, the ongoing movement to informational capitalism is about much more than ownership of intellectual property and control of code. It also entails other important changes that involve both inputs to production and the organization of economic activity. Second, informational property rights are emergent institutional formations. Over time, patterns of dealing in intangibles can cause the contours of traditional doctrines to shift. Finally and importantly, none of the shifts now underway as part of the movement to informational capitalism is organic; rather, they are the results of the self-interested, strategic activities of many different players.

Yet the investigation in this chapter also has surfaced additional questions: Where do the new raw materials that constitute the fourth factor of production in the emerging informational economy come from, and who decides on their allocation? Who or what determines the proper allocation of accountability for harms flowing from datafication and platformization? What accounts for the startling power of platforms to command adherence to their terms, and have any countervailing obligations emerged that platforms are bound to respect? As we will see in the remainder of Part I, answering those questions requires moving beyond investigations of rights and correlative duties to respect them. The remaining chapters in Part I examine other ongoing processes of decomposition and recomposition in the landscape of information-economy legal entitlements.

The Biopolitical Public Domain

In the beginning all the World was America.
John Locke, Second Treatise of Government, § 49

Chapter 1 described the emergence of the platform as the core organizational logic of the political economy of informational capitalism. Platforms have become both key drivers of the datafication of important resources and active legal entrepreneurs, pursuing powerful strategies for ensuring their continued access to and de facto control of the data on which they rely. That exploration, however, also raised an important question that sits outside the frame of propertization-through-control and that concerns the origins of the presumptive entitlement that platforms and other information businesses assert to appropriate and use data flows extracted from people. That presumptive entitlement is the subject of this chapter.

Scholarship on the relationship between law and the collection and processing of personal data typically considers such activities as raising problems of privacy or data protection, and typically has focused on regulation of such activities after the fact. But the legal framework within which collection, processing, and use of personal data occur is not simply a reactive framework, nor is it simply concerned with the relationship between commercial or law enforcement activities and privacy. The data flows extracted from people play an increasingly important role *as raw material* in the political economy of informational capitalism. Personal data processing has become the newest form of bioprospecting, as entities of all sizes—including most notably both platforms and businesses known as data brokers—compete to discover new patterns and extract their marketplace value.

Understood as processes of resource extraction, the activities of collecting and processing personal data require an enabling legal construct. This chapter identifies that construct—one foreign to privacy and data protection law but commonplace within intellectual property law—and traces its effects. Contemporary practices of personal data extraction and processing constitute a new type of public domain, which I will call the *biopolitical public domain*: a source of raw materials that are there for the taking and that are framed as inputs to particular types of productive activity. The raw materials consist of data identifying or relating to people, and the public domain made up of those materials is biopolitical—rather than, say, personal or informational—because the productive activities that it frames as desirable are activities that involve the description, processing, and management of populations, with consequences that are productive, distributive, and epistemological.

A public domain is not a naturally occurring phenomenon. It is first and foremost an idea: a culturally situated way of understanding patterns of resource ownership and availability. But a public domain also is much more than an idea. The construct of a public domain both designates particular types of resources as available and suggests particular ways of putting them to work. In Hohfeldian terms, a public domain is a zone of legal privilege: it demarcates conduct as to which no one has a right to object. It thereby legitimates the resulting patterns of appropriation and obscures the distributive politics in which they are embedded.[1] The biopolitical public domain conforms to these patterns, constituting the field for appropriation and use of personal data in two complementary and interrelated ways. First, it constitutes personal data as *available and potentially valuable*: as a pool of materials that may be freely appropriated as inputs to economic production. That framing supports the reorganization of sociotechnical activity in ways directed toward extraction and appropriation. Second, the biopolitical public domain constitutes the personal data harvested within networked information environments as *raw*. That framing creates the backdrop for culturally situated techniques of knowledge production and for the logic that designates those techniques as sites of legal privilege. It thereby catalyzes the emergence of a complex set of economic and social relations.

My purpose in naming the biopolitical public domain and exploring its material and conceptual entailments is to construct a genealogy of legal privilege-in-the-making. The emerging patterns of privilege and disentitlement now coalescing around the construct of the biopolitical public domain have far-reaching implications in the domains of both political economy and law. They undergird new business-to-business markets based on patterning, prediction, and targeted surplus extraction, and those markets profoundly alter other economic and social relationships. As legal institutions confront choices about whether to validate or constrain the practices that make such markets possible, it is important to recognize the extent to which law is already implicated in the construction and assertion of information power.

Logics of Abundance and Extraction

The process of constructing a public domain begins with an act of imagination that doubles as an assertion of power. An identifiable subject matter—a part of the natural world or an artifact of human activity—is reconceived as a resource that is unowned but potentially appropriable, either as an asset in itself or as an input into profit-making activity. The biopolitical public domain is an act of imagination tailored to the political economy of informational capitalism; it constitutes the field of opportunity for a particular set of information-based extractive activities.

To the contemporary mind, the idea of a public domain is most closely associated with regimes of intellectual property, but it has older roots in the era of global exploration and conquest. For the early explorers and the European sovereigns who financed their voyages, the act of naming and staking claim to hitherto undiscovered lands marked those lands as ownable resources and their contents as available for harvesting or capture.[2] Later, for the fledgling government of the United States, the idea of a public domain available to be claimed by the state and then parceled out to deserving claimants gave tangible purchase to narratives of inevitable and productive westward expansion and manifest destiny.[3] The copyright and patent regimes that emerged during the nineteenth century in Europe and the United States depend centrally on the idea of the intellectual public domain as a repository of raw materials upon which future authors and inventors can build. One may not lay exclusive claim to resources in the intellectual public domain, but resources in the public domain may be freely appropriated as inputs to profitable activity.

In both real property law and intellectual property law, the idea of a public domain thus both emphasizes and assumes two conditions. The first is abundance. As political philosopher John Locke put it in 1690, "in the beginning all the World was America."[4] That framing is revelatory; it depends for its intelligibility on an understanding of America as terra nullius, unowned and available for occupation. Formulated at a historical moment when the world still seemed limitless enough to satisfy all conceivable sources of demand, it expresses a heady sense of infinite possibility. In contemporary intellectual property debates about the exploitation of intangibles, which are nonrivalrous, the constraints of scarcity have seemed even more remote. Ideas, facts, and scientific principles are understood as paradigmatic examples of renewable resources; it is thought inconceivable that we could ever run out.

The second condition that the idea of a public domain presumes is the absence of prior claims to the resource in question. America in 1690 was not terra nullius to its native inhabitants, but their traditions of occupancy and use were not understood as ownership claims by European explorers and colonists. Similarly, intellectual property regimes traditionally have taken a dismissive stance toward those claiming interests in folk art and traditional knowledge. In the modern era that stance has encouraged the intellectual equivalent of a land rush by the mass culture industries, pharmaceutical companies, and other information businesses. The resulting patterns of exploitation have predictable geographies. Legal scholars Anupam Chander and Madhavi Sunder, who study the global intellectual property system, have mapped a distinctive pattern of information flow, in which resources extracted from the global South flow north twice: once as indigenous resources extracted and appropriated by intellectual property industries headquartered in the global North and a second time as payments exacted for products based on those resources.[5]

The idea of a public domain thus reflects an implicit distributive politics, with important, real-world consequences for the distribution of economic wealth. The idea of the biopolitical public domain conforms to that pattern.

Contemporary descriptions of the commercial future of personal data processing contain numerous examples of framing in terms of abundance and infinite possibility. In marketing brochures and prospectus statements, information businesses of all sorts describe in glowing terms the ways that processing of data about people will open new and profitable lines of exploration. Data broker Intelius boasts: "Intelius has a robust and proprietary technology platform that gathers over 20 billion public records from a large network of publicly- and commercially-available sources." TowerData (formerly Rapleaf) promises "80% of email or postal addresses in batch or via a real-time API," and CoreLogic touts its access to "more than 4.5 billion records" and its focus on "turning mountains of data into valuable insights," while according to Recorded Future, it "continuously processes billions of data points in multiple languages from technical, open, and closed (dark web) sources."[6] These optimistic pronouncements, which herald the dawn of a new age of data science, constitute the ever-expanding universe of personal data as a terra nullius for enterprising data developers, an unexplored frontier to be staked out, mapped, and colonized.

Those descriptions also reflect a familiar distributive politics. Commercial surveillance practices deploy powerful new data processing techniques to map and monetize subject populations, and those who undertake that project speak and behave in ways that express unquestioned assumptions about their rights to appropriate and exploit that which is freely available. According to Experian, "Marketing data differs in important ways from consumer credit data. Experian's marketing data is drawn primarily from public records and other publicly available sources."[7] Google Chief Economist Hal Varian reports: "Google runs about 10,000 experiments a year in search and ads. There are about 1,000 running at any one time, and when you access Google you are in dozens of experiments."[8] In these and similar statements, all the world is America again, and doubly so: the information resources extracted from populations worldwide flow into the databanks of the new information capitalists, who then use those resources to devise new profit-making strategies. And both in the United States and worldwide, U.S. information companies are in the forefront of the race to harvest the resources of the biopolitical public domain and make them productive.

Imagining the universe of personal data as a commons ripe for exploitation is only the beginning, however. For the idea of a public domain to fulfill its imagined destiny as a site of productive labor it must be linked to more concrete logics of extraction and appropriation. By that standard, the biopolitical public domain is a construct of extraordinary power. As this section describes, the idea of a public domain of personal data has catalyzed far-reaching reorganizations of sociotechnical activity to facilitate harvesting personal data "in the wild" and to mark such data, once collected, as owned.

Prologue: Fair Credit Reporting and Walled Gardens

The personal data processing economy derives its structure partly from the activities of the platform businesses described in Chapter 1 and partly from those of a different group of information businesses known as data brokers. Today, the commercial data broker industry is a multibillion-dollar industry that, according to a 2013 study by the U.S. Senate Committee on Commerce, Science, and Transportation, "largely operates hidden from public view."[9] Its origins, however, are both more modest and more public. As we saw in Chapter 1, platforms trace their roots to developments in advertiser-driven target marketing that began in the early twentieth century. The data broker industry originated in practices of customer profiling and target marketing developed by and for members of the financial services industries—and in the empty spaces left by incomplete legal regulation of those practices.

Ironically, one impetus for the emergence of consumer profiling and target marketing within the financial services industry was a law intended to protect consumers. By the mid-twentieth century, both consumer advocates and legislators had become alarmed by the free-wheeling nature of the emerging credit reporting industry. Lenders and third-party consultants were building dossiers that demonstrated scant regard for accuracy and disseminating them with even scanter regard for the value of confidentiality and the potential for harm. The Fair Credit Reporting Act of 1970 (FCRA) created both substantive and procedural safeguards, including limits on the purposes for which a "consumer report" could be provided, informed consent provisions for the release of certain kinds of information, and procedures by which consumers could gain access to the records compiled by consumer reporting agencies and correct any errors.[10]

The FCRA's drafters, however, also had other goals in mind. The law imposed no duty on consumer reporting agencies to verify reported information or reconcile discrepancies between conflicting reports, but instead simply required them to respond to consumer complaints once raised. It provided automatic, statutory damages only for willful violations, and preempted any state law causes of action that might have imposed stricter duties or more significant deterrent liability. In short, the much-heralded federal law with "fair" in its title was designed with the significant purpose of ensuring smooth sailing for the fledgling consumer reporting industry.[11] In that purpose it succeeded. As electronic processes for credit reporting and approval emerged, the uniform federal limitation on liability and the relatively weak, post hoc guarantees of procedural fairness facilitated the emergence of nationwide, automated credit reporting agencies and a vast and profitable consumer credit industry.

Notably, the drafters of the FCRA did not attempt to develop a new, comprehensive definition of a "consumer reporting agency," but instead employed recursive definitions: consumer reports are communications of credit-related information by consumer reporting agencies, while consumer reporting agencies are entities that assemble and evaluate consumer credit information for the purpose of furnishing consumer reports.[12] That approach likely made sense for both practical and political reasons; it avoided the difficult task of generating consensus on the precise coverage of a sweeping new law intended to govern still-emerging entities and practices. At any rate, the project of amassing comprehensive, searchable nationwide databases still confronted large logistical and technical challenges. All parties seem to have assumed that when the dust settled after an inevitable period of consolidation, consumer reporting agencies would be few in number and easy to identify by the nature of the reports their resources enabled them to prepare. The statutory circularity, however, created an important point of entry for the nascent consumer profiling industry. From early on, the structure of the statute's definitions seems to have encouraged both consumer reporting agencies and other entities to experiment with data-based products and services that could be offered for sale without triggering the FCRA's requirements.[13]

The FCRA also did not impose any special legal obligations on financial institutions that submitted information about consumers' payment behavior to consumer reporting agencies. Submitters, Congress likely assumed, would not be in position to compile comprehensive reports using only the discrete items of information each possessed. As we saw in Chapter 1, however, one consequence of the intensified financialization that began in the late twentieth century was a rapid increase in consumer reliance on revolving credit, and credit card issuers' proprietary databases grew commensurately. Jockeying for competitive advantage in an increasingly crowded field that now included American Express charge cards, major payment brand networks, and independent credit issuers, card issuers began to mine their databases in an effort to identify different market segments and possible co-branding opportunities.[14]

One important structural limitation constrained experimentation with consumer profiling. As practices of consumer profiling evolved within the consumer reporting and credit card industries, the databases used to generate consumer reports and profiles remained walled gardens. The three major consumer reporting agencies received data directly from banks, credit card companies, and other financial institutions that had preexisting relationships with consumers and followed statutorily prescribed procedures in granting access to the reports they compiled. Consumer credit issuers built databases of their own cardholders' transactions. As the twentieth century drew to a close, however, the information-gathering landscape changed decisively.

Digital Breadcrumbs

The discovery of the biopolitical public domain dates to 1994, when a researcher at the Netscape Corporation named Lou Montulli developed a protocol for identifying visitors to websites. The protocol involved insertion of a small piece of code—which Montulli named a "cookie"—into the user's browser. This enabled so-called stateful interactions, such as transactions involving use of a virtual shopping cart. Implemented in "persistent" form, it also could enable reidentification of those users when they returned to the site later on.[15] Netscape and other technology companies quickly recognized that cookies could play a key role in transforming the internet into an infrastructure for commercial communications. Netscape implemented the technology in its Navigator browser and filed a U.S. patent application in Montulli's name. In 1995, recognizing the promise of cookie technology as a standard for state management and seeking to avert technical inconsistency in implementation, the Internet Engineering Task Force (IETF) formed a working group to develop a formal specification.[16]

Initial implementations of cookie protocols by both Netscape and Microsoft were nontransparent to users, but the technology was open in an entirely different sense: it dramatically expanded the opportunity to participate in commercial surveillance activity. Anyone with a server connection to the internet could become a data collector, and cookies also could be served and collected by third parties providing hosting, payment, or marketing services.

The significance of this restructuring of surveillance capacity is evident from the dramatic nature of the marketplace response. Although the commercial internet was in its infancy, marketers and advertisers rushed to adopt and improve upon the new technology. By mid-1996, when articles in the *Financial Times* and the *San Jose Mercury News* revealed to the general public the existence of cookies for online tracking, experiments with the use of cookies as persistent identifiers were already underway.[17] That same year, the Federal Trade Commission (FTC) held public hearings about "consumer privacy in the global information infrastructure" during which the use of cookies to collect information about internet users was a topic of lively discussion.[18]

Over the ensuing decade, the increasing public and regulatory scrutiny of cookies did nothing to dampen commercial enthusiasm for the technology. As Chapter 1 described, new capabilities for intermediation and legibility intersected with the pursuit of commercial viability in an increasingly fragmented media environment. Advertisers who might provide revenue wanted results and so, increasingly, did users. Personalized tracking seemed the logical way to satisfy both imperatives.

As the push for more user control intensified, Netscape and other browser developers began to build greater transparency and control into subsequent iterations of their browsers. At the same time, however, the commercial web resisted. Willingness to accept at least some kinds of cookies became an increasingly necessary precondition for transacting online and participating in online communities. In addition, marketers and technologists in their employ developed a set of less-visible tracking techniques, known variously as "clear GIFs" or "web bugs," for surreptitiously collecting information about internet users' behavior.[19] The IETF working group had identified the privacy issues raised by cookies very early on, but efforts to write a uniform level of heightened user control into the standard met with pushback. Technology companies preferred a more minimal standard that would afford greater flexibility in implementation, and members of the rapidly growing online advertising industry sought to preserve the possibility of a promising new business model. More generally, the IETF standards process had not previously experienced intensive public policy scrutiny. Working group members unused to evaluating and responding to political and policy objections had difficulty bringing the standards process to closure, and the delay allowed the more minimal standard to become entrenched within industry practice.[20]

Meanwhile, new platform-based environments for social sharing and massively multiplayer gaming were taking shape in ways that relied on techniques for keeping track of users. The earliest online communities were organized around chat rooms, listservs, and communal bulletin boards, and had neither the desire nor the capability for built-in surveillance. Similarly, the original online massively multiplayer games were not-for-profit enterprises organized around communities of enthusiasts rather than around the quality of the multimedia experiences they provided. In the late 1990s and early 2000s, however, the first true multimedia gaming platforms and social networking platforms began to emerge: graphically rich, hypertext-based environments that enabled customizable member profiles and relied on cookies to manage login information.[21] As they moved beyond the startup phase and sought stable sources of financing from capital markets, both kinds of platforms gradually became entangled within the biopolitical public domain's commercial and extractive logics. In particular, venture capital investors encouraged high tech startups to pursue business models that might generate the revenue streams needed to attract additional capital.[22]

Among the companies on the receiving end of investor pressure was Silicon Valley darling Google, which was in search of a formula for ensuring its continued survival following the end of the "dot-com bubble," and which had already built the most powerful engine for online search that the world had ever seen. Gradually, following the lead of its digital advertising team, it began developing, patenting, and acquiring new methods for generating online advertising revenues that relied on comprehensive information about users to target ads.[23] In that effort it was soon joined by new kid on the block Facebook, which was working to develop methods of monetizing a new form of digital asset that it called the "social graph."[24]

At the same time, both old and new data brokers were developing the capability to combine multiple databases and search across them to amass more complete dossiers on individuals. As a wider variety of data began to be digitized, automated, and offered for sale or license—including directory listings, property records, tort judgments, divorce decrees, arrest records, and many more—data brokers were well positioned to acquire and exploit them.[25] Data brokers and emerging platform firms also contracted with or acquired new Web-based analytics firms that relied on cookies and web bugs to monitor users' activities, gathering valuable information that could be used to personalize content, sell ads, and generate revenue streams in transactions with subscribing clients. Google and Facebook pursued especially aggressive acquisition strategies, targeting both established and start-up firms and assimilating both competing and complementary functionalities.[26]

Last but not least, digital advertising ventures, data brokers, and emerging digital platform firms began to exploit new capabilities for data analysis. Those capabilities combined new configurations of information processing hardware capable of sifting, sorting, and interrogating vast quantities of data in very short times with new automated techniques for identifying patterns, distilling the patterns into predictions, and continually adjusting the patterns and predictions in response to new data. The result, popularized under the moniker "Big Data," was a fast-evolving group of techniques for converting voluminous, heterogeneous flows of physical, transactional, and behavioral information about people (or about anything else) into a particular, highly data-intensive type of knowledge.[27]

Efforts to extend consumer protection frameworks to encompass the new developments were largely ineffective. During the first decade of the new century, attempts to enact legislation restricting the use of so-called spyware failed repeatedly. Merchants and communications providers that deployed cookies for what they saw as legitimate purposes balked at definitional language extending labels such as "spyware" and "cybertrespass" to their own activities. Both the venerable Direct Marketing Association and the newly formed Network Advertising Initiative lobbied strongly on behalf of the advertising industry against language that would sweep in too many uses of the new techniques. Technology and information businesses urged Congress to move cautiously in order not to foreclose innovative market responses.[28] Data brokers also worked assiduously to avoid meaningful FCRA oversight by exploiting the recursivity of the statute's definitional structure, representing that their products were just incomplete enough or anonymized enough or aggregated enough not to count as "consumer reports" and cautioning their subscribers not to use them that way.[29]

In the absence of a regulatory framework specifically tailored to the problems of surreptitious tracking and "behavioral advertising," the FTC attempted to fill the regulatory gap by asserting its general authority to police unfair and deceptive practices in commerce. As a practical matter, this meant that the construct of notice and consent became the dominant regulatory framework for evaluating online businesses' use of tracking techniques, and the "privacy policy"—a lengthy, turgid document disclosing information about an online entity's collection and processing of personal data—became the de facto vehicle for ensuring compliance.[30]

At the same time, the quest to track internet users by less transparent means continued, pushing ever more deeply into the logical and hardware layers of consumers' devices. Digital advertising companies ranging from emerging platform giants Google and Facebook to new start-up firms began developing techniques for identifying and tracking the MAC numbers that are permanently associated with all network-capable digital devices. As smart mobile platforms emerged and as additional techniques for device tracking and fingerprinting developed, tracking by both persistent, surreptitious cookies and permanent hardware identifiers became routine.[31] Telecommunications providers also got into the act. In 2014, Verizon customers were surprised to learn that Verizon had been tracking their online activities by means of a deeply embedded, invisible, and undeletable "supercookie" even after they had set their account preferences to reject such tracking; four years later, such revelations have come to seem ordinary.[32]

The Sensing Net

The radical expansion of surveillance capability via cookie technology was an unintended consequence of the search for a viable protocol for commercial transactions, but subsequent continuing extensions of surveillance capability have been more deliberate. The primary vehicles for those extensions have been the marketplace shifts toward smart mobile devices, wearable computing, and the internet of things. As a result of those developments, commercial data collection has become a nearly continuous condition. Communications networks have been transformed into sensing networks, organized around always-on mobile devices and embedded, networked sensors that collect and transmit an astonishingly varied and highly granular stream of data about user behavior to powerful, interconnected platforms.

In the relatively short time since the first true smartphone was introduced by Motorola in 2004, internet-ready mobile devices have become ubiquitous and ordinary. In January 2017, the Pew Research Center reported that 77 percent of U.S. adults own a smartphone.[33] Even when used simply for one-to-one voice communications, mobile devices collect more kinds of data than tethered landlines do, for the simple reason that mobile devices use geolocation to route calls to their intended destinations. But smart mobile devices also collect and transmit text messages, internet searches, social networking updates, personalized news and entertainment feeds, and interactions with dedicated apps for traffic, transit, shopping, investment and personal finance, fitness, and much more. And mobile application usage has grown exponentially. In January 2012, Apple's online App Store reported that downloads had reached 25 billion; by 2016, total downloads from the Apple, Android, Google, and Amazon online app stores exceeded 149 billion.[34]

In parallel with the increasingly widespread penetration of smart mobile devices and the continual expansion of those devices' capabilities, infrastructures for Web tracking have become complex and robust. In 2016, researchers attempting to catalog tracking techniques and map tracker networks uncovered a vast infra-structure, comprised of a heterogeneous and continually evolving assortment of techniques, overlaid on a million of the Web's most popular sites. Dominant plat-form firms Google, Facebook, and Twitter maintain especially large networks, but a variety of other digital analytics firms also engage in pervasive and undisclosed device fingerprinting and tracking.[35]

Data harvested from people also flows through sensors embedded in ordinary artifacts and dispersed widely throughout the built environment. Transit passes and highway toll transponders record daily travels; smart home thermostats, alarm sys-tems, and building access cards create digital traces of comings and goings; special-purpose "wearables" collect and upload biometric data to mobile apps that sync with cloud-based services. Fingerprint readers and facial recognition systems col-lect and process biometric information to authenticate access to devices, places, and services. Still other sensing systems, such as license plate readers and facial recog-nition technologies embedded in visual surveillance systems, are operated by state actors.[36]

Formally, commercial sensor networks require enrollment—apps must be installed and configured for location awareness, social sharing, push notifications, and the like. Particularly to those versed in the legal language of privacy and data protection, it might appear that the legal rules enabling the ongoing construction of the sensing net are those relating to notice and consent, just as the FTC's en-forcement practice has suggested. According to that way of reasoning about the col-lection and processing of personal data, data subjects have rights to control such activities but may exercise those rights by consenting to collection and processing.

As a practical matter, though, information businesses have powerful incentives to configure the world of networked digital artifacts in ways that make enrollment seamless and near-automatic. Even when users do have choices to prevent col-lection of certain types of data, the design of user interfaces, menu options, and accompanying disclosures systematically obscures those choices, guiding users instead toward options that involve more intensive data extraction.[37] And many important details about the kinds of behavioral data that the sensing net extracts simply are not disclosed to users at all. Within the sensing net, practices of data are continuous, immanent, complex, and increasingly opaque to ordinary users. For some technologists and legal scholars, these characteristics have suggested an analogy to the autonomic nervous system, which automatically and responsively mediates basic physiological functions such as respiration and digestion. Like the autonomic nervous system, the sensing net is designed to operate invisibly and automatically in a way that is exquisitely attuned to environmental and behavioral conditions.[38]

The conception of consent emerging from that default condition is unprece-dented in the law of contracts or any other body of law. Consent to data extrac-tion is being sublimated into the coded environment, and along the way it is being effectively redefined. In the contemporary networked marketplace, consent flows from status, not conduct, and attaches at the moment of marketplace entry. Under those circumstances, the lawyerly emphasis on such things as disclosure, privacy dashboards, and competition over terms becomes a form of Kabuki theater that distracts both users and regulators from what is really going on.

The construction of the sensing net and the accompanying sublimation of consent work both to generate large quantities of data and to make public domain status the default condition for the data that are generated. Or, as data broker Acxiom (now rebranded as LiveRamp) puts it: "To drive value from the new opportunities presented by the Internet of Things, companies must be able to connect these new data feeds with their existing CRM [customer relations management] systems to distill enhanced insights and better understand their customer's needs beyond just the data from a connected device."[39] Unlike land, which exists in finite quantity, data flows extracted from people are (in theory) subject to uncertainties: their seeming bounty depends heavily on both technical design and user agency. The sublimation of consent within the sensing net is a technique for supply chain management and is designed to ameliorate those uncertainties. It operates to call the biopolitical public domain into being and to define it as a zone of free and productive appropriation.

The Postcolonial Two-Step

It is tempting to understand the biopolitical public domain as a developed-world phenomenon—or, less charitably, as a "first-world problem"—but it would be a mistake to do so. Today, the most valuable data is that collected from wealthier consumers in developed countries, who have readier access to networked information and communications technologies and more consumer surplus to be extracted. Additionally, among less privileged consumers and in less developed nations, lower economic resources and literacy levels translate into lower penetration rates for internet use and mobile device ownership. Even so, the future of personal data processing is global. The push to exploit the biopolitical public domain is a contest over a postcolonial terrain, in which global networked elites seek to harness the power of populations worldwide. The drive to explore and colonize the global public domain of personal data has produced a pattern that I will call the postcolonial two-step: initial extensions of surveillance via a two-pronged strategy of policing and development, followed by a step back as the data harvests are consolidated and absorbed.

In some global contexts, data collection and processing initiatives have arisen within the context of policing operations. The bulk communications surveillance programs disclosed by Edward Snowden in 2013 had their origin in an asserted need to combat terrorist threats originating abroad. U.S. military battalions in Afghanistan and Iraq have used portable fingerprinting devices to gather biometric data from individuals suspected of ties to insurgency or simply seeking access to U.S. installations, and some Latin American countries have begun using electronic access cards and biometric technologies for policing and security purposes. A special strike force convened within the United States currently uses communications metadata to target drone strikes against suspected terrorist leaders.[40]

Critics of these and other initiatives have argued that they are incompatible with international human rights obligations, and also have stressed the likelihood of "mission creep" into domestic policing and deployment against vulnerable and minority populations. Both history and recent events suggest that those fears are well founded. Historian Alfred McCoy has documented the U.S. military's use of the Philippines as a test bed for surveillance techniques that subsequently migrated to the United States via the army's newly formed Military Intelligence Division during the years surrounding World War I.[41] In the post-9/11 environment, biometric identification first of noncitizens and subsequently of citizens has become an increasingly routine part of crossing the U.S. border; more recently, a number of state and local police departments have begun programs for biometric identification of suspects using facial recognition technologies trained on databases of driver license photographs.[42] Federal, state, and local law enforcement agencies have conducted prolonged, intrusive surveillance of Muslim and Latino communities, relying on a range of surveillance techniques including algorithmic analysis of communications metadata.[43] As Chapter 8 will discuss in more detail, a notable feature of these and other contemporary policing initiatives is the way they incorporate participation by for-profit providers of surveillance data, techniques, and platforms.

In other global contexts, however, initiatives for personal data collection and processing are framed as development projects aimed at improving the living standards and prospects of the world's least fortunate peoples. In India, the Aadhaar system, which assigns an universal identification (UID) number based on biometric data, was conceived as a way of solving the enormous logistical challenges associated with providing government benefits (such as rice allotments and health services) to a population with high rates of poverty and illiteracy.[44] Other initiatives attempt to use biometric and wireless technologies to compensate for the lack of developed financial and communications infrastructures. For example, in a number of African nations including Nigeria and South Africa, financial institutions are conducting experiments with biometric identification cards that do double duty as banking tools, allowing direct access to various services but also generating streams of information that can be used to develop and market new services.[45] In developing countries around the world, the Facebook Free Basics app supplies mobile handset users with curated lists of websites and services, including Facebook's own newsfeed. Use of those sites and services does not trigger data charges; meanwhile, Facebook collects comprehensive data about users and their activities.[46]

Among scholars and activists, a rich debate has unfolded about whether these initiatives and others like them should be understood as empowering or commodifying.[47] The fairest answer to this question probably is that the evidence is mixed and that it is too early to say for certain. Yet some of the factors that make the impacts of such projects difficult to assess are worth considering carefully. Development of new surveillance infrastructures, such as those for the Aadhaar system, typically is contracted to multinational data processing companies. The terms of those contracts are difficult to discover, and the countries in which such initiatives are sited may lack open-government laws that would force disclosure. As Chapter 1 described, new infrastructures for cashless payment also have deep connections to private finance capital. Facebook does not disclose information about its uses of data extracted via the Free Basics program at all. In addition, developing countries may have rudimentary data protection laws or weak enforcement (or both), and may be under pressure to accede to bilateral or multilateral free trade agreements mandating free flows of data across borders.[48]

The distinctive pattern of the postcolonial two-step also is visible in policing and social welfare initiatives directed at wholly domestic populations within the United States. Felony convicts are subject to mandatory DNA collection, and 28 states and the federal government require DNA collection from felony arrestees. In a decision upholding Maryland's felony arrestee testing law against a constitutional challenge, Supreme Court justices disagreed hotly about both the extent of the privacy interest in DNA and the potential for such laws to become templates for testing obligations directed at other segments of the population.[49] But other biometric identification schemes already are in widespread use to identify recipients of government welfare programs, to conduct background checks of applicants for government jobs and security clearances, to monitor certain categories of temporary visa recipients, and in many other contexts involving vulnerable populations.[50] Meanwhile, new data mining initiatives being developed, with the federal government's blessing, in the education and healthcare contexts are touted for their potential to improve the delivery of public services and funding.[51]

Both globally and domestically, important questions remain about the trajectories of data flows for policing and data flows for development, and about the relationships between the two kinds of data flows. Other questions concern the relationships between data collection efforts directed at favored and disfavored populations. Different kinds of surveillance generate different kinds of data streams, and the differences can lead to adverse inferences when the data flows are combined. To take one example, some U.S. cities and states—colloquially known as "ban the box" jurisdictions—prohibit employers from asking job applicants about their arrest and imprisonment histories, but the information may be readily available from commercial sources, and the presence or absence of certain other kinds of data (for example, unexplained gaps in debit or credit card purchase history) can obviate the need to ask. Platform differences also shape "ordinary" commercial surveillance practice. Both domestically and abroad, those of lower economic means are more likely to use smartphones for all of their internet access, and data collection via mobile devices is less transparent and less easily customized.[52] The potential of relatively inexpensive mobile platforms to foster economic development and social inclusion is celebrated in the international development literature, but data collected from and about vulnerable populations also can be put to other, less salutary uses.

Secrecy as Enclosure

For both commentators and lawmakers, perhaps the most noteworthy attribute of the personal data economy has been its secrecy, which frustrates the most basic efforts to understand how the internet search, social networking, and consumer finance industries sort and categorize individual consumers.[53] The secrecy imperative overrides even official demands to produce information about data extraction practices and related agreements. In 2014, a Senate committee seeking to discover information about industry structure and contracting practices found itself effectively stonewalled as three of the nine largest data brokers in the country politely refused to answer questions about their data sources and their customers; the remaining six made voluminous submissions about their data sources and products but did not provide specific detail about their contract terms, their data processing techniques, or the extent to which they enforce policies assertedly put in place to protect consumers against abuse.[54] In enforcement proceedings before the FTC and in hearings before Congress, the dominant platform firms have pursued a strategy of deliberate obfuscation about the data flows that they collect, deflecting questions with vague and general responses and claiming inability to locate requested documents.[55]

In the context of the biopolitical public domain's productive logics, however, secrecy performs a function that is straightforward: Realizing the profit potential of commercial surveillance activity requires practices that mark data flows with indicia of ownership. The networks of secret agreements that constitute markets for personal data and information derived from it are acts of enclosure that complement the user-facing techniques explored in Chapter 1. They represent strategies for perfecting the appropriation of valuable resources from the (imagined) common.

In recent years, intellectual property scholars have invoked enclosure metaphorically to characterize legislative extensions of intellectual property rights, most notably copyright term extension intended to delay passage of copyrighted works into the public domain. So used, the term traces its origin to the Enclosure Movement in seventeenth century Britain, during which wealthy landholders erected physical fences to assert their control and ownership of common lands formerly used for grazing, hunting, and passage.[56] Inspired by that work, surveillance theorist Mark Andrejevic uses "digital enclosure" to denote the pervasive informational exposure that occurs within commercial surveillance environments and the consequent loss of control over self-articulation. Both uses of the metaphor situate acts of enclosure on a grand scale as a way of underscoring their connections to economic and political power.[57]

But enclosure as a strategy also proceeds on a level that is more small-bore and ordinary than contemporary usage suggests. Information-related transactions routinely involve strategic uses of contractually mandated secrecy. In particular, although intellectual property theory places "facts" permanently in the public domain, intellectual property practice traditionally has recognized a need for gap-filling protection in certain industries, and has looked to trade secrecy and contract law to fulfill that need. Participants in data-intensive industries, including both platforms and data brokers, routinely deploy trade secrecy law and contract to achieve a measure of exclusive control over the data that they collect. As we saw in Chapter 1, such practices of contractual enclosure are both strategic and performative: they simultaneously consummate processes of data appropriation and constitute those processes as lawful and foreordained.

Strategic uses of secrecy by platforms and data brokers also underscore the difference between public domain and commons as resource governance strategies. Governance as commons entails rules for maintaining a resource as open to community members. It also may involve rules imposing duties to use the resource sustainably and sanctions for abusing the privilege of membership.[58] Advocates for scientific and nonprofit research uses of collected personal data have sometimes argued (or have been happy to concede) that such collections should be governed as commons and that membership should be subject to various data protection obligations.[59] The public domain framing entails no comparable set of obligations; it functions and is intended to function as a backdrop for appropriation and private profit-seeking activity. Put differently, although the new information capitalists have worked hard to construct the sociotechnical conditions for the biopolitical public domain, they have not done this so all could share equally in its fruits. The race to harvest and profit from the public domain of personal data is intensely contested.

In short, the networks of secret agreements that characterize the emerging personal data industry, and that have frustrated observers seeking to map data flows and uses more precisely, are entirely intelligible within the discourses of property and intellectual property law. They work to establish quasi-property entitlements enforceable against competitors in the event of misappropriation and against counterparties in the event of breach. They represent strategies through which resources extracted from the biopolitical public domain are made to function as marketable assets and as sources of competitive advantage.

From Raw to Cooked: A Political Economy of Patterns and Predictions

As it mobilizes sociotechnical activity to facilitate extraction and enclosure, the idea of a public domain of personal data also frames an approach to knowledge production that underwrites the processing of personal data on an industrial scale. That process begins with a set of conventions for cultivating and collecting personal data, within which the data to be collected are posited as "raw" even when they are elicited in carefully standardized fashion. Cultivated and extracted data enter an industrial production process during which they are refined to generate data doubles—information templates for generating patterns and predictions that can be used to optimize both online and physical environments around desired patterns of attention and behavior. Data doubles are not marketed individually, but rather in groups with similar behavioral and risk characteristics; the participants in the data economy trade in people the way one might trade in commodity or currency futures. The new data refineries—and especially the dominant platforms that have reconstituted data markets around their own protocols for intermediation and legibility—infuse the data flows extracted from people with an epistemology optimized for surplus extraction. At the same time, they mark their operations and outputs with indicia of legal privilege. The public domain construct supports those processes from beginning to end.

Data Cultivars

In press releases, marketing materials, and other public statements, data brokers and platform firms frame the data harvested from individual users of networked information and communications technologies as raw streams of observation that are parsed, enhanced, and systematized through their own productive labor. Thus, for example, Acxiom (now LiveRamp) promises "meticulous data cleansing," while Oracle describes its "DaaS for Social" service as providing "categorization and enrichment of unstructured social and enterprise data." Less specifically but more famously, Google's self-proclaimed mission is "to organize the world's information and make it universally accessible and useful."[60]

In scholarly and policy communities, the "raw data" framing has generated considerable pushback. Scholars who study information systems argue that the "raw data" framing is not, and never could be, entirely accurate. Inevitably, data collection activities are structured by basic judgments about what to collect, what units of measurement to use, and what formats and metadata will be used to store and tag the data that are collected.[61] That is true of data gathered in disciplines far removed from personal data processing, such as geology and oceanography, and it is also true of data collected from and about people. For example, the decision to collect information about patterns of attention in automated gambling environments or patterns of "social reading" in platform environments, and to collect that information in a particular way, imposes a structure of sorts on the resulting data set.[62]

In theory, at least, the new, data-driven surveillance processes do differ importantly from earlier forms of commercial surveillance in terms of the way that flows of data are collected and processed. Scholars have long criticized the use of artificial categories to sort and segment populations of consumers, but new data mining techniques that emphasize pattern recognition and behavioral forecasting can move well beyond predefined categories.[63] In addition, because such techniques can combine and synthesize heterogeneous data sets, an analyst looking for patterns is not constrained to search only in the ways for which any single data set is coded. Some legal scholars argue that the inherent dynamism of data mining for pattern recognition and prediction undercuts the traditional scholarly narrative of surveillance as imposing an artificial and often invidious discipline.[64]

Particularly in light of the processes described earlier in this chapter, however, it is equally inaccurate to say that the data collected for processing just happen to be there. The flexible and adaptive techniques used within contemporary surveillance environments are—and are designed to be—productive of particular types of information. An algorithm for pattern detection may be formally agnostic about the content of a user's preferences—say, for burgers or sushi, for golf or bowling, for *Game of Thrones* or *ESPN College Football*, for scientifically vetted information about climate change projections or other narratives framing climate change as a conspiracy propagated by mainstream media and liberal elites—but it is not agnostic as to the kinds of information it collects and produces.

The technologies of the sensing net are designed to modulate surveillant attention, offering options tailored to what is known or inferred about data subjects' habits, beliefs, and inclinations. As social psychologist Shoshana Zuboff explains, that goal demands ever more detailed behavioral patterning. To achieve maximum accuracy and minimum uncertainty, the sensing net must plumb the depths of users' experiences, interpreting minute behavioral cues to ferret out underlying cognitive and emotional patterns.[65] To achieve maximum yield, the sensing net must keep users logged in and responsive to its harvesting mechanisms. As designers of mobile interfaces, social networking environments, and their embedded apps work to maximize opportunities for behavioral data extraction, research on the pathways of addiction has become an explicit lodestar.[66]

Processes of data extraction within the sensing net are also and importantly participatory. Platform-based, massively intermediated environments enable people seeking connection with each other to signal their affinities and inclinations using forms of shorthand—"Like," "Follow," "Retweet," and so on—that simultaneously enable data capture and extraction.[67] Sometimes, processes of technologically intermediated signaling also call upon individual consumers to sort themselves into more definite categories by selecting various descriptors or categories—for example, "Professional," "Alumni," "Engaged," "Female Seeking Male," "Social Drinker"— informed by analysts' and marketers' sense of the types of patterns they are seeking.

Techniques for participatory data extraction are intended to cultivate habits of self-identification in a very particular way. In Scott Lash's formulation, these processes represent power becoming ontological: power expressed not through hegemonic control of meaning but rather through techniques for making the crowd known to itself.[68] They constitute the subjects of data-driven surveillance as knowing agents who attain freedom through a focused and purposeful—and often playful—consumerism that incorporates continual, automatic self-documentation. To the extent that self-sorting requires sets of choices within structured fields, it also effects a partial return to a more rigid patterning, undercutting the characterization of predictive analytics as protean and dynamic.

As these processes operate, they generate new informational byproducts that are themselves artifacts of the patterns with which their designers are concerned. The processes of harvesting and culling "raw" consumer personal data resemble the harvesting of raw materials within an industrial system of agriculture. Just as agriculture on an industrial scale demands grain varieties suited to being grown and harvested industrially, so the collection of personal data on an industrial scale inevitably adopts an active, curatorial stance regarding the items to be gathered.[69] Strains of information are selected and cultivated precisely for their durability and commercial value within a set of information processing operations. The data are both raw and cultivated, both real and highly artificial.

Data Refineries

After personal data have been cultivated and harvested, they are processed to generate patterns and predictions about data subjects' preferences and behaviors. Like the data extraction and contracting practices discussed previously, the data processing practices of platform firms and data brokers also are shrouded in secrecy.[70] Here again, however, one does not need access to the technical details in order to understand the role that such processes play within the imagined narrative of the biopolitical public domain. Within the political economy of informational capitalism, sites for large-scale, automated processing of data flows extracted from people function as information-age refineries, converting those flows into the forms best suited for exploitation on an industrial scale.

Investigations of systems for automated, predictive processing of personal data through the lenses of privacy and data protection law typically have criticized such systems for offering artificial and instrumental forms of personalization based on externally determined logics. I have offered that characterization in my own work and have no quarrel with it. Modulation of surveillant attention is both a mode of privacy invasion and a mode of social control; it seeks "to produce tractable, predictable citizen-consumers whose preferred modes of both consumption and self-determination play out along predictable and profit-generating trajectories."[71] It therefore has profound implications both for individuals pursuing self-determination and for society more generally.

Even when scholarly critics of personal data processing focus on its larger social welfare implications, however, the view from privacy scholarship remains one that is both informed and limited by an individualistic frame of reference. Rights, including privacy and data protection rights, are tautologically individualistic, and scholarly preoccupation with the relationship between privacy and social shaping also testifies powerfully to anxiety about subjectivity's absence. The new data refineries, in contrast, operate on an entirely different scale. The agribusinesss model again supplies a useful analogy: the processing of data flows extracted from people within contemporary data refineries is comparable to the milling of corn and wheat to generate stable, uniform byproducts optimized for industrial food production.[72] Data refineries refine and massage flows of personal data to produce virtual representations—data doubles—optimized for modulating human behavior systematically.

Data doubles correlate to identifiable, flesh-and-blood human beings—they are sets of data that derive from and pertain to particular individuals and that can be used to simulate individual behavior at a very high level of granularity—but their function within the emerging political economy of personal information is to subsume individual variation, idiosyncrasy, and self-awareness within a probabilistic and radically behaviorist gradient. Their purpose is to make human behaviors and revealed preferences calculable, predictable, and profitable *in aggregate*. As long as that project is effective on its own terms—an outcome that can be measured in hit rates or revenue increments—partial (or even complete) misalignments at the individual level are irrelevant. (Despite glowing rhetoric about the promise of personalization in the digital era, we saw in Chapter 1 that this approach owes as much to Nielsen as it does to Page and Brin; the idea of analyzing current and target markets using demographic analysis reflects the influence of advertising models that are decades old.)

Data doubles are, in other words, biopolitical in character: they are designed to enable the statistical construction, management of, and trade in populations. The idea of biopolitics more typically has been articulated in contexts involving the overt assertion of state power—thus, for example, when the government establishes performance metrics for allocating special education resources to some schoolchildren but not others, or when it promulgates standards for ideal body mass and recommended nutrition, we can identify a kind of biopolitical power at work.[73] Yet it has become equally important to trace the emergence and articulation of biopolitical power in contexts where state authority plays a more general and constitutive role in constructing the conditions of possibility for private activity. Data doubles afford a form of aggregated, population-based knowledge that enables participants in the political economy of informational capitalism to engage in "the management of fluctuating processes in an open field."[74] Indeed, in the era of ascendant neoliberal governmentality, it is data refineries' very privateness that gives their outputs normative and epistemological authority.[75]

Within the political economy of informational capitalism, the data refinery is a centrally important means of economic production. Its principal functions include not only knowledge production but also—and perhaps more importantly—data productivity. It promises new ways of making the data flows extracted from people economically productive within the framework of a capitalist political economy. That framing in turn suggests the importance of studying markets for the outputs of data refineries as markets—that is, as sites of economic exchange with concrete institutional manifestations.

Consider the agribusiness analogy again: Corn can be milled directly into flour for human consumption, but most of the principal markets for corn are the intermediate and derivative ones—markets for livestock feed and for chemical subcomponents, derived in industrial laboratories, that are used as sweeteners and preservatives.[76] Those markets reflect extraordinary innovation of a sort, but they also operate to conceal the extent of our dependence on monoculture and to entrench that monoculture in ways that make addressing its external effects on human and environmental health extremely difficult. In similar fashion, data doubles have given rise to complex, derivative products traded in specialized markets with institutional lives of their own.

Data Markets

Understanding the markets for the outputs of data refineries requires probing beyond the economist's very general definition of a market as an economic system in which pricing and allocation of goods and services are determined as a result of the aggregate of exchanges between participants, without central direction or control. That definition treats the market mechanism as a black box; it begs both the question of what might come to qualify as a good or service and that of how transactions might be made intelligible as exchanges. And it ignores entirely the question of supervening organizational logics imposed by the platforms within which data markets are increasingly embedded. An adequate description of the origins and operation of emerging markets in personal data requires investigation of precisely those questions.

As a general, abstract matter, markets are institutional structures for calculated exchanges. As elaborated by sociologists Michel Callon and Fabian Muniesa, that concise definition has three principal parts: First, a functioning market requires a subject matter that is capable of being valued so that it can be traded. Put differently, the subject matter traded in markets must be conceived as a "calculable good": a good detached from its context in a way that enables it to be objectified, manipulated, and valued.[77] Because calculable goods must be marketed to prospective buyers, buyers participate in that process, whether by serving as audiences for marketing campaigns or more actively by providing feedback or other input.

Second, a functioning market requires a widely distributed "calculative agency": a framework that mobilizes calculative power using a set of common techniques and methods. For example, the supermarket system of price labels, barcode scanners, and coupons and the online system of a virtual "shopping cart," cookies for state management, and promotion codes or loyalty discounts both embed forms of calculative agency that enable the distributed valuation of calculable goods. Calculative agency may be distributed asymmetrically—consumers, for example, do not play an active role in determining the price of shampoo, but do participate in its purchase and in the consumption of advertising that positions shampoo as a desirable purchase.[78]

Third, a functioning market requires a commonly understood institutional structure within which exchanges can occur. The institutional structure must be capable of bringing would-be participants together and enabling them to engage in what Callon and Muniesa call a "calculated encounter": an encounter generally mediated by distributed, materially embedded techniques and practices that all parties understand as transactional.[79] Thus, for example, the procedures followed on the trading floor of the New York Stock Exchange, in Japanese tuna markets, and in the Amazon. com online marketplace each command unquestioned, deeply embedded assent as ways of ordering distribution and allocation.[80]

Although the terms and conditions of business-to-business transactions over the data refinery's inputs and outputs have proved astonishingly difficult to locate and bring into the light of day, the multibillion-dollar trade in the byproducts of personal data processing speaks volumes about the emergence of each of these institutional components. To understand the process by which calculable goods are defined in markets served by the new data refineries, however, we must contend with two sets of complications, one hermeneutic and one organizational.

First, although it is customary in public-facing rhetoric about personal data collection and processing to refer to data subjects as individuals with singular wants and needs—and therefore to position them as the consumers whose desires are being served—that framing misdescribes the uses to which data doubles are put. The data-driven, predictive operations of the data refinery produce tranches of data doubles with probabilistically determined behavioral profiles. Businesses and other organizations of all sorts can then purchase different forms of access to those tranches as inputs (refined materials) to their own production processes.[81] Notably, Callon and Muniesa use the frame of singular wants and needs to denote not actual personalization but rather the performance of personalization via marketing strategy. In their terminology, marketers seek to "singularize" goods for consumers, and often may do so by appealing to ideals of individualization.[82] Public-facing rhetoric about personal data harvesting and processing is most usefully understood in an analogous way, as an example of marketing-speak designed to encourage enrollment in the services that make up the sensing net (we will delve more deeply into such enrollment strategies in Chapter 3).

Behind the public-facing rhetoric about individualization and personalization, the data refinery's operators offer services that operate on populations. Generally speaking, those services advance two distinct but complementary types of profit-making strategies. One strategy identifies groups of high-value consumers as targets for surplus extraction by platform firms, data brokers, and their customers, including advertisers of all sorts but also employers, app developers, and others.[83] The other facilitates surplus extraction strategies optimized for riskier groups of consumers. For example, a principal cause of the 2008 financial crisis was risky subprime lending to high-risk buyers, and predatory lenders used tranches of data doubles to identify and target vulnerable populations.[84] As described in Chapter 1, the Dodd-Frank Act and implementing regulations established new, tighter standards for residential mortgage lending, but the use of data-driven predictive profiling to facilitate targeted risk-taking is gaining ground in other credit-related markets.[85] Together, strategies for targeting high-value and high-risk consumer pools offer powerful new formulas for market segmentation. Using the information supplied by the new data refineries, marketers can position their goods and services for target populations of consumers more effectively—and, in the process, can choose to target different offers to consumers with different profiles or to exclude consumers viewed as undesirable from viewing their offers at all.[86]

Second, the theory of markets as institutional structures for calculated exchanges predates the era of dominant information platforms, so it does not contend with the emergence of the platform as the core organizational logic of informational capitalism. As we saw in Chapter 1, platform-based, massively intermediated environments increasingly have colonized and rematerialized markets, placing themselves, their protocols for information exchange, their proprietary algorithms, and their massive computing resources at the center of a wide and growing variety of activities. Tellingly, major data brokers are now attempting to follow suit, rebranding themselves as platforms for specialized services—so, for example, LiveRamp (formerly Acxiom) now holds itself out as an "identity platform" for "powering the people-based marketing revolution."[87] Platforms are data refineries given specific material and institutional form. The most dominant platforms enjoy direct access to vast populations of data subjects and have exploited that access to develop extractive relationships with seemingly limitless scope.

In sum, data markets are markets for calculated exchanges over tranches of data doubles derived probabilistically via behavioral patterning, and the calculable goods at the center of those exchanges are not the data doubles themselves but rather access to particular pools of data doubles constructed for particular purposes. The calculative agency required to power the exchanges consists of special-purpose frameworks for digital advertising, "customer relations management," "identity resolution," human resources management, and the like, and those frameworks increasingly are embedded in and structured by platform protocols.

Consuming Consumers

Scholarly investigations of techniques for processing personal data tend to frame the construction and manipulation of data doubles as knowledge production processes with secondary economic and legal-institutional implications, rather than as economic and legal-institutional processes with secondary knowledge production implications.[88] Those critiques are trenchant, and yet there is an important way in which they miss the point. The data refinery is only secondarily an apparatus for producing knowledge; it is principally an apparatus for producing wealth. It facilitates new and unprecedented surplus extraction strategies within which data flows extracted from people—and, by extension, people themselves—are commodity inputs, valuable only insofar as their choices and behaviors can be monetized.

The overriding goal of data refineries and data markets is not understanding but rather predictability in pursuit of profit. Data refineries are designed to offer powerful, high-speed techniques for matching populations with particular strategies calibrated for surplus extraction. The techniques operate on "raw" personal data to produce "refined" data doubles and use the data doubles to generate preemptive nudges that, when well executed, operate as self-fulfilling prophecies, eliciting the patterns of behavior, content consumption, and content sharing already judged most likely to occur.[89] Such operations have a very particular economic purpose: They work to maintain and stabilize the available pool of consumer surplus so that it may be more reliably identified and easily extracted.

By virtue of their widening control over the sensing net's endpoints and the processes of data extraction and appropriation that occur there, the dominant platform-based purveyors of search, social networking, and connectivity enjoy correspondingly great control over the design and implementation of data-driven surplus extraction strategies. From the consumer perspective, the results of such processes in platform-based, massively intermediated environments may appear as reductions in search and transaction costs. Those strategies, however, have ripple effects on other market and social institutions, and indeed that is exactly their point. Both the material logics of data extraction and appropriation discussed earlier in this chapter and the epistemological logics of data cultivation and processing operate to submerge important exchange-related features of transactions and relationships in business-to-consumer markets. They produce calculated exchanges that are increasingly etiolated and social processes that are increasingly colonized by privatized data flows.[90]

This description of the personal data economy, which posits users of networked information and communications technologies as resources to be themselves cultivated, processed, and consumed, has a science fiction quality to it, and yet within intellectual property circles its form is entirely commonplace. In 1984, John Moore sued the Regents of the University of California and a UCLA doctor who had treated his leukemia for conversion, or wrongful appropriation of his personal property. The property identified in his complaint was his cancerous spleen, which had been removed from his body and used to develop a valuable, patented cell line. The lawsuit reached the California Supreme Court, which rejected Moore's conversion theory on the ground that diseased tissue removed from the human body could not be the subject of a property interest (though it allowed Moore to maintain an action for failure of informed consent).[91] Among lawyers, the *Moore* opinion is famous. It is routinely included in first-year property casebooks, where it stands for the principle that anti-commodification values can (sometimes) prevent the propertization of human tissue.

The *Moore* court, however, did not hold that human tissue could not be the subject of any proprietary claims; rather, it contrasted Moore's claim to that of the research scientists who had labored to develop the patentable byproduct. And, even as it took for granted the wisdom of granting patents on medical research byproducts, it worried fretfully about the costs to innovation of allowing proprietary claims to the raw materials used in medical research.[92] In short, the court's famous anti-commodification opinion articulated a powerful *logic of productive appropriation* that rendered Moore's asserted right to control the disposition of resources extracted from his body simply incoherent.

One can trace a similar elaboration of relative privilege and disentitlement in the evolving debates about data harvesting, processing, and use. Data brokers proudly tout their "unprecedented," "proprietary," and sometimes "patented" analytic techniques, while platform firms boast of their massive computing power and the cutting-edge algorithms that power their search engines, ad placement services, and newsfeeds.[93] Claims such as those situate ownership of personal data at the heart of the data refinery, vesting it in those who (supposedly) create value where none previously existed. They work to create and perpetuate a narrative of romantic authorship that unfolds in counterpoint to that of the public domain, and that is old and familiar.[94] Other narratives about innovative exploitation of the biopolitical public domain locate romance in the technologies themselves—in their power to find patterns, unlock new sources of competitive advantage, and enable new strategies for surplus extraction and accumulation—and that power is at its most romantic when its reach is most sweeping.[95] As we will see in Chapter 3, romantic narratives about data processing as innovation also do powerful normative work in political and regulatory arenas.

In short, there is more at stake here than a new model of knowledge production. The idea of a public domain of personal data alters the legal status of the inputs to and outputs of personal data processing. Its animating logic of productive appropriation is relational and distributive: it both suggests and legitimates a pattern of appropriation by some, with economic and political consequences for others.

The Power of Appropriative Privilege

The idea of a public domain of personal data sets in motion a familiar and powerful legal and economic just-so story. As it justifies the pervasive redesign of networked environments for data harvesting and positions the new data refineries as sites of legal privilege, it naturalizes practices of appropriation by information platforms and data brokers. It subtly and durably reconfigures the legal and economic playing field, making effective regulation of its constituent activities more difficult to imagine.

One of the Hohfeldian framework's most important lessons is that legal privilege does not exist in a vacuum. It is always-already relative, entailing disempowerment on the part of someone else.[96] In the case of the biopolitical public domain, users of networked information and communications technologies have no right to contest the harvesting of their data, no right to fully informed participation in the proprietary knowledge production processes of the new data refineries, and no right to contest the preemptive superimposition of predictions derived from data doubles upon their activities, their social and emotional lives, and their aspirations.

For individuals and communities, the change in status from users and consumers to resources is foundational. The problem is not simply that the biopolitical public domain facilitates commodification (though it does) or that it enables discrimination (though it does that too), but more fundamentally that it subordinates considerations of human well-being and human self-determination to the priorities and values of powerful economic actors. The legal-institutional construct of the biopolitical public domain alienates consumers from their own data as an economic resource and from their own preferences and reservation prices as potentially equalizing factors in economic transactions. The emerging system of data-driven predictive profiling is designed to strip away opportunities for bargaining and arbitrage, producing a set of wholly nontransparent exchange institutions that reconfigure demand to match supply. It seeks, in wholly unironic fashion, a commercial future in which consumer surplus is extracted "from each according to his ability" while goods and services flow "to each according to his [manufactured] needs."[97]

The systemic implications of pervasive data harvesting and predictive profiling are equally profound. Reimagining consumer markets as sites of unilateral technosocial sorting undermines both their utility as markets and their legitimacy as decentralized governance processes. At least according to theory, in a capitalist society, market transactions function as an essential mode of governance. The conception of the biopolitical public domain expressed by the commercial surveillance economy is a hierarchical conception that sits in fundamental tension with the market-libertarian ideal. Despite the popularity of transactional consent as a frame for neoliberal policy discourse, the surveillance economy leaves consent—and, for that matter, volition—with very little work to do.

As we are about to see next, the sensing net and the data refinery have also catalyzed systemic changes in the operation of networked digital media ecologies. Those changes too have inspired new forms of legal-institutional entrepreneurship by the actors that they benefit.

3

The Information Laboratory

So what I told you was true ... from a certain point of view.
Obi-Wan Kenobi in *Star Wars, Episode VI: Return of the Jedi* (1983)

The emergence of the platform as the core organizational logic of the networked information economy and the accompanying proliferation of infrastructures for data harvesting and predictive profiling have profoundly reshaped both patterns of information flow and capabilities for participation in social and commercial life. The changes upend settled ways of understanding the nature and social function of media technologies—and challenge conventional wisdom about the appropriate roles(s) for law in relation to media and information.

For several hundred years, political philosophers and legal theorists have conceptualized media technologies as "technologies of freedom," arguing that access to information and to the means of communication promotes reason, self-determination, and democratic self-government.[1] Some things about that equation have not changed; certainly, access to information, self-determination, and democratic self-government are inescapably interrelated. But aspects of the interrelationship have changed beyond recognition. As communications theorist Mark Andrejevic explains, our most deeply rooted instincts about the role of information in a democratic society "took shape during an era of relative information scarcity," and so many defining political battles "revolve[d] around issues of scarcity and the restriction of access to information."[2] Today's networked digital information infrastructures have different and more complicated affordances. In the contemporary era of *infoglut*—of "an unimaginably unmanageable flow of mediated information ... available to anyone with Internet access"—new political and epistemological dilemmas flow instead from abundance and algorithmic intermediation.[3] The problem is not scarcity but rather the need for new ways of cutting through the clutter, and the re-siting of power within platforms, databases, and algorithms means that meaning is easily manipulated.

As the volume of information available online has mushroomed, the quest for data-intensive surplus extraction described in Chapter 2 has spurred development of a fast-evolving collection of techniques designed to undercut the exercise of informed reason by users of networked information services. Contemporary, platform-based information infrastructures and ecosystems are being optimized to detect behavioral cues and to appeal to motivation and emotion on a subconscious level. That gradual but seemingly inexorable shift has begun to produce object lessons in the law of unintended consequences. Widespread harvesting of personal data has engendered new patterns of reputational anxiety, manipulation, and insecurity. Algorithmically mediated processes designed to create tight stimulus-response feedback loops have exposed and deepened social divides on a variety of cultural and political issues, reinforced the power of conspiracy theories and junk science, and amplified toxic currents of bigotry, nationalism, and ideological extremism.

Debates about *how law should respond* to the emergence of massively intermediated media environments have generated more heat than light. Many accomplished and well-meaning observers misread contemporary media ecologies, applying time-tested syllogisms about media freedom, reasoned public discourse, and rational self-determination to situations for which they are no longer well suited. Meanwhile, powerful information-economy actors have mobilized new kinds of arguments about freedom of expression to stave off protective regulation and deflect accountability for both old and new kinds of harm. Those arguments give the traditional First Amendment metaphor of a "marketplace of ideas" a modern and distinctly neoliberalized inflection, positing a virtuous alignment between economic and expressive liberty. They also introduce a powerful new metaphoric frame—that of the information laboratory, a site of beneficial and constitutionally privileged innovation and experimentation that functions as a depoliticized engine of truth production. Meanwhile, a combination of expertly fanned anxiety about censorship and exquisitely calibrated political gamesmanship about what constitutes noninterference with freedom of expression works to foreclose discussion of viable (and speech-regarding) alternative pathways. The result of those efforts is a growing constellation of de jure and de facto legal immunities that predominantly bolsters private economic power, that magnifies the vulnerability of ordinary citizens to manipulation, exploitation, and political disempowerment, and that threatens profound collective harm.

The Emergent Limbic Media System

It is useful to begin by exploring patterns of information flow within the platform-based, massively intermediated information environment. As we saw in Chapter 2, the construct of the biopolitical public domain and its accompanying logic of productive appropriation have both catalyzed and justified large-scale sociotechnical shifts toward datafication, data harvesting, and the construction of powerful new data refineries. But Chapter 2 did not delve deeply into questions about the *kinds* of data that information businesses collect or the *mechanisms* by which algorithmic intermediation operates on the data to produce results. This section takes up those questions. Both to structure the discussion and by way of provocation, I offer the following analogy: The operation of the digital information environment has begun to mimic the operation of the collection of brain structures that mid-twentieth-century neurologists christened the limbic system and that play vital roles in a number of precognitive functions, including emotion, motivation, and habit-formation.[4]

I do not mean to suggest that anything about the configuration or operation of the digital information environment is natural or organically determined. I seek simply to focus the reader's attention on the mismatch between the "technologies of freedom" frame that dominates legal discussions about media law and policy and the kinds of responses that platform-based, massively intermediated information infrastructures work to produce. By design and as operated, the emergent limbic media system supplies the information laboratory with responsive experimental subjects.

Rather than predominantly stimulating the development and exercise of conscious and deliberate reason, today's networked information flows are optimized to produce what social psychologist Shoshana Zuboff calls instrumentarian power: They employ a radical behaviorist approach to human psychology to mobilize and reinforce patterns of motivation, cognition, and behavior that operate on automatic, near-instinctual levels and that may be manipulated instrumentally.[5] To similar effect, but focusing on the subjects of datafication, legal philosopher Mireille Hildebrandt traces the emergence of a new form of "data-driven agency" that is "mindless," algorithmically mediated, and constituted by "ubiquitous anticipation."[6] The result is an emergent form of collective consciousness that is primed for precognitive activation and manipulation at scale. To an extent, that reflects deliberate design, but experiments in data-driven, algorithmic intermediation also have proved powerful in ways their designers likely did not intend or expect. They portend far-reaching collateral effects on the emerging information society and the subjects who inhabit it.

Reputation as Capital and Stigma

An important forerunner of the emergence of data-driven agency was the gradual reinvention of digital reputation as both an explicit locus of self-management and a distributed mechanism for behavior modification. As twentieth-century sociologist Erving Goffman documented, self-presentation is an enduring human concern. Individuals have always devoted time to reputation work of one sort or another, building, cementing, and sometimes undermining their standing in their communities.[7] In the networked information age, however, reputation has become increasingly quantified and datafied, and reputational data and metrics are widely dispersed, flowing through channels far removed from individual control. As those shifts have occurred, the mechanisms for building and maintaining reputational capital and attempting to repair reputational damage have changed almost beyond recognition.[8]

Today's quantified, datafied reputation metrics trace their origins to two mid-twentieth-century developments. The first, discussed in Chapter 2, was the emergence of the consumer reporting industry. The types of socially mediated, inherently local judgments about reputation that historically had guided credit and employment decisions could not perform that function well in an increasingly urbanized, national economy, and so practices of reputation assessment began to evolve to meet changing needs.[9] The earliest consumer reporting entities were simply clearinghouses for collection and exchange of the sorts of information traditionally monitored by local lenders—salary, repayment history, and so on. As the volume of information mushroomed and as technological development produced new methods for storing and processing the information, market actors began to experiment with more efficient ways of formulating and expressing judgments about consumer creditworthiness and reliability. Those efforts led ultimately to metrics for quantified credit scoring.[10]

Consumer reputation scoring was initially the province of a small, specialized group of initiates, but that is no longer the case. To participate in reputation scoring markets, one needs both computing resources and access to flows of relevant information. The revolution in processing power that began during the late twentieth century, and that continues today with the development of cloud-based data processing services, has put the necessary computing resources within general reach. And, as we saw in Chapter 2, the emergence of networked information architectures and the reconfiguration of those architectures to enable pervasive tracking and data harvesting have made flows of personal data ubiquitous and easy to capture. The relevance of those flows to predictive scoring is both an article of faith and the foundation of a multibillion-dollar industry. Today, consumer reputation metrics include a wide range of correlations, inferences, and predictions generated by data mining and analysis.[11]

Another historical precursor of contemporary quantified, datafied reputation metrics was the ratings systems developed during the mid-twentieth century to demystify markets in consumer goods and services. As mass-marketed goods and services increasingly displaced more local options, and as those goods and services became increasingly more complex and difficult for consumers to evaluate at the point of purchase, ratings systems such as those developed by *Consumer Reports* and *Good Housekeeping* emerged.[12] Those systems, often consisting of simple, 5-point scales for communicating the results of more complicated product testing, are the conceptual antecedents of the customer satisfaction ratings that today are seemingly everywhere. Like credit scoring, however, ratings production is no longer the sole province of trained experts. Many contemporary ratings systems claim a different kind of epistemic authority, located in the personal experiences of consuming subjects. Information businesses—including both general-purpose platforms such as Google and Yelp and specialized sites such as TripAdvisor and OpenTable—compete with each other to develop crowd-sourced ratings and present them to consumers as valuable sources of information.

Within platform-based information environments, the ratings craze has spread beyond businesses and products to individuals themselves. An early pioneer in this regard was eBay, which developed the first widely publicized system for aggregating user feedback on buyers and sellers. Contemporaneously, news and information sites such as Slashdot began using feedback systems to help users make sense of the rapidly proliferating participatory universe. Slashdot designed its interface both to push more highly rated comments to the top and to identify those users whose postings tended to be rated more highly.[13] Both models spread rapidly to other platform-based commercial and discussion fora, which developed variants suited to their own purposes. Sites as varied as Twitter, Reddit, and Amazon all rely heavily on both crowd-sourced content and data designed to enable participating users to evaluate the value of contributions by other participating users. Meanwhile, computer scientists and legal academics have gravitated to the idea of crowd-sourced, peer-produced ratings as a panacea for a wide variety of social coordination problems ranging from driving to dating.[14]

Both the personal data used for consumer reputation scoring and publicly available reputation metrics are increasingly widely dispersed, and that has made network users vulnerable to new kinds of reputational harm. Crowd-sourced ratings systems and similar participation metrics are expressly designed to enable reputation-at-a-distance and to allow users to dispense with the need for repeat interaction before forming judgments. For exactly those reasons, though, such systems create new possibilities for abuse ranging from self-interested gaming to targeted sabotage.[15] The consequences of the latter can be especially drastic for individuals and small businesses, which may lack both the resources to counter sabotage campaigns and the reputational security to ignore them. The design and operation of social networking platforms also magnifies reputational vulnerability. Although in recent years social networking platforms such as Facebook have allowed users to indicate their preferences about sharing certain items and about identification and tagging in photos posted by others, it is impossible to prevent information posted to a social network from spreading beyond its point of origin.

Neither the growing importance of datafied reputational constructs nor the new vulnerabilities they generate have been lost on network users. Literatures from marketing to self-help to media studies reflect the emergence of an acutely reputation-inflected sensibility of self-presentation. Social media updates, for example, are less spontaneous and more carefully curated to accentuate the positive and enviable. Younger, "born digital" network users in particular have developed and internalized elaborate rules of self-presentation.[16] Many older users, meanwhile, cultivate techniques of online reputation building that are highly instrumentalized, straightforwardly acknowledging that their point is to craft reputation as a factor of production. In part, that approach reflects the changing nature of production in the dematerialized, platform-based labor markets described in Chapter 1. Self-promotion is an essential survival skill for freelance information workers, and new data-based metrics of reputation—numbers of followers on Twitter or Instagram, number of views on YouTube, and so on—matter for success. It has become common to see self-proclaimed experts on self-management and self-promotion tutoring their readers on the best ways of maximizing and refining their own public exposure.[17]

The paradoxical combination of heightened reputational sensibility and diminished control over reputational development creates and feeds a continual need for reputational maintenance and repair.[18] Predictably, maintenance and repair themselves have become business models. One model, euphemistically titled "search engine optimization" (SEO) has emerged to serve the needs of both individuals and businesses seeking to burnish their public images and improve their visibility. Another, dedicated to credit monitoring and credit repair, responds to the prevalence of credit fraud and identity theft by offering individuals the promise of protection for a small monthly fee.[19]

Although the language of reputation management and self-management is the language of individual choice, the new economies of reputation and reputation modeling distribute reputational authority and vulnerability unevenly. Information about reputation is plentiful, but decoding and effective intervention require specialized expertise. The technologies of curation and repair that offer to return some measure of control also change the nature of that control. Prior to the era of datafied, dispersed reputation, repairing damaged commercial and social reputation demanded sustained relational and communal engagement. The new processes of curation and repair substitute an individualized, commodified vision of reputation management as a market-centered activity pursued by individual neoliberal subjects.

Surveillance as Play and Self-Betterment

Techniques for motivating enrollment and participation in the surveillance economy also have contributed importantly to the emergence of data-driven, instrumentarian power and the formation of data-driven agency. Within commercial surveillance environments, the themes of play, games, and participation are increasingly prominent. The forms of play and gaming are highly organized and strategic and revolve around the idea of gamification, defined in business texts as the application of concepts and techniques from games to drive consumer "engagement" that promotes business objectives in other areas of activity.[20] In gamified commercial surveillance environments, personal data collected from subscribers—both at enrollment and on a continual basis during the course of play—are used both to deliver rewards and to engage in various forms of targeted marketing.

FourSquare, a social networking application used for sharing information about one's whereabouts, is generally credited with popularizing the idea of gamification as a data collection technique. For the first four years of its existence, FourSquare offered subscribers opportunities to compete for rewards, which took the form of badges that might designate a subscriber "Mayor" of her favorite bar (for being a regular visitor) or "Player Please" (for checking into the bar with three or more members of the opposite sex). The success of that initial experiment inspired a broad and durable marketplace shift. For example, discount fashion retailer H&M, in partnership with an online gaming company, has used gamification to bring customers off the street and into its stores, offering those who are playing the game items that can be scanned in the store to generate discounts. Nike+, a personal fitness tool, uses gamification to help its users set fitness goals, monitor their own progress, and track their progress relative to that of other users.

As these examples illustrate, the gamification of commercial surveillance has roots in customer loyalty programs that are decades old, but gamification rewards customer loyalty in ways that generate public, social recognition. The field of crowd-sourced promotion its own cautionary tales. Facebook's ill-fated Beacon service, which automatically coopted its members' social updates as promotion tools, sparked outrage that led to high-profile class action litigation.[21] Contrast, however, the experience of gamified promotion ventures that are shopping-oriented first and foremost. Groupon, a social shopping site, uses gamification—in the form of an anthropomorphic icon named "Clicky" that entices users to pursue access to additional content and exclusive discounts—to incentivize bargain-hunters to visit the site more frequently. Groupon's early success can be traced to its founders' recognition that customers could absorb producer surplus and reveal information about their resources, their patterns of discretionary spending, and their social networks at the same time. After settling the Beacon litigation, Facebook used its newly developed "Like" button to similar (but far more wide-ranging) effect.[22]

The gamification of commercial surveillance environments also has roots in the Quantified Self (QS) movement, which was founded in 2007 by a group of technology evangelists seeking better living through data. The initial impetus behind the QS movement was aggressively populist. QS entrepreneurs and communities offered participants the opportunity to shift control of health, diet, and fitness away from impersonal providers offering cookie-cutter recommendations and back toward individuals, and promised to keep participants' data safe within walled gardens.[23] Predictably, however, commercial providers of QS technologies and applications entered the field, offering services like the Nike+ fitness tracker described previously. As they have done so, the dialogue around QS has shifted, de-emphasizing control over data and emphasizing instead the need to provide and share data to gain tools for controlling other aspects of one's life, including health, diet, and fitness, but also work habits, sex life, sleep patterns, and so on. Where the populist QS discourse was earnest and geeky, commercial QS products speak to lifestyle concerns in the language of marketing.[24]

Gamified surveillance environments are not games, but they are like games. They manifest both actions taken by the subject of gamified surveillance to perform the in-world rituals of gameplay—for example, to unlock benefits or "level up" membership—and background machine actions that establish the environment for gameplay—for example, the repetitive background displays of status updates from other users or ticker updates offering a continual stream of discount opportunities. They also establish an external frame of reference for the gameworld—for example, by establishing a process for enrollment, defining tiers of membership and corresponding benefits, and imposing "gamic death" upon logout.[25] But there are also profound differences between games and gamified surveillance environments. The gameworld purports to be the social world, or some segment of it, but its focus is on targeting and nudging patterns of discretionary spending and leisure mobility. Gamification techniques reconfigure their participants as depoliticized subjects who achieve both self-expression and self-realization through the purposive and playful exercise of consumptive freedom.[26]

Gamified surveillance environments therefore constitute powerful mechanisms for behavioral conditioning. The "token economies" characteristic of gamified surveillance environments have been used as a form of behaviorist therapy for psychiatric patients, preparing them for reintegration into society by giving them sets of situation-specific rituals to perform.[27] In commercial surveillance environments, gamification takes on a similarly ameliorative gloss, inculcating repetitive behavior patterns oriented toward self-betterment. As Jennifer Whitson describes it, "becoming the victorious subject of gamification is a never-ending leveling-up process, guided by a teleology of constant and continual improvement, driven by an unending stream of positive feedback and virtual rewards, and fuelled by the notion that this process is playful."[28]

Like the sublimation of consent, discussed in Chapter 2, gamification is a technique for supply chain management that works to keep the surveillance economy's data harvesting pipelines full and flowing. Its rapid spread reflects by the same financialization dynamics that Chapter 1 explored. FourSquare emerged as social networking platforms were migrating into the economic mainstream and seeking sources of financing in capital markets. Its use of rewards as incentives for participants was both a strategy for achieving market penetration and a way of responding to potential investors' demands for a plausible revenue model. Foursquare is also a cautionary tale, because its gamification strategy proved unable to hold subscriber interest over the longer term, and in 2013 it announced that it was abandoning its badge system.[29] Different and more durable examples of gamification within social networking platforms are the unending competition for followers, favorites, and retweets on Twitter and for followers and likes on Facebook and Instagram.

While Foursquare's badge system proved in the end to be a passing fad, on Twitter, Facebook, and Instagram the rewards leverage a more intrinsic motivation for recognition and influence.

Recall from Chapter 2, moreover, that the user interfaces that mediate access to gamified surveillance environments also are designed with behavioral conditioning in mind. Both the dominant platforms that sit atop data harvesting ecologies and lesser designers of app-based services rely on insights gleaned from addiction research to maximize users' "time on device."[30] More time on device means more data, and more data translate into a wider range of potential surplus extraction opportunities.

The Rise of Behavioral Microtargeting

The newest commercial surveillance techniques are designed to bypass individual awareness altogether, detecting behavioral cues and using them to target precisely calibrated flows of promotional, informational, and cultural content. From one perspective, such activities are broadly consistent with marketing's decades-long effort to claim for itself the status of a behavioral science.[31] From another, techniques for behavioral microtargeting represent radical departures from the traditional marketing canon. As Zuboff describes, today's cutting-edge behavioral surveillance techniques trace their origins to two sets of mid-twentieth-century research initiatives: one in experimental social psychology that was predicated on absolute denial of the possibility of free will, and another on the behavior of animal herds that emphasized behavioral "tuning" to modulate group behavior in desired ways.[32] As applied to human beings, such techniques eschew persuasion in favor of direct behavioral conditioning, and they target not only consumptive preferences but also cultural, political, and religious affiliations and even basic frames for scientific, historical, and journalistic understanding.

From the perspective of purveyors of goods and services, behavioral microtargeting responds to the dilemma of abundance that characterizes the contemporary era of infoglut. Strategies for capturing market share using branding and gamification have become both more powerful and more demonstrably incomplete. As we saw in Chapter 1, branding has assumed ever-increasing economic and legal importance in the informational economy. Modern branding is memetic and compelling, exploiting compact, graphically intensive signifiers and catchy slogans and sound bites carefully designed to take root in consumers' subconscious minds.[33] Platform-based media environments enable brands to become even further detached from the goods and services to which they notionally refer and to take on expressive lives of their own. The modern corporation does not simply advertise its wares. It develops a "social media presence" on platforms such as Facebook and Twitter, streaming updates to its followers about developments that might implicate its market or enhance its brand cachet, and uses social media to recruit certain types of consumers as brand evangelists. And, as we have just seen, it uses gamification strategies in an attempt to capture and hold consumers' attention.

Ultimately, however, brand-related strategies for consumer surplus extraction confront inherent limitations. First, consumers are not simply passive recipients of brand-related messaging. Some simply resist brand-related messaging, while others appropriate and remix logos, jingles, and other promotional material to subvert such messaging in powerful and creative ways.[34] The same platform-based media infrastructures that enable businesses to reach consumers also enable consumers to assign new meanings to brands and advertising copy and distribute their own messages widely. Second, even highly effective brand-related messaging must contend with the condition of infoglut, which makes even those messages that (some) consumers want to receive difficult to distinguish from the millions of other pieces of information competing for their attention. As David Murakami Wood and Kirstie Ball have explained, even the more certain access to consumer preferences that databases combining demographic information with information about buying behavior appeared to promise is in important respects a mirage; like other techniques of governance, the constructed "brandscapes" informed by such databases remain "messy, contingent, and subject to failure."[35]

Techniques for behavioral surveillance and microtargeting promise solutions to these problems. Chapter 2 traced the emergence of the sensing net as a distributed assemblage for harvesting vast quantities of behavioral data for industrial-scale refinement, analysis, and deployment. From a behaviorist standpoint, unmediated behavioral data—data that are not self-reported or otherwise subject to conscious manipulation by data subjects—are the holy grail, promising previously unequaled accuracy in predictive forecasting and commensurate levels of profit. That logic dictates continuous experimentation with methods for sensing, measuring, and modeling consumer interests, affinities, and aversions.

Like gamification, behavioral microtargeting is not the exclusive province of platform firms and data brokers. As Joseph Turow has described, supermarkets in particular have been pioneers in the use of techniques for tracking consumers' progress through physical stores and correlating patterns of movement and browsing with coupons and personalized discount offers.[36] The siren song of behavioral microtargeting also has attracted a wide and varied assortment of academic researchers focused on improving the state of the art. Burgeoning literatures in marketing, psychology, and data science describe new research programs designed to test the efficacy of existing microtargeting techniques and develop new ones.[37]

Within platform-based, massively intermediated environments, however, techniques for behavioral surveillance and microtargeting have opened vast new horizons of opportunity, furthering the intertwined platform strategies of intermediation and legibility that Chapter 1 described. Both dominant platform firms such as Amazon, Facebook, and Google and smaller, more specialized entities are continually experimenting with techniques designed to detect and record the minutest of pauses on a page view or news item or the movements of a cursor hovering over a link, creating detailed simulacra of attention patterns and inferred personality traits that can be folded into existing systems for algorithmic intermediation.[38] Other new microtargeting initiatives deployed within platform-based environments attempt to detect users' mental and emotional states and personalize promotional messages accordingly. Facebook in particular has acknowledged conducting various experiments involving use of linguistic analysis to detect users' emotional states.[39]

Meanwhile, providers of online content have pursued methods of competing for attention and mindshare that harness both the insights of behavioral psychology and the properties of network organization. The reigning method of content optimization for user engagement, pioneered by the founders of sites such as BuzzFeed and UpWorthy, involves a technique colloquially known as clickbait—"a style of headline that explicitly tease[s] readers, withholding just enough information to titillate them into reading further."[40] According to behavioral psychologists, clickbait exploits a nearly universal human dislike of being uninformed about something that everyone else already knows. Users will engage with the content by clicking through the headline in order not to be left out of the loop, and they will share what they find with their networks as a way of signaling inclusion to others.[41]

Like so much else in the online environment, the emphasis on content optimization for engagement reflects the importance of digital advertising revenues. Page views and clicks generate revenues, and when users share an item with others in their social networks, it may begin to spread virally, eliciting more page views and more clicks. In the wake of platform-driven cycles of consolidation and retrenchment in the print media industry, even long-established outlets for news and commentary now rely on services such as Chartbeat, a platform for tracking clicks, likes, and retweets, to help them refine their abilities to drive Web traffic. One result is that media outlets of all types increasingly rush to cover the same topics, lean heavily on techniques for manufacturing instant outrage, and frame their appeals for attention in the same breathless, you-won't-believe-what-happened-next tone.[42]

Platform-based providers of search, content aggregation, and social networking services operate at the intersection of behavioral microtargeting and content optimization for engagement. So, for example, Google's search engine uses behavioral cues together with its accumulated wealth of data about users to anticipate the type of content users want to find and adjust both autocomplete recommendations and search results accordingly.[43] Its content aggregation platform YouTube uses similar information to target video content; social networking providers such as Facebook and microblogging platforms such as Twitter function as de facto aggregators for a wide range of content and deliver feeds optimized to everything that is known or inferred about particular users' opinions and beliefs. By design, all of those algorithms incorporate feedback effects, and so their operation both reflects and continually reinforces the powerful economic motivation to pursue viral spread. That is where the law of unintended consequences kicks in. Within platform-based, massively intermediated environments, the digital unconscious becomes a device for manipulating and activating subjectivity at scale. Platform-based intermediation alters collective behavior in ways that have begun to produce large-scale societal effects.[44]

Amplifying Collective Unreason

Some of the most transformative effects of networked, platform-based media infrastructures concern the ways that they alter and amplify the capabilities and behaviors of groups. Networked, platform-based architectures enhance the ability to form groups and share information among members, to harness the wisdom and creativity of crowds, and to coalesce in passionate, powerful mobs. They also, however, magnify the dark side of each of those forms of affiliation, collective meaning-making, and collective action. In particular, the spread of behavioral surveillance techniques into the domains of search and content distribution has produced powerful affordances for volatility, polarization, and public unreason.

Platform-based digital infrastructures' affordances for collective meaning-making are widely recognized. Just as networked digital platforms have lowered the costs of identifying and connecting with commercial counterparties, they also have lowered the costs of forming affinity groups of all kinds. Platform users can more easily find and connect with others who share their hobbies, their political affiliations, their identity perspectives, their affiliations with real-world communities (such as neighborhood or parent-teacher associations), and so on. Like their counterparts in real space, online affinity groups provide friendship, intellectual and emotional affirmation, and shared organizational capacity. Unlike their real space counterparts, online affinity groups can extend over great distances and also can bridge other kinds of divides, connecting many who otherwise would not have met. The internet era has witnessed the emergence of a vast, diverse, and eclectic range of peer-based cultural production, ranging from open source software developed according to the maxim "given enough eyeballs, all bugs are shallow" to wikis and fanworks reflecting multiple contributions.[45] Search engines and crowd sourcing sites exploit the "wisdom of crowds," basing judgments about relevance and importance on the searching, linking, and upvoting behavior of millions of users.[46]

Platform-based digital infrastructures also both facilitate collective action and enable new forms of collective action. The landscape of networked collective action encompasses everything from spontaneous flash mobs to social action campaigns coordinated via Facebook pages, Twitter hashtags, and reddits to digital infrastructures for facilitating both traditional charitable giving and new types of "pay-it-forward" generosity. Networked information and communication technologies also have enabled rapid organization of mass protests, such as those mobilized by the Occupy Wall Street and Black Lives Matter movements and by pro-democracy activists during the political uprisings of the Arab Spring.[47]

The dominant cultural narratives about these cultural and political effects of platform-based interconnection have been celebratory, but other implications of the platform-based digital environment's affordances for collective meaning-making and collective action are less rosy. Distributed communities of peers have created and sustained thriving exchanges for malware and stolen personal information, as well as robust and seemingly impermeable alternate realities rooted in misinformation, junk science, and virulent forms of ideological extremism. Crowd-based judgments about the relevance, credibility, and urgency of online information can create cascades that lend sensationalized, false, and hatred-inciting online material extraordinary staying power, and those cascades can engender behaviors that cause both private and social harms.[48]

Platform-based, massively intermediated environments both expose and intensify political and ideological polarization around multiple, assertedly equivalent truths. Cultural and ideological polarization themselves are not new phenomena; in fact, social scientists who study political polarization have found that the percentages of Americans holding sharply opposing views on major political and cultural issues have remained fairly constant over the decades. What has changed is that percentages of respondents reporting strongly negative feelings about those with opposing views have skyrocketed.[49] That result stands in jarring contradiction to the utopianism of the early internet pioneers, who assumed that expanded access to information online would usher in a new era of cosmopolitanism and enlightened tolerance. Platform-based intermediation promotes cosmopolitanism only to those users already inclined in that direction; to other users, it promotes other values.

A wealth of social science research shows that more homogenous groups—whether online or off—more readily become polarized in both their beliefs and their perceptions of reality. Algorithmic mediation of information flows intended to target controversial material to receptive audiences intensifies in-group effects, reinforcing existing biases, inculcating resistance to facts that contradict preferred narratives, and encouraging demonization and abuse of those who hold opposite beliefs and political goals. People do encounter other perspectives online, but exposure to opposing views is more likely to trigger automatic, instinctual rejection and anger than it is to promote reasoned engagement.[50] And platform affordances for volatility, engagement around sensationalized content, and ideological polarization have fueled the emergence of a vast alternative media ecosystem organized around conspiracist theorizing and hyperpartisan political outrage.[51]

Relatedly, platform-based information feeds flatten communicative hierarchies in a way that underscores the relative unimportance of claims to objective and/or empirical authority. A Facebook or Twitter feed, for example, presents the reader with a continuous stream of content within which all sources appear to be equivalent. That diminishes the privileged position once held by the three major broadcast networks and by national newspapers of record and invites both relativization and rejection of the possibility of objectivity; "all so-called experts are biased, any account partial, all conclusions the result of an arbitrary and premature closure of the debate."[52] Relativization fortifies alternate realities such as climate change denialism and anti-vaccination narratives and the echo chambers that support them. Relativization and infoglut also generate new types of power asymmetries that revolve around differential access to data and to the ability to capture, store, and process it on a massive scale. Under such conditions, techniques of critique and deconstruction increasingly become tools of powerful interests seeking to advance their own agendas.[53]

Platform affordances for cascade-based diffusion, polarization, and relativization are easily manipulated and weaponized. As is now widely known, in the months preceding the 2016 U.S. presidential election, websites peddling "fake news" stories—such as allegations that Democratic candidate Hillary Clinton and her campaign manager, John Podesta, were running a child pornography ring out of the basement of a Washington, DC, pizza restaurant—earned their distributors millions of dollars in advertising revenues. According to their own statements, some distributors had no particular political axe to grind, but instead were simply circulating content carefully designed to earn the clicks, views, shares, and retweets that generate advertising revenue. Other stories were sponsored by hostile state actors, and still others were sponsored by wealthy and highly motivated domestic interests seeking to reinforce and widen existing partisan divides. As they had hoped, groups predisposed to believe the worst of Clinton and her team shared, upvoted, and retweeted the stories.[54] Experts in election law and digital voting, watching carefully for signs of fraudulent tampering with digital voting machines, were unprepared for new kinds of digital disinformation and misinformation that took aim directly at voters' minds. Arguably, however, no one should have been surprised; the weeks leading up to both the earlier "Brexit" vote in the United Kingdom and the 2014 Russian incursions into Ukraine had followed similar patterns.[55]

Platform affordances also have fueled upsurges in ethnic nationalism, ideological extremism, identity-based harassment, and mob aggression. Affordances for networked collective action enable the rapid, ad hoc formation of angry, vengeful mobs, eager to shame real or apparent transgressors. Pioneering work by Danielle Citron in law and by Whitney Phillips in media studies explores the ways that networked, massively intermediated spaces reinforce and magnify the power of crowds to target selected individuals and groups. Women and members of racial, religious, and sexual minorities are especially frequent targets of crowd-sourced hate and intimidation.[56] More generally, investigations by multiple teams of researchers have explored the ways that platform-based, massively intermediated environments amplify bigotry and hate, intensify narratives about threats to national, racial, and religious purity, and propel coded memes into the limelight.[57] As a result of its increasing ubiquity and its algorithmically mediated normalization, nativist and white supremacist hate-mongering bleeds inexorably into political discourse and public life. The pro-Brexit vote was influenced in part by narratives about the cultural and economic consequences of uncontrolled migration, and similar themes continue to shape elections and political debates across Europe and the United States. Activists affiliated with extremist movements have adopted cutting-edge content targeting techniques and sophisticated and ironic modes of outreach, and those efforts have gradually but inexorably shifted the tenor of public discourse, gaining in strength as outraged responses generate new information cascades and bringing bigotry and xenophobia into the mainstream.[58]

The increasingly unreasoning and often vicious character of interaction in online, platform-based digital environments complicates accounts of the democratizing potential of information networks. Networked, platform-based information and communication technologies are crowd-enhancers; they boost the amplitude of collective actions and counter-actions. Undeniably, such technologies have important affordances for bottom-up organizing, collective creativity, and crowd-sourced, democratic action. Collective meaning-making and collective action, however, can be directed toward a variety of ends. The particular configurations that networked information technologies have assumed within the political economy of informational capitalism also make them sites of extraordinary divisiveness and manipulability, creating new risks to the human project of democratic, inclusive, sustainable coexistence. Accounts of the promise or peril of networked communication and production have tended to downplay one or the other face of networked communication and collective action, but—at least for the present—the two are inextricably linked.

Can't Touch This: The Unbearable Lightness of Intermediation

As the platform-based, massively intermediated information environment has evolved toward ever-greater efficiency as a tool for behavioral and cognitive conditioning, powerful information-economy actors have worked to craft narratives that make unaccountability for certain types of information harms seem logical, inevitable, and right. One important narrative mobilizes the idea of innovation to clothe commercial information processing operations in a presumption of virtue. The discourse of information processing as innovation signals an important shift in the political economy of surveillance: the emergence of a *surveillance-innovation complex* within which advances in information processing are privileged for their own sake and regulatory oversight is systematically marginalized.

Two other important narratives mobilize the idea of freedom of expression to imbue information processing and data-driven, algorithmic intermediation with constitutional privilege. During the closing decades of the twentieth century, businesses of all sorts began to appropriate and repurpose the strand of the

U.S. First Amendment tradition that characterizes the public sphere as a *market-place of ideas* to support robust anti-regulatory narratives that encompass a wide range of information-related activities. Information businesses have continued and expanded upon those efforts, and they also have begun to develop a new metaphoric frame that positions the networked information and communications environment as a depoliticized, self-regulating apparatus for truth production—an *information laboratory* that is, and should be, untouchable by protective regulation. Those efforts have proceeded in almost willful disregard of the fact that the networked digital information environment is neither neutral nor self-regulating, and they have catalyzed tectonic shifts in relations of accountability.

Within the Hohfeldian framework of entitlements and disentitlements with which this part of the book is concerned, the developments chronicled here are most aptly characterized as emergent legal immunities and correlative disabilities. Legal scholars exploring the meaning of the immunity-disability dyad have tended to focus on questions about the accountability of government actors.[59] In the networked information economy, at least, that approach is too hasty. Law entrenches informational immunity and correlative disability not only when it constrains or empowers the state, but also when it alters the legal relationships between private parties. We will see in this section that the intertwined *logics of innovative and expressive immunity* underwrite broad regimes of de jure and de facto insulation from accountability for internet intermediaries and other information businesses. They also deeply infuse the ongoing dialogues among policymakers and academics about the appropriate extent of accountability for information harms.

Innovation Jumps the Shark

Our story begins with a concerted effort by information businesses to recast discourses about information processing and its potential benefits and harms as discourses about innovation and the type of regulatory environment that it requires. In government proceedings and in the popular press, the information processing industries have worked to position innovation and protective regulation as intractably opposed. That strategy has produced a discursive process that infuses "innovation" with a particular, contingent meaning linked to economic liberty and the absence of government oversight.

Over the past decade or so, in proceedings convened by the Federal Trade Commission (FTC), the Department of Commerce, and the White House, in the debates that preceded the replacement of the European Data Protection Directive with the General Data Protection Regulation, and in ongoing discussions about the prospects for new U.S. legislation, members of the information processing industries—including platform firms, data brokers, and others—have advanced a carefully crafted narrative organized around the themes of innovation and deregulation. Urging that "data-driven innovation can only occur if laws encourage use and reuse of data,"[60] they have argued that "industry self-regulation is flexible and can adapt to rapid changes in technology and consumer expectations, whereas legislation and government regulation can stifle innovation."[61] The rhetoric of freely flowing innovation as the lifeblood of the economy, and of regulation as its enemy, has been taken up by the libertarian think tanks and technology blogs, whose contributors work to offset what they view as alarmist narratives about the extent of commercial surveillance.[62] Meanwhile, commentators concerned to preserve the full range of potential benefits from future information processing—whatever those may be—worry that rights to withdraw one's data from databases or curtail uses of one's data, if widely exercised, would compromise the utility of those databases as resources for pattern identification.[63]

Implicit in rhetoric linking innovation with deregulation is a conception of innovation as an autonomous and inevitably beneficial process that is the natural result of human liberty. Importantly, that conception is relatively invulnerable to the standard science studies critique of public debates about technology policy, for it does not depend on deterministic assumptions about the inevitable, linear nature of scientific and technical progress. In the early twenty-first century, the idea of technological development as autonomous has been thoroughly debunked. Instead, both industry leaders and policymakers speak the language of diffusion studies, which emphasizes all of the contingent factors that can affect the market uptake of technological developments.[64] The understanding of diffusion studies that is current in business and regulatory circles, however, is a specifically market-centered one, and it puts a different kind of autonomy in play, which resides in the market itself. According to that understanding, invention may be historically and technologically contingent, but innovation is not. Innovations rise to the top of the pack as a result of the choices of self-interested actors, catalyzing a continual and inherently depoliticized process of social and economic betterment. And if innovation is autonomous, then what is produced is what should be produced. Regulators can only get in the way, and when they do we are all worse off, so they should not meddle.

Regulators, for their part, have responded to the rhetoric of autonomous, market-centered innovation by embracing the concept of a balance between two opposing goods. While rejecting the premise that regulation should simply defer to innovation in the digital era, they have accepted the more general proposition that privacy and innovation are in tension, and have turned back to conceptions of choice and consent as offering a way out of the resulting dilemma. In a series of reports expressly framing the privacy-innovation relationship as one of conflict, they have argued that a predictable legal framework for privacy protection is necessary to create user trust and foster the right climate for market acceptance.[65] U.S. regulators and diplomats have worked to soften the European Commission's regulatory stance on data protection, articulating justifications in which the theme of innovation is uppermost.[66]

The view of innovation as both inevitable and riskless is all the more remarkable because it is an anomaly. In the domains of environmental regulation and food and drug regulation, regulatory regimes have long endorsed the precautionary principle, which dictates caution in the face of as-yet-unknown and potentially significant risks. Importantly, rather than stifling "innovation," the precautionary approach is widely recognized as creating incentive effects of its own, encouraging research and development in areas such as clean manufacturing and energy production, safe drug delivery, and the like.[67]

We will return to the problem of how to conduct precautionary regulation of information processing activities in Chapter 6; for now, I simply want to underscore that the understanding of information and information processing as definitionally exempt from precautionary regulation has persisted even as it has become increasingly difficult to maintain. Information processing has jumped the shark, running far ahead of the twentieth-century logic that animates our current, largely hands-off regulatory philosophy. There is mounting evidence about a wide variety of systemic threats created by digital infrastructures optimized for commercial surveillance: threats to the security of data transmission protocols and data reservoirs, predatory pricing and discrimination in markets for financial services and consumer goods, large-scale manipulation of electoral processes, amplification of junk science, organized hate, and virulent nationalism, and a more basic and pervasive corruption of public discourse.[68] As we saw in Chapter 1, the financial transactions that produced the economic bubble of the 2000s and the ensuing global financial collapse were triumphs of complex information processing. Before and after the crash, both financial leaders seeking to avoid regulation and the government officials charged with oversight responsibility invoked "innovation" to justify regulatory restraint.[69]

The rhetoric of information processing as innovation has been particularly powerful in the United States because it both derives from and mobilizes a distinctively American ideology about the power and promise of technology. Scholars such as Vincent Mosco and David Nye have documented the American inclination to believe that technology will subdue unruly nature and usher in an age of transcendent reason. For information industry thought leaders, faith in the "technological sublime" is a powerful motivator, reinforcing virtuous narratives about automated, data-driven surveillance and, for some, informing the confident expectation of a "singularity" waiting in our soon-to-be-realized future.[70] For economists and business scholars, it justifies confidence in a process that economist Joseph Schumpeter termed creative destruction: the sudden emergence of new forms of economic activity that both displace existing incumbents and disrupt the structure of existing markets.[71] For both groups, the way forward is clear: innovate first and clean up the mess (if any) later. (Or, put differently, move fast and break things, and then consider damage control strategies.)

The equation of innovation with economic liberty is not solely an American phenomenon, however. That framing of innovation has won adherents in some of the world's most important developing economies. As we saw in Chapter 2, India is embroiled in a bitter struggle over the future of data harvesting facilitated by the Aadhaar biometric identification system, and proponents of opening the "India Stack" to private innovation have included both multinational corporations and Indian entrepreneurs.[72] As Chapters 7 and 8 will discuss, the global platform firms Tencent and Alibaba are leading exponents of an emerging Chinese brand of informational capitalism characterized by closer and more openly acknowledged public-private partnerships in surveillance and control of information flow. For its part, the European technology sector has produced few firms that can rival their U.S.- and China-based counterparts, and some scholars and policymakers on both sides of the Atlantic have concluded that the European data protection regime is at least partly to blame.[73]

Scholars who study surveillance have worked to draw attention to a surveillance-industrial complex in Western political economy: a symbiotic relationship between state surveillance and private-sector producers of surveillance technologies.[74] The surveillance-industrial complex encompasses a set of essential production relations: for surveillance technologies to be available, they must be produced, and for a market to exist, the technologies must be lawful and sought-after. Politically, however, the idea of a mutually beneficial relation between the state and producers of surveillance technologies has always been problematic, underscoring the degree to which systematic, focused observation of individual activities can threaten fundamental civil liberties. In the era of the "war on terror," support for government information gathering has become widespread, but the view that supervision and transparency are essential to minimizing surveillance abuses is also widely shared across the political spectrum.

The emerging *surveillance-innovation complex* represents a new, politically opportunistic phase of the symbiosis between surveillance and political economy, one that casts surveillance in an unambiguously progressive light and repositions it as a modality of economic growth. The surveillance-innovation complex is far more than a set of production relations. It is also a discursive formation that has as its purpose and effect not simply to legitimate surveillance but more fundamentally to give it sex appeal. Within the surveillance-industrial complex, surveillance is a necessary evil; within the surveillance-innovation complex, it is a force for unalloyed good. The resulting model of surveillance is light, politically nimble, and relatively impervious to regulatory constraint.

From Persuasion to Experimentation

A second strand of the ongoing legal and policy discussion about accountability for information harms involves attempts to constitutionalize data harvesting and processing activities. In recent decades, a campaign has been underway to insulate all forms of commercial information processing from regulatory oversight by invoking the First Amendment's protection for freedom of speech. It has mobilized two powerful metaphoric frames: the familiar conception of the public sphere as a *marketplace of ideas*—a site where the laws of supply and demand produce high-quality information—and a newer conception of the platform-based, massively intermediated public sphere as an *information laboratory*—a site where beneficial experimentation yields new forms of datafied and depoliticized truth.

Historically speaking, a striking aspect of the campaign to constitutionalize all information-related regulation is the relative novelty—even for the United States—of the theory of expressive liberty that it seeks to enshrine. As has been ably chronicled elsewhere, corporate attainment of constitutional personhood did not follow inevitably from constitutional text or history but rather was the fruit of a long and carefully strategized legal and public relations campaign.[75] Even so, for almost two centuries, the First Amendment was considered largely irrelevant to regulation of speech advancing commercial activities because such regulation was understood to be directed fundamentally at commerce rather than at public discourse.

In the late twentieth century, an anti-regulatory agenda refined in law review articles and strategy sessions at libertarian and neoliberal think tanks began to produce a steady stream of First Amendment challenges to regulatory activity.[76] The initial cases challenged regulations targeting various types of complex corporate and professional messaging. They produced what became known as the commercial speech doctrine—a type of intermediate constitutional scrutiny that attempted to strike a balance between protecting speech interests and preserving room for the protective regulation necessary in complex, increasingly informationalized markets.[77] Meanwhile, the various internal information processing activities that firms had begun to undertake—activities afforded by new technologies for computing and data storage—were not on constitutional litigators' radar screens at all. Today, both parts of that equation have changed. The test developed by the courts for evaluating the legitimacy of commercial speech regulation is under sustained assault for being too lenient, and information processing is in the spotlight.

The contemporary First Amendment agenda blends rigid doctrinal logic and entrepreneurial, expansionist expressions of neoliberal governmentality together in a potent cocktail. According to the most widely held definition, "commercial speech" includes only direct-to-consumer communications—communications that "propose a commercial transaction." When other types of corporate information processing activities were not considered speech at all, a narrow definition of commercial speech simply would have excluded them from the First Amendment landscape. If those other activities do count as speech, however, the fact they are not "commercial speech" bolsters arguments for stricter scrutiny of regulations that burden them. In particular, regimes of economic regulation generally begin with scope limitations identifying particular types of content and/or particular actors. Other strands of First Amendment jurisprudence, however, label such distinctions as requiring compelling justification and the narrowest possible tailoring, and that doctrinal structure has enabled arguments for regulatory minimization to find easy points of entry.

The contemporary First Amendment anti-regulatory agenda also relies on a particular, distinctively neoliberal reading of the marketplace-of-ideas metaphor. As originally elaborated by judges and commentators conversant with liberal political theory, the metaphor connoted an arena for deliberate, reasoned exchange, where the ideas on offer could be evaluated on their merits. The neoliberal anti-regulatory reading is more literal: the marketplace of ideas is an arena where the volume and quality of information are—and should be—regulated only by the laws of supply and demand, and where those making decisions about the quality of information function as separate, individual nodes of rationality.[78] So, for example, businesses challenging mandatory disclosure and labeling requirements argue that the government is simply interposing its own opinions about what information consumers ought to want before making marketplace decisions, and businesses challenging regulations on other kinds of information processing argue that the regulations distort the natural and normal operation of the marketplace.

In a notable recent victory for both the campaign to constitutionalize information processing and the neoliberal reading of the marketplace metaphor, a majority of the Supreme Court ruled that a Vermont statute prohibiting pharmaceutical companies' use of prescriber-identifying information for marketing purposes—a practice known as "detailing"—must survive strict scrutiny because the restriction was both content- and speaker-based.[79] The state legislature had enacted the law because it feared that allowing detailers to conduct data mining operations in the state's prescription drug database and use the information to market more costly proprietary drugs would drive up the cost of its Medicaid prescription drug program. The majority, however, saw the state's action as an attempt to undermine the persuasive force of pharmaceutical marketers' speech.[80]

Sorrell, however, also suggests the marketplace metaphor's logical limits. The detailing activities in *Sorrell* targeted physicians rather than their patients, so the issue was not squarely joined, but data-driven targeting is different from persuasion along a critical dimension that has to do with transparency and manipulation. As we saw in Chapter 2, the operative principle behind predictive data processing is the preemptive nudge rather than the reasoned comparison among alternatives, and its point is surplus extraction, pure and simple. Its goal is to minimize the need to persuade by targeting those potential customers most strongly predisposed to buy and crafting appeals based on their habits and predilections. Constitutional challenges to mandatory labeling and disclosure requirements similarly ignore that direct-to-consumer information is pervasively manipulated. Today, even basic consumer products increasingly come with a bewildering amount of information attached—consider, for example, nutrition-related marketing claims and the conflicting recommendations that they engender. In markets for information-related goods and services, and in online marketplaces for goods and services of all sorts, consumer awareness is even easier to manipulate because the purchase interaction can be designed in ways that lead consumers to overlook or minimize crucial terms of the deal.[81]

Platform-based, massively intermediated processes of search, content aggregation, and social networking strain the marketplace metaphor past the breaking point. As this chapter has explained, platform-based environments optimized for behavioral surveillance and microtargeting operate—and are systematically designed to operate—in ways that preclude even the most perceptive and reasonable consumer from evaluating the goods, services, and information on offer. Advertisers use platforms' services precisely to ensure that different users see different offers. Techniques for behavioral microtargeting and content optimization attempt to bypass reason and persuasion altogether—and, as we have also seen, those techniques produce other harmful effects that manifest at scale. At minimum, information businesses are complicit in fostering the information cascades that draw eyeballs and generate ad revenues—and some have been silent partners in fostering the conspiracy theories, extremism, and violence that they officially disclaim.[82]

Unfazed by mounting scrutiny on these issues, platform businesses have worked to recast their pervasive manipulations of the information environment in the service of profit extraction as scientific truth-discovery processes. Platform-based media infrastructures, they argue, are laboratories, in which providers of information services experiment to see which types of information are most useful and most responsive to consumers' needs.[83] So, for example, Google's chief economist has explained that at any given time Google and competing search engines are running millions of experiments on their users, designed to determine how we respond to information so that search results can be optimized.[84] A 2014 paper coauthored by a Facebook data scientist described varying items in users' newsfeeds and then using automated discourse analysis tools on those users' own subsequent posts to gauge the effects of the newsfeeds on their emotional states. When critics decried Facebook's failure to give users prior notice of the experiment, Facebook's defenders pointed out that marketing is inherently a science of experimentation. In a stark demonstration of its own power to influence political processes, Facebook also has acknowledged, and has seemed to expect public approbation for, experimenting with ways of delivering "get out and vote" messages.[85]

The metaphoric frame of the information laboratory appropriates and repurposes the neoliberalized, innovation-centered trope of the surveillance-innovation complex as a constitutional trump. It solidifies the positioning of surveillance as an activity that is virtuous, productive, and therefore rightly exempted from legal and social control. Within the frame of the information laboratory, the fact that online information intermediaries manipulate meaning in ways and for purposes that they do not disclose is of little moment. Similarly, the recent troubling demonstrations that platform-based, massively intermediated media infrastructures have played pivotal roles in fostering and amplifying deeply entrenched political polarization that extends all the way down to bedrock narratives about reality and scientific fact becomes a matter best left to the experts in the white lab coats to sort out.

In short, the information laboratory is a First Amendment metaphor optimized for what platforms do. From Google's description of its mission to "organize the world's information and make it universally accessible and useful" to Mark Zuckerberg's insistence that Facebook represents a space for people to build community and resolve their differences, platform firms' self-descriptions imagine a public sphere continually structured and restructured for optimal utility by enlightened stewards.[86] In those formulations, the platform is the solution to all of the world's information needs, and if it is the solution, it cannot possibly be the problem.

The Most Important Law

Debates about whether and when platform providers and other information intermediaries should be accountable to private plaintiffs for information-related harms are pervasively structured by the logics of innovative and expressive immunity. In the United States, efforts to insulate information intermediaries from liability bore early fruit in section 230 of the Communications Decency Act (CDA), which was enacted as part of the Telecommunications Act of 1996 and granted broad immunity to providers of "interactive computer services" for their roles in distributing speech produced by others. A broad coalition of information businesses and digital civil liberties advocates has worked strenuously to defend that institutional settlement, mobilizing the interlocking frames of the surveillance-innovation complex, the marketplace of ideas, and the information laboratory and downplaying the extent to which intermediaries shape both the content that users see and the contexts within which that content is offered.

After early court decisions in defamation cases against internet access providers suggested a risk of significant liability for an emerging industry that promised to create unprecedented opportunities for both expression and commercial development, early internet intermediaries and their supporters pushed Congress to establish clear rules precluding liability for those merely furnishing conduits or platforms for speech by third parties. Invoking the familiar idea of media technologies as technologies of freedom, they prophesied that a broad grant of immunity would promote both the spread of online commerce and the flowering of public discourse. Sympathetic members of Congress obliged by inserting into a comprehensive telecommunications reform bill language that not only granted information intermediaries immunity for defamatory speech published by others but also extended that immunity well beyond the bounds of existing defamation law to encompass an open-ended group of information-related harms.[87]

The language and legislative history of the CDA showcase both the marketplace and laboratory frames that now dominate debates about information and communications policy—and illustrate their uneasy juxtaposition. The language of section 230—titled "protection for private blocking and screening of offensive material"—expressed the hope that internet access providers, acting as "good Samaritans," would develop and make available to consumers tools for filtering out undesirable content. (As Chapter 4 will discuss, the new law also included an ill-fated attempt to establish broad liability for those directly providing indecent content online.) At the same time, both in the legislative history and in individual statements, members of Congress endorsed the marketplace metaphor as a principal justification for section 230's broad grant of immunity, stating their belief that immunity for infrastructure providers would foster and preserve the emerging network as a vibrant marketplace of ideas.[88] That language framed still-emergent networked information architectures as neutral speech engines that would simply reflect and transmit what people wanted to say. In other words, it implicitly posited the internet as a neutral space lacking the sorts of specific affordances that might themselves shape communicative practices and communicative content, even as the good Samaritan language both invited manipulation and invested it with innovative virtue.

The impact of section 230 on the litigation landscape has been stark. Courts have interpreted the statutory language as eliminating not only traditional publisher liability for defamation but also distributor liability for intermediaries possessing knowledge of falsity and ongoing harm. Today, defamation lawsuits against information platform providers are routinely found to be preempted by the statute, as are many other kinds of claims involving actionable falsity—for example, business tort claims alleging an intermediary's participation in false advertising or unfair competition. In addition, because the statutory language sweeps well beyond defamation in ways that implicate many other types of expressive conduct, it has supplied defenses in lawsuits alleging a wide variety of other harms ranging from discrimination to market manipulation.[89] Although some commentators have questioned whether Congress really intended to grant such broad insulation to a business model whose shape was still unknown, others have criticized the current regime because it does not yield dismissals quickly enough.[90]

Two features of the contemporary debate about intermediary immunity are especially striking. One is the widespread refusal by judges, policymakers, and legal scholars to pay careful attention to what platform-based online intermediaries do. Views about the unassailable rightness of intermediary immunity have solidified even as time and technological change have undermined the presumptions of truth production and technological neutrality that section 230's proponents emphasized. As we saw earlier in this chapter, today's platform-based, massively intermediated information environment has attributes that Congress in 1996 could not have imagined; it is continually manipulated by techniques for detecting and predicting predilections, calibrating commercial and affective appeal, and structuring information feeds accordingly.

Attempts to focus judicial attention on these issues are rapidly hijacked by injured protestations of innocence and expressive virtue. As James Grimmelmann has painstakingly demonstrated, search engines have become adept at insisting on their neutrality for purposes of section 230 even while claiming that their search results are their own constitutionally protected speech.[91] For the most part, courts have uncritically accepted both sets of arguments, concluding both that algorithmic intermediation doesn't make an intermediary a publisher of other people's speech and that the same processes of intermediation are speech-like in their own right. Digital civil liberties organizations, meanwhile, have christened section 230 the internet era's "most important law" and have argued that altering the terms of the balance struck in 1996—near-complete immunity in exchange for voluntary self-oversight—would spell disaster for both freedom of expression and the internet economy. That proposition has commanded broad consensus even among commentators otherwise inclined to be critical of platforms, the speech environments they provide, and their approaches to self-governance.[92]

The second striking feature of the contemporary debate about intermediary immunity concerns the widespread consensus about what intermediary companies are not: they are not "media companies."[93] Intermediaries' continued insistence on that distinction may seem increasingly disingenuous, but it is carefully crafted to maintain a strategic distance between the activities of content provision and data-driven, algorithmic intermediation.

From one perspective, the attempted distinction between a content provider such as Disney, HBO, Fox News, or the *New York Times* and a giant platform provider such as Facebook or Google's YouTube is powerfully anachronistic. Despite the Supreme Court's relatively recent pronouncement that "television networks and major newspapers" are "the most important means of mass communications in modern times," internet platforms play an increasingly important and multifaceted role in structuring the universe of information that people see.[94] For some people, online services long ago eclipsed television networks and major newspapers as information sources. Both the continuing collapse of the print newspaper industry and the continuing dramatic increases in mobile device ownership suggest that the proportion of the population that relies on television and print newspapers for current events coverage will continue to decline.[95] There is also a pervasive interplay between Web-based content and mainstream media content that attempts to distinguish between the two sources of content typically overlook. Many people who rely on traditional news sources also rely on giant platform businesses to serve as news aggregators. Traditional media cover topics that are trending online and use techniques for maximizing user engagement once that coverage migrates back online, and political interest groups seeking to influence mainstream media coverage of particular topics exploit that dynamic for their own purposes.[96]

From another perspective, maintaining a bright-line distinction between content providers and online intermediaries is essential to avoiding closer scrutiny of the ways that data-driven, algorithmic intermediation shapes content. Within the U.S. constitutional tradition, media companies are paradigmatic speakers, and Supreme Court decisions in cases challenging both media and election regulation have positioned ownership of the means of communication as the ultimate touchstone of expressive freedom.[97] Consistent with that orientation, the dominant approach to media regulation holds that technological distribution bottlenecks are the principal obstacles to market entry by new media owners. As the concentrated broadcast markets of the middle twentieth century gave way to more complex infrastructures for cable and satellite distribution, that approach became a recipe for deregulation, and the deregulatory consensus has endured even as consolidation in both local and nationwide media markets has become increasingly pronounced.[98] That might change, however, if public and legislative attention were to focus on intermediated newsfeeds and the distributed sociotechnical systems that enable giant platform firms to control and manipulate them. As things stand, media law and policy in the United States have almost nothing to say about the activities of online intermediaries, and platform firms would like to keep it that way.

So read, the internal contradictions in intermediaries' descriptions of what they are and are not have a very particular purpose. They work to define a new category of information-related activity that consists of non-content-based expression—that is simultaneously in-between users and content (and therefore not content) and useful to users who want content (and therefore expressive). Because its purveyors are not providing content, they are both definitionally exempt from legacy regimes of media regulation and beneath the radar of enterprising regulators who might be seeking to update those regimes. Because what they provide gives the torrent of online information a more definite structure, it can be described as advancing the information laboratory's experimental mission, and it can be named in a way that comports with that mission—as providing both utility and *moderation*.[99] The language of moderation simultaneously proclaims intermediaries' virtue—signaling that they have become the good Samaritans that Congress envisioned—and diverts attention from questions about why flows of online information are *im*moderate to begin with. It therefore represents a significant narrative triumph.

European legal regimes have demanded more from information businesses, but those demands also have presented the opportunity for more intensive and opaque self-regulation of information flows in networked spaces. The evolution of the so-called "right to be forgotten" for data subjects is illustrative. Led by Google, which lost a key decision in the European Court of Justice on delinking of old, potentially damaging information, information businesses bitterly criticized the initial articulations of the right by European jurists and officials. Relying heavily on the frame of the information laboratory as depoliticized truth engine, they characterized takedown requests as efforts to subtract information from the historical record, making the remaining information less authentic and complete. In the media, they also pursued a strategy of widely publicizing the inevitable outrageous requests while barely acknowledging the many legitimate ones.[100] Reading the headlines, one would not understand that both the European Court of Justice and the Commission had clearly articulated the need to consider public interests in freedom of speech and access to information and had carefully distinguished between linking and indexing by search engines and online archiving by originating sites.[101] When the dust settled, though, Google itself had put in place takedown procedures that performed the very same role it had claimed was both impossible and unwise.[102] As Chapter 4 will discuss in more detail, European debates about platforms' roles in the circulation of terrorist and hate speech have begun to follow a similar path.

Identity and Authentication in the Cloud

A final set of emergent informational immunities is de facto rather than de jure, and is more broadly distributed. As an increasing amount of commercial and government activity moves onto the network, providers of networked information services—including information platform businesses but also financial institutions, healthcare providers, retailers, and government agencies—have become custodians of valuable and sensitive personal information. Nearly everyone, whether knowingly or not, is a user of networked services, and poor security for confidential personal information magnifies users' vulnerability to fraud and identity theft. Custodians of sensitive personal information share a common need to protect against both malicious actors and accidental leaks—and common interests in shifting the risks of losses onto consumers and each other. As they have labored to minimize their exposure to direct regulatory oversight, they have developed a common playbook that involves mobilizing the logic of innovative immunity to justify private governance of data risk.

According to both marketers and policymakers, the future of paperless transactions and networked, remotely controlled devices is rosy. Ad campaigns entice consumers to do their banking by phone, to control their home security systems and personal health records remotely, and to rely on networked medical devices to keep their hearts pumping or their insulin at appropriate levels. They promise convenient and fail-safe storage of personal documents and data in the cloud and offer cloud-based computing services as cheap and powerful substitutes for local computing power. In the very near future, we are told, driverless cars will ferry us to our destinations, leaving even more time for productive intangible labor, while driverless trucks and drones will ensure the just-in-time delivery of those physical goods that we still require.[103]

The sunny optimism of ads and policy discussions about the future of the networked informational economy belies a seemingly continuous stream of major data breaches and epidemic levels of fraud and identity theft. For any particular user, vulnerability is a given, and eventual loss seems only a matter of time.[104] Distributed information architectures protect against localized data losses but at the same time create new and unprecedented systemic and personal vulnerabilities. Large data reservoirs make enticing targets, and widespread norms of promiscuous data harvesting and processing undercut incentives to minimize collection and maximize security at the front end.

Information businesses do not dispute the large and growing threats to the security of personal information; they just do not seem to think the law can or should provide much help. Invoking the narrative of the surveillance-innovation complex, they stress the "burdensome" nature of formal legal obligations, insisting that security should be left in the domain of private best practices.[105] A second and related strand in the campaign against legal accountability invokes the concept of acceptable losses; tighter security practices, they argue, would be "wasteful," though the baseline for that determination is left unspecified.[106] A third strand invokes the language of fault and moral responsibility; blameless information providers, we are told, should not be called to account for the criminal acts of third parties.[107] Last, and in ironic tension with the marketplace-of-ideas frame, business interests argue that disclosures about data breaches and system vulnerabilities would be "confusing" to consumers.[108]

Among policymakers and academics, there has been a long-running debate over whether the de facto standard of care for entities holding consumer or citizen personal information can be raised simply by enacting so-called data breach notification laws mandating disclosure of incidents. Proponents of the notification approach maintain that disclosure will enable the market to penalize vendors with poor security practices. Opponents object that that prediction lacks foundation in reality. Consumers' abilities to police the terms of online transactions are extremely limited. Data security in particular is a highly complex dimension of transactions that people enter for other reasons, and security levels are not subject to a la carte variation, so it's hard to imagine that greater disclosure would lead to greater consumer empowerment.[109] Put differently, although information businesses' sudden upsurge of concern about consumer confusion is deeply disingenuous, there is more than a grain of truth to it.

Whether data breach notification laws will "work," however, does not really seem to be the point of debates about whether to enact them. Instead, debates about the power of information in an idealized marketplace of custodial services for personal data distract lawmakers from questions about whether and how to impose more substantive security obligations. Perhaps unsurprisingly, most of the laws that have been enacted are weak. Of the 47 U.S. states that have enacted data breach notification laws, about one-third have afforded consumers a private right of action, but the right of action covers only failure to notify. (Additionally, as we will see in Chapter 5, consumer suits alleging privacy harms face many other hurdles.) Provisions authorizing enforcement by state attorneys general similarly focus narrowly on the problem of adequate notification; none defines substantive security-related obligations that data custodians must meet.[110] Congress so far has not acted at all. In contrast, the European Union's new General Data Protection Regulation adopts both data breach notification requirements and substantive data security obligations, although the content of the latter remains to be determined.[111]

In the United States, the Federal Trade Commission has stepped into the breach, asserting authority to police data security practices as an offshoot of its more general jurisdiction over unfair and deceptive acts and practices in commerce. The FTC's Consumer Protection Division has sought and won a series of high-profile consent decrees establishing commitments to meet industry standard best practices. The National Institute of Standards and Technology has endorsed a data security standard reflecting a composite of industry best practices, and that standard now informs FTC enforcement activity. We will consider those efforts more closely in Chapter 6. Some affected industries, however, have resisted even that relatively relaxed level of oversight, mounting court challenges asserting that the FTC lacks jurisdiction to oversee data security at all.[112]

Financial institutions also have sought to hold retailers to higher standards, but the baseline presumptions of private ordering and private governance of security standards have powerfully shaped the discourse around the kinds of obligations that information businesses reasonably can be expected to assume. New payment provider rules incentivize brick-and-mortar retailers to adopt microchip-based credit card readers by shifting liability to merchants who do not use the technology. As Adam Levitin explains, however, the various interests involved in existing and emerging payment systems markets have principally sought to shape rules about risk allocation in ways that enhance their own competitive position vis-à-vis one another.[113] And financial institutions acting as plaintiffs are poorly placed to vindicate the more significant harms flowing from pervasive insecurity, which concern the loss of control over personal identifiers that are difficult or impossible to change.

The result for consumers is utter powerlessness. Anyone who has ever received a data breach notification and thought about the extent of his or her ability to respond knows that there is very little to be done. The recommended strategy—to double down on the personal information economy by handing over one's personal financial information to a credit monitoring service that will be happy to charge a monthly fee for monitoring accounts and trolling online black markets—does not inspire confidence. Ultimately, the business lobbies are right that debates about security standards are about acceptable losses, but the losses have names and faces. The logics of innovative and expressive immunity dictate a high baseline level of tolerance for human vulnerability in the interest of unfettered commerce.

The Culture of Capture

The interlocking frames of the surveillance-innovation complex, the marketplace of ideas, and the information laboratory express a distinctively neoliberal ideology within which profit-motivated private enterprises are appropriate and morally virtuous guarantors of social progress, expressive liberty, and robust debate about matters of public importance. Over time, that ideology has produced a powerful anti-regulatory force field that affords information businesses an extra layer of insulation against efforts to create new forms of legal accountability. A helpful framework for understanding that force field is the idea of "deep capture," or capture on the level of ideology.[114] The intertwined frames of the information marketplace and the information laboratory have attained the status of ground truths, and the mainstream of thought about optimal public policy has come to reflect their unquestioned rightness.

Scholars who study the relationships between regulators and regulated entities have recognized for some time that morality tales in which regulatory capture proceeds via naked assertions of economic power are far too simple. Generally speaking, regulators understand themselves as acting in the public interest and care about underlying legal and policy narratives of right and obligation. Powerful actors also use their resources to reshape those narratives, however, supplying a range of inputs that include legal arguments, economic models, empirical studies, opinion polls testing public responses to carefully crafted questions, and compelling rhetorical and metaphoric devices for framing descriptions and arguments. Those inputs function as information subsidies, supplying policymakers who have limited resources of their own with ready access to a trove of facts, anecdotes, theories, and narrative frameworks from which to draw.[115] Information-economy actors are no different.

Platform-based information infrastructures have provided unprecedented opportunities for advocacy groups to communicate their visions for a future unencumbered by regulatory meddling directly and simultaneously to policymakers, journalists, and the public. The landscape is busy and complex, characterized by a dense and interlocking network of ties between and among for-profit firms, wealthy individuals, industry trade associations, and ostensibly nonprofit entities with grand- and objective-sounding names.[116] A flood of research output, carefully burnished with a shiny patina of objectivity but of varying quality, circulates continually via press releases and social media, deluging regulators, commentators, and the public in a glut of messaging. Innovation and the deregulatory climate ostensibly necessary to foster and sustain it are popular topics, and claims about autonomous innovation, productive experimentation, and virtuous moderation gain legitimacy in part through their incessant repetition.

Alarmist rhetoric about the downside risks of government intrusion into processes better managed by the private sector also plays an important role in shaping regulatory and public opinion. Consider again the disputes about the scope and wisdom of the statutory immunity afforded by section 230. Another interesting feature of those debates is the stridency of section 230's defenders. Attempts to bring legislative and technological creativity to bear on the increasingly incontrovertible evidence of platform affordances for hate, unreason, harassment, and intimidation are routinely met with carefully tended hysteria about censorship. Libertarian tech policy pundits have trumpeted their alarm about purported attacks on "The Most Important Law about the Internet," painting proposals by thoughtful scholars and commentators as stalking horses for censorship and authoritarian rule. Female proponents of legislation addressing such issues as cyberstalking and revenge porn have come in for particularly scathing ridicule.[117]

A different and more subtle example of the effects of framing on public discourse about information policy is the rise and fall of the "information superhighway" metaphor that dominated information policy discourse in the 1990s and early 2000s. Formerly ubiquitous, the metaphor is now widely mocked as outdated and technically unsophisticated.[118] Yet it invited regulatory scrutiny and oversight in a way that the cloud metaphor does not. To take just one example of a comparison that the superhighway metaphor invites, we don't define passive restraint obligations solely by reference to industry-determined best practices in automotive design or by relying on financial intermediaries to sue automakers for manufacturing and design defects. The cloud metaphor, by contrast, actively resists regulatory oversight; the essence of clouds lies precisely in their ability to evade our grasp.[119] The move to the cloud asserts the primacy of private ordering, and the results are far from ethereal. The vulnerabilities resulting from inadequate security may be informational rather than physical, but they are both real and pervasive.

As these examples suggest, deep capture strategies are concerned not only with results in particular cases but also with crafting and reinforcing master narratives that become deeply internalized, and they do not target only regulators but also cultural influencers, public intellectuals, and academic thought leaders.[120]

Some deep capture strategies, however, have targeted the scholarly community specifically. Google/Alphabet in particular has spent lavishly to fund academic centers and research fellowships; other platform giants, most notably Microsoft, have built affiliated research groups and recruited leading scholars in new media, information studies, and technology studies to staff them.[121] Data-mining company Palantir has constituted a blue-ribbon advisory board composed of prominent privacy scholars while continuing to offer a core suite of products and services designed to give federal, state, and local law enforcement the ability to conduct pervasive, collaborative, long-term dataveillance of populations.[122] More generally, scholars in a variety of fields, but especially in law, public policy, and economics, have eagerly embraced both new platform-based tools for reputation-building and new opportunities funded by technology companies to mingle face-to-face with journalists, public intellectuals, government officials, and prominent entrepreneurs.[123]

In the case of Google/Alphabet, a 2017 scandal involving the firing of the entire competition group at a Google-funded policy think tank made especially clear that the massive outlays in support of policy research do have a few strings attached.[124] Allegations of influence-manufacturing levied by Google's competitors, however, often ring hollow. One recent loudly publicized effort to raise questions about Google's investments in scholarly production fell flat after it was revealed that funding for the initiative had come from a company embroiled in litigation with Google and that the data quality was poor and the allegations of bias unsubstantiated and scattershot.[125] Google is simply very good at a game that is much more widely played, and whose tacit rules and conditions are well understood.

As channels for influencing public and policymaker opinion have proliferated and the quest to become an influencer has intensified—and as the intermingling of academic and corporate-funded information policy research has become more pervasive—the boundaries of scholarship as a category have become correspondingly less clear. Policy interventions in the domain of information policy exist on a continuum that encompasses everything from scholarly books and articles to think-tank-funded books, position papers, and amicus briefs to op-eds and opinion columns to blogs and tweets. Many pieces of legal and economic scholarship in particular are versioned in all of these forms, making it hard to tell where on the continuum and from what stance relative to the policy process they originated.

For their part, scholars who have benefitted personally or institutionally from the largesse of information-economy firms bristle at the suggestion that they might have been co-opted as a result. Their research agendas and opinions, they insist, remain their own. That answer is not wrong so much as it is incomplete. The power of cultural conditioning is deep. Like the divine right of kings in the age of exploration, or like manifest destiny during the westward settlement of the Americas, the logics of innovative and expressive immunity are fast on the way to becoming constitutive ideologies of the economic age. They are both inextricably intertwined with the reigning governmentality and experienced by those invoking them as simply just so.

Law and the Construction of Information Power, Revisited

As patterns of immunity for informational harms have crystallized, they have begun to reflect an increasingly stark imbalance. Information platforms and other information businesses are largely unaccountable for behavioral manipulation, for practices of behavioral microtargeting and content optimization that amplify collective unreason, and for the security vulnerabilities that distributed architectures for data harvesting, storage, and processing engender. Ordinary individuals, meanwhile, are left essentially unprotected against a wide range of very real harms, and processes that have worked for centuries to foster deliberative dialogue and democratic self-government are revealed to be newly fragile and unthinkably vulnerable.

Defenders of free speech at any cost are right to note that throughout history, moral panics about new communication technologies have produced calls for censorship and control. As we are about to see in Chapter 4, that pattern continues today.

But the history of information and communication technologies—like that of other new technologies—is not simply a history of moral panics, legal overcorrections, and heroic libertarian struggles. New sociotechnical relations surrounding communication, participation, and power have both challenged and reinforced economic and political power, and those struggling to define the conditions of information exchange and control have advanced a diverse variety of goals and interests. In the contemporary information economy, the ongoing construction of constitutional, statutory, and de facto immunities for information-processing activities principally benefits powerful economic interests in their quest to construct a device for jacking directly into the volatile and fractious collective id.

The communicative spaces produced by platform-based, massively intermediated information infrastructures are not neutral spaces. They are spaces optimized for eliciting automatic, instinctual reactions and for engendering, amplifying, and exploiting cascade-based diffusion, polarization, and relativization. Public discourse in a democratic society is, and should be, contentious and unruly, but there is also a difference between bending and breaking. Constitutional and policy precepts formulated under different sociotechnical conditions do not automatically port to the conditions that now exist; they must be translated. Conceptual frameworks that begin by defining the problems away do not simply disable courts and policymakers from crafting appropriate forms of regulatory oversight. They make the possibility of finding a different way forward difficult even to imagine.

4

Open Networks and Closed Circuits

Sovereign is he who decides on the exception.
—Carl Schmitt, *Political Theology*

Platforms are not the only powerful entities with interests in shaping flows of information, and logics of intermediation are not the only kinds of logics that networked digital information infrastructures enable. Such infrastructures also offer new possibilities for interrupting and blocking information flows, and those capabilities can be deployed to serve a variety of interests. In particular, both nation-states and digital content providers have sought to impose interdiction obligations on network intermediaries—and network intermediaries have responded to those efforts in ways that leverage and solidify their own operational authority.

This chapter considers the extent to which efforts to optimize networked digital information infrastructures for interdiction and control have begun to coalesce into more definite patterns. One organizing theme for that inquiry is the idea of the exception in political theory. The idea of the exception originates in the tradition of emergency authority. For millennia, legal theorists have reasoned that in true emergencies, including most notably in wartime, the state has some leeway to suspend operation of the ordinary rules and procedures that characterize the rule of law. For twentieth-century political theorist Carl Schmitt, whose theories became key pillars of the National Socialist regime in 1930s Germany, that tradition pointed to an insight about the nature of sovereignty more generally. Schmitt reasoned that because it is the emergency—the state of exception—that legitimates the exercise of absolute power, true sovereignty consists in the power to say when the exception exists.[1] That conclusion profoundly challenged the liberal tradition in political theory, which conceives sovereignty in terms of consent, ordered liberty, and fidelity to the rule of law.

Nominally, the postwar constitutional order has rejected Schmittian theorizing about sovereign power in favor of renewed commitments to constitutionalism and legal process.[2] And yet matters are not quite so simple. The state of exception may be integrated into the legal and political fabric in less obvious ways. As political theorist

Giorgio Agamben argues, some actions are lawlike in form but not in substance; they manifest the bare force of law stripped of the features that give the rule of law legitimacy.[3] For some constitutional theorists, that argument resonates especially well with the narratives about security and control that have emerged in the context of the post-9/11 "war on terror" and aptly describes the new kinds of authoritarian legal structures those narratives are invoked to justify.

In the networked, massively intermediated information environment, the themes of exception and bare force of law also take on a new kind of meaning. Sovereignty consists in the power to say what information will flow and what will not, and the party making that determination need not be a state sovereign at all. As emergent *logics of fiat interdiction* have encountered those of intermediation and legibility, powerful new platform entities have resisted the imposition of formal mandates, seeking arrangements that better serve their own interests. And so a second organizing theme for the discussion in this chapter is that of contest and compromise between competing authorities.

The chapter begins by identifying and exploring the logics that are claimed to justify fiat interdiction of particular kinds of networked information flows. It traces the intertwined development of three themes: threats to public safety, threats to information property, and threats to state authority. In each case, traditional narratives according enforcement imperatives some limited leeway have morphed into expansionist accounts of existential threat that are thought to justify correspondingly broad countermeasures. Those accounts are more than just a series of instrumentalist arguments for drawing legal lines differently. They are efforts to mobilize, cultivate, and normalize systemic reflexes equating (some kinds of) uncontrolled information flow with danger and hard-coded control with safety. Next, the chapter traces the processes by which mechanisms for combating existential threats have begun to crystallize, producing effective lacunae within which absolute authority over information flow is both unaccountable and unquestioned.

Processes of contest and compromise between and among state actors, intellectual property owners, and platform intermediaries have unfolded in a variety of different settings and with varying amounts of publicity, transparency, and public participation. In terms of law on the books, those struggles have produced a still-shifting patchwork of regulatory obligations and political stalemates. In some contexts, the struggles among competing authorities to dictate the terms of the exception have produced institutional settlements that involve strong legal mandates. In particular, contests over intellectual property enforcement and state secrecy have produced versatile, expansionist templates for control of information flow. In other contexts, platform-based, algorithmically mediated "self-regulation" has emerged as the path of least resistance. In tension with the logics of fiat interdiction—but in keeping with the logics of innovative and expressive immunity that Chapter 3 explored— dominant platforms enjoy increasing autonomy to determine for themselves how various enforcement imperatives are met. Meanwhile, logics of fiat interdiction have become progressively normalized within legal and policy discourses.

Logics of Fiat Interdiction

State actors have always sought to control information flows, and all states permit some such controls. For example, even in countries that traditionally have recognized broad protection for freedoms of speech and association, there is broad consensus that neither child pornography nor step-by-step instructions for producing weapons-grade plutonium should circulate freely. Democratic, speech-regarding countries also have long-standing disagreements about other free speech exceptions. For example, U.S. courts have interpreted the First Amendment as sheltering hate speech, but the post-World War II European constitutional order views hate speech as undermining protection for fundamental human rights and therefore unworthy of protection. In the United States, free speech doctrine sharply limits potential liability for defamation and publication of private facts; European countries with stronger traditions of legal protection for dignitary interests allow both tort theories broader scope. For the most part, however, until the dawn of the internet era, the areas of agreement and disagreement about the scope of free speech protection were well understood and relatively stable.

In mid-1990s, amid dawning realization that decentralized digital networks facilitated the uncontrolled and radically democratic spread of all kinds of information, long-stable areas of consensus about state control of information flows began to destabilize and shift. Traditionally authoritarian states such as China, Iran, and Saudi Arabia responded to networked digital communications infrastructures by mandating backbone-level filtering for certain kinds of undesirable content and by enlisting internet access and search providers to perform additional filtering and surveillance.[4] Other countries began to confront new kinds of disputes about prohibited information flow. In the United States, public fears about uncontrolled flows of dangerous information coalesced around a set of threats that tech pundits dubbed the "Four Horsemen of the Infocalypse": terrorism, drug dealers, pedophiles, and organized crime.[5] The Four Horsemen represented existential threats to the fabric of society and the rule of law: threats in response to which ordinary procedures might be suspended in favor of extraordinary measures. They were quickly joined by two more: large-scale, networked infringement of intellectual property rights that threatened powerful information-economy interests and large-scale, networked leaking and whistleblowing that threatened state secrecy. The articulation of those threats set the stage for a shift in the legal understanding of the relationship between speech and danger—and consequently for the emergence of new logics of interdiction justified by conditions of permanent emergency.

Dangerous Knowledge

Debates about the government's ability to prevent the spread of information that threatens public safety predate the internet era by many decades. The First Amendment doctrines that evolved over the course of the twentieth century, however, allowed the government to label speech "dangerous" and prohibit it on that ground only after showing a sufficiently direct connection to physical harm or the threat of harm. Rising fears about the uncontrolled, viral spread of existential threats have prompted steady erosion of that relatively bright line in favor of a standard that is both much more deferential to executive threat assessments and much more open-ended about the sorts of information that can qualify as threatening. The catalyst for that process of doctrinal erosion has been the idea of *culpable facilitation*. Activities that might seem speech-like are framed instead as taking on more material and culpable qualities by virtue of their connection to other activities seen as posing threats to public safety and security. Over time, the culpable facilitation construct has become both powerful and capacious.

An early dispute about the circumstances under which executable computer code could qualify as dangerous knowledge subject to government control illustrated the potential power of the idea of culpable facilitation as the basis for interdiction. Executable code changes the behavior of digital networked systems to produce results. For many commentators, that capacity distinguished code from more traditional forms of expression and made the assertion of a regulatory interest only logical. During the Cold War, the State Department had adopted export control regulations covering not only munitions but also certain dual-use technologies, and had classified cryptographic techniques, without reservation, as covered technologies.[6] Within just a few decades, however, the personal computer revolution had put unprecedented processing power within general reach, and the internet had enabled widespread distribution of executable code and, eventually, encryption technologies suitable for widespread adoption to ensure communications privacy and security.[7] To those who worried about code's powerful functional capabilities, extension of the cryptography export controls into the modern era of widely distributed computer power seemed wise. Others, however, underscored code's dual-purpose and communicative aspects and worried about the potential for overbreadth and chill.

In the mid-1990s, litigants in a pair of cases challenged the application of federal export control regulations to restrict internet-based distribution of encryption technologies and won rulings acknowledging that human-readable source code is speech and that even machine-readable object code has an important expressive dimension.[8] Following the general rule established in other cases involving expressive conduct, both courts concluded that intermediate First Amendment scrutiny of the challenged regulations was appropriate. Generally speaking, that conclusion seems both inevitable and right given the close nexus between cryptographic code and confidential communication, and it proved sufficient to dispose of the underlying disputes. By any standard, the prohibition was not narrowly drawn. Rather than risk an adverse ruling on either the validity of the prohibition or the particular classification decisions that it had made, the government announced that it would amend the regulations in a way that excluded the source code at issue.[9] After the amendment, the disputes ended and the wider public controversy died away.

From a different perspective, though, that outcome shows the culpable facilitation construct beginning to function as an entering wedge for assertions of government need to control dangerous knowledge that were relatively open-ended. Rather than targeting implementations of code to destroy or penetrate critical systems, the cryptography export rules rested on a broad application of the idea of culpable facilitation: they targeted code that could be used to conceal communication. Identification of the proper standard for review of government regulations stopped several steps short of answering some rather important questions about how to craft and administer more well-balanced rules. The amended export-control regulations exclude over-the-counter, non-customizable implementations designed for installation by users but specify that, "when necessary," unspecified "details" must be made available to help determine whether those criteria are met. That phrasing is a recipe for government leverage without transparency or accountability. According to some reports, it is now routinely used to help ensure that communications providers afford desired levels of accessibility for government investigations.[10]

Consider now a less specialized and more open-ended set of prohibitions that repeats the same pattern of asserted existential threat, culpable facilitation rubric, and discretionary enforcement. During the 1990s, after years of debate about the appropriate response to an upsurge in terrorist activity around the world, Congress first amended the immigration laws to exclude those who had provided material support to terrorist activities from entering the country and then enacted a new law criminalizing the knowing provision of material support for terrorism. The idea that provision of support might itself be criminally punishable was not new. Criminal prohibitions against aiding and abetting violators have existed for centuries, and a statute first enacted in 1790 forbids those owing a duty of loyalty to the United States—including both members of the military and other government officers and employees—from giving "aid and comfort" to its enemies.[11] The new law, however, appears to have been the first time that a prohibition specifically directed toward the idea of "aid and comfort" had been incorporated into the general criminal code, and the prohibition expanded on that eighteenth-century framing of the idea of culpable facilitation by listing a variety of covered activities, including financial services, training, provision of lethal substances, and transportation.[12] An exception allowed humanitarian assistance to those not directly involved in violent conduct, but two years later, in the aftermath of the 1995 bombing of the Oklahoma City federal building by domestic terrorists, Congress eliminated the humanitarian assistance provision and also extended the material support prohibition to encompass assistance to designated foreign terrorist organizations.

In *Holder v. Humanitarian Law Project*, a majority of the Supreme Court rejected a First Amendment challenge to the amended material support law.[13] The entity challenging the law had provided human rights advocacy training to certain Kurdish and Tamil dissident organizations designated as terrorist organizations by the State Department. Under the previous version of the ban, its activities would have been lawful; now, it feared prosecution. According to mid-twentieth century jurisprudence about speech and danger, which allowed punishment of speech only when sufficiently linked to direct threats of violence, *Humanitarian Law Project* should have presented an easy case for invalidation.[14] But both the world and narratives about the threats it presented had begun to change rapidly.

The statute challenged in *Humanitarian Law Project* did not single out computer code or computer-based training as especially dangerous, but it nonetheless reflected a contemporary sensibility about the materiality of certain kinds of expressive conduct. As the lawsuit wound its way through the courts, Congress amended the definition of "material support or resources" to include "expert advice or assistance," and then amended the definition of "expert advice or assistance" to include "advice or assistance derived from scientific, technical or other specialized knowledge."[15] Expert speech, Congress seemed to be saying, has a kind of power that ordinary speech does not, and it can be restricted on that basis—which, both Congress and the courts seemed to think, is a different proposition than making invidious distinctions among kinds of speech or kinds of speakers. In a world in which the line between speech and computer-mediated action had become vanishingly thin, the idea that expert legal training produced material consequences could begin to seem entirely credible.

The statute also did not single out networked, digital communication as especially problematic, but the majority opinion by Chief Justice Roberts nonetheless reflects a contemporary sensibility about the threats posed by uncontrolled online spread of potentially damaging information. The Court held oral argument in February 2010. In April 2010, the news broke that WikiLeaks.org, a self-described open government organization founded in 2006, had published a video of a 2007 attack by a U.S. military helicopter in Baghdad that killed a number of civilians, including children, and two Reuters employees. The video, which WikiLeaks titled "Collateral Murder," received extensive coverage by U.S. newspapers of record, which noted the organization's history of leaking hidden information about government and corporate operations.[16] WikiLeaks attracted its share of defenders, but its critics saw a textbook case of advocacy run amok and threatening to disrupt the orderly flows of policing and nation-building. A *New York Times* article on WikiLeaks published only a few weeks beforehand had quoted a Pentagon report as concluding that information of the sort routinely published by WikiLeaks "could be used by foreign intelligence services, terrorist groups and others to identify vulnerabilities, plan attacks and build new devices."[17]

The Court decided *Humanitarian Law Project* two months after WikiLeaks published the "Collateral Murder" video and two days after the *New York Times* reported as front-page news that U.S. Army Specialist Bradley Manning had been arrested on suspicion of having leaked the video and other information to WikiLeaks.[18] At oral argument and in its briefs, the government had asserted that expert training in human rights advocacy could work to legitimize dangerous organizations.[19] By traditional First Amendment standards, the argument was laughable; rhetorical battles over legitimacy are exactly the sorts of contests that belong in the realm of persuasion. The majority accepted it uncritically, and also noted that terrorist organizations could rely on such training to "threaten, manipulate, and disrupt" the international legal system.[20] Additionally, it cautioned about the risks of "straining the United States' relationships with its allies and undermining cooperative efforts between nations to prevent terrorist attacks."[21]

The exercise of situating the justices within a larger cultural context is inevitably speculative; even so, the justices live in the same world that the rest of us do. Read in context, the *Humanitarian Law Project* decision is a product of its time, and not only because the majority's observations about materiality, risk, and danger expressed the deference to asserted national-security imperatives that had become the norm in the post-9/11 environment.[22] Those observations also dovetail neatly with the fears about the uncontrollable viral spread of damning and damaging information that were suddenly coming to loom so large in the public view.

Both the *Humanitarian Law Project* litigation and the saga of the cryptography export rules supply object lessons in the expansionist trajectory of the logic of culpable facilitation in times of perceived exceptional threat. As domains of expertise far removed from violence and lawlessness were recast as inextricably entwined with threats to the body politic, government practices that the courts of an earlier era would have recognized instantly as overbroad and politically suspect came to seem both apolitical and existentially justified. In the case of the material assistance statute, that double shift in meaning has vastly expanded the universe of activities potentially meriting prosecution, sweeping in everything from human rights training to religious instruction to remittances sent by would-be migrants via private payment networks.[23] In the case of the export control regulations, the continuing provisional assertion of authority to verify the eligibility of cryptographic products for general distribution has enabled the government both to assert an ongoing interest in the capabilities of networked communications products and services and to further that interest in ad hoc and unaccountable ways.

Other People's Property

A second strand of the contemporary discourse about speech and existential threats concerns the copyright pirate, and the appearance of this "fifth horseman" is in itself a development worth remarking. Initially, legislative anxieties about online immorality—in particular, pornography and drug dealing—promised to play a far more significant role in policymaking for the internet. Ultimately, however, the influence of powerful new information-economy actors and the economic logics of digital property and *digital contraband* proved both more durable and more difficult to cabin.

In 1996, fears about proliferation of online pornography and pedophilia became the focus of a short-lived and controversial legislative campaign to clean up the internet. Among other things, the proposed legislation provided an early illustration of the power of "alternative facts" to fuel outrage. In addition to horror stories and alarmist rhetoric, the bill's main sponsor in the Senate relied on an academic study that purported to measure the quantity and evaluate the nature of pornographic content available online, but that had serious methodological deficiencies. Its author had avoided traditional processes of peer review by seeking and winning publication in a student-edited law journal. Although his sensationalized claims were quickly discredited, that seemed to make little difference to the bill's supporters and did not slow its momentum.[24] As eventually enacted, the Communications Decency Act's prohibitions were broad and vague, establishing criminal penalties for the knowing preparation or solicitation and transmission of "indecent" content.[25]

As its opponents had foreseen, the CDA's core prohibitions could not withstand judicial scrutiny. Anxiety about sexually explicit speech is a traditional theme within First Amendment discourse, and precisely for that reason, claims that the internet was simply an out-of-control smut factory encountered well-established case law mandating very skeptical review. The federal courts swiftly invalidated both the initial legislation and the first revision that Congress attempted.[26] The effort to ban online smut became another chapter in a history of moral panic, legislative overreach and judicial correction that extends over many decades. (As we saw in Chapter 3, that history creates its own risks, powerfully shaping civil libertarian thinking about current problems bedeviling platform-based speech environments.) In subsequent years, traditional First Amendment narratives have remained robust enough to quell periodic alarm about online smut and crime, and law enforcement officials have used traditional enforcement tactics to combat trafficking in unsavory materials.[27]

At the same time, however, alarm about the uncontrolled online spread of a different kind of information began to command the attention of law- and policymakers. Over the course of the twentieth century, the publishing, music, television, and motion picture industries had coalesced into a politically savvy interest group accustomed to exerting powerful influence over the shape of copyright legislation. By the 1990s, the software industry also had emerged as a force to be reckoned with in legislative debates. Both old and new copyright industries and their respective trade associations began a systematic campaign to frame online copyright infringement as an existential threat to society in its own right.

In Congress and in the media, entertainment and software industry represent-atives worked to position online copyright infringement, and particularly peer-to-peer file-sharing, as morally objectionable and socially insidious. In a blizzard of press releases and media interviews, and in a variety of more formal interventions ranging from conference remarks to congressional testimony, they equated online copyright infringement with theft, piracy, communism, plague, pandemic, and ter-rorism.[28] They attempted to link peer-to-peer technologies with the rapid spread of pornography and with increased risk of exposure to viruses and spyware.[29] And they urged enactment of new laws designed to prevent unauthorized flows of digital content and to keep authorized flows secure.

During the 1990s, the convergence of economic power, legislative access, and moral panic rapidly produced a series of enactments expanding the duration of copyrights and prohibiting unauthorized access to and appropriation of valuable digital resources. New statutes included the Copyright Term Extension Act, which added 20 years to the terms of both new and already-subsisting copyrights; the Uruguay Round Agreements Act, which restored copyright protection to many for-eign works then residing in the public domain; the Digital Millennium Copyright Act (DMCA) of 1998, which authorized new interdiction-based strategies for countering online copyright infringement; and the Economic Espionage Act, which criminalized the misappropriation of valuable trade secrets. Additionally, a series of amendments to the Computer Fraud and Abuse Act extended statutory prohibitions on unauthorized access to computing resources to encompass many more types of computer systems and a much wider range of conduct.[30]

Rejecting a steady stream of constitutional challenges to the new legislation, the federal courts concluded that, in general, new protections for proprietary informa-tion resources did not trigger the First Amendment at all. So, for example, in *Eldred v. Ashcroft* and *Golan v. Holder*, the Court held that laws retrospectively extending copyright terms and resurrecting lapsed foreign copyrights from the public domain required no special free speech scrutiny. That was so because, as Justice Ginsburg explained for the majority in *Eldred*, there is no "right to make other people's speeches."[31] Reasoning that copyright itself performs a constitutional function by incentivizing production and distribution of speech, the Court indicated that Congress has nearly unlimited leeway to expand the footprint of the copyright re-gime as long as it leaves certain traditional limits on copyright scope undisturbed. In cases challenging the DMCA's interdiction-related provisions, lower courts invoked the rhetoric of pandemic alongside that of piracy, framing online infringement as a threat to both the rule of law and the survival of the body politic.[32]

More generally, alarmist rhetoric about online infringement of intellectual property rights worked to alter the tenor of public discussions about ownership of and access to digital resources. Terms such as "piracy" and "theft," formerly rare in intellectual property discourse, have become commonplace. Public service advertisements funded by copyright industry organizations portray those downloading music and movies as selfish, immoral, and criminal.[33] As the new narratives about digital contraband have become ordinary and familiar, they have worked to legitimate exceptional enforcement measures.

State Secrets and State Secrecy

A final important strand of the contemporary discourse about information contraband involves ever-expanding logics of *operational secrecy* surrounding government activities. Governments have always kept secrets, but the kind of secrecy that the logic of the exception justifies is different. With increasing frequency, the government has sought not only to punish unauthorized disclosures of particular information but also and more generally to develop institutional structures for "deep secrecy"—structures that free some government actors from the obligation to provide any account of their actions at all.[34]

Unlike rules prescribing export controls for munitions or targeting online copyright infringement, the state secrets doctrine is centuries old. Framed broadly in terms of the overlapping imperatives of national and domestic security, the doctrine has long been understood to shield certain kinds of information about executive branch operations from disclosure.[35] In the contemporary legal system, the state secrets doctrine underlies a variety of rules and practices, including the rules for classifying certain types of information as confidential, statutes that specify penalties for unauthorized disclosure, and procedures for in camera review of secret executive branch actions by special legislative oversight committees and courts. Those rules, statutes, and procedures exist in tension with others purporting to guarantee openness and transparency, including freedom of information laws and whistleblower protection statutes. Leaks and leaking in violation of state secrecy rules also are well-established practices with their own complex institutional sociologies.[36]

In the networked information era, however, anxieties about the dangers of uncontrolled information flow have elicited free-floating and seemingly unconstrained logics of operational secrecy that attach to a wide variety of government functions with asserted connections to national security. That shift has engendered intense debates about government accountability, lending momentum to an ongoing legal campaign to shed light on the far-flung operations of the modern surveillance state and also to diverse and creative efforts to create new institutionalized structures for facilitating leaking. In response, the government pursuit of operational secrecy has grown ever more determined.

By the turn of the twenty-first century, a diverse collection of scholars, tech industry observers, and legal advocates had become worried about vast, secret expansions in government surveillance activities and capabilities. Following the 9/11 attacks on the World Trade Center and the Pentagon, investigations into intelligence failures leading up to the attacks focused public attention on a set of special surveillance procedures authorized by the Foreign Intelligence Surveillance Act (FISA) and on a secret court constituted under the FISA to oversee surveillance requests.[37] Soon, however, the evidence began to suggest that surveillance programs authorized in the aftermath of 9/11 extended more broadly than even that statute permitted. In 2004, U.S. Treasury agents investigating Al-Haramain, a Muslim charity headquartered in Oregon, for alleged links to terrorist activities abroad inadvertently disclosed to Al-Haramain's attorneys a document indicating that the government had undertaken lengthy warrantless surveillance of the charity's telephone calls.[38] In 2005, the *New York Times* published an investigative report revealing that, following the 9/11 attacks, the administration had authorized a program of warrantless mass communications surveillance, and in 2006, a technician who had recently retired from AT&T's San Francisco Bay Area operations center disclosed the existence of a long-term, secret government data-collection operation housed directly within the center itself.[39]

Litigation arising from these indirect and partial disclosures, however, led nowhere. After the Electronic Frontier Foundation filed a class action lawsuit against AT&T on behalf of customers who objected to the company's apparent facilitation of routine government monitoring, Congress hastily amended the FISA statute, authorizing the government to make warrantless demands for interception of communications with parties located abroad and granting retroactive immunity from civil liability to communications intermediaries that assisted with such interception. Because it now lacked authority to grant the relief plaintiffs had requested, the court dismissed the lawsuit.[40] A group of human rights advocates who believed that their calls with vulnerable clients and witnesses were being monitored filed a different lawsuit asserting that warrantless government surveillance under the amended statute chilled the exercise of their constitutional rights and those of their clients. Reasoning that plaintiffs could not prove that they or their clients had been targeted or that any of their communications had been collected and read, the court ruled that they had not alleged any actual injury and lacked standing to sue.[41] While that lawsuit worked its way through the appeals process, the massive scale of government communications surveillance was becoming something of an open secret. In 2012, *Wired* magazine published a detailed piece of investigative reporting by journalist James Bamford that described a new data center being built by the government in the middle of the Nevada desert and drew the obvious conclusions about the center's purpose.[42] Even so, a majority of the Supreme Court upheld dismissal of the constitutional claims, characterizing plaintiffs' arguments as based on speculations and assumptions.[43]

Then, in June 2013, the world learned that former National Security Agency contractor Edward Snowden had copied and disclosed to reporters for *The Guardian* and the *Washington Post* voluminous files documenting the NSA's extralegal surveillance of communications worldwide. The documents revealed that the major

U.S. telecommunications and internet access providers were operating under on-going demands for bulk production of accountholder information and session metadata. They provided irrefutable, documentary proof of both the vast scope of the government's surveillance operations and the lawlessness of many of the component programs.[44]

The Snowden revelations led to new legislation ostensibly designed to rein in government excesses. After learning about the government's post-9/11 warrantless wiretapping, Congress had created a Privacy and Civil Liberties Oversight Board (PCLOB) but had given it very little authority; after Snowden, it gave the PCLOB independent status and charged it with evaluating the legality of the programs that Snowden had exposed and recommending additional reforms and best practices.[45] Additionally, it added language to the FISA statute restricting the scope of permissible queries to telecommunications providers, thereby limiting the government's ability to submit new requests for bulk metadata production. It also created a small corps of advocate-advisors authorized to participate in FISA court proceedings on the public's behalf.[46]

From one perspective, the legislative response to the Snowden revelations continued a pattern of secretive government overreach and eventual legislative correction begun much earlier in the modern era. The Snowden episode was not the first revelation about massive unsanctioned government surveillance programs. In the 1970s, disclosures about the COINTELPRO (COounter INTelligence PROgram) operation—a surveillance and disinformation program devised by the Pentagon to discredit the American Communist Party, leaders of the civil rights movement, and members of a variety of other protest and social justice movements—had prompted a detailed congressional investigation and the enactment of the country's first modern electronic surveillance laws.[47]

From another perspective, however, the official response to the Snowden revelations both confirmed the inadequacy of post-COINTELPRO reforms and was far more anemic than the response to COINTELPRO had been. Unlike the Church Commission, constituted by the Senate to investigate COINTELPRO, the PCLOB lacked authority to compel the production of documents and witnesses, and its recommendations were purely advisory.[48] After it concluded that the bulk metadata program was unlawful and recommended that the program be discontinued and its stored data destroyed, the government took almost two years to comply.[49] Powerful legislators resisted enacting all of the reforms that the PCLOB recommended to provide more comprehensive public accountability, and public opinion remains starkly polarized about how much surveillance authority the government should have.[50] Last and importantly, as in the case of COINTELPRO, the enacted reforms both sanctioned many of the surveillance techniques formerly employed without express authority and institutionalized new processes for secret authorization.[51]

Litigation over government surveillance and related counterterrorism activities in the wake of the Snowden leaks and their legislative aftermath increasingly resembles trench warfare. Courts have become more willing to concede that the government conducted dragnet communications surveillance. However, they have then cited other justifications either for dismissal or for allowing only limited "jurisdictional discovery" that feature logics of fiat interdiction at their core, including both the need to defer to the executive branch in national security matters and the imperative of protecting state secrets.[52] Additionally, the government's litigation strategy has relied on the prevalence of sunset clauses and reauthorization requirements in national security surveillance statutes. Government officials have argued that courts should avoid ruling on the constitutionality of grants of surveillance authority that have since been amended, an argument that, if accepted, would effectively convert such provisions into strategies for evading judicial review.[53]

Litigation over government surveillance practices also has shown the government increasingly willing to experiment with new tactics involving refusal to follow ordinarily applicable procedural and evidentiary rules. Recall Al-Haramain, the Muslim charity whose attorneys accidentally received a confidential document in discovery. The attorneys promptly returned the document, but later sought to introduce testimony about it in litigation challenging the charity's designation as terrorist-affiliated. The government argued that the state secrets doctrine barred the testimony. The courts ultimately agreed with that interpretation of the doctrine but noted that the FISA statute authorizes courts (though not parties or their attorneys) in subsequent litigation to inspect documents relating to secret government surveillance. The district court therefore ordered the document produced for inspection subject to appropriate protective constraints.[54] Over a period of many months and multiple court orders, the government simply declined to comply. Ultimately, it was rewarded for its stonewalling. Although the attorneys for the now-defunct charity were able to obtain a ruling that the government's conduct had violated FISA, the litigation was dismissed on sovereign immunity grounds.[55] Prosecutors in later cases have followed the same playbook, stonewalling in litigation by individuals wrongly placed on the no-fly list rather than disclose information about the criteria for adding or retaining someone on the list, dragging out litigation over gag orders and then dropping demands for secrecy rather than risk an unfavorable ruling on constitutionality, and dismissing minor criminal charges rather than reveal the confidential and possibly ultra vires investigative techniques that led to them.[56]

Struggles over Facilitation and Control

Within the networked information environment, the logics of culpable facilitation, digital contraband, and operational secrecy work to justify the development and implementation of new enforcement strategies directed at unauthorized information flows. Network intermediaries represent attractive targets for such strategies. As noted earlier in this chapter, the idea that otherwise lawful acts sometimes can trigger liability for culpable facilitation is not new. That idea underlies criminal "aiding and abetting" liability, theories of indirect infringement in intellectual property law, and a variety of statutory prohibitions. The dominant justification for imposing liability on facilitators is instrumental. Such prohibitions exploit valuable cost efficiencies and, when effective, work to dry up the market for assistance to violators. If enforcement efficiency were the only relevant standard, it might make sense to treat network intermediaries as essential partners in a wide variety of network-based malfeasance. Most commentators and judges, however, have thought efficiency-based reasoning insufficient to serve as the sole justification for imposing liability. To avoid unfairness and preserve the social benefits that third-party activities often provide, theories of culpable facilitation typically have incorporated substantive protections that incorporate tests of moral responsibility, such as requirements of culpable knowledge or intent, and have been invoked in settings where procedural and evidentiary safeguards are available.[57]

The new interdiction rules are different in both form and effect. Within the Hohfeldian framework that has guided the inquiry in this part of the book, entitlements to pursue third-party facilitators of unlawful conduct are not simply rights, although they are often justified that way, because they do not simply impose correlative duties. Instead, they confer authority to require such facilitators to perform their own activities differently to avoid civil or criminal liability. In Hohfeldian terms, interdiction mandates are most aptly classified as powers to alter the legal obligations of others and to impose liability for noncompliance.[58] Those powers, moreover, increasingly are defined and implemented in ways that de-emphasize traditional substantive and procedural protections and emphasize instead the bare force of legal authority. As the logics of fiat interdiction have begun to work themselves into information law and policy, they have melded and recombined to produce hybrids that reflect origins in both national security and intellectual property enforcement practice.

At the same time, however, struggles over interdiction rules have come to reflect the unexpected power and influence of network intermediaries, and particularly of the dominant platform firms. Recall from Chapter 3 that during the drafting of the Communications Decency Act, opponents of the proposed anti-smut law achieved what seemed to be a limited victory in the form of an immunity provision for internet access providers that simply redistributed speech made by others. Described as a "good Samaritan" provision, section 230 of the CDA was intended to encourage internet access providers to develop and voluntarily adopt measures for filtering out undesirable content or enabling users to do so.[59] As we saw in Chapter 3, section 230 has become the cornerstone of a legal regime that shelters internet service providers of all sorts—including platform providers that play very active roles in shaping the universe of information that users see—from accountability for both old and new information harms. And the nascent industry that it was designed to protect has become one of the most powerful in the world.

As network intermediaries have resisted efforts to write the logic of the exception into law, they have become masters at both public relations and inside-the-Beltway political positioning. The result is a legal and media landscape characterized by complex power struggles among the dominant interests. In those struggles, platforms do not simply play defense. Rather, they have worked to position themselves as both essential partners and competing sovereigns in the quest to instantiate states of exception algorithmically.

Finding and Paying for Contraband

In the domain of copyright, the logics of digital contraband and culpable facilitation have melded to produce a deep and seemingly permanent shift in the nature of enforcement activity. Thirty years ago, the principal enforcement tool was the civil infringement lawsuit. Criminal enforcement was relatively rare, and capabilities for technical enforcement were virtually nonexistent.[60] Today, all that has changed. Third-party facilitators have become principal targets of efforts to block unauthorized flows and eliminate unauthorized channels. The interdiction game is played on multiple fronts simultaneously: in courtrooms, legislative hearings, rulemakings, and treaty negotiations—and targets every stage in the process of finding and paying for digital content. Efforts to impose broad mandates fail with some regularity but often are followed by private initiatives that achieve similar results and that enable platforms to assert their own authority over the terms and conditions of information flow.

On the civil enforcement side, one important strategy for interrupting flows of digital contraband relies on a statutory "notice and takedown" regime for obtaining removal of publicly posted content. Enacted as part of the Digital Millennium Copyright Act of 1998, the regime exploits the interplay between the statutory procedures and background doctrines governing indirect infringement liability. Generally speaking, indirect infringement liability requires some form of culpable knowledge. Compliance with the notice and takedown regime confers safe harbor from liability, but failure to remove infringing material after learning of it vitiates the safe harbor—and, given the scope of many online intermediaries' operations, threatens crushing liability. The regime therefore encourages speedy removal triggered by notice without prior judicial review. (To help make this work, interdiction imperatives relating to digital contraband also figure prominently within neighboring legal regimes. Intellectual property enforcement is a categorical limitation on the immunity granted to online service providers under section 230 of the CDA, and it has been a categorical exception to both net neutrality rules adopted by the Federal Communications Commission (FCC).[61]) Although the notice and takedown regime regularly elicits significant numbers of meritless or legally questionable takedown notices (many generated by automated processes for detecting infringement), it has been implemented around the world as a result of pressure exerted by U.S. trade negotiators.[62]

The emergence of the platform business model at the turn of the twenty-first century placed the copyright industries and the internet industries on a collision course with regard to the scope of the statutory safe harbors. The DMCA's separate safe harbors for hosting and information location services were drafted before the emergence of automated search, content aggregation, and social networking technologies began to blur such easy distinctions. From the copyright industry perspective, new platform-based technologies for storing, indexing, and sharing uploaded information seemed designed to encourage infringement. In a series of high-profile lawsuits, powerful copyright owners have argued that the platform business model falls outside the scope of the safe harbors, and that the venture capitalists, law firms, and payment processors that work with platforms to facilitate access to digital content also should be held accountable for the widespread availability of digital contraband. In Congress, they have pressed their case for affirmative filtering obligations and other new mandates.

Copyright industry efforts to impose stricter obligations on platforms, however, have failed repeatedly. Over and over again, litigation designed to win rulings unambiguously extending indirect infringement liability to platforms and other alleged third-party facilitators of infringement failed to produce the desired results.[63] Meanwhile—and partly as a result of the copyright wars—the internet industry gradually found its political voice. Although internet businesses did not play a major role in the debates over the notice and takedown provisions, as dominant platforms began to emerge, the political landscape began to shift. The events surrounding enactment of the DMCA had sparked a vibrant, populist backlash against maximalist copyright enforcement, out of which emerged both new organizations constituted to speak on behalf of the public domain and new entrepreneurial ventures, such as the Creative Commons movement, offering alternative legal platforms for content distribution. In addition to emphasizing the now-familiar theme of permissionless innovation, the new platform firms learned to appropriate other strands of antimaximalist rhetoric for their own purposes, latching onto the themes of commons, open content, and fair use to advance their own interests. And as platforms became more adept at flexing their political muscle, defeating wave after wave of proposed new legislation, the copyright legislative juggernaut began to lose momentum.[64]

Matters came to a head in 2011, when the motion picture, recording, and major league sports industries convinced several members of Congress to propose legislation that would empower courts to cut off the services provided by payment processors and other infrastructure providers upon ex parte application by an aggrieved rightholder. The Stop Online Piracy Act (SOPA) and its companion bill, the Protect Intellectual Property Act (PIPA), were expected to pass by a wide margin. Instead, Google and other platform firms coordinated a massive mobilization of the online community that effectively shut down many of the internet's most popular sites. Shortly thereafter, Congress tabled the legislation and has not revived it.[65] The SOPA and PIPA debacle signaled a sea change in the politics of intellectual property—the end of uniform and unwavering support for the protectionist leg-islative agenda that dominated the 1990s and 2000s. In subsequent years, the rate of proposals for new legislation has slowed dramatically—although, as Chapter 7 will discuss, attempts to ensure that new trade agreements include strengthened en-forcement obligations have continued.[66]

Yet this recounting of legislative and litigation failures to impose mandates for what legal theorist Jack Balkin calls "digital prior restraint" overlooks the extent to which interdiction of infringing content by search, social networking, and pay-ment providers increasingly has become the norm. Every major platform that hosts user-provided content uses automated filtering technology to prevent the posting of infringing content, and the major payment providers increasingly have followed suit, entering agreements with the major copyright trade associations that obligate them to restrict access by entities and sites identified as infringing.[67] Similarly, fol-lowing its successful campaign against legislated domain-blocking requirements, Google announced that it would begin demoting or removing entirely from search results sites that generate repeated takedown notices.[68] Platforms such as Google's YouTube also offer copyright owners the opportunity to monetize unauthorized uses of their content by claiming a portion of the advertising revenues.

From the platform perspective, decisions to institute voluntary automated filtering represent a pragmatic response to background legal doctrines that es-tablish indirect liability for contributing to infringement. Although courts have resisted interpreting those doctrines in ways that would make liability flow near-automatically to platforms or payment providers, they have indicated that the details of platform design and behavior matter. Copyright litigation between the major in-dustry players can be prolonged and expensive—litigation between Viacom and Google over infringing videos on YouTube dragged on for seven years—and, as already noted, the penalties for guessing wrong include statutory damages poten-tially running into millions of dollars.[69] But automated filtering also does not simply amount to capitulation; platforms have declined to disclose their methods or to give copyright industries a say in their implementation.

To similar effect, the enforcement playbook that eventually emerged for addressing the widespread use of peer-to-peer file-sharing technologies is pragmatic and relies heavily on the voluntary actions of service providers. Because peer-to-peer file-sharing technologies are designed to eliminate central indexing, winning indirect infringement lawsuits against their providers has proved difficult, and when claims do succeed, they tend to result in remedial orders that are impossible to enforce. Additionally, the notice and takedown regime applies only to hosting and information location providers, not to internet access providers whose serv-ices are used to engage in file-sharing. Some copyright owners have used automated investigative tools to discover and attempt to identify individual users of peer-to-peer technologies who appear to be downloading proprietary files, but suing users directly has never been the preferred enforcement strategy.[70] Additionally, although U.S. courts have rejected privacy challenges to subpoenas for production of subscriber information, within the more privacy-protective European legal environment, there is ongoing tension between interdiction and privacy imperatives. Consensus on the appropriate balance remains elusive, with directives concerning intellectual property enforcement and data protection imposing arguably conflicting mandates.[71]

Many peer-to-peer downloads, however, eventually come to rest in cloud storage, and cloud storage providers are vulnerable to both civil suits for contributory infringement and criminal enforcement proceedings. Both in the United States and around the world, criminal copyright enforcement has become far more frequent. Over the course of the 1990s and 2000s, in response to rising panic about the uncontrolled spread of information contraband, Congress amended the criminal provisions of the federal intellectual property laws nine times, expanding the categories of conduct eligible for prosecution, increasing penalties, and giving both prosecutors and copyright owners new and powerful tools for site-wide blocking and domain forfeiture.[72] At the urging of trade negotiators from the United States and other developed countries, similar provisions have spread throughout the world.[73] For companies seeking to establish themselves as providers of legitimate services, the possibility of prosecution is more than just theoretical. Federal prosecutors have issued several indictments against cloud storage providers, including the widely publicized proceedings against MegaUpload and its colorful principal, Kim Dotcom, for criminal copyright violations. Unsurprisingly, major cloud storage firms serving the U.S. market have implemented automated systems for scanning clients' stored content to detect files with cryptographic signatures (or "hashes") that match those supplied by rightholders.[74]

Circumventing Digital Barriers

Another important strategy for online copyright enforcement involves new prohibitions on circumvention of technical access protections, trafficking in circumvention technologies, and knowingly obtaining valuable trade secrets through improper means. Through these strategies, which meld the logics of culpable facilitation and digital contraband with that of operational secrecy, copyright enforcement efforts have become efforts to rearrange information flows within circuits of authorization. Legal prohibitions target both unauthorized access and dissemination of technical expertise that might disrupt secure channels for information flow.

In addition to establishing a notice-and-takedown regime for removal of content posted without authorization, the DMCA included other provisions prohibiting circumvention of technologies applied to protect copyrighted works against unauthorized access and banning trafficking in circumvention technologies.[75] According to the internal logic of those provisions, circumvention technologies themselves are dangerous knowledge. Those distributing such technologies are culpable facilitators, as are those who attempt to understand circumvention protocols and share information about them without following proper procedures.

Following their enactment, the anti-trafficking provisions became the cornerstone of a litigation campaign designed to deter the unauthorized development of systems for accessing and rendering copyrighted content. Unlike litigation against platform providers based on theories of indirect infringement, that campaign has been an unqualified success. A series of court rulings interpreting the provisions to bar the development of unauthorized devices for rendering content, even if the content itself was lawfully acquired, gives copyright holders and their licensed technology developers comprehensive de facto control over the design and functionality of digital media players, video recorders, and gaming systems.[76] As a result, licensing of access control protocols has become widespread. The major commercially available systems for delivering and playing audio and audiovisual content now incorporate functionality designed to defeat unauthorized copying and prevent retransmissions to unauthorized platforms and devices.[77] Like interdiction imperatives directed at digital contraband, struggles between copyright interests and communications providers over secure digital protocols also have spilled over into neighboring legal regimes; most recently, a rule proposed by the FCC to enable competition in the provision of cable set-top boxes was defeated after copyright lobbyists mobilized against it.[78]

Exceptions to the anti-trafficking provisions for software reverse engineering, security research, and encryption research do exist but are crafted in ways that largely precludes their use by ordinary members of the public. Those conducting encryption research must make "a good faith effort to obtain authorization" and can claim exemption from anticircumvention liability only if factors including their purpose and their credentials suggest that it is warranted. Those engaged in software reverse engineering may share operational information about technical protection systems with others only for the purpose of creating a separate interoperable computer program, and those conducting computer security testing must use their findings "solely" to promote the network owner's security.[79] The overall—and likely intended—effect of these provisions is twofold. The restrictions on information sharing conflict with the foundational commitments of open source software communities and therefore burden those communities in particular. More generally, the emphasis on credentialing and tightly controlled sharing operates to foreclose unauthorized experimentation and innovation of all sorts.[80]

The DMCA's anticircumvention provisions, meanwhile, authorize the Copyright Office to declare exceptions on a case-by-case basis, but only if it finds that users are likely to be "adversely affected" in their ability to make use of "particular classes" of works.[81] Those criteria, and the procedure more generally, sit in substantial tension with the innovative ethos that supposedly defines the information era. Although "ask forgiveness, not permission" has become a Silicon Valley mantra, those wishing to engage in acts of circumvention must ask permission, not forgiveness, and must agree to stay within narrow, well-defined limits. The lists of exceptions requested and granted since the process began, which includes items such as transferring a mobile phone between cellular networks and repairing automotive components, reveal that the anticircumvention provisions have been invoked not simply to protect copyrights but also and more fundamentally to stifle competition in important consumer markets.[82]

A related frontier for struggles over interdiction authority is the concept of a "right to repair" the software in consumer devices, vehicles, and appliances. Assuming that one can gain access to the software in one's mobile phone, car, or tractor under an exception to the circumvention ban, the process of diagnosis and repair may create the factual predicate for a copyright infringement claim. The Copyright Act permits owners of copies of software to take the necessary steps to repair those copies, but software copyright owners typically structure end-user transactions as licenses and argue that the statutory protections for owners do not apply. A "right to repair" movement has begun to emerge at the state level; so far, however, it has produced little momentum for change at the federal level.[83]

Platform firms have an ambivalent relationship to the anticircumvention and anti-trafficking provisions. The DMCA does not mandate use of any particular technical protection system or standard but rather encourages private development of technical protection measures and, ultimately, private standard-setting. As a practical matter, those processes have different effects on established firms that are major players in content distribution markets and smaller or start-up firms. Participation in industry-driven standards processes is costly and tends to require both long-term commitment and a preexisting organizational track record. Such processes therefore tend to favor established providers, including dominant platform firms such as Apple and Microsoft that are also personal computing and consumer electronics firms. More generally, the rise of "walled gardens" for access to proprietary content is compatible with the "rich-get-richer" principle of network organization (discussed in Chapter 1) and reinforces the platform business model. Smaller and start-up firms have difficulty gaining access to processes dominated by industry insiders and confront higher litigation risk when they try to design around existing case law.[84]

The momentum to entrench technical protection of digital content appears to be accelerating at the global level. As Chapter 7 will discuss, at least some internet standards organizations have begun to look more favorably on efforts to develop network standards that are compatible with technical protection protocols. According to the official positions of the United States and other developed countries, strong intervention in the online environment on behalf of intellectual property owners is entirely consistent with solicitude for freedom of speech.[85] Technical protection protocols, though, can be deployed in many different ways— for example, to privilege content authorized by state sovereigns and disfavor dissident content or content circulated anonymously. As a practical matter, then, as democratic states have intensified their commitments to technical protection measures for copyright enforcement, that stance opens the door to other kinds of hard-coded interdiction as well.

Keeping Unauthorized Secrets

In the context of the government's desire to stop dangerous information from flowing, the logic of culpable facilitation disfavors concealment and suggests instead that network intermediaries should provide government investigators with unimpeded access to private communications. That logic has set in motion cycles of reaction and counterreaction that are increasingly extreme. Technologists and activists have worked to develop techniques for more effective digital privacy and security; additionally, as Chapter 8 discusses in more detail, in the networked information era, anonymous online action has become a potent and unruly source of political power. The prospects of enhanced concealment and anonymous direct action in turn have inspired more intensive and often lawless surveillance practices. As government officials have pushed for more seamless access to private communications, network intermediaries have pushed back, citing both civil liberties and network security considerations. And yet platform interventions in debates about surveillance reform often have seemed calibrated first and foremost to preserve their own authority vis-à-vis threatened intrusions by government actors.

From one perspective, the most effective way of enabling governments to detect transmissions of dangerous information would involve modifying core internet standards and protocols to make them surveillance-ready. As noted earlier in this chapter, many authoritarian states already require internet intermediaries operating within their borders—including backbone providers, search engines, and social networking sites—to block a broad array of content deemed subversive. Embedding capabilities for surveillance and policing more deeply within the internet's protocol stack might seem a logical next step. Countries with democratic political traditions, however, have regarded that approach as inconsistent with core commitments to fundamental human rights. In global internet standards proceedings, they have opposed proposals for surveillance-ready standards introduced by some authoritarian governments.[86]

In democratic states, the logic of the exception has pushed surveillance policy and practice in the opposite direction, toward development of interception capabilities that can be deployed at the network's endpoints in particular cases. Following the failure of early attempts to control the spread of encryption code, law enforcement agencies have worked continuously to preserve lines of access into networked communications systems and devices. In 1994, Congress enacted legislation requiring telecommunications providers to design and maintain wiretap capability, but efforts to legislate similar "back door" capabilities for digital microprocessors were defeated after strong opposition from both the computer industry and academic computer scientists.[87] Continued technological evolution has disrupted that fragile equilibrium, however. The intercept capabilities mandated by statute are increasingly obsolete in an era in which communications by voice, text, and email all travel over digital networks and in which capabilities for strong communications encryption are increasingly widespread.

The political equilibrium briefly attained after the "crypto wars" of the 1990s has also become unstable. The Snowden leaks did not simply expose mass surveillance programs conducted under color of law based on overbroad interpretations of existing statutes. They also revealed a variety of equally long-standing but far more clearly lawless government surveillance practices that included hacking into overseas data centers to scoop up communication flows outside the territorial United States, remotely accessing privately owned computers and installing keyloggers or commandeering built-in cameras and microphones, and compromising network security protocols to permit repeated access.[88] Subsequent leaks from other sources have also revived the specter of COINTELPRO, revealing that the government has conducted routine ongoing surveillance of civil rights and social justice activists even as it has downplayed the large and growing problem of domestic terrorism and discontinued an official program to track homegrown extremist groups that actually advocate violence.[89]

Unlike the surveillance debates of the 1990s, however, contemporary debates about the scope of government surveillance authority have unfolded against a backdrop of ongoing struggle between governments and dominant global platform firms, with each vying for both the moral high ground and the practical upper hand. In 2008, after several widely-publicized capitulations by platform firms to authoritarian regimes' demands for censorship, a coalition of platform firms, academics, and nongovernmental organizations formed the Global Network Initiative, the website for which proudly proclaims: "Privacy is a human right and guarantor of human dignity. Privacy is important to maintaining personal security, protecting identity and promoting freedom of expression in the digital age."[90] The documents leaked by Snowden, however, revealed both traditional telecommunications providers and new digital platform firms to be essential participants in ongoing and seemingly unconstrained government surveillance operations. Subsequently, the dominant global platform firms have worked hard to restore and burnish their civil libertarian public personae, publicizing their legal challenges to government surveillance efforts and positioning themselves as the principal line of defense for individuals and groups concerned about government overreach.[91]

As a practical matter, meanwhile, two of the principal strategies that have been deployed to check national security surveillance strengthen the privileged position of private-sector communications intermediaries. One strategy involves control over data retention. As noted previously, post-Snowden, Congress enacted legislation narrowing the government's authority to request production of telecommunications metadata; as amended, the FISA statute now requires such requests to be structured by appropriately defined selectors and effectively bans bulk collection.[92] Self-evidently, the amendments do not limit communications intermediaries' power to collect and retain data for their own purposes, but rather depend on their continuing to do exactly that. The year beforehand, the Court of Justice of the European Union had invalidated a European Union directive mandating data retention by communications providers, ruling that the mandate imposed a disproportionate burden on citizen's fundamental rights. That ruling, however, did not speak directly to purportedly consensual platform activities that result in equally comprehensive collection and retention of data about users, and a separate directive governing data collection and processing for law enforcement purposes unambiguously authorizes governments to compel production of such data.[93]

A very different strategy for limiting communications surveillance by state actors involves platform provision of strong communications encryption. After the Snowden revelations, platform giant Apple spearheaded a push to make strong encryption the marketplace default for both voice and text communications. That campaign received an important boost when Facebook agreed to enable encryption by default for users of its WhatsApp messaging service, used by billions of people worldwide.[94] Once again, however, questions about lines of access for government investigations have become hotly contested. In the wake of the 2015 terrorist attack in San Bernardino, California, after which investigators acquired but could not readily access one terrorist's iPhone, law enforcement and national security officials mounted an aggressive campaign, still continuing as of this writing, to convince both Congress and the courts to impose decryption mandates on communications firms that provide strong encryption capabilities to their users. Technology experts, in turn, have renewed their earlier arguments that mandatory decryption "back doors" will make the network less secure for everyone, and the rising tide of data breach incidents has made those arguments even more compelling.[95]

Notably, strong encryption is an increasingly toothless safeguard against *commercial* surveillance, so even a complete shift to strong encryption for communications would not disrupt the platform business model much, if at all. As we saw in Chapters 2 and 3, that model revolves around the application of machine learning techniques to the digital traces of people's activities in real and virtual spaces. Communications data provide useful inputs to that process, but those inputs are neither the only nor the most important kinds of information on which the platform business model relies. To the contrary, within the behaviorist framework that animates platform logics, what people say to each other matters far less then what they do. Even with strong communications encryption, digital traces of what people do remain available to the platform provider—location-based information collected from mobile devices, sensor-based techniques for tracking cursor movements, click-through information for items in newsfeeds and social network status updates, DNS level information for tracking web browsing, and so on.

Network architectures constructed for widespread, sensor-based data harvesting in turn have affordances that facilitate opportunistic data grabs by state actors, and when such data grabs occur, laws purporting to safeguard communications privacy do not interpose significant obstacles. The surveillance economy and the surveillance state are inextricably intertwined in more ways than one. As the sensing net extends more broadly throughout and deeply into the everyday lives of ordinary people, the scope for unauthorized secret-keeping narrows.

Publicizing Forbidden Knowledge, Part 1: Enforcing Government Secrecy

Government efforts to preserve and expand operational secrecy, meanwhile, have harnessed a variant of the logic of digital contraband, within which the government's quasi-proprietary interest in secret information trumps the public's right to know. Just as the idea of digital property has come to signal a definitional exception to protections for expressive freedom, so the strategies deployed to block flows of information that the government wishes to keep secret have begun to signal equally absolute exceptions to ordinary principles of due process and government accountability.

Consider first the WikiLeaks/Manning and Snowden episodes described earlier in this chapter. The historical precedent most directly comparable to the leaks by Manning and Snowden is the Pentagon papers episode. In 1971, Daniel Ellsberg, a high-ranking analyst for the RAND Corporation, had become increasingly disillusioned with the Johnson administration's publicly stated justifications for continuing the Vietnam War. Ellsberg copied documents revealing previously undisclosed information about the extent of U.S. military involvement in Southeast Asia and shared them with the *New York Times*, which began publishing selected excerpts.[96] The government indicted Ellsberg for violations of the Espionage Act and sued the *Times* in an attempt to enjoin additional disclosures of classified information. The episode did not, however, end with Ellsberg imprisoned and the *Times* cowed into submission; instead, it revealed a judicial system that was fiercely independent and robustly accountable to overarching principles of expressive freedom and the rule of law. The Supreme Court handed the *New York Times* a sweeping victory, ruling that freedom from prior restraint was essential in order for the press to "fulfill its essential role in our democracy" and that the government had not met the very heavy burden that would be necessary to override that freedom.[97] (Three justices, however, thought that the government's assertion of national security considerations warranted greater deference.) Subsequently, after revelations that government investigators seeking to discredit Ellsberg had themselves committed multiple criminal acts, the government's attempted prosecution of Ellsberg ended in dismissal.[98]

Decades later, the prosecution of then-Bradley Manning for distributing classified materials to WikiLeaks and the controversy over the Snowden leaks have unfolded very differently. Ellsberg had been a civilian; Manning was a member of the U.S. armed forces and was court-martialed before a panel of military judges, a tribunal relatively insulated from the influence of public opinion. The Espionage Act criminalizes willful publication of classified information detrimental to the United States without regard to the motive underlying publication, which over the years has made it a convenient vehicle for prosecution of whistleblowers attempting to shed light on government misdeeds.[99] In an effort to mitigate the eventual punishment, defense counsel called Harvard Law professor and internet law expert Yochai Benkler to testify that WikiLeaks should be regarded as a legitimate journalistic endeavor and that the charges against Manning threatened to chill the practice of investigative journalism. Observers were unsurprised, however, when Manning was convicted and sentenced to 35 years in prison.[100] Edward Snowden, who had fled the country before sharing the documents about bulk NSA surveillance, faces charges that carry the death penalty, and remains in Russia on the advice of counsel.[101] Meanwhile, the pattern of prosecuting leakers and whistleblowers has continued. Most recently, Reality Winner, a national security contract employee and former military officer, now faces a 10-year prison sentence for providing the press with a document prepared by the NSA confirming Russian attempts to compromise U.S. digital voting systems before the 2016 presidential election.[102]

Perhaps because the *New York Times* precedent so clearly shields media organizations from criminal liability for publishing materials of public concern, no charges were brought against the long list of established media organizations that published excerpts from the Manning and Snowden leaks, but other organizations and individuals have been less fortunate. Documentary filmmaker Laura Poitras, who later served as one of Snowden's initial contacts, was subjected to systematic surveillance and repeated border detentions after having filmed an Iraqi family watching an American military operation from the roof of their home. Freelance journalist Barrett Brown, who embedded himself with hackers to research the operation of the hacker collective Anonymous, was tried and convicted for violating the federal computer fraud and abuse laws and served four years in prison. Federal prosecutors secretly filed charges against WikiLeaks founder Julian Assange and have pursued his extradition to the United States, even though he is not a U.S. citizen and was not within U.S. territory when he took the actions that incurred the government's displeasure.[103] Leaving nothing to chance, organizations such as the *Times*, the *Washington Post*, and *The Guardian* have worked to distance themselves from WikiLeaks and its methods, stating publicly that they do not simply publish information received from whistleblowers, but instead conduct due diligence to guard against endangering covert agents or undermining military operations.[104]

The logic under which the government asserts a free-floating interest in operational secrecy often blurs state and private economic interests, giving the secrecy claims a distinctly proprietary cast. Since its enactment in 1966, the Freedom of Information Act has exempted trade secret information submitted by private parties from the disclosure obligations that ordinarily attach to information about how the government operates.[105] As digital technologies and capabilities furnished to the government by private contractors have become more central to national security and law enforcement operations, both the privileged status of trade secrets and the legal justifications asserted for protecting secrecy have changed. The criminal prohibitions in the Economic Espionage Act of 1996 explicitly refer to both private economic and national security concerns stemming from the misappropriation of valuable information.[106] As Laura Donohue has shown, many post-9/11 cases in which the state secrets privilege is asserted involve government contractors. Many of those cases are really disputes about trade secrecy, in which the state secrets privilege functions as a tool for preserving economic advantage. Similarly, in ordinary criminal proceedings, federal and state prosecutors have begun to assert contractual obligations to respect trade secrecy as a way of shielding from disclosure information about privately sourced surveillance technologies.[107]

A newer collection of techniques used by state actors to protect operational secrecy also echoes the intellectual property enforcement playbook. After it published the cache of diplomatic cables provided by Manning, WikiLeaks suddenly found itself without DNS and Web hosting providers and without a way to process donations. Although government officials denied that official pressure on EveryDNS.net, Amazon.com, and PayPal, which formerly had provided those services to WikiLeaks, caused those sites to terminate their relationships, industry observers who had watched the developments closely concluded otherwise.[108] In 2009, British law enforcement conducted a warrantless raid and seizure of computer equipment at premises owned by the operator of a Web server used by IndyMedia, an independent journalism collective founded to provide an alternative perspective on current events to that offered by giant media corporations. The stated purpose was to obtain removal of personal information posted about a judge, but the information had already been removed by the site operator.[109] The national security letters that demand production of communications and financial records include nondisclosure provisions that mimic those commonly found in trade secrecy licensing agreements. State authorities also have deployed credentialing tactics to suppress unwanted criticism of the way they do their jobs; recently, an Oregon administrative board fined a critic of its traffic light timing protocols for practicing engineering without a license.[110]

Platform firms have publicly resisted some government efforts to protect operational secrecy, but here again both the extent and the purpose of that resistance are hotly debated and difficult to parse. Google, Twitter, and other communications intermediaries have filed lawsuits to challenge the secrecy surrounding government programs for communications surveillance, and have scored some important victories. Although, as already noted, courts remain reluctant to second-guess government threat assessments, they have treated demands to maintain secrecy indefinitely with greater skepticism. Arguing that the public has a right to be informed about the fact of government surveillance activity, communications intermediaries also have developed a "warrant canary" system to circumvent the nondisclosure requirements in national security letters. These actions have garnered accolades from digital civil liberties groups. Other commentators, more skeptical, observe that platforms challenge only a very small number of the orders they receive and that important information about the level and nature of the cooperation between platform firms and law enforcement entities remains undisclosed and undiscovered.[111]

Publicizing Forbidden Knowledge, Part 2: Competing Sovereignties

Other government efforts to prevent the spread of forbidden information involve materials distributed by terrorist, extremist, and organized hate groups. Here the logics of dangerous information and culpable facilitation collide more directly with platforms' interest in maintaining their own operational secrecy—and also with the logics of innovative and expressive immunity that Chapter 3 explored. Government efforts to enlist platforms in efforts stop dangerous information from flowing have triggered protracted, still-unresolved struggles over the nature of platforms' obligations, the adequacy of their disclosures, and the extent of their power.

It is useful to begin by noting an obvious disconnect within emerging logics of fiat interdiction: Despite the increasingly draconian nature of such logics and the undeniable fact that platform-based intermediation works to target flows of information toward recipients identified as especially willing to receive them, nobody has prosecuted platforms for, say, material facilitation of terrorism. In the United States, although the possibility of prosecution undoubtedly has been the subject of private discussions both at the Department of Justice and in platform C suites, the *public* struggles over the extent of platforms' interdiction obligations generally have concerned whether and under what conditions platforms must permit communications to flow, not whether and under what conditions they should be required to block them. Civil suits filed against platforms for facilitating the spread of terrorist information have been quickly dismissed. As we saw in Chapter 3, that result follows straightforwardly from the language of section 230 of the Communications Decency Act and its accompanying logic of expressive immunity, and it has been greeted with widespread approbation.[112]

In Europe and elsewhere around the globe, debates about platform obligations have followed a somewhat different path. Following a series of terrorist attacks in Europe and Britain by homegrown perpetrators who had been radicalized in part by online recruiting materials, government authorities began publicly pressing platforms to block certain types of content more aggressively and effectively. As of this writing, Germany has enacted legislation requiring platforms to remove "unlawful content" within a period of time ranging from 24 hours to seven days. Russia has proposed legislation requiring deletion of "illegal content" within 24 hours, and the European Commission has issued a proposed regulation that would impose liability for failure to remove "terrorist content" within one hour. Predictably, these developments have elicited howls of protest and dire warnings about the incipient triumph of state censorship from U.S. commentators.[113]

The dominant U.S. platform firms initially resisted pressure from European governments to alter their content removal policies, invoking the "technologies of freedom" ideal and the logics of innovative and expressive immunity. As it became clear that European policymakers had no intention of emulating their American counterparts' pliability on matters of platform autonomy, however, they gradually became more amenable to negotiation and compromise. In 2017, Facebook, YouTube, Microsoft, and Twitter announced plans to begin developing a shared registry of content identified as terrorist-affiliated and marked for removal—and framed the initiative as a voluntary act of good corporate citizenship.[114] In 2018, Facebook announced that it would host a delegation of French authorities for closed-door discussions about possible improvements to its content removal protocols.[115]

Under pressure from European governments, U.S. platform firms also become more amenable to discussing aspects of their content removal policies publicly. From time to time, journalists and scholars had extracted bits of information about platforms' policies and practices for content flagging, review, and removal, and in May 2017, leaked Facebook training manuals and other documents afforded a more comprehensive picture of then-existing policies regarding harassing, suicide-related, hate-related, and terrorist-related content. Subsequently, Facebook and other platforms began to release more detail about their "content moderation" policies and practices.[116]

At the same time, however, platforms have mobilized both their own logics of operational secrecy and narratives about heroic civil libertarian opposition to state censorship to manage the terms of the public debate about content removal, mandated and otherwise. We have already seen in Chapter 3 that releases of takedown information can be highly selective and strategic. So, for example, Google and other platform firms have labored both to provide information about takedowns pursuant to the European "right to be forgotten" and to do so in ways that express their opposition to the new requirements. The major platform firms also have developed new "transparency reports" to publicize information about takedown notices served by copyright owners and firms acting on their behalf. Platform responses to demands for interdiction of terrorist and extremist content have followed the same general pattern. Information about takedown statistics for other unlawful content is a core component of the new strategy of engagement with European governments, and so are efforts to publicize politically motivated requests for content removal.[117]

Other interventions by platforms assert their own innovative and technical authority over the logistics of content moderation and content removal. Conference presentations by representatives of a number of leading firms play up themes of technical and managerial expertise, stressing the scale of their operations, the technical and contextual difficulties that surround identifying the relevant content, and the human resources challenges entailed in managing the workers tasked to review it.[118] Notably, however, when discussions about interdiction of terrorist and hate speech turn toward the operational details of platforms' content *recommendation* practices, the newfound commitment to openness ends. As earlier chapters have described, platforms work hard to keep information about the ways in which their intermediation practices foster *im*moderation out of court and out of public view.

My goal here is not to litigate whether platforms are doing enough or too much (or, perhaps, not enough and too much at the same time) but rather to focus the reader's attention on the ways that the outcomes just described are both inconsistent with the logics of existential threat and fiat interdiction that this chapter has traced and entirely consistent with the larger patterns explored in earlier chapters. The complex interplay between law and private economic power is reshaping both information-related entitlements and practical enforcement realities across a variety of contexts. To the ledger listing reasons for U.S. authorities' relatively hands-off approach to platforms must be added tacit acknowledgment of the central organizational role that platforms play in the political economy of informational capitalism and deep internalization of the neoliberalized logics of innovative and expressive immunity that platforms and other information businesses have so vigorously asserted. Interdiction mandates arising outside the United States, meanwhile, exist in unavoidable tension with platforms' day-to-day operational control—and dominant platform firms' pockets are very deep indeed.

Information Power and the Reconstruction of Law (and Order)

Commentators have disagreed vigorously about how to evaluate each of the developments that this chapter has described. Some warn of rapidly metastasizing government overreach, while others worry that the government should be doing more to protect the security of borders, critical infrastructures, and civilian populations. Some argue that technology-based copyright enforcement initiatives threaten both expressive freedom and creative experimentation, while others worry about the social and economic costs of the copying that evades existing protections. Meanwhile, those attempting to evaluate the complex landscape of platform behavior have debated whether to count platforms as civil libertarians, rapacious appropriators of creative labor, obstructors of justice, or privatized extensions of the surveillance state.

Those debates are important, but it is also essential to consider the larger patterns that are emerging as a result of the repeated, strategic interactions between and among the competing interests. For my purposes here, two aspects of that pattern are especially worth underscoring.

First, the "new normal" in the platform-based, massively intermediated information economy is a condition in which fiat-based prohibitions on information flow are both increasingly routine and increasingly inscrutable. Even as state actors, intellectual property owners and platform firms have struggled to claim the moral high ground in particular disputes, the logics of fiat interdiction have become more closely intertwined and more resistant to disruption. Across a wide variety of contexts, the combination of powerful secrecy rules, privatization of interdiction functions, and exceptionalist procedural tactics works to shield such logics from critical interrogation.

Second, and relatedly, the landscape of arrangements for interdiction and control of information flows is only partly comprised of state mandates. Compromises that involve voluntary filtering shift much day-to-day authority over management of information flows to platforms and at the same time make such decisions more difficult to contest. The "new normal" in the platform-based, massively intermediated information economy is a condition in which platform businesses enjoy increasing autonomy both to define the terms of their own compliance with mandates promulgated by state actors and to create and refine their own operational arrangements. The normative and practical authority of platforms—including, increasingly, their sovereign power to determine the exception—has become both something taken for granted and a powerful force reshaping the law in its own image. In Part II, we will explore the consequences of that transformation unfolding across multiple institutional domains.

PART II

PATTERNS OF
INSTITUTIONAL CHANGE

The chapters in this part of the book are about the processes that are reshaping the structure and operation of legal institutions. They highlight three sets of effects that together are shaping emerging institutional settlements.

To begin with, legal institutions are backward-looking, or artifactual, in two different senses. First and most obviously, they are creatures of procedure. Courts and regulatory bureaucracies follow jurisdictional and procedural rules that define the kinds of matters they can entertain and the kinds of actions they can take. More generally, the legal institutions that evolved during the industrial era reflect certain basic presumptions about constraints on institutional design and action that are artifactual in the ideological sense—that are intertwined with distinctively liberal governmentalities and reflect corresponding ideas about the rule of law. Presumptions dictating, for example, that courts cannot investigate complaints or render advisory opinions and that administrative agencies can wield discretion only pursuant to a formal delegation of executive authority and only subject to judicial oversight are artifactual in the second, ideological sense. Procedural rules and animating ideologies generate powerful path dependencies that shape both the horizons of possibility for institutional change and *perceptions* about where those horizons are located.

A second set of structuring effects is political and economic. Patterns of institutional change are not neutral. To use Marc Galanter's memorable phrase, in institutional processes structured by procedural rules, the "haves" tend to come out ahead because, as repeat players with disposable resources to spare, they can play for rules in addition to results.[1] To a far greater extent than other parties, repeat players can both choose their battles and determine how they will be fought. The chapters in this part highlight constellations of rules and practices that have begun to emerge as the informational economy's powerful repeat players—platform firms, data brokers, financial firms, owners of large intellectual property portfolios, and others—have developed, iterated, and refined their litigation, regulatory, and government relations strategies.

Relatedly, processes of institutional realignment also tend to reflect background allocations of rights, privileges, and other entitlements. So, for example, as Morton Horwitz demonstrated in his classic study of the evolution of private and commercial law prior to the constitutional battles of the *Lochner* era, during the nineteenth century, economic regulation developed in ways that reinforced emerging concentrations of industrial power, and judges came to understand the common law as a tool for promoting commerce and economic development. Those relatively recent developments established the distributive backdrop against which the high-profile constitutional disputes of the *Lochner* and New Deal eras were litigated.[2] Similarly, we will see in this part of the book that the patterns of entitlement and disentitlement described in Part I—and the accompanying logics of performative enclosure, productive appropriation, innovative and expressive immunity, and fiat interdiction—produce powerful normative force fields, inclining courts, regulators, and policymakers toward particular views about which private-sector actions merit responses and what those responses ought to be.

A final set of structuring effects is sociotechnical. Technological capabilities originally envisioned as facilitating the activities of existing institutions have begun to catalyze deeper institutional transformations. Here I mean not only to refer to the general proposition that networked information and communications technologies and infrastructures alter the background conditions for having and exercising power, but also to argue that those technologies' capabilities and affordances have more concrete procedural and institutional entailments. The same sociotechnical shifts that have enabled more fine-grained control of economic and communicative activities are also producing complementary patterns of legal-institutional evolution and change. Those patterns, moreover, are not necessarily neutral. Recall that the core strategy of neoliberal governmentality involves bringing market techniques and methods into government, infusing processes of legal and regulatory oversight with a competitive and capitalist ethos.[3] Patterns of institutional change in the networked information era reflect beliefs and unquestioned assumptions about the best uses of new technological capabilities to *manage* legal and regulatory processes. Often (though not always), those beliefs emanate from an ideology—managerialism—that is closely entwined with neoliberal governmentality. The melding of new technical capabilities with neoliberal ideologies and the deployment of those capabilities toward managerialist ends have both accelerated and altered the trajectories of institutional evolution.

5

The End(s) of Judicial Process

"But what of the Castle in the Air?" the bug objected, not very pleased with the arrangement.
"Let it drift away," said Rhyme.
"And good riddance," added Reason, "for no matter how beautiful it seems, it's still nothing but a prison."

Norton Juster, *The Phantom Tollbooth*

We begin with institutions for resolving disputes and vindicating (or declining to vindicate) claims about harm. Within the industrial-era legal system, civil litigation was the principal mechanism for dispute resolution. Over the past several decades, however, the landscape of remedial litigation has undergone a number of much-remarked shifts. Liberalized institutional features dating from an earlier, more reformist era—including the pleading standards inaugurated by the Federal Rules of Civil Procedure, federal class action procedures, standards of tort liability capable of reaching the manufacture of complex consumer products, and statutory regimes intended to help courts reach and remedy a variety of marketplace harms—have been systematically ratcheted back. Alternative dispute resolution systems have proliferated. Meanwhile, due in part to the volume of case filings and in part to the increasing complexity of some types of litigation, the judicial system now seems to function principally to funnel disputes toward settlement. The judicial pursuit of efficiency has produced the model that Judith Resnik, over three decades ago, labeled "managerial": a system focused on processing mass claims efficiently through its various stages and largely disinclined to entertain questions about structural or systemic injustice.[1]

This chapter recontextualizes those familiar stories. Courts are one piece, albeit the most visible and contested one, of a larger puzzle that concerns the design of dispute resolution systems and institutions for the era of informational capitalism. As we saw in Part I, the movement to informational capitalism puts new resources, new economic logics, and new technological affordances into play. There is no particular reason to think either that the kinds of disputes requiring resolution should remain the same or that information-era dispute resolution mechanisms should function the same way that their predecessors did. But there is also no reason to think that the patterns now emerging are the fairest or most effective. The ongoing processes of judicial retrenchment and reconfiguration are the products of a complex encounter between the liberal-individualist paradigm underlying the traditional, court-centered system of procedural justice, the affordances that networked digital technologies offer for large-scale information aggregation and processing, and the ascendant ideology of neoliberal governmentality.

The gradual but accelerating movement to informational capitalism has confronted the judicial system with two large and interrelated problems: a proliferation of asserted harms that are intangible, collective, and highly informationalized; and an unmanageably large and ever-increasing number of claimants and interests. I will call these problems, respectively, the *problem of harm* and the *problem of numerosity*. In the abstract, both problems might seem easy enough to solve. For example, confronted with an accelerating proliferation of complex, intangible harms, one might systematically investigate whether and how current doctrines limiting the justiciability of those harms should evolve in response, equipping courts to respond more effectively to the patterns of power and vulnerability that characterize the contemporary, informational economy. Similarly, one might logically conclude that an effective response to the problem of numerosity should entail the development of wholly new mechanisms for aggregating, sequencing, and processing disputes, and attempt to develop such mechanisms. But judges cannot simply proclaim that courts are to be remade as institutions for resolving mass disputes involving intangible, collective harms without colliding headlong with long-standing institutional traditions. For some commentators, meanwhile, the logics of information-driven modernization have seemed fundamentally irreconcilable with the traditional emphasis on individualized claims, harms, and remedies.

Other factors shaping the evolution of judicial processes are much newer, however, and here the critique of judicial managerialism merits very careful consideration. As understood by its proponents, the critique also signifies intellectual dismissal. The label "managerial" denotes a stance toward procedural justice that is simultaneously totalizing and theoretically lightweight.[2] That is a great mistake. Managerialism is not simply an orientation but rather a flourishing discipline that has been called "the first neo-liberal science."[3] It is founded on a specific body of knowledge that is the subject of large and growing literatures in fields such as management theory and organization studies, and both managerial theories and the knowledge practices that they have elicited are deeply entangled with ideologies of neoliberal governmentality.

More specifically, *management* is the practice of deploying informational techniques to reshape organizations along competitively efficient lines; *managerialism* refers to the ideological framework that both posits such reshaping as desirable and prescribes how it may best be achieved.[4] Managerial theories incorporate both ideologies about the nature of effective governance and assumptions about the universe of feasible institutional strategies and practices. Such theories both presume and work to reproduce a particular type of subjectivity; the ideal subject of managerialism is self-interested but understands his or her self-interest to be aligned with the organization's larger goals. Such theories also presume and privilege managerial elites with the skills needed to coordinate productive competition, to discipline participant subjectivity in the interest of efficient production, and to keep wasteful bureaucracy in check.[5] The tradition of critical legal studies, which equates managerialism with bureaucracy, overlooks or elides this last point, but it is fundamental to understanding the implications of the managerial turn for the design of dispute resolution systems. Neoliberal managerialism does not value bureaucracy but rather efficient administration of lean and nimble production, a very different thing.[6]

We will see in this chapter that the turn toward neoliberal managerialism in dispute resolution reinforces certain aspects of the liberal-individualist procedural tradition and undermines others, producing hybrid doctrinal and procedural formations that resonate with one another in unexpected and potent ways. Most notably, the traditional emphasis on individualized claims and individuated process resonates with neoliberalism's emphasis on marketized, individualized choice. Reconceiving judicial process within the ideology of neoliberal governmentality thus appears as a reassertion of tradition while at the same time drastically narrowing the courts' ability to address the conditions of contemporary market and commercial life. Judicial retrenchment also lends momentum to informationalized processes of organizational innovation occurring both within the court system and elsewhere in the dispute resolution landscape. Through those processes, courts are being decentered and repositioned as components within a larger assemblage for dispute resolution that also incorporates other major systems.

In short, a process of institutional reinvention is underway. The judicial system—conceived throughout the industrial era as a monolithic dispenser of one-size-fits-all justice—is being reconceived and re-engineered along streamlined and diversified lines. Fundamental to that process is the conviction—incoherent from the traditional, procedural-justice perspective but pellucid from a managerialist perspective—that different kinds of disputes should be managed differently. At the same time, the rules that govern the sorting, classification, routing, and processing of disputes are being optimized to the interests of powerful information-economy actors. Some kinds of claims—most notably those for recognition and enforcement of intellectual property rights and similar proprietary interests—are afforded extensive and creative process, while others—most notably those for recognition and vindication of information privacy, data protection, consumer, and worker claims—are afforded only minimal or notional process. Scholarly critiques of judicial retrenchment and differentiation in the quality of procedural justice have remained largely court-centric and nostalgic, thereby effectively ceding questions about what an effective and just dispute resolution system for the political economy of informationalism ought to look like.

Who's Harming Who? Legal Constructions of Injury and Justiciability

Litigating information-era harms requires framing them as justiciable injuries—that is, injuries that courts can recognize and redress. According to current doctrine, to establish standing to litigate in federal court, a would-be plaintiff must establish "injury in fact," which requires a showing of harm that is concrete and particularized, actual or imminent rather than conjectural or hypothetical, fairly traceable to the defendant's activity, and likely to be redressed by a favorable decision.[7] Although state courts don't impose identical requirements, would-be plaintiffs still must allege cognizable injury. Finally, in either court system, litigants who succeed in establishing standing must then establish harm if they want to recover.

As Seth Kreimer has shown, the injury-in-fact doctrine is a mid-twentieth-century invention, constructed by the Supreme Court in response to cases in which the claimed injuries were predominantly informational and seemed too general and intangible to count as redressable wrongs.[8] Put differently, the injury-in-fact doctrine is a generally reactionary (i.e., noninterventionist) institutional response to the problem of harm. Confronted with a variety of situations involving complex, informationally mediated activities and correspondingly complex harms, the judicial system erected jurisdictional bulwarks against certain kinds of claims.

In operation, the injury-in-fact construct functions as a black box, simultaneously regulating access to the courts and deflecting attention from its own internal logics. Its constituent propositions about harm, imminence, causal connection, and redressability rest on tightly constructed syllogisms that verge on circularity—a justiciable "controversy" requires actual, concrete injury; the requirement of actual, concrete injury enables courts to avoid issuing advisory opinions; courts should avoid issuing advisory opinions because their core competence lies in the resolution of actual controversies; and so on. Whether or not that reasoning can stand on its own regarding what actually qualifies as a "controversy" is not really the point, however. Like the processes of entitlement redefinition explored in Part I, the injury-in-fact inquiry is performative; it redefines the appropriate institutional role of courts at a moment of economic transformation even as it denies the possibility that courts themselves might participate in such reshaping.

We will see in this section that the injury-in-fact inquiry enshrines a distinctively neoliberalized conception of the judicial role in which courts function principally to discipline deviations from marketplace norms rather than to correct more systematic marketplace excesses. That stance foregrounds harms that are discrete, individuated, and preferably monetizable. (As we will see later in the chapter, emerging resolutions of the problem of numerosity then systematically devalue such harms, effectively reducing them to operating costs.) It positions more diffuse, systemic market and sociotechnical dynamics as presumptively normal—an approach that is calculated to leave most complaints about accountability for economic activity at the courthouse door. For courts, that approach promises a reliable strategy for avoiding the uncertainties that attend intervention in complex, far-flung activities. For litigants, it underscores the sociotechnical intractability and "facts on the ground" character of economic power. And so judicial consensus about the nonjusticiability of certain kinds of claims begins to harden in ways that appear neutral and inevitable but cannot help being ideologically inflected.

Concreteness and the Problem of Intangibility

One set of objections to justiciability concerns the asserted intangibility and generality of many information-era legal claims. Suits asserting environmental claims and, more recently, information privacy claims have been frequent targets of this objection. Citizen claims alleging environmental harm often fail because environmental protection statutes define harms that are collective and difficult to personalize.[9] In information privacy litigation, defendants argue that the ordinary acts of information collection and use that have become routine background conditions in the information environment create no cognizable injury both because tiny bits of personal information have no inherent value and because the asserted consequences of personal data processing and profiling are too nebulous. Information privacy claims, they conclude, are really no more than generalized claims about the perceived unfairness of economic and technological processes that people have not yet learned to accept.[10]

Whether such assessments are right, of course, depends importantly on baselines. Therefore, it is useful to begin by reconsidering the kinds of injuries that serve as implicit (and sometimes explicit) reference points for the managerial project of narrowing access to the courts. Over the years we have come to think of the theories of recovery commonly employed in more traditional tort contexts involving bodily injury as concrete and precise, and in the process we have learned to overlook the fact that they are neither.[11] Both bodily injury and the seemingly more nebulous categories of "pain and suffering" and "mental anguish" serve as proxies for other types of harms that are inherently anticipatory: lost wages, loss of consortium, lost future happiness, and so on. Over time, inquiries about impairment and suffering have come to function conceptually as ways of black-boxing complex processes by which an unknowable future is translated into a calculable present.[12]

One certainly could do at least as well (if not better) at valuing and compensating privacy injury. For example, data-driven predictive profiling offers employers tools designed to predict which prospective employees will be difficult to retain for personal reasons and which current employees may be looking for work else-where. Armed with that information, employers can decline to hire candidates characterized as high turnover risks and can use the pool of money available for raises to retain those employees most at risk of leaving.[13] In a suit for employment discrimination, breach of contract, or violation of other applicable labor and em-ployment laws, a court could instruct the jury to consider what an individual's serv-ices would be worth if the factors suggesting turnover risk had not been considered or if raises were distributed solely based on performance. We saw in Chapter 2 that data-driven predictive profiling enables merchants and lenders to target particular consumer populations and tailor pricing for goods and services to different kinds of attributes.[14] In a suit for violation of the consumer protection or fairness-in-lending laws, the jury could consider evidence about the services offered and the prices charged to consumers with different attributes.

These suggestions are neither far-fetched nor hypothetical; in fact, courts attempting to quantify damages in copyright and patent infringement cases already engage in very similar reasoning. They assign damages based on hypothesized rea-sonable licensing fees for imagined transactions and posit menus of licensing rates for nascent or nonexistent markets.[15] They determine the profits attributable to infringing activity by means of arithmetically convenient fictions—for example, awarding one-seventeenth of the profits earned by an entire album as damages for sampling a few bars of a copyrighted song on one of the album's 17 tracks.[16]

Some types of asserted intellectual property harm are impossible to quantify with any accuracy, but the copyright system has an answer for that, too: It provides statutory damages as an alternative measure for the rightholder to elect. For or-dinary (i.e., nonwillful) infringement, a court may in its discretion award up to $30,000 for "all infringements involved in the action, with respect to any one work"; for willful infringement, the upper bound increases to $150,000.[17] Courts have exercised their discretion broadly, awarding damages that often seem to be based on little more than their intuitive sense of the rightness or wrongness of the challenged conduct. And the courts of appeal have uniformly rejected the argument that some such awards are so excessive that they violate due process, reasoning that even very large awards simply serve the deterrence function that Congress intended.[18]

Statutory damages also feature in many twentieth-century remedial schemes, including statutes that regulate electronic surveillance, consumer credit re-porting, health information privacy, and government information practices. When interpreting these statutes, however, courts have been notably less generous. For ex-ample, the Supreme Court has read the statutory damages provisions of the federal Privacy Act as authorizing awards only to plaintiffs who can prove actual pecuniary or economic harm.[19] More recently, in a lawsuit against data aggregator Spokeo for statutory damages under the Fair Credit Reporting Act, the Court vacated and remanded an appellate judgment recognizing standing to sue, ruling that al-though violations of statutorily defined individual interests may be sufficiently particularized, some such violations—including both "bare procedural violations" and putatively small data quality errors—still may not be "concrete" enough to count.[20]

Again, one certainly could derive an account of concrete information privacy injury that meets the lenient standard set in copyright cases awarding statutory damages to plaintiffs who cannot prove actual damages. Just as the copyright plaintiff whose works are included in a karaoke DVD has lost a licensing opportunity (though the defendant might never have taken the license and it's impossible to say with any certainty how much it would have paid), so the FCRA plaintiff whose profile contained errors has lost appropriate employment opportunities (though he may never have been offered the job and it's impossible to say with any certainty what he would have earned).[21]

As these examples illustrate, both particularity and concreteness are socially constructed attributes. Judgments about the sufficiency of a claim reflect conclusions about both the locus of experienced harm and the extent of desirable accountability. Some types of asserted harms to copyright interests are extraordinarily abstract, yet the legal system assigns them concrete and particular value. We can tell both that data processing generates consequences of some sort—if it didn't, nobody would spend the resources to engage in it—and that the market considers collected reservoirs of personal data to be valuable, yet the legal system treats the possibility of harm skeptically. Both conclusions, moreover, reflect the gravitational pull of the distributive baselines explored in Part I of this book. The logic of fiat interdiction militates in favor of liability for defendants in intellectual property disputes, while the logics of appropriative privilege and innovative and expressive immunity militate against liability for information privacy defendants.

Imminence and the Problem of Risk

Another set of objections to justiciability concerns whether the plaintiff can state a plausible connection to some actual or reasonably imminent harm. In the case of the federal courts the bar is framed as jurisdictional, but state courts also are reluctant to assign liability based on risk alone. The idea is that the courts should not be called upon to issue advisory opinions about problems that may never materialize. So, for example, defendants in cases involving exposure to toxic chemicals argue that exposure does not invariably lead to illness, and defendants in information privacy cases argue that plaintiffs who object to the harvesting and exploitation of their personal data have alleged no more than generalized fears about possible future events that may never occur.

To evaluate the argument that risk is not injury, it is important to begin by acknowledging the extent to which the injury-in-fact doctrine is itself oriented toward the future. The "imminence" formulation implicitly recognizes that there may be categories of harms that are felt before they have finished arriving. It opens the door to addressing at least some claims about nascent harm and at the same time designates such claims as a focal point for judicial anxiety. In so doing, it underscores the doctrine's dual character as simultaneously reactionary and thoroughly modern.

The heightened sensitivity to nascent harm that the imminence prong of the injury-in-fact doctrine both expresses and attempts to police is in turn the product of a more general conceptual shift toward risk awareness and risk management that has occurred over the course of the modern era. In the eighteenth and nineteenth centuries, developments in statistical and actuarial modeling began to give governments and businesses new tools for measuring, defining, and profiting from populations.[22] Those developments both expressed a newly abstract, probabilistic sensibility toward concepts such as harm and loss and promised to offer ways of making such concepts more concrete and tractable. As constructs based on probability and risk crystallized, they also began to reshape the law, infusing the operation of both old and new legal institutions. We will consider administrative responses to risk sensibility in Chapter 6. In the courts, risk sensibility gave rise to new categories of damages that signified new understandings of harm. We have already seen one small example of this, in the idea of damages for "pain and suffering," discussed previously.

The promise of probabilistic reasoning about harm and liability has never been fully realized within the judicial system, however, and the problem of heightened risk remains one of the flashpoints.[23] Efforts to infuse risk sensibility into tort law have been hotly contested. Over the second half of the twentieth century, as awareness of nascent, systemic harms became more widespread, litigants began to assert new theories of injury predicated on heightened risk of future disease and/or earlier death. In a number of states, courts ruled that exposure to a toxic chemical with a known and sufficiently predictable risk profile can create liability for the costs of ongoing medical monitoring. Other courts, however, declined to follow suit, and the defense bar assailed the development of risk-based liability for toxic tort exposure as unprincipled and potentially ruinous.[24]

Decisions in information privacy cases have begun to follow the pattern established in the toxic exposure cases. The federal courts have cautiously begun developing an account of standing to sue following a data breach based on determinate levels of increased risk. Plaintiffs in data breach cases typically allege not only that they have lost time and money resolving fraudulent charges and instituting credit monitoring but also that they face a heightened risk of future fraudulent charges and identity theft. Reasoning that "customers should not have to wait until hackers commit identity theft or credit-card fraud," courts increasingly have allowed both kinds of claims to proceed in cases manifesting an "objectively reasonable likelihood" of future harm.[25] They tend to think, however, that risks flowing from increased vulnerability to data-driven predictive profiling are too remote and speculative to count as actionable injuries.[26]

At the same time, though, following the pattern described previously, courts have been consistently more receptive to risk-based reasoning about injury to digital property interests. In cases about unauthorized access litigated under the federal

Computer Fraud and Abuse Act, which defines "loss" as including "any reasonable cost to any victim, including the cost of responding to an offense [or] conducting a damage assessment," courts have allowed recovery for the costs of evaluating and mitigating the risks created by system intrusions.[27] The test for injunctive relief in intellectual property cases is predicated in part on the threat of continuing harm that cannot be remedied adequately by a monetary award. Although courts no longer presume irreparable harm from the mere fact of infringement, they have been especially willing to weigh the risk of future infringement in cases with large structural implications.[28]

I will return to the objection about the nonredressability of structural harms, which is fundamentally about institutional competence, at the end of this chapter; for now, I simply want to highlight the way in which this pattern of reasoning about risk frames the background sociotechnical landscape—including all of the factors that embed vulnerability systemically—as risk-neutral. The purported difference between data breach cases and other cases about data collection and processing is that a data breach requires immediate, discrete mitigation measures, whereas in other cases there is nothing (yet) to mitigate. But the sense of emergency that surrounds data breaches has been carefully manufactured in a particular way. Large data breaches now receive widespread media coverage, and entire industries have sprung up to serve the needs of data breach victims.[29] Media coverage of data breaches also tends to point fingers at particular culprits—the data custodian, its purportedly ham-fisted employees, and/or the nameless hackers that perpetrated the theft—rather than at the background condition of widespread, "ordinary" data harvesting and processing. There are no vested interests in creating a comparable sense of emergency about processes that underlie a multibillion-dollar industry. And yet many instances of payment fraud and identity theft do not stem from mass data breaches. Rather, they are the foreseeable results of design choices that privilege convenience and speed over data integrity and security.[30]

The problem, in other words, is that framing the data breach or the exposure to a chemical with a known risk profile as the exception warranting emergency response has enabled courts to ignore the extent to which background norms and design practices work to enshrine vulnerability as a marketplace norm. That result gives the logics of productive appropriation and innovative and expressive immunity broad preemptive scope, categorically foreclosing accountability for entire categories of marketplace activity.

Traceability and the Problem of Causation

A third argument sometimes levied against litigants asserting informational-era harms, as an objection either to standing or to liability, concerns causation. A hallmark of many information-era harms is their causal complexity. When someone develops cancer 10 years after exposure to a known carcinogen but also after exposure to many other potential contributing factors, or when the stock of a company about which false information has been circulated later declines in price, it can be difficult (and often impossible) to trace the harm precisely to one cause rather than another. This seems to stand in stark contrast to the precision of the causal connection that exists when, for example, automobile brakes fail or a defective tire explodes. Time exacerbates the problem of attribution; cancers and other diseases may develop many years after harmful exposure, and in the interim many other potentially contributing factors may have come into play. Here again, courts have been more willing to innovate in some contexts than in others, and the contingent solutions under construction reflect the imperatives of the managerial turn.

Like the problem of risk, the dilemma of probabilistic causation has been one of the defining challenges of the modern era. The two problems are, of course, related; conduct that is linked to harm probabilistically may be difficult to link to particular cases of harm that has materialized. In both cases, the link between the conduct and the harm requires modeling to understand, and the impossibility of gaining unmediated access to the relevant relationships opens the way for politicization of the problem and possible responses.

To appreciate the fact that causation, like concreteness, is a constructed concept, it is useful to begin by reconsidering the examples of defective brakes and tires with which this section began. The causal connection was not always so obvious. In the earliest days of the product liability revolution, the conventional ways of framing causes of action insulated mass-market manufacturers from claims brought by both end users and unlucky bystanders injured by their products. Theories of privity foreclosed claims by parties lacking a prior commercial relationship with the manufacturer.[31] More fundamentally, as noted in the previous section, the tort system had little experience thinking through the issues of complex, probabilistic harm raised by industrial processes and distribution chains. The traditional tort paradigm demanded an individualized inquiry into cause and effect, but many industrial-era injuries were predictable only in the aggregate.[32] Eventually, in a pair of influential opinions, then-judge Cardozo constructed a now-familiar doctrinal device—foreseeability—for bridging the gap between statistically predictable harms and particular claimants. Following Cardozo's lead, courts gradually learned to understand industrial processes as amenable to inspection with regard to notions of fault and later also to see those processes as appropriate sites for interventions directed toward risk-spreading.[33]

Later in the twentieth century, the court system began to confront cases in which individuation and aggregation could not be so easily reconciled using legal fictions such as foreseeability because the identity of the proper defendant was also unclear. In a series of cases involving asserted manufacturing defects in generic pharmaceutical products that could not be traced with certainty to a particular manufacturer, courts in some states concluded that participation in a well-defined market could justify assigning partial liability based on overall market share.[34] Most courts, however, have balked at extending enterprise liability theories to cases in which different manufacturers' products contain different amounts of the substance challenged as harmful, or in which epidemiological modeling implicates both the challenged substance and other causes.[35] Concurrently, defendants in antitrust litigation and in fraud-on-the-market lawsuits filed under the federal securities laws have challenged sophisticated econometric models developed to identify and isolate price effects, arguing that price fluctuations in consumer and securities markets reflect the influence of too many factors to permit precise attribution.[36] Most recently, information privacy claims have seemed to present extreme iterations of both kinds of traceability problems. Many such claims present both probabilistic plaintiffs (i.e., plaintiffs as to whom more discrete privacy injuries, such as loss of job opportunities, are absolutely certain in aggregate but difficult to predict on an individual level) and probabilistic defendants (i.e., defendants whose conduct contributes in an epidemiological sense to those injuries). Defendants argue that plaintiffs cannot link the asserted injuries to the actions of any particular firm, and courts usually agree.[37]

As these disputes have unfolded, theories of probabilistic causation also have engendered ever more intense political and ideological pushback against the very idea of broadly distributed liability for harms flowing from economic development. Political pressure by powerful industries has produced legislation designed to limit the tort system's reach. Additionally, firms seeking to minimize their own liability have deliberately and systematically exploited the overlap between their self-interest and individualized paradigms of procedural justice, working to discredit the evidentiary value of scientific conventions for communicating about probabilistic knowledge and inviting policymakers, judges, and the public to understand judicial insistence on atomistically precise causal explanations as natural and proper.[38] Legal scholars, for their part, have been both uncertain about how tort understandings of cause-in-fact might better accommodate contemporary realities and divided as to the wisdom of such accommodation.[39]

Yet resistance to assigning liability in cases involving complex, probabilistic causation is not uniform. And here again, the intellectual property system may be leading the way toward a more expansive approach to judicially enforced accountability. Consider *Columbia Pictures v. Fung*, a copyright case involving allegations of contributory infringement against a defendant who maintained BitTorrent sites. The court of appeals observed that "where other individuals and entities provide services identical to [the defendant's], causation . . . cannot be assumed, even though fault is unquestionably present."[40] That did not end the matter, however. Instead, the court indicated that the plaintiff still might manage to show a "sufficient causal connection" between the defendant's conduct and infringement of the plaintiffs' copyrights. It left open what that showing would need to entail but noted other evidence clearly suggesting that the defendant knew of and encouraged the use of his sites for infringement.[41] *Fung* raises the prospect of something akin to enterprise liability for (some types of) information intermediaries that threaten major copyright interests. The question of traceability did not arise, and does not even appear to have been contemplated, as an objection to standing to sue.

As these disputes about complex causation illustrate, a decision that a claimed injury is fairly traceable to the defendant's conduct is only partly about causation in the cause-in-fact sense. More generally, such decisions are about how to interpret and reconcile competing instincts about accountability and fairness. Today, those decisions often must be made in the context of emerging categories of networked, probabilistic harms that cannot be traced to any single cause to the exclusion of all others. Societal understandings of harm have evolved to encompass the long-term, systemic effects of industrial development and the growing informationalization of economic activity, but judicially defined constructs of causation often continue to operate at cross purposes to those changes.

Alone/Together: The Evolving Institutional Forms of Mass Justice

In addition to questions about harm and injury, courts—and the judicial system more generally—now routinely confront questions about how to adapt a predominantly individuated model of procedural justice to a world in which justice must deal in large numbers. The judicial system has already undergone one process of partial retrofitting as an institutional vehicle for mass justice claims. That process began in the early twentieth century and gathered momentum later when new class action procedures were devised to handle claims of injury stemming from mass-manufactured and mass-marketed consumer goods. As both consumer products and services and related theories of personal and economic harm have become more complex, however, and as the number of complaints has mushroomed, the judicial system has come under acute logistical and political strain. The orientation that Resnik has labeled "managerial"—including expedited discovery rules and an orientation toward settlement—is a response, in part, to the problem of numerosity.[42]

Among legal scholars and policymakers, reactions to the emergence of managerial justice have been mixed. Some have celebrated the new emphasis on efficiency; some, including Resnik, lament the demise of the aspiration to provide individualized justice but have appeared to hold out hope for the possibility of reinvigorating the traditional paradigm. Others argue the system is simply broken— too expensive, too slow, too focused on the needs of the few and wealthy and unable to serve the needs of the many.[43]

My project in this section is different and entails taking managerialism seriously as a form of institutional discipline that has gradually but inexorably swept the judicial system into its orbit. The judicial system is one component (albeit a very visible and important one) of a larger landscape that also includes other significant mechanisms and processes. Dispute resolution problems are problems of production at scale, to be addressed using techniques for input sorting and supply chain management.

In what follows, I tell three interrelated stories about the management of scale in processes of dispute resolution. Broadly speaking, each story involves reoptimization of the dispute resolution supply chain for systemically significant classes of disputes. But the stories also reveal that dispute resolution processes have evolved very differently for different types of disputes, in ways that reflect the imprint of emergent economic power. High-volume, low-value claims and ancillary knowledge production issues associated with those claims increasingly are regarded as noncore competencies to be managed via outsourcing. Claims for vindication of large-scale, aggregate harm are handled internally but in ways that increasingly route around the relatively rigid class action framework in favor of alternative production methods that are flexible and highly informationalized, Claims for enforcement of intellectual property rights, meanwhile, have elicited creative experimentation with processes for modular production of important intermediate outputs.

Outsourced Production: Boilerplate and Beyond

The first story involves a set of procedural devices that are designed to remove certain kinds of disputes and ancillary knowledge production issues from the judicial system and assign responsibility for managing them to other actors. One controversial and much-remarked feature of the contemporary litigation landscape is the increasing use of private dispute resolution mechanisms as substitutes for judicial process. Legal scholars have focused primarily on the use of boilerplate waivers to deflect civil complaints away from courts and into arbitration. Many high-volume, low-dollar-value disputes, however, are resolved via wholly privatized processes that do not involve either judges or arbitrators, and privatization has begun to reshape the landscape of criminal dispute resolution as well. Other kinds of high-volume, low-dollar-value disputes are delegated to specialized tribunals with narrow but deep expertise in the particular questions requiring resolution, and still others are managed by courts using knowledge frameworks developed partly or wholly outside the judicial system. The literatures in management theory and organization studies supply a perspective on those developments that moves beyond the objections typically raised by legal scholars and suggests the need for more comprehensive, systemic redesign.

We begin with civil litigation. In a wide variety of contexts ranging from employment contracts to service contracts to one-off consumer transactions, courts have become increasingly willing to enforce boilerplate clauses that constrain access to judicial process.[44] Some courts initially resisted such arrangements, but as form contracts became both more ordinary and more central to information-economy business arrangements, they gradually allowed themselves to become re-educated. Economic arguments about the efficiency of such arrangements came to seem familiar and unremarkable, and judges confronted with unthinkable numbers of transactions and relationships mediated by boilerplate lost interest in parsing their terms. Emboldened by judicial inattention, businesses of all sorts now routinely use boilerplate terms to rearrange default entitlements and obligations covering a wide variety of matters relating to their dealings with both consumers and workers.[45]

The current climate of extreme deference to (presumed) individual waiver has produced a powerful historical irony. As noted earlier in this chapter, firms seeking to minimize their liability to those injured by defective products used privity of contract as a mechanism of exclusion. Today, a new generation of firms deploys a (radically reenvisioned) concept of privity to keep consumers and workers close, invoking narratives about consent to bar them from asserting a variety of claims that the law otherwise might support. As in the data sensing and harvesting arrangements studied in Chapter 2, the underlying conception of individual agency is vanishingly thin, consisting of little more than the ability to decline a transaction or employment relationship.

Critiques of waiver-based litigation avoidance strategies by legal scholars have emphasized their distributive justice and rule-of-law implications. As a practical matter, boilerplate waivers effectively instantiate private regulation of employment relationships and consumer rights and remedies. Systematic removal of certain kinds of claims from the courts also freezes the gradual, iterative evolution of legal doctrine. Even when such claims proceed to arbitration, arbitral decisions generally are not published, and so it becomes increasingly difficult to know how the law in practice corresponds to the law on the books.[46]

The lens of managerialism, however, suggests a complementary perspective that situates boilerplate waivers of judicial process within the contemporary turn to outsourcing in the interest of lean and nimble production. Businesses and other organizations now routinely identify various functions for outsourcing to contract providers. Generally speaking, outsourcing involves obtaining inputs to production that a firm previously produced internally from external suppliers in order to realize some sort of competitive gain.[47] That summary definition, however, elides the influence of a variety of sociotechnical, ideological, and cultural factors. To begin with, outsourcing will be efficient only if the savings in production costs outweigh the increase in communication and coordination costs; the turn to outsourcing therefore both assumes the availability of networked information and communication technologies to coordinate far-flung production and deepens reliance on such technologies. Increased informational complexity in turn necessitates increased investment in capabilities for monitoring and oversight; the shift to outsourcing therefore also reflects neoliberal managerialism's emphasis on coordination of production and extraction of rents by elite management. Lastly, the turn to outsourcing reflects the influence of theories of firm value that prize lean organization over various countervailing considerations—such as, for example, shallower carbon footprints or more robust duties of care toward employees—and that rely on market-based shareholder action as the principal disciplinary mechanism. From that perspective, the functions that are ripest for outsourcing are those that lie outside the firm's core extractive competencies.[48] As a practical matter, that category often includes support functions that can be purchased as commodities, including both those performed on-site, such as custodial and food services work, and those capable of being performed remotely in time and space, such as customer support. The increasingly routine outsourcing of such functions both relies upon and intensifies the informationalization of labor described in Chapter 1.[49]

Legal scholarship on managerial judging has applied the outsourcing label to boilerplate litigation waivers but has not carefully considered the lessons the analogy has to teach for the study of dispute resolution systems more generally.[50] From a supply chain management perspective, consumer and employee disputes have many of the attributes that the theoretical and critical literatures on outsourcing identify: they represent significant cost centers, they have many features that are amenable to routinization using networked information and communication technologies and elite management, and their resolution involves discrete and mundane competencies that elite judges may be inclined to view as largely outside their core domains. The logics underlying those judgments are self-reinforcing. Once a particular kind of dispute has been outsourced, any larger policy issues that such disputes implicate may seem irrelevant, extraneous, or simply above the pay grade of the managerial employees to whom oversight is assigned, and such issues may therefore persist unaddressed unless other internal controls are in place.

When changes in the dispute resolution landscape are considered through the lens of outsourcing as managerial discipline, moreover, boilerplate litigation waivers are just one aspect of a much larger movement toward functional disaggregation and reconfiguration of institutional mechanisms for resolving high-volume, low-dollar value disputes. For the vast majority of consumers who become involved in disputes with providers of goods and services, the first and last stop is the provider's internal process for resolving customer complaints. Corporate customer relations personnel follow customized procedural templates that include both scripts for responding to complaints and quasi-appellate processes for escalating more difficult matters up the chain of command; human resources personnel follow similar templates for dealing with employment matters.[51] A similar process of disaggregation and reconfiguration is underway in the criminal justice system. Many businesses that confront repeated, low-level criminal conduct—for example, theft by employees or shoplifting by customers—resolve such matters using privatized processes that do not involve the law enforcement system. Like privatized customer relations proceedings, privatized quasi-criminal dispute proceedings are simple, standardized, and administered by specialized personnel.[52]

Significant private-sector investments in dispute resolution might appear to pose something of a conundrum for the outsourcing framework. From the firm's perspective, privatization represents a significant insourcing of complexity and cost. Developing and implementing regularized dispute resolution processes for customer relations and human relations disputes is a resource-intensive project. For that reason, such processes typically involve a second layer of outsourcing to contract providers of customer relations and human resources services.[53] The processes established by platform firms to handle content removals, discussed in Chapters 3 and 4, follow a similar pattern.[54] Double outsourcing, however, exacerbates the systemic fairness and accountability problems that privatized dispute resolution raises.

The outsourcing rubric also illuminates a diverse set of trends in the contemporary dispute resolution landscape that involve the production and application of specialized knowledge for judges and quasi-judicial officers to apply. From the managerialist perspective, the questions surrounding the optimal use of outsourcing in knowledge production are complex. Certain inputs that are both knowledge-intensive and discrete have long been considered prime candidates for outsourcing. So, for example, firms other than technology firms often hire document management and information technology specialists on a contract basis. Firms also hire outside auditors and lawyers, although the "outsourcing" label generally is not applied to such highly professionalized functions (and, notably, outsourcing financial and legal oversight also serves broader public accountability concerns). The wisdom of outsourcing research and development processes that are more central to the firm's mission is hotly disputed, however. Some argue that, for any firm wishing to remain competitive, research and development are and should remain core competencies. Others take a more nuanced view, arguing that in the globalized information economy, decisions about the optimal allocation of knowledge production should consider both the availability of skilled researchers in lower-cost locations and the extent to which knowledge production processes can be modularized and codified to facilitate exchange within and across organizational boundaries.[55]

Consistent with these trends, the U.S. legal system increasingly relies on specialty tribunals to hear certain kinds of high-volume, low-dollar value cases requiring expertise outside the core competency of generalist judges. They include, among others, administrative tribunals for adjudicating benefits claims, employment disputes, and immigration and tax enforcement matters; administrative bodies charged with distributing mass tort awards and judgments collected in agency enforcement actions; and specialty criminal courts for hearing drug cases and mental health cases.[56] These systems differ from each other in a variety of ways, but all perform explicitly managerial and biopolitical functions. They employ population-based frameworks to evaluate claims to government benefits and private payouts and to determine appropriate responses to certain common pathological or disfavored behaviors.

Consider next uses of externally-developed information frameworks to stream-line criminal dispute resolution. Like legal scholars who study changes in civil dispute resolution, those who study shifting patterns of criminal dispute resolution have been preoccupied principally with the disappearing trial; most criminal charges today result in plea arrangements entered before trial proceedings have begun.[57] Increased reliance on plea bargaining, however, is only one piece of a larger puzzle that also includes substitutes for and supplements to judicial production of criminal justice. In the federal system, the use of such substitutes in sentencing has been routine for many decades. The United States Sentencing Commission, however, is a public entity overseen by current and former criminal justice officials, so its sentencing guidelines represent only a flirtation with outsourced knowledge protection. More recent initiatives using privately designed analytic systems to guide policing, charging, bail, sentencing, and parole decisions are different and raise the prospect of more comprehensive functional disaggregation.[58]

Last but not least is a group of initiatives that involve new electronic systems for resolving high-volume, low-dollar disputes. In Canada, Australia, Europe, and the United States, public programs for alternative dispute resolution increasingly are experimenting with platforms for online dispute resolution. Some such platforms are designed and provisioned with public funding. Mirroring the trend toward outsourcing of knowledge production by the criminal justice system, however, many other experiments involve systems designed and furnished by private contractors.[59]

My purpose in developing this account of outsourcing processes now underway in the production of civil and criminal dispute resolution is neither to signal endorsement of any of the developments just described nor to express opposition to the very idea of functional differentiation. Rather, it is to situate the systematic decentering of litigation for certain categories of disputes within the neo-Polanyian framework of institutional change that this book has developed. From that perspective, the problem is not that legal institutions are changing, but rather that they are changing in ways that leave systemic justice issues and associated problems of institutional design unaddressed. Without question, it is neither feasible nor desirable to convene a full-dress judicial proceeding for every instance of consumer dissatisfaction, every employment-related disagreement, every benefits dispute, or even every instance of alleged theft or fraud. That observation, though, should not end discussion of the possibility of designing procedures that are efficient and scalable but also justice-affording.

Flexible Production: Aggregate Litigation Reconsidered

The second story is about the aggregation and management of claims for asserted large-scale harm. Within the model of remedial litigation developed early in the twentieth century, the principal device for pursuing aggregate relief was the class action, but the primacy of the class device is waning, and newer multidistrict litigation procedures afford judges powerful, flexible tools for managing and resolving aggregated tort and statutory claims. Meanwhile, in both aggregate litigation and public enforcement actions, versatile templates for consent-based structural relief have emerged. Juxtaposing the two sets of developments—once again in light of perspectives afforded by developments in management theory and organization studies—yields valuable insights into emerging systems for the production of legibility and finality in mass dispute resolution.

The American class action device is cited enviously by consumer advocates in other countries, but over the past half century it has been under sustained attack. The courts and Congress have systematically restricted access to class action procedures, and those procedures also have proved insufficiently adaptable to new kinds of claims for networked, intangible harm. The result, as Maria Glover has explained, is a distribution of outcomes that belies aspirations to transsubstantive procedural uniformity.[60] Claims for violation of remedial statutes that define specific wrongs and prescribe uniform remedies have a relatively smooth road to certification, and plaintiffs may use statistical evidence to fill certain types of well-defined gaps in the evidentiary record. Putative class claims involving "the invocation of markets as the source of some common wrong" also achieve certification relatively easily, but only to the extent that the economic harm to each plaintiff is relatively easy to calculate.[61] Certification may be avoided if the market is complex and the plaintiff's expert economic report does not isolate the alleged harm with sufficient precision. Class complaints asserting broader, structural theories of civil wrongdoing not specifically delineated by statute face an uphill battle to both certification and admission of statistical evidence. Notably, those outcomes also reflect the influence of the atomistic approach to causation and responsibility explored in the first half of this chapter.

Contests over standards for class certification and uses of statistical evidence to substantiate claims and calculate remedies are becoming increasingly irrelevant, however, because class action litigation has gradually been subsumed within a different and more flexible rubric for managing and resolving mass claims. The federal courts increasingly rely on consolidated multidistrict litigation (MDL) proceedings to aggregate certain types of individual claims for more efficient processing. Relative to class actions, MDL proceedings allow courts more flexibility in identifying common issues, grouping cases, and crafting comprehensive settlement decrees, a comparative advantage that has steadily grown as access to class actions has narrowed. MDL proceedings also are far more opaque than class action proceedings, which are subject to regularized procedural rules.[62] Once inside the MDL process, even formerly headline-grabbing lawsuits have seemingly vanished. Many putative class actions move into MDL before being certified and most cases settle while still in the preliminary stages, so the certification decision is made, if at all, in the context of a motion to certify a settlement class.

Mass tort litigation has been a significant driver of the turn to MDL, but in recent years new types of information-economy disputes—in particular data breach and information privacy litigation—also have become significant drivers, and platform defendants in particular have developed a suite of powerful strategies for avoiding or drastically limiting both class certification and the scope of available remedies. Those strategies exploit the narratives about entitlement and disentitlement that Part I explored, leveraging the logics of performative enclosure and appropriative privilege to minimize possible monetary exposure and deflect meaningful structural relief.[63] Aggregate litigation against platform firms also confronts obstacles stemming from the technologically opaque nature of data-driven algorithmic processes. Interactions involving consumers' personally identifying information often are embedded deeply within the operating protocols of a mobile phone or Web browser, and may involve complex commercial relationships among multiple companies. That enables platform firms to argue both that the methods proposed for ascertaining the group of consumers affected by any particular practice are just too imprecise and that including all users of a particular service would threaten crippling liability—an objection that ultimately boils down to the argument that some classes are just "too big to certify."[64] Courts reject some of those arguments, but they also routinely decline requests to define classes broadly and refuse to craft discovery orders far-reaching enough to enable plaintiffs to understand the challenged patterns of information flow.[65]

Consider now a very different group of examples that also involve the attempted use of litigation to produce large-scale structural reform. Beginning in the mid-twentieth century, courts charged with resolving constitutional claims against government entities for large-scale equal protection violations improvised on the relatively limited remedial forms available to them, developing templates for ongoing oversight that were formally injunctions but that extended far into the future and asserted an interest in the day-to-day operation of the entities under supervision. Beginning with the enforced desegregation of school districts and continuing with orders designed to remedy civil rights violations by other government entities, courts imposed remedial orders on a wide variety of public institutions. Subsequently, litigation under new federal civil rights statutes extended the model of the supervisory injunction to private corporations as well. Initial academic assessments credited the resulting model of public law litigation with enormous upside potential for reform of entrenched structural inequality and argued that direct judicial supervision was the key ingredient for producing institutional transformation.[66]

But there is a parallel story about public law litigation, in which the supervisory injunction—eventually restyled as the consent decree—gradually began to impose a new form of institutional discipline on the courts as well. Like claims asserted as putative class actions, most viable claims for injunctive relief against both corporate and public defendants now eventually settle, producing lengthy consent decrees that specify the details of commitments to come into compliance with the applicable requirements. Along the way, the project of structural transformation has gradually been subsumed within more prosaic managerialist rubrics. Structural reform orders styled as consent decrees incorporate standard time periods, benchmarks for improvement, and methods of compliance monitoring, and compliance monitoring is intensively informationalized.[67] In parallel with those changes, contemporary reappraisals of the efficacy of structural-reform litigation as a catalyst for institutional transformation have become far less glowing. In particular, critics argue that, after the publicity generated by the initial filing and the settlement has died away, reappraisals to track durable institutional change are rare.[68]

The same general pattern—an initial wave of litigation successes followed by a shift toward settlement and a concomitant shift toward routinization, diminishing returns, and heightened informational complexity and opacity—has characterized public enforcement practice involving corporate defendants. Like public law litigation, most enforcement actions for violation of securities, antitrust, and consumer protection laws tend to culminate in consent decree proceedings. Such decrees generally require changes to certain business practices and impose obligations to submit to periodic or ongoing audits of those practices. Although the defendants sometimes agree to pay fines, they generally need not admit fault. Advocates of such arrangements argue that changing firm behavior is more important than extracting formal acknowledgment of responsibility. Judges and academic commentators studying such no-fault arrangements, however, have raised pointed questions about their efficacy as catalysts for longer-term behavioral change.[69]

Information-economy bellwether firms—platform companies such as Google and Facebook and financial firms such as Citigroup and JP Morgan Chase—have proved particularly adept at incorporating consent decree compliance into their regular business practices with only minimal disruption. A few additional managerial controls are imposed; additional consumer disclosures are incorporated into the already-existing documents that most consumers do not read; and the necessary reports are generated, reviewed by auditors, and filed with regulators. The occasional fines levied in civil and criminal proceedings are relatively small compared to annual revenues and can be lumped with other expenses of doing business.[70]

Together, these trends—the de facto marginalization of the class action device, the emergence of MDL as the principal vehicle for awarding monetary relief in aggregate litigation, and the routinization of consent decree practice in both aggregate litigation and public enforcement actions—exemplify another prominent theme in management and organization studies, which has to do with changing approaches to mass production over the course of the twentieth century. Even as the justice system has been pressed to assume greater and greater responsibility for the mass production of litigation outcomes, the conventional wisdom about the optimal design of mass production processes has undergone a revolution. Over the course of the twentieth century, the lock-step system of industrial production pioneered by

Frederick Winslow Taylor and embraced by industrial giants such as Ford, General Motors, and U.S. Steel gradually gave way to the flexible production system developed by W. Edwards Deming and pioneered in practice by the Toyota Motor Corporation in Japan. The "Toyota Production System" envisions a production process that is lean, flexible, and motivated by pursuit of both continual product improvement and continual cost reduction. As firms worldwide have moved to adopt more flexible workflow configurations, moreover, those configurations often have prioritized finance-based "innovation" and improved organization for maximum surplus extraction as principal goals.[71]

From the traditional legal perspective, the emerging solutions to the production of mass dispute resolution are "unorthodox."[72] As the label suggests, however, that perspective is itself the product of a particular, historically and ideologically contingent understanding of the nature and purpose of judicial process. Class actions, MDL proceedings, and consent decrees are modern inventions, but so is the underlying ideal of individualized justice against which unorthodox instrumentalities for affording collective justice have been defined.[73]

From a managerialist perspective, the emergence of MDL and the routinization of consent decree practice embody parallel shifts toward flexible production of legibility and finality in the resolution of mass claims. In contrast to the class action framework, which favors standardized production of common outcomes, both MDL settlements and consent decrees use common templates as points of departure for more tailored resolutions that can be produced on a just-in-time basis. Emerging conventions for processing and accounting for mass claims and settlement payouts and conducting ongoing monitoring and compliance reporting enable flexible production practices to be tracked and subjected to regularized cost accounting.[74] The flexible production of compensation and structural reform also reflects neoliberal managerialism's commitment to supervision of production by (and for the benefit of) managerial elites. Even as aggregate litigation now largely fails to achieve meaningful structural reform, it has become structural in a different sense, comprising the principal revenue model for burgeoning and profitable practices in aggregate litigation and corporate compliance.[75]

Here again, in theory there is nothing wrong with the use of flexible procedures for producing tailored litigation outcomes in situations involving large numbers of parties, large structural implications, or both. To the contrary, both the theory and the practice of flexible production have revealed considerable transformative potential, and it is reasonable to consider what the lessons learned from and about flexible production in other contexts might teach the law. Writing about emergent systems for transnational regulation, William Simon has invoked the Toyota method as metaphoric inspiration for the project of producing new governance structures that are both democratically responsive and critically reflexive.[76] One might envision an analogous pathway for the project of complex litigation reform.

In practice, however, the flexible production of compensation and oversight has played out toward quite different ends, evolving in ways that have systematically minimized the likelihood of meaningful structural reform of market and public institutions. The growing practices of settlement without responsibility and oversight without accountability valorize market institutions as the principal source of structural discipline in the informational economy. Bargain-basement resolution of claims for aggregate monetary relief expresses and reinforces managerialism's commitment to reproducing the neoliberal subject, who practices self-expression principally through consumptive choice and who has been disciplined to stand alone in the marketplace.

Modular Production: Intellectual Property Experimentalism (and Its Limits)

The third and final story, which concerns intellectual property litigation, showcases a third (and overlapping) family of managerial solutions to dispute resolution problems. In disputes involving enforcement of intellectual property rights, which generally do not involve the MDL system, courts have devised a variety of strategies for sequencing issues and aggregating and streamlining claims. The landscape of intellectual property dispute resolution also includes various nonjudicial intermediaries, including specialty administrative tribunals and collective rights organizations, but outsourcing strategies cover only certain kinds of issues, and courts generally have retained high-level oversight.

Consider first decisions about the sequencing of issues and claims in litigation. As we have just seen, shifting aggregate litigation into MDL proceedings gives courts more flexibility to determine the order of proceedings and to experiment by defining bellwether parties and claims. Both trends have excited cautious interest on the part of commentators but also a fair amount of criticism, in large part because the MDL system is opaque and unaccountable. In contrast, both courts and commentators have openly embraced a variety of strategies for sequencing and streamlining intellectual property litigation. In litigation involving large numbers of patents or copyrights, they encourage the parties to select representative patents, patent claims, or copyrights to use in evaluating the parties' arguments.[77] In software copyright litigation, they conduct detailed preliminary proceedings to evaluate the copyrightability of the programs in suit.[78] Patent litigation has gradually been restructured around the *Markman* hearing, a preliminary proceeding in which the court construes the claims of the patents in suit and determines their scope.[79]

Consider next decisions about the aggregation of parties and claims. Intellectual property class action litigation is relatively rare, although class claims alleging large-scale unauthorized exploitation of copyrighted works have become somewhat more common in the networked digital era. In stark contrast to the relatively restrictive approach to class definition in information privacy disputes, the courts have been generous toward putative copyright class claimants. Although an individual plaintiff must obtain a federal registration before filing suit for infringement, a putative class claim for injunctive relief may encompass unregistered copyrights.[80] More importantly, copyright litigation also regularly involves a different kind of aggregation strategy. In suits against platform firms, distributors of circumvention technologies, and other new information intermediaries, joinder of plaintiffs that together represent entire industries has become routine. The result is effectively class litigation as to the copyrights involved, but without the restrictions that the requirements for class certification would impose.[81]

Specialized administrative tribunals also do important work within the intellectual property system, but courts monitor the outputs of such tribunals more closely than they do the outputs of the various specialty tribunals that handle benefits determinations, mass tort payouts, and so on. Administrative patent and trademark judges and copyright examiners apply specialized expertise to questions about patent grants and the issuance of federal trademark and copyright registrations, but their determinations are subject to judicial review.[82] Most members of the Federal Circuit, a specialized federal appellate court that has exclusive jurisdiction of patent appeals, have some technical expertise, but patent litigation originates in the federal district courts and may return to the Supreme Court after the experts have had their say. In the copyright system, specialized rate courts determine statutory licensing rates for certain activities involving large-scale uses of copyrighted works, but the federal courts retain ultimate authority to interpret the scope of the statutory licenses.[83]

Last but not least, licensing intermediaries play key roles in the copyright and patent systems. Collective rights organizations, patent pools, and other licensing intermediaries administer standardized menus of rights and obligations, processing large numbers of low-dollar-value transactions covering certain uses of copyrighted works and coordinating and pricing industry-wide uses of certain patented inventions. Such systems are primarily transactional, but they also eliminate entire categories of repetitive litigation. Here too, however, courts retain basic supervisory capabilities. The performance rights intermediaries ASCAP, BMI, and SESAC are subject to continuing antitrust oversight pursuant to consent decrees entered in the mid-twentieth century, and antitrust law sets outer limits on the activities of patent pools as well.[84]

An apt lens through which to explore these and other trends in intellectual property litigation is the enthusiasm for modular production that has dominated corporate boardrooms and management theory scholarship for the last two decades. The theoretical framework underlying modular production derives from the work of Herbert Simon, who observed that modular organization can facilitate efficient performance of complex activities because it obviates the need for direct supervision of many constituent processes.[85] He argued, moreover, that modular organization also facilitates both gradual improvement and more dramatic innovation for the same reason; some modules can change while others remain stable. Modules cannot be fully autonomous. Managers must receive enough information and retain enough oversight authority to ensure that the interaction between modules furthers the organization's overall goals. Simon therefore characterized modular organization as "nearly decomposable."[86] The challenge for managers is to design oversight processes that permit optimal information flow while ensuring that individual modules have sufficient adaptive leeway. Modularity has become the gold standard in the design of networked digital products and services.[87] The turn to modularity also has accelerated some of the less salutary trends described in Part I, reinforcing extractive strategies based on the datafication of important resources and lending additional normative heft to labor outsourcing arrangements in particular.

Taken as a whole, the complex assemblage of institutions and procedures for intellectual property dispute resolution and collective licensing approximates a system for modular production of outcomes in which the federal courts play the central managerial role. Just as the growing body of scholarship on modular management would recommend, the intellectual property dispute resolution system makes strategic use of both outsourcing and flexible production arrangements. Particularly where outsourcing is involved, courts generally do not concern themselves much with the operational details of the processes in question. At the same time, the principle of near decomposability dictates that an indissoluble quantum of control be retained at the center.

The modularization of intellectual property dispute resolution is also emergent, incomplete, and contested, however. In part that reflects perceived limits on the institutional authority of courts to produce modular outcomes. So, for example, in litigation over Google's Book Search service, the district court refused to approve a settlement agreement that purported to cover future claims, works, and authors and that included provisions regarding so-called orphan works whose copyright owners could not be located. It did so on the ground that it lacked authority to approve forward-looking changes in entitlement configuration.[88] A subsequent fair use ruling sheltered the Book Search program comprehensively from infringement liability, but at the cost of the institutional texture that the settlement would have provided. Although Google voluntarily implemented measures to restrict the size of search results returned to users, it chose not to implement some of the other arrangements for safeguarding both authors' interests and the public interest that had been included in the proposed settlement.[89]

Other reasons for contesting the turn to modular production in intellectual property dispute resolution relate to broader concerns about whether the system as a whole inappropriately elevates enforcement and licensing over other goals. So, for example, a persistent criticism of the Markman hearing is that claim construction cannot proceed in a vacuum but rather must consider matters of context, tacit knowledge, and ordinary practice that may appear only on a full development of the evidentiary record. *Markman* sequencing militates against such development and instead invites gamesmanship.[90] In copyright infringement cases involving programmatic institutional copying, the use of bellwether works and claims to narrow the issues similarly advances the goal of concreteness while downplaying larger considerations of intellectual exploration and creative flow.[91]

The modularization of intellectual property dispute resolution also has systematically marginalized the interests of individual users of copyrighted works and patented inventions. As already noted, modularization and outsourcing strategies complement one another, and outsourcing has become the principal method of managing users and their asserted needs. Boilerplate waivers circumscribe permitted uses of copyrighted content and prohibit repair, resale, and sometimes reuse of patented inventions.[92] As Chapter 4 described, disputes about online copyright infringement are managed using an array of procedures that includes the statutory notice-and-takedown process but also automated filtering and purely private enforcement programs. Although critics have raised persistent and significant rule-of-law objections to such procedures, so far there has been little creative thinking about how to design integrated dispute resolution systems that are more transparent and accountable not only to rightholders but also to users and the public generally.[93] In copyright industry litigation with online intermediaries, users and their concerns typically go unrepresented. Notably, courts also have largely rejected attempts by so-called copyright trolls to file so-called reverse class actions against large numbers of asserted online infringers with the purpose of encouraging waiver into settlement. Their objections have sounded principally in abuse of process but may also reflect a sense of institutional mismatch, born of a growing conviction that disputes involving individual users or groups of users simply do not belong in the courts.[94]

My purpose in drawing attention to the modular production of dispute resolution in intellectual property cases, however, is not to express blanket disapproval of modularity-based strategies. As with the other strategies discussed in this section, it is simply to note that a great deal more work is needed before those strategies can fairly be said to be effective ways of advancing the full range of relevant goals.

Reimagining Dispute Resolution for the Era of Networked Harms and Large Numbers

Emerging resolutions of the problem of harm and the problem of numerosity are framed as the neutral results of existing doctrines and rules, but they also map neatly to distributions of power within the emerging political economy of informational capitalism. In particular, arguments from tradition and institutional competence sit uneasily alongside the ongoing managerial reconfiguration of systems for dispute resolution. As we have seen in this chapter, powerful information-economy actors have seized upon traditional tropes of discreteness and individuation to deflect claims about intangible collective harms while advancing creative new claims for enforcement of informational property rights, and they have worked to develop new managerial structures for dispute resolution that advance both goals. Under the circumstances, exhortations to rally behind traditional divisions of institutional authority ring more than a little hollow. The questions on the table should concern the best paths for institutional evolution now.

As we saw in the first half of this chapter, the *conceptual* challenges now confronting the courts are less unfamiliar than they appear. It is true that the patterns of harm and benefit in the networked information economy are complex and difficult to unravel. But both the products liability revolution and the emergence of mass torts also required courts to develop facility with new types of inquiries, and their decisions helped to produce a societal shift toward a thicker notion of industrial responsibility that also included regulatory components.[95] We will consider the conceptual and institutional challenges surrounding regulatory settlements of information-era problems in Chapter 6; for present purposes, the point simply is that remedial litigation is—or can be—an important catalyst of institutional change in its own right.

The *structural* challenges confronting courts are more difficult. The traditional, individuated model of procedural justice and its narrowly defined mass-justice exceptions are simply ill-suited to a world in which processes for dispute resolution must deal in large numbers. As we have seen in this chapter, disputes about information-economy problems are calling forth a variety of new solutions to the problem of numerosity. Those solutions are best understood and evaluated as contingent institutional formations. Casting about for new ways of handling unfamiliar logistical and conceptual problems, courts are responding to strategic interventions by powerful repeat players interested first and foremost in shielding their business models and information-processing practices from judicial oversight. Through their efforts, a new model of procedural justice is taking shape—one that comports in some respects with the demands of the networked information economy but that also reflects both the more parochial concerns of information capitalists and the pervasive influence of managerial logics.

Charting the course of a Polanyian countermovement for the courts, and for the landscape of dispute resolution more broadly, requires more careful attention to a wider range of values. How, for example, might one design processes for alternative dispute resolution to flag and escalate systemic questions about harm and responsibility for judicial attention? In contexts involving aggregate relief and/or structural reform, how might one harness principles of flexible production to allocate judicial attention most effectively? In both contexts, how might one structure information flows to deepen institutional accountability and ensure access to justice?[96] While these and other important questions remain unanswered, invoking traditions about form to take options off the table is a mistake. If the emerging, functionally differentiated landscape of dispute resolution is to yield institutions for the production of *justice*, a more comprehensive process of institutional reinvention will be necessary.

6

The Regulatory State in
the Information Age

A European says: I can't understand this, what's wrong with me? An
American says: I can't understand this, what's wrong with him? I make
no suggestion that one side or other is right, but observation over many
years leads me to believe it is true.

—Terry Pratchett, interview

In Chapter 5, we saw that the movement to informational capitalism and the emergence of neoliberal governmentality are reshaping legal institutions for dispute resolution; here, we will see that an equally significant reconstruction of the regulatory state is underway. The design of regulatory institutions reflects prevailing legal wisdom about fair and effective process, but it also responds—and indeed, is designed to respond—to problems created by prevailing modes of economic production and resulting alignments of economic and political power. The institutions that we now have were designed around the regulatory problems and competencies of an era in which industrialism was the principal mode of development. The ongoing shift from an industrial mode of development to an informational one, and to an informationalized way of understanding development's harms, has created existential challenges for regulatory models and constructs developed in the context of the industrial economy. At the same time, the ascendancy of neoliberal managerialism has produced new strategies for disciplining the regulatory state, reshaping its constituent frameworks and processes in ways that align with overarching ideological commitments to privatization, financialization, and expert, informationalized oversight.

Consider the following example: In September 2015, the public learned that European automotive giant Volkswagen had designed the emissions-control software for its diesel engines to comply with prescribed emissions limits only when the software detected that a vehicle was being subjected to emissions testing. At all other times, the software employed a "defeat device" to disable emissions-control functionality, resulting in emissions that vastly exceeded applicable regulatory limits. The scandal resulted in the resignation of Volkswagen's CEO, a precipitous drop in the company's stock value, and a wave of fines and recalls spanning three continents.[1]

The Volkswagen scandal neatly encapsulates many of the challenges that the shift from industrialism to informationalism has presented for regulators. From one perspective, the automobile industry is a paradigmatic industrial-era formation. Modern regimes of emissions regulation, however, are the product of an information-era realignment in societal understanding of the harms flowing from economic development. Additionally, computer software resides at the core of the modern automobile and regulates nearly everything about its performance. The story of the defeat device revealed a regulatory apparatus pushed beyond its capabilities by the cumulative impact of these developments.

To begin with, the striking success of Volkswagen's defeat device—which escaped detection for six years and ultimately was discovered not by regulators but by independent researchers—illustrates a large and troubling mismatch between regulatory goals and regulatory methods. Debates over emissions targets have long been deeply politicized, but the now-undeniable need for emissions regulators to move into the software audit business adds new and unfamiliar methodological and procedural problems into the mix. If regulation of automotive emissions— and thousands of other activities ranging from loan pricing to derivatives trading to gene therapy to insurance risk pooling to electronic voting—is to be effective, policymakers must devise ways of enabling regulators to evaluate algorithmically embedded controls that may themselves have been designed to detect and evade oversight.

The Volkswagen scandal also illustrates the pervasive institutional influence of economic power—and shows that influence operating on levels that are both political and ideological. In the weeks after the news broke, press coverage documented Volkswagen's systematic efforts to stave off more intrusive regulation in the European Union and probed its close ties with the private European emissions testing laboratories that act as regulatory surrogates.[2] Such efforts and ties are not unusual, however. Scholars and policymakers have long recognized that regulated industries are intensely interested in matters of regulatory capacity and institutional design. More noteworthy are Volkswagen's apparent justifications for designing and installing the defeat device: it was deemed necessary to enable improved engine performance, which in turn enabled Volkswagen to maintain and burnish its glowing reputation as an innovator in the field of automotive design.[3] Also noteworthy is European regulators' choice to devolve primary responsibility for emissions testing to private entities that certified compliance.

The themes of innovative flexibility and privatized oversight have gained increasing traction within regulatory settings as the movement to informational capitalism has gathered speed. For the last several decades, advocacy emanating from Wall Street and Silicon Valley has pushed for deregulation and devolution of governance to the private sector, invoking asserted imperatives relating not only to market liberty but also and more fundamentally to innovation and economic growth. The particular formulations advanced often are more accurately characterized as capital's imperatives, and yet the intertwined themes of liberty, innovation, and growth have proved extraordinarily powerful in structuring public debate about regulatory goals and methods.

The chapter begins by identifying some important areas of disconnect between information-era activities and industrial-era regulatory constructs. Industrial-era regimes of economic regulation presumed well-defined industries, ascertainable markets and choices, and relatively discrete harms amenable to clear description and targeted response. The shift to an informational political economy has disrupted those presumptions, making it more difficult to articulate compelling accounts of what precisely should trigger compliance obligations, enforcement actions, and other forms of regulatory oversight.

Next, the chapter explores the connections between information-era regulatory problems and ongoing changes in the design of regulatory institutions. Among U.S. legal scholars, there is fairly widespread consensus that administrative law is in crisis but substantially less agreement on the reason. Perhaps unsurprisingly, administrative law scholars focus primarily on the disintegration of the legal process paradigm that has animated the regulatory state since its inception.[4] As is now widely recognized, much current regulatory activity follows nontraditional institutional models. Such activity may blend policymaking and enforcement, involve public-private partnerships in rulemaking and standard setting, and/or devolve responsibility for assessing compliance to private auditors. Nontraditional regulatory models are particularly prominent in areas such as privacy, telecommunications, health, food and drug regulation, and finance, all of which are information-intensive. This is (or should be) unsurprising. As we have just seen, auditing a compliance algorithm to detect embedded cheats is a different and more difficult task than simply assessing engine outputs. Similarly, auditing a credit rating algorithm, interrogating the health implications of a new food additive, or evaluating the competitive implications of a dominant platform firm's acquisition of an information aggregator is a different and more difficult task than evaluating a proposed merger between two grocery chains or inspecting a factory assembly line. For these and other reasons, scholars in a variety of fields, including cyberlaw, telecommunications, information privacy, and finance, have argued that regulatory processes have failed to respond—and perhaps cannot in their nature respond adequately—to the regulatory problems created by information markets and networked information and communications technologies.[5]

As we will see, the information-era regulatory approaches that have begun to emerge reflect the distinctive imprint of neoliberal managerialism. They are procedurally informal, standard-based, mediated by expert professional networks, and increasingly financialized. Theoretically, at least some of those attributes might make the new models better suited to addressing information-era regulatory problems. In reality, institutional disruption has provided new points of entry for economic power. Emergent, nontraditional regulatory models have tended to be both opaque to external observation and highly prone to capture. New institutional forms that might ensure their legal and political accountability have been slow to develop.

Seeing Like a (Regulatory) State

Regulating information-era activities requires frameworks for making sense of the activities being regulated—for understanding how they work and identifying their legitimate and illegitimate modes of operation. The movement to informational capitalism, and especially the growing centrality of platforms and algorithms as modes of organization and governance, has disrupted many of the basic legibility rubrics that underlie and inform regulatory activity.

Generally speaking, economic regulation in the era of industrial capitalism has had two principal concerns: facilitating fair competition in markets and preventing harms to the public health and safety. Where markets are concerned, scholars and policymakers traditionally have defined impermissible results in terms of concepts such as market power, discrimination, and deception—benchmarks that are relatively easy to assess when markets are distinctly ascertainable, goods have fixed properties, and information about consumers is limited. In the platform-based, massively intermediated information economy, none of those things is true. Markets are fluid and interconnected and information ecologies have complex and often opaque path dependencies. Debates about how to address the health and safety harms flowing from economic activity similarly reflect both the pervasive influence and the disruptive effects of new informational capabilities. Beginning in the late twentieth century, networked digital information technologies supplied new tools for conceptualizing and modeling a wide variety of complex, systemic harms. At the same time, however, the displacement of preventive regulation into the realm of models and predictions has complicated, and unavoidably politicized, the projects of identifying and addressing such harms.

In each of these contexts, neoliberal governmentality interposes its own legibility rubrics, which revolve around the presumed existence of competition, the presumptively beneficial effects of private innovative activity, and the presumptive superiority of utilitarian methods for assessing costs, benefits, and trade-offs. Those rubrics in turn reflect the pervasive influence of the logics of performative enclosure, appropriative privilege, and innovative and expressive immunity that Part I explored.

From Market Power to Platform Power

A core concern of economic regulation is identifying the circumstances in which economic power requires oversight. Power in markets for goods or services can translate into predatory pricing or barriers to competitive entry, while power embedded in the structure of particular distribution channels or relationships can facilitate other types of inefficient or normatively undesirable behavior. Platform-based, massively intermediated media infrastructures introduce bewildering new variations on these themes. Understanding economic power and its abuses in the era of informational capitalism requires discussions about the new patterns of intermediation and disintermediation that platforms enable, and about the complexity and opacity of the services they provide.

The industrial-era regulatory toolkit includes a number of regulatory schemes that are concerned with the illegal acquisition and maintenance of market power. In the United States, that group includes most notably the antitrust laws but also other, more specific regimes, such as the Federal Trade Commission (FTC)'s unfair and deceptive acts and practices authority. Both regimes presume the ability to define markets in the first instance, and both also presume the ability to isolate discrete practices that harm consumers in direct and observable ways. Finally, they traditionally have presumed that the ability to tie separate markets together is both rare and suspect.

Platform-based, massively intermediated media infrastructures disrupt conventional understandings of market power and market harm. Recall from Chapter 1 that the economics of two- and multi-sided markets differ in important ways from those of traditional, one-sided markets. Because platforms can define terms for each user group separately, pricing is not a reliable sign of market power, and secondary heuristics such as the competition regulator's basic distinction between horizontal and vertical integration strategies also do not translate well to the platform-based environment.[6] The complexity and opacity of platform-based, massively intermediated exchange structures have stymied courts and policymakers used to working with more traditional economic models.

An early harbinger of the conceptual difficulties that platforms create for antitrust law was the antitrust litigation against Microsoft Corporation for bundling the Internet Explorer browser with its operating system. Microsoft's software licenses with its original equipment manufacturers (OEMs) required that personal computers be shipped with Internet Explorer preinstalled. Competing browser manufacturers argued that given Microsoft's undisputed dominance in the personal computing market, that requirement created unfair barriers to entry. From the standpoint of antitrust doctrine formulated for the industrial era, however, the market for browsers was unusual. To begin with, it was hard to discover a price advantage that accrued to Microsoft because the leading competitors offered their software free of charge. Microsoft also asserted copyrights in its operating system and browser software, and it invoked traditions of rightholder control over licensing to bolster its defense. Finally, and importantly, although Microsoft's licenses prohibited OEMs from removing Internet Explorer and its desktop icons, the licenses did not prohibit either OEMs or consumers from installing and using competing browsers. In the traditional language of antitrust law, they were vertical restrictions rather than horizontal restrictions and therefore less suspect. As those who developed and prosecuted the Microsoft case recognized, however, Microsoft's desktop environment also created powerful path-dependencies.[7] Although the government ultimately obtained a judgment against Microsoft requiring it to unbundle its licensed products, the judgment issued 10 years after the complaint had been filed, and the proceedings lumbered to their conclusion without the benefit of a coherent framework for determining harm.[8]

In the intervening years, platform-based information ecosystems have grown ever larger and more complex. Dominant platform firms such as Alphabet (Google), Facebook, and Amazon have thrived by developing ways to offer both individual and business users a wide variety of information services while controlling both advertising markets and the harvesting and processing of user data. Many platform services are available to users at no direct financial cost, but that does not make them costless. As Chapters 2 and 3 described, loss of control over personal information creates a variety of near-term and longer-term risks that are difficult for individuals to understand—and, importantly for antitrust purposes, therefore impossible for them to value.[9] As Chapter 1 explained, business users of platform services— ranging from small mom-and-pop storefronts to businesses with nationwide name recognition—also cannot easily value or monitor the quality of the services that they have purchased. The doctrinal landscape also has become more complex; as we saw in Part I, platforms use contract and trade secrecy to create and sustain competitive advantages and assert free speech interests to avert regulatory oversight.

Although antitrust doctrine and theory traditionally have prided themselves on being attuned to economic realities, they have lagged behind these rapid changes in the economic landscape. Business scholars were quick to recognize the importance of the platform business model, but antitrust thinking is far more rigidly circumscribed by preexisting conventions for economic modeling that have become enshrined in case law and government enforcement practice, so it evolves more slowly. As of this writing, there is no generally accepted definition of *platform power* that might replace the antitrust construct of market power and no consensus on how to remedy the effects of platform-based manipulation of the competitive environment. Only within the last few years have antitrust economists and legal scholars started working to develop a methodology for identifying the competitive injuries that platform-based environments enable. Those efforts, moreover, have met with intense pushback from neoliberal economic thinkers and think tanks.[10]

Other industrial-era regulatory schemes address circumstances in which high fixed costs make monopoly provision of certain services more efficient. Public utility regulation and common carrier regulation are the two principal examples. It would be inefficient, for example, to install multiple sets of water pipes or electric cables to residential neighborhoods, or to build parallel sets of railroad tracks to move freight around the country. Instead, special regulatory regimes have emerged that take a different approach to the question of market structure. Such regimes, which date to the early twentieth century and reflect Progressive-Era and New Deal concerns about both market access and market fairness, typically incorporate both rate-setting restrictions and nondiscrimination obligations.[11]

Whether and when communications platforms and other information intermediaries should be subject to common-carrier or public-utility obligations is a controversial topic, and debates about those questions also have lagged behind the emergence of platform power. In the United States, the debate over "net neutrality"—or the obligation to "treat all content, sites, and platforms equally"[12]— has followed a tortuous path dictated in part by an obsolete statutory framework to which we will return later in this chapter. On a conceptual level, however, the net neutrality debate raises questions about the best way of adapting industrial- era notions of common-carriage and/or public utility provision to information services that are much more complex. Unlike earlier twentieth-century debates about public utility and common-carrier regulation, the net neutrality debate has not squarely addressed more general questions about the extent to which commu- nications regulation should incorporate considerations of fairness and economic justice.[13]

To begin with, it is important to recognize that the "net neutrality" rubric is it- self a neoliberally inflected way of answering questions about economic power and public access, because it assumes that market forces operating on an intraplatform basis will produce services of adequate variety and quality as long as access providers are prevented from blocking or throttling such services. Notably, each side in the net neutrality debate has attempted to claim for itself the mantle of innovative liberty and economic growth. Large telecommunications companies argue that freedom to experiment with high-bandwidth delivery of premium services will foster eco- nomically productive innovation. Supporters of a net-neutrality mandate, including internet companies, digital civil liberties groups, and consumer advocates, argue that price discrimination within closed platforms will threaten both widely distributed innovation and freedom of expression.

Provider incentives to engage in blocking and throttling are not the only factors affecting equal access to information services, however. There are many online serv- ices that privileged consumers take for granted, but that less privileged consumers struggle to obtain because they require higher bandwidth or more versatile platforms to be delivered effectively. The Federal Communications Commission (FCC) has long overseen a program to offer basic telephone service to the poorest consumers, and more recently developed a parallel program for broadband internet access. Both in the United States and globally, however, many lower-income users rely exclusively on mobile platforms that are less versatile, less amenable to user customization and control, and designed to maximize data sensing and harvesting.[14]

From the internet access provider's perspective, the ability to discriminate among different types of network traffic is valuable in part because it enables access providers to compete more effectively in data harvesting economies. The logics of performative enclosure (described in Chapter 1) and productive appropriation (Chapter 2) reinforce arguments framing network traffic discrimination as a business and innovative necessity. The same logics also increasingly infuse discussions about provision of essential services. At least some wireless internet providers would prefer to handle the essential-services problem via the practice of zero rating, in which usage of a designated suite of applications is not counted for billing purposes. Such arrangements—which, from the platform perspective, simply represent another permutation of the access-for-data bargain—are more affordable, but they are not neutral. They incentivize consumers to use zero-rated applications more heavily, and providers may grant zero rating designations in exchange for access to data about users' in-app behavior or other favorable terms. Internet providers seeking to build their user bases in developing economies have relied heavily on zero rating schemes, and the net neutrality rules briefly adopted in the United States permitted zero rating subject to case by case analysis of reasonableness.[15] In U.S. communications policy circles, thinking about the connections between network control, platform power, and data harvesting is still rudimentary.

By comparison, European regulators have engaged with the problem of platform power and its complex embeddedness in data harvesting arrangements far more aggressively. Over the past two decades, competition regulators have initiated several investigations of Microsoft, Google, and Facebook for alleged anticompetitive actions. In 2017, the European Commission announced that it had fined Google a staggering 2.4 billion euros for abusing its dominant position in search to the advantage of its own online shopping service, though whether that fine will survive review is yet to be determined.[16] Data protection authorities, although willing to experiment with coregulation and to allow some leeway for consumer consent to data processing, have steadfastly insisted that guarantees of transparency and purpose limitation should be meaningful and that consumer consent has limits.[17] As to network neutrality, European regulators generally have been inclined to view internet access as a type of public utility. They have exempted both certain high-bandwidth "specialised services" such as internet TV and zero-rating schemes deployed by European internet providers from the full force of neutrality obligations, but European telecommunications policy also incorporates strong privacy and data protection obligations.[18]

European policymakers also have made more concerted and thoughtful efforts to understand the economic logics underlying the platform business model and the various kinds of external costs that platform power can create. One component of the digital single market strategy announced by the European Commission in

2015 is a research initiative on online platforms that includes investigation of those questions.[19] Although it is too early to judge the success of that effort, it reflects comparatively greater openness to new ways of seeing and describing logics of economic domination.

In U.S. legal and policy discussions, to offer European regulatory actions as valid alternative models is to risk vehement and at times nearly unhinged ridicule. The historical U.S. antipathy to European-style bureaucracy does not fully explain the level of contemporary vitriol, levied indiscriminately against actions that appear to privilege dominant information providers and those that seek to restrain them.[20] A more accurate explanation simply may be that the behavior of European regulators contradicts the reigning neoliberal account of optimal regulatory behavior. As we saw in Chapter 3, that account paints "regulation" as innovation's mortal enemy. U.S. critics also charge European regulators with attempting to institute a regime of economic protectionism that would give European businesses an unfair advantage. Protectionism can flow from underregulation as well as from overregulation, however. It is true that European regulators make no secret of their desire to see domestic businesses gain ground, but it is also true that U.S. stances on antitrust and data protection have permitted a race to the bottom, fueling the rise of the dominant U.S. platform giants and hastening the accumulation of platform power.

From Market Distortion to Infoglut and Intermediation

Regimes of economic regulation also include anti-distortion rules—rules intended to ensure that flows of information about the goods, services, and capabilities on offer are accurate and unbiased. Some anti-distortion rules are information-forcing; rules in that category include those requiring disclosure of material information to consumers or investors. Other anti-distortion rules are information-blocking; examples include prohibitions on discrimination, false advertising, and insider trading. The difficulty currently confronting regulators is that contemporary conditions of infoglut and pervasive intermediation disrupt traditional anti-distortion strategies. To achieve meaningful anti-distortion regulation under those conditions, a different regulatory toolkit is needed.

The rationales behind information-forcing and information-blocking rules are straightforward. According to standard microeconomic theory, transactions between willing buyers and sellers generally will produce prices that accurately reflect the characteristics of goods and services, including any nonprice terms that meaningfully affect the quality of the good or experience.[21] Sometimes, however, goods and services may have latent, complex or highly technical characteristics that consumers cannot understand fully or value accurately. In other cases, power imbalances or other structural imbalances may undercut or frustrate efforts to obtain more comprehensive and accurate information. Disclosure mandates represent attempts to correct for market failures by closing information gaps. Examples of such mandates include food and drug labeling requirements and truth-in-lending rules. Other kinds of information flows reflect or enable systematic bias or favoritism that society views as normatively undesirable. For example, discrimination in housing, lending, and employment violates foundational commitments to equal opportunity, and insider trading and false advertising undermine confidence in the overall fairness of markets. Modern systems of economic regulation typically include numerous rules targeting both the undesirable conduct and the information flows that facilitate it.

From a regulatory perspective, the problem with infoglut is that it makes information-forcing rules easy to manipulate and information-blocking rules easy to evade. Both information-forcing and information-blocking rules are premised on the assumptions that information is scarce and costly to obtain and convey and that regulatory mandates therefore can produce meaningful changes in the nature and quality of information available to economic actors. Information-forcing rules additionally presume that consumers and investors are in a position to benefit from required disclosures. Under conditions of infoglut and pervasive intermediation, all of those assumptions fail. Recall from Chapter 3 that infoglut—or information overload resulting from unmanageable, mediated information flows—creates a crisis of attention.[22] The massively intermediated, platform-based environment promises solutions, offering network users tools and strategies for cutting through the clutter. At the same time, however, it enables information power to find new points of entry outside the reach of traditional anti-distortion regimes.

Consider first the problem of how to conduct meaningful antidiscrimination regulation and enforcement under conditions of infoglut and pervasive intermediation. To enforce existing antidiscrimination laws effectively, the various agencies with enforcement authority need the ability to detect and prove discrimination, yet that task is increasingly difficult when decisions about access to credit, employment, and housing are made via criteria deeply embedded in complex algorithms used to detect patterns in masses of data. Markers for protected class membership can be inferred with relative ease and near-impunity from other, seemingly neutral data. Data-intensive methods also may seem naturally to support arguments about legitimate business justifications for decisions denying access or offering it only on unfavorable terms.[23]

In an era when decision-making is mediated comprehensively by so-called big data, regulators seeking to fulfill antidiscrimination mandates must learn to contend with the methods by which regulated decisions are reached—with data and algorithms as instrumentalities for conducting (regulated) activity. In general, the existing regulatory toolkit is poorly adapted for scrutinizing data-driven algorithmic models. One rudimentary gesture toward algorithmic accountability is the Federal Reserve's Regulation B, which lists criteria for the Consumer Financial Protection Bureau (CFPB) to use in determining whether credit scoring systems are "empirically derived [and] demonstrably and statistically sound."[24] The list relies heavily on "accepted statistical principles and methodology," but leaves unexplained what those principles and methods might be and how they ought to translate into contexts involving automated, predictive algorithms with artificial intelligence or machine learning components.

Infoglut and pervasive intermediation also impair the ability to conduct effective consumer protection regulation. Consumer protection regulation typically involves both information-forcing and information-blocking strategies. Regulators seek to require disclosure of material information about quality and other nonprice terms, and they also attempt to prevent marketing practices that are deceptive or that prey upon vulnerable populations. In the era of information overload, however, more comprehensive disclosures do not necessarily enhance understanding. Market researchers and consumer advocates have long recognized that the increasing amounts of information associated with even basic consumer products such as prepackaged foods and over-the-counter pharmaceuticals can be bewildering. More complex goods and services often are amenable to versioning in ways that embed material nonprice terms—for example, access to technical support services, different processor speeds, amounts of digital storage, and so on—within price discrimination frameworks.[25] Additionally, the traditional regulatory focus on the *content* of disclosures is far too limited. The way that choices are presented also matters. Techniques for nudging consumer behavior become even more powerful in platform-based, massively intermediated environments, which incorporate "choice architectures" favoring the decisions that platform or application designers want their users to make.[26]

Disclosures and choice architectures, moreover, are far from the only issues of concern to consumers. As Chapters 2 and 3 described, platform-based, massively intermediated online environments raise profound economic justice questions. Predictive profiles can convey valuable information about consumers' priorities and reservation prices. Targeted advertising can ensure that consumers see only certain options, and cutting-edge behavioral microtargeting techniques that identify points of vulnerability can be used to shape and refine targeting strategies. Scholars and social justice advocates have begun to draw attention to the linkages between the new types of pattern-based discrimination enabled by data-intensive profiling and the emergence of a seemingly permanent economic underclass.[27] Current consumer protection paradigms framed in terms of notice and choice are ill-suited to address these issues.

In similar fashion, infoglut and pervasive intermediation create barriers to effective financial regulation. As Chapter 1 described, financial markets have become increasingly complex in the networked information era. Networked information and communication technologies have greatly increased overall levels of access to investment-related information, and yet access also is mediated by a growing number and variety of information providers. The resulting increase in *differential* access to market information has prompted market regulators to push for more regularized transparency to investors in traditional areas of investor concern—hence, for example, the SEC's Regulation FD, which attempts to place all investors on an equal footing with regard to major corporate announcements and disclosures by publicly traded companies.[28]

Contemporary investors, however, have access to such a wealth of information and such a variety of investment vehicles that an equally pressing problem concerns how to make sense of it all. On that question, financial regulators have been silent. As we saw in Chapter 1, datafication and platformization have profoundly changed financial activity, disintermediating traditional points of exchange and catalyzing the emergence of markets for new, synthetic products invented by sophisticated institutional investors and traded amongst themselves. Putting investors on an equal footing with respect to data processing, analytic capacity, and access to private trading venues and investment vehicles is far less feasible—and many new financial instruments are so complex that they defy efforts to describe the associated risks.[29] Increasingly, it has begun to seem as though there is one set of rules for the ordinary consumer and institutional investors serving that consumer and a very different set for the financial cognoscenti, and it also seems beyond dispute that piecemeal reforms simply encourage well-resourced investors to seek new opportunities for regulatory arbitrage.

Last and importantly, although economic regulators traditionally have not concerned themselves with election integrity, in the platform-based, massively intermediated information economy, the domains of economic and election regulation have converged. As Chapter 3 described, platform-based information environments optimized for behavioral microtargeting and user engagement have enabled new strategies for voter manipulation that exploit infoglut to sow and magnify distrust and discord. By and large, election regulators use the same information-forcing and information-blocking strategies that consumer protection regulators and financial regulators do. Candidates for office typically must make certain disclosures, and campaign finance laws set limits on campaign funding and political advertising. The ease with which campaigns of election manipulation have unfolded demonstrates that conditions of infoglut and pervasive intermediation disrupt those strategies as well. Proposals to double down on the same methods—for example, by devising new transparency requirements and extending prohibitions on advertising purchases by foreign entities to online ads—are vanishingly unlikely to achieve their stated aims.[30]

As with platform power, European policymakers have been far more open to comprehensive study of the challenges that infoglut and pervasive intermediation present to regulatory regimes that incorporate anti-distortion rules. The Commission's ongoing research project on online platforms includes both technical research on mechanisms for achieving algorithmic accountability and exploration of possible new regulatory mechanisms for ensuring fairness and transparency for both individual and business users of online environments.[31] In the United States, media attention to such initiatives has been notable chiefly for its absence, and the logics of productive appropriation and innovative and expressive immunity that Chapters 2 and 3 described have effectively foreclosed comparable domestic efforts. Even policy initiatives widely heralded as both progressive and too adventurous to be politically feasible lean heavily on traditional methods and gesture only timidly, if at all, toward the problem of unaccountable algorithmic intermediation.[32]

From Discrete Harms to Systemic Threats

A final major concern of economic regulation involves collective health and safety harms arising as byproducts of economic activity. Such harms are a long-standing concern, but new informational capabilities have gradually reshaped ways of both seeing harms and formulating possible responses. For example, at the turn of the nineteenth century, the harms that concerned regimes of food and drug and workplace safety regulation were relatively clear and concrete—deaths caused by adulterated foods and medicines, dismemberments caused by industrial machinery, and the like. By the mid-twentieth century, policymakers had begun to recognize other types of complex and emergent harms—for example, environmental pollution caused by industrial waste and diseases caused by carcinogenic or teratogenic chemicals. They also had assimilated lessons from the 1929 stock market crash and the Great Depression about threats to the stability of financial systems.[33] As societal understandings of harm evolved to encompass a wider range of systemic effects of industrial and informational development, regulatory methods evolved to include techniques for measuring, communicating about, and responding to those effects. Yet even as new informational resources and capabilities have oriented regulators toward systemic harms to be realized in the future—toward the problem of *systemic threat*—they also have exposed the extent to which regulatory models are politically constructed.

Systemic threats are accessible—to regulators, affected industries, and members of the public—only through modeling and representation, and techniques of modeling and representation are not neutral. Models depend on assumptions about variables and parameters that are open to contestation. Representation of a systemic threat as more or less threatening also requires the use of narratives and metaphoric frames to communicate the likelihood and magnitude of impending systemic changes. As threatened future harms have become more abstract, diffuse, and technologically complex, disputes about appropriate regulatory responses have become struggles for control over both modeling and representation. The contemporary condition of infoglut exacerbates those struggles. Finding firm regulatory footing amid a welter of conflicting models, frames, assertions and opinions—and, more recently, amid a growing torrent of misinformation, disinformation, and simulated citizen engagement—has become increasingly difficult.

In terms of regulatory methodology, the need to contend with systemic threats creates two problems. Both are well recognized within the legal literature on regulation, but neither has been systematically conceptualized as a potential lever for institutional change in response to shifting modes of economic and technological development.

The first problem arises because threats of future harm are inevitably probabilistic. Methods for modeling and assessing a range of possible future scenarios now inform regulatory approaches in fields ranging from environmental protection to financial regulation, but the shift to a probabilistic sensibility underscores a tension between two very different approaches to evaluating asserted dangers. One approach, based on the concept of risk, emphasizes formal modeling and quantification; the other, based on uncertainty, holds that not all factors bearing on the probability of future harm can be modeled and quantified.[34] The discourse of risk is conceptually crisper than that of uncertainty, and supplies a way of both describing probabilistic future harms and quantifying—and sometimes pricing—acceptable risk thresholds. For that reason, it has won influential adherents in government and business circles.[35] Sometimes, however, experts in the relevant technical fields argue that risk modeling is insufficient. For example, vulnerability to data security breaches depends in part on technical configuration, in part on organizational configuration, and in part on human error, and these factors are heterogeneous and incommensurable. Computer security experts therefore have developed threat modeling protocols that explicitly incorporate both risk and uncertainty.[36]

The tension between risk-based and uncertainty-based approaches to evaluating systemic threats is political as well as epistemological. When risk discourses dominate threat modeling, they can become ways of black-boxing areas of uncertainty, displacing contradictory or otherwise inconvenient scientific authority, and ratifying existing distributions of resources.[37] Reliance on risk assessment and risk management discourses also can induce unwarranted complacency and encourage excessive risk-taking. The financial instruments and transactions that produced the economic bubble of the 2000s and the ensuing crash incorporated extensive risk calculations, but the calculations were based on self-serving assumptions and did not model the scenarios that could lead to systemic collapse. The sheer level of complexity also introduced new uncertainties and new possibilities for market failure.[38] Post-crash disputes about the Federal Reserve's protocols for administering stress tests to financial institutions have been disputes about precisely whether formal risk assessment tools can adequately model vulnerability to future catastrophic collapse.[39]

If regulators are to develop effective tools for avoiding systemic breakdowns, comprehensive engagement with uncertainty-based threat modeling protocols is essential, but even good threat modeling protocols cannot tell regulators how to resolve the second problem, which arises when regulatory responses to systemic threats are crafted. The reorientation toward systemic threats underscores a tension between two very different approaches to identifying and analyzing the trade-offs that such models inevitably present: a cost-benefit approach, which assesses proposed regulations largely in terms of their concrete, monetizable impacts, and a precautionary approach, which holds that regulators seeking to avoid foreseeable, significant harms should err on the side of caution and should consider a broader range of factors relating to human wellbeing. To its adherents, cost-benefit analysis promises a neutral, rational discourse for evaluating regulatory proposals and for charting a course between the Scylla of regulatory capture and the Charybdis of bureaucratic inefficiency. Skeptics charge that cost-benefit analysis persistently undervalues threatened harms that are diffuse, cumulative, and difficult to describe in monetized, present-value terms and persistently overstates the costs of compliance with new obligations.[40] Additionally, experts in the behavior of complex systems have begun to urge more careful attention to tipping points—points at which gradual change suddenly produces a discontinuous jump.[41] Within a precautionary paradigm, it is easier to justify interventions designed to prevent the system from tipping.

The tension between cost-benefit and precautionary approaches to countering systemic threats also is political as well as epistemological. As with conventions for modeling and pricing risk, conventions for analyzing regulatory trade-offs can become ways of black-boxing the harshest consequences of systemic failure and justifying regulatory deference to the self-interested decisions of private economic actors. Cost-benefit analysis is associated with an era of notable deregulation, and in practice it tends to be inflected by a distinctively neoliberal vision of regulatory minimization that seeks to downplay collective or intangible harms arising from market activities. As Frank Ackerman, Lisa Heinzerling, and Rachel Massey show, many environmental regulations now regarded as foundational would not have been adopted under the approach to cost-benefit analysis currently ascendant.[42]

Contestation between adherents of cost-benefit and precautionary approaches—and of the different regulatory ideologies that each has come to signify—has emerged as a defining feature of the information-era regulatory landscape. Environmental law is a paradigmatic example: it is fundamentally concerned with systemic threats accessible only via information-intensive modeling. Over the past half century, growing awareness of the acute systemic threat presented by climate change has catalyzed calls for aggressively precautionary responses—and equally aggressive pushback by threatened interests.

Similar dynamics now infuse many other regulatory domains. Federal new drug approval processes are precautionary in character, but the regulatory stance toward software in medical devices has been different. The now-discredited separation between commercial and investment banks, instituted after the Great Depression to protect the financial system against the risk of catastrophic failure, was a precautionary safeguard, and in the wake of the global financial collapse of 2008, some banking and finance scholars have proposed reintroducing structural safeguards into financial markets.[43] European data protection regulators have attempted to maintain a generally precautionary stance toward personal data protection, and some scholarly interventions call for explicit adoption of the precautionary paradigm. In the United States, where cost-benefit analysis and the logics of innovative and expressive immunity are more deeply entrenched, some participants in policy and scholarly debates about information privacy have begun to deploy environmental analogies as they seek to explain whether and how to regulate data harvesting economies more comprehensively.[44] Meanwhile, expressing different regulatory and ideological sensibilities, the financial and internet industries and libertarian and neoliberal tech policy pundits have advanced a carefully crafted narrative that paints precautionary regulation as rigid, "Mother, may I?" policymaking that threatens to stifle both liberty and economic growth.[45]

Even when regulators can muster the will to make difficult trade-offs, however, the way to do so effectively may be less clear. In part the problem is methodological. In particular, regulatory schemes that rely on fixed targets for harmful private-sector activities—for example, dosage limits for prescription drugs, chemical contaminant thresholds for consumer products and industrial byproducts, and particulate emissions thresholds for factories and automobiles—sit in growing tension with accumulated learning about the behaviors of complex, networked systems. So, for example, existing regimes of threshold-based environmental regulation have failed to avert the continuing degradation of pollination networks, water systems, and marine ecologies, and fixed thresholds for capital adequacy and data deidentification have proved elusive. Other important dimensions of the problem concern institutional design. Countering systemic threats effectively requires more than just techniques for modeling complex, dynamic processes. As we are about to see, it also requires new thinking about implementation of such techniques and about oversight modalities.

Enacting Governmentality: Evolving Practices for Oversight and Accountability

As the story of the Volkswagen defeat device illustrates, a regulatory state optimized for the informational economy requires not only new rubrics for making sense of the activities being regulated but also new institutional mechanisms for defining obligations and overseeing compliance. It is no coincidence that settled ways of thinking about the appropriate modalities of administrative lawmaking have come under challenge with increasing frequency over the past half century. And it is no coincidence that the regulatory problems of the emerging informational economy have proved particularly disruptive. Information-intensive fields of economic activity—telecommunications, privacy, health care delivery, and finance—have become especially active sites of experimentation with new institutional models.

Emergent institutional models share some important family resemblances. They are procedurally informal; they emphasize ongoing compliance with performance-based standards intended to guide complex, interdependent sets of practices; they are mediated by expert professional and technical networks that define relevant standards and manage compliance systems, and they are increasingly financialized. For all of these reasons, however, they also create new accountability challenges and afford new opportunities for powerful actors to shape institutional design.

Like the ongoing transformations in the judicial system studied in Chapter 5, the ongoing transformations within the regulatory state reflect the powerful shaping influence of neoliberal governmentality. Newly powerful information-economy actors and mushrooming professional constituencies dedicated to auditing and compliance monitoring have engaged in highly creative forms of institutional entrepreneurship, developing new frameworks for self-regulation and self-certification while resisting less congenial forms of institutional innovation. The ascendancy of neoliberal managerialism also has deterred legislative action to resolve the most urgent problems of regulatory mismatch, reinforcing political gridlock and investing structural obsolescence with deregulatory virtue.

The Regulatory State as Norm Entrepreneur

In the United States, the institutional model established by the Administrative Procedure Act of 1946 contemplates two general types of regulatory activity: rulemaking and adjudication. According to the modernist, legal process-based vision that animated the model at its creation, the two types are opposites: Rules of general application are to be promulgated in orderly, quasi-legislative proceedings and later applied to specific disputes in orderly, quasi-judicial proceedings. For quite a long time, however, it has been evident that rulemaking and adjudication represent endpoints on a continuum and that a great deal of activity occurs with markedly less formality in the space between them.[46] The new informality is a particularly striking feature of regulatory oversight of highly informationalized activity. Regulators have worked to develop new methods of nudging and cajoling regulated entities toward more public-regarding behavior, while regulated entities have worked to shape the new informality to their own ends.

Over the last several decades, formal agency policymaking processes have become progressively more and more hobbled by breakdown and interest group capture. The suite of rulemaking procedures available to administrative agencies is widely acknowledged to be insufficiently nimble for many types of regulatory problems created by networked information technologies and processes. Internet business models in particular evolve so rapidly that a proposed rule can be obsolete before the time period for submitting comments has closed (or even before the printed notice of proposed rulemaking has been published).[47] In addition, processes initially envisioned as neutral fora for consideration of expert evidence have come to reflect the dominating influences of interest group participation and normative deep capture. Agencies too suffer the effects of infoglut; notices of proposed rulemaking on controversial issues can elicit many thousands of submissions—including, most recently, automated comments submitted using faked names and email addresses.[48] We saw in Chapter 3 that for-profit actors supply regulators with a variety of information subsidies. One way for regulators to cut through the clutter is to focus on the relatively well-researched submissions by trade associations representing affected industries.[49] Partly for these reasons, and partly because many information-age regulatory problems push the boundaries of existing, often decades-old statutory regimes, issued rules often bog down for years in legal challenges.

Within the space created by the limited utility and efficacy of rulemaking, scholars who study administrative governance have chronicled the emergence of other, relatively unstructured and often substantially privatized processes through which agencies make policy. Many U.S. federal agencies now routinely issue "guidances" that are intended to signal regulated entities about their interpretations of governing statutes and rules and their likely enforcement stances. Although courts are not required to defer to agency guidances, they may give them substantial weight. Some agencies also routinely publicize staff interpretations that are characterized as nonbinding but that have enormous practical impact on the conduct of regulated entities.[50] Finally, regulated entities have enjoyed new types of informal input into agency policymaking. Increasingly, agencies make policy in ways that incorporate privatized information subsidies openly and directly, engaging regulated entities in dialogues intended to produce consensus on industry "best practices" and structuring some oversight functions as public-private partnerships.[51]

In scholarly and policy discourses, the turn toward privatization in policymaking has acquired a name—the "new governance"—and a set of justifications that express what Jodi Short has called the "paranoid style" in regulatory reform: an intense worry about the risks of state coercion and/or bumbling, combined with relative insensitivity to the ramifications of private power. The new governance paradigm distills neoliberal governmentality into "a regulatory reform discourse that is antithetical to the very idea of government regulation."[52] Particularly in highly informationalized domains, informal, coregulatory processes may produce regulatory standards more reflective of current technological practice and therefore less costly to implement and administer. But coregulatory processes also can emphasize inside baseball over participation by a broad range of affected interests, and at their most lopsided risk devolving into self-regulation with minimal oversight. Over time, such approaches have produced significant devolution of regulatory authority to the private sector.[53]

Even as agency policymaking activities devolve increasingly toward informality, enforcement activity is becoming more rule-ish. A leading example of this phenomenon is the FTC's practice of lawmaking through adjudication. In the domain of information privacy, the FTC has used its enforcement authority vigorously but unconventionally, filing unfair and deceptive acts and practices actions and then negotiating and publicizing consent decrees that include suites of ongoing compliance requirements. According to Daniel Solove and Woodrow Hartzog, the corpus of consent decrees constitutes a new common law jurisprudence of unfair and deceptive conduct.[54] Institutionally speaking, the FTC's enforcement posture reflects an especially complex calculus. The agency has no general Administrative Procedure Act rulemaking authority and no specific authority to issue general information privacy rules, so it relies on its consent decree practice to fill the regulatory gaps.[55] But the FTC is not the only example of an agency creatively using its enforcement powers to engage in gap-filling and norm entrepreneurship on information-economy issues. For example, amidst an ongoing dispute over its jurisdiction to promulgate net neutrality regulation that spanned nearly a decade, the FCC used both its general enforcement authority and its merger review authority to advance net-neutrality-related goals.[56]

The turn to rule-ishness in enforcement, however, also incorporates a significant and largely unheralded privatization component. As Chapter 5 described, the consent decree has become an important vehicle for the managerial reconfiguration and privatization of dispute resolution, and that is true in regulatory enforcement contexts as well. So, for example, boilerplate provisions in the FTC's data privacy and data security consent decrees impose new monitoring and reporting obligations that as a practical matter demand new managerial competencies. Consent decrees in agency enforcement actions also follow the temporal arc that Chapter 5 sketched: newly approved decrees are announced with great fanfare, but their longer term efficacy is less clear.[57] In some regulatory domains, the increasing reliance on consent decrees also raises concerns about the accessibility of law that mirror those created by the shift to privatized and outsourced dispute resolution. Although privacy practitioners read the FTC's privacy consent decrees carefully and regard published decrees as quasi-precedential, some entities, such as the Equal Employment Opportunity Commission, do not publish their consent decrees, so interested parties cannot easily monitor evolving enforcement practices.[58]

More informal enforcement strategies also reflect the shaping influence of private power. Ian Ayres and John Braithwaite coined the term "responsive regulation" to describe a range of extrajudicial sanctions available to regulators, beginning with persuasion and escalating through formal warnings to fines and other penalties.[59] U.S. regulatory agencies make extensive use of the responsive regulation toolkit. For example, even when it chooses not to bring litigation, the SEC from time to time issues "reports of investigation" that it styles as providing it with an opportunity to "clarify" and "amplify" its views about various industry practices, and the FTC uses persuasion, investigation, threats of enforcement action, and the threat of fines for violations of existing orders to shape the ongoing evolution of industry best practices regarding information privacy.[60] Similar methods have long played central roles in European regulatory practice, which places relatively lower emphasis on litigation and relatively greater emphasis on other strategies.[61] The success of responsive regulation methods, however, depends importantly on cooperation by regulated entities, and consistent resistance can force regulatory oversight into a holding pattern, unable to make meaningful headway in shifting patterns of industry behavior. As we saw in Part I, platforms and information businesses in particular have effectively stonewalled regulators seeking more detail about their information harvesting and processing practices.

The Regulatory State as Auditor

A more telling barometer of institutional disruption is the increasing prominence of regulatory activities that do not seem to fall on the rulemaking-to-enforcement continuum at all. William Simon identifies a set of emergent regulatory practices that he characterizes as "post-bureaucratic": that are based on proactive planning rather than reactive rulemaking and on compliance monitoring rather than reactive enforcement.[62] Notably, the new regulatory modalities are intensively informational and technical in character. From a political economic standpoint, they are not so much post-bureaucratic as they are postindustrial, products of the "control revolution" that began with the introduction of automated information systems into industrial-era factories and businesses and continued with the increasing informationalization of economic development.[63] As implemented, they are also intensively managerial in orientation. They rely heavily on regulatory competencies such as auditing and technical standard-setting that involve specialized corps of professional experts and impose new technical challenges to public accountability.

Compliance monitoring and reporting play increasingly important roles in the contemporary regulatory landscape. Many regulatory schemes, including most notably those governing the financial system and the various markets for publicly traded securities, mandate periodic reporting on various matters. In other areas, including most notably consumer privacy, consent decrees requiring periodic reporting are an increasingly common component of enforcement practice. Compliance monitoring and reporting may entail demonstrated satisfaction of highly technical performance targets. For example, entities covered under the Health Insurance Portability and Accountability Act (HIPAA) Privacy Rule that wish to release data sets to the public must demonstrate that the data sets have been deidentified in a way that ensures sufficiently low risk of reidentification. Compliance monitoring and reporting also frequently involve audits conducted by specialized, private-sector professionals. Professional financial auditors play central roles in the modern system of financial regulation, and privacy and data security audits are becoming increasingly routine.[64]

A second strand in the emerging narrative of professionalized, informationalized regulation involves algorithmically mediated compliance with regulatory mandates.

As Kenneth Bamberger has detailed, regulatory regimes relying on information-systems mandates have become commonplace in a variety of information-intensive fields. Notably, most of the research and development activity surrounding algorithmic enforcement and software audit originates in the private sector, where so-called "government, regulation, and compliance" technologies and services comprise a large and growing market.[65] Also notably, some industries have developed similar technologies and systems absent any regulatory mandate to do so. For example, as we saw in Chapter 4, large platform companies generally rely on automated detection and filtering systems to avoid liability for facilitating copyright infringement.

A third type of regulatory activity that is increasingly common involves technical standard-setting. Both domestically and internationally, governments have long been involved in standards policy. In the United States, the National Institute of Standards and Technology (NIST) was established in 1901 to facilitate the development of measurement conventions that would enhance the global competitiveness of U.S. manufacturing and transportation industries. On a global scale, the International Telecommunication Union (ITU) has been active since 1865 in setting standards for telegraph interoperability.[66] In the digital era, however, technical standards have gone mainstream: they are core components of many regulatory regimes and appear as agenda items in the work of multiple agencies and transnational entities. Here too, privatization plays an important role. In the United States, federal law mandates public-private collaboration in standards policy. Agencies must use "technical standards that are developed or adopted by voluntary consensus standards bodies" unless that course of action "is inconsistent with applicable law or otherwise impractical."[67] NIST coordinates agency interaction with private standards bodies, and its mission has expanded to encompass everything from climate change measurement and standards for alternative energy technologies to metrics for food and drug safety and data privacy and security standards. To similar effect on a global scale, the ITU (now a specialized agency of the United Nations) has seen its mission expand to encompass telephone, radio, and television broadcast technologies and internet telephony protocols, and it has been joined by an alphabet soup of other standards bodies and initiatives that we will consider more carefully in Chapter 7.

The new regulatory modalities offer techniques for structuring, supervising, and certifying information flows. They therefore have at least the potential to address information-economy regulatory problems more effectively than older, command-and-control modalities. Whether they can fulfill that potential, however, depends on the details of their institutional implementation.

Each of the regulatory modalities just described encompasses many different possible implementation approaches, but, as noted previously, there are often pervasive mismatches between regulatory goals and necessary methods. Regulators and the public may have particular results in mind, but adequate performance in the realm of pollution control or financial accounting or data security or antibiotic resistance, for example, cannot simply be a matter of meeting discrete, fixed targets. To be effective, standards of adequacy must apply dynamically and must incorporate consideration of a wide and heterogeneous assortment of variables that bear on the behaviors of complex systems.[68] In addition, such standards generally will be technically complex, requiring special kinds of expertise to decipher.

For these reasons, the new postindustrial regulatory modalities tend to defy standard ways of thinking about regulatory accountability.[69] Terminology developed by Lauren Willis to describe new types of information products and services is useful as a way of summarizing the difficulty: traditional agency rules have dashboard complexity—they may consume many pages in the Code of Federal Regulations—but they are not especially complex under-the-hood.[70] Their provisions are developed via open proceedings to which multiple parties have input and their key terms are defined to supply publicly available points of common reference. The new regulatory modalities, in contrast, have dashboard simplicity but are complex under-the-hood. Reporting conventions and standards-related nomenclature can make it easy to know at a glance whether a regulated entity has met performance benchmarks or produced technically compliant products or services. The considerations and judgments that those results reflect, however, are harder to translate into forms suitable for general public understanding.

Other types of opacity reflect the private-sector origins of many performance assessment standards and practices. Consensus regarding the requirements for satisfactory performance may develop among members of a professionalized auditor class, but regulators and members of the public typically lack good access to the processes by which private-sector professionals hold themselves accountable. In rapidly changing fields, agreed standards may be nonexistent or disputed, and so the idea of "best practices"—whether for regulated entities or for the auditors purporting to supervise them—may mean very little.[71] In addition, private-sector compliance regimes may involve asserted trade secrets. Statutory open government regime typically contain trade secrecy exceptions, so they are poorly adapted to ensuring transparency where a significant privatization component is involved.[72]

Two well-known examples of how things can go badly wrong in highly professionalized regulatory domains come from the financial context. Professional consensus on so-called "generally accepted accounting principles" (GAAP) and on criteria for issuing and revising credit ratings proved inadequate to constrain rapid changes in accounting practice that led ultimately to the 2001 bankruptcy of billion-dollar energy company Enron. The Enron scandal exposed the need for a mechanism to ensure the accountability of those providing audit and credit rating services to publicly traded companies to limit moral hazard and self-dealing.[73] More recently, the global financial crisis of 2007–2008 exposed the inadequacy of mechanisms designed to ensure that large financial institutions participating in capital markets maintained adequate capital reserves. The applicable standards relied on banks and credit rating agencies to conduct their own assessments of capital adequacy and creditworthiness using complex and often proprietary algorithms, and many components of the system were not subject to capital-adequacy requirements at all.[74]

Both crises triggered increased oversight, but the regimes that resulted still have been criticized for deferring too greatly to accounting and finance professionals. The Sarbanes-Oxley Act of 2002 created the Public Company Accounting Oversight Board (PCAOB) to oversee compliance with public accountancy standards, but the accounting profession retained its authority over the substance of the GAAP, and the processes by which regulators and industry representatives negotiate capital requirements remain largely opaque to the public.[75] The Credit Rating Agency Reform Act of 2006 imposed a registration requirement on credit rating agencies, but that requirement failed to constrain the practice of issuing inflated ratings, including investment-grade ratings for securitizations of subprime mortgages in the run-up to the 2007–2008 crisis.[76] Finally, the Dodd-Frank Act of 2010 imposed additional requirements on credit rating agencies and gave federal regulators authority to prescribe minimum capital requirements for entities that engage in swap transactions, but as of this writing, the effects of those reforms are unclear and their future is in jeopardy.[77]

Automation of critical compliance functions adds another layer of opacity that inheres in the code through which compliance is measured and enforced. Automated processes have obvious efficiency advantages, but such processes may not align well (or at all) with applicable legal requirements that are couched in shades of gray.[78] As the example of the Volkswagen defeat device illustrates, the push to take human judgment out of the enforcement loop also raises a variety of difficult questions about how to define and audit compliance. Cary Coglianese and Jennifer Nash have observed that reliance on encoded, algorithmically enforced performance standards encourages gaming through a process they analogize to "teaching to the test"; firms have incentives to achieve a passing grade but not necessarily to do so in a way that fulfills the purpose the test was meant to serve.[79] As noted at the start of this chapter, regulators charged with overseeing emissions-control regimes now must learn to audit software if they wish to do their jobs effectively.

Mastering the processes by which technical standards are developed also requires both new kinds of regulatory expertise and new public accountability mechanisms. The language of data security, digital content management, and the like is dense and technical. It resists both public comprehension and public input, and even regulatory personnel themselves may not understand the key issues well. Many U.S. agencies now employ technical experts in key positions, but their work must be translated adequately for other agency staff. In addition, anti-regulatory advocacy has coalesced around a narrative about the foolhardiness and futility of regulatory intervention in highly technical, rapidly evolving fields. As agencies such as the FCC and FTC have begun to take up more technically complex issues, industry groups and pro-business think tanks have argued that direct government supervision of standards development will stifle innovation and slow economic development.[80] Industry standard-making processes, meanwhile, are lengthy, secretive, and notoriously resistant to public interest oversight. To take just one example, the ongoing negotiations over digital copy protection standards for high-definition audiovisual content are conducted on an invitation-only basis. Groups not invited to the table have been forced to rely on black-box testing and complaints from disgruntled consumers to gain information about the protocols as implemented.[81]

As this brief summary suggests, however, the current regulatory landscape also includes important innovations with respect to accountability and oversight. From a traditional "administrative law" perspective, the new regulatory bodies and competencies mentioned in this Section—the PCAOB, the still-emerging constellation of rules governing credit rating agencies, the administrators at the Federal Reserve who oversee bank stress testing, the administrators within the Department of Health and Human Services' Office of Civil Rights who oversee implementation of the HIPAA rules, and some components within NIST—seem to sit on the periphery of the regulatory state. Each oversees arcane and highly technical subject matter, and each sits within and is subject to the oversight authority of a larger and more traditionally configured administrative body. In terms of their core competencies, however, they are paradigmatic information-era regulatory bodies, with at least some amount of front-line authority over decisions that have enormous systemic impact.[82] Each has important lessons to teach about the possible futures of the regulatory state, and for that reason they merit more careful study by administrative law scholars generally.

The Regulatory State as Manager

A functioning government requires a budget, and budgetary decisions therefore provide another locus for the exercise of regulatory authority. As the regulatory state has grown larger, more complex, and more expensive, budgetary controls have become more and more important. Once again, this should be unsurprising. Financial controls are another paradigmatic postindustrial regulatory technique: they are intensively informational and their effective implementation requires both constructed (informational) measures of soundness and technical information-processing capacity. Like audits and technical protocols, however, financial controls have generated unfamiliar public accountability challenges. In addition, their congeniality to concrete, cost-benefit modeling has provided new points of entry for managerial efforts directed first and foremost toward regulatory minimization.

In the United States, budgetary authority is centralized in the Office of Management and Budget (OMB), which was created in 1970 to assume functions formerly performed by the Treasury Department. Within administrative law scholarship, interest in the OMB's activities and methods is a relatively recent development.

Beginning in the 1980s, scholars began to pay close attention to the role that the Office of Information and Regulatory Affairs (OIRA), a subdivision within OMB, plays in cost-benefit analysis of proposed regulations. As Eloise Pasachoff explains, however, OIRA is the tip of a much larger iceberg. A suite of activities, including not only cost-benefit analysis but also budget oversight, grant-making authority, and various other efficiency mandates, involves OMB pervasively in executive branch regulatory activities and enables it to assert new modes of financialized control over those activities. Some efficiency mandates, most notably the Paperwork Reduction Act, give OMB leverage over even formally independent agencies.[83]

Institutionally speaking, OMB's expertise is non-topical. Although program officers in its resource management offices are assigned to particular substantive areas, appointment within OMB does not require, for example, detailed familiarity with climate science, spectrum policy, or consumer finance. Instead, it traditionally has required training in "public policy, public administration, business, economics, etc."[84] The issue here is not that OMB staff lack familiarity with the technical and policy issues that are specific to the particular activities being regulated. As Pasachoff's description makes clear, OMB staff assigned to particular areas acquire expertise over time and reflect institutional memory the same way that staffers at agencies do. What is significant is simply that OMB's mission calls for the involvement of a cadre of professionals whose expertise is principally oriented toward efficient management. OMB therefore has become an important fulcrum point for the ongoing managerial reconfiguration of the regulatory state.

Like the managerial reconfiguration of dispute resolution systems, the managerial reconfiguration of regulatory activity has tended to elevate values such as efficiency and technocratic oversight over others such as fairness and public-facing accountability. Accounting and management methodologies rest on sets of assumptions about how to describe, measure, and account for program costs and benefits. Those assumptions are neither transparent nor inherently neutral, and merit careful scrutiny based on both the values that they enshrine and those that they elide or omit. And, precisely because they rest on assumptions about the inherent neutrality of management-based approaches, statutory provisions designed to facilitate public oversight of government effectiveness do not join these methodological issues effectively.[85] OMB's often-technical review and approval processes also exacerbate the problems of differential access and cumulative opacity described in the previous sections. As a result, OMB oversight sometimes has seemed merely to provide additional opportunities for regulated entities to exert influence over agency outputs.[86]

The ongoing centralization of regulatory functions in the OMB has meshed especially well with the turn to cost-benefit analysis described earlier in this chapter, and here the ideological and political undercurrents become more powerful. Academic proponents tout cost-benefit analysis as a neutral tool for centralized, politically accountable oversight of regulatory activity, but cost-benefit rhetoric—and particularly rhetoric emphasizing the purportedly intractable conflict between burdensome regulation on one hand and innovation and economic growth on the other—also has become a preferred mode of public policy discourse among scholars and policymakers who advocate regulatory minimization and privatization. Because cost-benefit analysis contemplates that even serious harms may be outweighed by higher levels of overall economic benefit, and because it tends to weigh the concrete costs of regulatory implementation more heavily than the more diffuse and often external benefits to be realized from compliance, it offers a particularly congenial technique for achieving that result. The increasingly tight conflation of cost-benefit review with regulatory rationality has meant that critics of regulatory minimization and privatization have found themselves placed in the unenviable role of Luddites, advancing complex conceptions of fairness and collective interdependence to counter a simpler, more accessible narrative about getting government out of the way.

The upshot is that the modern OMB has extended its influence over thinking about regulatory efficiency and efficacy in ways both institutional and cultural. In the absence of comprehensive scholarly and public scrutiny of the values encoded in government efficiency imperatives, the neoliberal hostility to regulation increasingly fashionable on both sides of the political aisle has enacted a kind of regulatory double movement, detaching regulatory authority from the various agencies to which it is assigned and re-embedding it under the oversight of a new, corporatized/managerial class concerned chiefly with minimizing the impact of regulation on economically productive activity. During the 2012 presidential campaign, a refrain oft-repeated by Republican candidate Mitt Romney concerned the business expertise that a former management consultant would bring to the executive branch. But Democrats also have gotten into the act: every administration for the last four decades has imposed new initiatives to be implemented within OMB.[87]

In the informational era, thinking about the proper relationship between government and management requires a more measured and constructively critical approach. The modes of financialized control practiced by OMB have not been embraced and systematically studied *as core regulatory modalities*—as much a part of the regulatory canon as the notice-and-comment rulemaking or the enforcement action. Put differently, financialized controls are not simply tools for achieving greater regulatory accountability. They represent a new information-era modality for the managerial exercise of regulatory power. In an enterprise as large and complex as the modern executive branch, developing the capacity for efficient management of taxpayer resources is important, but how exactly financialized controls should be incorporated within regulatory institutions attuned to the information economy is open to debate. Exercising financialized authority responsibly and fairly, and with appropriate attention to new rubrics constructed around the organizing problems of platform power, infoglut, and systemic threat, requires corresponding institutional innovation.

The Regulatory State as Artifact

The increased emphasis on centralized management and budget oversight in contemporary U.S. regulatory practice also points to a final kind of mismatch between the regulatory state and information-era regulatory problems and practices, which is structural: The jurisdictional boundaries of the existing administrative framework were drawn with industrial-era activities in mind. Information-economy activities have developed in utter disregard of the executive branch organization chart, cascading around and across existing lines of authority. The resulting overlaps and gaps underscore the need for new oversight modalities but also the need for new approaches to matters of high-level structure and organization.

Many contemporary regulatory disputes are artifacts of outdated statutory grants of authority. Consider net neutrality again. The last set of major amendments to the statutory framework governing "telecommunications" dates from 1996, when internet services were still-emergent and not yet understood as central components of modern communications architecture and policy. Initially, the FCC classified cable broadband services as information services under the statute, but after the D.C. Circuit ruled that the statute did not permit imposition of nondiscrimination obligations on such services and invalidated an initial set of net neutrality rules, it recharacterized broadband access providers as common carriers subject to regulation under a different title of the statute and then issued new rules, now themselves revoked.[88]

As we have already seen, however, the telephone-based communications paradigm is too narrow to encompass all of the service-related questions that digital networked communications raise. The parts of the statute that regulate designated common carriers were designed for basic telephone service; for example, common carriers must route all calls to their destinations without blocking or playing favorites.[89] Internet access providers routinely engage in traffic management for a diverse set of purposes ranging from network optimization to spam control to network security, and some network uses require higher bandwidth than others. Commercial internet access providers typically have defined tiers of pricing based on network speed and data usage rather than on the services consumers plan to use, but they also have experimented by selectively slowing or prioritizing traffic in ways that serve their own narrower interests.[90] Net neutrality regulation takes aim at the latter sort of conduct, but needs to say something about the former sort and to provide guidelines for distinguishing between the two, and the complexity of that project multiplies opportunities for rent-seeking. A modern enabling statute would not eliminate all of these problems but could address some of the more obvious difficulties.

The Telecommunications Act of 1996 is hardly unusual; many agency enabling statutes are much older. The Food and Drug Administration regulates computerized medical devices pursuant to a statutory definition of "device" enacted in 1976, the

Copyright Act of 1976 contains separate broadcast retransmission provisions for cable and satellite systems and does not speak to internet retransmission at all, the Magnuson-Moss Warranty Act, which granted the Federal Trade Commission limited rulemaking authority relating to unfair and deceptive acts in commerce, dates from 1975, decades before anyone had contemplated the necessary components of privacy and data security policies; and so on.[91] In many cases, political gridlock has defeated efforts to rethink obsolete statutory frameworks, but the cultural dynamic of deep capture (described in Chapter 3) also plays an important role in fostering regulatory stagnation. In a policy climate increasingly oriented toward neoliberal governmentality, even well-intentioned policymakers are relatively disinclined to embark on the complex task of designing new administrative structures better matched to information-economy activities.

Both new and old economic actors have treated obsolete laws as invitations to create business arrangements that route around existing points of regulatory control. As we saw in Chapter 1, high-profile, platform-based "disruptors" of existing work arrangements—including labor-matching sites such as Mechanical Turk and TaskRabbit and transportation-matching sites such as Uber and Lyft—argue that existing regulatory regimes do not apply to them. Instead, they recruit user-workers into arrangements that are styled as licenses to access the platform's resources. As critics have detailed, however, provisions in those licenses cover matters more commonly addressed in employment agreements.[92] And platforms' self-interested description of their operations is incomplete; they are also structures for converting the labor of user-workers and their customers into flows of monetizable data and finance capital. Outdated statutory frameworks do not address these issues at all, and the logics of performative enclosure, productive appropriation, and innovative and expressive immunity work to make them seem both less salient and less important from a regulatory standpoint. Meanwhile, long-established industrial-economy employers also have relied on networked information and communications technologies to restructure patterns of work in ways that avoid protective regulation. So, for example, corporate giant Fedex uses sophisticated information systems to match drivers with parcels and delivery routes and structures its relationships with drivers as independent-contractor arrangements. Employers of all sizes use scheduling software to limit employees' hours in order to avoid triggering various regulatory requirements.[93]

In other cases, business models designed around obsolete statutory frameworks have become entrenched in ways that systematically disadvantage new entrants. For example, in the field of music copyright, some entities administer reproduction rights in musical compositions while others administer public performance rights in those same compositions. Rights in sound recordings are held by a third group of actors. Some rights are subject to statutory licenses, but the technical details create many pitfalls for digital music services that must clear multiple rights for large numbers of works. Rent-seeking to preserve existing allocations of entitlements and obligations has produced a powerful inertial effect, compromising efforts to clear the way for continued innovation in digital delivery of content.[94]

Each of the examples just given involves a single regulator, but in other cases, efforts to devise modern frameworks for regulating information-era activities confront jurisdictional difficulties that are even more intractable. Many kinds of information-related activities simply were not contemplated when the divisions of authority among the various executive branch, legislative, and independent agencies were established. Activities such as digital broadcast content protection, pharmaceutical patenting, data-driven predictive profiling, regulation of health-related information services, and regulation of financial services implicate the jurisdiction of multiple entities. Assertions of incomplete and poorly defined regulatory authority both add to the overall confusion and embolden critics of regulatory overreach.[95]

Consider net neutrality again. An ideal enabling statute for the modern FCC would acknowledge the full range of considerations that attend the provision of internet access and provide guidance on how to weigh them. But even if Congress managed to transcend its dysfunctions and enact such a statute, the current regulatory structure still does not permit any regulator to consider the full group of actors whose activities determine the neutrality or nonneutrality of access to networked digital communications capabilities and services. The FCC's short-lived rules applied straightforwardly to broadband and wireless internet providers, with some exceptions for certain voice-over-internet services, and not at all to platforms such as Facebook and Twitter that do not provide internet access directly to U.S. consumers. If the question is whether an entity provides telecommunications services of the general sort contemplated by Congress in the most recent iteration of the Telecommunications Act, those distinctions may make sense. If the question is whether platforms' self-interested mediation of the networked information environment ought to be subject to some basic nondiscrimination obligations, they seem both arbitrary and laughable.

Platforms and their government relations firms have exploited the fact that regulatory authority over their activities is incomplete and fragmented by pointing to isolated instances of apparent unfairness. For example, Google has adopted the posture of a supplicant seeking nondiscriminatory access to connection points for its Google Fiber initiative, even though it dominates the market for search and, together with other dominant platform firms, "already benefit[s] from what are essentially internet fast lanes, and this has been the case for years."[96] Proposals to create a regulatory authority empowered to impose comparable neutrality obligations on search providers, meanwhile, have drawn criticism from commentators all along the political spectrum.[97] The FCC's net neutrality rulemakings also have systematically excluded privacy-related concerns. After the Obama-era FCC issued separate rules requiring internet access providers to protect the privacy of subscriber personal information, access providers argued that those obligations were duplicative in light of the FTC's enforcement activities. After the acting chair of the Trump-era FTC endorsed that position, Congress invoked a new anti-regulatory instrument, the Congressional Review Act, to rescind the privacy rules and prevent their re-enactment. Meanwhile—and while challenging the Obama-era FCC's authority to issue net neutrality rules—access provider AT&T attempted to defend against an FTC privacy enforcement action by arguing that, because it performs common carriage functions and the FTC lacks enforcement jurisdiction over issues relating to common carriage, the FTC had no authority over it at all.[98]

Patterns of regulatory oversight in some industries reflect a more considered commitment to regulatory fragmentation. That approach accords with the reigning neoliberal anti-regulatory ideology and its emphasis on bringing competition into government; as we have seen throughout this chapter, however, it has been notably ineffective at countering systemic threats. Consider, for example, financial regulation, which emanates from multiple agencies, commissions, and specialized boards. While fragmentation may have seemed sensible as a method of avoiding capture during the years when the financial industry also was subject to statutorily imposed fragmentation, the demise of those restrictions has opened the way for banks and other financial services firms to amass extraordinary power over both national and global financial systems. Through multiple rounds of reform legislation, commitments to fragmentation have persisted and have disabled regulators from mounting effective systemic responses.[99] Similarly, regulatory fragmentation has become a salient attribute of food and drug law. Even as the range of considerations that affects systemic safety and sustainability has grown increasingly large and complex, regulators have worked to keep lines of authority distinct and limited.[100]

Notably, the executive branch sometimes has responded to structural obsolescence and jurisdictional overlap by creating interagency task forces and working groups. Those experiments have inspired a new subgenre of administrative law scholarship focused on developing procedures and lines of accountability for interagency entities. Such proposals, however, also promise to add new layers of regulatory complexity and magnify the scope for bureaucratic infighting.[101] (The European Commission, meanwhile, has constituted a separate Directorate-General for the sole purpose of studying information-economy needs and attempting to coordinate solutions, but regulators in other directorates have not necessarily welcomed its interventions.[102])

Like the new templates for large-scale dispute resolution studied in Chapter 5, interagency entities are best understood and evaluated as contingent institutional formations. They gesture toward the possibility of a different structure for the administrative state, but they are also stopgap measures that take existing structures for granted. True blueprints for a regulatory state optimized for the informational economy have yet to emerge.

Reinventing Regulatory Practice for the Era of Algorithmic Governance

As the basis of our political economy shifts, corresponding shifts in the nature of regulatory concepts and processes are to be expected. From that standpoint, some of the changes I have described may usefully be understood through the lens of creative destruction; outdated regulatory formations are and should be vulnerable to the winds of change just as outdated products and irrelevant monopolists are. Regulatory institutions are stickier than market arrangements, however, and not only because so many aspects of their operation are codified. Regulatory institutions also have at least the potential to perform protective functions that market institutions cannot—to interpose friction where it is most needed and most justified. And for that reason, regulatory institutions also are important sites of innovation.

It is too soon to say precisely what a regulatory state optimized for the era of informational capitalism ought to look like, but it is nonetheless essential to understand current regulatory disputes as contests over that question. Transformation in political economy demands corresponding transformation in regulatory logics. Reinvigorating market oversight in the era of informational capitalism requires a willingness to rethink both competition law and public utility law from the ground up. Additionally, if protections against discrimination, fraud, manipulation, and election interference are to be preserved in the era of infoglut, regulators will need to engage more directly with practices of data-driven, algorithmic intermediation and their uses and abuses. Both projects demand more careful investigation of the kinds of power that information platforms wield and more open-minded consideration of possible corrective measures. Effective regulation in the information era also requires creative, interdisciplinary thinking about the design of regulatory methods for modeling and countering systemic threats.[103]

If the dysfunctions now confronting the regulatory state are to be addressed effectively, however, scholars and policymakers also must be willing to entertain the prospect of paradigm shifts in the design of regulatory institutions and in the deep structure of "administrative law" more generally. In that process, it will be important not to confuse the demands of informational capitalism, understood as a distinct system of political economy requiring effective oversight and guidance, with the demands of information capitalists. The pervasive mismatch between the regulatory instrumentalities that we have and the ones that we need does not simply call for new cadres of auditors and more cutting-edge managerial techniques but rather for creative thinking about how new structures for oversight and public accountability might develop. And even new enabling statutes for existing agencies will not necessarily address problems requiring deeper restructuring.

In the current U.S. political climate, comprehensive overhaul of the regulatory state may seem infeasible. As of this writing, all branches of government seem intent instead on presiding over its destruction. If that approach has a silver lining, it may be that it clears the way for subsequent administrations and Congresses to rebuild and in the process to reimagine the regulatory state in a form better suited to the tasks at hand.

7

Networks, Standards, and Transnational Governance Institutions

The Net interprets censorship as damage and routes around it.
—John Gilmore, Interview, *Time Magazine*

The story of law's reoptimization to the demands of the informational economy is not just about the reconfiguration of old, familiar legal institutions but also about the emergence and configuration of new ones. Over the last half century, institutions for transnational governance have multiplied. The landscape of world trade agreements and enforcement processes has grown increasingly complex. New structures for transnational regulation of economic activity have emerged that seem to operate according to their own rules in ways influenced by states but not controlled by them. Other new institutions, created to govern the internet and its constituent protocols and processes, do not operate based on state representation at all.

Each set of transnational processes has met perceived needs arising from the ongoing transformation of the global political economy, and each set of processes also has accelerated that transformation. Their successes and failures and half-completed projects reflect themes that will have become familiar to readers of this book: the importance of global flows of resources and corresponding logics of extractive privilege; the increasingly insistent assertion of logics of interdiction directed at particular, assertedly dangerous flows and the countervailing, equally insistent assertion of logics of platform immunity; the emergence of highly informationalized, managerial techniques and strategies for coordinating global flows; and contestation over the design of institutions for rendering such flows accountable.

This chapter juxtaposes the various governance processes and treats them explicitly as iterations of a new—or, more precisely, emergent—networked legal-institutional form. Although the new institutions differ from each other in many ways, they share a common structure: they are organized as networks constituted around legally or practically mandated standards. And the role of standards within those arrangements is both vitally important and especially easy for legal scholars accustomed to other types of governance texts to overlook.

Each of the scholarly literatures that has grown up around the various institutions described in this chapter has grasped some essential aspects of the network-and-standard dynamic but not others. Legal scholars who study world trade and transnational business regulation have conducted long-running and vigorous debates about the legitimacy and accountability of networked governance processes, and they also have explored the political issues that inevitably complicate the work of transnational standards bodies. Even so, they have paid less attention to the distinctive ways that standards bind such networks together, and so the two conversations do not fully join up.[1] In part that may be because legal theory traditionally has drawn a distinction between rules and standards that drives in the opposite direction. Within that scholarly tradition, "rules" are granular and demand precise compliance, while "standards" are more flexible and are fleshed out via norms and interpretative conventions.[2] The standards at the core of transnational legal-institutional arrangements are different creatures entirely.

Legal scholars who study "code as law" are familiar with different literatures about networks and standards, including literatures on how technical standards structure the markets organized around them, and they also have raised persistent, serious concerns about the relationships between and among automated enforcement, lock-step conformity and authoritarian modes of governance. They have tended, however, to situate standards processes within market-based governance frameworks and to understand code's mandatory nature as an example of the way that code *differs from* law; consequently, they have not taken network-and-standard-based governance seriously as a new legal-institutional type.[3] And, for the most part, the two scholarly communities have not engaged in much dialogue with one another.

To posit network-and-standard-based governance institutions as an emergent category of legal institutions is, of course, to beg some basic questions about what makes an institution distinctively legal. One traditional set of answers has to do with the ways that the outcomes produced by such institutions are linked to rulemaking and enforcement authority. Many human activities rely on networks and standards, but legal ordering bites on such activities differently. Violation of a community standard may trigger gossip or ostracism, and departure from a commercial or technical standard may consign the violator to irrelevance or spark a productive standards war, but noncompliance with a legal standard will incur sanctions backed by the full force of state authority.[4] Another traditional set of answers is more explicitly normative: what makes an institution distinctively legal is its adherence to regular procedural rules and associated rule-of-law values. Communities are accountable only to themselves and markets may mete out consequences that seem arbitrary. According to a thick conception of what makes a legal institution, law's authoritarian bite is (or should be) mitigated by procedural fairness and conformance with principles of public reason.[5]

As we are about to see, network-and-standard-based governance institutions satisfy each of these definitions in some respects while challenging them in others. For some, that means they are not legal institutions at all, but I think that answer is too pat. We will see that the shift to a networked and standard-based governance structure reshapes modes of lawmaking and enforcement, patterns of contestation over lawmaking authority, and structures for participation and accountability in ways that pose important challenges both to the realizability of traditional rule-of-law values and to traditional conceptions of the institutional forms that those values require. But the rule-of-law constructs that legal theorists traditionally have articulated are themselves artifactual in precisely the two senses with which this book has been concerned. They are the products of earlier contests over the forms of legal authority, and they are outgrowths of the era of text-based communication and of accompanying assumptions about the feasible mechanisms for formulation, justification, and transmission of claims of authority that are now rapidly being outpaced by sociotechnical change.[6] If the new network-and-standard-based governance institutions are to serve the overarching institutional functions that traditionally have informed thicker versions of rule-of-law thinking—functions that, to borrow Martin Krygier's formulation, temper the arbitrary exercise of power—both institutions and constructs will need to adapt.[7]

Global Assemblages for Economic and Technical Coordination

The processes of world trade regulation, transnational business regulation, and internet governance span many different subject areas and involve many different participants and interests. The institutions through which those forms of regulation are conducted also vary considerably from one another in terms of their rules for membership and participation. Even so, juxtaposing the various institutions and processes reveals important resemblances. In what follows, I borrow from and expand upon the frameworks sketched by Terence Halliday and Greg Shaffer in the domain of legal theory and by Heather McKeen-Edwards and Tony Porter in the domain of political economy. Network-and-standard-based governance institutions are situated within larger assemblages for transnational legal ordering. Their operations reflect complex and mutually interpenetrating sets of relationships and practices that involve a heterogeneous array of public, private, and public-private actors and associations.[8] Even formally multilateral arrangements are increasingly multistakeholderist as a practical matter, and standards and expert standard-making activities play increasingly prominent roles in constituting the substance of governance arrangements.[9] Information-economy flows and assets have become focal points for transnational governance activities, and information-economy disputes about cross-border information flows increasingly have brought different networked governance arrangements into contact, and conflict, with one another.

The Emergence and Metamorphosis of World Trade

Global institutions for world trade play a central role in the story of informational capitalism's emergence and continuing evolution. The global logics of production and extraction that have become characteristic of informational capitalism rely heavily on legal frameworks for facilitating cross-border flows of goods, materials, people, and information, and those logics have elicited corresponding changes in the structure and operation of the world trade system. For most of the twentieth century, the system of world trade governance revolved around the framework established under the General Agreement on Tariffs and Trade (GATT). Policymaking within that framework was dominated for the most part by the United States. In the 1990s, however, the landscape of world trade governance began to change rapidly. New multilateral instruments dramatically expanded the scope and reach of the existing regime, and competing avenues for trade policymaking also began to emerge. Last but not least, giant transnational corporations have become powerful players in the world trade landscape.

In terms of coverage, three features of the emergent constellation of trade-related governance arrangements are especially important. First, norms of liberalization do not simply relate to manufactured goods or even to cross-border flows of raw materials and intermediate inputs to more complex products. Following the important Uruguay Round of negotiations, which concluded in the 1990s and produced both the World Trade Organization (WTO) as a powerful new enforcement body and the General Agreement on Trade in Services (GATS), liberalization of cross-border trade in services has emerged as a separate, powerful logic driving the articulation and expansion of trade obligations.[10] That logic is intimately bound up with the patterns of resource reconceptualization described in Chapter 1. As we saw there, networked information and communication technologies have catalyzed the dematerialization and informationalization of labor and finance, which in turn facilitate the cross-border provision of many types of information-based services and accelerate cross-border flows of capital and investment.

Second and relatedly, imperatives relating to intellectual property protection and enforcement have become more pronounced and more pressing. The Uruguay Round also produced a new protocol on Trade-Related Aspects of Intellectual Property Rights (TRIPS), and the United States and other developed countries have continued to advance additional initiatives designed to strengthen protections, deepen enforcement obligations, and rationalize ownership of intellectual goods across borders. Political economists studying post-TRIPS treaty-making efforts have found that the presence or absence of new intellectual property terms has become an important factor prompting business interests to support new proposed international agreements.[11] For their part, however, developing countries have grown increasingly resistant to proposals for stronger enforcement and protection emanating from the global North. Such proposals, they argue, reflect rent-seeking by already-powerful industries rather than good-faith efforts to help developing economies engage in capacity-building; consequently, they are far more likely to widen existing wealth disparities than to narrow them. Protection of indigenous groups' interests in biological and cultural resources also has become an important point of contention in such negotiations.[12]

Third, multilateral arrangements for technical standard-making play increasingly prominent roles within the world trade apparatus. The Uruguay Round produced two new agreements on technical standardization, one relating to global food safety and another to standardization as a strategy for minimizing technical barriers to trade. Adherence to relevant international standards is now mandatory unless deviation can be justified—and the extent to which domestic protective considerations may justify deviations on matters viewed as "technical" first and foremost has become an important point of contention. Because the WTO does not develop standards itself, the turn toward technical standardization also entails considerable de facto reliance on the outputs of transnational standard-setting bodies. For all of these reasons, questions about the politics of standard-setting and of standards-based governance have become important recent additions to the scholarly research agendas of international trade scholars and policymakers.[13]

Although the Uruguay Round was intended to strengthen and extend the existing multilateral trade regime, its conclusion also marked the start of a pronounced and unanticipated shift in the institutional structure of world trade governance. The process of reaching new agreements under the established multilateral framework slowly ground to a halt as efforts to negotiate additional trade liberalization requirements encountered a variety of obstacles. Those included violent protests against the human costs of globalization (in Seattle in 1999), disagreements over access to patent-protected medicines in the developing world (in Doha in 2001), and differing views of agricultural protection measures adopted by developed countries (in Cancun in 2003).[14] Meanwhile, trade negotiators from developed economies began to shift their efforts toward framing and securing new bilateral free trade agreements. The thickening network of bilateral agreements in turn shaped proposals for new multilateral and regional instruments that included both new substantive obligations and mandates for new and powerful dispute resolution processes.[15]

The United States spearheaded the initial move toward bilateral and multilateral agreements negotiated outside the WTO framework, but the so-called

Washington Consensus on trade liberalization subsequently has begun to fragment, and other significant initiatives have emerged. Many interpreted the U.S.-led negotiations over the Trans Pacific Partnership (TPP), which did not include China, as an effort to constrain emergent Chinese economic power. Partly in response, the Regional Coalition for Economic Participation (RCEP) launched an effort to negotiate a new, pan-Asian trade protocol in which China has played a significant role. Meanwhile, after the Trump administration withdrew the United States from negotiations over the TPP, the remaining nations finalized the agreement but changed some of its provisions to fit their own priorities.[16]

In parallel with these changes in institutional structure, the landscape of world trade governance and world trade activism also has broadened to include a more heterogeneous assortment of actors and interests. In particular, transnational corporations and cooperative business associations wield increasing de facto power in setting trade policy priorities. In part this power flows through traditional channels of influence. Powerful economic actors have long enjoyed privileged access to national policymakers and have learned to exploit that access to demand stronger and more effective protection for their global supply chains.[17] But global logics of production and extraction also have elicited new networked models of influence that flow outside state-sanctioned channels. A giant transnational corporation with operations in many countries can assert interests within all of them and can formulate and advance a unified strategy for furthering those interests.[18] Increasingly importunate assertions of corporate interest also have catalyzed experimentation with new forms of dispute resolution, most notably procedures for so-called investor-state dispute settlement that allow corporations to assert claims directly against states whose domestic regulations allegedly violate trade liberalization obligations.[19] Last and importantly, as the next section describes, transnational corporations and their business associations actively participate in national, international, and private standard-setting processes.

A final cross-cutting strand in the increasingly complex landscape of world trade governance involves the emergence of an active transnational community of civil society activists seeking to broaden access to and participation in governance processes. Exploiting the same networked connectivity that has enabled global concentrations of economic power, civil society NGOs have worked to build alliances with one another and to coordinate their efforts for maximum effect. Civil society groups have worked to draw public attention to failures of transparency and accountability at all stages of the trade governance cycle, from domestic discussions about agenda-setting to negotiations over new trade instruments to dispute resolution. At each stage, they have advocated for greater attention to the broader public interests served (or disserved) by both existing and prospective governance arrangements.[20]

Collapsing Hierarchies in Transnational Regulation

The transnational economic governance landscape also includes a large and varied group of regulatory arrangements, some well established and others more emergent, that extend through and around the boundaries of nation-states. Some arrangements originate with the United Nations (UN) or its member agencies. Others are cooperative ventures among subnational regulators or among other entities that play well-established quasi-regulatory roles, such as central banks. Others involve subnational regulators in collaboration with private industry oversight bodies and trade associations, and still others involve coordination directly among nonstate actors. Like world trade governance processes, transnational regulatory processes produce complex standards intended to structure the behaviors of both corporations and governments. And, as in the case of world trade, a pervasive and cross-cutting theme in both the theory and the practice of transnational regulation is the increasing power of private "stakeholders" in the domains of both standard-making and dispute resolution.

Providing a full catalog of transnational regulatory processes is a project well beyond the scope of this chapter. For my purposes here, it is useful simply to draw the reader's attention to four broad and general categories of activity that are formally distinct but increasingly convergent as a practical matter.

The first category includes formal, multilateral, bureaucratic processes conducted by the UN and agencies within its organizational umbrella or by independent multilateral entities. Some of those processes involve negotiating and drafting new treaties. For example, since 1990, the UN has shepherded to completion several major environmental accords, including the 1992 United Nations Framework Convention on Climate Change, the 1997 Kyoto Protocol, and the 2015 Paris Climate Agreement. The World Intellectual Property Organization (WIPO) has finalized several new agreements intended to extend and harmonize aspects of the intellectual property laws of member states. Other processes involve standard-making for areas within the organizational remits of existing agencies or agreements. So, for example, the International Labor Organization superintends the development of standards for fair labor practices, the United Nations Forum on Sustainability Standards coordinates the work of five UN member agencies on standards for environmentally responsible manufacturing, and the United Nations Global Compact coordinates the UN's efforts to implement standards for corporate social responsibility generally. The International Organization for Standardization (ISO), an independent nongovernmental entity in which states are represented by their national standards organizations, also engages in standard-making on a variety of business-related matters, including corporate social responsibility.[21]

Although membership in the UN is state-based, participation in the policymaking and regulatory processes unfolding under its aegis reflects the increasingly pervasive influence of nonstate actors and especially commercial actors. In 1996, the

UN liberalized the criteria that civil society organizations and other nongovernmental organizations must meet to gain consultative status. As Melissa Durkee has explained, the revised criteria have afforded business interests the opportunity to gain entry into those processes via NGOs of their own. Commercial NGOs have systematically exploited that opportunity, navigating with relative ease the bureaucratic requirements that some civil society organizations have found trickier.[22] Additionally, many of the standard-making initiatives mentioned in the previous paragraph are formally structured as public-private collaborations.[23]

A second category of transnational regulatory processes involves specialized, freestanding accords between and among subnational regulators and other established sectoral institutions. For example, financial regulators and central bankers engage in extensive, cooperative cross-border governance of financial market activities, and data protection regulators work collaboratively on various policy issues.[24] Such arrangements comprise a thickening network of "soft law" that structures and coordinates industry activities. Here again, public-private collaboration, delegation of oversight authority to private economic actors, and standard-making are recurring themes. For example, global money center banks have played major roles in the development of risk assessment algorithms and capital adequacy standards; private transnational associations spanning fields from securities to insurance to accounting perform a wide variety of governance functions both on their own and in cooperation with government actors; and technical standards play important roles in facilitating transnational financial flows.[25]

There is a notable and steadily increasing overlap between processes in the first two categories and those in the third, which consists of standard-making that emanates from the private sector in the first instance. The universe of private standard-making activities is large and diverse. Transnational corporations engage in standard-making to facilitate their own operations and those of their supply chains, and industry associations coordinate standardization activities in areas that their members perceive as mutually beneficial. Service professionals such as accountants, engineers, and information technology consultants employ extensive and well-developed standards to guide their work, which in turn informs financial, technical, and information systems design practices more generally. Compliance with private standards is formally voluntary, but standard-making processes produce distinctive sociotechnical configurations—reporting formats, performance benchmarks, and so on—that work to channel industry behavior into compliant patterns.[26]

Also notably, the outputs of both private standard-making processes and public-private standard-making collaborations have begun to migrate into the domain of world trade. As noted in the previous section, the WTO framework includes two agreements mandating reliance on relevant international technical standards. In addition new bilateral and multilateral trade agreements covering labor, environmental regulation, and corporate social responsibility often refer to privately developed standards in those domains.[27] As a result, standard-making activities constitute a new avenue for private firms and associations to shape the formulation of trade obligations, including especially provisions intended to delineate the appropriate reach of domestic protective mandates.

The fourth and final template for transnational business governance involves assemblages for private arbitral dispute resolution. This form of transnational regulation mirrors the outsourcing experiments discussed in Chapter 5, but with an important difference. In domestic litigation, parties to commercial contract disputes generally do not opt out of court entirely but instead use contract to develop customized procedural rules.[28] In the transnational context, such parties rely heavily on arbitration when disputes arise. Private power is starkly evident in the operation of these systems, which some commentators have likened to the *lex mercatoria* through which medieval merchants and craftsmen resolved their own disputes. Three different commercial conventions, one sponsored by the UN and the other two freestanding, supply default rules for interpreting cross-border agreements and resolving disputes before arbitrators drawn from the international business bar. Parties to a transaction may alter the default rules and procedures by contract, and the results of dispute resolution generally remain private. The conventions and their associated arbitral bodies compete with one another for clientele and strive to produce results that client communities will find sensible and congenial.[29] Not all political regimes have proved equally hospitable to that system, but "new legal hubs"—exceptional zones sited within such regimes but governed by separate institutions—have emerged to fulfill dispute resolution demands.[30]

Order without Law? From Rough Consensus to Internet Multistakeholderism

A final important site of transnational legal-institutional entrepreneurship is the internet and its constituent protocols and processes. Among cyberlaw scholars, the emergence, formalization, and ongoing evolution of governance arrangements for the internet have excited intense interest. Those scholars, however, have relied heavily on conceptual frameworks that locate internet governance principally within the realms of technical design and private ordering rather than that of law.[31] The literatures on transnational governance, meanwhile, have paid relatively little attention to internet governance institutions, treating them as instances of purely technical oversight or, in one notable example, as manifestations of a modern-day *lex mercatoria* that information technology businesses and trademark owners use to govern themselves.[32] As we will see in this section, those characterizations are too simple to describe either the origins of internet governance or what internet governance has become. Institutional structures for global network governance add to our growing catalog of emergent transnational legal-institutional models, supplying new templates for the configuration and exercise of network-and-standard-based governance authority.

One important constellation of governance arrangements relates to the information transfer protocols used to move information from one node on the network to another. Most prominently, the Internet Engineering Task Force (IETF), a voluntary membership organization of computer technologists, oversees the continuing evolution of the TCP/IP protocols, which serve as the internet's foundational standards for information transmission. Notably, the IETF originated in a struggle over technical merit and bureaucratic turf but also political philosophy. Most experts viewed the TCP/IP protocols as technically superior, but the ISO preferred a different standard that it had helped to develop and had a greater expectation of continuing to control. The IETF was the brainchild of a group of computer scientists determined that the evolution of standards for networked digital communication would follow a different path. Their rejection of the ISO's proposed standard was also a rejection of an institutional process that they perceived as slow and bureaucratic and a deliberate embrace of participatory direct democracy by those with the necessary technical qualifications to contribute to the project of building and maintaining the best possible network.[33] In the words of founding IETF member David Clark: "We reject: kings, presidents and voting. We believe in: rough consensus and running code."[34] The particular brand of idealism that Clark expressed resonated with the meritocratic orientation and libertarian political leanings of many of his fellow computer technologists, and it became the IETF's operating credo.

Another important constellation of arrangements relates to the internet's namespaces. To avoid Balkanization of the internet into incompatible networks, the tables used to link internet addresses to definite nodes and map human-readable domain names to those addresses must be identical. Initially, the internet's core addressing and routing functions were managed by a researcher at the University of Southern California pursuant to an agreement with the U.S. Department of Defense. As internet connectivity began to spread beyond government and educational institutions, however, it became apparent that a more formalized and robust set of governance arrangements was required. Once again, those most directly involved in the development and oversight of the relevant protocols resisted proposals for formalizing namespace governance that would have vested control in established government or multilateral institutions, and once again, the reasons were not only technical but more fundamentally political and ideological. After a period of intense turmoil, the most visible result of those struggles was a new legal-institutional formation, the Internet Corporation for Assigned Names and Numbers (ICANN), a not-for-profit transnational governance corporation chartered under California law but accountable via its constitutive documents to a global community of stakeholders. Controversially, the U.S. Department of Commerce retained residual authority over namespace governance until 2016.[35]

The disputes that surrounded the formation of ICANN reflected a complex set of political and ideological cross-currents. According to some, the internet could not become a truly global information infrastructure while still under U.S. oversight because such oversight would work to enable, or more minimally preserve space for, the assertion of U.S. geopolitical and economic hegemony. According to others, the internet had emerged and thrived precisely because of its embeddedness in U.S.-style free expression values and norms. According to some, established pathways for transnational governance, including especially those under the aegis of the UN, boasted both unblemished legitimacy and the capacity to address the full range of relevant policy issues, including especially those relating to economic development and inclusiveness. According to others, the protocol wars of the 1980s had decisively established that legacy entities such as the ISO and the UN were inadequate to the task of stewarding cutting-edge technological protocols that must evolve in real time. According to some, U.S.-based operational oversight was too prone to co-optation by capitalist and neoliberal economic and political ideologies. According to others, UN-based oversight would be too vulnerable to holdup engineered by authoritarian states wishing to assert greater control over internet traffic for their own political reasons. The eventual form that ICANN assumed is conventionally understood as a compromise resolution of those disputes (although, as we are about to see, observers differ on the extent of the compromise).[36] For its part, although the UN has continued to assert an interest in the institutional arrangements for namespace governance, it also has tacitly acknowledged the critiques leveled at it, constituting a new Internet Governance Forum as both a venue for ongoing high-level policy discussions and a bully pulpit for those attempting to ensure greater attention to democratic and distributive values.[37]

For U.S. legal scholars and members of the nascent technology policy community, both the IETF's rejection of governance by governments and the disputes that surrounded the formation of ICANN resonated with other prominent themes in scholarly and contemporary thought. To legal scholars steeped in the traditions of liberal political theory, the IETF was enlightened self-government brought to improbable life. Its existence in seeming defiance of the dysfunctions of other ostensibly democratic institutions demonstrated that direct, deliberative democracy could function and flourish.[38] Judged by that standard, ICANN represented a fundamentally unaccountable privatization of oversight authority, so those scholars labored to convince ICANN to adopt additional mechanisms for public input and participation.[39] Other scholars of a more libertarian bent were attracted by the rejection of regulatory oversight in favor of enlightened, meritocratic self-rule; for these scholars, ICANN's organization illustrated the potentially transformative power of contract and incorporation to supplant state-based lawmaking.[40]

But as the rejection of governance by governments become more solidly entrenched, something strange began to happen: Disputes over process and representation began to catalyze the emergence of more formal governance structures and the codification of rules and procedural conventions to guide their operation. Several decades in, the new governance institutions are both like and unlike more traditional legal institutions. Their outputs are paradigmatically not "law" in the sense that they have not been codified by legislators and regulators or distilled into precedential nuggets by courts, and they are not (directly) accountable to states. Both their outputs and their operations, however, have become both more recognizably lawlike and more like those of the other institutions this chapter has described.

As ICANN has matured, it has undergone considerable institutional hybridization, developing more regularized pathways for policymaking and participation. Its public meetings are attended by a diverse and vocal group of stakeholders, and membership in its working groups—where much of its real business is done—is formally open to all comers. It has adopted formal consultative procedures for governments and civil society organizations and, following the issuance of a report by the Council of Europe interrogating ICANN's compliance with human rights guarantees, has become somewhat more attentive to input from the latter.[41] ICANN's evolution, however, also reflects other themes that this section has explored. ICANN was chartered as a California public benefit corporation not only to "promot[e] the global public interest in the operational stability of the Internet" but also to "lessen[] the burdens of government."[42] As the internet's constitutive liberalization norms have been filtered through the lens of neoliberalized and explicitly multistakeholderist institutional design, they have produced institutional responses optimized to the needs of ICANN's most active and well-resourced stakeholders. As we will see later in this chapter, ICANN's most notable characteristic is its extreme solicitude for intellectual property interests. ICANN's rules also encode policy decisions about a variety of other issues ranging from registrant privacy to freedom of expression, and those decisions tend to reflect the policy preferences of powerful corporate and government actors.

The IETF's original simple, flat structure also has undergone dramatic change. Today, although membership remains voluntary and policymaking consensus-based, the IETF comprises two principal divisions made up of over 100 working groups, overseen by two steering groups and advised by two different boards. Working groups follow elaborate protocols for documenting their activities, communicating with other groups, and reporting to the steering groups and advisory boards. There is a process (so far, never used) for administrative appeals.[43] Although many members would strenuously resist the characterization, the IETF has taken on some characteristics of the sorts of governance processes that it initially had rejected, with its system of RFCs and administrative oversight functioning in a way roughly analogous to the system of guidances, advisories, and internal oversight adopted by federal administrative agencies.[44] Along the way, the IETF membership also has needed to learn how to identify, understand, and address a broad range of policy questions. In particular, issues relating to tracking and filtering—and, therefore, to privacy, surveillance, censorship, intellectual property enforcement, and freedom of expression—have complicated ostensibly technical discussions and taxed the commitment to decision-making based on rough consensus about technical merit alone.[45]

Last and importantly, as Laura DeNardis explains, although the IETF and ICANN have commanded an outsize share of scholarly attention, the assemblages for global network governance within which those entities are situated are more complex.[46] Many other entities perform standard-making activities relevant to information transfer across nodes and connected devices, and those entities are heterogeneous in structure and composition. Some are formally multilateral, others are private technical associations, and still others more closely resemble private standards bodies. For example, the World Wide Web Consortium (W3C), a private membership organization, oversees the development of the hypertext protocols that constitute the Web. The W3C has different tiers of membership for different types of stakeholders, with large technology corporations paying the highest fees and wielding corresponding influence. The International Telecommunications Union (ITU), a UN-affiliated entity that oversees standards relating to broadcast technologies, supervises standards for internet telephony, and the Institute of Electrical and Electronic Engineers, a technical professional organization, coordinates the evolution of standards for wireless interconnection.[47] ICANN's highly visible processes for policing domain name allocation similarly represent only one component of a more complex assemblage for namespace governance. The databases that map human-readable domain names, however allocated, to network addresses are far more vital to operational continuity. A small group of entities—including universities, research consortia, government entities, and private corporations—maintains those databases pursuant to agreements with the Internet Assigned Numbers Authority (IANA), an organization whose operations are now administered by an affiliate of ICANN. Those agreements constitute a form of privatized governance by a tightly knit community of technical peers.[48] Internet governance does not occur at any single site but rather emerges via the interlinked outputs of a wide variety of sites and processes.

Colliding Mandates: Global Assemblages and Cross-Border Information Flows

Within the emergent landscape of institutions and assemblages for transnational legal ordering, governance problems involving cross-border flows of intellectual property and data have become flashpoints, in part because of rapid technological change but in part because such problems tend to implicate multiple governance regimes. In an era when many services are provided via digital information and communications networks, cross-border information flows seem to fall squarely within the province of regimes governing trade in services. The new information-economy actors that profit from those services—including global platform companies and financial services firms but also any firm that engages in offshoring of functions such as customer support and human resources—have interests in defining and controlling their own global operations in ways that may include transfers of data for processing, cloud storage spanning multiple jurisdictions, and cross-border provision of services to end users. Data flows between networked devices—ranging from personal communications devices to industrial sensors—are central concerns of internet governance processes. Cross-border flows and operations also may implicate a variety of other transnational regulatory concerns and instruments, including those relating to financial stability, fair labor practices, privacy, intellectual property protection, and national security, to name just a few. Unsurprisingly, controversies over regulation of cross-border flows are now frequent occurrences and have become powerful catalysts of continuing institutional evolution.

To begin with, cross-border information flows that relate to trade in services introduce a baseline level of institutional complexity that flows from the way the GATS protocol was drafted. Although the GATT protocol encompasses all physical goods and materials that are not expressly excluded, the GATS protocol was drafted to cover only those categories of services that signatory states expressly designate. Disputes before the WTO about alleged barriers to trade therefore must begin by considering whether the challenged practices are covered.[49] The United States and other developed countries have worked to expand treaty coverage for various types of information services via bilateral and multilateral agreements, both by enumerating specific categories and by including so-called "free flow" provisions.[50]

Consider next the ways that cross-border flows complicate intellectual property enforcement. From one perspective, flows of content are information services that are covered only if the parties to the dispute have agreed to liberalization; from another, they may be substitutes for physical goods whose importation would be subject to the nondiscrimination obligations of the GATT; from a third, they require respect for territorial distribution arrangements negotiated by rightholders and their domestic licensees; from a fourth, they may implicate criminal law enforcement provisions.[51] Contests over how far to extend logics of intellectual property interdiction within trade regimes have led to protracted battles. The global entertainment industries have pushed repeatedly for stronger interdiction requirements, while platform firms and other information businesses wishing to make new kinds of information services available have opposed such requirements. (All industries, however, have supported strengthened protection for trade secrets.) Trade negotiators and law enforcement officials acting within the frameworks established by multilateral cooperative agreements have seemed especially unsure how to understand the implications of cloud storage. As we will see later in this chapter, contests over interdiction capabilities also have become regular features of internet standards processes.[52]

Conflicts over global flows of personal data are even more complex. Generally speaking, differences in data protection obligations create incentives for organizations to collect and process data in jurisdictions with more lenient rules and to transfer data collected elsewhere to those jurisdictions for processing. Exploiting a dynamic that Anu Bradford has termed the "Brussels Effect," the European Union has worked to export its higher standards for personal data protection to the rest of the world by setting strict limits on cross-border transfers of data relating to its citizens.[53] The U.S. government, loath to commit to the European model but seeking access to data both on its own behalf and on behalf of U.S. companies, has sought compromise arrangements that would permit data to flow. A viable compromise has proved elusive, however. In 2015, following the Snowden revelations about widespread, systematic communications surveillance by the U.S. government, the European Court of Justice invalidated a safe harbor agreement covering data transfers to the United States that had required laborious negotiations between the U.S. State Department and the European Commission. As of this writing, that court is considering a legal challenge to the replacement agreement, styled the U.S.-E.U. Privacy Shield and finalized in 2016.[54] Meanwhile, bilateral trade negotiations between the United States and the European Union over a series of agreements intended to expand liberalization requirements for trade in services have periodically threatened to upend the compromises negotiated by data protection and law enforcement interests. The diplomatic struggles over cross-border data flows also reflect the growing influence of U.S.-based information businesses, including especially the dominant global platform firms, seeking a regulatory environment more hospitable to their interests and activities.[55]

Importantly, moreover, although the various U.S.-E.U. negotiations over flows of personal data have commanded the lion's share of scholarly and media attention, they are not the only relevant regulatory and institutional developments on the global scene. In the years following enactment of the European Union's 1995 Data Protection Directive, the Asia-Pacific Economic Cooperation bloc, which includes the United States, formulated its own set of privacy principles. In form, those principles resemble certain aspects of the European data protection framework; in substance, however, they are friendlier to the cross-border flows upon which the regional economies of the Pacific Rim increasingly rely.[56] As described earlier in this chapter, those economies have become a significant force driving the evolution of new mega-regional trade agreements that include new provisions designed to liberalize restrictions on cross-border data flows. Both the post-U.S. version of the TPP and the RCEP include such provisions.[57]

Members of the BRICS (Brazil, Russia, India, China, and South Africa) group of countries, meanwhile, have pursued different kinds of authority over cross-border flows for their own, varied reasons. In the case of Russia, which aspires to recapture its former geopolitical power, the motivations for control appear straightforwardly political. As we will see in more detail later in this chapter, Chinese motivations and behavior are more complex. The Chinese state has sought both to control information flows for political reasons and to further China's status as a rising global economic powerhouse, and the latter goal has entailed more systematic attention to global coordination mechanisms. In Brazil, concern about the growing power of giant global information businesses prompted the introduction of comprehensive digital economy legislation, the Marco Civil. Ultimately, however, an active lobbying campaign by those businesses successfully defeated data localization requirements that had been intended to protect Brazilians' rights of privacy vis-à-vis foreign technology companies and their governments.[58] The Indian relationship to informational capitalism has been even more complicated. Indian companies spanning the gamut from giant transnationals to small start-ups are deeply involved in the emerging global information processing economy, both as participants in outsourcing chains and as developers in their own right. At the same time, however, a growing chorus of civil society advocates concerned about vulnerability to data harvesting has made India one of the most active locations for legal struggles over both data protection and the conditions of internet access.[59]

Points of Convergence: Six Problematics of Network-and-Standard-Based Governance

As noted at the start of this chapter, transnational governance processes are organized as networks constituted around standards. Recall from Chapter 1 that a *network* is a mode of organization in which hubs and nodes rather than fixed hierarchies structure the flows of transactions and interactions. The legal and political implications of that mode of organization are vigorously debated. Some commentators have characterized structures for networked participation and governance as radically democratizing, while others have worried about the massive, fluid, and seemingly ungovernable concentrations of power that network organization enables.[60] Two important recent books about power and global political economy explore the importance of networked organization for political economy generally, articulating new theoretical models of networked social, political, and communication power.[61] The idea of a "flat" world—in which everything is connected to and affects everything else—also has captured the imagination of pundits and commentators.

Networked governance arrangements, however, are not simply networks; they are also institutions.[62] And *standards*—structured protocols for conforming the activities of multiple nodes in a network—play an important and undertheorized role in their structure and operation. This section explores the various points of mismatch between the rule-of-law tradition in legal theory and the operation of the network-and-standard-based legal-institutional form. It begins by reconsidering two points of conventional wisdom about network organization and its relationship to power.

First, the assertion that network organization is inherently more democratic than other forms of organization because it facilitates the expression and circulation of dissenting views is open to serious question. It is true that, because network organization is nonhierarchical, even an enormously powerful hub cannot prevent information from flowing around it through other nodes.[63] Additionally, scholars affiliated with the new governance movement in transnational legal theory have rightly noted that network-and-standard-based governance has many potential benefits. It is resilient and flexible, offering stability while permitting localized experimentation and innovation, and depending on the details of implementation it can be extraordinarily inclusive.[64] Yet the turn to network-and-standard-based governance also invites certain predictable dysfunctions. Within networked governance arrangements, the ability to route around interruptions works most reliably to the benefit of the powerful. The same networked affordances that enable the dissident to evade the censor also enable economically or politically dominant parties— parties that enjoy hub status—to work around inconvenient negotiating stalemates and avoid inconvenient regulatory burdens in particular locations or within particular regulatory regimes. Put more succinctly, power interprets regulatory resistance as damage and routes around it.

Second, the observation that network organization is nonhierarchical can be somewhat misleading. From an internal perspective, network organization around a standard imposes a form of hierarchical ordering that inheres in the standard itself. If other networks organized around other standards are available, the nature of any particular standard may not matter much. But a standard invested with legal significance is not *just* a standard because participants lack the authority to depart from it. So too with a standard such as the basic internet protocol that exacts universal adherence as a practical matter. Network organization under conditions of legally or practically mandated standardization signals a de facto relocation of legal authority into the standard. That authority may be quite exacting as to the forms of compliance, and it also may afford new opportunities for the exercise of economic and political power.

The powerful critiques of transnational governance arrangements that have emerged within legal scholarship still have not fully assimilated the hybridity of the networked legal-institutional form. Both the ability of power to route around inconvenient regulatory resistance and the relocation of authority into the standard strain traditional accounts of *law*, reliably eliciting institutional features that seem very different from those that a system of the rule of law would require. The same developments also strain conventional understandings of *standards* and *standardization*, reliably foreclosing the kinds of pathways that facilitate competition, correction, and stabilization in the contexts where standards are more usually studied.

It has become vitally important to understand the ways that the intersecting vectors of governance, law, and standardization are transforming one another. This section identifies and develops six important directions for inquiry, which relate to the nature of standard-making authority; the available pathways for contesting and changing the reigning standard; the available pathways for coopting network-and-standard-based governance mechanisms to serve authoritarian political and geopolitical interests; the mechanisms for political accountability; the vernaculars in which mandatory standards are articulated, applied, and contested; and the possibility of nonstate yet functionally sovereign power.

Dominance as Hegemony: The Problem of Unchecked Authority

One distinctive characteristic of emergent transnational legal-institutional arrangements is the way that network-and-standard-based organization reshapes the exercise of policymaking authority. Within such arrangements, policy dominance—or the ability to shape the content and direction of policy without interference—is both more absolute than it typically is within more traditional legal settings and more immediate than it typically is in technology standards markets. When instituted against a background of vastly unequal geopolitical power, networked organization under conditions of mandated standardization has resulted in policy hegemony relatively unchecked by political or structural constraints.

In democratic societies with rule-of-law traditions, legal institutions are recognizable as such in part because of their adherence to regular, reasoned processes for making, enforcing, and contesting rules.[65] This is not to suggest that such processes work perfectly or even well. As of this writing, idealistic pronouncements about the redemptive power of democratic politics and democratic constitutionalism have become increasingly difficult to credit. But certain high-level constraints on institutional behavior—and in particular the principles of separation of powers, procedural due process, and public reason—have commanded widespread adherence in democratic societies and have limited arbitrary exercises of official power.

Dominance in technology standards markets confronts different kinds of limits. Although networks do exhibit lock-in effects, various forms of competition remain possible (we will consider those forms more closely in the next section). Consumers who feel that exit is not a reasonable option retain the option of voice; even monopolists can and do respond to public shaming.[66] And of course, if those conditions fail, antitrust or consumer protection authorities may intervene to restore them. Most importantly for the point I wish to make here, in paradigmatic, discrete technology standards markets, the connection between market dominance and policy dominance tends to be indirect. In the era of copper wires and common carriage requirements, telephone carriers could not filter out undesirable or unlawful conversations. The standards governing such matters as the layout of a typewriter keyboard or the arrangement of prongs on an appliance plug are thoroughly agnostic as to their users' political beliefs and policy commitments.

Many contemporary disagreements over technology policy arise precisely because the emergence of networked information and communications technologies has set protocol and policy on converging paths. Generally speaking, dominant hubs within digital communications networks possess enormous power to block or structure flows of activity. Technology critics often posit that the operator of a dominant operating system, social network, or search platform might use (or is already using) its power over interconnection standards to shape the substance of what is communicated, while technology evangelists tend to downplay that possibility. The frequent and widely publicized disagreements between members of the two camps conceal some important common ground: If a private commercial entity (or indeed any entity) did have the power to leverage its control of an interconnection standard into policy-setting power over unrelated matters, that would be undesirable.

Network-and-standard-based legal-institutional arrangements connect protocol and policy directly to one another and eliminate separation between them. Within such arrangements, the point of mandated standardization is exactly to specify the kinds of flows that must, may, and may not travel via the network. The policy is the standard and vice versa. Power over one translates directly into power over the other. Under background conditions of vastly unequal geopolitical power, that equivalence sets up the two interlocking dynamics that produce policy hegemony. On one hand, a dominant network enjoys *network power*—which David Grewal defines as the self-reinforcing power of a dominant network and Manuel Castells explains as a power that is "exercised not by exclusion from the networks, but by the imposition of the rules of inclusion"—simply by virtue of its dominance.[67] On the other, if a particular hub within a dominant network exercises disproportionate control over the content of the standard, then networked organization will amplify that hub's authority to set policy and legally mandated standardization will amplify it still further. When network-and-standard-based legal-institutional arrangements are instituted under background conditions of vastly unequal geopolitical power, network power translates into policy hegemony. And policy hegemony is power that may be exercised without regard for the basic, high-level rule-of-law constraints that obtain in more traditional institutional settings.

Developments in the domains of world trade governance and transnational business regulation over the second half of the twentieth century mapped straightforwardly to this theoretical model (we will consider some more recent anomalies in the next section). The magisterial study of emergent global business law completed in 2000 by John Braithwaite and Peter Drahos traced the emergence and consolidation of U.S. policy hegemony across a wide and varied set of domains. A decade later, Grewal's explication of the concept of network power in the context of the world trade system again spotlighted that hegemony and linked it to control of the standards mandating trade liberalization.[68]

The case of internet governance is more complicated. To ordinary observers, internet governance processes might appear to be chiefly concerned with technical matters—with protocol first and foremost and policy only secondarily. And for U.S. observers, internet governance processes additionally might appear to have avoided the problem of U.S. policy hegemony precisely because of their sui generis, multistakeholder design. But neither perception is entirely accurate. Technical governance functions and policy choices are inextricably intertwined, and the choices made by internet governance bodies are invariably infused with ideological commitments that reflect those of the organizations' memberships.[69] Although IETF membership is formally individual, U.S.-based technology companies are heavily represented in the IETF's working groups, and the W3C's corporate membership tier is dominated by U.S.-based technology companies. The choice to constitute ICANN as a California corporation tethers it to a peculiarly American set of operational conventions, and ICANN's multistakeholder design reflects a long-standing and largely bipartisan U.S. preference for a strong private-sector role in internet governance—that is, for corporatized multistakeholderism over state-based multilateralism.[70] And the responses of all three institutions to the policy problems that have repeatedly bedeviled them—from privacy and surveillance to content regulation and censorship to intellectual property enforcement to network security—have tended to reflect the particular norms of flow enshrined in U.S. information law and policy. In short, although internet governance processes were designed to avoid state-based control, network power and resultant policy hegemony are difficult to outrun.

Legal Standards Wars: The Problem of Regulatory Arbitrage

A second striking characteristic of emerging global networked legal-institutional arrangements relates to the mechanisms available for changing a governing standard. Networked organization under legally or practically mandated standardization is simultaneously sclerotic and unstable at the margins. On the one hand, mandated standardization intensifies lock-in to the current standard by foreclosing many of the pathways for change that ordinarily would exist. On the other, it incentivizes efforts at regulatory disintermediation by those favoring a different or modified standard, and those efforts may gain purchase to the extent that the network remains open to new patterns of interconnection.

It is useful to begin by considering the mechanisms through which standards can change over time in market settings. Carl Shapiro and Hal Varian distinguish between evolution and revolution, with the former consisting of gradual change while maintaining backward compatibility with the original standard and the latter involving a sharp, disjunctive break between new and old standards.[71] Such changes may be implemented cooperatively, or two (or more) parties may seek conflicting changes, as in the case of the Blu-ray and HD DVD standards for digital video storage and playback, which maintained backward compatibility with the regular DVD format but were incompatible with one another. If the parties cannot agree on which course is best, a standards war may ensue. As Shapiro and Varian explain, the decision whether to precipitate a standards war is an economic and strategic one. Even a disjunctive break without backward compatibility may succeed if it can be justified to the proponent's installed base of customers.

In struggles to shape the future of a legally mandated standard, the mandatory structure of networked legal-institutional arrangements narrows the universe of possible outcomes. Gradual evolution is most feasible when it moves in directions that are compatible with the dominant standard's underlying policy commitments. In theory, gradual retrenchment from the hegemonic norm is also possible; in practice, however, one cannot fall below the threshold level of compliance that the standard requires absent cooperative agreement to extend forgiveness. Consider ICANN's 2007 decision to expand the number of top-level internet domains. In theory, that decision provided an opportunity to broaden the base of second-level domain ownership; in reality, the new top-level domains were rapidly subjected to rules for allocating second-level domains that incorporated existing, pro-trademark logics.[72] In the domain of world trade, some commentators have thought that the trade negotiations commenced by the Asian nations under the auspices of the RCEP might offer an opportunity to chart a gradual path away from U.S.-dominated intellectual property norms toward new norms better calibrated to stimulate economic development across the region. As Anupam Chander and Madhavi Sunder show, however, certain provisions of the underlying WTO framework militate against such a departure; for example, under the "most favored nation" rule, Asian nations seeking to grant one another preferable treatment would also need to grant such treatment to the United States and the member states of the European Union.[73]

Revolution against a background of mandated standardization is more difficult still. Absent cooperative agreement to depart from the dominant standard, revolutionary change—or, in the language of technologists, forking the standard—requires not only confidence in one's installed base but also willingness to court diplomatic or even geopolitical instability. In the domain of world trade, disjunctive changes without backward compatibility risk starting trade wars; in the various domains of transnational business regulation, departure or threatened departure from agreed conventions can roil markets and create diplomatic incidents. Internet governance institutions have powerful norms against forking network standards. When such proposals have originated—generally from states that are geopolitical outsiders—they have commanded little sympathy or support and have been unable to generate networked momentum of their own.[74] A systemic shock can create impetus for a mutually agreed disjunctive break; so, for example, as Chapter 6 discussed, the 2008 financial crisis generated momentum to tighten standards for measuring bank capital adequacy both in the United States and globally. Absent such a shock, however, revolutionary change is unlikely.

Standards wars can be horizontal or vertical, however, and this means that even dominant standards are characterized by their potential amenability to disintermediation by a rival standard that sits closer to the relevant activity. So, for example, although Microsoft's Windows operating system still holds a significant share of the personal computing market, it is no longer the most important interface for those wishing to market applications to personal computer users. Web browsers provide an alternative interface for many applications, as do social networks and mobile operating systems. Techniques for object-oriented programming have introduced "write once, run everywhere" practices and norms to the world of software development, shifting the locus of competition to rival software developer kits and to online app stores curated by a variety of old and new technology companies.[75] Most recently, the "internet of things" and the emergent market for smart products have opened new channels for companies seeking to become the intermediary of choice for as many online interactions as possible.[76]

Networked governance arrangements organized around legally mandated standardization are similarly vulnerable to disintermediation by adjacent governance arrangements. When developing nations began to balk at additional extensions to the WTO regime, which they saw as entrenching the already considerable advantages accruing to intellectual property-producing industries based in developed economies, U.S. trade negotiators simply routed around the WTO, negotiating new bilateral and multilateral agreements incorporating the stronger provisions they wanted to see enshrined as new network standards.[77] Developing nations fought back with a different routing strategy, gradually organizing around a proposed "development agenda" for the WIPO and lobbying successfully to make it part of WIPO's official program. The WIPO Development Agenda thereby briefly became an entry in the ongoing intellectual property standards war.

In legal standards wars, however, opportunities for regulatory disintermediation more reliably benefit already-powerful interests that can move quickly to exploit potential regime workarounds. As Laurence Helfer has described, developing nations' effort at "regime shifting" via WIPO enjoyed only temporary success.[78] Developed countries returned to WIPO in force and ensured that the only subsequent agreement that WIPO has managed to shepherd to completion, the 2013 Marrakesh Treaty on access to published works for the visually impaired, contains language constraining developing countries' ability to enact access-promoting exceptions.[79] Meanwhile, the copyright industries of the global North have appropriated regime-shifting tactics to their own ends, lobbying both ICANN and the W3C to introduce interdiction mandates into both the internet domain registration rules and the basic protocols for exchanging information via the World Wide Web.[80]

As a different example, consider evolving arrangements for governance of cross-border transfers of personal information. As discussed earlier in this chapter, the European Union has worked to institutionalize stronger data protection norms around the world but has been stymied by the policy hegemony of the United States and by the rising economic influence of Asian nations. Faced with increasingly aggressive demands for data protection emanating from the European Union, parties seeking liberalization have shifted their emphasis toward inserting strengthened mandates for cross-border flow in trade agreements. Privacy NGOs have worked to thwart trade workarounds for data protection obligations, but that project has become more difficult as the center of gravity has shifted into trade governance, which had not traditionally been a focus of transnational privacy activism, and toward Asia, where civil society organizations focused on privacy and data protection had not traditionally maintained a significant presence. And here again, ICANN has emerged as an important focus of regime-shifting efforts; even European data protection authorities have largely acquiesced in the organization's continuing failure to require protection of WHOIS registry data that complies with applicable data protection standards.[81] Each of these developments destabilizes settled expectations about where authority to regulate data protection and cross-border transfers of personal data resides and about what the reigning standard is and what it requires.

A final example involves disintermediation of protective labor regulation. Scholars who study global and transnational labor regulation have long recognized that domestic protective mandates are vulnerable to reconceptualization as non-tariff barriers to trade.[82] Although other transnational regulatory arrangements might function as a meaningful counterweight to obligations emanating from trade governance arrangements, transnational protective labor regulation also is in the process of being disintermediated from within. The parallel turns toward private standard-making for global supply chains and public-private collaboration in standard-making more generally work to shift the center of gravity of such activities, making the development of standards for global fair labor practices increasingly a private affair.[83] As a result, the push to incorporate externally developed labor standards within free trade agreements, noted earlier in this chapter, probably is best understood as an attempted colonization of protective labor regulation by trade rather than vice versa.

In theory at least, a system of the rule of law is not supposed to work this way. An important principle associated with the ideal of the rule of law is that legal rules should be applied consistently, and the ideal of consistency in turn implies a degree of constancy. Put simply, legal rules should be relatively stable, and so should procedures for changing them.[84] In fact, the ideal of legal constancy has been under siege since the complex legal ecologies of the late twentieth century began to offer a wider and more complex array of possibilities for regulatory arbitrage than those within which the rule-of-law ideal was first articulated. Domestically as well as transnationally, both regulated entities and local sovereigns have learned to identify and exploit gaps and loopholes. Even so, however, in domestic settings each strategy confronts built-in limits. At the end of the day, there is an institutional actor with the power to exercise jurisdiction over the challenged conduct, to superintend a reasoned but finite process of contestation over what the law ought to be, and then to say with authority what the law is. Relative to that benchmark, the new networked governance arrangements manifest both frustrating path-dependence and a destabilizing failure of finality. Rule-of-law constructs developed for hierarchical legal systems have little to say about criteria for ensuring consistency and constancy within network-and-standard-based governance institutions.

Network Power and Moral Hazard: The Problem of the Authoritarian End Run

A third distinctive attribute of global network-and-standard-based governance arrangements is a particular kind of moral hazard that concerns the relative importance of economic and political liberalization. In the era of ascendant neoliberal governmentality, as economic liberalization has become the primary driver of innovation in transnational legal ordering, the overriding importance often ascribed to facilitating flows of cross-border economic activity sets up the conditions for a dynamic that I will call the authoritarian end run. In brief, an authoritarian regime wishing to stint its liberalization obligations in the interest of maintaining its political control often may do so with impunity because of the dominant network's interest in maintaining and consolidating its economic dominance.

Recall that network power operates by harnessing and disciplining the desire for inclusion. That mechanism presents trade-offs for the policy hegemon—the party that enjoys dominant hub status—as well as for other network participants. Simply put, there are downsides to sanctioning or expelling members for standards violations, and those downsides may lead both the policy hegemon and other network participants to overlook certain types of infractions—especially those that can plausibly be characterized as purely domestic in scope—to preserve flows of goods, services, and information across borders and within corporate supply chains. So, for example, developed nations historically have been willing to minimize the importance of certain labor practices in developing countries, to overlook local restrictions on religious and press freedoms, and to excuse certain endemic forms of gender discrimination.[85]

Above all else, authoritarian states seek to control unwanted flows of information within and across their borders. In the early years of the internet era, maintaining such control required assistance from foreign technology providers. So, for example, China imposed filtering requirements on Western platform companies such as Google and Yahoo! as a condition of operating within its borders. Less visibly, many regimes seeking to capture the benefits of networked digital communications while minimizing the perceived political costs sought out technology vendors willing to develop and implement surveillance and filtering capabilities at the backbone and server levels. Western governments anxious to negotiate and expand free trade agreements did nothing to discourage such arrangements and ignored arguments that the resulting restrictions violated existing trade-in-services agreements and undercut liberalization norms.[86]

To the extent that the authoritarian end run entails subverting the dominant standard for purposes dictated by conflicting political goals, it is broadly consistent with the dynamic of the legal standards war described in the previous section, but it is also different. In the short term, it is a shirking strategy available to entities lacking the power or the motivation to provoke a standards war. In the longer term, it is a strategy that implicates what Castells calls *network-making power*—the power to constitute a rival network by establishing alternative conditions of interconnection.[87] The authoritarian end run is a strategy for alternative network-making around standards that blend elements of economic liberalization with elements of mercantilist central planning and political control.

In the contemporary geopolitical landscape, the principal author of the authoritarian end run is China. Chinese trade policy and information technology policy have emerged as powerful and mutually reinforcing components of a larger strategy for pursuing policy hegemony over standards for global economic, technical, and information exchange.

China is a member of the WTO and an important participant in the mega-regional RCEP negotiations, but it also practices an alternative form of network-making directed toward development and control of physical and digital infrastructures. Now known in English as the Belt and Road initiative, the Chinese program for physical infrastructure development seeks to facilitate flows of labor, goods, and raw materials across continents and oceans under conditions that advance Chinese economic interests. Relying on bilateral investment treaties and contracts negotiated with host governments and other local counterparties, the Chinese state and Chinese firms have financed and built roads, railway and shipping lines, and ports and terminals across the Asian continent and throughout East Africa and Europe. Belt and Road projects have opened new distribution channels for Chinese-manufactured goods and new markets for Chinese labor. In the longer term, the Chinese vision for the initiative also envisions it underpinning new, China-centered global supply chains.[88] Developing economies, most notably India, have begun to object that they incur all of the debt for Belt and Road projects and receive very little of the economic gain.[89] Some developed economies, however, appear to be hedging their bets. In another example of the legal standards war dynamic, the China-led Asian Infrastructure Investment Bank (AIIB), a principal vehicle for financing Belt and Road projects, has positioned itself as an alternative to the Western-led International Monetary Fund. Although the United States has declined to join the AIIB, citing concerns about China's refusal to include rule-of-law and human rights benchmarks in its financing agreements, powerful economies such as Germany and Canada have chosen differently.[90]

Chinese information technology policy also has become a powerful tool for alternative network-making. Over the last decade, the Chinese information technology sector has grown rapidly and (as of this writing) includes two firms that rank among the world's 20 largest: search and social networking firm Tencent and e-commerce giant Alibaba.[91] Whereas the United States fostered the growth of new information intermediaries by granting them broad legal immunities, the Chinese strategy for developing a domestic information technology sector combined draconian restrictions on foreign technology companies with highly enterprising—and, U.S. companies have alleged, coercive and underhanded—technology acquisition programs. Meanwhile, the Chinese government invested heavily in homegrown alternatives, providing early-stage funding, tax subsidies, and other incentives, and it also waived or overlooked limits on foreign direct investment to attract other investors.[92] As Chinese technology firms moved out of the start-up stage and began building market share, they also benefited from the relative absence of domestic antitrust and consumer protection oversight, engaging in rapid and strategic diversification both horizontally and vertically. In particular, the leading Chinese platform firms offer fully integrated mobile payment systems, and large numbers of Chinese citizens who previously lacked access to credit cards, bank accounts, and other developed world financial conveniences have flocked to their services.[93]

As the Chinese information technology sector has matured and turned toward new markets, affordances for both economic development and state control of communications infrastructure have emerged as central elements in the Chinese state's pursuit of global economic dominance. Tencent, Alibaba, and other Chinese platform companies have begun to make inroads in developing markets across Asia, Africa, and the Middle East, and Chinese hardware manufacturers such as Huawei and Xiaomi sell equipment ranging from backbone servers to mobile phones across the developing world. In terms of development, capabilities for mobile payment, banking, and credit have driven rapid penetration within populations hungry for modernization.[94] For client states inclined to control information flows to their own populations, meanwhile, Chinese firms' relative willingness to work with host governments to implement filtering and surveillance in their own markets is a selling point—and a powerful rebuttal to those Western observers who initially believed that the Chinese insistence on censorship and surveillance mandates would prove self-defeating.[95]

The combined result of these technology policy initiatives is "a geopolitical enclave in which computational architectures and informational actors are coming together into what could be deservedly termed the Red Stack"—a networked communications infrastructure offering the ability to layer separation and control on top of the underlying connectivity afforded by the basic internet protocols.[96] Notably, because the Red Stack leverages powerful and preexisting economic and political motivations, its expansion does not depend on the success or failure of efforts by other BRICS countries, most notably Russia and Brazil, to encourage development of a separate BRICS internet, nor is a separate internet necessary as a technical matter.[97]

Although one benefit of the Red Stack is the capacity for more effective state censorship, the technology companies whose offerings comprise the Red Stack benefit handsomely from other types of cross-border information flows and from transnational governance arrangements designed to facilitate them. More generally, the authoritarian end run differs from the legal standards war in a critical respect that relates to the degree to which it entails courting open conflict with the dominant network that it seeks to displace. Because the dominant network and its dysfunctions afford important benefits, the authoritarian end run seeks to deepen ties, not to make waves.[98]

At the same time, the authoritarian end run also involves the use of soft power to deepen moral hazard by strengthening intellectual ties. As China has grown wealthier, so have its state-funded universities and research institutions. Where previously the principal connections between Chinese and Western universities were the Chinese students who traveled to Western universities to learn and the Western scholars who traveled to China to teach and conduct research, newly wealthy Chinese institutions now reach out directly to their Western counterparts, funding programs for research cooperation and intellectual exchange. Other outreach programs target journalists in developing countries, offering resources that include all-expenses-paid trips and access to state-of-the-art media facilities. Like the tech-industry political outreach programs that Chapter 3 described, Chinese outreach programs have implicit conditions attached. In particular, they discourage attention to matters related to internal control of information flows and suppression of dissent for political reasons. Scholars and journalists involved with such programs have begun to report that they are changing the discussion about China, its political economy, and its global role in meaningful ways.[99]

The authoritarian end run has an ambivalent relationship to the rule of law. On one hand, both Chinese trade policy and Chinese technology policy emphasize centralized control by state institutions. One byproduct of China's accession to membership in the WTO and its movement toward greater economic liberalization has been modernization of domestic courts and other formal governance institutions along the lines that the WTO's obligations require. To the extent that concerns about the rule of law in the era of networked governance hinge on the disintegration of sovereign authority, one might argue that some components of the Chinese strategy are more compatible with traditional, hierarchical governance models. On the other, the rule-of-law construct that Chinese global governance initiatives enshrine is thin, emphasizing regularity and predictability over transparency and contestability—features that Chinese information technology policy, in particular, works to eliminate. And for those reasons, the authoritarian end run does not offer new mechanisms for tempering arbitrary power but instead creates new obstacles to the project of developing such mechanisms.

Extreme Multistakeholderism: The Problem of Public Accountability

A fourth striking characteristic shared by the processes described in this chapter is their unusual mechanisms for political accountability. Emergent network-and-standard-based governance arrangements are strikingly inhospitable to traditional mechanisms for instilling accountability within legal institutions, and they also have invited powerful new variations on rent-seeking by nonstate actors. The success of those rent-seeking strategies in turn has inspired new networked tactics for civil society mobilization, but civil society actors seem continually to be outmaneuvered by transnational business interests. Both developments mark the emergence of a new model of public participation in governance, which I will call extreme multistakeholderism. It is amenable to practice by those entities or coalitions that are both sufficiently well-resourced to monitor governance processes unfolding concurrently at multiple sites and sufficiently well connected to gain access to processes and documents that may be shrouded in secrecy.

In theory, many of the transnational regulatory processes described in this chapter incorporate delegation-based accountability mechanisms.[100] In the United States for example, trade policy is the domain of the executive, and the executive in turn is accountable to the Senate, which must consent to ratification of new treaties, and to the voting public, which may repudiate an administration's trade policies at the ballot box. Interventions in transnational business regulatory processes also emanate from the executive branch and its constituent agencies and commissions, many of which are headed by political appointees.

In practice, both trade policy processes and transnational regulatory processes are far more accountable to private economic interests than to either of their official constituencies. The reasons are partly structural. In general, network-and-standard-based transnational governance arrangements have grown up between and around more traditional legal institutions in ways that have rendered them both relatively impervious to the sorts of checks and balances that those institutions are accustomed to exercising and relatively receptive to assertions of economic power. In the United States, for example, members of the industries affected by trade agreements sit on trade advisory councils that operate outside the purview of open-government laws, and new "fast-track" procedures have been devised to move newly ratified agreements through the congressional approval process without opening them up to bothersome second-guessing. Both arrangements are thought to be justified by the executive's broad authority to conduct diplomatic relations with foreign countries.[101] Both in the United States and worldwide, trade negotiators routinely withhold information about the texts under discussion from citizens and media organizations in their own countries.[102] Like the domestic regulatory mechanisms studied in Chapter 6, transnational regulatory processes are procedurally entrepreneurial and may also incorporate substantial privatization components—as was the case, for example, with bank capital regulation before the 2008 crash—so traditional mechanisms for political accountability tend not to reach them directly.[103] The courts, for their part, are inclined to regard both trade policy choices and transnational regulatory undertakings as nonjusticiable because they involve matters committed to the discretion of political actors.[104]

Other reasons for the pervasive influence of private economic interests are ideological. Narratives about the virtues of "multistakeholderism" as a modality of governance have become a pervasive and cross-cutting theme in scholarly and policy discussions about the design of transnational governance arrangements. Both in theory and in practice, multistakeholder processes can involve a wide variety of actors.[105] Multistakeholderist narratives, however, typically express neoliberal ideologies about governance as an arena for regulatory entrepreneurship by affected interest groups.

Internet governance processes that rely on delegation-based accountability work differently and somewhat better. The particular form of incorporation chosen for ICANN—that of a California public benefit corporation—imposes a set of accountability mandates that break down loosely into three types: directors must consider the interests of all stakeholder groups rather than just a narrower group of shareholders, the corporation must prepare annual reports that create an adequate level of transparency about its operations, and directors or shareholders who feel that the corporation has deviated from its public-regarding mandate may sue the corporation.[106] As noted previously, ICANN attempts to fulfill its multistakeholder mandate principally via representation; board nominations are made by an independent committee and are subject to regional diversity mandates, anyone may join the working groups that generate policy proposals, and there are formal consultative processes for certain important constituencies. ICANN also takes its transparency mandate seriously. In addition to reporting annually on various dimensions of its performance and operations, it has adopted a variety of other measures to keep its constituencies informed, some taken from the corporate toolkit (e.g., quarterly performance calls) and others from the transnational governance toolkit (e.g., multilingual reporting).[107]

In practice, though, the choice of a multistakeholder-based model for public input has produced—and was intended to produce—a significant policy tilt toward relatively well-resourced interests concerned chiefly with protection of trademarks and other intellectual property. The capture of policy decisions relating to allocation of second-level domain names by trademark interests has been widely remarked. Courts in the United States and other countries around the world may set aside particular decisions favoring mark owners but lack authority in the context of such proceedings to pass judgment on the legitimacy of the dispute resolution processes more generally.[108] ICANN's continuing resistance to implementing data protection measures for the rich trove of personal information contained in the WHOIS domain registry databases reflects the demands of intellectual property interests and national law enforcement authorities—and those of information businesses engaged in data aggregation and data mining—for unimpeded access to that information.[109] In theory, the California court system retains jurisdiction of lawsuits challenging ICANN's fulfillment of its public mission, but it is difficult to imagine such a suit producing meaningful change in any of ICANN's policies.

The other traditional mechanism for political accountability involves direct participation. Some internet standards governance arrangements adopt this model, but here too underlying patterns of power and access can operate to impede participatory democracy. As noted previously, although membership in the IETF and its constituent working groups is exercised on an individual basis, as a practical matter participation is heavily corporatized. At the W3C, which recognizes organizational membership, corporate influence over policymaking is an acknowledged fact.

From a theoretical perspective, these developments are unsurprising. Within networked governance arrangements, one would expect both assertions of power and assertions of counterpower to exhibit returns to scale.[110] The networked governance processes described in this chapter bear out that expectation. The lengthy, intricate, and globally distributed nature of transnational legal-institutional processes sets an effective lower bound on the kinds of entities that can participate effectively. Entities that are both vertically integrated and operationally nimble—in general, large transnational corporations and their trade associations—have the easiest time surmounting the threshold requirements for policy influence. The affordances of networked media and communication infrastructures offset geographical limits to some extent but also favor those best positioned to make use of them to coordinate interventions across multiple, far-flung sites.

Civil society organizations too have learned to play the multistakeholder game within network-and-standard-based governance processes. They have formed transnational networks that enable them to pool their resources and act cooperatively. We have seen that in the context of intellectual property, those alliances proved powerful enough to route around unresponsive institutions for trade policymaking and find leverage elsewhere—but only temporarily. Similarly, a transnational network of privacy organizations has coordinated efforts both to achieve greater transparency about ongoing regulatory and diplomatic initiatives and to expose and challenge unfavorable provisions under discussion in trade negotiations.[111] Even as civil society organizations have discovered regime shifting, however, corporate actors and business NGOs such as the International Chamber of Commerce and the International Trademark Owners Association have followed suit, mobilizing the comparatively greater resources of their memberships to shift policymaking efforts into more congenial arenas. Where processes for NGO consultation are more formalized, as in the case of UN-sponsored standard-making initiatives, well-resourced business NGOs have rapidly mastered the diplomatic and bureaucratic skills required to make their voices heard loudly.[112]

The flip side of procedures guaranteeing both orderly contestation and finality is a political culture prepared to honor their requirements and abide by their results. The political culture of extreme multistakeholderism is different. The practice of extreme multistakeholderism within networked legal-institutional environments is best understood via a videogaming metaphor, as a never-ending process of "leveling up." Within that process, the rewards flow to those who can access the most up-to-date information and marshal it most effectively on a global playing field. Those who lack comparable resources are doomed to play catch-up, pursuing a threshold of influence that remains continually out of reach.

Technocracy and Its Discontents: The Problem of Publicly Available Law

A fifth distinctive attribute of emergent arrangements for global business governance and global network governance is their highly technocratic character. As we saw in Chapters 5 and 6, the regulatory problems of the informational economy have begun to elicit complex, highly informationalized responses that are managerialist in orientation. The networked legal-institutional form continues both the turn toward flexible and often outsourced dispute resolution described in Chapter 5 and the turn toward privatized, audit-based oversight explored in Chapter 6. That is so in large part because the standards at the core of transnational legal institutional arrangements are managerial ur-texts—dense, complex, and transparent only to those with relevant expertise.

Legal scholars who study transnational regulatory processes have long worried that those processes lend themselves to capture by powerful global elites.[113] It is helpful to understand that tendency as bound up with essential but imperfectly assimilated shifts in the technologies and the media of regulation. Network-and-standard-based legal-institutional arrangements exemplify an approach to mandated standardization that scholars who study sociotechnical assemblages for financial regulation have called the numericization of governance.[114] They are developed via expert proceedings and encoded in lengthy, highly technical specifications whose implementation requires ongoing supervision by cadres of managerial elites and professional auditors. The resulting methodological and technical constraints on participation provide entry points for capture motivated by ideology or economic self-interest, but they also can produce subtler perspectival and ideological shifts that reflect the deep and unquestioned commitments of expert communities of practice.

The particular expert register in which transnational governance is conducted varies from setting to setting. In the internet governance context, the language of governance is produced by and for computer scientists and engineers. In world trade governance and transnational financial regulation, the language of governance is predominantly economic and, particularly in financial governance settings, highly quantitative. Environmental and food and drug regulatory processes incorporate technical vernaculars from fields such as climate science, marine ecology, and epidemiology. Other prevailing vernaculars are more generally managerial. For example, detailed operational standards geared to the rhythms of organizational processes and to the benchmarks and reporting conventions used by professional auditors are increasingly common features of transnational environmental and labor regulation.[115] Many of the transnational regulatory arrangements surveyed in this chapter also adopt approaches to dispute resolution that are decidedly managerial in orientation. Across multiple domains ranging from trade and foreign direct investment to international business transactions to domain name registration, arbitration superintended by elite members of the relevant private bars is the order of the day.[116]

In each case, reliance on technical vernaculars produces both some obvious entry barriers and some less obvious obstacles to broadly democratic policymaking. Even where participation in network governance processes is formally open to all comers, as in the case of the IETF's working groups, the learning curve for those without appropriate technical facility is often steep. Civil society organizations in particular have struggled to attain technical parity with their better-resourced counterparts in the business and technology communities.[117] Expertise is required, as well, to understand the ways in which methods and analytical commitments that are ostensibly technical also implicate, reflect, reinforce, and sometimes pre-determine policy commitments. Disentangling fact from value and understanding the social construction of technology are perennial problems in science and tech-nology policy, but network organization under legally or practically mandated standardization exacerbates them.[118] As substantive policy choices are folded into standards, they become more and more difficult to disentangle, and certain types of especially incommensurable concerns—for example, concerns relating to develop-ment of capabilities for human flourishing and protection of fundamental rights—may seem to disappear altogether. The midlevel frameworks for articulating such considerations within expert rubrics tend to be underdeveloped at best.[119] Both policy and methodological disagreements become more difficult for outsiders to frame and deploy.

A corollary is that, as technocratic oversight of regulatory functions becomes more solidly entrenched, the (explicit or implicit) political commitments of the ex-pert regulators themselves may become more difficult to identify, contest, and dis-lodge. So, for example, the pathbreaking "end to end" design of technical protocols for the internet reflected solid technical judgment about robustness to certain kinds of disruptions and also encoded the generally libertarian commitments of the orig-inal internet pioneers. As a result, although the internet overall is extraordinarily resistant to disruptions of service, it has proved extraordinarily hospitable to other kinds of threats that exploit networked interconnection.[120] As we saw in Chapter 6, discourses of risk management that play increasingly important roles in environ-mental and financial regulation may fail to reckon adequately with certain kinds of large systemic threats. Those discourses and their blind spots also have featured prominently in the corresponding transnational regulatory debates.[121] In the do-main of world trade, the leading theoretical models generally have viewed liberaliza-tion as an unqualified good, even though developing countries and their advocates charge that the models ignore or undervalue considerations relating to equitable distribution of resources and capability-building for future innovation. Additionally, ascendant discourses about technical standard-making purport to elevate the "sci-entific" over the political but often operate to submerge political considerations.[122]

An important element of the rule-of-law ideal is commitment to publicly accessible rules and publicly accessible reasoning about the justifications for particular decisions.[123] From that perspective, network organization under legally or practically mandated standardization creates a paradox: Effective control of highly informationalized processes requires governance institutions capable of responding in kind, but the very process of optimizing regulatory controls to highly informationalized processes makes governance processes more opaque and less accountable to broader global publics. The strain that the turn toward technocracy places on ideals of public accessibility and contestability is not confined to the institutions that this chapter has studied. The rule-of-law paradigm has long struggled with questions about how to frame contestation over proffered scientific or quasi-scientific expertise, and those struggles have intensified as debates about risk and injury have become more pervasively informationalized. The turn toward technocracy in transnational governance, however, exacerbates the problem of public impenetrability. As transnational network-and-standard-based governance arrangements have proliferated, their expert networks have become increasingly opaque, arcane, and self-reinforcing.

Standards, Hubs, and Platforms: The Problem of Private Sovereignty

So far, the discussion in this section has presumed that, within networked governance arrangements, nonstate entities act as stakeholders but only sovereign states function as policy hubs. But that implicit division of roles ignores both the leveling effects of network logics and the amenability of standards to disintermediation. Commentators have long puzzled over the undeniable fact that, although they are nominally stakeholders in transnational networked governance processes, transnational corporations speak with increasingly independent voices in their relationships with sovereign states and also wield considerable governance authority of their own over globally distributed labor and supply chains.[124] Because of their central importance for global communication and information exchange, the dominant global platform firms push both tendencies to new extremes. The growing power of platform firms has implications that are both conceptual and practical. It raises the possibility that the Westphalian international legal order may be giving way to a hybrid order characterized by interlocking spheres of practical sovereignty and that disintermediation strategies targeting legally or practically mandated standards may in some circumstances reach beyond particular standards to target their associated policy hubs.

From the traditional international relations perspective, it makes no sense to speak of platforms or any other private corporations as sovereigns. Within the Westphalian international legal order, a sovereign state is, most minimally, an entity with a defined territory and a permanent population, the authority to govern its territory, and the capacity to enter into relations with other states.[125] Platform firms own premises within the territories of nation-states and provide services to citizens of those states. Unlike state sovereigns, they lack authority to use physical force to assert the primacy of their laws or defend the sanctity of their borders. Yet the growing practical sovereignty of platforms over many aspects of their users' everyday lives blurs the boundaries that those criteria impose.

Dominant platforms are unmatched by other transnational corporations in the extent of the authority they wield over the day-to-day experiences and activities of their users. Here again, the terminology developed by Castells in his exploration of communication power in the networked digital era is useful for explicating the various kinds of power that dominant platforms possess. By virtue of their privileged and infrastructural access to flows of information, such platforms wield both network power—which, as we have seen, inheres in the self-reinforcing power of a dominant network and by extension in its standards—and network-making power—or the power to constitute the network and perhaps to reconstitute it along different lines by altering the conditions of interconnection.[126]

The network power and the network-making power of dominant platforms are rooted in the very considerations of territory, population, and enforcement authority that platforms supposedly lack. Platform territories are not contiguous physical spaces but rather are defined using protocols, data flows, and algorithms. Both technically and experientially, however, they are clearly demarcated spaces, and, as we saw in Part I, platforms guard their virtual borders vigilantly.[127] Put differently, network-making power is not just theoretical. Dominant platform firms have used combinations of boilerplate and technical protocols to structure the commercially important layers of their operations as walled gardens within which the conditions of interconnection are strictly controlled, and they have gradually but inexorably reconfigured the networked information environment in ways that reinforce their dominance over the conditions of data collection and knowledge production.

As to population, dominant platforms such as Facebook, Google, and Apple have user populations that number in the billions, vastly eclipsing the populations of all but the largest nation-states.[128] To be sure, there are differences between platform usership and citizenship: Citizenship is constitutive of juridical identity, whereas platform usership is not. Nation-states make citizenship difficult to attain and easy to relinquish, while for digital platforms the reverse is true. The logic of platform membership is a network logic that relies on lock-in, and it persistently undercuts the strategies of exit and voice through which users police more ordinary commercial relationships. The increasingly indispensable nature of the services that platforms provide makes exit practically infeasible for many users. Voice is also less feasible precisely because the enforcement authority of platforms is real and immediate. Platforms govern their domains with a quiet tenacity, using protocols and interface design to structure permitted conduct—for example, sponsored search results, Facebook "likes" and "tags," Twitter retweets—and imposing internal sanctions ranging from content removal to account suspension or cancellation for disfavored conduct.[129]

Sovereign authority also must be recognized as such by other sovereigns, and here the picture is muddier. As we have seen throughout the book, the sovereignty of platforms is emergent and performative. The dominant U.S. platform firms acting in their capacity as surveillance intermediaries actively and theatrically resist certain kinds of incursions by nation-states on their own governance authority. In court systems around the world, they have simultaneously defended against production requests for data stored domestically and declined to comply with production requests for data stored overseas. In regulatory fora, they have engaged in protracted negotiation with competition regulators, transportation and labor regulators, data protection authorities, and tax authorities.[130]

Although some of these controversies also implicate users' rights of privacy, expression, and association, platforms more often seem to be principally concerned with establishing their own regulatory independence. Platforms also increasingly practice diplomacy in the manner of sovereign actors. Facebook's privacy team travels the world meeting with government officials to determine how best to satisfy their concerns while continuing to advance Facebook's own interests, much as a secretary of state and his or her staff might do. Such efforts recently bore unprecedented fruit when Denmark announced the appointment of a digital ambassador whose portfolio focuses on relations with the giant platform companies. That decision in turn may inform discussions now underway in various other European settings about the desirability of appointing new government "ministers for digital."[131]

The nature of the sovereignty that dominant platforms claim to exercise and the extent of the policy disintermediation to which their ambitions extend are also unclear. Speaking at a recent network security conference, Microsoft's president crystallized one version of that ambition, sketching a future in which platform firms function as "a trusted and neutral digital Switzerland."[132] As we saw in Chapter 4, however, networked information and communication providers, including the dominant platform firms, have pursued more collaborative relationships with governments on both matters of national security and law enforcement, and they also have at times forged such relationships on matters of technology policy more generally.[133] And as discussed previously, the dominant Chinese platforms have been more amenable to partnering with national governments on a wide variety of policy and governance initiatives.

It is worth noting that, within transnational governance arrangements, the emergent authority of platforms is greatest precisely where the links to state sovereignty are most tenuous: within the interlinked complex of internet governance processes. As already noted, in general the major information technology firms and their employees play active roles in network governance processes. Google and Facebook each operate substantial privatized internet "backbone" infrastructures—the interconnection facilities that link different pieces of the global network together—and

Google and Amazon have acquired extensive domain name portfolios that map to other elements of their market expansion strategies.[134] But platform firms also have begun to assert their preferences more directly within trade and transnational regulatory settings, most notably with regard to arrangements for governing cross-border data flows. They have played a central role in crafting the case for stronger trade-related protection of data flows that might counteract European-style data protection mandates.[135]

In sum, concentrated stakeholder control of the networked communications infrastructure can produce and perhaps is beginning to produce an inversion of law- and policymaking authority, through which some stakeholders become policy hubs in their own right. Theories of international relations that deny the possibility of private sovereignty are ill-equipped to respond to that possibility. Reconceptualizing the arena for transnational governance in a way that expressly accounts for both network-and-standard-based governance and the network-making power of dominant platforms has become an increasingly important project.

Designing Institutional Forms for Rule of Law 2.0

Just as contests over accountability for industrial-age harms shaped the forms of legal institutions and the content of legal doctrine in an earlier era, so the contests now playing out within network-and-standard-based legal-institutional settings will determine the structure of the legal system in the emerging, globalized, postindustrial era. The new transnational processes follow network laws and standardization dynamics, and that organization explains a great deal about their inconsistency with traditional rule-of-law formulations. Network power actively routes around inconvenient sources of friction, whatever their origin, and network organization around mandated standardization resists conventional mechanisms for direct contestation and public accountability.

Taking networks and standards seriously as organizing principles for law raises urgent questions about whether and how network-and-standard-based governance institutions might be configured differently—and underscores the high costs of failing to pursue such efforts. The disconnects between network-and-standard-based governance and rule-of-law ideals point to the beginning of an important institutional design project that emphasizes both the ultimate problem of arbitrary power and the ultimate goal of accountability to global networked publics. That project also must contend with both the power of the authoritarian end run and the growing practical sovereignty of platforms, offering new and more effective strategies to address the challenges those developments pose for the realization of rule-of-law aspirations in the networked information era.

The Future(s) of Fundamental Rights

Your legal concepts of property, expression, identity, movement, and context do not apply to us. They are all based on matter, and there is no matter here.
—John Perry Barlow, "A Declaration of the Independence of Cyberspace"

For some commentators on the emerging informational economy, the prospect of continued and ever more severe regulatory destabilization is a joyous one—a necessary period of disruption en route to a more perfectly free (and substantially deregulated) digital future. Although many digital entrepreneurs and information-economy pundits self-identify as iconoclasts, that view of the digital networked world has a very traditional pedigree. Writing at the dawn of the digital era, self-appointed cyber-philosopher John Perry Barlow proclaimed cyberspace to be a new domain of pure freedom. Addressing the nations of the world, he cautioned that their laws, which were "based on matter," simply did not speak to conduct in the new virtual realm.[1] As Barlow himself recognized, that was not so much a statement of fact as it was an exercise in deliberate utopianism. But it has proved prescient in a way that he certainly did not intend. The "laws" that increasingly have no meaning in online environments include not only the mandates of market regulators but also the guarantees that supposedly protect the fundamental rights of internet users, including the expressive and associational freedoms whose supremacy Barlow asserted.

This chapter considers the effects of digital disruption on the recognition and enforcement of fundamental human rights. It maps three overlapping and mutually reinforcing sets of trends.

First, traditional mechanisms for defining and enforcing human rights have begun to unravel. New, hybrid modes of infringement that involve private economic power and privately developed surveillance infrastructures and information services play an important part in that shift, but other changes set in motion by the movement to informational capitalism are equally important. Highly informationalized forms of rights discourse and practice that link human rights to development and sustainability have confronted difficult implementation challenges, and new techniques for data-driven, algorithmic surveillance and control also have proved powerfully resistant to traditional forms of human rights oversight. Meanwhile, like the other evolving institutional formations that Part II has studied, evolving institutional formations for human rights practice have been progressively overtaken by the managerial turn, increasingly emphasizing "corporate social responsibility" over more stringent accounts of moral and legal obligation and deferring to opaque and often privatized arrangements for expert supervision of algorithmic processes.

Second, the vision of a cyberutopian golden age that Barlow so vividly described has proved a mirage. The internet activists and communities that took up Barlow's call quickly grasped the transformative potential of new technological capabilities for expression, association, and bottom-up organization. As we have seen throughout this book, however, they failed to reckon with the equally transformative potential of informational capital, and they also have consistently ignored or downplayed the human capacity for malice and mayhem. The chapter's middle section revisits those failures. Networked digital information technologies enable new kinds of communication but also supply new infrastructural points of control; platform-based, massively intermediated media infrastructures both facilitate and co-opt bottom-up cultural and political production; and algorithmic intermediation processes optimized for behavioral tuning and user engagement amplify both benevolence and malevolence. It has become increasingly apparent that functioning legal institutions have an indispensable role to play in protecting and promoting fundamental human rights in the networked information era.

Finally, the chapter considers a cluster of emergent discourses about the nature and importance of fundamental rights that reinforce the normative authority of powerful, nonhuman actors. Within the political economies of the global North, the turn to neoliberal governmentality has produced forms of rights discourse that invite cooptation by corporate entities seeking to privilege their own profit-making activities. An alternative way of conceptualizing the political economy of informationalism, ascendant in China and gaining ground globally, emphasizes instead the virtues of publicness, accountability, and cooperation with state authority. Under both approaches, the fundamental rights of human beings and communities—to flourishing, self-determination, and the hope of a sustainable future—are afterthoughts.

Institutions Unmoored

In the networked digital age, protections for fundamental human rights have begun to fail comprehensively. Practically speaking, private economic interests wield increasing power over the conditions of human freedom. In particular, surveillant assemblages that combine private and public elements have effectively disintermediated traditional, state-centered mechanisms for protecting rights to privacy, freedom of expression, and freedom of association while at the same time facilitating new modes of infringement with unprecedented scope and reach.[2] Other challenges are conceptual and institutional. Critics of traditional, liberty-based rights frameworks have asserted (or reasserted) the importance of resource distribution, collective self-determination, and environmental sustainability for human flourishing. At the same time, platform-based, massively intermediated information systems have destabilized long-standing assumptions about the material conditions of possibility for privacy, intellectual freedom, and political self-determination. Both developments have underscored the inadequacies of traditional, court-centered approaches to defining and vindicating rights claims, and they also have created points of entry for new discourses and practices organized around managerial and technical expertise and neoliberalized assertions of corporate social responsibility.

Intermediating Freedom and Evading Review

Around the world, new patterns of mobility, networked communication, and networked economic power have thrown traditional, state-centered paradigms for human rights definition and enforcement into disarray. Embodied subjects encounter threats to life and liberty as they move across borders and between sovereign territories. Flows of networked communications also cross borders, and states can act remotely on those communications and their traces in ways that affect the people with whom they are associated regardless of where in physical space those people happen to be located.[3] Powerful transnational corporations that channel global flows of information and other resources wield increasing power, including sometimes the power of life or death, over the individuals and communities whom those flows affect. And the pervasive *entanglement* of corporate and state surveillance activity has left existing treaty and constitutional frameworks unable to constrain either public or private surveillance power in any meaningful way.

Concern about the unaccountability of private economic power is a long-standing theme within human rights scholarship and activism. Within domestic and international discourses about fundamental human rights, the paradigmatic legal guarantees are those that structure sovereign states' dealings with embodied subjects located within their territorial borders. According to theory, state obligations to protect fundamental rights flow from the sovereign monopoly over the use of violence, simultaneously acknowledging that monopoly and subjecting it to limits.[4] That way of reasoning about the primacy of state power does not allow for the possibility of private power over the conditions of human freedom, and it has produced human rights institutions that speak to private power indirectly, if at all. In some countries, including the United States, constitutional restrictions apply only to government actors. Although some human rights instruments, such as the European Convention on Human Rights, purport to encompass both state and private conduct, they do not authorize enforcement directly against private companies.

In 2008, the United Nations Secretary-General appointed a Special Representative to supervise the development of a framework and a set of guiding principles intended to nudge multinational corporations toward behavior more consistent with existing human rights norms. Guiding principles and special reports intended to constrain corporate conduct have no independent legal force, however, and the unprecedented power of capital over the conditions of human freedom has continued to grow.[5] In particular, giant transnational corporations that construct global networked supply chains wield vast power over their workers and the surrounding communities.

More recently, the unaccountability of private communications intermediaries has become a topic of special concern. By the mid-2000s the importance of the internet for communication, political self-determination, and economic opportunity—and the correspondingly powerful positions enjoyed by internet intermediaries—had become impossible to ignore. At the same time, a growing chorus of industry observers had begun to argue that internet platforms' easy adaptability to networked surveillance was an urgent global problem. Pointing to a series of unnerving events—including the Chinese government's enlistment of Yahoo! and Google to identify dissenters and block communication about prohibited topics, the Saudi and Iranian regimes' use of server-level firewalls to control internet traffic into and out of their countries, and Egyptian and Libyan governments' use of server-level surveillance capabilities to identify and target citizens using social media for political organizing—they urged technology firms, democratic regimes, and transnational human rights institutions to institute more effective protections for communicative rights and freedoms in the networked digital environment.[6] The Global Network Initiative (GNI), founded in 2008 by a coalition of platform firms, academics, and human rights NGOs, represented an attempt both to coordinate resistance to censorship demands by authoritarian states and to respond to criticisms levied at platforms for acceding to such demands. The United Nations also initiated what become a series of special reports dealing with the power of information intermediaries and the threats that counterterrorism efforts pose to fundamental rights and liberties.[7] Compliance with the GNI's principles and the special rapporteurs' recommendations, however, remains voluntary and inconsistent.

Some academic commentators argue that privately operated communications providers fulfill an important separation of powers function without which the potential for human rights abuses would be far greater, but the evidence supporting that proposition is mixed at best.[8] As we saw in Chapter 4, to the extent that courts have engaged at all with questions about the legality of programmatic state surveillance of networked communications, resistance by communications intermediaries has been instrumental in helping to frame the legal challenges. Information technology firms also have rightly chastised governments for developing (and, inevitably, losing control of) exploits that jeopardize network security.[9] But communications intermediaries—including especially the dominant global platform firms—also have complied with surveillance and censorship requests by host governments around the world.

Even more basically, arguments about the essential structural role of communications intermediaries fail to consider those intermediaries' roles in the construction of sociotechnical assemblages for data harvesting, behavioral microtargeting, and maximizing user engagement. State-centered conceptions of protection for fundamental rights and freedoms sit uneasily alongside a reality in which flows of information to, from, and about network users are intermediated by and through privately owned and operated communications infrastructures and platforms, and in which those flows encompass information of an astonishing variety, granularity, and intimacy.

The vast and growing extent of commercial surveillance facilitates a pervasive entanglement of public and private power, producing a practical reality within which each feeds off the other and neither can be effectively constrained. Post-Snowden, bulk collection and analysis of data generated by networked communications intermediaries have become acknowledged pillars of national security surveillance. The ready availability of data generated by networked communications intermediaries also has begun to alter ordinary law enforcement practice. In the United States, for example, police have begun issuing subpoenas to communications intermediaries to identify the owners of all mobile devices who were near the scenes of crimes in progress, and police departments in a growing number of cities have used predictive policing tools supplied by private vendors to predict the likelihood of individuals' becoming involved in violent crimes.[10] New data-driven assertions of power that blend private self-interest and public force in varying combinations range from intensive surveillance and repression of minority and dissident populations to state-sponsored disinformation campaigns designed to weaken democratic institutions and regimes.[11] Private employers, meanwhile, use a variety of networked digital surveillance technologies to monitor the productivity, health, communications, and political activities of their employees and contractors, and private economic interests and political organizations exploit platform-based capabilities for content targeting for their own purposes.[12]

The continued ascendancy of private economic power and the deepening entanglement of public and private surveillance power leave populations worldwide simultaneously exposed to new threats and cut off from traditional institutional mechanisms for vindicating the rights that are threatened. These developments are combining to constitute the spaces of transnational economic activity and networked digital communication as spaces devoid of protections for vital human rights and freedoms—even as the activities conducted in those spaces become more and more fundamental to the exercise of those rights and freedoms.

Networks and Standards Revisited

Other challenges to traditional paradigms for human rights definition and enforcement involve alternative forms of rights discourse and contestation over the practices those discourses might require. In particular, important strands of discourse about the necessary conditions for human flourishing and a sustainable future hold that securing human rights for all of the world's peoples requires moving beyond liberty-based, individualistic formulations of fundamental rights to frameworks that encompass a broader variety of economic, institutional, and environmental factors. Within the model of network-and-standard-based governance developed in Chapter 7, those discourses represent efforts to redefine the standards at the core of transnational human rights practice. Such efforts have struggled, however, to gain an institutional foothold. Traditional, court-centered mechanisms for rights enforcement are unresponsive (by design) to certain kinds of economic and self-determination claims, and processes for standard-making and enforcement within legal-institutional arrangements for transnational economic and network governance have evolved in directions that increasingly decouple them from human rights considerations. Efforts to develop new forms of human rights discourse and practice organized around capabilities for human flourishing also have confronted new forms of co-optation rooted in the logics and imperatives of the managerial turn.

Scholars, activists, and advocates for marginalized communities worldwide have long argued that it is one thing to articulate formal statements of fundamental rights and quite another to guarantee freedom and self-determination for all peoples. The leading human rights instruments developed and ratified in the post–World War II era consisted for the most part of relatively simple, aspirational statements of the various civil and political or social and economic liberties to which individuals should be entitled.[13] To some, those statements represented important, albeit incompletely realized progress toward a more humane international order. To others, the emphasis on individual civil and social liberties reflected a deliberate effort to disempower more radical, anticolonialist movements emanating from the global South while bolstering the emergent neoliberal global order.[14] At minimum, it has long been clear that exercising fundamental rights and freedoms—whether civil and political or economic and social—also requires resources and capabilities that many lack, particularly (but not only) in the world's least developed countries.

Gradually, claims sounding in distributive justice have engendered alternative forms of human rights discourse within which individual rights, collective self-determination, and economic and institutional development are inextricably intertwined. One such discourse is based on philosophical theories about capabilities for human flourishing—a formulation that encompasses the resources required for physical well-being, intellectual development, cultural participation, and political self-determination.[15] Another concerns the relationship between human flourishing and systemic environmental degradation. Environmental scientists, legal scholars, activists, and advocates have long argued that environmental threats represent acute threats to the future of humanity that require a strong collective response. In 1988, the UN established a permanent intergovernmental panel on climate change to collect and synthesize information on the effects of climate change and recommend mitigation options. In 2015, it formally endorsed the Sustainable Development Goals, a set of recommendations that is widely understood as having important human rights implications.[16]

Human rights discourses organized around capabilities and sustainable development, however, underscore the defects of existing institutional approaches to rights enforcement. The problem is not simply that transnational tribunals charged with enforcing international instruments lack authority to compel signatory states to remedy violations or that signatory states lack the will to do so.[17] More fundamentally, considerations relating to capabilities and sustainability have been difficult to recast as concrete obligations amenable to judicial enforcement.[18] In part the reasons are political and ideological and involve resistance to large-scale redistributive change. Legal reasoning about the privileged status of civil and political rights and the purported conceptual unruliness of economic and social rights also has played an important role in discouraging doctrinal and process innovations designed to advance substantive economic equality.[19]

Last and importantly, network power also matters. Within emergent legal-institutional arrangements for network-and-standard-based transnational governance, human rights courts and their concerns are increasingly marginalized. As a practical matter, then, the network-and-standard-based institutions for transnational economic and network governance described in Chapter 7 have become the front lines for many struggles to realize capabilities and sustainability goals. In theory, such institutions are well equipped to advance those goals, both because they operate via highly informationalized standard-making and because the mechanisms of network power obviate the need for legal compulsion. Other features of network-and-standard-based economic governance, however, cut the other way.

We saw in Chapter 7 that the mandatory structure of networked legal-institutional arrangements favors efforts to shape the governing standard in directions that are compatible with the dominant standard's underlying policy commitments and disfavors efforts to reorient those commitments. So, for example, legal-institutional arrangements for trade governance privilege global flows of extractive activity and for the most part treat local protective regulation as network damage. In many cases, claims about capabilities- and sustainability-related imperatives must be framed as justifiable deviations from scientifically derived international standards that are more lenient. Other types of networked economic governance institutions have a relationship to rights enforcement that is simply haphazard. For example, financial stability standards have indirect implications for a range of capabilities- and sustainability-related goals, but making those connections takes work that the customary practices of financial standard-making organizations may not accommodate.

Meanwhile and perhaps predictably, as human rights discourses and practices organized around capabilities and sustainability have encountered transnational legal-institutional arrangements for economic and network governance, they have undergone other kinds of transformation. New forms of human rights-related economic development practice emphasize efforts to make measurable improvements in the human condition, and those practices exemplify the themes of sociotechnical change and informationalization that this book has explored. They make intensive use of both technological capabilities for collecting, communicating, and processing large quantities of information, and they rely on compact, information-intensive indicators to facilitate measuring, monitoring, and communicating about progress toward identified goals.[20] Those characteristics in turn have invited informationalism's distinctive institutional failure modes.

One long-standing critique of development discourse engages the turn to neoliberal managerialism that earlier chapters have explored. As new enterprise models for development have emerged, those models sometimes have seemed more concerned with proper management of development efforts and development-based business plans than with whether those efforts and plans are producing meaningful change on the ground. Activists, advocates, and scholars have raised persistent concerns about the methodological tyranny of utilitarianism in the articulation of development goals and benchmarks.[21] As, development discourses have become increasingly expert-driven and inaccessible to the populations whose futures they affect, they also exacerbate the problem of public reason that Chapter 7 explored.

More recently, human rights discourses and practices addressed to private economic power also have undergone a novel form of institutional co-optation that relocates them inside corporations themselves. Within network-and-standard-based economic governance contexts, a fast-growing sector of corporate-facing human rights practice has become "corporate social responsibility" (CSR) practice. As Chapter 7 noted, CSR standard-making has become a principal mechanism through which the UN attempts to govern the conduct of private actors on a variety of matters relating to human rights, economic well-being, and sustainability. In particular, the United Nations Global Compact, a framework for encouraging sustainable development, has worked in partnership with both public and private entities to formulate and encourage implementation of standards for corporate social responsibility covering a wide variety of topics, many of which intersect with human rights.[22] CSR discourses and initiatives have begun to proliferate and have spawned new academic journals and new practices of their own. Yet those discourses and initiatives also have sparked resistance; as one pair of scholars puts it, some argue that "CSR is bad capitalism" and others contend that "weak CSR is bad development."[23]

As those criticisms suggest, CSR advocates and initiatives occupy a uniquely equivocal position within corporate decision-making processes and network-and-standard-based governance arrangements. They seek to inform and shape a wide variety of corporate decisions and actions, but mechanisms for exacting compliance are weak. From one perspective, initiatives such as the UN Global Compact represent pragmatic and flexible solutions to pressing global governance problems; from another, they are powerful expressions of neoliberal governmentality. They rely exclusively on political and hortatory strategies to extract commitments that may or may not be honored. At the same time, they project an image of consensus around virtuous privatization of rights enforcement.[24] It remains to be seen whether efforts to incorporate CSR standards into other standard-making processes can achieve higher levels of compliance and whether, if so, compliance with CSR standards actually translates into concrete progress toward development and sustainability goals.

Ghosts in the Machine

New technologies for data-driven, algorithmic surveillance and intermediation raise different conceptual and institutional challenges for human rights enforcement that resides in the realm of the sociotechnical rather than the socioeconomic. Even if fundamental rights guarantees extended unambiguously and enforceably across the public-private divide, and even if network-and-standard-based institutions for transnational economic governance were ready and willing to accommodate such guarantees, such technologies alter the material conditions of possibility for the exercise of fundamental rights in ways that both liberty-based and capabilities-based formulations fail to capture. And they operate in ways that both traditional modes of court-centered enforcement and new modes of network-and-standard-based governance fail to constrain.

Until relatively recently, discourses about fundamental rights have relied on a set of unstated and unexamined assumptions about the material environment's affordances—the conditions of possibility that the material environment offers for individual, collective, and organizational activity.[25] So, for example, large-scale surveillance of telephone communications was impossible, and surveillance of movements in physical space was resource-intensive and could be difficult to conceal. Personalized targeting of information and advertising was something about which marketers could only dream, and microtargeting based on such considerations as political views, personality types, or emotional states was inconceivable. Relatively limited capabilities for surveillance and targeted intermediation engendered correspondingly open-ended possibilities for privacy, association, and intellectual and personal exploration.

Advances in networked digital communication and information have exposed the contingency of those assumptions, making clear that it is a mistake to take materiality for granted. As we have seen throughout this book, networked digital information and communications technologies have radically expanded the horizons of possibility for communication, association, and intellectual exploration, but they also have expanded the horizons of possibility for surveillance, control of expression and association, and highly granular, microtargeted intermediation of the information environment.

The rapid and dramatic changes in affordances for surveillance, control, and targeted intermediation pose novel challenges for traditional ways of conceptualizing and detecting rights violations. Legal scholars have paid special attention to the relationships between algorithmic pattern-detection and unlawful discrimination in violation of fundamental rights to equal treatment, so it is useful to begin there. As we saw in Chapter 2, data-driven algorithmic epistemologies sort and classify individuals probabilistically in ways that are simply inconsistent with traditional ways of thinking about the kinds of reasoning necessary to justify, for example, decisions about investigation, sentencing, and eligibility for parole in criminal cases or decisions about access to important economic resources such as employment, housing, and credit. Data-driven epistemologies that rely on machine learning also optimize and reoptimize in ways that persistently elude review. Those processes can produce additional examples of the phenomenon that we encountered in Chapter 1: a systematic dismantling of the Polanyian protective countermovements instituted to protect workers and consumers in an earlier economic era. For example, a system forbidden to use race as a variable might use other data, such as media consumption or purchases of hair care products, to infer race and adjust the offered pricing or services accordingly, and it might use factors that themselves reflect preexisting patterns of discrimination, such as lower scores on standardized tests or longer commuting distances to the site of a new job, as decision-making proxies.[26] Machine-learning epistemologies also may embed discrimination in policing more systematically while clothing it in a veneer of automated neutrality. For example, facial recognition software trained on predominantly white faces does poorly at recognizing nonwhite faces, and the increasingly widespread use of such technologies renders individual members of racial minority groups more vulnerable to misrecognition and mislabeling.[27]

The problem of discrimination, however, is merely one manifestation of a more complex rule-of-law problem that inheres in the networked, algorithmically intermediated communications environment. Smart digital technologies operate continually and immanently, producing decisions that are ad hoc, personalized, and pattern-based rather than principled and generalizable. They don't give reasons for—or even draw attention to—the choices they make. And they are designed to learn, producing outcomes that their designers did not directly specify. As Mireille Hildebrandt explains, these attributes contradict the principles of generality, stability, equality, and publicness that are foundational to the idea of the rule of law— and that establish predicate conditions for human rights protection. Pointing to the ways that printing facilitates stability, replication, deliberation, and universal application, Hildebrandt contends that the rule of law is itself an artifact of sociotechnical relations organized around print and text.[28] That conclusion may prove too much— it is possible that new rule-of-law criteria for evaluating the effects of networked digital technologies could be developed (and, as we saw in Chapter 7, new rule-of-law criteria capable of constraining the operation of network-and-standard-based governance institutions also are urgently needed). But algorithmic processes optimized for particular goals continually assert and reassert their own internal logics, which will resist interpolation of other values unless they are redesigned to incorporate new parameters.

Here again, institutional deficits compound the conceptual and operational difficulties. Consider policing again: For generations of lawyers and policymakers, the paradigmatic form of police work has been the individualized investigation. A crime is committed, and afterward investigators search for clues that may enable them to identify the perpetrator(s) and prove the connection in court beyond a reasonable doubt. Modern police work, however, increasingly relies on the ability to access information collected through techniques for routine, population-wide surveillance. When courts attempt to resolve disputes about use of information acquired via population-wide surveillance using legal rules developed in the context of traditional, targeted investigations, they confront a mismatch that is both temporal and doctrinal. Judicial review is retrospective by design. Even a request for a warrant presupposes an already-committed crime and a discrete investigation that has produced results to which a judicial decision-maker can respond. And the questions that constitutional law empowers courts to ask—Is there probable cause? Was there a search? Was the search reasonable?—demand simple, yes-or-no answers that do not mesh well with a reality in which surveillance practices are ongoing. Doctrinal frameworks that focus on the moment of collection and impose few (if any) restrictions on subsequent access and use are poorly calibrated to address questions about the governance of contemporary, data-driven investigative methods and techniques.[29]

In the United States, some of the reasons for courts' refusal to supervise programmatic surveillance are historical and ideological. During the early twentieth century, police work became increasingly professionalized, shift that sprang in part from a Progressive-Era ethos of scientific improvement. Law reformers saw criminal behavior as presumptively amenable to systematic study and criminal investigation as presumptively amenable to expert management.[30] As Progressive-Era ideologies about scientific management of the criminal justice process have given way to neoliberal managerialism, beliefs about the appropriate roles of professional discretion, informationalized management, and technical expertise in law enforcement have become ever more deeply entrenched. Narratives about the linear, depoliticized nature of technological progress do important background work, suggesting, for example, a neutral and generally optimistic stance toward the outputs of pattern-detection algorithms and biometric matching techniques.[31]

More generally, however, the same characteristics that defy traditional rule-of-law formulations make the new modes of programmatic surveillance highly resistant to the institutional concerns and competencies of courts. Courts and other institutions tasked with enforcing human rights guarantees traditionally have focused on impermissible *reasons* or *results*, but trying to govern algorithmic processes of surveillance and intermediation by focusing on discrete and particular outputs—whether one is contesting the results of a predictive policing search, a denial of employment or credit, or the results of a process for content removal—is like trying to produce sustainable improvements in water quality by removing individual impurities with a sieve. The design of automated machine-learning processes includes a number of steps that prohibitions directed to reasons and results do not capture. Data collection, data cleaning, algorithm design, and algorithm training all entail value-laden choices. The goals to be served must be defined computationally, and designers typically must choose which one(s) to prioritize by defining trade-offs among different training parameters. Eliminating or minimizing undesirable results is possible only if the tools are subject to continual audit and retraining.[32] Institutions unable to oversee those processes are almost perfectly optimized to leave programmatic surveillance initiatives and the intermediaries that operate them unaccountable for the real and very consequential roles that they play in defining the material conditions of possibility for human freedom.

Viable alternatives or complements to judicial oversight, however, have yet to emerge. In the United States, the tradition of relying on courts has discouraged experimentation with new institutional forms for administrative oversight of law enforcement activity.[33] Paradoxically, such forms are somewhat better developed in the national security context. As we saw in Chapter 4, the logic of secrecy that surrounds and permeates national security operations disrupts conventional processes for ex post judicial oversight of investigations. Even the FISA court has found it necessary to rely more heavily on oversight by senior law enforcement officials, and over the years Congress has tasked those officials more explicitly with developing and formalizing certain types of oversight procedures.[34] The lessons such procedures might teach about the design of criminal administrative procedure more generally are largely hypothetical, however, because of the pervasive secrecy that surrounds their day-to-day use. In jurisdictions where ex ante regulation of programmatic surveillance is more extensive, there is little consensus about what might constitute effective operational oversight of policing activities. Courts seem to limit themselves to determining whether the laws as written include certain basic safeguards, and structures for operational oversight are unclear.[35]

As described in the previous section, network-and-standard-based institutions for transnational economic and network governance are for the most part neither accountable for human rights consequences nor directly concerned with fulfilling human rights mandates. But it is also unclear what standards those institutions would apply to ensure algorithmic accountability if they were so inclined. A baseline requirement of network-and-standard-based governance arrangements is the ability to define an applicable standard and invite compliance with it, and regulatory toolkits for ensuring algorithmic accountability are rudimentary.

As in the case of the capabilities and sustainability discourses described in the previous section, the resulting competency gap has invited new forms of governance that reflect well-known pathologies of managerial oversight. External oversight of the national security establishment now increasingly consists of production, publication, and review of aggregate performance data—numbers of production orders requested and granted, numbers of nefarious plots successfully thwarted, and so on. As in other contexts, however, such reporting is itself a type of performance, designed to express a generic commitment to accountability without exposing the types of operational information that might enable meaningful scrutiny of the underlying processes.[36] The operational secrecy surrounding national security and law enforcement uses of networked digital capabilities remains endemic.

Emergent arrangements for privatized governance of algorithmic content moderation processes similarly privilege expert management over public accountability. Debates about content moderation in a wide variety of contexts—copyright takedowns, the emergent right to be forgotten, child pornography, terrorist recruiting videos, and hate speech—increasingly revolve around the aggregate performance metrics prepared and released by communications intermediaries.[37] Some intermediaries, including notably Facebook, have produced "community guidelines" and have shared those guidelines with regulators and with the public.[38] External observers are forced to rely on those disclosures—which are mostly about results and to some extent also about reasons—because no intermediary has provided operational detail about its algorithmic moderation processes, and none has been willing to allow interrogation of underlying practices of optimizing for *im*moderation in the first place. As practiced by the dominant platform firms and a host of smaller ones, algorithmic governance via "content moderation at scale" depends on elite management to define its parameters and oversee its operation, and it also asserts the sufficiency of elite management to correct for the ensuing and inevitable errors.

Power from Below?

In the face of these developments, broad coalitions of technologists, internet users, and digital rights activists have pursued two complementary sets of strategies for production and protection of fundamental rights and freedoms, one involving decentralized cultural and political production and the other involving anonymous resistance to and disruption of political and economic power. In platform-based, massively intermediated information environments, however, both sets of digital-rights strategies have encountered a variety of obstacles. Platform-based, massively intermediated environments magnify the effects of distributed, peer-produced cultural, social, and political activity but also co-opt the processes and outputs of distributed production in the service of data-driven profit strategies. Networked digital communications technologies afford new opportunities for anonymous resistance but also new points of control for state surveillance and censorship.

More fundamentally still, the results of anonymous online activism and distributed cultural and political production are not inevitably democracy-promoting, and predictions to the contrary have, in retrospect, come to seem extraordinarily naïve. Technological protections for anonymous online communication have enabled powerful new forms of resistance but have been far less successful at underwriting new institutional forms dedicated to ensuring more widespread protections for all people.

The Gift That Keeps on Giving

At the dawn of the internet era, some scholars and activists prophesied that decentralized production of various social, cultural, and political goods by communities of peers would largely displace centralized, top-down coordination and control in a wide variety of domains, with transformative and broadly freedom-promoting effects. In the ensuing years, decentralized production strategies have expanded access to information and political capacity-building for peoples all around the world and have come to be regarded as essential tools for fostering human freedom in the networked information era.[39] The grander visions of whole-sale transformation in political economy and in politics have not materialized, however. Instead, strategies for decentralized cultural and political production have reinforced platform logics and business models, fueling the emergence of dominant information platforms and affording new vantage points for data harvesting, surplus extraction, and manipulation of information flows.

Chapters 1 and 3 described some of the new forms of decentralized, collective cultural production that networked information and communication technologies have enabled. The two most well-known examples, the open source software movement and the Creative Commons movement, were self-consciously designed as efforts to develop sustainable, "copyleft" alternatives to the existing copyright regime—arrangements that would permit and encourage open access, copying, sharing, tinkering, repurposing, and remixing content created by others.[40] The trailblazing crowd-sourced encyclopedia, Wikipedia, uses Creative Commons licensing to keep its content open and freely accessible. Open source software has been at the forefront of efforts to make computing resources widely available to people in developing economies.

Networked information and communication technologies also have catalyzed new approaches to grass-roots political organizing. Some of the most transformative gains from such approaches have come in the global South. Grass-roots organizers around the world have appropriated networked, platform-based communication tools—including Facebook pages, Twitter hashtags, applications for multiparty messaging, and many more—for a wide variety of purposes, ranging from the storied uprisings of the Arab Spring to voter-registration drives in emerging African democracies to efforts to organize workers in Asian garment and high technology factories to local struggles over failure to provide municipal services.[41]

Some of the obstacles to commons-based cultural and political production were predictable or at least familiar. Leading software firms waged public and creative campaigns against open source software, labeling it unreliable, insecure, and a point of entry for organized crime. Although open source products and accompanying services eventually achieved widespread penetration in certain industry sectors and some once-formidable opponents have become adherents, persistent, thorny issues continue to surround the interfaces between open source and proprietary systems and modules.[42] The major content industries have resisted commons-based production and open-access distribution strategies for educational and cultural materials, and as Chapter 4 described, they have devised a continuing stream of legal and technological methods for asserting control over their products and business models.[43]

Political activists, for their part, quickly learned that the networked digital information environment afforded not only unprecedented scope for circulating dissenting ideas and coordinating political resistance but also new, hidden control points for state censorship and surveillance. Surveillance capabilities built into backbone servers and similar equipment—some of it supplied by Chinese technology firms but some sourced from the United States and other Western countries—have given governments across the Middle East, Africa, and Asia leverage to counter uses of social media to fuel popular protests and uprisings. In most of the countries where the Arab Spring uprisings occurred, they were quickly followed by government crackdowns that exploited networked surveillance capabilities, and that pattern has continued elsewhere.[44] In the United States, where communications intermediaries generally have resisted installing "back doors" for law enforcement and national security officials, electronic surveillance laws nonetheless afford only limited protections to communications metadata, and the relative ease of acquiring such data has enabled law enforcement to monitor and track activists and social movement organizers.[45]

Other failure modes for commons-based production were wholly unanticipated. In terms of political economy, openness has proved a double-edged sword. Platform protocols invite commons-based production arrangements and commons-based production arrangements in turn reinforce platform logics of datafication, data harvesting, and proprietary, algorithmic knowledge production. Like the gig workers and creative freelancers discussed in Chapter 1, content developers within open content ecosystems gain an extra measure of agency and content users an extra measure of information access, but both groups also double as voluntary information workers for platforms and their business affiliates.[46] And the peer-based quality control mechanisms that keep open source software robust and secure and Wikipedia reliable and (mostly) objective work far less well within massively intermediated environments that are optimized to advertiser-driven platform revenue models.

More fundamentally, algorithmic processes optimized to manufacture out-rage, boost click-through rates, prompt social sharing, and enhance capabilities for behavioral microtargeting are agnostic as to underlying political and ideolog-ical commitments. As Chapter 3 explained, networked, massively intermediated communication technologies are crowd enhancers—they amplify whatever the crowd wants, while at the same time making the crowd easier to manipulate. Under such conditions, power from below becomes power directed toward whatever purpose its organizers want to advance, and crowdsourcing strategies for polit-ical consciousness-raising and political action lend themselves to actors pursuing a wide variety of ends. One result is that platform-based, massively intermediated environments have become fertile breeding grounds for virulent forms of ethnic na-tionalism and ideological extremism. Around the world, authoritarian regimes and nationalist movements use social media cascades to warn majority groups that they are under threat, spreading rumors and lies designed to provoke fear, incite small-scale acts of hatred and violence, and catalyze more systematic campaigns of ethnic cleansing.[47] At the same time, and paradoxically, the increasingly pronounced ori-entation toward manufactured outrage and political polarization within such environments also dissipates other kinds of political energy. As Zeynep Tufecki explains, in the networked information era, it has become easy to organize a protest (or simply to elicit cascades of viral sharing) but more difficult to enlist networked publics in the work of democratic capacity-building in the real world.[48]

Among scholars and commentators who write about digital media, a debate has raged about whether it is fair to blame platforms for these problems. According to Siva Vaidhyanathan, "the problem with Facebook is Facebook," and more spe-cifically the combination of Facebook's global reach, its optimization-based business model, and the ways that its information feeds have displaced other, po-tentially moderating sources of information.[49] By similar reasoning, the problem with WhatsApp is WhatsApp, which offers secure encryption but permits contact harvesting and message chaining to reach large groups; the problem with Twitter is Twitter, which boosts the visibility of trending topics and selectively amplifies them based on predictive profiling; the problem with Google is Google, which elevates search results to positions of supremacy and purported objectivity if they are pop-ular enough; and the problem with YouTube is YouTube, which facilitates targeted and extraordinarily effective audiovisual indoctrination by conspiracy theorists of all stripes. Others argue that such explanations unfairly blame platforms for long-standing dysfunctions that are not of their creation.[50] Part of the problem with Facebook (and WhatsApp and so on) is the preexisting social and cultural divisions that information cascades amplify—white supremacist politics in the United States, Hindu-Muslim tensions in India, and so on.

For my purposes here, the important point (which Vaidhyanathan also makes) is that debates about the root causes of popular bigotry and irrationality and the overriding importance of free information flow tend to elide the essential roles of other institutions, both public and private, that might modulate and selectively amplify or dampen features of public discourse. Part of the problem with Facebook (and WhatsApp and so on) is people, easily distracted, highly susceptible to misinformation, and prone to herd behavior. And part of the problem is the systematic disintermediation and delegitimation of the other legal and social institutions that formerly debunked unfounded rumors, suppressed public expressions of bigotry, and moderated populist excesses. In the networked information era, preserving fundamental rights and freedoms for all people requires an institutional foundation that encompasses not only rights to speak, to access information, and so on but also other structural safeguards—safeguards designed to preserve a well-functioning networked public sphere and inoculate it sufficiently against cascading misinformation and hatred.[51] The idea that digital direct democracy will produce the latter seems increasingly difficult to countenance.

Anonymity, Trust, and the Problem of Scale

Other scholars and activists who took up Barlow's call for enlightened cyberlibertarianism focused on building capabilities for distributed, anonymous communication and coordination. Although many of the developments discussed in this book have made anonymity in daily life illusory for most ordinary people, deliberately constructed online anonymity has become a site of ongoing research and activism. Several decades into that project, however, persistent and intractable questions remain about the extent to which behaviors that historically have functioned as safety valves can assume more central roles in the project of securing fundamental rights and freedoms for all people. Some anonymous online actors have worked to advance democracy, equality, and broadly distributed enjoyment of civil rights and liberties in contexts all around the world, and others have worked just as hard to subvert those goals. The challenge of designing infrastructures and institutions for anonymous action that are reliably democracy-promoting remains unanswered.

Discussions about the promise or peril of anonymity often are framed in terms of absolutes. So, for example, some argue that persistent identification enables censorship and oppression, while anonymity shelters dissent and fosters the capacity for criticism and political self-determination. Others contend that identification engenders trust and fosters beneficial accountability, while anonymity encourages irresponsibility and antisocial behavior.

In reality, a wealth of historical and contemporary evidence supports *both* sets of arguments, suggesting that the relationships among anonymity, democratic self-determination, and social benefit depend very much on context. The virtues of anonymity are not just theoretical. Throughout history, anonymous and pseudonymous advocates, activists, and whistleblowers have catalyzed public debate about vital issues of political accountability, and in the modern era, state surveillance and human rights abuses have been closely linked.[52] In other contexts, however, there is broad consensus that easy anonymity would strain the social compact too far. So, for example, corporations must register with the state and disclose the names and addresses of their directors. Transfers of corporate stock must be registered by the purchaser or the purchaser's agent, as must transfers of internet domains. Applicants for professional licenses must provide identifying information. Systemic incentives to record real property purchases are so pervasive that registration is essentially mandatory.[53] There are good reasons for all of these rules, which enable government to provide for the public safety and welfare and to hold accumulations of private economic power accountable in certain basic ways.

The spectrum of anonymous online action mirrors these complexities. Around the world, anonymous online actors have used networked communication capabilities to name and challenge abuses of political and economic power. They organize political protests and acts of civil disobedience and maintain networks and sites for unmonitored exchange of information, anonymous discussion of forbidden topics, and anonymous publication of dissident and whistleblower content. Activists pursuing social change and journalists reporting on controversial topics rely on capabilities for anonymous communication to protect themselves and their sources.[54] In the wake of the Snowden revelations, the general public also has shown more sustained interest in such capabilities. Some information businesses, including most notably Apple but also others, have come to view market offerings designed to enable secure, anonymized communication as a point of competitive advantage.[55]

But the story of online anonymity also is more complicated than romanticized narratives equating anonymity with press freedom and democratic self-determination make it out to be. In networked spaces, cadres of technological cognoscenti wield anonymity as a new and potent source of social and political power to be deployed toward a wide variety of ends. They orchestrate large-scale whistleblowing, operate safe channels for journalists, and distribute samizdat on behalf of political dissidents—and also spread hate speech, disinformation, and fascist and nationalist ideologies. They hack into government and corporate networks to expose corruption and disrupt secrecy—and also to obtain and release the private documents and photographs of those who incur their displeasure. The counterpower of anonymity can expose and discomfit the powerful, and it also can be deployed to profoundly antisocial and destructive ends.

Additionally, the trajectories of projects designed to scale up certain types of anonymous interaction demonstrate that breaking things is easier than building them. So, for example, in Chapter 1, we encountered the blockchain, a technical protocol for enabling distributed, secure authentication of transactions. Because blockchain-supported transactions can be executed without relying on centrally certified intermediaries, the technology has been heralded as a promising vehicle for restoring trust in online environments. In theory, such technologies might be deployed within existing institutional fabrics to eliminate opportunities for corruption, waste, and rent-seeking.[56] But uses for private surplus extraction and self-interested (and environmentally destructive) speculation are far more widespread, and some argue that the highest and best uses of blockchain technologies involve the creation of alternative currencies to displace state-sponsored fiat currency and ultimately the state itself. Meanwhile, a continuing series of implosions by private cryptocurrency experiments has demonstrated that sustainable private cryptocurrency systems have institutional as well as technical dimensions and that the institutional structures underlying such systems do not automatically scale.[57]

As a second example, consider the online organization WikiLeaks, which we encountered in Chapter 4. Among digital civil liberties advocates, WikiLeaks and its flamboyant founder, Julian Assange, rapidly attained heroic status for their stated commitment to facilitating anonymous whistleblowing about powerful wrongdoers.[58] The media organizations with which WikiLeaks shared information about U.S. military operations and diplomatic cables were more circumspect. Because some kinds of leaks really can endanger lives, they engaged in careful review to determine what to publish and what to withhold, and they also made efforts to draw WikiLeaks into a conversation about how to construct institutional mechanisms for responsible whistleblowing. Without question, that conversation was complicated by the virulence of U.S.-led efforts to deprive WikiLeaks of Web hosting and payment services, label it a criminal organization in the court of international opinion, and bring its leaders to trial in the United States. But differences of opinion among WikiLeaks' principals also undermined efforts to draw the organization into discussions about institutional design questions. Assange in particular had a deeply ingrained fascination with disruption for its own sake and an equally deep distaste for the liberal, globalist commitments of his establishment interlocutors.[59] WikiLeaks has continued to pursue government transparency and to publish important leaks, but it also has been linked to state-sponsored disinformation campaigns designed to discredit competing regimes.[60]

As these examples suggest, although anonymous online action has played and will continue to play an important role in efforts to secure fundamental rights and freedoms for all people, arguments equating scope for anonymous action with the preservation of human freedom are far too simple. Some of the relevant factors are cultural. Experiments with scaling up anonymity have tended to express complex sets of political commitments that bear closer examination. Understood as anti-institutionalist projects, WikiLeaks and many blockchain-based cryptocurrency schemes reflect ideologies that are powerfully utopian but not particularly democratic. They express and reproduce a particular kind of moral and ideological purity that is both unrealistic and inconsistent with a broadly inclusive social compact. More generally, as anthropologist Gabriella Coleman has shown, hacker culture speaks the intertwined languages of liberal individualism and libertarianism, which prize freedom from state-imposed limitations and posit enlightened self-reliance and, by necessary implication, technical meritocracy as cardinal virtues.[61]

Barlow's famous declaration of independence for cyberspace resonated with those commitments, but the views it so vividly expressed have complicated efforts to transform digital anonymity from a tool for resistance to the foundation of a stable democratic framework. In any functioning system of the rule of law, dissent and opposition play vital structural roles, and anonymity therefore is an indispensable safety valve. But achieving durable, effective protection for fundamental rights and freedoms requires a broader and more diverse institutional foundation.

Taking Liberties: The New Normative Authority of Capital

A third set of significant shifts in discourses and practices relating to fundamental rights involves entrepreneurial appropriation of discourses about fundamental human rights to describe the rights and privileges of corporate entities. One form of corporate rights entrepreneurship concerns protections for corporate foreign direct investment. The rapid spread of investor-state dispute settlement provisions within the world trade system has enabled firms to frame complaints about burdensome local regulation as claims for impairment of their private property rights. Other forms of corporate rights entrepreneurship concern rights of free speech and privacy. We saw in Chapter 3 that information intermediaries based in the United States rely on the First Amendment's protection for freedom of speech to shelter their information-processing activities, but the co-optation of rights discourses about free speech and privacy by powerful commercial entities also takes other forms, and the story about the emerging global economy of personal data processing is not only a story about the expanding global footprint of powerful U.S. technology companies. Two other permutations—a European story about the entailments of individual autonomy and a Chinese story about virtuous corporate citizenship as one pillar of the rule of law—are also in play.

Property Goes Rogue: The Emerging Global Law of Regulatory Takings

The network-and-standard-based institutions for world trade governance studied in Chapter 7 have facilitated a powerful form of corporate rights entrepreneurship that revolves around the asserted primacy of private property rights. Investor-state dispute settlement (ISDS) provisions in many treaties governing foreign direct investment permit nonstate investors, typically multinational corporations, to challenge various kinds of state actions that threaten their investments and to bring their claims before panels of private arbitrators rather than in the host country's courts. Over the last several decades, those provisions have become vehicles for an effort to protect the asserted private property rights of corporations against domestic regulations that would lower the value of their transnational investments.

First created in the mid-twentieth century, ISDS mechanisms were envisioned as necessary incentives for investment in developing economies because they promised to protect investing firms, typically headquartered in the global North, against corruption, favoritism toward local competitors, and possible direct expropriation of corporate assets. So understood, ISDS provisions expressed a modernized ethos of colonial expansion updated for the era of trade liberalization; they replaced claims by colonial sovereigns (though not their involvement) with claims by private capital investors.[62]

As with the processes that Chapter 7 explored, however, the decentering of state institutions laid the groundwork for other kinds of changes. Beginning in the 1990s, the ISDS landscape began to change rapidly. Today, ISDS provisions encompassing both direct and "indirect"—that is, regulatory—expropriations exist in tens of thousands of bilateral and multilateral agreements that extend around the globe and that are expressly designed to enable their assertion in any country.[63]

In large part due to the dynamics of network-and-standard-based governance studied in Chapter 7, emerging global frameworks for ISDS have begun to reflect the influence of U.S. constitutional doctrine relating to so-called regulatory takings of private property rights. In the 1990s, following implementation of the North American Free Trade Agreement (NAFTA), U.S. scholars and policymakers grew concerned that the language of the treaty's ISDS chapter, which referred to state actions that were "tantamount to nationalization or expropriation," could support a variety of investor demands for relief from local, state, or federal laws imposing regulatory burdens. That possibility materialized in 2000 in the form of a multimillion-dollar arbitral award against the Mexican government on behalf of Metalclad, a U.S. corporation whose application to operate a hazardous waste landfill had been denied for environmental reasons.[64]

Following the *Metalclad* award, the U.S. Trade Representative urged Congress to amend the ISDS mechanism to refer to the standard used in regulatory takings cases so that the results in any future arbitral proceedings against the United States would mirror those that could be obtained in the federal courts. According to that standard, first articulated in a case called *Penn Central*, a proposed regulatory change that interferes too greatly with distinct investment-based expectations regarding private property can be deemed a taking without just compensation unless it is justified as a generally applicable exercise of the state's traditional police power to protect the public welfare.[65] After Congress complied, the Trade Representative drafted a new model bilateral investment treaty that included language directly incorporating key terms from the regulatory takings case law, including the idea of government interference with "distinct, reasonable investment-backed expectations." It then began using the treaty as a template in negotiations over other bilateral and multilateral trade agreements worldwide.[66]

The U.S. attempt to discipline the ISDS mechanism by tethering it to regulatory takings doctrine but also to export clauses modeled on the NAFTA ISDS provision to the rest of the world reflects more than just protectionism. Here it is useful to consider the political and ideological history of the doctrine as it has evolved domestically. Over the past several decades, U.S. legal scholars who study property law have chronicled the emergence of a movement to limit land use regulation by expanding constitutional protection for private property rights. Like the movement to expand constitutional protection for commercial speech that Chapter 3 described, the property rights movement originated in libertarian and neoliberal think tanks and began to take shape as a coordinated litigation agenda during the 1980s.[67] As interpreted by the federal courts, the *Penn Central* standard embodies some resistance to that agenda—it is highly malleable and courts have resisted interpretations that would allow vested interests to trump all forms of protective environmental and land use regulation—but the idea of "reasonable investment-backed expectations" also came to be understood as reifying a baseline level of protection against changing public sensibilities about economic development risks and harms.[68]

The decisions to insert the *Penn Central* standard into the NAFTA investor-state dispute mechanism and subsequently to pursue its incorporation within the thickening network of bilateral and multilateral investment treaties to which the United States is party must be read in light of that history. Viewed against the backdrop of decades of coordinated resistance to environmental regulation in the name of sacrosanct property rights, the campaign to orient the network-and-standard-based processes of world trade governance to the investment-backed expectations of multinational corporate actors cannot be characterized simply as an effort to preserve space for protective regulation. Looking to the longer term and to the transnational arena for legal standard-making, it was also a stance calculated to privilege relatively concrete and monetizable extractive interests over changing public needs.

Consistent with the increasing importance of intangible assets in the informational economy, the ISDS landscape has gradually widened to include asserted takings of intangible intellectual property interests, including patent interests and trade secrecy interests relating to research and development activities.[69] In Chapter 1, we saw that, over the last half century, both intellectual property doctrines and their accompanying narratives of justification have gradually aligned with the goals and desires of corporate rightholders. ISDS proceedings concerning intellectual property interests continue that evolutionary arc. As Rochelle Dreyfuss and Susy Frankel have observed, the outcomes of investor-state proceedings turn on narratives that do not require human creators or their creative incentives at all, but instead reframe intangible intellectual progress as the product of investment.[70] It seems sensible to predict that, over time, corporate "investors" will invoke ISDS mechanisms to protect other types of intangible interests covered under trade in services agreements. As of this writing, there is no report of any investor-state proceeding arising out of asserted state interference with cross-border flows of personal data, but such disputes seem certain to materialize.

All has not been smooth sailing for the transnational corporate property rights movement. As arbitral rulings identifying unlawful indirect expropriations have begun to emerge, public outrage and calls for reform have mounted. Opinions differ strikingly, however, on the sort of reform that is needed. The 2016 presidential election in the United States produced a number of reversals of well-established trade policy positions, including an effort to eliminate ISDS from NAFTA altogether. Canada, Mexico, and the powerful U.S. Chamber of Commerce all opposed elimination, and, as of this writing, the finalized U.S.-Mexico-Canada Agreement preserves ISDS, but only for a drastically narrowed class of disputes.[71] European debates reflect similar disagreements. In a 2018 decision in a case challenging an arbitral award against Slovakia under a bilateral investment treaty with the Netherlands, the European Court of Justice held that the treaty provision creating the ISDS procedure impermissibly impaired the autonomy of European law. Meanwhile, the European Commission has been attempting to design a new ISDS mechanism with more robust rule-of-law characteristics, including publicly appointed judges, public proceedings, prescribed grounds for invalidating state regulatory determinations, and provisions for an appellate body. It also has proposed multilateral negotiations on a new convention establishing a multilateral dispute settlement court.[72]

Both the sheer number of ISDS provisions in existing treaties and their distributive politics, however, suggest that investor-state dispute resolution in some form is here to stay. Within the liberty-based approach to conceptualizing fundamental rights that still characterizes transnational discourses about nonnegotiable baseline obligations to persons, rights talk about investment expectations functions and is intended to function as a normative trump card. It is a way of inoculating network-and-standard-based legal-institutional arrangements for transnational economic governance against the destabilizing effects of legal standards wars that threaten to inject other, more explicitly public-regarding considerations into the standard-setting calculus.

Free Speech and Privacy through the Looking Glass: Escalating the Battle to Control Global Data Flows

For the last two decades, the United States and Europe have been engaged in protracted struggles to define and calibrate corporate obligations regarding privacy, data protection, and removal of online content, and those struggles have showcased two other forms of corporate rights entrepreneurship. In the United States, the predominant form of corporate rights entrepreneurship about privacy involves asserted corporate free speech rights. We have already explored contemporary U.S. thinking about the free speech rights of information intermediaries, and I will revisit it here only briefly. In Europe, which does not recognize corporate free speech interests to a similarly broad extent, the predominant mode of corporate rights entrepreneurship concerns the autonomy of individual data subjects.

As Chapter 3 described, the United States has for many decades been ground zero for efforts to enshrine an expansive approach to corporate free speech rights, and those efforts have begun to bear substantial fruit. Cases about the contours of the contemporary First Amendment have constructed a broad equivalence between information processing and speech, and platform entities in particular have mobilized both the traditional First Amendment frame of the marketplace of ideas and the new frame of the information laboratory to underwrite broad immunities from regulatory oversight. Internet intermediaries also enjoy broad statutory immunity from liability for civil wrongs, and conventional wisdom about the relationship between media technologies and human freedom justifies that arrangement on both speech- and innovation-related grounds.

As we have seen throughout this book, European and U.S. legal traditions differ markedly on many privacy- and speech-related issues. European human rights law enshrines both privacy and data protection as fundamental rights, while U.S. constitutional law is more grudging, according protection to narrower interests in more piecemeal fashion.[73] The two legal traditions also differ on the circumstances that justify speech restrictions. European legal systems generally prohibit hate speech, while the United States does not, and European legal systems are less tolerant of unauthorized publication of personal information about private individuals. Last but not least, although European courts sometimes have permitted media companies and other fictional entities to assert interests in protecting and promoting freedom of expression, they have done so in a comparatively restrained and context-specific way.[74]

Among U.S. legal commentators and tech policy pundits, it is conventional to think that European law's relative receptiveness to certain kinds of restrictions on speech and information processing makes European citizens less free, but that conclusion does not withstand close scrutiny. In general, European nations have both robust media ecosystems and courts willing to block legislative and prosecutorial overreach. There have been some notable exceptions, but that is true on both sides of the Atlantic.[75] When European courts need to resolve asserted conflicts between one person's rights to privacy and another's freedom of speech, they use doctrines requiring interest balancing that are similar to those developed in the U.S. constitutional context, and information intermediaries sometimes benefit from that balancing. Decisions about matters such as the right to be forgotten and the scope of obligations to remove various kinds of harmful content have begun to establish clearer parameters for information intermediaries to use in structuring their operations. Contrary to alarmist predictions by some U.S. commentators, those parameters do not insulate public figures from criticism, nor do they prohibit reporting and commentary about hate groups or terrorist acts.[76]

Questions about individual consumers' rights to *authorize* the harvesting and processing of their personal data, however, have presented difficult challenges for European legal systems. Formally, European law reserves much greater control to consumers than U.S. law does. Both the General Data Protection Regulation adopted in 2016 (GDPR) and the regime it replaced adopt the paradigm of "privacy-as-control," which emphasizes the autonomy and dignity of data subjects.[77] In European privacy practice, however, important strands of discourse about individual autonomy present opportunities for co-optation by corporate claimants seeking to privilege the choices of European consumers, and the patterns of co-optation have begun to unfold in opposite but mutually reinforcing ways.

As a practical matter, there is an intractable tension between the regulatory goal of specific, explicit consent to data collection and processing and the marketplace drift toward convenience. Formally, European data protection law imposes a strict definition of consent and forbids processing personal data in ways incompatible with the purpose for which the data was initially collected. Renewed consent can justify later processing for a new, incompatible purpose, but rolling consent is not supposed to become a mechanism for evading purpose limitations entirely. An entity providing information services may not rely on consent to justify harvesting and processing if there is "a significant imbalance between the position of the data subject and the controller."[78] Practically speaking, however, individuals wanting access to the social media services offered by global (often U.S.-based) internet companies typically elect to grant consent to data processing in the ways that those services recommend. That result accords with neoliberal ideals of self-actualization through market and consumptive choices, and when it is permitted to stand, it substantially narrows the distances between U.S. and European regimes.[79]

Less obvious but equally important, in networked, algorithmically intermediated environments, the autonomy-based privacy-as-control paradigm confronts significant and potentially fatal implementation difficulties. For example, although the scope of the requirement is disputed, European law requires that data subjects be provided with meaningful information about the automated logics involved in processing personal data in at least some cases. Important questions remain, however, about whether it is possible to explain certain types of automated processes at all and whether such explanations, if available, constitute meaningful remedies for complaints that are, at bottom, complaints about unfair treatment. It is unclear what, if anything, individual data subjects might gain from the opportunity to navigate an additional layer of complexity in aid of making wide-ranging and imperfectly informed decisions about an uncertain future.[80] Additionally, as described earlier in this chapter, machine-learning-based algorithmic processes are resourceful at working around constraints, which means that even well-intentioned disclosures may be inaccurate and even clearly specified scope limitations may be ineffective. Placing individual data subjects and their choices at the center of debates about how far such processes should be authorized seems unlikely to produce either fairer markets or more coherent choices about the appropriate extent of data-driven surveillance and intermediation.[81] Operationalizing disclosure and access rights also promises to increase both overall levels of surveillance and the severity of associated data security threats.[82]

Much has been made of the fact that the GDPR's provisions for policymaking and enforcement depart from the previous data protection regime by centralizing data protection authority in the European Commission. Some reasons for that shift were enforcement-related. Arguably, to regulate global information businesses such as Google, Facebook, and Apple in a way that effectively counters American laxity, Europe must speak with a unified voice. But the details of the change reflect corporate entrepreneurship of a different kind. European and global businesses had found the previous regime's patchwork of national compliance requirements expensive and unwieldy. The GDPR provides a mechanism for achieving Europe-wide compliance via boilerplate clauses and binding corporate rules. In so doing, however, it narrows the list of targets for regulatory capture efforts. National regulators continue to wield front-line enforcement authority, but lack power to impose new substantive requirements; they cannot lower European data protection standards, but they also cannot attempt to raise them.

Taken together, these developments reflect a still-unresolved struggle between demands for meaningful substantive protection of fundamental rights of privacy, expression, and association and demands for reduction of barriers to global economic enterprise.[83] On one view, European legal institutions have embarked on a process of human rights experimentalism aimed at extending protections for fundamental rights gradually via iterative interactions among the Commission, the courts, and national regulators who wield front-line enforcement authority.[84] On another, the vaunted European data protection framework, and by extension the larger human rights framework within which it is embedded, are undergoing a (largely unacknowledged) moment of crisis whose resolution remains uncertain.

The success or failure of European-style data protection regulation therefore will depend only in part on the Commission's willingness to wield its enhanced enforcement powers under the GDPR in the service of thicker conceptions of individual autonomy and flourishing than the ones that global information businesses have preferred. It also will depend in part on development of new competencies for achieving algorithmic accountability that do not rely exclusively on individualized autonomy and control claims to secure their realization. Additionally, as we saw in Chapter 7, it will depend on whether European regulators and consumers can marshal sufficient network-making power to propagate heightened levels of protection throughout network-and-standard-based arrangements for global economic governance—and to reinforce such arrangements vis-à-vis the growing power of the authoritarian end run.

Accountability, Authority, and Corporate Virtue in the "Red Stack"

A final important strand of the evolving global contest over the rights and privileges of informational capital concerns Chinese information technology firms and Chinese information technology policy. Like their U.S. counterparts, Chinese firms also have surveillance-based business models; unlike the U.S. government, however, the Chinese government has maintained control over domestic implementations of those models. Domestically, Chinese information technology policy has embraced a vision of personal data collection and processing within which digital reputation is a central pillar not only of good citizenship but also of the rule of law—and in which cooperation in the construction of state-supervised reputation metrics is a marker of corporate virtue.

As noted earlier in this chapter, during the internet's early years, Western commentators marveling at the rapid growth and global spread of technology firms such as Microsoft, Yahoo!, Google, Facebook, and Apple appeared to believe that the emerging global communications network would have an inherently libertarian orientation. Users would exploit networked capabilities to evade state surveillance and censorship, consumers would demand unfiltered access to the open internet, and internet intermediaries would honor consumer preferences by resisting state demands for cooperation.[85] Time has shown those predictions to be incorrect. Although many determined Chinese citizens have resisted state surveillance, finding creative ways of discussing banned topics and circumventing filters and firewalls, the Chinese population more generally is relatively inured to state surveillance and control of permissible expression. And U.S. platform firms operating in China (and elsewhere) have largely acceded to host country demands for content filtering and identification of account users.[86]

Narratives about global information intermediaries' resistance to state surveillance also were problematic for a far more basic reason: they envisioned the nations of the global South as innovation bottom feeders—offering new markets and new data but not their own information platforms and services—and gave correspondingly little thought to what information platforms emerging from the global South might look like. As Chapter 7 described, that assessment has proved shortsighted. A coordinated campaign combining state investment, systematic technology acquisition, and end runs around transnational norms favoring liberalization of information flows has produced the "Red Stack"—a thriving Chinese information technology sector whose products and services have capabilities for surveillance and control built in at the core.

As Chinese technology companies have thrived, they have begun partnering with state and local government authorities to develop surveillance infrastructures and capabilities along a new, distinctively Chinese model. Within that model, communications, commerce, policing, and the provision of public services are fully integrated all the way down. Chinese citizens already accustomed to the need to provide identification documents have readily transitioned to using digital platforms for interacting with government offices and even participating in virtual public hearings. For some, at least, the ready availability of those services expresses both the state's care for its citizens and the public-spiritedness of Chinese industry.[87]

Chinese technology firms' commercial offerings have straightforward affordances for state filtering and surveillance. Search engines and internet access providers are supplied with lists of items and domains to be blocked, and equipment and software for the provision of internet services must straightforwardly accommodate such demands.[88] Consumer technologies and apps also are surveillance-friendly. For example, as a condition of selling iPhones in the Chinese market, the government required Apple to contract with a Chinese cloud storage provider to store customers' iCloud encryption keys locally. One review of leading instant messaging applications gave Tencent's WeChat application a security rating of zero because it does not attempt to counter third-party surveillance at all, and WeChat also engages in extensive, legally mandated image filtering.[89] Chinese platforms also have provided congenial environments for government-sponsored disinformation campaigns designed to distract Chinese networked publics from more serious pursuits, thereby stabilizing the ruling regime.[90]

Following the pattern described in the first half of this chapter, the thickening web of public-private surveillance also has begun to foster new state surveillance initiatives; in the Chinese model, however, the state has taken the lead in developing those initiatives, in crafting narratives about their reliability and legitimacy, and in enlisting private-sector cooperation. Among other things, it has announced its intent to develop and implement a nationwide system for "social credit scoring" by 2020, to equip its extensive network of surveillance cameras with facial recognition capabilities, and to integrate the two projects. Much Western coverage of these efforts has emphasized their potential for fostering social conformity, stifling dissent, and facilitating systematic oppression.[91] Perhaps most notably, field tests of state surveillance capabilities in the Xinjiang region have shown those capabilities being used to restrict the movements of members of the predominantly Muslim Uighur population as part of a more systematic campaign of social and cultural "reeducation."[92] In time, however, the state envisions providing every citizen with a score that encompasses far more than either past purchasing behavior or political activity and that mediates access to a wide variety of public and private privileges and services.[93]

Entrenching state political control is an undoubted goal of the emergent Chinese social credit scoring system, but there are also others that Western observers have tended to discount, and they reflect more complicated narratives about the nature and origins of both privacy rights and corporate virtue. As Xin Dai explains, other goals include both strengthening intra-governmental accountability and furthering economic development. In particular, systems for tracking and disclosing compliance with court orders and administrative fines are understood and represented to the public as advancing the rule of law. Yet another purpose is to assert state supremacy relative to what many Chinese have begun to see as the entirely unaccountable information practices of powerful Chinese platform providers.[94] Both Alibaba and Tencent were among a select group of companies initially approved by the state to develop pilot social credit scoring technologies, but both have incurred unprecedented popular criticism for their undisclosed data harvesting activities. In February 2018, the government ordered Tencent to cancel a nationwide test of its scoring project. In theory at least, the government's system will have the capacity to extend some basic data protection guarantees, including the opportunity to know one's ranking and to challenge the accuracy of particular items.[95] In both respects, the emergent Chinese regime of networked information governance stands in thought-provoking counterpoint to the neoliberal regime of reputation surveillance described in Part I, which locates both power and immunity from accountability differently.

As Chapter 7 described, the emergent Chinese regime of surveillance as state prerogative also is gaining ground globally. So far, the dominant Chinese platform firms have made only partial inroads into U.S. and European markets. Merchants that cater to Chinese tourists now accept mobile payments via WeChat and AliPay, and anecdotal evidence also suggests that an unknown number of small merchants that advertise on U.S. platforms such as Instagram use members of Alibaba's affiliated group of companies to source merchandise directly from China.[96] In developing economies and regions, Chinese firms have a much higher profile, in part because they offer services tailored to the distinctive needs and desires of both populations and governments. Populations that, like China's, are rapidly moving online using mobile devices as the primary access points are gravitating to relatively affordable Chinese-manufactured mobile devices and to the services that Chinese platform firms excel at providing, including instant messaging, e-commerce, and mobile payment systems. Governments, meanwhile, have gravitated to the built-in surveillance capabilities offered by Chinese technology firms and platform services.[97]

Together, these developments are underwriting the global expansion of a vision of the networked public sphere in which fundamental human rights play no discernible part. The Red Stack and the distinctive form of governmentality that it expresses must be acknowledged as an entrant in the ongoing legal standards war over the appropriate extent and uses of data-driven surveillance. The implications of that development and possible responses have yet to be systematically considered.

Rule of Law 2.0 Revisited

Among all of the problems that legal institutions have confronted in the modern era, that of guaranteeing fundamental human rights and freedoms for all people has been the most difficult, and the movement to informational capitalism has exacerbated the challenges that project now confronts. If legal protections for fundamental human rights are to remain relevant and meaningful in the networked digital age, three kinds of institutional change are urgently necessary.

First, and self-evidently, institutions for recognizing and enforcing fundamental rights should work to counterbalance private economic power rather than reinforcing it. Obligations to protect fundamental rights must extend— enforceably—to private, for-profit entities if they are to be effective at all. As an example, early in the twentieth century, the U.S. courts developed a new constitutional doctrine for responding to ascendant industrial power in the form of the "company town." Under the doctrine, a private employer that had completely subsumed public functions—furnishing not only the houses in which its employees lived but also the stores in which they shopped, the streets and sidewalks on which they traveled, and the town squares in which they could gather—thereby also subjected itself to an obligation to protect their First Amendment rights even when it did not like what they said.[98] The doctrine was narrow and its career short-lived, and in any event its emphasis on control of physical space and on state action as the conceptual baseline make it unsuited for direct transposition into the networked digital era. But the intuition that justified it is nonetheless instructive and has already begun to inform new ways of thinking about the legal responsibilities that should accompany the new forms of network power wielded by powerful information and communication intermediaries.[99]

Second, the importance of development, sustainability, and materiality for the conceptualization and enjoyment of fundamental rights points to the need to develop new modalities for oversight and enforcement that harness informational resources and tools without falling into managerialist traps. Important initial steps in that project are conceptual. Securing the predicate conditions for human flourishing requires development discourses that are context-sensitive and methodologically diverse, and securing the predicate conditions for privacy, intellectual freedom, and political self-determination in the networked information era requires other kinds of universally applicable material and operational guarantees.[100] Other steps are methodological and institutional. The task of ensuring progress toward broadly distributed development, sustainability, and algorithmic accountability is not one for courts alone or even primarily; it will also require new methods of administrative oversight and new thinking about the appropriate relationship(s) between administrators and courts.

Third and finally, protecting fundamental human rights in the networked information era requires more careful attention to the mechanisms of network-and-standard-based transnational governance, and particularly to the ways that powerful state and for-profit actors have exploited those mechanisms for their own benefit. The Red Stack is a clear threat to certain kinds of freedom, but it is also important to contend more systematically and effectively with its growing power and appeal worldwide, and it is simply wrong to think that populations worldwide see its principal competition, the U.S.-dominated regime of global informational capitalism, as a shining beacon of human freedom. The reality is both more complicated and simpler: building protection for fundamental human rights directly into institutions for economic and network governance has become an essential aspect of the rule-of-law project for transnational governance sketched at the end of the previous chapter.

Conclusion

Countermovements, Now and Then

Drowning people
Sometimes die
Fighting their rescuers.

—Octavia Butler, *Parable of the Sower*

This has been a book about both institutional transformation and institutional failure. It has mapped the evolution of legal entitlements and institutions in response to the demands of information capital, and it has also traced the failure of institutional strategies developed over the course of two centuries to constrain unbridled economic power. Two decades into the twenty-first century, the Polanyian countermovements and the others that came after them are increasingly outpaced, outflanked, and co-opted. It would be easy to conclude that the outlook for law as an instrument of reform is bleak. To reach that conclusion, however, would be to misunderstand the most important lesson that the rise and fall of countermovements has to teach.

Legal countermovements have a rich and varied history. The original Polanyian countermovements were crude but effective circuit breakers that interrupted market-driven logics of commodification by imposing basic worker-protection requirements. Beginning in the late nineteenth century and culminating with the administrative innovations of the New Deal and the constitutional and legislative innovations of the civil rights era, the U.S. legal system developed a host of other protective measures that ranged from simple prohibitions to complex institutional arrangements. Transnational human rights institutions represent yet another kind of legal countermovement, in which moral and normative components played especially prominent roles. Each countermovement was flawed and imperfect, but each changed the conversation about the kinds of institutional action that were possible. Eventually, all have invited new strategies for evasion, capture, co-optation, and arbitrage.

Next, consider the strong property and contract rights at which the Polanyian and U.S. countermovements took aim. Familiar narratives now connect the pernicious effects of unbridled economic power to expansive notions of property and contract. But strong property and contract rights were initially countermovements devised to limit monarchical authority, and legal innovations that expanded opportunities for property ownership and freedom of contract have played important democratizing roles in the United States as well. To similar effect, the first modern copyright statute—the British Statute of Anne—was expressly conceived as an author-centric reform to regimes of publisher licensing that kept the interests of both authors and the reading public subordinated to those of publishers and the Crown. The first modern patent statutes replaced royal charters granted to favorite businesses and revocable at whim with more durable legal protections for the fruits of human ingenuity. Natural-rights-based arguments for strong and undiluted property, contract, and intellectual property rights have an antediluvian whiff today, but they were progressive once.

Here it is useful to recall the functional description of power sketched briefly at the outset of this investigation: Power is both pragmatic and protean, defying efforts to describe its workings and cabin its reach. Given rules of engagement, it seeks out gaps; confronted with prohibitions, it finds workarounds. Durable countermovements disrupt the rhetorical and institutional logics that power has constructed, but if countermovements prove durable, they also become sources of opportunity and targets for co-optation.

In short, the most important lesson that the rise and fall of countermovements has to teach is that countermovements are inevitably temporary. But that does not make them futile nor their gains illusory. While they have force, countermovements produce both concrete improvements in the living conditions of ordinary people and less tangible but equally important benefits to human societies generally. Countermovements also engender expectations—for enjoyment of civil, political, and social rights, for equal and meaningful access to economic opportunities, and for the protection of the rule of law—and those expectations have a power of their own. Expectations that the law will find a way to do justice create pressure for continuing experimentation with the institutions and practices of governance. As law mediates between truth and power, the possibility for real, incremental improvement—and occasionally even for transformative improvement—exists in the windows of opportunity between institutional innovation and institutional capture.

Whether the effects of the transformations explored in this book will elicit meaningful countermovements is yet to be seen. What seems certain is that reforms that simply adopt yesterday's methods are unlikely to succeed. Just as the most effective institutional changes of a previous era engaged directly with the logics of commodification and marketization, so institutional changes for the current era will need to engage directly with the logics of dematerialization, datafication, and platformization, and will need to develop new toolkits capable of interrogating and disrupting those logics. In particular, data protection, algorithmic accountability, platform power, and network-and-standard-based governance have begun to emerge as essential modalities of oversight for the information age. Each oversight modality requires both new legitimating constructs and new institutional forms. Articulations of fundamental rights designed to defend and extend liberal individualism must be paired with others that engage directly with the logics of neoliberal governmentality and platform-based, data-driven, algorithmic power. And overarching rule-of-law constructs designed for a slower, more atomistic, and more court-centered era require rethinking and revision. Together, these goals define an essential agenda for institutional innovation within a new window of opportunity that now stands open.

ACKNOWLEDGMENTS

The ideas and arguments that form the basis for this book have been iterated gradually over the course of a number of years of scholarly work. Portions of the book are adapted from previously published work, as follows: Parts of the Introduction appeared as "Introduction: Information Platforms and the Law," *Georgetown Law Technology Review* 2 no. 2 (2018): 191–96. Parts of Chapter 1 are adapted from "Law for the Platform Economy," *U.C. Davis Law Review* 51 no. 1 (2017): 133–204; a short-form adaptation of portions of Chapter 1 also will appear as "Property and the Construction of the Information Economy: A Neo-Polanyian Ontology," in *The Handbook of Digital Media and Communication*, eds. Leah A. Lievrouw & Brian D. Loader (New York: Routledge, forthcoming). Chapter 2 is adapted from "The Biopolitical Public Domain: The Legal Construction of the Surveillance Economy," *Philosophy and Technology* 31 no. 2 (2018): 213–33. Parts of Chapter 3 are adapted from "The Surveillance-Innovation Complex: The Irony of the Participatory Turn," in *The Participatory Condition in the Digital Age*, eds. Darin Barney et al. (Minneapolis: University of Minnesota Press, 2016), 207–26; a short-form version of the first half of Chapter 3 also will appear as "The Emergent Limbic Media System," in *Life and the Law in the Era of Data-Driven Agency*, eds. Kieron O'Hara & Mireille Hildebrandt (Northampton, Mass.: Edward Elgar, forthcoming). Parts of Chapter 4 are adapted from "The Zombie First Amendment," *William and Mary Law Review* 56 no. 4 (2015): 1119–58. Parts of Chapter 5 are adapted from "Information Privacy Litigation as Bellwether for Institutional Change," *DePaul Law Review* 66 no. 2 (2017): 535–78. Chapter 6 is adapted from "The Regulatory State in the Information Age," *Theoretical Inquiries in Law* 17 no. 1 (2016): 369–414. A short-form version of Chapter 7 will appear as "Networks, Platforms, and Networked Governance," in *After the Digital Tornado*, ed. Kevin Werbach (New York: Cambridge University Press, forthcoming). Parts of Chapter 8 are adapted from "Turning Privacy Inside Out," *Theoretical Inquiries in Law* 20 no. 1 (2019): 1–32, and "Between Truth and Power," in *Information, Freedom, and Property: The Philosophy of Law*

Meets the Philosophy of Technology, eds. Mireille Hildebrandt & Bibi van den Berg (New York: Routledge, 2016), 57–80.

Many talented and perceptive colleagues gave freely of their time and effort to help me develop, test, revise, and refine the arguments presented here. For their generosity, wisdom, wit, and patience, I am profoundly grateful to Ifeoma Ajunwa, Lisa Austin, danah boyd, Yochai Benkler, Dan Bouk, Kiel Brennan-Marquez, Bill Buzbee, Ryan Calo, Anupam Chander, Danielle Citron, Gabriella Coleman, Nick Couldry, Kate Crawford, Laura DeNardis, Deven Desai, Kristen Eichensehr, Niva Elkin-Koren, Dan Ernst, Michael Froomkin, Oscar Gandy, Anna Gelpern, Andrew Glickman, Maria Glover, Christoph Graber, James Grimmelmann, Seda Gurses, Lisa Heinzerling, Mireille Hildebrandt, Chris Hoofnagle, Margaret Hu, Gordon Hull, Meg Jones, Emma Coleman Jordan, Margot Kaminski, Martin Kenney, Benedict Kingsbury, Greg Klass, Don Langevoort, Kyle Langvardt, Paddy Leerssen, Karen Levy, Michael Madison, Alice Marwick, Allegra McLeod, Naomi Mezey, Adam Mossoff, Deirdre Mulligan, Kali Murray, Christopher Newman, Helen Nissenbaum, Anne Joseph O'Connell, Paul Ohm, Ruth Okediji, Eloise Pasachoff, Frank Pasquale, Julia Powles, David Pozen, John Rappaport, Priscilla Regan, Joel Reidenberg, Neil Richards, Brishen Rogers, Tanina Rostain, Dan Schiller, Pierre Schlag, Andrew Selbst, Greg Shaffer, Jonathan Sterne, Thomas Streinz, Madhavi Sunder, Olivier Sylvain, Linnet Taylor, Rebecca Tushnet, Joseph Turow, Joris Van Hoboken, Rory Van Loo, David Vladeck, Joseph Weiler, Kevin Werbach, Robin West, Jennifer Whitson, and Lauren Willis.

During the intellectual journey that this project represents, I also benefited greatly from the opportunity to present both the various papers listed and draft book chapters at numerous workshops and conferences, including: the "Philosophers of Law Meet Philosophers of Technology" sessions at the 2013 and 2016 meetings of the International Conference on Computers, Privacy, and Data Protection; the 2013 Annual Meeting of the Association of Internet Researchers; the 2014, 2015, 2016, and 2018 Privacy Law Scholars Conferences; the 2015 and 2018 Amsterdam Privacy Conferences; the 2013 Media@McGill ymposium on The Participatory Condition in the Digital Age; the 2014 William and Mary Law Review symposium on The Contemporary First Amendment; the 2015 Law and Media and Communications Annual Lecture at the London School of Economics; the 2015 Information Law Cluster Seminar at the University of Sussex; the 2015 Mark Claster Mamolen Professorship Inaugural Lecture at the Georgetown University Law Center; the 2015 Theoretical Inquiries in Law symposium on The Constitution of Information: From Gutenberg to Snowden, held at the University of Toronto Law School; the 2015 Fordham Center for Law and Information Policy research workshop; the 2015 workshop on Responsible Use of Open Data at the New York University School of Law; the 2016 Clifford Symposium on Tort Law and Social Policy at DePaul University College of Law; the 2017 U.C. Davis Law Review Symposium on Future-Proofing Law; the 2017 Colloquium on

Philosophical Approaches to IP at George Mason University Scalia School of Law; the 2017 Public Law and Legal Theory Workshop at the University of Chicago Law School; the 2017 Wharton School Symposium on After the Digital Tornado; the 2018 Yale Law School Workshop on Law and Political Economy; the 2018 Fordham Colloquium on Civil Rights and Civil Liberties in the Digital Age; the 2018 Guarini Colloquium on the International Law of Global Digital Corporations at New York University School of Law; the University of Haifa Center for Cyber Law and Policy's 2017–2018 lecture series; and faculty workshops at Georgetown University Law Center, Northwestern University Pritzker Law School, Washington and Lee School of Law, and Washington University St. Louis School of Law. My thanks to participants in those events for their engagement, their collegiality, and their constructive criticism.

I thank Dean William Treanor of Georgetown Law, along with Associate Deans for Research Josh Teitelbaum (2015–2017) and John Mikhail (2017–present), for their generous support and encouragement, and Jorge Juarez, Barbara Monroe, Erie Taniuchi, and the staff of the Edward Bennett Williams Library at Georgetown Law for their assistance with an endless list of ordinary and strange requests. I am also profoundly grateful for the research assistance provided by a cadre of talented and dedicated Georgetown Law students: Aislinn Affinito, Kelley Chittenden, Jade Coppieters, Justin Erb, Natalie Gideon, Peter Gil-Montllor, Ben Hain, Alex Moser, Nur Lalji, Sean Quinn, Patrick Reid, Sherry Safavi, Thomas Spiegler, Alya Suleiman, Mario Trujillo, Apeksha Vora, and Alex Zajac. Thanks also to David McBride, my editor at OUP, for his wise and patient guidance.

Thanks and love always to Andrew Glickman and Eli Glickman for their love, their great patience, their mostly genuine enthusiasm for eating leftovers, and their confidence that I would eventually finish this project. This book is dedicated to my parents, Natalie and Donald Cohen, in profound gratitude for everything they have taught me about inquiry, integrity, and persistence.

NOTES

Introduction

1. American Friends Service Committee, "Speak Truth to Power: A Quaker Search for an Alternative to Violence" (Mar. 2, 1955), https://perma.cc/T7ER-L4LX.

2. The terminology derives from Ithiel De Sola Pool, *Technologies of Freedom* (Cambridge, Mass.: Harvard University Press, 1984). Influential statements of this view include John Perry Barlow, "A Declaration of the Independence of Cyberspace," Electronic Frontier Foundation (1996), https://perma.cc/GL7C-A3HB; David R. Johnson & David G. Post, "And How Shall the Net Be Governed?: A Meditation on the Relative Virtues of Decentralized, Emergent Law," in *Coordinating the Internet*, eds. Brian Kahin & James H. Keller (Cambridge, Mass.: MIT Press, 1997), 62–91; Philip Elmer-Dewitt, "First Nation in Cyberspace," *Time* (Dec. 6, 1993), 62 ("[A]s Internet pioneer John Gilmore puts it, 'The Net interprets censorship as damage and routes around it.'").

3. Lawrence Lessig, *Code and Other Laws of Cyberspace* (New York: Basic Books, 1998).

4. For examples, see Anupam Chander & Uyen Le, "Free Speech," *Iowa Law Review* 100 no. 2 (2015): 501–49; Eric Goldman, "Search Engine Bias and the Demise of Search Engine Utopianism," *Yale Journal of Law and Technology* 8 (2005): 188–200; Adi Kamdar, "EFF's Guide to CDA 230: The Most Important Law Protecting Online Speech" (Dec. 6, 2012), https://perma.cc/5Q9W-VCE8; Daphne Keller & Lee Rowland, "Private Companies, Public Squares," Panel at the Internet Summit (Sept. 14, 2017), https://perma.cc/Y8PY-5H6L; Daphne Keller, "Making Google the Censor," *New York Times* (June 12, 2017), https://perma.cc/ZP2J-867Z.

5. Manuel Castells, *The Information Age, vol. 1: The Rise of the Network Society* (Cambridge, Mass.: Blackwell, 1996), 14–18; see also Dan Schiller, *How to Think About Information* (Champaign: University of Illinois Press, 2007), 3–35.

6. Thomas Piketty, *Capital in the Twenty-First Century* (Cambridge, Mass.: Belknap Press, 2014); Schiller, *How to Think About Information*, 3–35.

7. Daniel Bell, *The Coming of Post-industrial Society: A Venture in Social Forecasting* (New York: Basic Books, 1973); Schiller, *How to Think About Information*, 3–35.

8. James R. Beniger, *The Control Revolution: Technological and Economic Origins of the Information Society* (Cambridge, Mass.: Harvard University Press, 1986).

9. See, for example, Frederic Gros, "Is There a Biopolitical Subject? Foucault and the Birth of Biopolitics," in *Biopower: Foucault and Beyond*, eds. Vernon W. Cisney & Nicolae Morar (Chicago: University of Chicago Press, 2016), 259–73; Shoshana Zuboff, "Big Other: Surveillance Capitalism and the Prospects of an Information Civilization," *Journal of Information Technology* 30 (2015): 75–89.

10. Klaus Schwab, *The Fourth Industrial Revolution* (New York: Crown Business, 2017).

11. Michel Foucault, *Security, Territory, Population: Lectures at the College de France 1977–78*, trans. Graham Burchell (New York: Picador, 2007), 108–10; Nikolas Rose, Pat O'Malley, & Mariana Valverde, "Governmentality," *Annual Review of Law and Social Science* 2006 no. 2 (2006): 83–104.

12. On liberal governmentality, see Michel Foucault, *The Birth of Biopolitics: Lectures at the College de France 1978—1979*, trans. Graham Burchell (New York: Picador, 2008), 65–69, 280–85; Peter Miller & Nikolas Rose, "Governing Economic Life," in *Foucault's New Domains*, eds. Mike Gane & Terry Johnson (New York: Routledge, 1993), 75–105, 78–81.

13. David Harvey, "Neoliberalism as Creative Destruction," *Annals of American Political and Social Science* 610 no. 1 (2007): 22–44, 22.

14. Wendy Brown, "Neo-liberalism and the End of Liberal Democracy," *Theory & Event* 7 no. 1 (2003): 15, http://muse.jhu.edu/journals/theory_&_event/; Thomas Lemke, "'The Birth of Bio-politics': Michel Foucault's Lecture at the College de France on Neo-liberal Governmentality," *Economy & Society* 30 no. 2 (2001): 190–207; Nikolas Rose & Peter Miller, "Political Power beyond the State: Problematics of Government," *British Journal of Sociology* 43 no. 2 (1992): 173–205, 198–201; see also Miller & Rose, "Governing Economic Life," 97–101; Philip Mirowski & Dieter Plehwe, eds., *The Road from Mont Pelerin: The Making of the Neoliberal Thought Collective* (Cambridge, Mass.: Harvard University Press, 2009).

15. Nicholas Gane, "The Governmentalities of Neoliberalism: Panopticism, Post-Panopticism, and Beyond," *The Sociological Review* 60 no. 4 (2012): 611–634, 625–29.

16. Simon Deakin et al., "Legal Institutionalism: Capitalism and the Constitutive Role of Law," *Journal of Comparative Economics* 45 no. 1 (2017): 188–200; David Singh Grewal, Amy Kapczynski, & Jedediah Purdy, "Law and Political Economy: Toward a Manifesto," *Law and Political Economy* (Nov. 16, 2017), https://perma.cc/NG8L-WDAB.

17. Karl Polanyi, *The Great Transformation: The Political and Economic Origins of Our Time* (Boston: Beacon Press, 1957).

18. Morton J. Horwitz, *The Transformation of American Law 1780–1860* (Cambridge, Mass.: Harvard University Press, 1977); Morton J. Horwitz, *The Transformation of American Law, 1870–1960* (Cambridge, Mass.: Harvard University Press, 1992).

19. For an overview, see David Singh Grewal & Jedediah Purdy, "Introduction: Law and Neoliberalism," *Law & Contemporary Problems* 77 no. 4 (2014): 1–23, and the symposium issue to which it pertains.

Part I

1. The literatures here are vast. On the politics and economics of enclosure and appropriation of informational resources, see James Boyle, *Shamans, Software, and Spleens: Law and the Construction of the Information Society* (Cambridge, Mass.: Harvard University Press, 1998); James Boyle, "The Second Enclosure Movement and the Construction of the Public Domain," *Law and Contemporary Problems* 66 nos. 1–2 (2008): 33–74; Madhavi Sunder, "IP³," *Stanford Law Review* 59 no. 2 (2006): 257–332. On the transformative potential of informational resources held as commons, see Yochai Benkler, *The Wealth of Networks: How Social Production Transforms Markets and Freedom* (New Haven, Conn.: Yale University Press, 2006); Brett M. Frischmann, *Infrastructure: The Social Value of Shared Resources* (New York: Oxford University Press, 2012); On the ways that intellectual property law and policy structure global dynamics of development and resource distribution, see Anupam Chander & Madhavi Sunder, "The Romance of the Public Domain," *California Law Review* 92 no. 5 (2004): 1331–73; Margaret Chon, "Intellectual Property and the Development Divide," *Cardozo Law Review* 27 no. 6 (2006): 2821–12. On the uses of code as a regulatory instrument, see Lawrence Lessig, *Code and Other Laws of Cyberspace* (New York: Basic Books, 1999); Joel R. Reidenberg, "Lex Informatica: The Formulation of Information Policy Rules through Technology," *Texas Law Review* 76 no. 3 (1998): 553–93.

2. Wesley Newcomb Hohfeld, "Some Fundamental Legal Conceptions as Applied in Judicial Reasoning," *Yale Law Journal* 23 no. 1 (1913): 16–59.
3. Pierre Schlag, "How to Do Things with Hohfeld," *Law and Contemporary Problems* 78 nos. 1–2 (2015): 185–234.

Chapter 1

1. Karl Polanyi, *The Great Transformation: The Political and Economic Origins of Our Time*. Boston: Beacon Press (1957).
2. Catherine L. Fisk, "Removing the 'Fuel of Interest' from the 'Fire of Genius': Law and the Employee-Inventor, 1830–1930," *University of Chicago Law Review* 65 no. 4 (1998): 1127–98; Catherine L. Fisk, "Working Knowledge: Trade Secrets, Restrictive Covenants in Employment, and the Rise of Corporate Intellectual Property, 1800–1920," *Hastings Law Journal* 52 no. 2 (2001): 441–535; Joshua L. Simmons, "Inventions Made for Hire," *New York University Journal of Intellectual Property and Entertainment Law* 2 no. 1 (2012): 1–50.
3. Catherine L. Fisk, "Authors at Work: The Origins of the Work-for-Hire Doctrine," *Yale Journal of Law and the Humanities* 15 no. 1 (2003): 1–70; Simmons, "Inventions Made for Hire."
4. Robert P. Merges, "One Hundred Years of Solicitude: Intellectual Property Law, 1900–2000," *California Law Review* 88 no. 6 (2000): 2187–240; P.J. Federico, "Commentary on the New Patent Act," *Journal of the Patent and Trademark Office Society* 75 no. 3 (1993): 161–231. By contrast, legislated expansions of patent rights in the nineteenth century primarily addressed narrower issues related to the scope and duration of individual patents. See Adam Mossoff, "Who Cares What Thomas Jefferson Thought About Patents? Reevaluating the Patent 'Privilege' in Historical Context," *Cornell Law Review* 92 no. 5 (2007): 953–1012.
5. Jessica Litman, *Digital Copyright* (Amherst, NY: Prometheus Press, 2001); Jessica Litman, "Copyright, Compromise, and Legislative History," *Oregon Law Review* 68 no. 2 (1987): 275–362.
6. James Boyle, *Shamans, Software, and Spleens: Law and the Construction of the Information Society* (Cambridge, MA: Harvard University Press, 1998); Oren Bracha, "The Ideology of Authorship Revisited," *Yale Law Journal* 118 no. 1 (2009): 186–271.
7. On the nineteenth-century American understanding of the purposes of patent and copyright protection, see B. Zorina Khan, *The Democratization of Invention: Patents and Copyrights in American Economic Development, 1790–1920* (New York: Cambridge University Press, 2005). For an exploration of the factors shaping patent law's understanding of social obligation during the Progressive Era, see Kali Murray, "Constitutional Patent Law: Principles and Institutions," *Nebraska Law Review* 93 no. 4 (2015): 901–49; on copyright and social obligation, see Twentieth Century Music Corp. v. Aiken, 422 U.S. 151, 156 (1975) ("The limited scope of the copyright holder's statutory monopoly, like the limited copyright duration required by the Constitution, reflects a balance of competing claims upon the public interest: Creative work is to be encouraged and rewarded, but private motivation must ultimately serve the cause of promoting broad public availability of literature, music and the other arts."). Early examples of the Chicago-style, incentives-based approach to intellectual property include Edmund Kitch, "The Nature and Function of the Patent System," *Journal of Law and Economics* 20 no. 2 (1977): 265–90; William M. Landes & Richard A. Posner, "An Economic Analysis of Copyright Law," *Journal of Legal Studies* 18 no. 2 (1989): 325–64. An influential contemporary articulation is William M. Landes & Richard A. Posner, *The Economic Structure of Intellectual Property Law* (Cambridge, Mass.: Harvard University Press, 2003). Today, even the harshest critics of broad intellectual property protection tend to be thoroughly steeped in the belief that the economic perspective is what matters most. See, for example, Mark A. Lemley, "Faith-Based Intellectual Property," *UCLA Law Review* 62 no. 5 (2015): 1328–47; Kal Raustiala & Christopher Sprigman, *The Knockoff Economy: How Imitation Sparks Innovation* (New York: Oxford University Press, 2012).

8. Compare "The Copyright Term Extension Act of 1995," Hearing Before the Senate Committee on the Judiciary, 104th Cong. 55–58 (1995) (statements of Bob Dylan, Don Henley, Carlos Santana, and Stephen Sondheim), and "Pre-1978 Distribution of Recordings Containing Musical Compositions; Copyright Term Extension; and Copyright Per Program Licenses," Hearing Before the Subcommittee on Courts and Intellectual Property of the House Committee on the Judiciary, 105th Cong. 27–29 (1997) (statement of Julius Epstein, screenwriter of "Casablanca"), with "The Role of Voluntary Agreements in the U.S. Intellectual Property System," Hearing Before the Subcommittee on Courts, Intellectual Property, and the Internet of the House Committee on the Judiciary, 113th Cong. 12–25 (2013) (statement of Cary Sherman, Chairman & CEO, Recording Industry Association of America), and "Music Licensing Under Title 17," Hearing Before the Subcommittee on Courts, Intellectual Property, and the Internet of the House Committee on the Judiciary, 113th Cong. (2014) (statement of David Israelite, President & CEO, National Music Publishers Association), http://perma.cc/DCK7-V3XE.

9. Golan v. Holder, 132 S. Ct. 873, 889 (2012) ("Full compliance with Berne, Congress had reason to believe, would expand the foreign markets available to U.S. authors and invigorate protection against piracy of U.S. works abroad, thereby benefitting copyright-intensive industries stateside and inducing greater investment in the creative process.").

10. Yochai Benkler, "Intellectual Property and the Organization of Information Production," *International Review of Law and Economics* 22 no. 1 (2002): 81–107; Gideon Parchomovsky & R. Polk Wagner, "Patent Portfolios," *University of Pennsylvania Law Review* 154 no. 1 (2005): 1–78.

11. The case that best encapsulates the older, more restrictive approach is the "Sam Spade" case: Warner Brothers Pictures, Inc. v. Columbia Broad. Sys., 216 F.2d 945 (9th Cir. 1954), *cert. denied*, 348 U.S. 971 (1955). Representative examples of the newer, lenient approach include Warner Brothers Entertainment v. X One X Productions, 644 F.3d 584 (8th Cir. 2011); Gaiman v. McFarlane, 360 F.3d 644 (7th Cir. 2004).

12. On enablement, see Dan L. Burk & Mark A. Lemley, "Is Patent Law Technology-Specific?," *Berkeley Technology Law Journal* 17 no. 4 (2000): 1155–206; Dan L. Burk, "Patent Silences," *Vanderbilt Law Review* 69 no. 6 (2016): 1603–30. On strategic disclosure, see Douglas Lichtman, Scott Baker, & Kate Kraus, "Strategic Disclosure in the Patent System," *Vanderbilt Law Review* 53 no. 6 (2000): 2175–218; Gideon Parchomovsky, "Publish or Perish," *Michigan Law Review* 98 no. 4 (2000): 926–52.

13. See, for example, Patrina Ozurumba, "Information Under-Load: Rethinking IP Valuation in the Context of U.S. Securities Regulation," *Journal of Law and Business Ethics* 19 no. 1 (2013): 89–104; Jerold L. Zimmerman, "The Role of Accounting in the 21st Century Firm," *Accounting and Business Research* 45 no. 4 (2015): 485–509; Charles Hodges & Lynn Fowler, "Tax Considerations of Acquiring Intellectual Property," *Journal of Taxation* (Oct. 2014): 157–63; Linda M. Beale, "Reining in Intellectual Property Tax Avoidance," *Tax Notes* (June 26, 2017): 1877–87; Ariel Glasner, "Making Something Out of 'Nothing': The Trend toward Securitizing Intellectual Property Assets and the Legal Obstacles That Remain," *Journal of Legal Technology Risk Management* 3 no. 2 (2008): 27–66.

14. Jennifer E. Rothman, "The Questionable Use of Custom in Intellectual Property," *Virginia Law Review* 93 no. 8 (2007): 1899–982; Daralyn J. Durie & Mark A. Lemley, "A Realistic Approach to the Obviousness of Inventions," *William and Mary Law Review* 50 no. 3 (2008): 989–1020; Lee Petherbridge, "On the Decline of the Doctrine of Equivalents," *Cardozo Law Review* 31 no. 4 (2010): 1371–406.

15. Daniel Crane, "Intellectual Liability," *Texas Law Review* 88 no. 2 (2009): 253–300; Mark A. Lemley, "Intellectual Property Rights and Standard-Setting Organizations," *California Law Review* 90 no. 6 (2002): 1889–980; Robert P. Merges, "Contracting into Liability Rules: Intellectual Property Rights and Collective Rights Organizations," *California Law Review* 94 no. 5 (1996): 1293–394.

16. Mark P. McKenna, "The Normative Foundations of Trademark Law," *Notre Dame Law Review* 82 no. 5 (2007): 1839–916.

17. On the rise of American mass manufacturing, see generally Vaclav Smil, *Made in the USA: The Rise and Retreat of American Manufacturing* (Cambridge, Mass: MIT Press, 2013).

18. Joseph Turow, *Breaking Up America: Advertisers and the New Media World* (Chicago: University of Chicago Press, 1997), 27–36.

19. Adam Arvidsson, "On the 'Pre-history of the Panoptic Sort': Mobility in Market Research," *Surveillance and Society* 1 no. 4 (2004): 456–74; Vance Packard, *The Hidden Persuaders* (New York: D. McKay, 1957).

20. For discussions of informational opacity in food and pharmaceutical labeling, see Jon Duke, Jeff Friedlin, & Patrick Ryan, "A Quantitative Analysis of Adverse Events and 'Overwarning' in Drug Labeling," *Archives of Internal Medicine* 171 no. 10 (2011): 945–46; Jane Kolodinsky, "Persistence of Health Labeling Asymmetry in the United States: Historical Perspectives and Twenty-First Century Realities," *Journal of Macromarketing* 32 no. 2 (2012): 193–207. On "Della," see Margaret Hartmann, "Dell Discovers Ladies Use Computers for More than Diet Tips," *Jezebel* (May 15, 2009), https://perma.cc/SX8V-UGK5.

21. Laurie Simon Bagwell & B. Douglas Bernheim, "Veblen Effects in a Theory of Conspicuous Consumption," *American Economic Review* 86 no. 3 (1996): 349–73; Mario Biagioli, Anupam Chander & Madhavi Sunder, "Brands R Us," in *The Luxury Economy and Intellectual Property: Critical Reflections*, eds. Haochen Sun, Barton Beebe, & Madhavi Sunder (New York: Oxford University Press, 2015), 77–92; Young Jee Han, Joseph C. Nunes, & Xavier Dreze, "Signaling Status with Luxury Goods: The Role of Brand Prominence," *Journal of Marketing* 74 no. 4 (2010): 15–30.

22. Douglas B. Holt, *How Brands Become Icons: The Principles of Cultural Branding* (Cambridge, Mass.: Harvard Business School Press, 2004); Luke McDonagh, "From Brand Performance to Consumer Performativity: Assessing European Trademark Law after the Rise of Anthropological Marketing," *Journal of Law and Society* 42 no. 4 (2015): 611–38; Rebecca Tushnet, "Gone in 60 Milliseconds: Trademark Law and Cognitive Science," *Texas Law Review* 86 no. 3 (2008): 507–68.

23. Ralph S. Brown, Jr., "Advertising and the Public Interest: Legal Protection of Trade Symbols," *Yale Law Journal* 57 no. 7 (1948): 1165–206.

24. Landes & Posner, *The Economic Structure of Intellectual Property Law*, 166–68; Mark A. Lemley & Stacey R. Dogan, "Trademarks and Consumer Search Costs on the Internet," *Houston Law Review* 41 no. 3 (2004): 777–838. Early accounts of the predominantly economic function of trademarks include William M. Landes & Richard A. Posner, "The Economics of Trademark Law," *Trademark Reporter* 78 no. 3 (1988): 267–306; see also Jack Hirshleifer, "Where Are We in the Theory of Information?," *American Economic Review Proceedings* 63 no. 2 (1973): 31–39; Phillip Nelson, "Advertising as Information," *Journal of Political Economy* 82 no. 4 (1974): 729–54.

25. Mark A. Lemley, "The Modern Lanham Act and the Death of Common Sense," *Yale Law Journal* 108 no. 7 (1999): 1687–716.

26. Beebe, "Intellectual Property and the Sumptuary Code," 851–55.

27. See, for example, Gabriela Salinas, *The International Brand Valuation Manual: A Complete Overview and Analysis of Brand Valuation Techniques, Methodologies, and Applications* (New York: John Wiley & Sons, 2011); Michael J. Freno, "Trademark Valuation: Preserving Brand Equity," *Trademark Reporter* 97 (2007): 1055–72.

28. Lemley, "The Modern Lanham Act and the Death of Common Sense"; Merges, "One Hundred Years of Solicitude."

29. Barton Beebe, "Intellectual Property Law and the Sumptuary Code," *Harvard Law Review* 123 no. 4 (2010): 809–89; see also Deven R. Desai, "From Trademarks to Brands," *Florida Law Review* 64 no. 4 (2012): 981–1044.

30. Steven Levy, "Secret of Googlenomics: Data-Fueled Recipe Brews Profitability," *Wired* (May 22, 2009), https://perma.cc/P6NE-V6LC.

31. Peter Lee & Madhavi Sunder, "The Law of Look and Feel," *Southern California Law Review* 90 no. 3 (2017): 529–92.

32. For the legal hybrids terminology and a prescient early treatment, see J.H. Reichman, "Legal Hybrids between the Patent and Copyright Paradigms," *Columbia Law Review* 94 no. 8 (1994): 2432–558.

33. For a sampling of perspectives on dilution, see Barton Beebe, "A Defense of the New Federal Trademark Antidilution Law," *Fordham Intellectual Property, Media & Entertainment Law Journal* 16 no. 4 (2006): 1143–74; Ronald A. Cass & Keith N. Hylton, *Laws of Creation: Property Rights in the World of Ideas* (Cambridge, Mass.: Harvard University Press, 2013), 140–43; Tushnet, "Gone in 60 Milliseconds."

34. Jessica Litman, "The DNS Wars: Trademarks and the Internet Domain Name System," *Journal of Small and Emerging Business Law* 4 no. 1 (2000): 149–66; Merges, "One Hundred Years of Solicitude."

35. U.S. Patent & Trademark Office, U.S. Patent Statistics Chart: Calendar Years 1963–2015, https://perma.cc/DE9K-PW8N (last visited Apr. 10, 2019).

36. Sarah Burstein, "Costly Designs," *Ohio State Law Journal* 77 no. 1 (2016): 107–58; Lee & Sunder, "The Law of Look and Feel."

37. James H.A. Pooley, Mark A. Lemley, & Peter J. Toren, "Understanding the Economic Espionage Act of 1996," *Texas Intellectual Property Law Journal* 5 no. 2 (1997): 177–230; James H.A. Pooley, "The Myth of the Trade Secret Troll: Why the Defend Trade Secrets Act Improves the Protection of Commercial Information," *George Mason Law Review* 23 no. 4 (2016): 1045–78.

38. For a summary and critique, see Orin S. Kerr, "Norms of Computer Trespass," *Columbia Law Review* 116 no. 4 (2016): 1143–84.

39. Robin Feldman, "Regulatory Property: The New IP," *Columbia Journal of Law and the Arts* 40 no. 1 (2016): 53–104.

40. Pamela Samuelson, "Intellectual Property and the Digital Economy: Why the Anti-circumvention Regulations Need to Be Revised," *Berkeley Technology Law Journal* 14 no. 2 (1999): 519–66.

41. For representative examples of innovation-based arguments, see Brief for Public Knowledge et al. as Amici Curiae supporting Petitioners, Samsung Electronics Co., LTD. v. Apple Inc., 136 S. Ct. 1453 (2016), 9–12, https://perma.cc/Q8QT-KZEX; Brief for Public Knowledge et al. as Amici Curiae supporting Petitioner, Star Athletica, LLC, v. Varsity Brands, Inc., 137 S. Ct. 1002 (2017), 22–33, https://perma.cc/Q6HW-BESJ. For representative examples of originalist arguments, see Brief for Intellectual Property Law Professors as Amici Curiae Supporting Petitioner, Dastar Corp. v. Twentieth Century Fox Film Corp., 539 U.S. 23 (2003), 3–7; Brief for 50 Intellectual Property Professors as Amici Curiae supporting Petitioners, Samsung Electronics Co., LTD. v. Apple Inc., 136 S. Ct. 1453 (2016), 2–3, https://perma.cc/7B6A-ZNFB.

42. Though not impossible. See, for example, Mariana Mazzucato, *The Entrepreneurial State: Debunking Public vs. Private Sector Myths* (New York: Anthem, 2013); Eric A. Von Hippel, *Democratizing Innovation* (Cambridge, Mass.: MIT Press, 2005).

43. The European Union enacted database protection, but there is widespread consensus that it did little or nothing to incentivize development of new information services. Mark Davison, "Database Protection: Lessons from Europe, Congress, and WIPO," *Case Western Reserve Law Review* 57 no. 4 (2016): 829–54; P. Bernt Hugenholtz, "Something Completely Different: Europe's Sui Generis Database Right," in *The Internet and the Emerging Importance of New Forms of Intellectual Property*, eds. Susy Frankel & Daniel Gervais (The Hague: Kluwer Law International, 2016), 205–22.

44. On the rise of finance capital and the ensuing financialization of global political economy, see Giovanni Arrighi, *The Long Twentieth Century: Money, Power, and the Origins of Our Times* (New York: Verso, 1994); Greta Krippner, *Capitalizing on Crisis: The Political Origins of the Rise of Finance* (Cambridge, Mass.: Harvard University Press, 2012); Natascha Van der Zwan, "Making Sense of Financialization," *Socio-Economic Review* 12 (2014): 99–129.

45. Joseph Santos, "A History of Futures Trading in the United States," *EH.Net Encyclopedia* (Mar. 16, 2008), https://perma.cc/L866-P5H2; K. Geert Rouwenhorst, "The Origins of Mutual Funds," in *The Origins of Value: The Financial Innovations That Created Modern Capital Markets*, eds. William N. Goetzmann & K. Geert Rouwenhorst (New York: Oxford University Press, 2005), 249–70.

46. Matthew P. Fink, *The Rise of Mutual Funds: An Insider's View* (New York: Oxford University Press, 2008); Jerry W. Markham, "Federal Regulation of Margin in the Commodity Futures Industry—History and Theory," *Temple Law Review* 64 no. 1 (1991): 59–143.

47. Bank for International Settlements, OTC Derivatives Settlements at End—December 2016 (May 2017), https://perma.cc/FFS7-9BE6; Securities Industries and Financial Markets Association, SIFMA 2017 Fact Book, 61–17, https://perma.cc/L3Z3-2RXM; Zoltan Pozsar et al., "Shadow Banking," Federal Reserve Bank of New York Staff Report no. 458, revised Feb. 2012, https://perma.cc/2KGV-3Z52.

48. On dual-class ownership, see Jill E. Fisch & Stephen Davidoff Solomon, "The Problem of Sunsets," *Boston University Law Review* 99 (forthcoming, 2019); Ronald J. Gilson, "Evaluating Dual Class Common Stock: The Relevance of Substitutes," *Virginia Law Review* 73 no. 5 (1987): 807–44. On venture capital arrangements and their beneficiaries, see Bernard S. Black & Ronald J. Gilson, "Venture Capital and the Structure of Capital Markets: Banks versus Stock Markets," *Journal of Financial Economics* 47 no. 3 (1998): 243–77; Ronald J. Gilson & David M. Schizer, "Understanding Venture Capital Structure: A Tax Explanation for Convertible Preferred Stock," *Harvard Law Review* 116 no. 3 (2003): 874–916; John F. Coyle & Gregg D. Polsky, "Acqui-Hiring," *Duke Law Journal* 63 no. 2 (2013): 281–346. On the roles played by hedge funds, see Marcel Kahan & Edward B. Rock, "Hedge Funds in Corporate Governance and Control," *University of Pennsylvania Law Review* 155 no. 5 (2007): 1021–93; Henry T.C. Hu & Bernard S. Black, "Hedge Funds, Insiders, and the DeCoupling of Economic and Voting Ownership: Empty Voting and Hidden (Morphable) Ownership," *Journal of Corporate Finance* 13 nos. 2–3 (2007): 343–67.

49. David Weidner, "The Secret Stock Market," *MarketWatch* (May 14, 2007), https://perma.cc/5734-AAG9; Chris Brummer, "Disruptive Technology and Securities Regulation," *Fordham Law Review* 84 no. 3 (2015): 977–1052; see also Iris H.-Y. Chiu, "Fintech and Disruptive Business Models in Financial Products, Intermediation and Markets: Policy Implications for Financial Regulators," *Journal of Technology Law and Policy* 21 no. 1 (2016): 55–112.

50. Lisa Servon, *The Unbanking of America: How the Middle Class Survives* (New York: Houghton Mifflin Harcourt, 2017), 29–25, 63–102; Anne Fleming, *City of Debtors: The History of Fringe Finance before the Subprime Crisis* (Cambridge, Mass.: Harvard University Press, 2018).

51. U.S. Federal Reserve System, The Federal Reserve Payments Study 2016 (Dec. 2016), https://perma.cc/Y37K-RFWZ; U.S. Federal Reserve System, The Federal Reserve Payments Study—2017 Annual Supplement (Jan. 25, 2018), https://perma.cc/Y8XQ-RMTA; Servon, *The Unbanking of America*, 32–33; Adam J. Levitin, "Pandora's Digital Box: The Promise and Perils of Digital Wallets," *University of Pennsylvania Law Review* 166 no. 2 (2018): 305–76.

52. Mark Anderson, "Digital Payments Could Help Billions of People without Access to Banks," *Guardian* (Aug. 28, 2014), https://perma.cc/T2TF-3HH5; Jerri-Lynn Scofield, "The Global War on Cash—India's Demonetization Debacle," *Naked Capitalism* (Dec. 31, 2016), https://perma.cc/WQ6M-XAML.

53. For good summaries, see Primavera Di Filippi & Benjamin Loveluck, "The Invisible Politics of Bitcoin: Governance Crisis of a Decentralized Infrastructure," *Internet Policy Review* 5 no.

3 (2016), doi: 10.14763/2016.3.427.; Alan Feuer, "The Bitcoin Ideology," *New York Times* (Dec. 14, 2014), https://perma.cc/F9X7-TFMT.

54. Cade Metz, "Wall Street Officially Opens Its Arms to Bitcoin Invaders," *Wired* (Sept. 11, 2015), https://perma.cc/R83Y-YP2K; see also Robert C. Hockett & Saule T. Omarova, "The Finance Franchise," *Cornell Law Review* 102 no. 5 (2017): 1143, 1201–11.

55. On finance as innovation, see Josh Lerner & Peter Tufano, "The Consequences of Financial Innovation: A Counterfactual Research Agenda," *Annual Review of Financial Economics* 3 (2011): 41–85. On neoliberalization and the dismantling of financial regulation, see Krippner, *Capitalizing on Crisis*. On the failure of efforts to minimize systemic risk, see Nassim Nicholas Taleb, *The Black Swan: The Impact of the Highly Improbable*, 2nd ed. (New York: Random House, 2010). We will return to the problem of systemic threat in Chapter 6.

56. Harry Braverman, *Labor and Monopoly Capital* (New York: Monthly Review Press, 1974), 125.

57. Braverman, *Labor and Monopoly Capital*, 251–69; Sanford Jacoby, *Employing Bureaucracy: Managers, Unions, and the Transformation of Work in the 20th Century*, rev. ed. (Mahwah, NJ: Lawrence Erlbaum, 2004).

58. James R. Beniger, *The Control Revolution: Technological and Economic Origins of the Information Society* (Cambridge, MA: Harvard University Press, 1986).

59. Guy Standing, *The Precariat: The New Dangerous Class* (New York: Bloomsbury, 2011); Arne L Kalleberg, "Precarious Work, Insecure Workers: Employment Relations in Transition," *American Sociological Review* 74 no. 2 (2009): 1–22. On the shifts toward just-in-time production, flexible accumulation, and correspondingly flexible corporate and labor force structures, see David Harvey, *The Condition of Postmodernity* (Malden, Mass.: Blackwell, 1990), 147–59.

60. For different perspectives on this issue, see Orly Lobel, "The Law of the Platform," *Minnesota Law Review* 101 no. 1 (2016): 96–101; Trebor Scholz, *Uberworked and Underpaid: How Workers Are Disrupting the Digital Economy* (New York: Polity Press, 2017).

61. Polanyi, *The Great Transformation*, 73.

62. See, for example, Jodi Kantor, "Working Anything but 9 to 5," *New York Times* (Aug. 13, 2014), https://perma.cc/AVF7-YUAL; Rebecca Greenfield, "For Seasonal Workers, Amazon's Grueling Working Conditions Are Only Temporary," *Atlantic* (Dec. 20, 2011), https://perma.cc/8RQL-C2R8; Joann Weiner, "The Hidden Costs of Being an Uber Driver," *Washington Post* (Feb. 20, 2015), https://perma.cc/56AV-YJQH; Molly McHugh, "Uber and Lyft Drivers Work Dangerous Jobs—But They're on Their Own," *Wired* (Mar. 10, 2016), https://perma.cc/89R4-E9QR; Natasha Singer, "In the Sharing Economy, Workers Find Both Freedom and Uncertainty," *New York Times* (Aug. 16, 2014), https://perma.cc/TX6T-XXFA.

63. Andrew Norman Wilson, *Workers Leaving the Googleplex, 2009–2011*, https://perma.cc/7A66-73FH.

64. Bryan Walsh, "The Surprisingly Large Energy Footprint of the Digital Economy," *Time* (Aug. 14, 2013), https://perma.cc/H9S7-3UVW.

65. For different perspectives on this issue, see Scholz, *Uberworked and Underpaid*; Juliet Schor, "Debating the Sharing Economy," *Great Transition Initiative* (Oct. 2014), https://perma.cc/SF3B-SDZY; Arun Sundararajan, *The Sharing Economy: The End of Employment and the Rise of Crowd-Based Capitalism* (Cambridge, Mass.: MIT Press, 2016).

66. Orly Lobel, "The New Cognitive Property: Human Capital Law and the Reach of Intellectual Property," *Texas Law Review* 93 no. 4 (2015): 789–854.

67. For a detailed exploration of one such contract, see Taffy Brodesser-Akner, "Kesha, Interrupted," *New York Times Magazine* (Oct. 26, 2016), https://perma.cc/Y9QU-L332. On precarious creative work, see Sara Horowitz et al., "The Rise of the Freelance Class: A New Constituency of Workers Building a Social Safety Net," Freelancers Union 2005 Report, https://perma.cc/C8H7-M5SP; David Hesmondhalgh & Sarah Baker, "'A Very Complicated Version of Freedom': Conditions and Experiences of Creative Labour in Three Cultural Industries," *Poetics* 38 no. 1 (2010): 4–20; Kate Oakley, "Good Work? Rethinking Cultural Entrepreneurship," in *Handbook of Management and Creativity*, eds. Chris Bilton &

Stephen Cummings (Northampton, Mass.: Edward Elgar, 2014), 145–59; Henrik Ornebring, "Journalists Thinking about Precarity: Making Sense of the New Normal," *#ISOJ* 8 no. 1 (2018): 109–26.

68. Thought-provoking explorations of these issues, include Charlotte S. Alexander S. & Elizabeth Tippett, "The Hacking of Employment Law," *Missouri Law Review* 82 no. 4 (2017): 973–1022; Scholz, *Uberworked and Underpaid*; Kate Andrias, "The New Labor Law," *Yale Law Journal* 126 no. 1 (2016): 2–100.

69. Mark Graham, Isis Hjorth, & Vili Ledonvirta, "Digital Labor and Development: Impacts of Global Digital Labor Platforms and the Gig Economy on Worker Livelihoods," *Transfer* 23 no. 2 (2017): 135–62; Todd C. Frankel, "The Cobalt Pipeline," *Washington Post* (Sept. 30, 2016), https://perma.cc/Q9RU-N6QA; Geoffrey A. Fowler, "How Was Your Smartphone Made? Nobody Really Knows," *Wall Street Journal* (July 8, 2016), https://perma.cc/AAN3-GLN6.

70. Valerio De Stefano, "The Rise of the 'Just-in-Time' Workforce: On-Demand Work, Crowdwork, and Labor Protection in the 'Gig-Economy,'" *Comparative Labor Law and Policy Journal* 37 no. 3 (2016): 471–504.

71. Martin Kenney & John Zysman, "The Rise of the Platform Economy," *Issues in Science and Technology* 32 no. 3 (2016): 61.

72. Adam J. Levitin & Susan M. Wachter, "The Public Option in Housing Finance," *U.C. Davis Law Review* 46 no. 4 (2013): 1111–74; Georgette Chapman Phillips, "An Urban Slice of Apple Pie: Rethinking Home Ownership in U.S. Cities," *Notre Dame Journal of Law, Ethics and Public Policy* 24 no. 1 (2010): 187–218.

73. Adam J. Levitin, "The Paper Chase: Securitization, Foreclosure, and the Uncertainty of Mortgage Title," *Duke Law Journal* 63 no. 3 (2013): 637–734, 671–76; Adam J. Levitin & Susan M. Wachter, "Explaining the Housing Bubble," *Georgetown Law Journal* 100 no. 4 (2012): 1177–258, 1233–44. On the roles that consumer data and credit scores played in that process, see Martha Poon, "From New Deal Institutions to Capital Markets: Commercial Consumer Risk Scores and the Making of Subprime Mortgage Finance," *Accounting, Organizations, and Society* 34 no. 5 (2009): 654–74.

74. Levitin & Wachter, "Explaining the Housing Bubble," 1228–52.

75. On the conceptual and institutional history of negotiability, see Morton J. Horwitz, *The Transformation of American Law 1780–1860* (Cambridge, Mass.: Harvard University Press, 1977), 212–26; Kurt Eggert, "Held Up in Due Course: Codification and the Victory of Form over Intent in Negotiable Instrument Law," *Creighton Law Review* 35 no. 2 (2002): 363–432; James Steven Rogers, *The End of Negotiable Instruments: Bringing Payment Systems Law out of the Past* (New York: Oxford University Press, 2011).

76. Christopher L. Peterson, "Two Faces: Demystifying the Mortgage Electronic Registration System's Land Title Theory," *William and Mary Law Review* 53 no. 1 (2011): 111–61, 114–121.

77. Levitin, "The Paper Chase," 680–83; Petersen, "Two Faces," 121–30; Michael Powell & Gretchen Morgenson, "MERS? It May Have Swallowed Your Loan," *New York Times* (Mar. 5, 2011), https://perma.cc/A2UC-FYCK.

78. For a trenchant analysis, see Jean Braucher, "Humpty Dumpty and the Foreclosure Crisis: Lessons from the Lackluster First Year of the Home Affordable Modification Program (HAMP)," *Arizona Law Review* 52 no. 3 (2010): 727–88.

79. For an overview of the post-crisis reforms, see David S. Huntington, "Summary of Dodd-Frank Financial Regulation Legislation," Harvard Law School Forum on Corporate Governance and Financial Regulation (July 7, 2010), https://perma.cc/9QKZ-B7TP.

80. See, for example, Kurt Eggert, "Not Dead Yet: The Surprising Survival of Negotiability," *Arkansas Law Review* 66 no. 1 (2013): 145–84.

81. See, for example, Eggert, "Not Dead Yet"; Levitin, "The Paper Chase"; Ronald J. Mann, "Searching for Negotiability in Payment and Credit Systems." *UCLA Law Review* 44 no. 4 (1997): 951–1007; Dale Whitman, "How Negotiability Has Fouled Up the Secondary Mortgage Market, and What to Do about It." *Pepperdine Law Review* 37 no. 2 (2010): 737–70.

82. Boris Emmet & John E. Jueck, *Catalogues and Counters: A History of Sears, Roebuck and Company* (Chicago: University of Chicago Press, 1950), 59–99, 100–13.

83. Hugh Malcolm Beville, Jr., *Audience Ratings: Radio, Television, Cable*, rev. ed. (Hillsdale, NJ: Lawrence Erlsbaum, 1988), 34–38, 70–75; Turow, *Breaking Up America*, 24–32.

84. Dan Bouk, "The History and Political Economy of Personal Data over the Last Two Centuries in Three Acts," *Osiris* 32 no. 1 (2017): 8–11; see Emmet & Jueck, *Catalogues and Counters*, 39–40.

85. Bouk, "The History and Political Economy of Personal Data over the Last Two Centuries in Three Acts," 12–16.

86. Ing Ang, *Desperately Seeking the Audience* (New York: Routledge, 1991), 53–57; Arvidsson, "On the 'Pre-history of the Panoptic Sort'. As this example illustrates, legibility rubrics incorporate both implicit epistemologies and associated action strategies. Legibility (of some sort) is a vital component of effective governance, but legibility rubrics also can do violence to complex and interdependent social processes and reify power imbalances. A thought-provoking exploration of these issues is James C. Scott, *Seeing Like a State: How Certain Schemes for Improving the Human Condition Have Failed* (New Haven, Conn.: Yale University Press, 1998).

87. Emmet & Jueck, *Catalogues and Counters*, 117–19, 150–68.

88. Ang, *Desperately Seeking the Audience*, 68–77.

89. Turow, *Breaking Up America*, 27–36.

90. Bouk, "The History and Political Economy of Personal Data over the Last Two Centuries in Three Acts," 17–20; see also Arvidsson, "On the 'Pre-history of the Panoptic Sort.'"

91. Albert-Laszlo Barabasi, *Linked: The New Science of Networks* (Cambridge, Mass.: Perseus, 2002).

92. On network externalities, see Michael L. Katz & Carl Shapiro, "Systems Competition and Network Effects," *Journal of Economic Perspectives* 8 no. 2 (1994): 93–115.

93. On the varied nature and provision of infrastructure, see Brett M. Frischmann, *Infrastructure: The Social Value of Shared Resources* (New York: Oxford University Press, 2012), 61–114.

94. On digital communications networks and economic organization, see Laurel Smith-Doerr & Walter W. Powell, "Networks and Economic Life," in *The Handbook of Economic Sociology*, eds. Neil J. Smelser & Richard Swedberg, 2d ed. (Princeton, N.J.: Princeton University Press, 2005), 379–401. On political economy, see Manuel Castells, *The Information Age, vol. 1: The Rise of the Network Society* (Cambridge, Mass.: Blackwell, 1996); Manuel Castells, *Communication Power* (New York, Oxford University Press, 2009). On human geography, see , Saskia Sassen, ed., *Global Networks, Linked Cities* (New York: Routledge, 2002). On social interaction, see Jose Van Dijck, *The Culture of Connectivity: A Critical History of Social Media* (New York: Oxford University Press, 2013).

95. See, for example, Fisch & Solomon, "The Problem of Sunsets"; Thomas Hellman & Manju Puri, "Venture Capital and the Professionalization of Start-Up Firms: Empirical Evidence," *Journal of Finance* 57 no. 1 (2002): 169–97.

96. Jean-Christophe Plantin, Carl Lagoze, Paul N. Edwards, & Christian Sandvig, "Infrastructure Studies Meet Platform Studies in the Age of Google and Facebook," *New Media and Society* (2016), doi: https://doi.org/10.1177/1461444816661553. 5–9.

97. Tarleton Gillespie, "The Politics of 'Platforms,'" *New Media and Society* 12 no. 3 (2012): 347–64, 358–59.

98. See, for example, Alexis C. Madrigal, "Silicon Valley's Big Three vs. Detroit's Golden-Age Big Three," *The Atlantic* (May 24, 2017), https://perma.cc/D3VR-2E4F. The dominant five platform firms—Alphabet (Google), Amazon, Apple, Facebook, and Microsoft—have a combined market capitalization that as of this writing exceeds $3.5 trillion. Google and Facebook together command approximately 20 percent of global advertising revenue, 65 percent of digital advertising revenue, and 85 percent of every new dollar spent on advertising. Lucy Handley, "Google and Facebook Take 20 Percent of Total Global Ad Spend, Top List of World's Largest Media Owners," *CNBC* (May 2, 2017), https://perma.cc/9MJU-3FEH;

Matthew Ingram, "How Google and Facebook Have Taken Over the Digital Ad Industry," *Fortune* (Jan. 4, 2017), https://perma.cc/S3LL-QZ9R; Peter Kafka, "Google and Facebook Are Booming. Is the Rest of the Digital Ad Business Sinking?," *Recode* (Nov. 2, 2016), https://perma.cc/CNN6-DK37.

99. On the rich-get-richer principle, see Barabasi, *Linked*, 79–92.

100. For additional discussion of this issue and citations, see Chapter 6, pp. 174–77.

101. Karla Lant, "Everything You Need to Know about Amazon Featured Merchant Status," *Informed.Co.* (July 7, 2015), https://perma.cc/P9KG-ZQ3K; Chuck Topinka, "How Exactly Does Google AdWords Work?," *Forbes* (Aug. 15, 2014), https://perma.cc/WD3U-TAS7.

102. Ariel Ezrachi & Maurice Stucke, *Virtual Competition: The Promise and Perils of the Algorithm-Driven Economy* (Cambridge, Mass.: Harvard University Press, 2016), 131–46; Berten Martens, "An Economic Policy Perspective on Online Platforms," Institute for Prospective Technological Studies Digital Economy Working Paper 2016/05, JRC 101501, 2016, https://perma.cc/Y7M6-B72P; Julia Angwin & Surya Mattu, "Amazon Says It Puts Customers First. But Its Pricing Algorithm Doesn't," *ProPublica* (Sept. 20, 2016), https://perma.cc/RMU2-LCHY; Benjamin Edelman, "Hard-Coding Bias in Google 'Algorithmic' Search Results," *Ben Edelman* (Nov. 15, 2010), https://perma.cc/CV7T-KWQE; Julia Greenberg, "Google Will Now Favor Pages That Use Its Fast-Loading Tech," *Wired* (Feb. 24, 2016), https://perma.cc/H6B4-WW6F.

103. Ezrachi & Stucke, *Virtual Competition*, 147–90; Nick Srnicek, *Platform Capitalism* (Malden, Mass.: Polity Press, 2017).

104. Jonas Andersson Schwarz, "Platform Logic: An Interdisciplinary Approach to the Platform Economy," *Policy & Internet* 9 no. 4 (2017): 374–94.

105. Margaret Jane Radin, *Boilerplate: The Fine Print, Vanishing Rights, and the Rule of Law* (Princeton, N.J.: Princeton University Press, 2013), 19–51; see also Nancy S. Kim, *Wrap Contracts: Foundations and Ramifications* (New York: Oxford University Press, 2013), 44–52.

106. Julie E. Cohen, "Property as Institutions for Resources: Lessons from and for IP," *Texas Law Review* 94 no. 1 (2015): 1–57, 11–15; Thomas W. Merrill & Henry E. Smith, "The Property/Contract Interface," *Columbia Law Review* 101 no. 4 (2001): 773–852.

107. On the performativity of legal entitlements more generally, see Nicholas Blomley, "Disentangling Law: The Practice of Bracketing," *Annual Review of Law and Social Science* (Nov. 2014), 133–48; Nicholas Blomley, "Performing Property: Making the World," *Canadian Journal of Law and Jurisprudence* 26 no. 1 (2013): 23–48.

108. On Facebook, see Anne Helmond, "The Platformization of the Web: Making Web Data Platform Ready," *Social Media and Society* (2015), doi: 10.1177/2056305115603080. On Google, see Benjamin Edelman, "Does Google Leverage Market Power through Tying and Bundling?," *Journal of Competition Law and Economics* 11 no. 2 (2015): 365, 389–91; Christian Sandvig, "Seeing the Sort: The Aesthetic and Industrial Defense of 'The Algorithm,'" *Journal of the New Media Caucus* 10 (2014), https://perma.cc/84U2-9RJD. On Amazon, see Valentina Palladino, "Amazon Opens Up Alexa Voice and Text Tech for Developers to Make New Chatbots," *Ars Technica* (Apr. 20, 2017), https://perma.cc/HDQ6-FTXE.

109. Google has led the fight—as of this writing, unsuccessfully—against compilation-based copyright protection for application programming interfaces. See Oracle Am., Inc. v. Google, Inc., 872 F. Supp. 2d 974 (N.D. Cal. 2012), *rev'd* 750 F.3d 1339 (Fed. Cir. 2014), *cert. denied* 135 S. Ct. 2887 (2014), *on remand*, 2016 WL 3181206 (N.D. Cal., June 8, 2016) and 2016 WL 5393938 (N.D. Cal., Sept. 27, 2016), *rev'd and remanded*, 886 F.3d 1179 (Fed. Cir. 2018).

110. See, for example, Jorge L. Contreras, "Technical Standards, Standards-Setting Organizations and Intellectual Property: A Survey of the Literature (with an Emphasis on Empirical Approaches)," in *Research Handbooks on the Economics of Intellectual Property Law, vol. 2—Analytical Methods*, eds. Peter S. Menell & David Schwartz (Northampton, Mass.: Edward Elgar, 2019), 185–235; David H. Hsu & Rosemarie H. Ziedonis, "Resources as Dual Sources of Advantage: Implications for Valuing Entrepreneurial-Firm Patents," *Strategic Management*

Journal 34 (2013): 761–81; Yongwook Paik & Feng Zhu, "The Impact of Patent Wars on Firm Strategy: Evidence from the Global Smartphone Industry," *Organization Science* 27 no. 6 (2016): 1397–416.

111. Jacob S. Sherkow, "Protecting Products versus Platforms," *Nature Biotechnology* 34 no. 5 (2016): 462–65.

Chapter 2

1. See Jessica Litman, "The Public Domain," *Emory Law Journal* 39 no. 4 (1990): 965–1023; Anupam Chander & Madhavi Sunder, "The Romance of the Public Domain," *California Law Review* 92 no. 5 (2004): 1331–73.

2. Within the U.S. legal system, the definitive treatment of these questions is Johnson v. M'Intosh, 21 U.S. 543 (1823).

3. See David Feller, *The Public Lands in Jacksonian Politics* (Madison: University of Wisconsin Press, 1984); Paul W. Gates, *The Jeffersonian Dream: Studies in the History of American Land Policy and Development* (Albuquerque: University of New Mexico Press, 1996).

4. John Locke, *Second Treatise of Government*, ed. C.B. Macpherson (Indianapolis: Hackett, 1980), 29.

5. Chander & Sunder, "The Romance of the Public Domain."

6. "Welcome to the People Connect Family of Products," Intelius, https://perma.cc/H5EK-4HZD (last visited June 24, 2018); "Get Data on 80% of Your Customers," Towerdata, https://perma.cc/9JTC-S2WS (last visited June 24, 2018); "Powering the Global Real Estate Economy," CoreLogic, https://perma.cc/K2X7-8YGD (last visited June 24, 2018); "The Only Universal Threat Intelligence Solution," Recorded Future, https://perma.cc/5YXW-J2RB (last visited June 24, 2018).

7. Hearing Before the Senate Committee on Commerce, Science, and Transportation, "What Information Do Data Brokers Have on Consumers, and How Do They Use It?," 113 Cong., 1st Sess. (Dec. 18, 2013) (statement of Tony Hadley, Senior Vice President of Government Affairs and Public Policy, Experian).

8. Hal R. Varian, "Beyond Big Data," *Business Economics* 49 no. 1 (2014): 27–31, 29.

9. U.S. Senate Committee on Commerce, Science, and Transportation, Office of Oversight and Investigations Majority Staff, "A Review of the Data Broker Industry: Collection, Use, and Sale of Consumer Data for Marketing Purposes" (Dec. 18, 2013), https://perma.cc/SEC4-GEGB. Other useful overviews of the data broker industry include Upturn, "Data Brokers in an Open Society" (Nov. 2016), https://perma.cc/AL2X-SUEM; U.S. Federal Trade Commission, "Data Brokers: A Call for Transparency and Accountability" (May 2014), https://perma.cc/K6FK-TJGA.

10. On the new legislation and the abuses that had prompted it, see Robert M. McNamara, Jr., "The Fair Credit Reporting Act: A Legislative Overview," *Journal of Public Law* 22 no. 1 (1973): 67–101.

11. See, for example, Hearings before Subcommittee on Consumer Affairs of the House Comm. on Banking and Currency on H.R. 16340, 91st Cong., 2d Sess. 108 (1970) (testimony of John L. Spafford, President, Associated Credit Bureaus Inc.). A useful summary of the legislative history on this point is National Consumer Law Center, *Fair Credit Reporting Act* 3rd ed., § 1.4.3 (Boston: National Consumer Law Center, 1994).

12. Fair Credit Reporting Act, 15 U.S.C. § 1681a(d)(1), (f) (2018).

13. Pauline T. Kim & Erik A. Hanson, "People Analytics and the Regulation of Information under the Fair Credit Reporting Act," *St. Louis University Law Journal* 61 no. 1 (2016): 17–34.

14. Oscar H. Gandy Jr., *The Panoptic Sort: A Political Economy of Personal Information* (Boulder, Colo: Westview, 1993); see also Robert D. Manning, *Credit Card Nation: The Consequences of America's Addiction to Credit* (New York: Basic Books, 2000), 106–24.

15. For a good explanation, see David M. Kristol, "HTTP Cookies: Standards, Privacy, and Politics," *ACM Transactions on Internet Technology* 1 no. 2 (2001): 152–56.

16. U.S. Patent 5,774,670, "Persistent Client State in a Hypertext Transfer Protocol Based Client-Server System"; Kristol, "HTTP Cookies," 159.

17. Tim Jackson, "This Bug in Your PC Is a Smart Cookie," *Financial Times* (Feb. 12, 1996), 15; Lee Gomes, "Web 'Cookies' May Be Spying on You," *San Jose Mercury News* (Feb. 13, 1996), 1C.

18. U.S. Federal Trade Comm'n, Public Workshop on Consumer Privacy in the Global Information Infrastructure, June 4–5, 1996, https://perma.cc/FSL4-SB7J.

19. Richard M. Smith, "The Web Bug FAQ" (Nov. 11, 1999), https://perma.cc/5HVY-FW6E.

20. Kristol, "HTTP Cookies."

21. On the evolution of massively multiplayer and social gaming, see Simon Egenfeldt-Nielsen, Jonas Heide Smith, & Susana Pajares Tosca, *Understanding Video Games: The Essential Introduction*, 3rd ed. (New York: Routledge, 2016), 108–13; Lauren Indvik, "The Fascinating History of Online Role-Playing Games," *Mashable*, Nov. 14, 2012, https://perma.cc/F68U-NHSN; Riad Chikhani, "The History of Gaming: An Evolving Community," *Tech Crunch* (Oct. 31, 2015), https://perma.cc/GRK3-SL7Y.

22. Rebecca Buckman, "Investors to Web Start-Ups: Where's the Advertising?," *Wall Street Journal* (Aug. 21, 2007), archived at CommercialAlert.org, https://perma.cc/V4WG-RMMU; see also Rebecca Greenfield, "2012: The Year Facebook Finally Tried to Make Some Money," *The Atlantic* (Dec. 14, 2012), http://perma.cc/DS6B-U7H9.

23. Steven Levy, *In the Plex: How Google Thinks, Works, and Shapes Our Lives* (New York: Simon & Schuster, 2011), 87–120; Shoshana Zuboff, *The Age of Surveillance Capitalism: The Fight for a Human Future at the New Frontier of Power* (New York: Polity, 2019), 71–85.

24. David Kirkpatrick, *The Facebook Effect: The Inside Story of the Company That Is Connecting the World* (New York: Simon & Schuster, 2010), 218–63.

25. Leanne Roderick, "Discipline and Power in the Digital Age: The Case of the U.S. Consumer Data Broker Industry," *Critical Sociology* 40 no. 5 (2014): 729–46; Chris Jay Hoofnagle, "Big Brother's Little Helpers: How ChoicePoint and Other Commercial Data Brokers Collect and Package Your Data for Law Enforcement," *North Carolina Journal of International Law and Commercial Regulation* 29 no. 4 (2004): 595–638.

26. "List of Mergers and Acquisitions by Alphabet," Wikipedia, https://perma.cc/8TKN-F3B8 (last visited Dec. 13, 2018); "List of Mergers and Acquisitions by Facebook," Wikipedia, https://perma.cc/YR76-RNDS (last visited Dec. 13, 2018).

27. McKinsey Global Institute, "Big Data: The Next Frontier for Innovation, Competition, and Productivity" (May 2011), https://perma.cc/C8X8-Q3SX; Jeff Kelly, "Big Data: Hadoop, Business Analytics and Beyond," Wikibon, Feb. 5, 2014, https://perma.cc/8U2W-RWAV.

28. See, for example, Hearing Before the Senate Committee on Commerce, Science & Transportation, "Spyware," 109th Cong., 1st Sess. (May 11, 2005) (statement of Trevor Hughes, Executive Director, Network Advertising Initiative); Hearing Before the House Committee on Energy and Commerce, "Combating Spyware: H.R. 29, the SPY Act," H.R. No. 109-10, 109th Cong., 1st Sess. (Jan. 26, 2005), 17–14 (statement of Ira Rubinstein, Associate General Counsel, Microsoft Corporation).

29. Sarah Jeong, "You Can't Escape Data Surveillance in America," *The Atlantic* (Apr. 29, 2016), https://perma.cc/Q4BM-CL98; Astra Taylor & Jathan Sadowski, "How Companies Turn Your Facebook Activity Into a Credit Score," *The Nation* (May 27, 2015), https://perma.cc/2RF9-J55W; Opinion, Julie Brill, "Demanding Transparency from Data Brokers," *Washington Post* (Aug. 15, 2013), https://perma.cc/2X95-G4GM.

30. Chris Jay Hoofnagle, *Federal Trade Commission Privacy Law and Policy* (New York: Cambridge University Press, 2016), 145–92. As Hoofnagle explains, the FTC also learned over time to draw on elements from its false advertising toolkit in policing companies' disclosures and interface designs.

31. Steven Englehardt & Arvind Narayanan, "Online Tracking: A 1-Million-Site Measurement and Analysis," in *Proceedings of the 2016 ACM SIGSAC Conference on Computer and Communications Security* (New York: ACM, 2016), 1388–401; Jeremy Gillula & Seth Schoen, "An Umbrella in a Hurricane: Apple Limits Mobile Device Location Tracking," EFF Deeplinks (June 11, 2014), https://perma.cc/2M85-BY2T.

32. Brian X. Chen & Natasha Singer, "Verizon Wireless to Allow Complete Opt-Out of Mobile 'Supercookies,'" *New York Times Online* (Jan. 30, 2015), https://perma.cc/XYR5-6DVC; Jon Brodkin, "AT&T Buying Company That Delivers Targeted Ads Based on Your Web Browsing," *Ars Technica* (June 25, 2018), https://perma.cc/AEF3-555C; Karl Bode, "Another Day, Another Massive Cellular Location Data Privacy Scandal We'll Probably Do Nothing About," *TechDirt* (Jan. 9, 2019), https://perma.cc/2FQX-X83T.

33. Aaron Smith, "Record Shares of Americans Now Own Smartphones, Have Home Broadband," Pew Research Center (Jan. 12, 2017), https://perma.cc/ZLQ3-ZBV2.

34. Lex Friedman, "The App Store Turns Five: A Look Back and Forward," *Macworld* (July 8, 2013), https://perma.cc/5TKN-EFSW; Arytom Dogtiev, "App Download and Usage Statistics 2017," Business of Apps (Oct. 16, 2017), https://perma.cc/W2X8-2UJ5.

35. Englehardt & Narayanan, "Online Tracking"; Timothy Libert, "Exposing the Hidden Web: An Analysis of Third-Party HTTP Requests on One Million Websites," *International Journal of Communication* 9 (2015): 3544–61; see also Ibrahim Altaweel, Nathaniel Good, & Chris Jay Hoofnagle, "Web Privacy Census," *Technology Science* (Dec. 15, 2015), https://perma.cc/H8WV-7T63; Kashmir Hill, "I Cut the 'Big Five' Tech Giants from My Life. It Was Hell," *Gizmodo* (Feb. 7, 2019), https://perma.cc/8HP4-9AFV.

36. For different perspectives on these developments, see McKinsey Global Institute, "The Internet of Things: Mapping the Value Beyond the Hype," June 2015, https://perma.cc/34UX-AJYX; Mark Andrejevic & Mark Burdon, "Defining the Sensor Society," *Television and New Media* 16 no. 1 (2015): 19–36; Kelly A. Gates, *Our Biometric Future: Facial Recognition Technology and the Culture of Surveillance* (New York: New York University Press, 2011).

37. See Alessandro Acquisti, Laura E. Brandimarte, & George Loewenstein, "Privacy and Human Behavior in the Age of Information," *Science* 347 (2015): 509–14; Woodrow Hartzog, *Privacy's Blueprint: The Battle to Control the Design of New Technologies* (Cambridge, Mass.: Harvard University Press, 2018), 21–55; Lauren E. Willis, "When Nudges Fail: Slippery Defaults," *University of Chicago Law Review* 80 no. 3 (2013): 1170–200.

38. Mireille Hildebrandt & Antoinette Rouvroy, eds., *Law, Human Agency and Autonomic Computing* (New York: Routledge, 2011); Julie E. Cohen, *Configuring the Networked Self: Law, Code, and the Play of Everyday Practice* (New Haven, Conn.: Yale University Press, 2012), 200–01; Jeffrey O. Kephart & David M. Chess, "The Vision of Autonomic Computing," *Computer* 36 no. 1 (2003): 41–50. On the sensing net as a mechanism for "passiv-izing" interactivity, see Andrejevic & Burdon, "Defining the Sensor Society..

39. Kamal Tahir, "Marketing in the Internet of Things (IoT) Era," Acxiom Perspectives (Apr. 9, 2015), https://perma.cc/2ZK9-UDM4.

40. On military use of biometric technologies, see for example Tanya Polk, "Handheld Device Helps Soldiers Detect the Enemy" U.S. Army, (Jan. 14, 2010), https://perma.cc/25VX-KCSG; George I. Seffers, "U.S. Defense Department Expands Biometrics Technologies, Information Sharing," *SIGNAL Magazine* (Oct. 2010). On biometric surveillance and policing in Latin America, see Nelson Arteaga Botello, "Surveillance and Urban Violence in Latin America," in *Routledge Handbook of Surveillance Studies*, eds. Kirstie Ball, Kevin D. Haggerty, & David Lyon (New York: Routledge, 2012), 259–66. On targeted drone strikes, see Jeremy Scahill & Glenn Greenwald, "The NSA's Secret Role in the U.S. Assassination Program," *The Intercept* (Feb. 10, 2014), https://perma.cc/8ZFR-EC22; David Cole, "We Kill People Based on Metadata," *New York Review of Books* (May 10, 2014), https://perma.cc/ERY2-Z44L.

41. Alfred McCoy, *Policing America's Empire: The United States, the Philippines, and the Rise of the Surveillance State* (Madison: University of Wisconsin Press, 2009).

42. Gates, *Our Biometric Future*; Clare Garvie, Alvaro Bedoya, & Jonathan Frankle, "The Perpetual Lineup: Unregulated Police Face Recognition in America," Center on Privacy and Technology, Georgetown Law (Oct. 18, 2016), http://perma.cc/DM3U-ZPYD); Harrison Rudolph, Laura M. Moy, & Alvaro M. Bedoya, "Not Ready for Takeoff: Face Scans at Airport Departure Gates," Center on Privacy & Technology, Georgetown Law (Dec. 21, 2017), http://perma.cc/V288-MCM4.

43. Matt Apuzzo & Joseph Goldstein, "NYPD Drops Unit That Spied on Muslims," *New York Times* (Apr. 16, 2014), A1, https://perma.cc/C7EC-489Q; Diala Shamas, "Where's the Outrage when the FBI Targets Muslims?," *The Nation* (Oct. 31, 2013), https://perma.cc/Q8DY-JAK8; Glenn Greenwald & Murtaza Hussein, "Meet the Muslim-American Leaders the FBI and NSA Have Been Spying On," *The Intercept* (July 9, 2014), https://perma.cc/HMC9-43BC; Adam Schwartz, "No Hunting Undocumented Immigrants with Stingrays," Electronic Frontier Foundation (May 19, 2017), http://perma.cc/YN63-6GRD.

44. Vjiay Sathe, "The World's Most Ambitious ID Project," *Innovations* 6 no. 2 (2011): 39–65; Manan Kakkar, "Companies, Processes and Technology behind India's UID Project, Aadhaar" (Oct. 1, 2010), https://perma.cc/96U3-CQBL; Glyn Moody, "Aadhaar—Soon, in India, Everyone *Will* Be a Number," *TechDirt* (July 7, 2015), https://perma.cc/2UKV-V6Z6.

45. "Press Release: MasterCard, MasterCard-Branded National eID Card Launched in Nigeria," MasterCard (Aug. 28, 2014), https://perma.cc/A5XF-FETC; Adam Oxford, "Nigeria Launches New Biometric ID Card—Brought to You by MasterCard," ZDNet (Aug. 29, 2014), https://perma.cc/9U3X-ZMUT; "SA Banks Begin Fingerprint Verification," South Africa: The Good News (Nov. 9, 2011), http://perma.cc/6FAA-23SR.

46. Advox, "Can Facebook Connect the Next Billion?," Global Voices (July 27, 2017), https://perma.cc/U9QR-8NTA.

47. See, for example, Amiya Bhatia & Jacqueline Bhabha, "India's Aadhaar Scheme and the Promise of Inclusive Social Protection," *Oxford Development Studies* 45 no. 1 (2017): 64–79; Shweta Punj, "A Number of Changes," *Business Today* (Mar. 4, 2012), https://perma.cc/LY3S-9Z86; Jean Dreze, "Unique Identity Dilemma," *The Indian Express* (Mar. 19, 2015), https://perma.cc/L4DB-9CYK; Manish Singh, "India's Database with Biometric Details of Its Billion Citizens Ignites Privacy Debate," Mashable (Feb. 13, 2017), https://perma.cc/4W4F-WQ78; P. Arun, "Uncertainty and Insecurity in Privacyless India: A Despotic Push towards Digitalization," *Surveillance and Society* 15 nos. 3/4 (2017): 456–64.

48. On the contracting of data infrastructure development to multinationals, see Linnet Taylor & Dennis Broeders, "In the Name of Development: Power, Profit and the Datafication of the Global South," *Geoforum* 64 (2015): 229–37. On the challenges of implementing data protection in developing countries, see Linnet Taylor, "Data Subjects or Data Citizens? Addressing the Global Regulatory Challenge of Big Data," in *Freedom and Property of Information: The Philosophy of Law Meets the Philosophy of Technology*, eds. Mireille Hildebrandt & Bibi van den Berg (New York: Routledge, 2016), 81–105. On free flow provisions in trade agreements, see Chapter 7, pp. 215–16, 223–24.

49. *Maryland v. King*, 569 U.S. 1958 (2013).

50. On the uses and implications of biometric identification techniques, see Gates, *Our Biometric Future*, 54–58; Michele Estrin Gilman, "The Class Differential in Privacy Law," *Brooklyn Law Review* 77 no. 4 (2012): 1389–445; Torin Monahan, ed., *Surveillance and Security: Technological Politics and Power in Everyday Life* (New York: Routledge, 2006).

51. U.S. Department of Education, Data.Ed.Gov, https://perma.cc/2CDB-8FYY (last visited Apr. 11, 2019); U.S. Department of Health & Human Services, HealthData.gov, https://perma.cc/QH8J-6GTU (last visited Apr. 11, 2019).

52. Pew Research Center, "The Smartphone Difference" (Apr. 2015), 16–19, https://perma.cc/KN9V-53EE.

53. For a comprehensive exploration, see Frank Pasquale, *The Black Box Society: The Secret Algorithms That Control Money and Information* (Cambridge, Mass.: Harvard University Press, 2015).

54. Senate Committee on Commerce, Science, and Transportation, "A Review of the Data Broker Industry," 10–11. See also Federal Trade Commission, "Data Brokers," 7–10 (describing results of a similar survey of a list of companies that partially overlapped the Senate committee's list).

55. Zuboff, *The Age of Surveillance Capitalism*, 145–48, 159–61; "Transcript of Mark Zuckerberg's Senate Hearing," *Washington Post* (Apr. 10, 2018), https://perma.cc/2UQ5-CWYD; "Transcript of Zuckerberg's Appearance before House Committee," *Washington Post* (Apr. 11, 2018), https://perma.cc/LSZ7-4ECA.

56. Yochai Benkler, "Free as the Air to Common Use: First Amendment Constraints on Enclosure of the Public Domain," *New York University Law Review* 74 no. 2 (1999): 354–445; James Boyle, "The Second Enclosure Movement and the Construction of the Public Domain," *Law and Contemporary Problems* 66 nos. 1–2 (1998): 33–74.

57. Mark Andrejevic, *iSpy: Surveillance and Power in the Interactive Era* (Lawrence: University Press of Kansas, 2007), 2–4, 104–11.

58. Yochai Benkler, *The Wealth of Networks: How Social Production Transforms Markets and Freedom* (New Haven, Conn.: Yale University Press, 2006), 60–61; Brett M. Frischmann, *Infrastructure: The Social Value of Shared Resources* (New York: Oxford University Press, 2012), 7–9, 91–95.

59. See, for example, Frederik Zuiderveen Borgesius, Jonathan Gray, & Mireille van Eechoud, "Open Data, Privacy, and Fair Information Principles: Towards a Balancing Framework," *Berkeley Technology Law Journal* 30 no. 3 (2015): 2073–130, 2098–101; Arthur W. Toga & Ivo V. Dinov, *Sharing Big Biomedical Data, Journal of Big Data* 2 (2015): 7, doi:10.1186/s40537-015-0016-1; Jane Yakowitz, "Tragedy of the Data Commons," *Harvard Journal of Law and Technology* 25 no. 1 (2011): 1–67, 42–50.

60. Acxiom, "Data Solutions," http://perma.cc/6AW3-7CWE; Oracle, Press Release, "New Oracle Data Cloud and Data-as-Service Offerings Redefine Data-Driven Enterprise" (July 22, 2014), http://perma.cc/V25M-8EHK; "About," Google AI (last visited Dec. 14, 2018), https://perma.cc/6XXX-UXZH.

61. danah boyd & Kate Crawford, "Critical Questions for Big Data: Provocations for a Cultural, Technological, and Scholarly Phenomenon," *Information, Communication & Society* 15 no. 5 (2012): 662–79; Lisa Gitelman, ed., *"Raw Data" Is an Oxymoron* (Cambridge, Mass: MIT Press, 2013).

62. Natasha Dow Schull, *Addiction by Design: Machine Gambling in Las Vegas* (Princeton, N.J.: Princeton University Press, 2012); Neil M. Richards, "The Perils of Social Reading," *Georgetown Law Journal* 101 no. 3 (2013): 689–724.

63. A leading critique of traditional, profile-based market segmentation is Gandy, *The Panoptic Sort*.

64. See, for example, Mark MacCarthy, "In Defense of Big Data Analytics," in *The Cambridge Handbook of Consumer Privacy*, eds. Evan Selinger, Jules Polonetsky, & Omer Tene (New York: Cambridge University Press, 2018), 47–78; Tal Zarsky, "Automated Prediction: Perception, Law, and Policy," *Communications of the ACM* 55 no. 9 (2012): 33–35; Tal Zarsky, "Transparent Predictions," *University of Illinois Law Review*, 2013 no. 4 (2013): 1527–28.

65. Zuboff, *The Age of Surveillance Capitalism*, 270–90; see also Kirstie Ball, "Exposure: Exploring the Subject of Surveillance," *Information, Communication and Society* 12 no. 5 (2009): 639–57. On surveillance as modulation, see John Cheney-Lippold, "A New Algorithmic Identity: Soft Biopolitics and the Modulation of Control," *Theory, Culture and Society* 28 no. 6 (2011): 164–81; Julie E. Cohen, "What Privacy Is For," *Harvard Law Review* 126 no. 7 (2013): 1915–18; Greg Elmer, *Profiling Machines: Mapping the Personal Information Economy* (Cambridge, Mass.: MIT Press, 2004), 41–50.

66. Bianca Bosker, "The Binge Breaker," *The Atlantic* (Nov. 2016), https://perma.cc/P7UJ-DEVD; Tristan Harris, "How Technology Is Hijacking Your Mind—from a Magician and Google Design Ethicist," *Thrive Global* (May 18, 2016), https://perma.cc/WG2Z-TLWJ; Adam Alter, *Irresistible: The Rise of Addictive Technology and the Business of Keeping Us Hooked* (University Park, Pa.: Penn State University Press, 2017). On design for addiction more generally, see Schull, *Addiction by Design.*

67. Jose van Dijck, *The Culture of Connectivity: A Critical History of Social Media* (New York: Oxford University Press, 2013), 46–65; Zuboff, *The Age of Surveillance Capitalism,* 457–61.

68. Scott Lash, "Power after Hegemony: Cultural Studies in Mutation?," *Theory, Culture & Society* 24 no. 3 (2007): 55–78; see also Cheney-Lippold, "A New Algorithmic Identity."

69. Michael Pollan, *The Omnivore's Dilemma: A Natural History of Four Meals* (New York: Penguin, 2007), 30–31, 36–37, 41–42, 45, 58–59.

70. Pasquale, *The Black Box Society,* 22–42, 64–80. As Zuboff explains, the secrecy imperative flows from the radical behaviorist premises underlying data-driven profiling; according to those premises, awareness that one's reactions and behaviors are being tracked is "the enemy" because it introduces confounding behavioral signals. Zuboff, *The Age of Surveillance Capitalism,* 88–89, 306–08.

71. Cohen, "What Privacy Is For," 1917.

72. Pollan, *The Omnivore's Dilemma,* 17–19, 85–99.

73. On biopower, biopolitics, and their relation to state power, see Michel Foucault, *The History of Sexuality, vol. 1: An Introduction,* trans. Robert Hurley (New York: Random House, 1978); see also, for example, Catherine Mills, "Biopolitics and the Concept of Life," in *Biopower: Foucault and Beyond,* eds. Vernon W. Cisney & Nicolae Morar (Chicago: University of Chicago Press, 2016), 82–101.

74. Thomas Nail, "Biopower and Control," in *Between Deleuze and Foucault,* eds. Nicolae Morar, Thomas Nail, & Daniel W. Smith (Edinburgh: University of Edinburgh Press, 2016), 247–63, 259; see also Cheney-Lippold, "A New Algorithmic Identity"; Frederic Gros, "Is There a Biopolitical Subject? Foucault and the Birth of Biopolitics," in *Biopower: Foucault and Beyond,* 259–73.

75. On neoliberal governmentality and its emphasis on the primacy of markets, see the Introduction, pp. 6–7.

76. Pollan, *The Omnivore's Dilemma,* 17–19, 73–79, 85–99.

77. Michel Callon & Fabian Muniesa, "Peripheral Vision: Markets as Calculative Collective Devices," *Organization Studies* 26 no. 8 (2005): 1229–50, 1232–36.

78. Callon & Muniesa, "Peripheral Vision," 1236–39.

79. Callon & Muniesa, "Peripheral Vision," 1239–43.

80. On the tuna market, see Eric A. Feldman, "The Tuna Court: Law and Norms in the World's Premier Fish Market," *California Law Review* 94 no. 2 (2006): 313–69.

81. On the representation of consumers as resources to be accounted for, see Greg Elmer, "IPO 2.0: The Panopticon Goes Public," *Media Tropes* 4 no. 1 (2013): 1–16; Mireille Hildebrandt, *Smart Technologies and the End(s) of Law* (Northampton, Mass.: Edward Elgar, 2015), 91–93.

82. Callon & Muniesa, "Peripheral Vision," 1235–36.

83. For examples of some of the categories into which high-value consumers are sorted, see U.S. Senate Committee on Commerce, Science, and Transportation, Office of Oversight and Investigations Majority Staff, "A Review of the Data Broker Industry: Collection, Use, and Sale of Consumer Data for Marketing Purposes"(Dec. 18, 2013), 24.

84. On the economic appeal of high-risk pools and the use of numerical credit scoring to construct such pools in the mortgage finance context, see Martha Poon, "From New Deal Institutions to Capital Markets: Commercial Consumer Risk Scores and the Making of Subprime Mortgage Finance," *Accounting, Organizations, and Society* 34 no. 5 (2009): 654–74. For other explorations of practices targeting vulnerable populations, see Virginia Eubanks, *Automating Inequality: How High-Tech Tools Profile, Police, and Punish the Poor* (New York: St. Martin's

Press, 2018); Seeta Pena Gangadharan, "Digital Inclusion and Data Profiling," *First Monday* 17 no. 5 (2012): 7, https://doi.org/10.5210/fm.v17i5.3821; Nathan Newman, "The Costs of Lost Privacy: Consumer Harm and Rising Economic Inequality in the Age of Google," *William Mitchell Law Review* 40 no. 2 (2014): 849–90. 876–82; Safiya Umoja Noble, *Algorithms of Oppression: How Search Engines Reinforce Racism* (New York: New York University Press, 2018); see also Senate Committee on Commerce, Science, and Transportation, "A Review of the Data Broker Industry," 24–27; Federal Trade Commission, "Data Brokers," 19–25.

85. On the rise of "behavioral credit scoring," see Robinson + Yu, "Knowing the Score: New Data, Underwriting, and Marketing in the Consumer Credit Marketplace" (Oct. 2014), https:// perma.cc/283P-FFGF; Mikella Hurley & Julius Adebayo, "Credit Scoring in the Era of Big Data," *Yale Journal of Law and Technology* 18 (2016): 148–216.

86. On exclusion, see Julia Angwin, Ariana Tobin, & Madeleine Varner, "Facebook Is (Still) Letting Housing Advertisers Exclude Users by Race," *ProPublica* (Nov. 21, 2017), http:// perma.cc/9K9C-JE6K; April Glaser, "Facebook Is Eliminating the Easiest Ways to Commit Housing and Employment Discrimination—but Not All the Ways," *Slate* (Mar. 20, 2019), https://perma.cc/JRL4-NKGK. On differential promotion and pricing, see Greg Petro, "Dynamic Pricing: Which Customers Are Worth the Most? Amazon, Delta Airlines and Staples Weigh In," *Forbes Online* (Apr. 17, 2015), https://perma.cc/RT63-MYDU; Jennifer Valentino-Devries, Jeremy Singer-Vine, & Ashkan Soltani, "Websites Vary Prices, Deals Based on Users' Information," *Wall Street Journal* (Dec. 24, 2012), https://perma.cc/HJ2V-PY3Y; Olga Kharif, "Supermarkets Offer Personalized Pricing," *Bloomberg News* (Nov. 15, 2013), https://perma.cc/BT6X-K963; Dana Mattioli, "On Orbitz, Mac Users Steered to Pricier Hotels," *Wall Street Journal* (Aug. 23, 2012), https://perma.cc/UQK9-XBGR; "Flexible Figures," *The Economist* (Jan. 30, 2016), https://perma.cc/9WZ2-C6CS; Carlo Longino, "SF Giants Test Dynamic Ticket Pricing," *TechDirt* (May 20, 2009), https://perma.cc/ L99T-KUMS; Mike Masnick, "Citizen Journalism Bites into Amazon's Attempts at Dynamic Pricing," *TechDirt* (Jan. 4, 2007), https://perma.cc/K5MW-Q72C.

87. See "About LiveRamp," LiveRamp, https://perma.cc/5LVM-VU62 (last visited Apr. 6, 2019).

88. An important early exception identifying Big Data as an expression of a logic of economic accumulation was Shoshana Zuboff, "Big Other: Surveillance Capitalism and the Prospects of an Information Civilization," *Journal of Information Technology* 30 no. 1 (2015): 75–89.

89. This terminology combines the concept of the nudge, imported from behavioral economics and now widely used by both critics and admirers of data-based analytics, with that of preemption as used by Hildebrandt, *Smart Technologies and the End(s) of Law*, 57–61, and Ian Kerr & Jessica Earle, "Prediction, Preemption, Presumption: How Big Data Threatens Big Picture Privacy," *Stanford Law Review Online* 66 (2013): 65–72, 68–70. The preemptive nudge simultaneously suggests and forecloses. See also Karen Yeung, "'Hypernudge': Big Data as a Mode of Regulation by Design," *Information, Communication, and Society* 20 no. 1 (2017): 118–26.

90. On data appropriation as a new iteration of the historic and political logics of colonialism, see Nick Couldry & Ulises A. Mejias, "Data Colonialism: Rethinking Big Data's Relation to the Contemporary Subject," *Television and New Media* (Sept. 2, 2018), https://doi.org/10.1177/ 1527476418796632.

91. Moore v. Regents of the University of California, 793 P.2d 479 (Cal. 1990).

92. For discussion of these points, see James Boyle, *Shamans, Software, and Spleens: Law and the Construction of the Information Society* (Cambridge, Mass.: Harvard University Press, 1998), 106–07.

93. "New Oracle Data Cloud and Data-as-Service Offerings Redefine Data-Driven Enterprise," *Oracle* (July 22, 2014), https://perma.cc/E6AR-4XH3 ("unprecedented intelligence"); Spokeo, "About," https://perma.cc/L78B-RZX6 (last visited June 24, 2018) ("proprietary merge technology"); Intelius, "Products," https://perma.cc/H5EK-4HZD (last visited June 24, 2018) ("proprietary technology"); ID Analytics, "Company Overview," https:// perma.cc/9PF7-ESSN (last visited June 24, 2018) ("patented analytics").

94. Boyle, *Shamans, Software, and Spleens*, 108–43; Chander & Sunder, "The Romance of the Public Domain," 1339–40.

95. For discussion of this point, see Cohen, "What Privacy Is For," 1921–23.

96. Wesley Newcomb Hohfeld, "Some Fundamental Legal Conceptions as Applied in Judicial Reasoning," *Yale Law Journal* 23 no. 1 (1913): 16–59, 32–44.

97. Karl Marx, "Critique of the Gotha Program," in *Marx: Later Political Writings*, ed. & trans. Terrell Carver (New York: Cambridge University Press, 1996), 208–26; see also Marion Fourcade & Kieran Healy, "Seeing Like a Market." *Socio-Economic Review* 15 no. 1 (2017): 9–29.

Chapter 3

1. Ithiel De Sola Pool, *Technologies of Freedom* (Cambridge, Mass.: Harvard University Press, 1983); see also Jack Balkin, "Digital Speech and Democratic Culture," *New York University Law Review* 79(1) (2004): 1–58.

2. Mark Andrejevic, *Infoglut: How Too Much Information Is Changing the Way We Think and Know* (New York: Routledge, 2013), 9–10.

3. Andrejevic, *Infoglut*, 9–10.

4. For an overview, see Paul D. MacLean, "The Limbic System ('Visceral Brain') in Relation to Central Gray and Reticulum of the Brain Stem: Evidence of Interdependence in Emotional Processes," *Psychosomatic Medicine* 17 no. 5 (1955): 355–66. Current models have moved beyond rigid functional segregation to recognize that, for example, the neurological processes that produce learning and memory extend across multiple brain regions. Within those models, however, the structures in the limbic region remain pivotal. See, for example, James L. McGaugh et al., "Involvement of the Amygdala in Memory Storage: Interaction with Other Brain Systems," *PNAS* 93 no. 24 (1996): 13508–14.

5. Shoshana Zuboff, *The Age of Surveillance Capitalism: The Fight for a Human Future at the New Frontier of Power* (New York: Hachette, 2019), 351–52, 376–97.

6. Mireille Hildebrandt, *Smart Technologies and the End(s) of Law: Novel Entanglements of Law and Technology* (Northampton, Mass.:, Edward Elgar, 2015), 41–46, 56–61, 66–67.

7. Erving Goffman, *The Presentation of Self in Everyday Life* (New York: Anchor Books, 1959).

8. Scholarly and popular commentary on reputation as a source of individual concern most often focuses on social and professional embarrassment when isolated facts or falsehoods can be taken out of context. See, for example, Daniel J. Solove, *The Future of Reputation: Gossip, Rumor, and Privacy on the Internet* (New Haven, Conn.: Yale University Press, 2007), 30–35; Jeffrey Rosen, *The Unwanted Gaze: The Destruction of Privacy in America* (New York: Random House, 2000). That fundamentally human-centered account of how reputation is created is only part of the story.

9. Josh Lauer, "From Rumor to Written Record: Credit Reporting and the Invention of Financial Identity in Nineteenth-Century America," *Technology and Culture* 49 no. 2 (2008): 301–24; Josh Lauer, "The Good Consumer: Credit Reporting and the Invention of Financial Identity in the United States, 1840–1940," *Enterprise and Society* 11 no. 4 (2010): 686–94.

10. "Statement of the Fair Isaac Corporation before the U.S. House of Representatives" (July 28, 2008), https://perma.cc/P3QW-7QSX; Martha Poon, "Scorecards as Devices for Consumer Credit: The Case of Fair, Isaac & Company Incorporated," *The Sociological Review* 55 no. s2 (2007): 284–306.

11. Robinson + Yu, "Knowing the Score: New Data, Underwriting, and Marketing in the Consumer Credit Marketplace" (Oct. 2014), https://perma.cc/283P-FFGF.

12. Mary L. Carsky, Roger L. Dickinson, & Charles R. Canedy III, "The Evolution of Quality in Consumer Goods," *Journal of Macromarketing* 18 no. 2 (1998): 132–44; Hayagreeva Rao, "Caveat Emptor: The Construction of Nonprofit Consumer Watchdog Organizations," *American Journal of Sociology* 103 no. 4 (1998): 912–61; Lauren Strach & Malcolm Russell,

"The Good Housekeeping Seal of Approval: From Innovative Consumer Protection to Popular Badge of Quality," *Essays in Economic & Business History* 21 (2003): 151–66.

13. Michele Knobel & Colin Lankshear, "What Am I Bid? Reading, Writing, and Ratings at eBay. com," in *Silicon Literacies: Communication, Innovation and Education in the Electronic Age*, ed. Ilana Snyder (New York: Routledge, 2002), 15–30; Axel Bruns, *Gatewatching: Collaborative Online News Production* (New York: Peter Lang, 2005), 31–52.

14. For a representative sampling of academic thought experiments, see Hasan Masum, Mark Tovey, & Yi-Cheng Zhang, *The Reputation Society* (Cambridge, Mass.: MIT Press, 2011).

15. Mihaly Heder, "A Black Market for Upvotes and Likes," Working Paper (Mar. 19, 2018), arXiv:1803.07029; Michael Luca & Giorgios Zervas, "Fake It Till You Make It: Reputation, Competition, and Yelp Review Fraud," *Management Science* 62 no. 12 (2016): 3412–27; Dina Mayzlin, Yaniv Dover, & Judith Chevalier, "Promotional Reviews: An Empirical Investigation of Online Review Manipulation," *American Economic Review* 104 no. 8 (2014): 2421–55.

16. danah boyd, *It's Complicated: The Social Lives of Networked Teens* (New Haven, Conn.: Yale University Press, 2014); Alice Marwick & danah boyd, "'It's Just Drama': Teen Perspectives on Conflict and Aggression in a Networked Era," *Journal of Youth Studies* 17 no. 9 (2014): 1187–204.

17. Ken Bolton, "Manage Your Online Reputation," *Information Outlook* 17 no. 4 (2013): 10–12; Stephanie Kelly, Scott Christen, & Lisa Gueldenzoph Snyder, "An Analysis of Effective Online Reputation Management: A Critical Thinking Social Media Activity," *Journal of Research in Business Education* 55 no. 1 (2013): 24–35. Notably, however, business models premised on more widespread use of portable ratings have yet to achieve durable success. See Rachel Pick, "Whatever Happened to Klout?" *Vice Motherboard* (Feb. 19, 2016), https://perma.cc/ 7DND-WH4M; Sarah Perez, "Controversial People-Rating App Peeple Goes Live, Has a Plan to Profit from Users' Negative Reviews," *TechCrunch* (Mar. 8, 2016), https://perma.cc/ W3U4-QCQB.

18. Allison Woodruff, "Necessary, Unpleasant, and Disempowering: Reputation Management in the Internet Age," in *Proceedings of the SIGCHI Conference on Human Factors in Computing Systems* (New York: ACM, 2015), 149–58.

19. On SEO, see Eric Enge, Stephan Spencer, Jessie Stricchiola, & Rand Fishkin, *The Art of SEO*, 2d ed. (Sebastopol, CA: O'Reilly Media, 2012); Jayson DeMers, "The Top SEO Trends That Will Dominate 2015," *Forbes Online* (Dec. 8, 2014), https://perma.cc/9HZV-EX9B. On credit repair, see James P. Nehf, "A Legislative Framework for Reducing Fraud in the Credit Repair Industry," *North Carolina Law Review* 70 no. 3 (2003): 781–821; Harland Clarke & Javelin Strategy and Research, "Fee Income Growth Opportunities in the Identity Protection Market" (2011), https://perma.cc/8F98-A6VP.

20. Rajat Paharia, *Loyalty 3.0: How Big Data and Gamification Are Revolutionizing Customer and Employee Engagement* (New York: McGraw Hill, 2013); Gabe Zichermann & Joselin Linder, *The Gamification Revolution: How Leaders Leverage Game Mechanics to Crush the Competition* (New York: McGraw Hill, 2013).

21. Ryan Singel, "Facebook Beacon Tracking Program Draws Privacy Lawsuit," *Wired* (Aug. 14, 2008), https://perma.cc/7NYS-UEWU.

22. David Kirkpatrick, *The Facebook Effect: The Inside Story of the Company that Is Connecting the World* (New York: Simon & Schuster, 2010), 218–63; Zuboff, *The Age of Surveillance Capitalism*, 159–61, 457–58.

23. Gary Wolf, "The Data-Driven Life," *New York Times* (Apr. 28, 2010), https://perma.cc/ QD3U-E2W7; Emily Singer, "The Measured Life," *MIT Technology Review* (June 21, 2011), https://perma.cc/6QD5-8ZF9.

24. See, for example, Jennifer Wang, "How Fitbit Is Cashing in on the High-Tech Fitness Trend," *Entrepreneur* (July 28, 2012), https://perma.cc/96VW-ZDNT; see also David Pierce, "Goodbye, Wearables. You Had a Stupid Name Anyway," *Wired* (Dec. 23, 2015), https:// perma.cc/3WSZ-9XNY.

25. Greg Sterling, "Foursquare to Move Check-ins Into 'Swarm' App, to Focus Better on Local Discovery," *Search Engine Land* (May 1, 2014), https://perma.cc/F5HE-PAG4

26. Alexander Galloway, *Gaming: Essays on Algorithmic Culture* (Minneapolis: University of Minnesota Press, 2006), 6–8, 91–104; see also Julie E. Cohen, "The Surveillance-Innovation Complex: The Irony of the Participatory Turn," in *The Participatory Condition in the Digital Age*, eds. Darin Barney et al. (Minneapolis: University of Minnesota Press, 2016), 207–26.

27. On the depoliticized self as the intended product of neoliberal ideology, see Wendy Brown, "Neo-liberalism and the End of Liberal Democracy," *Theory & Event* 7 no. 1 (2003): 15, https://perma.cc/SZ6K-2U6T; Todd May & Ladelle McWhorter, "Who's Being Disciplined Now? Operations of Power in a Neoliberal World," in *Biopower: Foucault and Beyond*, eds. Vernon W. Cisney & Nicolae Morar (Chicago: University of Chicago Press, 2016), 245–58.

28. Felix Raczkowski, "It's All Fun and Games . . . : A History of Ideas concerning Gamification," in *Proceedings of DiGRA 2013: DeFragging Game Studies*, 344–54 (Atlanta, Ga.: Digital Games Research Association, 2013).

29. Jennifer Whitson, "Gaming the Quantified Self," *Surveillance & Society* 11 nos. 1–2 (2013): 163–76, 169.

30. On addictive design and its connections to gaming and gambling, see Adam Alter, *Irresistible: The Rise of Addictive Technology and the Business of Keeping Us Hooked* (University Park, PA: Penn State University Press, 2017); Natasha Dow Schull, *Addiction by Design: Machine Gambling in Las Vegas* (Princeton: Princeton University Press, 2012).

31. D.G. Brian Jones & Eric H. Shaw, "A History of Marketing Thought," in *Handbook of Marketing*, eds. Barton A. Weitz & Robin Wensley (Thousand Oaks, Calif.: SAGE, 2002), 39–65; Robert Bartels, "The Identity Crisis in Marketing," *Journal of Marketing* 38 no. 4 (1974): 73–76.

32. Zuboff, *The Age of Surveillance Capitalism*, 204–12, 293–97, 361–75, 416–40.

33. See, for example, Syed Tariq Anwar, "Company Slogans, Morphological Issues, and Corporate Communications," *Corporate Communications: An International Journal* 20 no. 3 (2015): 360–74; S. Adam Brasel & James Gips, "Breaking Through Fast-Forwarding: Brand Information and Visual Attention," *Journal of Marketing* 72 no. 6 (2008): 31–48; Maxime Carron, Francoise Dubois, Nicolas Misdariis, Corinne Talotte, & Patrick Susini, "Designing Sound Identity: Providing New Communication Tools for Building Brands 'Corporate Sound,'" in *Proceedings of the 9th Audio Mostly: A Conference on Interaction with Sound* (New York: ACM, 2014), 15–22, https://perma.cc/3CTM-YGS7; Brigitte Muller, Bruno Kocher, & Antoine Crettaz, "The Effects of Visual Rejuvenation through Brand Logos," *Journal of Business Research* 66 (2011): 82–88.

34. Rosemary J. Coombe, *The Cultural Lives of Intellectual Properties: Authorship, Appropriation, and the Law* (Durham, N.C.: Duke University Press, 1998).

35. David Murakami Wood & Kirstie Ball, "Brandscapes of Control? Surveillance, Marketing, and the Co-construction of Subjectivity and Space in Neoliberal Capitalism," *Marketing Theory* 13 no. 1 (2013): 47–67, 57.

36. Joseph Turow, *The Aisles Have Eyes: How Retailers Track Your Shopping, Strip Your Privacy, and Define Your Power* (New Haven, Conn.: Yale University Press, 2017).

37. See, for example, Jeff Huang et al., "No Clicks, No Problem: Using Cursor Movements to Understand and Improve Search," *Proceedings of the SIGCHI Conference on Human Factors in Computing Systems* (New York: ACM, 2011), 1225–34; Michal Kosinski, David Stillwell, & Thore Graepel, "Private Traits and Attributes Are Predictable from Digital Records of Human Behavior," *PNAS* 110 no. 15 (2013): 5802–05; Wu Youyou, Michal Kosinski, & David Stillwell, "Computer-Based Personality Judgments Are More Accurate than Those Made by Humans," *PNAS* 112 no. 4 (2015): 1036–40; Hilke Plassmann, Vinod Venkatraman, Scott Huettel, & Carolyn Yoon, "Consumer Neuroscience: Applications, Challenges, and Possible Solutions," *Journal of Marketing Research* 52 no. 4 (2015): 427–35; Vinod Venkatraman, John A. Clithero, Gavan J. Fitzsimons, & Scott A. Huettel, "New Scanner Data for Brand Marketers: How

Neuroscience Can Help Better Understand Differences in Brand Preferences," *Journal of Consumer Psychology* 22 no. 1 (2012): 143–53.

38. See, for example, Natasha Lomas, "Amazon Patents 'Anticipatory' Shipping—To Start Sending Stuff before You've Bought It," *TechCrunch* (Jan. 18, 2014), https://perma.cc/8SK8-R2WS; Steve Rosenbush, "Facebook Tests Software to Track Your Cursor on Screen," *Wall Street Journal* (Oct. 30, 2013), https://perma.cc/X3XL-FEYK.

39. Robinson Meyer, "Everything We Know about Facebook's Secret Mood Manipulation Experiment," *The Atlantic* (June 28, 2014), https://perma.cc/YF8Q-LHEK; Paul Armstrong, "Facebook Is Helping Brands Target Teens Who Feel 'Worthless,'" *Forbes* (May 1, 2017), https://perma.cc/F62G-SNF7; see also "Comments on Research and Ad Targeting," *Newsroom, Facebook* (Apr. 30, 2017) ("Facebook does not offer tools to target people based on their emotional state. . . . Facebook has an established process to review the research we perform. This research did not follow that process, and we are reviewing the details to correct the oversight."), https://perma.cc/WG3D-JQX2. For a general survey of commercial mood-detection techniques in use or under development, see Tasha Glenn & Scott Monteith, "New Measures of Mental State and Behavior Based on Data Collected from Sensors, Smartphones, and the Internet," *Current Psychiatric Reports* 16 no. 12 (2014): 523–32, doi: 10.1007/s11920-014-0523-3. For an in-depth exploration of the feasibility and difficulties of sentiment mining, see Bo Pang & Lillian Lee, "Opinion Mining and Sentiment Analysis," *Foundations and Trends in Information Retrieval* 2 nos. 1–2 (2008): 1–35.

40. Franklin Foer, *World without Mind* (New York: Penguin, 2018), 139.

41. On the psychology of clickbait, see Bryan Gardiner, "You'll Be Outraged at How Easy It Was to Get You to Click on This Headline," *Wired* (Dec. 18, 2015), https://perma.cc/4QXK-5M56; George Loewenstein, "The Psychology of Curiosity: A Review and Reinterpretation," *Psychological Bulletin* 116(1) (1994): 75–98. On motivations for sharing, see Alice Marwick, "Why Do People Share Fake News? A Sociotechnical Model of Media Effects," *Georgetown Law Technology Review* 2 no. 2 (2018): 474–512, https://perma.cc/DT4C-94EU.

42. Foer, *World without Mind*, 144–46.

43. See, for example, Olivia Solon & Sam Levin, "How Google's Search Algorithm Spreads False Information with a Rightwing Bias," *The Guardian* (Dec. 16, 2016), https://perma.cc/Z8QZ-PUY7; Carole Cadwalladr, "Google, Democracy and the Truth about Internet Search," *The Guardian* (Dec. 4, 2016), https://perma.cc/A6UA-JKGA; Noam Cohen, "Google's Search Algorithm Isn't Biased; It's Just Not Human," *Wired* (Dec. 14, 2018), https://perma.cc/L35Q-Q3S3; see generally Lucas D. Introna & Helen Nissenbaum, "Shaping the Web: Why the Politics of Search Engines Matter," *The Information Society* 16 no. 3 (2000): 169–85.

44. For prescient work exploring the interconnections between subjectivity and scale, see Luke Stark, "Algorithmic Psychometrics and the Scalable Subject." *Social Studies of Science* 48 no. 2 (2018): 204–31; see also Nick Couldry & Andreas Hepp, *The Mediated Construction of Reality* (Malden, Mass.: Polity, 2017), 187.

45. Eric S. Raymond, *The Cathedral and the Bazaar* (Sebastopol, Calif.: O'Reilly Media, 1999), 30; see Yochai Benkler, *The Wealth of Networks: How Social Production Transforms Markets and Freedom* (New Haven, Conn.: Yale University Press, 2006), 59–90; Axel Bruns, *Blogs, Wikipedia, Second Life, and Beyond: From Production to Produsage* (New York: Peter Lang, 2008), 101–36; Karen Hellekson & Kristina Busse, eds., *Fan Fiction and Fan Communities in the Age of the Internet* (Jefferson, N.C.: McFarland Books, 2006); Aaron Delwiche & Jennifer Jacobs Henderson, eds., *The Participatory Cultures Handbook* (New York: Routledge, 2012).

46. James Surowiecki, *The Wisdom of Crowds: Why the Many Are Smarter than the Few and How Collective Wisdom Shapes Business, Economies, Societies and Nations* (New York: Anchor, 2004); see also Clay Shirky, *Here Comes Everybody: The Power of Organizing without Organization* (New York: Penguin, 2008); Amy N. Langville & Carl D. Meyer, *Google's PageRank and Beyond: The Science of Search Engine Rankings* (Princeton, N.J.: Princeton University Press,

2012), 25–30; David Easley & Jon Kleinberg, *Networks, Crowds, and Markets: Reasoning about a Highly Connected World* (New York: Cambridge University Press, 2010), 258–362.

47. See Rebecca MacKinnon, *Consent of the Networked: The Worldwide Struggle for Internet Freedom* (New York: Basic Books, 2012); Zeynep Tufecki, *Twitter and Tear Gas: The Power and Fragility of Networked Protest* (New Haven, Conn.: Yale University Press, 2017); Deen Freelon et al., "Beyond the Hashtags: #Ferguson, #BlackLivesMatter, and the Online Struggle for Offline Justice," *Center for Media & Social Impact* (2016), https://perma.cc/UWR4-6SUN.

48. See Timur Kuran & Cass R. Sunstein, "Availability Cascades and Risk Regulation," *Stanford Law Review* 51 no. 4 (1999): 683–768; Mara Barton, "Application of Cascade Theory to Online Systems: A Study of Email and Google Cascades," *Minnesota Journal of Law, Science, and Technology* 10 no. 2 (2009): 473–502.

49. Matthew Gentzkow, "Polarization in 2016," *Toulouse Network of Information Technology White Paper* (2016), https://perma.cc/5AVV-PPFP.

50. On homogeneity and polarization, see Cass Sunstein, *Going to Extremes: How Like Minds Unite and Divide* (New York: Oxford University Press, 2009). On algorithmically reinforced polarization in the networked digital information environment, see Andrejevic, *Infoglut*, 42–61; Marwick, "Why Do People Share Fake News?"; Walter Quattrociocchi, Antonio Scala, & Cass R. Sunstein, "Echo Chambers on Facebook," John M. Olin Center for Law & Economics, Harvard Law School, Discussion Paper No. 877 (2016). The term "filter bubble" has entered the popular lexicon as a way of conveying these effects, but to the extent it suggests that people are completely insulated from encounters with opposing narratives and views, it may also be misleading.

51. Yochai Benkler, Robert Faris, & Hal Roberts, *Network Propaganda: Manipulation, Disinformation, and Radicalization in American Politics* (New York: Oxford University Press, 2018); Russell Muirhead & Nancy Rosenblum, "The New Conspiracists," *Dissent* (Winter 2018), https://perma.cc/4CAX-BLQ6.

52. Andrejevic, *Infoglut*, 12; see, for example, Alfred Hermida et al., "Share, Like, Recommend: Decoding the Social Media News Consumer," *Journalism Studies* 13 no. 5–6: 815–24; Jason Turcotte, et al., "News Recommendations from Social Media Opinion Leaders: Effects on Media Trust and Information Seeking," *Journal of Computer-Mediated Communication* 20 no. 5 (2015): 520–35.

53. Andrejevic, *Infoglut*, 15–18; see, for example, Jonathan Albright, "Untrue-Tube: Monetizing Misery and Disinformation," *Medium* (Feb. 25, 2018), https://perma.cc/Y6BM-CQCD; Bill Scher, "Why the NRA Always Wins," *Politico* (Feb. 19, 2018), https://perma.cc/SC7Y-UA7U; Julia Carrie Wong, "How Facebook and YouTube Help Spread Anti-Vaxxer Propaganda," *Guardian* (Feb. 1, 2019), https://perma.cc/68GE-8TJL.

54. On the "pizzagate" story, see David A. Graham, "The 'Comet Pizza' Gunman Provides a Glimpse of a Frightening Future," *The Atlantic* (Dec. 5, 2016), https://perma.cc/J9L8-DEZL. On the various origins of efforts to spread misinformation and disinformation online, see, for example, Samanth Subramanian, "Inside the Macedonian Fake-News Complex," *Wired* (Feb. 15, 2017), https://perma.cc/528F-F48Q; "Tall Tales Spread by Alex Jones Breed Dangerous Plots," *Southern Poverty Law Center: Intelligence Report* (Feb, 15, 2017), https://perma.cc/28A8-ZFWR; Olivia Solon & Sabrina Siddiqui, "Russia-Backed Facebook Posts 'Reached 126m Americans' during U.S. Election," *Guardian* (Oct. 31, 2017), https://perma.cc/6REY-NMDX; Carole Cadwalladr & Emma Graham-Harrison, "Revealed: 50 Million Facebook Profiles Harvested for Cambridge Analytica in Major Data Breach," *Guardian* (Mar. 17, 2018), https://perma.cc/92UL-VMU8.

55. Katherine Viner, "How Technology Disrupted the Truth," *Guardian* (July 12, 2016), https://perma.cc/K6AU-YZYR; Carole Cadwalladr, "The Great British Brexit Robbery: How Our Democracy Was Hijacked," *Guardian* (May 7, 2017), https://perma.cc/UZ6R-BBQU; Christopher Paul & Miriam Matthew, "The Russian 'Firehose of Falsehood' Propaganda

Model: Why It Might Work and Options to Counter It," *RAND Corporation: Perspectives* (2016), https://perma.cc/CLB5-A5AG.

56. Danielle Keats Citron, *Hate Crimes in Cyberspace* (Cambridge, Mass.: Harvard University Press, 2014); Whitney Phillips, *This Is Why We Can't Have Nice Things* (Cambridge, Mass.: MIT Press, 2015).

57. Rebecca Lewis, "Alternative Influence: Broadcasting the Reactionary Right on YouTube," Data & Society (Sept. 18, 2018), https://perma.cc/63H4-QJAL; Alice Marwick & Rebecca Lewis, "Media Manipulation & Disinformation Online," *Data & Society* (2017), https://perma.cc/356L-XZQA; Kenneth Roth, "World Report 2017: The Dangerous Rise of Populism," Human Rights Watch (2017), https://perma.cc/Q7AC-VKYS; "The Online Hate Index," Anti-Defamation League, https:/perma.cc/SZ8A-B2CU (last visited Apr. 11, 2019); Julia Angwin, Madeleine Varner, & Ariana Tobin, "Facebook Enabled Advertisers to Reach 'Jew Haters," *ProPublica* (Sept. 14, 2017), https://perma.cc/9UD8-L9KG; see also Snigdha Poonam & Samarth Bansal, "Misinformation Is Endangering India's Election," *The Atlantic* (Apr. 1, 2019), https://perma.cc/V5WQ-2SHJ; Amanda Taub & Max Fisher, "When Countries Are Tinderboxes and Facebook Is a Match," *New York Times* (Apr. 21, 2018), https://perma.cc/LBC4-WGZQ.

58. "Europe's Rising Far Right: A Guide to the Most Prominent Parties," *New York Times* (Dec. 4, 2016), https://perma.cc/7XYU-RHKP; Sasha Polakow-Suransky, "The Ruthlessly Effective Rebranding of Europe's New Far Right," *The Guardian* (Nov. 1, 2016), https://perma.cc/5GNT-CYLM; Ben Schreckinger, "The Alt-Right Comes to Washington," *Politico* (Jan./Feb. 2017), https://perma.cc/2BEJ-6UB3; Jason Wilson, "Hiding in Plain Sight: How the Alt-Right Is Weaponizing Irony to Spread Fascism," *Guardian* (May 23, 2017), https://perma.cc/T7UK-S8E9; George Hawley, "The Alt-Right Is Not Who You Think They Are," *American Conservative* (Aug. 25, 2017), https://perma.cc/LG6M-PB5Q. For more in-depth explorations of the alt-right's cultural origins, see Angela Nagle, *Kill All Normies: The Online Culture Wars from Tumblr and 4chan to the Alt-Right and Trump* (Washington, D.C.: Zero Press, 2017); Phillips, *This Is Why We Can't Have Nice Things*, 95–136. On extremist techniques for hijacking mainstream media coverage, see Whitney Phillips, "The Oxygen of Amplification: Better Practices for Reporting on Extremists, Antagonists, and Manipulators," Data & Society (May 22, 2018), https://perma.cc/S8HZ-BKEM.

59. Frederick Mark Gedicks, "Incorporation of the Establishment Clause against the States: A Logical, Textual, and Historical Account," *Indiana Law Journal* 88 no. 2 (2013): 693–96; John Harrison, "Power, Duty, and Facial Invalidity," *University of Pennsylvania Journal of Constitutional Law* 16 no. 2 (2013): 501–47, 509–12; Henry M. Hart Jr. & Albert M. Sacks, *The Legal Process: Basic Problems in the Application of Law*, eds. William N. Eskridge, Jr. & Philip P. Frickey (St. Paul, Minn.: West Academic, 1994), 135.

60. Daniel Castro, Director, Center for Data Innovation, Letter to Nicole Wong, White House Office of Science and Technology Policy (Mar. 31, 2014), https://perma.cc/Y3T5-EJ3D.

61. Michael Zaneis, Senior Vice President and General Counsel, Interactive Advertising Bureau, Testimony Before the Subcommittee on Commerce, Manufacturing, and Trade of the House Committee on Energy and Commerce, Hearing on Balancing Privacy and Innovation: Does the President's Proposal Tip the Scale?, (Mar. 29, 2012), https://perma.cc/HS68-THGG; see also, for example, Bob Liodice, President and CEO, Association of National Advertisers, Inc. on Behalf of the Digital Advertising Alliance, Testimony Before the Senate Committee on Commerce, Science, and Transportation, Hearing on the Need for Privacy Protections: Is Industry Self-Regulation Adequate? (June 28, 2012), https://perma.cc/T5VY-ZWQ4; Randall Rothenberg, President and CEO, Interactive Advertising Bureau, Testimony Before Subcommittee on Information Technology of the House Oversight and Government Reform Committee, Hearing on Oversight of Federal Political Advertisement Laws and Regulations (Oct. 24, 2017), https://perma.cc/4CDA-LP4H.

62. See, for example, Berin Szoka & Adam Thierer, "Targeted Online Advertising: What's the Harm and Where Are We Heading?," *Progress on Point* 16 no. 2 (Feb. 26, 2009), http://perma.cc/CRU4-GZYE; Larry Downes, "A Rational Response to the Privacy 'Crisis,'" *Cato Institute Policy Analysis,* No. 716 (Jan. 7, 2013), https://perma.cc/U4B8-BZHP; Alan McQuinn, "The Economics of 'Opt-Out' versus 'Opt-In' Privacy Rules" (Oct. 21, 2017), *Information Technology & Innovation Foundation,* https://perma.cc/V3Q6-YSTS; Alan McQuinn & Daniel Castro, "Why Stronger Privacy Regulations Do Not Spur Increased Internet Use," Information Technology and Innovation Foundation, July 2018, https://perma.cc/KC6E-H7Q4.

63. See, for example, Mark MacCarthy, "In Defense of Big Data Analytics," in *The Cambridge Handbook of Consumer Privacy,* eds. Evan Selinger, Jules Polonetsky, & Omer Tene (New York: Cambridge University Press, 2018), 47–78; Omer Tene & Jules Polonetsky, "Privacy in the Age of Big Data: A Time for Big Decisions," *Stanford Law Review Online* 64 (2012): 63–69.

64. Jacob Goldenberg, Donald R. Lehmann, & David Mazursky, "The Idea Itself and the Circumstances of Its Emergence as Predictors of New Product Success," *Management Science* 47 no. 1 (2001): 69–84.

65. See, for example, U.S. Department of Commerce, Internet Policy Task Force, "Commercial Data Privacy and Innovation in the Internet Economy: A Dynamic Policy Framework" (Dec. 16, 2010), https://perma.cc/9QXL-Q53S; U.S. Federal Trade Commission, "Protecting Consumer Privacy in an Era of Rapid Change" (Mar. 2012), https://perma.cc/PW3F-T5WB; White House, "Consumer Data Privacy in a Networked World: A Framework for Protecting Privacy and Promoting Innovation in the Global Digital Economy" (2012), https://perma.cc/XM53-RAKH; Subcommittee on Online Investigations of the Senate Committee on Homeland Security and Governmental Affairs, Hearing on Online Advertising and Hidden Hazards to Consumer Security and Data Privacy (May 15, 2014) (remarks of Senator John McCain), https://perma.cc/55DC-XWYN; see also FTC Staff Report, "Internet of Things: Privacy and Security in a Connected World" (Jan. 2015), 19–25, 47–48 (summarizing comments by workshop participants emphasizing the need for balance and for self-regulation), https://perma.cc/MR3R-2ZCM.

66. See, for example, Cameron F. Kerry, General Counsel, U.S. Department of Commerce, "Remarks to the European Parliament," Interparliamentary Committee Meeting on the Reform of the EU Data Protection Framework: Building Trust in a Digital and Global World (Oct. 10, 2012), https://perma.cc/P2NV-LQMF; William E. Kennard, U.S. Ambassador to the European Union, "Remarks at Forum Europe's Third Annual European Data Protection and Privacy Conference" (Dec. 4, 2012), https://perma.cc/C7C8-PX4V; Natasha Singer, "Data Protection Laws, an Ocean Apart," *New York Times* (Feb. 2, 2013), https://nyti.ms/2uBbzqa; Anthony Gardner, U.S. Ambassador to the European Union, "Facing Legal Challenges in U.S.–EU Relations," Mackenzie Stuart Lecture at Cambridge University (Jan. 29, 2015), https://perma.cc/7PRK-C4EL.

67. On the incentivizing effects of climate change policy, see American Energy Innovation Council, "Catalyzing American Ingenuity: The Role of Government in Energy Innovation" (2012), https://perma.cc/JNQ5-D9BD; Dennis Hirsch, "The Glass House Effect: Big Data, the New Oil, and the Power of Analogy," *Maine Law Review* 66 no. 2 (2014): 373–95.

68. On security threats flowing from data harvesting ecologies, see Paul Ohm, "Broken Promises of Privacy: Responding to the Surprising Failure of Anonymization," *UCLA Law Review* 57 no. 6 (2010): 1701–777; Danielle Keats Citron, "Reservoirs of Danger: The Evolution of Public and Private Law at the Dawn of the Information Age," *Southern California Law Review* 80 no. 2 (2007): 241–97.

69. For discussion of finance as innovation, see Chapter 1, pp. 26–29.

70. Vincent Mosco, *The Digital Sublime* (Cambridge, Mass: MIT Press, 2004); David Nye, *American Technological Sublime* (Cambridge, Mass.: MIT Press, 1994). On the singularity, see

Richard Dooling, *Rapture for the Geeks: When AI Outsmarts IQ* (New York: Crown, 2008); Ray Kurzweil, *The Singularity Is Near: When Humans Transcend Biology* (New York: Viking, 2006); Brandon Keim, "Will the Singularity Make Us Happier?," *Wired* (May 30, 2008), http://perma.cc/BE53-ZZ88.

71. Christian Schubert, "How to Evaluate Creative Destruction: Reconstructing Schumpeter's Approach," *Cambridge Journal of Economics* 37 no. 2 (2013): 227–50; John A. Dove & Russell S. Sobel, "Entrepreneurial Creative Destruction and Legal Federalism," in *The Law and Economics of Federalism*, ed. Jonathan Klick (Northampton, Mass.: Edward Elgar, 2017), 214–37.

72. Manish Singh, "India's Database with Biometric Details of Its Billion Citizens Ignites Privacy Debate," *Mashable* (Feb. 13, 2017), https://perma.cc/4W4F-WQ78; Usha Ramanathan, "Opinion: Data Is the New Gold and Aadhaar Is the Tool to Get It," *Scroll.in* (Dec. 30, 2016), https://perma.cc/BMK3-48UU; N.S. Ramnath, "Aadhaar: A Quiet Disruption," *Founding Fuel* (June 25, 2016), https://perma.cc/2QY8-F6VL; K.C. Deepika, "JAM and India Stack Will Push Innovation: Nandan Nilekani," *The Hindu* (Mar. 25, 2016), https://perma.cc/JE7B-XS7N; M. Rajshekhar & Anumeha Yadav, "How the Government Gains When Private Companies Use Aadhaar," *Scroll.in* (Mar. 24, 2016), https://perma.cc/LHP4-K7S9.

73. For discussions of this issue from differing perspectives, see Tal Z. Zarsky, "The Privacy/ Innovation Conundrum," *Lewis and Clark Law Review* 19 no. 1 (2015): 115–68; Helena Ursic & Bart Custers, "Legal Barriers and Enablers to Big Data Reuse: A Critical Assessment of the Challenges for the EU Law," *European Data Protection Review* 2 no. 2 (2016): 209–21.

74. Kirstie Ball & Laureen Snider, eds., *The Surveillance-Industrial Complex: A Political Economy of Surveillance* (New York: Routledge, 2013); Ben Hayes, "The Surveillance-Industrial Complex," in *Routledge Handbook of Surveillance Studies*, eds. Kirstie Ball, Keven D. Haggerty, & David Lyon (New York: Routledge, 2012), 167–75.

75. Adam Winkler, *We the Corporations: How American Businesses Won Their Civil Rights* (New York: W.W. Norton, 2018).

76. For discussion of the origins of the neoliberal First Amendment as an advocacy movement, see Amanda Shanor, "The New *Lochner*," *Wisconsin Law Review* no. 1 (2016): 133–206, 138–63. For policy papers addressing the specific issue of information privacy regulation, see Solveig Singleton, "Privacy as Censorship: A Skeptical View of Proposals to Regulate Privacy in the Private Sector, *Cato Institute Policy Analysis*, No. 295 (Jan. 22, 1998), https://perma.cc/B34M-NFS2; Adam Thierer & Berin Szoka, "What Unites Advocates of Speech Controls & Privacy Regulation?," *Progress on Point* 16 no. 19 (Nov. 2009), https://perma.cc/C9UX-HDF5. An influential article advancing the First Amendment challenge to information privacy regulation was Eugene Volokh, "Freedom of Speech and Information Privacy: The Troubling Implications of a Right to Keep People from Speaking about You," *Stanford Law Review* 52 no. 5 (2002): 1049–124. For a more recent analysis extending the argument to data-driven algorithmic processes, see Jane R. Bambauer, "Is Data Speech?" *Stanford Law Review* 66 no. 1 (2014): 57–120.

77. See Central Hudson Gas & Electric Corp. v. Public Service Commission, 447 U.S. 557, 561–66 (1980). For a useful overview of the doctrine and of scholarly perspectives on its coherence, see Felix T. Wu, "The Commercial Difference," *William & Mary Law Review* 58 no. 6 (2017): 2005–61.

78. The metaphor traces its origins to a famous dissent by Justice Holmes. See Abrams v. United States, 250 U.S. 616, 630 (1919) (Holmes, J., dissenting). For a sampling of perspectives on the meaning of the marketplace metaphor and its significance for free speech jurisprudence more generally, see Vincent Blasi, "Holmes and the Marketplace of Ideas," *The Supreme Court Review* 2004: 1–46; Stanley Ingber, "The Marketplace of Ideas: A Legitimizing Myth," *Duke Law Journal* 1984 no. 1 (1984): 1–91; Robert C. Post, "Reconciling Theory and Doctrine in First Amendment Jurisprudence," *California Law Review* 88 no. 6 (2000): 2353–74.

79. Sorrell v. IMS Health, Inc., 564 U.S. 552, 563–70 (2011).

80. *Sorrell*, 564 U.S. at 577–78.
81. For more detailed discussion of this issue, see Chapter 6, pp. 178–81.
82. Jesselyn Cook, "From Nazis to Incels: How One Tech Company Helps Hate Groups Thrive," *Huffington Post* (July 25, 2018), https://perma.cc/W4Z3-CF8X; Mark Bergen, "YouTube Executives Ignored Warnings, Letting Toxic Videos Run Rampant," *Bloomberg* (Apr. 2, 2019), https://gtownlaw.li/2I8KoZK.
83. For an especially rich articulation, which originated as a white paper commissioned by Google, see Eugene Volokh & Donald Falk, "First Amendment Protection of Search Engine Search Results," *Journal of Law, Economics and Policy* 8 no. 4 (2012): 883–99.
84. Hal R. Varian, "Beyond Big Data," *Business Economics* 49 no. 1 (2014): 27–31.
85. On the emotional contagion experiment, see Adam D.I. Kramer, Jamie E. Guillory, & Jeffrey T. Hancock, "Experimental Evidence of Massive-Scale Emotional Contagion through Social Networks," *Proceedings of the National Academy of Sciences* 111 no. 24 (2014): 8788–90; see James Grimmelmann & Leslie Meltzer Henry, Letter to Inder M. Verma, Editor-in-Chief of *Proceedings of the National Academy of Sciences* (July 17, 2014), https://perma.cc/KG6F-XDMQ; Duncan J. Watts, "Stop Complaining about the Facebook Study. It's a Golden Age for Research," *The Guardian* (July 7, 2014), https://perma.cc/7UMH-NZGG.On the voter mobilization experiment, see Robert M. Bond, Christopher J. Fariss, Jason J. Jones, Adam D. I. Kramer, Cameron Marlow, Jaime E. Settle, & James H. Fowler, "A 61-Million-Person Experiment in Social Influence and Political Mobilization," *Nature* 489 (2012): 295–29; Robinson Meyer, "How Facebook Could Skew an Election," *The Atlantic* (Nov. 4, 2014), https://perma.cc/ZN6D-PQL5/.
86. "About," Google AI, https://perma.cc/6XXX-UXZH (last visited Dec. 14, 2018); Mark Zuckerberg, "Building Global Community," Facebook (Feb. 16, 2017), https://perma.cc/LVJ7-LCRT; see also Abby Ohlheiser, "Mark Zuckerberg Denies That Fake News on Facebook Influenced the Elections," *Washington Post* (Nov. 11, 2016), https://perma.cc/LDU4-TWHT; Mark Zuckerberg, "I Want to Share Some Thoughts on Facebook and the Election," *Facebook* (Nov. 12, 2016), https://perma.cc/7TKZ-PNHZ; "Transcript of Mark Zuckerberg's Senate Hearing," *Washington Post* (Apr. 10, 2018), https://perma.cc/2UQ5-CWYD; Gary Price, "Now Available: Keyword Searchable Video of Google CEO Sundar Pichai's Testimony Before U.S. House Judiciary Committee," *InfoDocket* (Dec. 11, 2018), https://perma.cc/462J-JAMG; Colin Crowell, "Our Approach to Bots and Misinformation," *Twitter Blog* (June 14, 2017), https://perma.cc/K5AN-UACB.
87. Robert Cannon, "The Legislative History of Senator Exon's Communications Decency Act: Regulating Barbarians on the Information Superhighway," *Federal Communications Law Journal* 49 no. 1 (1996): 51–94.
88. Communications Decency Act of 1996, Pub. L. 104-104, title V, §509, 110 Stat. 137, codified as amended at 47 U.S.C. § 230(a)(3) (2018); see, for example, Congressional Record, Feb. 1, 1996, H1175 (statement of Rep. Gilchrest) ("And with the advent of the information age, we need to recognize the need for competition among information media so that the free marketplace of ideas can be communicated through a free marketplace of information outlets. This bill seeks to exploit the market's ability to maximize quality, maximize consumer choice, and minimize prices."), https://perma.cc/QJ5Y-QLL2; see also "Senator Wyden's Speech to the Section 230 Anniversary Conference," Ron Wyden (Mar. 4, 2011) ("The Internet is becoming a central platform for commerce and a means by which people and societies organize. It is the shipping lane of the 21st century, the marketplace of ideas and a democratic town square inside even the most repressive of nations. It was imperative in 1996 that the nascent Internet be protected from the interests of those that wanted to tax and control it. But now that we have seen the power and importance of the Internet—protecting it is that much more imperative."), https://perma.cc/9QBP-V2WA.
89. For a summary of the traditional rules and a comprehensive review of the case law through 2009, see David S. Ardia, "Free Speech Savior or Shield for Scoundrels? An Empirical Study of

Intermediary Immunity under Section 230 of the Communications Decency Act," *Loyola of Los Angeles Law Review* 43 no.2 (2010): 373–506.

90. Jane R. Bambauer & Derek E. Bambauer, "Vanished," *Virginia Journal of Law and Technology* 18 no. 1 (2013): 137–77.

91. James Grimmelmann, "Speech Engines," *Minnesota Law Review* 98 no. 2 (2014): 868–952.

92. Adi Kamdar, "EFF's Guide to CDA 230: The Most Important Law Protecting Online Speech," (Dec. 6, 2012), https://perma.cc/Z799-TY8P; see, for example, Anupam Chander, "How Law Made Silicon Valley," *Emory Law Journal* 63 no. 3 (2014): 639–94; Anupam Chander & Vivek Krishnamurthy, "The Myth of Platform Neutrality," *Georgetown Law Technology Review* 2 no. 2 (2018): 400–16, https://perma.cc/WLS6-CQ35; Cindy Cohn, "Bad Facts Make Bad Law: How Platform Censorship Has Failed So Far and How to Ensure that the Response to Neo-Nazis Doesn't Make It Worse," *Georgetown Law Technology Review* 2 no. 2 (2018): 432–51, https://perma.cc/9WDH-CMK5; Sarah Jeong, "Revenge Porn Is Bad. Criminalizing It Is Worse," *Wired* (Oct. 28, 2013), https://perma.cc/7AZP-P9VL; Daphne Keller, "Internet Platforms: Observations on Speech, Danger, and Money," Aegis Series Paper No. 1807, Hoover Institution (June 13, 2018), https://perma.cc/N43P-F89T. Two notable recent attempts to retheorize the problem of online speech regulation are Jack Balkin, "Free Speech in the Algorithmic Society: Big Data, Private Governance, and New School Speech Regulation," *U.C. Davis Law Review* 51 no. 3 (2017): 1149–210; Kyle Langvardt, "A New Deal for the Online Public Sphere," *George Mason Law Review* 26 no. 2 (forthcoming, 2019).

93. David Carr, "The Evolving Mission of Google," *New York Times* (Mar. 21, 2011), https://perma.cc/8UPE-N3BF; Deepa Seetharaman, "Facebook Leaders Call It a Tech Company, Not a Media Company," *Wall Street Journal* (Oct. 25, 2016), https://perma.cc/DY2N-QWL8.

94. Citizens United v. Federal Election Comm'n, 558 U.S. 310, 353 (2010). The beginnings of a more up-to-date appreciation of contemporary networked media appear in Packingham v. North Carolina, 137 S. Ct. 1730, 1735 (2017).

95. Elisa Shearer & Jeffrey Gottfried, Pew Research Center, "News Use across Social Media Platforms" (Sept. 7, 2017), https://perma.cc/2ZHT-PBFA; Amy Mitchell et al., Pew Research Center, "The Modern News Consumer" (July 7, 2016), 5–8, https://perma.cc/SJ5S-M93H; "Mobile Fact Sheet," Pew Research Center (Jan. 12, 2017), https://perma.cc/V84A-CAJD.

96. Marwick, "Why Do People Share Fake News?"; Benkler, Faris, & Roberts, *Network Propaganda*, 225–33.

97. Julie E. Cohen, "The Zombie First Amemdment," *William & Mary Law Review* 56 no. 4 (2015): 1119–58.

98. Ellen P. Goodman, "Media Policy Out of the Box: Content Abundance, Attention Scarcity, and the Failures of Digital Markets," *Berkeley Technology Law Journal* 19 no. 4 (2004): 1389–472; Tom Wheeler, "Trump FCC Deregulation Policy Threatens Local Broadcasting," *Techtank, Brookings Institution* (July 11, 2017), https://perma.cc/JP85-LXHB. On the growing concentration of media ownership, see Ben H. Bagdikian, *The New Media Monopoly* (Boston, Mass.: Beacon Press, 2004), 27–54.

99. On moderation as the essential commodity that platforms provide, see Tarleton Gillespie, *Custodians of the Internet: Platforms, Content Moderation, and the Hidden Decisions That Shape Social Media* (New Haven, Conn: Yale University Press, 2018).

100. Kent Walker, "A Principle That Should Not Be Forgotten," *Google Europe Blog* (May 19, 2016), https://perma.cc/TD5J-RGN6; Natasha Lomas, "Google Super Successful at Spinning Europe's Right to Be Forgotten Ruling as Farce," *TechCrunch* (July 4, 2014), https://perma.cc/6NYT-XXFG; see also Natasha Lomas, "Wikimedia Attacks Europe's Right to Be Forgotten Ruling as Threat to Its Mission," *TechCrunch* (Aug. 6, 2014), https://perma.cc/B83S-MECK.

101. Google Spain SL v. Agencia Espanola de Proteccion de Datos (AEPD), Case No. C-131/12 (ECJ 13 May 2014), 81, 85–86; see also European Commission Directorate-General for Justice and Consumers, Article 29 Data Protection Working Party, "Guidelines on Implementation of the Court of Justice of the European Union Judgment on 'Google Spain and Inc. v. Agencia

Espanola de Proteccion de Datos (AEPD) and Mario Costeja Gonzales, C-131/14,' " (Nov. 26, 2014) https://perma.cc/MJ54-WK55.

102. Julia Powles & Enrique Chaparro, "How Google Determined Our Right to Be Forgotten," *Guardian* (Feb. 18, 2015), https://perma.cc/A85M-Z43S.

103. See, for example, California HealthCare Foundation, "How Smartphones Are Changing Health Care for Consumers and Providers," (Apr. 2010), https://perma.cc/CQM9-U6XX; Federal Reserve, "Consumers and Mobile Financial Services," (Mar. 2015), https://perma.cc/55FA-MAUD; "Reinventing Wheels," Special Reports, *Economist* (Mar. 1, 2018), https://perma.cc/D44S-79TY; "Unlocking the Promise of a Connected World: Using the Cloud to Enable the Internet of Things," Oracle White Paper (Sept. 2015), https://perma.cc/ANP6-UMYA; "12 Benefits of Cloud Computing," *Salesforce: Hub* (last visited Aug. 6, 2018), https://perma.cc/TH35-RXYB.

104. See, for example, U.S. Bureau of Justice Statistics, Press Release, "17.6 Million U.S. Residents Experienced Identity Theft in 2014" (Sept. 27, 2015), https://perma.cc/A4VU-TRJN; Erika Harrell, "Victims of Identity Theft, 2014," U.S. Bureau of Justice Statistics Bulletin No. NCJ 248991 (Sept. 2015), https://perma.cc/7CXB-B6WT.

105. Brief Amicus Curiae of Electronic Transactions Association on Behalf of Appellant Wyndham Hotels and Resorts, LLC, Federal Trade Commission v. Wyndham Worldwide Corp, No. 14-3514, U.S. Court of Appeals, Third Circuit, Oct. 14, 2014; Statement of David Wagner, President, Entrust, Inc., Hearing Before the Senate Committee on Commerce, Science, and Transportation, "Protecting Personal Consumer Information from Cyber Attacks and Data Breaches" (Mar. 26, 2014), https://perma.cc/8SXS-8X73; Statement of Dan Liutikas, Chief Legal Officer, CompTIA, Hearing Before the House Subcommittee on Commerce, Manufacturing, and Trade, "Reporting Data Breaches: Is Federal Legislation Needed to Protect Consumers?" (July 18, 2013), https://perma.cc/S45B-ZV8L.

106. Statement of Rep. Fred Upton, House Subcommittee on Commerce, Manufacturing, and Trade, Markup of "Discussion Draft of H.R. ____, Data Security and Breach Notification Act of 2015," Mar. 24, 2015, https://perma.cc/3WTM-4QFK; Exhibit A to Statement of Geoffrey Manne, "The FTC at 100: Views from the Academic Experts," Hearing Before the House Subcommittee on Commerce, Manufacturing, and Trade (Feb. 28, 2014), https://perma.cc/79WP-XHAP; "California Bill Analysis, A.B. No. 710," Assembly Committee on the Judiciary (Apr. 29, 2014), https://perma.cc/XR9F-X98L.

107. U.S. Chamber of Commerce, "Hill Letter Regarding the Data Security and Breach Notification Act," (Apr. 15, 2015) ("Given the complexity and expense of responding to a data breach, the Chamber cautions that the bill's flawed liability provisions would further penalize an entity that is itself a victim of data breach by drawing away valuable resources necessary to fix the breach [and] notify customers."), https://perma.cc/V452-55X8.

108. California Bill Analysis, A.B. No. 1710, Assembly Committee on the Judiciary (Apr. 29, 2014) (summarizing arguments by opponents that protective data breach legislation "would result in over-notification that would ultimately confuse California consumers").

109. Paul Schwartz & Edward Janger, "Notification of Data Security Breaches," *Michigan Law Review* 105 no. 5 (2007): 913–84; Sasha Romanosky, Rahul Telang, & Alessandro Acquisti, "Do Data Breach Disclosure Laws Reduce Identity Theft?," *Journal of Policy Analysis & Management* 30 no. 2 (2011): 256–86.

110. Steptoe & Johnson, LLP, "Comparison of US State and Federal Security Breach Notification Laws," (Aug. 26, 2015), https://perma.cc/92J3-RMR3.

111. Regulation (EU) 2016/679, Art. 33, 2016 O.J. (L 119).

112. See FTC v. Wyndham Worldwide Corp., 10 F. Supp. 3d 602 (D.N.J. 2014) (denying motion to dismiss on the ground that FTC lacked UDAAP enforcement authority over data security practices), *aff'd*, 799 F.3d 236 (3d Cir. 2015); LabMD v. FTC, 894 F.3d 1221 (11th Cir. 2018) (invalidating cease and desist order because it did not describe the data security practices prohibited as substandard so requirements for compliance were unclear).

113. Adam J. Levitin, "Private Disordering? Payment Card Fraud Liability Rules," *Brooklyn Journal of Corporate, Financial & Commercial Law* 5 no. 1 (2010): 1–48; Adam J. Levitin, "Pandora's Digital Box: The Promise and Perils of Digital Wallets," *University of Pennsylvania Law Review* 166 no. 2 (2018): 305–76.

114. Jon Hanson & David Yosifon, "The Situation: An Introduction to the Situational Character, Critical Realism, Power Economics, and Deep Capture," *University of Pennsylvania Law Review* 152 no. 1 (2003): 129–346, 212–30.

115. Oscar H. Gandy Jr., *Beyond Agenda Setting: Information Subsidies and Public Policy* (New York: Ablex, 1982).

116. See, for example, Copia Institute, https://copia.is/; Information Technology and Innovation Foundation, https://itif.org/; Tech America, https://www.techamerica.org/; Tech Freedom, http://techfreedom.org/; see also Donald E. Abelson, "Think Tanks in the United States," in *Think Tanks across Nations: A Comparative Approach*, eds. Diane Stone et al. (Manchester, UK: Manchester University Press, 1998), 107–26; Thomas Medvetz, *Think Tanks in America* (Chicago: University of Chicago Press, 2012), 1–22, 47–129.

117. For a sampling of reform proposals, see Danielle Keats Citron & Benjamin Wittes, "The Internet Will Not Break: Denying Bad Samaritans § 230 Immunity," *Fordham Law Review* 86 no. 2 (2018): 401–24; Grimmelmann, "Speech Engines," 893–936; Frank Pasquale, "Reforming the Law of Reputation," *Loyola University Chicago Law Journal* 47 no. 2 (2015): 515–40. For some responses, see Mike Masnick, "Law Professor Pens Ridiculous, Nearly Fact-Free, Misleading Attack on the Most Important Law on the Internet," *TechDirt* (Nov. 3, 2015), https://perma.cc/53W5-S9WS (attacking Ann Bartow and Danielle Citron); Mike Masnick, "Federal Revenge Porn Bill Will Look to Criminalize Websites," *TechDirt* (Apr. 2, 2014), https://perma.cc/KPU9-PXJ9 (attacking Mary Anne Franks); "Law Professor Claims Any Internet Company 'Research' on Users without Review Board Approval Is Illegal," *TechDirt* (Sept. 24, 2014), https://perma.cc/8W2E-TPCC (criticizing James Grimmelmann); Eric Goldman, "Congress Is about to Ruin Its Online Free Speech Masterpiece (Cross-Post)," *Technology & Marketing Law Blog* (Sept. 24, 2017), https://perma.cc/8EA7-VQ2Z; Sarah Jeong, "Revenge Porn Is Bad. Criminalizing It Is Worse," *Wired* (Oct. 28, 2013), https://perma.cc/7AZP-P9VL.

118. See, for example, Declan McCullagh, "The Mother of Gore's Invention," *Wired* (Oct. 17, 2000), https://perma.cc/ZC76-8MFU; Donna Wentworth, "What's Stupider than Calling the Internet an 'Information Superhighway'?," *Electronic Frontier Foundation* (July 5, 2005), https://perma.cc/4X5D-JET2; Nate Anderson, "Time Capsule: The Rough Guide to the Internet . . . from 1999," *Ars Technica* (Dec. 15, 2009), https://perma.cc/7MD9-TYRF.

119. Tung-Hui Hu, *A Prehistory of the Cloud* (Cambridge, Mass.: MIT Press, 2015).

120. On corporate public relations strategies as deep capture strategies, see generally Kirk Hallahan, "Political Public Relations and Strategic Framing," in *Political Public Relations: Principles and Applications*, eds. Jesper Stromback & Spiro Kiousis (New York: Routledge, 2011), 177–213; see also Robert L. Heath & Damian Waymer, "Corporate Issues Management and Political Public Relations," in *Political Public Relations*, 138–56.

121. Brody Mullins & Jack Nicas, "Paying Professors: Inside Google's Academic Influence Campaign," *Wall Street Journal* (July 14, 2017), https://perma.cc/3QLE-75PG.

122. "Announcing the Palantir Council on Privacy and Civil Liberties," *Palantir*, https://perma.cc/2KQH-AX5B (last visited June 16, 2018); Mark Harris, "How Peter Thiel's Secretive Data Company Pushed Into Policing," *Wired* (Aug. 9, 2017), https://perma.cc/R9X8-268W.

123. Examples include South by Southwest (SXSW), https://www.sxsw.com/, the Consumer Electronics Show (CES), https://www.ces.tech/, and the Virtuous Circle Summit, https://vc.internetassociation.org/.

124. Kenneth P. Vogel, "New America, a Google-Funded Think Tank, Faces Backlash for Firing a Google Critic," *New York Times* (Sept. 1, 2017), https://perma.cc/Y5VG-46XY; Kashmir Hill, "Yes, Google Uses Its Power to Quash Ideas It Doesn't Like—I Know Because It Happened

to Me," *Gizmodo* (Aug. 31, 2017), https://perma.cc/VCK5-AU5X; Danny Vinik, "Inside the New Battle against Google," *Politico* (Sept. 17, 2017), https://perma.cc/6L3U-XSVW.

125. Joe Mullin, "Anti-Google Research Group in Washington Is Funded by Oracle," *Ars Technica* (Aug. 19, 2016), https://perma.cc/8M2L-RMC4.

Chapter 4

1. Carl Schmitt, *Political Theology*, trans. George Schwab (Cambridge, Mass.: MIT Press, 1985), 5.

2. Kim Lane Scheppele, "Law in a Time of Emergency: States of Exceptions and the Temptations of 9/11," *University of Pennsylvania Journal of Constitutional Law* 6 no. 5 (2004): 1001–83.

3. Giorgio Agamben, *Homo Sacer: Sovereign Power and Bare Life*, trans. Daniel Heller-Roazen (Stanford, Calif.: Stanford University Press, 1998), 51–52; see also David Dyzenhaus, "*Schmitt v. Dicey*: Are States of Emergency Inside or Outside the Legal Order?," *Cardozo Law Review* 27 no. 5 (2006): 2005–40 (elaborating a theory of legal "grey holes").

4. Rebecca MacKinnon, *Consent of the Networked: The Worldwide Struggle for Internet Freedom* (New York: Basic Books, 2012), 31–61.

5. For what appears to have been the first use of the term, see Timothy C. May, "Crypto Anarchy and Virtual Communities," in *Crypto Anarchy, Cyberstates, and Pirate Utopias*, ed. Peter Ludlow (Cambridge, Mass.: MIT Press, 2001), 65–79, 67.

6. Executive Order 12356: National Security Information, 47 Fed. Reg. 14874 (Apr. 2, 1982).

7. Philip R. Zimmermann, "Cryptography for the Internet," *Scientific American* 279 no. 4 (1998): 110–15. For a comprehensive history of U.S. government cryptography policy, see Whitfield Diffie & Susan Landau, *Privacy on the Line: The Politics of Wiretapping and Encryption* (Cambridge, Mass.: MIT Press, 2007).

8. Junger v. Daley, 209 F.3d 481, 484–85 (6th Cir. 2000); Bernstein v. U.S. Dep't of State, 922 F. Supp. 1426, 1435 (N.D. Cal. 1996), *aff'd sub nom.*, Bernstein v. U.S. Dep't of Justice, 176 F.3d 1132 (9th Cir. 1999), *withdrawn and reh'g granted*, 192 F.3d 1308 (1999).

9. Bernstein v. U.S. Dep't of Commerce, No. C 95-0582 MHP, 2004 WL 838163, at *2, *5 n.2 (N.D. Cal. Apr. 19, 2004).

10. For the regulations, see 15 C.F.R. § 734.17 (2017); 15 C.F.R. Pt. 774, Supp. 1, Cat. 5, Part 2 (2017). On government use of the regulations for ongoing leverage, see Avidan Y. Cover, "Corporate Avatars and the Erosion of the Populist Fourth Amendment," *Iowa Law Review* 100 no. 4 (2015): 1441–502, 1473–76; Michael Hirsch, "How America's Top Tech Companies Created the Surveillance State," *National Journal* (July 25, 2013), https://perma.cc/Z5T8-MSVW; Shane Harris, "Google's Secret NSA Alliance: The Terrifying Deals between Silicon Valley and the Security State," *Salon* (Nov. 16, 2014), https://perma.cc/DFR2-U3ZZ.

11. Charles Warren, "What Is Giving Aid and Comfort to the Enemy?," *Yale Law Journal* 27 no. 3 (1918): 331–47; Gillars v. United States, 182 F.2d 962, 966 (1950). For the current version of the law, see 18 U.S.C. § 2381 (2018).

12. For a good history of the evolution of federal antiterrorism legislation, see Robert M. Chesney, "The Sleeper Scenario: Terrorism Support Laws and the Demands of Prevention," *Harvard Journal on Legislation* 42 no. 1 (2005): 1–89. For the current version of the material support law, see 18 U.S.C. § 2339A(b) (2018).

13. Holder v. Humanitarian Law Project, 561 U.S. 1 (2010).

14. David Cole, "The First Amendment's Borders: The Place of *Holder v. Humanitarian Law Project* in First Amendment Doctrine," *Harvard Law and Policy Review* 6 no. 1 (2012): 147–78.

15. For discussion of the amendments, see *Humanitarian Law Project*, 561 U.S. at 10-13 (2010).

16. Elisabeth Bumiller, "Video Shows U.S. Killing of Reuters Employees," *New York Times* (Apr. 5, 2010), https://perma.cc/5U6U-DRQ3; Noam Cohen & Brian Stelter, "Airstrike Video Brings Attention to Whistle-Blower Site," *New York Times* (Apr. 6, 2010), https://perma.cc/

AL47-CFP5; Garance Franke-Ruta, "Web Site Releases Video of Baghdad Attack That Killed 2 Journalists," *Washington Post* (Apr. 5, 2010), https://perma.cc/PF35-KQG5.

17. Stephanie Strom, "Pentagon Sees a Threat from Online Muckrakers," *New York Times* (Mar. 17, 2010), https://perma.cc/2XQA-EDNU.

18. Elisabeth Bumiller, "Army Leak Suspect Is Turned in, by Ex-hacker," *New York Times* (June 7, 2010), https://perma.cc/X5BE-7HPR.

19. Transcript of Oral Argument, at 42–46, *Humanitarian Law Project*, 561 U.S. 1 (Nos. 08-1498, 09-89), 2010 WL 621318; Brief for the Respondents at 56, *Humanitarian Law Project*, 561 U.S. 1 (Nos. 08-1498, 09-89).

20. *Humanitarian Law Project*, 561 U.S. at 37.

21. *Humanitarian Law Project*, 561 U.S. at 32.

22. On the construction of terrorism as an existential threat, see Wadie Said, "*Humanitarian Law Project* and the Supreme Court's Construction of Terrorism," *Brigham Young University Law Review* 2011 no. 5 (2011): 1455–508.

23. David Cole, "The New McCarthyism: Repeating History in the War on Terrorism," *Harvard Civil Rights-Civil Liberties Law Review* 38 no. 1 (2003): 1–30; Steven Schulman, "Victimized Twice: Asylum Seekers and the Material-Support Bar," *Catholic University Law Review* 59 no. 4 (2010): 949–64.

24. Peter H. Lewis, "New Concerns Raised over a Computer Smut Study," *New York Times* (July 16, 1995), https://perma.cc/YC5K-MG9L; Peter H. Lewis, "The Internet Battles a Much-Disputed Study on Selling Pornography On Line," *New York Times* (July 17, 1995), https://perma.cc/8TFF-XYY6. For the study, see Marty Rimm, "Marketing Pornography on the Information Superhighway: A Survey of 917,410 Images, Descriptions, Short Stories, and Animations Downloaded 8.5 Million Times by Consumers in over 2000 Cities in Forty Countries, Provinces, and Territories," *Georgetown Law Journal* 83 no. 5 (1995): 1849–934.

25. Communications Decency Act of 1996, Pub. L. No. 104-104, title V, § 502(a)(1)(A)-(B), 110 Stat. 133, 134–35, codified at 47 U.S.C. § 223, repealed, Higher Education Amendments of 1998, Pub. L. No. 105-244, Part H § 981, 112 Stat. 1581.

26. Reno v. ACLU, 521 U.S. 844 (1997); Shea v. Reno, 930 F. Supp. 916 (S.D.N.Y. 1996), *aff'd*, 521 U.S. 1113 (1997). The second revision was narrowly tailored to match the contours of existing case law on obscenity, and survived. Nitke v. Gonzales, 413 F. Supp. 2d 262 (S.D.N.Y. 2005), *aff'd*, 547 U.S. 1015 (2006).

27. See, for example, James Ball, "Silk Road: The Online Drug Marketplace That Officials Seem Powerless to Stop," *Guardian* (Mar. 22, 2013), https://perma.cc/X5K6-TAH3; Jake Swearingen, "A Year after the Death of Silk Road, Darknet Markets Are Booming," *The Atlantic* (Oct. 2, 2014), https://perma.cc/C5HL-7GFZ; Cyrus Farivar, "DOJ Announces Official Takedown of AlphaBay, World's Largest Dark Web Market," *Ars Technica* (July 20, 2017), https://perma.cc/9KKL-Y57F; Samuel Gibbs & Lois Beckett, "Dark Web Marketplaces AlphaBay and Hansa Shut Down," *Guardian* (July 20, 2017), https://perma.cc/KND3-B65Y.

28. For work collecting and analyzing these statements, see Tarleton Gillespie, *Wired Shut: Copyright and the Shape of Digital Culture* (Cambridge, Mass.: MIT Press, 2007); John Logie, *Peers, Pirates, and Persuasion: Rhetoric in the Peer-to-Peer Debates* (Anderson, S.C.: Parlor Press, 2006).

29. See, for example, Protecting Digital Broadcast Content: Hearing Before the House Committee on the Judiciary, Subcommittee on Courts, the Internet, and Intellectual Property, 109th Cong., 1st Sess. (Nov. 4, 2005) (testimony of Mitch Bainwol, CEO, Recording Industry Association of America); Copyright Infringement and File Sharing: Hearing Before the Senate Committee on the Judiciary, 109th Cong., 1st Sess. (Sept. 28, 2005) (testimony of Ali Aydar, CEO, SNOCAP); Peer-to-Peer Piracy: Hearing Before the House Committee on the Judiciary, Subcommittee on Courts, the Internet, and Intellectual Property, 109th Cong., 1st Sess. (Sept. 22, 2005) (testimony of Richard Taylor, Senior Vice President, Motion Picture Association of America).

30. For the copyright and trade secrecy enactments, see Uruguay Round Agreements Act, Pub. L. No. 103-465, title V, § 104(A), 108 Stat. 4809, 4976 (1994), codified as amended at 17 U.S.C. § 104A (1998); Economic Espionage Act of 1996, Pub. L. No. 104-294, title I, § 101, 110 Stat. 3488, 3488–91 (1996), codified as amended at 18 U.S.C. §§ 1831–1839 (2018); Sonny Bono Copyright Term Extension Act, Pub. L. No. 105-298, §§ 101–102, 112 Stat. 2827, 2827–28 (1998), codified at 17 U.S.C. §§ 302–304 (1998); Digital Millennium Copyright Act, Pub. L. No. 105–304, §§ 1201–1204, 112 Stat. 2860, 2863–76 (1998), codified as amended at 17 U.S.C. §§ 1201–1204 (1999). For the Computer Fraud and Abuse Act amendments, see Violent Crime Control and Law Enforcement Act of 1994, Pub. L. No. 103-322, title XXIX, § 290001, 108 Stat. 1796, 2097–98, codified as amended at 18 U.S.C. § 1030 (2018); Economic Espionage Act of 1996, Pub. L. No. 104-249, title II, § 201, 110 Stat. 3488, 3491, codified as amended at 18 U.S.C. § 1030 (2018).

31. Eldred v. Ashcroft, 537 U.S. 186, 221 (2003); see also Golan v. Holder, 565 U.S. 302, 329 (2012).

32. For the most well-known series of rulings, see Universal Studios, Inc. v. Reimerdes, 111 F. Supp. 2d 294, 332 (S.D.N.Y. 2000), aff'd sub nom., Universal Studios, Inc. v. Corley, 273 F.3d 429, 434–35, 450–52 (2d Cir. 2001). On the framing of copyright infringement as an existential threat, see Julie E. Cohen, "Pervasively Distributed Copyright Enforcement," *Georgetown Law Journal* 95 no. 1 (2006): 1–48.

33. Tarleton Gillespie, "Characterizing Copyright in the Classroom: The Cultural Work of Antipiracy Campaigns," *Communication, Culture and Critique* 2 no. 3 (2009): 274–318, doi:10.1111/j.1753-9137.2009.01039.x.; Logie, *Peers, Pirates, and Persuasion.*

34. David E. Pozen, "Deep Secrecy," *Stanford Law Review* 62 no. 2 (2010): 257–340.

35. On the origins of the privilege, see Robert M. Chesney, "State Secrets and the Limits of National Security Litigation," *George Washington Law Review* 75 nos. 5–6 (2007): 1249–332; on its contemporary uses, see Laura K. Donohue, "The Shadow of State Secrets," *University of Pennsylvania Law Review* 159 no. 1 (2010): 77–216.

36. The modern state is so sprawling and complex that neither secrecy nor transparency is entirely feasible. Instead, as Mark Fenster shows, both secrecy and transparency are essentially performative; the state withholds or provides information according to complex sets of rules, but the results do not predictably shed light on what the state actually does. See Mark Fenster, "The Implausibility of Secrecy," *Hastings Law Journal* 65 no. 2 (2016): 309–62; Mark Fenster, "Seeing the State: Transparency as Metaphor," *Administrative Law Review* 62 no. 3 (2010): 617–72. On leaks and leaking, see David E. Pozen, "The Leaky Leviathan: Why the Government Condemns and Condones Unlawful Disclosures of Information," *Harvard Law Review* 127 no. 2 (2013): 512–635.

37. Lee Tien, "Foreign Intelligence Surveillance Act: Frequently Asked Questions (and Answers)," *Electronic Frontier Foundation* (Sept. 27, 2001), https://perma.cc/46A2-3JRV; Philip Shenon, "Traces of Terror: Counterintelligence; 'Paper Court' Comes to Life over Secret Tribunal's Ruling on Post-9/11 Police Powers," *New York Times* (Aug. 27, 2002), https://perma.cc/KJ6N-4TMU; National Commission on Terrorist Attacks Upon the United States, "The 9/11 Commission Report" (July 22, 2004), chapter 3, https://perma.cc/CH6M-LARB.

38. Al-Haramain Islamic Found. v. Bush, 507 F.3d 1190, 1195 (9th Cir. 2007).

39. James Risen & Eric Lichtblau, "Bush Lets U.S. Spy on Callers without Courts," *New York Times* (Dec. 16, 2005), https://perma.cc/56M4-7ZKU; Nate Anderson, "AT&T Engineer: NSA Built Secret Rooms in Our Facilities," *Ars Technica* (Apr. 12, 2006), https://perma.cc/45U5-74L8; see also Julia Angwin, Charlie Savage, Jeff Larson, Henrik Moltke, Laura Poitras, & James Risen, "AT&T Helped U.S. Spy on Internet on a Vast Scale," *New York Times* (Aug. 15, 2015), https://perma.cc/2XHK-YPNQ.

40. See Hepting v. AT&T Corp., 539 F.3d 1157 (9th Cir. 2008); Hepting v AT&T Corp., 671 F.3d 881 (9th Cir. 2012).

41. Amnesty Int'l v. McConnell, 646 F. Supp. 2d 633 (S.D.N.Y. 2009), *vacated and remanded sub nom.*, Amnesty Int'l v. Clapper, 638 F.3d 118 (2d Cir. 2011), *rev'd*, 568 U.S. 398 (2013).

42. James Bamford, "The NSA Is Building the Country's Biggest Spy Center (Watch What You Say)," *Wired* (Mar. 15, 2012), https://perma.cc/LM2L-SS4S.

43. Clapper v. Amnesty Int'l USA, 568 U.S. 398, 402 (2013).

44. For a helpful overview of the different programs, see Julia Angwin & Jeff Larson, "The NSA Revelations All in One Chart, *ProPublica*, June 30, 2014, https://perma.cc/WA9Q-SUSB.

45. Garrett Hatch, Congressional Research Service Report No. RL34385, "Privacy and Civil Liberties Oversight Board: New Independent Agency Status," 1–9 (Aug. 27, 2012), https://perma.cc/7H2F-KDSP.

46. USA Freedom Act, Pub. L. No. 114-23, title I, § 101 & title IV, § 401, 129 Stat. 268, 270 & 279, codified as amended at 50 U.S.C. §§ 1861(b)(2), (c)(3) & 1803(i) (2018).

47. David Cunningham, *There's Something Happening Here: The New Left, the Klan and FBI Counterintelligence* (Berkeley: University of California Press, 2004): 27–41; Loch K. Johnson, "Congressional Supervision of America's Secret Agencies: The Experience and Legacy of the Church Committee," *Public Administration Review* 64 no. 1 (2004): 3–14, 5–12.

48. Jay Stanley, "What Powers Does the Civil Liberties Oversight Board Have?," *ACLU* (Nov. 4, 2013), https://perma.cc/3HQN-TUFA; Nicholas M. Horrock, "How Deeply Should the C.I.A. Be Looked Into," *New York Times* (June 22, 1975), 182.

49. Privacy & Civil Liberties Oversight Board, "Report on the Telephone Records Program Conducted under Sec. 215 of the USA Patriot Act & on the Operations of the Foreign Intelligence Surveillance Court" (Jan. 23, 2014), https://perma.cc/WM3Z-86NQ; Ellen Nakashima, "Independent Review Board Says NSA Phone Data Program Is Illegal and Should End," *Washington Post* (Jan. 23, 2014), https://perma.cc/R36W-UFME; Dan Roberts, "FISA Court Grants Extension of Licence for Bulk Collection of US Phone Records," *The Guardian* (June 20, 2014), https://perma.cc/5BFL-RP5F; Privacy and Civil Liberties Oversight Board, "Recommendations Assessment Report," (Jan. 29, 2015), http://perma.cc/8WZ5-MG32; Spencer Ackerman, "Obama Must Finally End NSA Phone Record Collection, Says Privacy Board," *The Guardian* (Jan. 29, 2015), https://perma.cc/6BK5-HRXQ; Cody M. Poplin, "NSA Ends Bulk Collection of Telephony Metadata under Section 215," *Lawfare* (Nov. 30, 2015), https://perma.cc/E4KZ-RXUR; Privacy & Civil Liberties Oversight Board, "Recommendations Assessment Report" (Feb. 5, 2016), http://perma.cc/3ZR2-S3KP.

50. Conor Friedersdorf, "NSA Surveillance Divides the Republican Party," *The Atlantic* (Jan. 27, 2014), https://perma.cc/D3GZ-N8ED; George Gao, "What Americans Think about NSA Surveillance, National Security, and Privacy," Pew Research Center (May 29, 2015), https://perma.cc/F726-8HCL.

51. On the ultimate effects of the post-COINTELPRO reforms, see Brian Hochman, *All Ears: A History of Wiretapping in the United States* (Cambridge, Mass.: Harvard University Press, forthcoming).

52. Wikimedia Found. v. NSA, 857 F.3d 193, 209–11, 213–15 (4th Cir. 2017); Schuchardt v. President, 839 F.3d 336, 349–54 (3d Cir. 2016); Obama v. Klayman, 800 F.3d 559, 563–64 (D.C. Cir. 2015) (opinion of Brown, J.); ACLU v. Clapper, 959 F. Supp. 2d 724, 751–56 (S.D.N.Y. 2013), *rev'd on other grounds*, 785 F.3d 787 (2d Cir. 2015); Jewel v. NSA, 2015 WL 545925 (N.D. Cal. Feb. 10, 2015), *appeal dismissed*, 810 F.3d 622 (9th Cir. 2015).

53. Doe v. Ashcroft, 334 F. Supp. 2d 471 (S.D.N.Y. 2004), *vacated as moot sub nom.*, Doe v. Gonzales, 449 F.3d 415 (2d Cir. 2006). This tactic has encountered limits, however. See Doe v. Gonzales, 500 F. Supp. 2d 379 (S.D.N.Y. 2007), *aff'd in part and rev'd in part sub nom.*, Doe v. Mukasey, 549 F.3d 861 (2d Cir. 2008).

54. Al-Haramain Islamic Found. v. Bush, 451 F. Supp. 2d 1215 (D. Ore. 2006), *rev'd*, 507 F.3d 1190 (9th Cir. 2007), *transferred by the Judicial Panel on Multidistrict Litigation, In re* National Security Agency Telecommc'ns Records Litig., 564 F. Supp. 2d 1109 (N.D. Cal. 2008).

55. In re National Security Agency Telecommc'ns Records Litig., 700 F. Supp. 2d 1182 (N.D. Cal. 2010), rev'd sub nom., Al-Haramain Islamic Found. v. Obama, 705 F.3d 845 (9th Cir. 2012).

56. Tim Cushing, "Government Drops Facebook Search Warrant Gag Order at Eleventh Hour," *TechDirt* (Sept. 18, 2017), https://perma.cc/855K-NQ47; Raymond Bonner, "The FBI Checked the Wrong Box and a Woman Ended Up on the Terrorism Watch List for Years," *ProPublica* (Dec. 15, 2015), https://perma.cc/L2ZH-ZBUZ; Jessica Glenza & Nicky Woolf, "Stingray Spying: FBI's Secret Deal with Police Hides Phone Dragnet from Courts," *The Guardian* (Apr. 10, 2015), https://perma.cc/7AZ2-6KB5; see also Human Rights Watch, "Dark Side: Secret Origins of Evidence in US Criminal Cases" (Jan. 9, 2018), https://perma.cc/L54M-ELZB.

57. Rodney A. Smolla, "Information as Contraband," *Northwestern University Law Review* 96 no. 3 (2002): 1099–176.

58. Wesley Newcomb Hohfeld, "Some Fundamental Legal Conceptions as Applied in Judicial Reasoning," *Yale Law Journal* 23 no. 1 (2013): 16–59, 44–54.

59. Robert Cannon, "The Legislative History of Senator Exon's Communications Decency Act: Regulating Barbarians on the Information Superhighway," *Federal Communications Law Journal* 49 no. 1 (1996): 51–94.

60. Trotter Hardy, "Criminal Copyright Infringement," *William and Mary Bill of Rights Journal* 11 no. 1 (2002): 305–42.

61. 47 U.S.C. § 230(e)(2) (2018); Federal Communications Commission, Protecting and Promoting the Open Internet, 80 Fed. Reg. 19,738, ¶¶ 113, 304 (Apr. 13, 2015), *repealed by* Restoring Internet Freedom, 83 Fed. Reg. 7852 (Feb. 22, 2018); Preserving the Open Internet, 25 F.C.C.R. 17905, ¶¶ 107, 111 (Dec. 23, 2010), *vacated in part by* Verizon v. FCC, 740 F.3d 623 (D.C. Cir. 2014).

62. On the characteristics of takedown notices, see Laura Quilter & Jennifer Urban, "Efficient Process or 'Chilling Effects'? Takedown Notices under Section 512 of the Digital Millennium Copyright Act," *Santa Clara Computer and High Technology Law Journal* 22 no. 4 (2005): 621–94; Wendy Seltzer, "Free Speech Unmoored in Copyright's Safe Harbor: Chilling Effects of the DMCA on the First Amendment," *Harvard Journal of Law and Technology* 24 no. 1 (2010): 171–232. On the trade strategy, see Markham Erickson & Sarah C. Leggin, "Exporting Internet Law through International Trade Agreements: Recalibrating U.S. Trade Policy for the Internet Age," *Catholic University Journal of Law and Technology* 24 no. 2 (2016): 317–68.

63. See, for example, UMG Recordings v. Shelter Capital Partners LLC, 718 F.3d 1006 (9th Cir. 2013); Viacom Int'l, Inc. v. YouTube, Inc., 676 F.3d 19 (2d Cir. 2012); Perfect 10, Inc. v. Visa Int'l Service Ass'n, 494 F.3d 788 (9th Cir. 2007).

64. On the populist backlash against maximalist copyright, see Bill Herman, *The Fight over Digital Rights: The Politics of Copyright and Technology* (New York: Cambridge University Press, 2013). On platforms' appropriation of anti-maximalist rhetoric, see Sean M. O'Connor, "Creators, Innovators, & Appropriation Mechanisms," *George Mason Law Review* 22 no. 4 (2015): 991–96; Tom Slee, *What's Yours Is Mine: Against the Sharing Economy* (New York, OR Books, 2017), 109–38; see also Guy Pessach, "Beyond IP—The Cost of Free: Informational Capitalism in a Post IP Era," *Osgoode Hall Law Review* 54 no. 1 (2016): 225–51. For examples of failed legislative efforts, see Consumer Broadband and Digital Television Promotion Act of 2002, Proposed Bill No. S. 2048, 107th Congress, 2nd Session; Digital Transition Content Security Act of 2005, Proposed Bill No. H.R. 4569, 109th Congress, 2nd Session; and Audio Broadcast Flag Licensing Act of 2006, Proposed Bill No. H.R. 4861, 109th Congress, 2nd Session. But see Federal Communications Commission, Commercial Availability of Navigation Devices and Compatibility between Cable Systems and Consumer Electronics Equipment, 68 Fed. Reg. 66,728 (Nov. 28, 2003) (incorporating copy-protection requirement into cable plug-and-play standard).

65. See Jonathan Weisman, "In Fight over Piracy Bills, New Economy Rises against Old," *New York Times* (Jan. 18, 2012), https://perma.cc/6UDK-WEVQ; "SOPA/PIPA: Internet Blacklist

Legislation," *Electronic Frontier Foundation*, https://perma.cc/L8BA-MVFB (last visited Apr. 12, 2019).

66. In 2014, the American Bar Association's Intellectual Property Section issued a report that included recommendations for stricter interdiction mandates, which Congress uncharacteristically has ignored. Section of Intellectual Property Law, American Bar Association, "A Section White Paper: A Call for Action for Online Piracy and Counterfeiting Legislation" (2014), http://perma.cc/9GCY-3D3D; see also Mike Masnick, "The Rebranding of SOPA: Now Called 'Notice and Staydown,'" *TechDirt* (Mar. 14, 2014), https://perma.cc/GHC9-JQUX.

67. Jack Balkin, "Free Speech in the Algorithmic Society: Big Data, Private Governance, and New School Speech Regulation," *U.C. Davis Law Review* 51 no. 3 (2017): 1149–210, 1177–79. On the implications of private-sector automated enforcement initiatives in copyright and other areas, see Annemarie Bridy, "Internet Payment Blockades," *Florida Law Review* 67 no. 5 (2015): 1524–68; Annemarie Bridy, "Graduated Response and the Turn to Private Ordering in Online Copyright Enforcement," *Oregon Law Review* 89 no. 1 (2010): 81–132.

68. "An Update to Our Search Algorithms," *Inside Search, Google* (Aug. 10, 2012), https://perma.cc/RG4F-B3US; see also "Continued Progress on Fighting Piracy," *Public Policy Blog*, Google (Oct. 17, 2014), https://perma.cc/5J2M-Y5WB; Adi Robertson, "Google Rolling Out New Search Update to Downrank 'Most Notorious' Pirate Sites," *Verge* (Oct. 17, 2014), https://perma.cc/R6HZ-ZQYC; James Titcomb, "Google and Microsoft Agree Crackdown on Illegal Downloads," *Telegraph* (Feb. 20, 2017), https://perma.cc/NA4V-FQSV.

69. Joe Silver, "Viacom and Google Settle $1 Billion YouTube Lawsuit," *Ars Technica* (Mar. 18, 2014), https://perma.cc/8RSV-5V7H.

70. Between 2004 and 2009, the Recording Industry of America filed over 30,000 lawsuits against individual users, settling most of the lawsuits for an average of $3,500–$4,500 each. See Steve Karnowski, "Facing the Music," *USA Today* (June 19, 2009); Justin Hughes, "On the Logic of Suing One's Customers and the Dilemma of Infringement-Based Business Models," *Cardozo Arts and Entertainment Law Journal* 22 no. 3 (2005): 725–66.

71. Scarlet Extended SA v. Societe belge des auteurs, compositeurs et editeurs SCRL (SABAM), [2012] E.C.D.R. 4, ¶ 45 (discussing conflicting legal directives and concluding that courts "must strike a fair balance" between them).

72. Copyright Felony Act, Pub. L. No. 102-561, 106 Stat. 4233 (1992), codified as amended at 18 U.S.C. § 2319 (2018); Violent Crime Control and Law Enforcement Act of 1994, Pub. L. No. 103-322, § 320104, 108 Stat. 1796, 2110–11 (1994), codified as amended at 18 U.S.C. § 2320 (2018); Anticounterfeiting Consumer Protection Act of 1996, Pub. L. No. 104-153, § 5, 110 Stat. 1386, 1387 (1996), codified as amended at 18 U.S.C. § 2320 (2018); No Electronic Theft (NET) Act, Pub. L. No. 105-147, § 2, 111 Stat. 2678, 2678–80 (1997), codified as amended at 18 U.S.C. §§ 2319, 2319A, 2320 (2018); Intellectual Property Protection and Courts Amendments Act of 2004, Pub. L. No. 108-482, § 102, 118 Stat. 3912, 3912–15 (2004), codified as amended at 18 U.S.C. § 2318 (2018); Family Entertainment and Copyright Act of 2005, Pub. L. No. 109-9, §§ 102–103, 119 Stat. 218, 218–21 (2005), codified as amended at 18 U.S.C. §§ 2319, 2319B (2018); Stop Counterfeiting in Manufactured Goods Act, Pub. L. No. 109-181, 120 Stat. 285 (2006), codified as amended at 18 U.S.C. § 2320 (2018); Prioritizing Resources and Organization for Intellectual Property Act, Pub. L. No. 110-403, §§ 202–206, 122 Stat. 4256, 4260–63 (2008), codified as amended at 18 U.S.C. §§ 2318–2320, 2323 (2018); Food and Drug Administration Safety and Innovation Act, Pub. L. No. 112-144, § 717, 126 Stat. 993, 1076–77 (2012), codified as amended at 18 U.S.C. § 2320 (2018); see also Digital Millennium Copyright Act, Pub. L. No. 105-304, §§ 1201–1204, 112 Stat. 2860, 2863–76 (1998), codified as amended at 17 U.S.C. § 1204 (2018).

73. For a critical analysis, see Christophe Geiger, "Towards a Balanced International Legal Framework for Criminal Enforcement of Intellectual Property Rights," in *TRIPS Plus 20: From Trade Rules to Market Principles*, eds. Hans Ullrich et al. (New York: Springer, 2016), 645–79.

74. See Philip S. Corwin, "MegaBust's MegaQuestions Cloud the Net's Future," *CircleID* (Feb. 13, 2012), https://perma.cc/BF7Y-BLE3; Greg Kumparak, "How Dropbox Knows When You're Sharing Copyrighted Stuff (Without Actually Looking at Your Stuff)," *TechCrunch* (Mar. 30, 2014), https://perma.cc/XF2W-SU2F. For reports on criminal intellectual property enforcement activities in the United States., see U.S. Dept. of Justice, "Pro-IP Act: Annual Report FY 2016," (Jan. 12, 2017), https://perma.cc/6EUN-2FHG; U.S. Dept. of Justice, "Pro-IP Act Annual Report FY 2015," (Apr. 29, 2016), https://perma.cc/8D7X-9AZH; Fed. Bureau of Investigation, "FBI Fiscal Year 2015 Report to Congress on Intellectual Property Rights Enforcement," (Apr. 8, 2019), https://perma.cc/W9D3-F7TG; Fed. Bureau of Investigation, "Federal Bureau of Investigation Pro-IP Act Annual Report 2014," (Apr. 8, 2019), https://perma.cc/NX5C-8RTV.

75. Digital Millennium Copyright Act, Pub. L. No. 105-304, § 1201, 112 Stat. 2860, 2863–65 (1998), codified as amended at 17 U.S.C. § 1201 (1999).

76. Julie E. Cohen, *Configuring the Networked Self: Law, Code, and the Play of Everyday Practice* (New Haven, Conn: Yale University Press, 2012), 202–207.

77. For an overview (and a call for more empirical investigation), see Justin Hughes, "Motion Pictures, Markets, and Copylocks," *George Mason Law Review* 23 no. 4 (2016): 941–66; on the processes by which technical protection systems become implemented and normalized, see Cohen, *Configuring the Networked Self*, 158–64, 193–99.

78. Cecilia Kang, "FCC Delays Vote on Cable Set-Top Boxes," *New York Times* (Sept. 29, 2016), https://perma.cc/LUT7-RAD6; Jon Brodkin, "FCC Chairman Pai Takes Wheeler's Set-Top Box Plan off the Table," *Ars Technica* (Jan. 30, 2017), https://perma.cc/92RD-8FUM.

79. 17 U.S.C. § 1201(f), (g), (j) (2018).

80. Wendy Seltzer, "The Imperfect Is the Enemy of the Good: Anticircumvention versus Open User Innovation," *Berkeley Technology Law Journal* 25 no. 2 (2010): 909–72; see also Cohen, *Configuring the Networked Self*, 209–13.

81. See 17 U.S.C. § 1201(a)(1) (2018); U.S. Copyright Office, Exemption to Prohibition on Circumvention of Copyright Protection Systems for Access Control Technologies: Final Rule, 65 Fed. Reg. 64,556, 64,558 (Oct. 27, 2000).

82. For the results of the triennial rule-makings, see U.S. Copyright Office, "Rulemaking Proceedings under Section 1201 of Title 17," https://perma.cc/N4UQ-9QHS (last visited June 12, 2019).

83. David Kravets, "Industry, and Apple, Opposing 'Right to Repair' Laws," *Ars Technica* (Mar. 7, 2017), https://perma.cc/F8BY-V955; Kyle Wiens, "You Bought That Gadget, and Damnit, You Should Be Able to Fix it," *Wired* (Mar. 22, 2017), https://perma.cc/CW6E-AMQM. For analysis of the underlying legal and philosophical issues, see Joshua T. Fairfield, *Owned: Property, Privacy, and the New Digital Serfdom* (New York: Cambridge University Press, 2017), 186–99; Aaron Perzanowski & Jason Schultz, *The End of Ownership: Personal Property in the Digital Economy* (Cambridge, Mass.: MIT Press, 2016), 121–54

84. The Supreme Court has identified intent to profit from infringement and platform design as factors to be considered in contributory infringement analysis. Large, diversified technology companies can point to all of the different services that they offer; see Metro-Goldwyn-Mayer Studios, Inc. v. Grokster, Ltd., 545 U.S. 913, 939–40 (2005), but smaller firms tend to be optimized for the functionality that prompted litigation in the first place.

85. See, for example, Macon Phillips, "Obama Administration Responds to We the People Petition on SOPA and Online Piracy," *White House Blog* (Jan. 14, 2012), http://perma.cc/TRS-8Y4A; Letter from Hillary Rodham Clinton, Sec. of State, to Rep. Howard L. Berman (Oct. 25, 2011), http://perma.cc/K9LP-SYRA.

86. See, for example, Chris Welch, "Russia, China, and Other Nations Draft Proposal to Give ITU Greater Influence over the Internet," *Verge* (Dec. 9, 2012), https://perma.cc/M8RY-QLDL; Matt Smith, "Russia Backs Down on Proposals to Regulate the Internet," *Reuters* (Dec. 10, 2012), https://perma.cc/X5FJ-TF43.

87. Steven Levy, "Battle of the Clipper Chip," *New York Times Magazine* (June 12, 1994), https://perma.cc/AE2C-36L4; Danielle Kehl et al., "Doomed to Repeat History? Lessons from the Crypto Wars of the 1990s," New America Cybersecurity Initiative (June 17, 2015), 5–11, https://perma.cc/M56H-9HUZ.

88. Ryan Gallagher, "Operation Auroragold: How the NSA Hacks Cellphone Networks Worldwide," *Intercept* (Dec. 4, 2014), https://perma.cc/A64Z-DKLJ; Ryan Gallagher & Glenn Greenwald, "How the NSA Plans to Infect 'Millions' of Computers with Malware," *Intercept* (Mar. 12, 2014), https://perma.cc/B4KE-UD5E; Barton Gellman & Ashkan Soltani, "NSA 'Hacked Google and Yahoo's Data Centre Links', Snowden Documents Say," *Independent* (Oct. 30, 2013), https://perma.cc/KR9E-5XTS.

89. George Joseph, "Exclusive: Feds Regularly Monitored Black Lives Matter since Ferguson," *Intercept* (July 24, 2015), https://perma.cc/9F9M-BBUP; Glenn Greenwald & Murtaza Hussain, "Meet the Muslim-American Leaders the FBI and NSA Have Been Spying On," *Intercept* (July 9, 2014), https://perma.cc/3GFB-PFKF; Michael German & Sara Robinson, "Wrong Priorities on Fighting Terrorism," Brennan Center for Justice at New York University School of Law (Oct. 31, 2018), https://perma.cc/MKP6-T24A.

90. "GNI Principles on Freedom of Expression and Privacy," Global Network Initiative (Apr. 8, 2019), https://perma.cc/J32J-GMXB; see MacKinnon, *Consent of the Networked*, 138–39, 179–82.

91. Julian Hattem & Mario Trujillo, "Silicon Valley Fights to Lift 'Gag Orders,'" *The Hill* (Oct. 11, 2014), http://perma.cc/WD7B-TDSR; Tim Cook, Apple CEO, "A Message to Our Customers" (Feb. 16, 2016), http://perma.cc/9VYP-WCLZ.

92. USA Freedom Act, Pub. L. 114-23, §101, 129 Stat. 270 (2015), codified as amended at 50 U.S.C. § 1861(b)(2) & (c)(3) (2018).

93. Digital Rights Ireland Ltd. v. Minister for Communications, Marine and Natural Resources, ECLI:EU:C:2014:238 (2014) (Grand Chamber, CJEU); Directive 2016/680 of the European Parliament and of the Council of 27 April 2016 on the protection of natural persons with regard to the processing of personal data by competent authorities for the purposes of the prevention, investigation, detection or prosecution of criminal offences or the execution of criminal penalties, and on the free movement of such data, and repealing Council Framework Decision 2008/977/JHA, O.J. L 119/89.

94. Kevin Poulsen, "Apple's IPhone Encryption Is a Godsend, Even if Cops Hate it," *Wired* (Oct. 8, 2014), https://perma.cc/GC98-YGPL; Joseph Cox, "Encryption Is Going Mainstream, but Will People Actually Use It?," *Vice Motherboard* (Aug. 21, 2014), https://perma.cc/8CKX-3XBZ; Matthew Panzarino, "Apple's Tim Cook Delivers Blistering Speech on Encryption, Privacy," *TechCrunch* (Jun. 2, 2015), https://perma.cc/98LT-5JF4; Cade Metz, "Forget Apple vs. the FBI: WhatsApp Just Switched on Encryption for a Billion People," *Wired* (Apr. 5, 2016), https://perma.cc/CJF4-9ZGK.

95. "An Encryption Tightrope: Balancing Americans' Security and Privacy," Hearing Before the House Committee on the Judiciary, 114th Cong., 2d Sess. 14–15 (2016) (statement of James Comey, Director, FBI); American Civil Liberties Union, "All Writs Act Orders for Assistance from Tech Companies," https://perma.cc/V8B8-XTU2 (last visited June 17, 2018); Harold Abelson et al., "Keys under Doormats: Mandating Insecurity by Requiring Government Access to All Data and Communications," *Journal of Cybersecurity* 1(1) (2015): 69–79; Sara Sorcher, "The Battle between Washington and Silicon Valley over Encryption," *Christian Science Monitor: Passcode* (July 7, 2015), http://perma.cc/B6Y4-DFHQ.

96. Neil Sheehan, "Pentagon Study Traces 3 Decades of Growing U.S. Involvement," *New York Times* (June 13, 1971), 1; Floyd Abrams, *Friend of the Court: On the Front Lines with the First Amendment* (New Haven, Conn.: Yale University Press, 2013), 137–46.

97. New York Times Co. v. United States, 403 U.S. 713, 717 (1971).

98. Martin Arnold, "Pentagon Papers Charges Are Dismissed; Judge Byrne Frees Ellsberg and Russo, Assails 'Improper Government Conduct,'" *New York Times* (May 12, 1973), 1; Abrams, *Friend of the Court*, 143.

99. Espionage Act of 1917, Pub. L. 104-294, title VI, § 602(c), 110 Stat. 3503, codified as amended at 18 U.S.C.A. § 798 (2018).

100. Charlie Savage, "Soldiers' Lawyers Rest Case with Defense of WikiLeaks' Journalistic Role," *New York Times* (July 10, 2013), https://perma.cc/BR8B-RE9R; Ed Pilkington, "Bradley Manning Verdict: Cleared of 'Aiding the Enemy' but Guilty of Other Charges," *The Guardian* (July 31, 2013), https://perma.cc/79RR-ZVQN; Paul Lewis, "Bradley Manning Given a 35-Year Prison Term for Passing Files to Wikileaks," *The Guardian* (Aug. 21, 2013), https://perma.cc/347C-X9V3. President Obama later commuted the sentence to the seven years Manning had already served. Charlie Savage, "Chelsea Manning to Be Released Early as Obama Commutes Sentence," *New York Times* (Jan. 17, 2017), https://perma.cc/Z2DC-467X. On the ways that the Espionage Act has functioned as a tool for censorship and preservation of government secrecy, see Yochai Benkler, "A Free Irresponsible Press: Wikileaks and the Battle over the Soul of the Networked Fourth Estate," *Harvard Civil Rights-Civil Liberties Law Review* 46 no. 2 (2011): 311–98; Cole, "The New McCarthyism."

101. Ewen MacAskill, "The Long Arm of US Law: What Next for Edward Snowden," *The Guardian* (Dec. 2, 2013), https://perma.cc/VB9G-AW6K; Shaun Walker, "Edward Snowden's Leave to Remain in Russia Extended for Three Years," *The Guardian* (Jan. 18, 2017), https://perma.cc/PQV5-D8AA.

102. Krishnadev Calamur, "Who Is Reality Winner?," *The Atlantic* (June 6, 2017), https://perma.cc/4RYZ-C9GY.

103. Andy Greenberg, "Snowden's Chronicler Reveals Her Own Life under Surveillance," *Wired* (Feb. 4, 2016), https://perma.cc/W2S2-8VFZ; Andy Greenberg, "Anonymous' Barrett Brown Is Free—And Ready to Pick New Fights," *Wired* (Dec. 21, 2016), https://perma.cc/7J56-FYE4; David Gilbert, "Wanted Man: The U.S. Now Says Arresting Julian Assange Is a Priority," *Vice News* (Apr. 21, 2017), https://perma.cc/NTR6-EJP9; Charlie Savage, Adam Goldman, & Michael S. Schmidt, "Assange Is Secretly Charged in U.S., Prosecutors Mistakenly Reveal," *New York Times* (Nov. 16, 2018), https://perma.cc/V8HQ-CVDA.

104. Alan Rusbridger, WikiLeaks: "The Guardian's Role in the Biggest Leak in the History of the World," *The Guardian* (Jan. 28, 2011), https://perma.cc/LU6R-F8RT; Bill Keller, "Dealing with Assange and the WikiLeaks Secrets," *New York Times* (Jan. 26, 2011), https://perma.cc/XP5Y-S2SZ; "A Note to Readers: Piecing Together the Reports, and Deciding What to Publish," *New York Times* (July 25, 2010), https://perma.cc/Q9B6-P7DS. For additional discussion of those efforts and of the institutional design questions surrounding WikiLeaks more generally, see Chapter 8, pp. 254–57.

105. 5 U.S.C. § 552(b)(4) (2018).

106. 18 U.S.C. §§ 1331–1331 (2018).

107. Donohue, "The Shadow of State Secrets"; Rebecca Wexler, "Life, Liberty, and Trade Secrets: Intellectual Property in the Criminal Justice System," *Stanford Law Review* 70 no. 5 (2018): 1343–429.

108. Ashlee Vance, "WikiLeaks Struggles to Stay Online after Attacks," *New York Times* (Dec. 3, 2010), https://perma.cc/HJ2S-SLFY; Bianca Bosker, "PayPal Admits State Department Pressure Caused It to Block WikiLeaks," *Huffington Post* (Dec. 8, 2010), https://perma.cc/V8BU-TCN5.

109. See Sian Sullivan, Andre Spicer, & Steffen Bohm, "Becoming Global (Un)Civil Society: Counter-hegemonic Struggle and the IndyMedia Network," *Globalizations* 8 no. 5 (2011): 703–17.

110. On the provisions of national security letters, see. Hannah Bloch-Webha, "Process without Procedure: National Security Letters and First Amendment Rights," *Suffolk University Law Review* 39 no. 3 (2016): 367–408, 374–77. On state licensing, see George F. Will, "Oregon

Is Suing Engineers for . . . Speaking Up about Engineering?," *Washington Post* (June 7, 2017), https://perma.cc/3A6M-VYNU.

111. Compare Nate Cardozo et al., "Who Has Your Back? 2017," Electronic Frontier Foundation (July 2017), https://perma.cc/S8YH-K9NN, with Cover, "Corporate Avatars"; Niva Elkin-Koren & Eldar Haber, "Governance by Proxy: Cyber Challenges to Civil Liberties," *Brooklyn Law Review* 82 no. 1 (2017): 105–62. On warrant canaries, see Naomi Gilens, "The NSA Has Not Been Here: Warrant Canaries as Tools for Transparency in the Wake of the Snowden Disclosures," *Harvard Journal of Law and Technology* 28 no. 2 (2015): 525–48; Rebecca Wexler, "Warrant Canaries and Disclosure by Design: The Real Threat to National Security Letter Gag Orders," *Yale Law Journal Forum* 124 (2014): 158–79. On national security letters more generally, see Bloch-Webha, "Process without Procedure."

112. Quinta Jurecic, "EDNY Dismisses Suits against Facebook on Hamas Attacks," *Lawfare* (May 18, 2017), https://perma.cc/P9YE-NW2J; Alexis Kramer, "Google Not Liable for Placing Ads Next to IS Videos," *Bloomberg* (Oct. 24, 2017), http://perma.cc/6CW2-V4X6; Eric Goldman, "Fourth Judge Says Social Media Sites Aren't Liable for Supporting Terrorists–Pennie v. Twitter," *Technology & Marketing Law Blog* (Dec. 10, 2017), http://perma.cc/AG5B-6JL4; David Kimball-Stanley, "Summary: Ninth Circuit Dismisses Civil Suit against Twitter for ISIS Attack," *Lawfare* (Feb. 6, 2018), http://perma.cc/ZSJ5-8GRJ.

113. For a summary of the German legislation and links to the texts of the German legislation and the proposed Russian law, see "Germany: Flawed Social Media Law," *Human Rights Watch* (Feb. 14, 2018), https://perma.cc/K77K-5EE3; for the European proposal, see Proposal for a Regulation of the European Parliament and of the Council on Preventing the Spread of Terrorist Content Online, COM(2018) 640 final, https://perma.cc/3MJ4-QABY. For a representative example of the U.S. response with links to some other examples, see Mike Masnick, "If You're Worried about Bad EU Internet Regulation, Just Wait Till You See the New Terrorist Regulation," *TechDirt* (Dec. 13, 2018), https://perma.cc/5VQA-BN7X; Citron, "Extremist Speech, Compelled Conformity, and Censorship Creep," *Notre Dame Law Review* 93 no. 3 (2018): 1035–71.

114. Mario Trujillo, "Tech Groups Try to Kill Terrorist Reporting Mandate in Spy Bill," *The Hill* (Aug. 5, 2015), http://perma.cc/J6C9-ADH3; Julian Hattem, "Spy Panel Drops Controversial Mandate on Web Firms, Amid Pressure," *The Hill* (Sept. 21, 2015), http://perma.cc/37HY-7NPG; Devlin Barrett & Damian Paletta, "Top U.S. Officials to Meet with Tech CEOs on Terror Concerns," *Wall Street Journal* (Jan. 7, 2016), https://perma.cc/LJC4-JQPC; Matt Burgess, "Facebook, YouTube, Twitter, and Microsoft Have Teamed Up to Fight Online Terrorism," *Wired* (June 27, 2017), https://perma.cc/YQT8-9H93; Sam Levin, "Tech Giants Team Up to Fight Extremism Following Cries That They Allow Terrorism," *The Guardian* (June 26, 2017), https://perma.cc/X7FZ-ZKDH.

115. Cyrus Farivar, "French Investigators to Work Directly with Facebook to Monitor Hate Speech," *Ars Technica* (Nov. 12, 2018), https://perma.cc/DCJ6-RMQA.

116. See, for example, Casey Newton, "Facebook Makes Its Community Guidelines Public and Introduces an Appeals Process," *The Verge* (Apr. 24, 2018), https://perma.cc/Q63V-AVSU; For the leaked documents, see "How Facebook Guides Moderators on Terrorist Content," *The Guardian* (May 24, 2017), https://perma.cc/Q28S-HL2X. On earlier, piecemeal disclosures, see Jeffrey Rosen, "Google's Gatekeepers," *New York Times Magazine* (Nov. 28, 2008), https://perma.cc/99Z2-JRL3; Sarah T. Roberts, "Social Media's Silent Filter," *The Atlantic* (Mar. 8, 2017), https://perma.cc/4DPE-4ATH; Gillespie, "Governance of and by Platforms"; Kate Klonick, "The New Governors: The People, Rules, and Processes Governing Online Speech," *Harvard Law Review* 131 no. 6 (2018): 1598–670. For more recent and comprehensive disclosures, see "Community Standards," Facebook, http://perma.cc/33YQ-UM82; "Video, Photos & Presentations," Content Moderation at Scale, https://perma.cc/XNF3-6ULW.

117. On copyright takedowns, see, for example, "Transparency Report," Google (Apr. 8, 2019), http://perma.cc/R9BZ-G372; "Search: Twitter," Lumen, (224,467 results through June 26,

2018) (Apr. 8, 2019), https://perma.cc/A6TJ-2PUE. On other takedowns, see Sarah Perez, "Facebook's New Transparency Report Now Includes Data on Takedowns of 'Bad' Content, Including Hate Speech," *TechCrunch* (May 15, 2018), http://perma.cc/YCV9-UM2F.

118. For those presentations, see "Video, Photos & Presentations," Content Moderation at Scale (Apr. 8, 2019), https://perma.cc/XNF3-6ULW.

Part II

1. Marc Galanter, "Why the 'Haves' Come Out Ahead: Speculations on the Limits of Legal Change," *Law and Society Review* 9 no. 1 (1974): 95–160.

2. Morton J. Horwitz, *The Transformation of American Law, 1780–1860* (Cambridge, Mass.: Harvard University Press, 1977), 47–54, 78–97, 116–26, 186–210, 218–26.

3. Nicholas Gane, "The Governmentalities of Neoliberalism: Panopticism, Post-Panopticism, and Beyond," *The Sociological Review* 60 no. 4 (2012): 611–634, 627–29.

Chapter 5

1. Judith Resnik, "Managerial Judges," *Harvard Law Review* 96 no. 2 (1982): 374–442; see also J. Maria Glover, "The Federal Rules of Civil Settlement," *New York University Law Review* 87 no. 6 (2012): 1713–1778.

2. See, for example, Todd D. Peterson, "Restoring Structural Checks on Judicial Power in the Era of Managerial Judging," *U.C. Davis Law Review* 29 no. 1 (1995): 41–114; Elizabeth G. Thornburg, "The Managerial Judge Goes to Trial," *University of Richmond Law Review* 44 no. 4 (2010): 1261–326; Stephen C. Yeazell, "The Misunderstood Consequences of Modern Civil Process," *Wisconsin Law Review* 1994 no. 3 (1994): 631–78.

3. Gerard Hanlon, "The First Neo-liberal Science: Management and Neo-liberalism," *Sociology* 52 no. 2 (2018): 298–315. To my knowledge, the only works of procedure scholarship that engage more deeply with management theory are Orna Rabinovich-Einy & Yair Sagy, "Courts as Organizations: The Drive for Efficiency and the Regulation of Class Action Settlements," *Stanford Journal of Complex Litigation* 4 no. 1 (2016): 1–46 and Brian Z. Tamanaha, *A Realistic Theory of Law* (New York: Cambridge University Press, 2017), 118–50. The argument presented in this chapter is the obverse of that in Lauren B. Edelman, *Working Law: Courts, Corporations, and Symbolic Civil Rights* (Chicago: University of Chicago Press, 2016). Edelman defines the managerialization of law as symbolic colonization of legal logics via internalized judicial deference to corporate compliance structures. I am concerned with the emergent managerial reconfiguration of institutions for the production of dispute resolution catalyzed by interrelated sociotechnical and ideological shifts.

4. Hanlon, "The First Neo-liberal Science," 7–11; Robert R. Locke & J.-C. Spender, *Confronting Managerialism: How the Business Elite and Their Schools Threw Our Lives out of Balance* (New York: Zed Books, 2011), 1–21.

5. Hanlon, "The First Neo-liberal Science"; see also Locke & Spender, *Confronting Managerialism*; Alexander Styhre, *Management and Neoliberalism: Connecting Policies and Practices* (New York: Routledge, 2014). On neoliberal subjectivity more generally, see Todd May & Ladelle McWhorter, "Who's Being Disciplined Now? Operations of Power in a Neoliberal World," in *Biopower: Foucault and Beyond*, eds. Vernon W. Cisney & Nicolae Morar (Chicago: University of Chicago Press, 2016), 245–58.

6. For extended development of this point, see Corinne Blalock, "Neoliberalism and the Crisis of Legal Theory," *Law and Contemporary Problems* 77 no. 4 (2015): 71–103; see also Gane, "The Governmentalities of Neoliberalism."

7. Lujan v. Defs. of Wildlife, 504 U.S. 555, 560–61 (1992).

8. Seth Kreimer, "Spooky Action at a Distance: Intangible Injury in Fact in the Information Age," *University of Pennsylvania Journal of Constitutional Law* 18 no. 3 (2016): 745–796.

9. Jan G. Laitos, "Standing and Environmental Harm: The Double Paradox," *Virginia Environmental Law Journal* 31 no. 1 (2013): 55–101.

10. See, for example, Dwyer v. Am. Express Co., 652 N.E.2d 1351, 1356 (Ill. App. Ct. 1995) ("[A] single, random cardholder's name has little or no intrinsic value to defendants (or a merchant). Rather, an individual name has value only when it is associated with one of defendants' lists. Defendants create value by categorizing and aggregating these names."); Brief for Experian Info. Sols., Inc. as Amicus Curiae Supporting Petitioners, at 1–2, First Am. Fin. Corp. v. Edwards, 132 S. Ct. 2536 (2012) (No. 10-708) ("Such suits are possible because the [Fair Credit Reporting] Act permits plaintiffs to sue for . . . what may be a wholly technical violation. Indeed, it is not uncommon in these cases for significant numbers of class members to have actually *benefited* from the alleged violations.").

11. Privacy claims can seem especially vague by comparison to claims for bodily injury, but it is not clear that bodily injury cases should be the touchstone when so many other kinds of intangible claims (tort and otherwise) are cognizable. For discussion, see Danielle Keats Citron, "Reservoirs of Danger: The Evolution of Public and Private Law at the Dawn of the Information Age," *Southern California Law Review* 80 no. 2 (2007): 241–98, 289–96; Kreimer, "Spooky Action at a Distance," 754–57; see also Ryan Calo, "Privacy Harm Exceptionalism," *Journal of Telecommunications and Technology Law* 12 no. 2 (2014): 361–64.

12. Randall R. Bovbjerg, Frank A. Sloan, & James F. Blumstein, "Valuing Life and Limb in Tort: Scheduling 'Pain and Suffering,'" *Northwestern University Law Review* 83 no. 4 (1989): 908–76; Philip L. Merkel, "Pain and Suffering Damages at Mid-Twentieth Century: A Retrospective View of the Problem and the Legal Academy's First Responses," *Capital University Law Review* 34 no. 3 (2006): 545–80. For good general introductions to the sociological processes by which forms of economic and quantitative knowledge are constructed, see Karin Knorr Cetina & Alex Preda, "The Epistemization of Economic Transactions," *Current Sociology* 49 no. 4 (2001): 27–44; Peter Miller, "Governing by Numbers: Why Calculative Practices Matter," *Social Research* 68 no. 2 (2001): 379–96.

13. See Pauline T. Kim, "Data-Driven Discrimination at Work," *William and Mary Law Review* 58 no. 3 (2017): 857–861, 861–64.

14. See discussion in Chapter 2, pp. 69–70.

15. On hypothesized per-transaction rates, see Jonathan S. Masur, "The Use and Misuse of Patent Licenses," *Northwestern University Law Review* 110 no. 1 (2015): 115–58; David Nimmer, "Investigating the Hypothetical 'Reasonable Royalty' for Copyright Infringement," *Boston University Law Review* 99 no. 1 (2019): 1–57. For examples of courts positing menus of rates, see Bridgeport Music, Inc. v. Dimension Films, 410 F.3d 792, 804 (6th Cir. 2005); Princeton Univ. Press v. Mich. Document Servs., Inc., 99 F.3d 1381, 1386–88 (6th Cir. 1996); Am. Geophysical Union v. Texaco Inc., 60 F.3d 913, 929–31 (2d Cir. 1995).

16. Bridgeport Music, Inc. v. Justin Combs Publ'g, 507 F.3d 470, 483 (6th Cir. 2007).

17. 17 U.S.C. § 504(c)(1)–(2) (2012).

18. Capitol Records, Inc. v. Thomas-Rasset, 692 F.3d 899, 907–08 (8th Cir. 2012), *cert. denied*, 133 S. Ct. 1584 (2013); Sony BMG Music Entm't v. Tenenbaum, 660 F.3d 487, 509 (1st Cir. 2011). For a comprehensive review of the case law on statutory damages, see Pamela Samuelson & Tara Wheatland, "Statutory Damages in Copyright Law: A Remedy in Need of Reform," *William and Mary Law Review* 51 no. 2 (2009): 439–512.

19. FAA v. Cooper, 132 S. Ct. 1441, 1453 (2012); Doe v. Chao, 540 U.S. 614, 618 (2004).

20. Spokeo, Inc. v. Robins, 136 S. Ct. 1540, 1548–50 (2016).

21. On the award of damages in the karaoke case, see Zomba Enters., Inc. v. Panorama Records, Inc., 491 F.3d 574, 583-84 (6th Cir. 2007).

22. Ian Hacking, *The Taming of Chance (Ideas in Context)* (New York: Cambridge University Press, 1990).

23. Kim Lane Scheppele, "Law without Accidents," in *Social Theory for a Changing Society*, eds. Pierre Bourdieu & James S. Coleman (Boulder, Colo.: Westview Press, 1991), 267–93.

24. See George W.C. McCarter, "Medical Sue-Veillance: A History and Critique of the Medical Monitoring Remedy in Toxic Tort Litigation," *Rutgers Law Review* 45 no. 2 (1993): 227–84; Victor E. Schwartz & Cary Silverman, "The Rise of 'Empty Suit' Litigation. Where Should Tort Law Draw the Line?," *Brooklyn Law Review* 80 no. 3 (2015): 599–676; see also James A. Henderson Jr. & Aaron D. Twerski, "Asbestos Litigation Gone Mad: Exposure-Based Recovery for Increased Risk, Mental Distress, and Medical Monitoring," *South Carolina Law Review* 53 no. 4 (2002): 815–50.

25. Remijas v. Neiman Marcus Grp., LLC, 794 F.3d 688, 693 (7th Cir. 2015) (quoting Clapper v. Amnesty Int'l USA, 133 S. Ct. 1138, 1147 (2013)). For a detailed exploration of the ways that heightened risk and anxiety following a data breach translate into real, concrete, and present harms, see Daniel J. Solove & Danielle Keats Citron, "Risk and Anxiety: A Theory of Data Breach Harms," *Texas Law Review* 96 no. 4 (2017): 737–86.

26. Some scholars agree. See M. Ryan. Calo, "The Boundaries of Privacy Harm," *Indiana Law Journal* 86 no. 3 (2011): 1131–62, 1139–40, 1156–61; see also Jane R. Bambauer, "The New Intrusion," *Notre Dame Law Review* 88 no. 1 (2012): 205–276, 242; Adam Thierer, "The Pursuit of Privacy in a World Where Information Control Is Failing," *Harvard Journal of Law and Public Policy* 36 no. 2 (2013): 409–456, 417–21.

27. 18 U.S.C. § 1030(e)(11) (2012); see, for example, EF Cultural Travel BV v. Explorica, Inc., 274 F.3d 577, 584–85 (1st Cir. 2001); United States v. Middleton, 231 F.2d 1207, 1213 (9th Cir. 2000).

28. eBay Inc. v. MercExchange, L.L.C., 547 U.S. 388, 391 (2006); see, for example, Metro-Goldwyn-Mayer Studios, Inc. v. Grokster, Ltd., 518 F. Supp. 2d 1197 (N.D. Cal. 2007).

29. Harland Clarke & Javelin Strategy & Research, Fee Income Growth Opportunities in the Identity Protection Market (2011), https://perma.cc/TD2W-Y4FJ; see also James P. Nehf, "A Legislative Framework for Reducing Fraud in the Credit Repair Industry," *North Carolina Law Review* 70 no. 3 (1992): 781–821.

30. Sasha Romanosky, Rahul Telang, & Alessandro Acquisti, "Do Data Breach Disclosure Laws Reduce Identity Theft?," *Journal of Policy Analysis and Management* 30 no. 2 (2011): 256–86; Erika Harrell, U.S. Bureau of Justice Statistics, "Victims of Identity Theft, 2014," at 2 (Sept. 2015), https://perma.cc/D3TT-6CNF.

31. Vernon Palmer, "Why Privity Entered Tort—An Historical Reexamination of *Winterbottom v. Wright*," *American Journal of Legal History* 27 no. 1 (1983): 85–98; see also Robert L. Rabin, "The Historical Development of the Fault Principle: A Reinterpretation," *Georgia Law Review* 15 no. 4 (1981): 925–62. For an important mid-century judicial discussion of the privity requirement's unsuitability to the modern economy, see Henningsen v. Bloomfield Motors, Inc., 161 A.2d 69, 80–84 (N.J. 1960).

32. Scheppele, "Law without Accidents," 269–72.

33. George L. Priest, "The Invention of Enterprise Liability: A Critical History of the Intellectual Foundations of Modern Tort Law," *Journal of Legal Studies* 14 no. 3 (1985): 461–528. For the two opinions, see Palsgraf v. Long Island R.R. Co., 162 N.E. 99, 100 (N.Y. Ct. App. 1928); MacPherson v. Buick Motor Co., 111 N.E. 1050, 1051 (N.Y. 1916).

34. George L. Priest, "Market Share Liability in Personal Injury and Public Nuisance Litigation: An Economic Analysis," *Supreme Court Economic Review* 18 (2010): 109–33; Aaron D. Twerski, "Market Share—A Tale of Two Centuries," *Brooklyn Law Review* 55 no. 3 (1989): 860–82.

35. M. Stuart Madden & Jamie Holian, "Defendant Indeterminacy: New Wine into Old Skins," *Louisiana Law Review* 67 no. 3 (2007): 785–822; Allen Rostron, "Beyond Market Share Liability: A Theory of Proportional Share Liability for Nonfungible Products," *UCLA Law Review* 52 no. 1 (2004): 151–216. Notable judicial experiments with epidemiological modeling in tort cases are Zuchowicz v. United States, 140 F.3d 381 (2d Cir. 1998) (Calabresi, J.); Alder v. Bayer Corp., AGFA Div., 61 P.3d 1068, 1086–90 (Utah 2002).

36. Jill E. Fisch, "Cause for Concern: Causation and Federal Securities Fraud," *Iowa Law Review* 94 no. 3 (2009): 811–72, 815–29; American Bar Association, Section of Antitrust Law,

"Proving Antitrust Damages: Legal and Economic Issues, 3rd ed. (Chicago: ABA Book Publishing, 2017).

37. Here again, data breach cases are emerging as the exception. See Remijas v. Neiman Marcus Grp., LLC, 794 F.3d 688, 696 (7th Cir. 2015); In re Anthem Data Breach Litig., No. 15-MD-02617-LHK, 2016 WL 589760, at *20 (N.D. Cal. Feb. 14, 2016).

38. On legislation, see Thomas O. McGarity, *Freedom to Harm: The Lasting Legacy of the Laissez Faire Revival* (New Haven, Conn.: Yale University Press, 2013). On scientific knowledge in court, see Lisa Heinzerling, "Doubting *Daubert*," *Journal of Law and Policy* 14 no. 1 (2006): 65–84.

39. The most sustained academic flirtation with a more complex understanding of causation has been Richard Wright's proposed "necessary elements of a sufficient set" test. See Richard W. Wright, "Causation in Tort Law," *California Law Review* 73 no. 6 (1985): 1735–828. After criticism by some of the academy's most preeminent tort logicians, Wright later abandoned some of the more far-reaching implications of his own theory. See Richard W. Wright, "Liability for Possible Wrongs: Causation, Statistical Probability, and the Burden of Proof," *Loyola Los Angeles Law Review* 41 no. 4 (2008): 1295–344. For a sampling of other perspectives on probabilistic causation, see Kenneth Abraham, "Self-Proving Causation," *Virginia Law Review* 99 no. 8 (2013): 1811–54; Danielle Conway-Jones, "Factual Causation in Toxic Tort Litigation: A Philosophical View of Proof and Uncertainty in Uncertain Disciplines," *University of Richmond Law Review* 35 no. 4 (2002): 875–942; Steve C. Gold, "When Certainty Dissolves into Probability: A Legal Vision of Toxic Causation for the Post-genomic Era," *Washington and Lee Law Review* 70 no. 1 (2013): 237–340; Alex Stein, "The Domain of Torts," *Columbia Law Review* 117 no. 3 (2017): 535–612.

40. Columbia Pictures Industries v. Fung, 710 F.3d 1020, 1038–39 (9th Cir. 2013).

41. See Columbia Pictures Industries, 710 F.3d at 1037–39 ("[I]f one provides a service that can be used to infringe copyrights, with the manifested intent that the service actually be used in that manner, that person is liable for the infringement that occurs through the use of the service."); see also Mark Bartholomew & Patrick F. McArdle, "Causing Infringement," *Vanderbilt Law Review* 64 no. 3 (2011): 675–746.

42. See Resnik, "Managerial Judges," 386–414.

43. On the beneficial efficiencies of managerial justice, see Nancy J. King & Ronald F. Wright, "The Invisible Revolution in Plea Bargaining: Managerial Judging and Judicial Participation in Negotiations," *Texas Law Review* 95 no. 2 (2016): 325–98; Steven Baicker-McKee, "Reconceptualizing Managerial Judges," *American University Law Review* 65 no. 2 (2015): 353–98; Barry R. Schaller, "Managerial Judging: A Principled Approach to Complex Cases in State Court," *Connecticut Bar Journal* 68 no. 1 (1994): 77–97; Robert F. Peckham, "A Judicial Response to the Cost of Litigation: Case Management, Two-Stage Discovery Planning and Alternative Dispute Resolution," *Rutgers Law Review* 37 no. 2 (1985): 253–78; Robert F. Peckham, "The Federal Judge as a Case Manager: The New Role in Guiding a Case from Filing to Disposition," *California Law Review* 69 no. 3 (1981): 770–805. For arguments by Resnik and others urging a return to a more traditional approach to litigation, see Judith Resnik, "Reinventing Courts as Democratic Institutions," *Daedalus* 143 no. 3 (2014): 9–27; Thornburg, "The Managerial Judge Goes to Trial," 1324–25; Peterson, "Restoring Structural Checks on Judicial Power in the Era of Managerial Judging," 43–46. For more recent work by Resnik probing the managerial reconfiguration of courts along the dimensions of both access to justice and access to information about mechanisms for dispensing justice, see Judith Resnik, "Diffusing Disputes: The Public in the Private of Arbitration, the Private in Courts, and the Erasure of Rights," *Yale Law Journal* 124 no. 8 (2015): 2804–939; Judith Resnik, "A2J/A2K: Access to Justice, Access to Knowledge, and Economic Inequalities in Open Courts and Arbitrations," *North Carolina Law Review* 96 no. 3 (2018): 605–78; Judith Resnik, "The Functions of Publicity and of Privatization in Courts and Their Replacements (from Jeremy Bentham to #MeToo and *Google Spain*)," in *Open Justice: The Role of Courts in a Democratic*

Society, eds. Burkhard Hess & Ana Koprivica Harvey (Baden-Baden: Nomos, 2019). On the need for reinvention from the ground up, see Gillian K. Hadfield, *Rules for a Flat World: Why Humans Invented Law and How to Reinvent It for a Complex Economy* (New York: Oxford University Press, 2017).

44. For comprehensive discussions of this trend and its substantive implications for law, see Myriam Gilles, "The Day Doctrine Died: Private Arbitration and the End of Law," *University of Illinois Law Review* 2016 no. 2 (2016): 371–424; J. Maria Glover, "Disappearing Claims and the Erosion of Substantive Law," *Yale Law Journal* 124 no. 8 (2015): 3052–93; J. Maria Glover, "The Structural Role of Private Enforcement Mechanisms in Public Law," *William and Mary Law Review* 53 no. 4 (2012): 1137–218.

45. Conventional economic wisdom holds that such strategies benefit both firms and consumers because they limit potentially ruinous litigation costs and therefore enable companies to offer a wide variety of goods and services on a more cost-effective basis. See, for example, Christopher R. Drahozal, "Arbitration Costs and Forum Accessibility: Empirical Evidence," *University of Michigan Journal of Law Reform* 41 no. 4 (2008): 813–42; Jason S. Johnston, "The Return of Bargain: An Economic Theory of How Standard-Form Contracts Enable Cooperative Negotiation between Businesses and Customers," *Michigan Law Review* 104 no. 5 (2006): 857–98; Steven J. Ware, "Paying the Price of Process: Judicial Regulation of Consumer Arbitration Agreements," *Journal of Dispute Resolution* 2001 no. 1 (2001): 89–100. For preliminary efforts to collect numbers on uses of boilerplate waivers in various contexts, see Alexander J.S. Colvin, "The Growing Use of Mandatory Arbitration," Economic Policy Institute (Sept. 27, 2017), https://perma.cc/RFB9-X3HY; Jean R. Sternlight, "Disarming Employees: How American Employers Are Using Mandatory Arbitration to Deprive Workers of Legal Protection," *Brooklyn Law Review* 80 no. 4 (2015): 1309–356, 1310 n.9, 1344–45; U.S. Consumer Financial Protection Bureau, "Arbitration Study: Report to Congress, pursuant to Dodd-Frank Wall Street Reform and Consumer Protection Act § 1028(a)" (Mar. 2015), https://perma.cc/7SY7-VW9V.

46. On the distributive and moral implications of boilerplate, see Margaret Jane Radin, *Boilerplate: The Fine Print, Vanishing Rights, and the Rule of Law* (Princeton, N.J.: Princeton University Press, 2013); see also Nancy S. Kim, *Wrap Contracts: Foundations and Ramifications* (New York: Oxford University Press, 2013). On the arrested development of law, see Gilles, "The End of Doctrine"; Glover, "Disappearing Claims and the Erosion of Substantive Law." In parallel with these developments, an increasing number of judicial opinions are designated as unpublished and non-precedential. David C. Vladeck & Mitu Gulati, "Judicial Triage: Reflections on the Debate over Unpublished Opinions," *Washington & Lee Law Review* 62 on. 4 (2005): 1667–708.

47. Ronan McIvor, *The Outsourcing Process: Strategies for Evaluation and Management* (New York: Cambridge University Press, 2005), 7–10.

48. On the theoretical underpinnings of outsourcing and its implications for firm value, see McIvor, *The Outsourcing Process*, 40–59.

49. Lauren Weber, "Some of the World's Largest Employers No Longer Sell Things, They Rent Workers," *Wall Street Journal* (Dec. 28, 2017), https://perma.cc/D268-RLEM; Don Lee, "Behind Shrinking Middle Class Jobs, A Surge in Outsourcing," *Los Angeles Times* (June 30, 2016), https://perma.cc/G2H6-KVJF; Deloitte's 2016 Global Outsourcing Survey (May 2016), https://perma.cc/E9MC-3VT6.

50. Resnik's recent work undertakes more systematic appraisal of outsourcing-based strategies for dispute resolution. See Resnik, "A2J/A2K"; Resnik, "The Functions of Publicity and of Privatization in Courts and Their Replacements."

51. Lauren B. Edelman & Mark Suchman, "When the 'Haves' Hold Court: Speculations on the Organizational Internalization of Law," *Law and Society Review* 33 no. 4 (1999): 941–92; Rory Van Loo, "The Corporation as Courthouse," *Yale Journal on Regulation* 33 no. 2 (2016): 547–602.

52. John Rappaport, "Criminal Justice, Inc.," *Columbia Law Review* 118 no. 8 (2019): 2251–321.

53. Rappaport, "Criminal Justice, Inc.," 2272–76; Michael Graf et al., "Outsourcing of Customer Relationship Management: Implications for Customer Satisfaction," *Journal of Strategic Marketing* 21 no. 1 (2013): 68–81; Howard Gospel & Mari Sako, "The Unbundling of Corporate Functions: The Evolution of Shared Services and Outsourcing in Human Resource Management," *Industrial and Corporate Change* 19 no. 5 (2010): 1367–96.

54. Adrian Chen, "The Laborers Who Keep Dick Pics and Beheadings out of Your Facebook Feed," *Wired* (Oct. 23, 2014), https://perma.cc/QB2T-YEKR; Nick Statt, "Facebook Pledges to Improve Oversight of Contractor Firms Amid Rising Criticism," *The Verge* (Feb. 25, 2019), https://perma.cc/U88J-KJ4A.

55. For discussion of the various considerations and of trends in R&D outsourcing, see Farok J. Contractor et al., eds. *Global Outsourcing and Offshoring: An Integrated Approach to Theory and Corporate Strategy* (New York: Cambridge University Press, 2011).

56. On administrative courts generally, see Kent Barnett, "Against Administrative Judges," *U.C. Davis Law Review* 49 no. 5 (2016): 1634–718; Chris Guthrie, Jeffrey J. Rachlinski, & Andrew J. Wistrich, "The Hidden Judiciary: An Empirical Examination of Executive Branch Justice," *Duke Law Journal* 58 no. 7 (2009): 1477–530. On administrative supervision of enforcement payouts, see Michael D. Sant'Ambrogio & Adam S. Zimmerman, "The Agency Class Action," *Columbia Law Review* 112 no. 8 (2012): 1992–2067; Adam S. Zimmerman, "Distributing Justice," *New York University Law Review* 86 no. 2 (2011): 500–72; Administrative Conference of the United States, "Aggregation of Similar Claims in Agency Adjudication, June 10, 2016, 3–6, https://perma.cc/4525-V9F7. On administrative hybrids in mass tort litigation, see Richard A. Nagareda, "Future Mass Tort Claims and the Rule-Making/Adjudication Distinction," *Tulane Law Review* 74 nos. 5–6 (2000): 1781–808, 1788–92; Richard A. Nagareda, "Turning from Tort to Administration," *Michigan Law Review* 94 no. 4 (2009): 899–981. On specialty criminal and drug courts, see James L. Nolan Jr., ed., *Drug Courts in Theory and in Practice* (New York: Routledge, 2002); Allegra M. McLeod, "Decarceration Courts: Possibilities and Perils of a Shifting Criminal Law," *Georgetown Law Journal* 100 no. 5 (2011): 1587–674.

57. A recent, large-scale study situating contemporary plea bargaining practice within the managerial paradigm is King & Wright, "The Invisible Revolution in Plea Bargaining."

58. U.S. Sentencing Commission, "2016 Guidelines Manual" (Nov. 1, 2016), https://perma.cc/B8PR-GFR6; John Logan Koepke & David G. Robinson, "Danger Ahead: Risk Assessment and the Future of Bail Reform," *Washington Law Review* 93 no. 4 (2018): 1725–807; Jeff Larson, Surya Mattu, Lauren Kirchner, & Julia Angwin, "How We Analyzed the COMPAS Recidivism Algorithm," ProPublica (May 23, 2016), https://perma.cc/JPR7-GMNY; Rebecca Wexler, "Life, Liberty, and Trade Secrets: Intellectual Property in the Criminal Justice System," *Stanford Law Review* 70 no. 5 (2018): 1343–429.

59. Ethan Katsh & Orna Rabinovitch-Einy, *Digital Justice: Technology and the Internet of Disputes* (New York: Oxford University Press, 2017), 158–65, 178–79.

60. J. Maria Glover, "The Supreme Court's Non-trans-Substantive Class Action," *University of Pennsylvania Law Review* 165 no. 7 (2017): 1625–68.

61. Richard A. Nagareda, "Class Certification in an Age of Aggregate Proof," *New York University Law Review* 84 no. 1 (2009): 97–173, 133–35. Class claims for violation of statutory information privacy rights generally are treated as falling within this category. Julie E. Cohen, "Information Privacy Litigation as Bellwether for Institutional Change," *DePaul Law Review* 66 no. 2 (2017): 535–78, 562–70.

62. See Elizabeth Chamblee Burch, "Judging Multidistrict Litigation," *New York University Law Review* 90 no. 1 (2015): 71–142; J. Maria Glover, "Mass Litigation Governance in the Post-Class Action Era: The Problems and Promise of Non-removable State Actions in Multi-district Litigation," *Journal of Tort Law* 5 no. 1 (2014): 3–46; Samuel Issacharoff, "Private Claims, Aggregate Rights," *Supreme Court Review* 2008: 183–222. For a thought-provoking exploration of MDL as institutional innovation, see Abbe Gluck, "Unorthodox Civil Procedure: Modern

Multidistrict Litigation's Place in the Textbook Understandings of Procedure," *University of Pennsylvania Law Review* 165 no. 7 (2017): 1669–710.

63. See Cohen, "Information Privacy Litigation," 562–70.
64. For example, in litigation alleging that media streaming service Hulu's technical protocols violated the Video Privacy Protection Act by disclosing viewing selections and personally identifying information to third parties, the arguments about class definition required detailed expert analysis of the technical protocols used by both Hulu and Facebook to keep track of users. In re Hulu Privacy Litig., 2014 WL 2758598 (N.D. Cal. Nov. 18, 2014). For a theoretical analysis of the argument against certifying very large classes, see Bert I. Huang, "Surprisingly Punitive Damages," *Virginia Law Review* 100 no. 5 (2014): 1027–60.
65. Cohen, "Information Privacy Litigation," 562–67.
66. The most well-known exposition of this argument is Abram Chayes, "The Role of the Judge in Public Law Litigation," *Harvard Law Review* 89 no. 7 (1976): 1281–316.
67. For a general description of the process—and an optimistic assessment of its transformative potential—see Charles F. Sabel & William H. Simon, "Destabilization Rights: How Public Law Litigation Succeeds," *Harvard Law Review* 117 no. 4 (2004): 1016, 1069–73, 1077–81.
68. See, for example, Jason Parkin, "Aging Injunctions and the Legacy of Institutional Reform Litigation," *Vanderbilt Law Review* 70 no. 1 (2017): 167–220; Margo Schlanger, "Civil Rights Injunctions over Time: A Case Study of Jail and Prison Court Orders," *New York University Law Review* 81 no. 2 (2006): 550–630; Michael Selmi, "The Price of Discrimination: The Nature of Class Action Employment Discrimination and Its Effects," *Texas Law Review* 81 no.5 (2003): 1249–336. For more equivocal assessments, see Nancy Levit, "Megacases, Diversity, and the Elusive Goal of Workplace Reform," *Boston College Law Review* 49 no. 2 (2008): 357–430; Zachary Powell, Michele Bisaccia Meitl, & John L. Worrall, "Police Consent Decrees and § 1983 Civil Rights Litigation," *Criminology and Public Policy* 16 no. 2 (2017): 575–606.
69. For an overview of the aggregate settlement phenomenon, see David M. Jaros & Adam S. Zimmerman, "Judging Aggregate Settlement," *Washington University Law Review* 94 no. 3 (2017): 545–606. For an influential judicial critique of securities enforcement consent decrees, see SEC v. Citigroup Global Markets, Inc., 827 F. Supp. 2d 328 (S.D.N.Y. 2011) (Rakoff, J.). On the provisions of consent decrees entered in information privacy enforcement actions brought by the FTC under its general consumer protection authority, see William McGeveran, "Friending the Privacy Regulators," *Arizona Law Review* 68 no. 4 (2016): 959–1026; Daniel J. Solove & Woodrow Hartzog, "The FTC and the New Common Law of Privacy," *Columbia Law Review* 114 no. 3 (2014): 583–676.
70. See, for example, David Kravets, "Judge Approves $9.5 Million Facebook 'Beacon' Award," *Wired* (Mar. 17, 2010), https://perma.cc/UZ3M-BQ5Y; Sewell Chan & Louise Story, "Goldman Pays $550 Million to Settle Fraud Case," *New York Times* (July 15, 2010), https://perma.cc/6VN7-HJ98; James B. Stewart, "Convictions Prove Elusive in 'London Whale' Trading Case," *New York Times* (July 16, 2015), https://perma.cc/9DXF-FA3H; Damon Darlin, "Google Settles Suit over Buzz and Privacy," *New York Times* (Nov. 3, 2010), https://perma.cc/A489-5GHN; see also Selmi, "The Price of Discrimination."
71. Darius Mehri, "The Darker Side of Lean: An Insider's Perspective on the Realities of the Toyota Production System, *Academy of Management Perspectives* 20 no. 2 (2006): 21–41; Hans Pruijt, "Teams between Neo-Taylorism and Anti-Taylorism," *Economic and Industrial Democracy* 24 no. 1 (2003): 77–80; Paul Thompson, "Financialization and the Workplace: Extending and Applying the Disconnected Capitalism Thesis," *Work, Employment and Society* 27 no. 3 (2013): 472–88.
72. Gluck, "Unorthodox Civil Procedure."
73. See Resnik, "Reinventing Courts as Democratic Institutions"; Judith Resnik, "The Democracy in Courts: Jeremy Bentham, 'Publicity', and the Privatization of Process in the Twenty-First Century," *NoFo* 10 (2013): 77–119; Resnik, "The Functions of Publicity and of Privatization in Courts and Their Replacements."

74. Abbe Gluck reports that judges who preside over MDL proceedings resist the idea of developing new rules to standardize them on the ground that each MDL proceeding is different. See Gluck, "Unorthodox Civil Procedure," 1702–03. On the FTC's use of flexible templates for information privacy consent decrees, see McGeveran, "Friending the Privacy Regulators," 998–99. On conventions for processing and accounting for mass claims and payouts, see Paul D. Rheingold, Litigating Mass Tort Cases, vol. 1, § 9:11–17 (Washington, D.C.: AAJ Press, 2018).

75. For discussion of the emergent model of aggregate litigation conducted and supervised by elites, Brooke D. Coleman, "One Percent Procedure," Washington Law Review 91 no. 3 (2016): 1005–71; Schlanger, "Civil Rights Injunctions over Time," 616–21; see also Gluck, "Unorthodox Civil Procedure," 1693–99 (discussing MDL judges' perceptions of themselves as judicial elites).

76. William Simon, "Toyota Jurisprudence: Legal Theory and Rolling Rule Regimes," in Law and New Governance in the E.U. and in the U.S., eds. Grainne de Burca & Joanne Scott (Portland, Ore.: Hartor. 2006), 37–64.

77. On patent litigation using representative works and/or claims, see Mark A. Lemley, "The Changing Meaning of Patent Claim Terms," Michigan Law Review 104 no. 1 (2005): 101, 114; P. E. Campbell, "Representative Patent Claims: Their Use in Appeals to the Board and in Infringement Litigation," Santa Clara Computer & High Technology Law Journal 23 no. 1 (2006): 55–87. For examples of copyright litigation using representative copyrights, see American Geophysical Union v. Texaco, Inc., 60 F.3d 913 (2d Cir. 1994), Princeton Univ. Press v. Mich. Document Servs., Inc., 99 F.3d 1381 (6th Cir 1996) (en banc). But see Cambridge Univ. Press v. Patton, 769 F.3d 1232, 1259–60 (11th Cir. 2014) (holding that "the fair use analysis is highly fact-specific and must be performed on a work-by-work basis") (citing Cariou v. Prince, 714 F.3d 694 (2d Cir. 2013) (same)).

78. For two high-profile examples, see Oracle Am. Inc. v. Google Inc., 872 F. Supp. 2d 974 (N.D. Cal. 2012), rev'd and remanded, 750 F.3d 1339 (Fed. Cir. 2014); Computer Assocs. Int'l, Inc. v. Altai, Inc., 775 F. Supp. 544 (E.D.N.Y. 1991), aff'd in part and vacated in part, 982 F.2d 693 (2d Cir. 1992).

79. See, for example, Dan L. Burk & Mark A. Lemley, "Fence Posts or Sign Posts? Rethinking Patent Claim Construction," University of Pennsylvania Law Review 157 no. 6 (2009): 1743–800; David L. Schwartz, "Pre-Markman Reversal Rates," Loyola Los Angeles Law Review 43 no. 3 (2010): 1073–108.

80. Reed Elsevier, Inc. v. Muchnick, 559 U.S. 154 (2010).

81. For some high-profile examples, see Metro-Goldwyn-Mayer Studios, Inc. v. Grokster, Ltd., 545 U.S. 913 (2005); A&M Records, Inc., v. Napster, Inc., 239 F.3d 1004 (9th Cir. 2001); Universal City Studios, Inc. v. Reimerdes, 273 F.3d 429 (2d Cir. 2001).

82. There is an ongoing debate about whether the standards of review that apply to administrative actions in other contexts apply in the same way in intellectual property contexts. For discussion, see Stuart Minor Benjamin & Arti K. Rai, "Administrative Power in the Era of Patent Stare Decisis," Duke Law Journal 65 no. 8 (2016): 1563–99; Dan L. Burk, "DNA Copyright in the Administrative State," U.C. Davis Law Review 51 no. 4 (2017): 1297–350. The emergence of different and somewhat less deferential standards supports the modularization thesis.

83. See, for example, Arista Records, LLC v. Launch Media, Inc., 578 F.3d 148 (2d Cir. 2009).

84. See Robert P. Merges, "Contracting into Liability Rules," California Law Review 84 no. 5 (1996): 1293–394. For a recent, much-publicized example of active judicial oversight of the collective licensing of music rights, see Pandora Media, Inc. v. Am. Soc'y of Composers, Authors, & Publishers, 785 F.3d 73 (2d Cir. 2015); In re Pandora Media, Inc., 6 F. Supp. 3d 317 (S.D.N.Y. 2014).

85. Herbert A. Simon, "The Architecture of Complexity," in Managing in the Modular Age: Architectures, Networks, and Organizations, eds. Raghu Garud, Arun Kumaraswamy, & Richard N. Langlois (Malden, Mass.: Blackwell, 2003), 15–38.

86. Simon, Managing in the Modular Age, 23–28.
87. Carliss Y. Baldwin & Kim B. Clark, *Design Rules: The Power of Modularity* (Cambridge, Mass.: MIT Press, 2000), 236–41; Raghu Garud, Arun Kumaraswamy, & Richard N. Langlois, *Managing in the Modular Age: Architectures, Networks, and Organizations* (Malden, Mass.: Blackwell, 2013); Andrew L. Russell, "Modularity: An Interdisciplinary History of an Ordering Concept," *Information and Culture: A Journal of History* 47 no. 3 (2012): 257–87.
88. Authors Guild v. Google, Inc., 770 F. Supp. 2d 666 (S.D.N.Y. 2011); on the quasi-legislative character of the proposed settlement, see Pamela Samuelson, "The Google Book Settlement as Copyright Reform," *Wisconsin Law Review* 2011 no. 2 (2011): 479–562.
89. Authors Guild v. Google, Inc., 804 F.3d 202 (2d Cir. 2015), *cert. denied*, 136 S. Ct. 1658 (2016).
90. See, for example, Burk & Lemley, "Fence Posts or Sign Posts?," 1751–61.
91. On the importance of exploration and flow and the ways that atomistic copyright definition and enforcement jeopardizes those values, see Julie E. Cohen, *Configuring the Networked Self: Law, Code and the Play of Everyday Practice* (New Haven, Conn.: Yale University Press, 2012), 80–104.
92. Joshua Fairfield, *Owned: Property, Privacy, and the New Digital Serfdom* (New York: Cambridge University Press, 2017); Aaron Perzanowski & Jason Schultz, *The End of Ownership: Personal Property in the Digital Economy* (Cambridge, Mass.: MIT Press, 2016).
93. On notice and takedown processes, see Laura Quilter & Jennifer Urban, "Efficient Process or 'Chilling Effects'? Takedown Notices under Section 512 of the Digital Millennium Copyright Act," *Santa Clara Computer and High Technology Law Journal* 22 no. 4 (2005): 621–94; Wendy Seltzer, "Free Speech Unmoored in Copyright's Safe Harbor: Chilling Effects of the DMCA on the First Amendment," *Harvard Journal of Law and Technology* 24 no. 1 (2010): 171–232. On the due process implications of private-sector automated enforcement initiatives in copyright and other areas, see Annemarie Bridy, "Graduated Response and the Turn to Private Ordering in Online Copyright Enforcement," *Oregon Law Review* 89 no. 1 (2010): 81–132; Annemarie Bridy, "Internet Payment Blockades," *Florida Law Review* 67 no. 5 (2015): 1524–68.
94. On absent users in infringement litigation, see Julie E. Cohen, "The Place of the User in Copyright Law," *Fordham Law Review* 74 no. 2 (2005): 347–74. On attempted aggregation of user-defendants, see Greg Reilly, "Aggregating Defendants," *Florida State University Law Review* 41 no. 4 (2014): 1011–66.
95. On the ways that litigation and regulation can facilitate complementary processes of knowledge production about risk of harm, see Mary L. Lyndon, "Tort Law and Technology," *Yale Journal on Regulation* 12 no. 1 (1995): 137–76. For an extended exploration of efforts over the last four decades to undo the mid-twentieth-century regulatory settlements in the domains of product safety, worker safety, and consumer protection, see McGarity, *Freedom to Harm.*
96. On the particular importance of the openness and transparency questions and the new obstacles that managerial processes now present, see Resnik, "A2J/A2K"; Resnik, "The Functions of Publicity and of Privatization in Courts and Their Replacements."

Chapter 6

1. Coral Davenport & Jack Ewing, "VW Is Said to Cheat on Diesel Emissions; U.S. to Order Big Recall," *New York Times* (Sept. 18, 2015), A1, https://perma.cc/P95U-UW8X; Melissa Eddy, "Volkswagen to Recall 8.5 Million Vehicles in Europe," *New York Times* (Oct. 15, 2015), B1, https://perma.cc/TKK6-DAFY; Choe Sang-Hun, "South Korea Fines Volkswagen and Orders Recall over Emissions Scandal," *New York Times* (Nov. 26, 2015), B3, https://perma.cc/3GLF-UXDZ.
2. Andrew Higgins, "Volkswagen Scandal Highlights European Stalling on New Emissions Tests," *New York Times* (Sept. 28, 2015), B1, https://perma.cc/69R2-BW9Z; Danny Hakim

& Graham Bowley, "VW Scandal Exposes Cozy Ties in Europe's New Car Tests," *New York Times* (Oct. 14, 2015), B1, https://perma.cc/URQ9-P6TA.

3. "Volkswagen Group to Reduce CO2 Emissions to 95 g/km by 2020," Volkswagen (Mar. 4, 2013), https://perma.cc/8NQL-KMVS; Davenport & Ewing, "VW Is Said to Cheat on Diesel Emissions"; see also Craig Smith, "The Problem with Those Who Cheat," *Financial Times* (Oct. 11, 2015), https://perma.cc/58TF-M6B9.

4. For especially rich discussions, see Daniel A. Farber & Anne Joseph O'Connell, "The Lost World of Administrative Law," *Texas Law Review* 92 no. 5 (2014): 1137–90; Edward Rubin, "It's Time to Make the Administrative Procedure Act Administrative," *Cornell Law Review* 89 no. 1 (2003): 95–190; and William H. Simon, "The Organizational Premises of Administrative Law," *Law and Contemporary Problems* 78 nos. 1–2 (2015): 61–100; see also Kenneth A. Bamberger, "Regulation as Delegation: Private Firms, Decisionmaking, and Accountability in the Administrative State," *Duke Law Journal* 56 no. 2 (2006): 377–468.

5. Particularly among scholars of financial regulation, the practical and political difficulties of regulating informational activities have been the organizing problems for the last decade. See, for example, Chris Brummer, "Disruptive Technology and Securities Regulation," *Fordham Law Review* 84 no. 3 (2015): 977–1052; Ronald J. Gilson & Reinier Kraakman, "Market Efficiency after the Financial Crisis: It's Still a Matter of Information Costs," *Virginia Law Review* 100 no. 2 (2014): 313–76; Henry T.C. Hu, "Disclosure Universes and Modes of Regulation: Banks, Innovation, and Divergent Regulatory Quests," *Yale Journal on Regulation* 31 no. 3 (2014): 565–666. On the breakdown of regulatory models in information privacy and telecommunications, respectively, see Paul Ohm, "Broken Promises of Privacy: Responding to the Surprising Failure of Anonymization," *UCLA Law Review* 57 no. 6 (2010): 1701–78; Philip J. Weiser, "The Future of Internet Regulation," *University of California Davis Law Review* 43 no. 2 (2009): 529–90.

6. For discussions of the difficulties that attend antitrust modeling of two- and multisided markets and reviews of the literature, see David S. Evans & Richard Schmalensee, "The Antitrust Analysis of Multi-Sided Platform Businesses." NBER Working Paper No. 18783, 2013, https://perma.cc/PNB4-DRTV; Jean-Charles Rochet & Jean Tirole, "Two-Sided Markets: A Progress Report." *RAND Journal of Economics* 37 no. 3 (2006): 645–67.

7. Robert J. Levinson, R. Craig Romaine, & Steven C. Salop, "The Flawed Fragmentation Critique of Structural Remedies in the Microsoft Case," *Antitrust Bulletin* 46 no. 1 (2001): 135–62.

8. See United States v. Microsoft Corp., 159 F.R.D. 318 (D.D.C.), rev'd, 56 F.3d 1448 (D.C. Cir. 1995), on remand, 87 F. Supp. 2d 30 (D.D.C. 2000), and 97 F. Supp. 2d 59 (D.D.C. 2000), *aff'd in part, rev'd in part, and vacated*, 253 F.3d 34 (D.C. Cir. 2001), *cert. denied*, 534 U.S. 952 (2001), *on remand*, 231 F. Supp. 2d 144 (D.D.C. 2002), *aff'd sub nom.*, Massachusetts v. Microsoft, 373 F.3d 1199 (D.C. Cir. 2004). While the litigation was underway, the Department of Justice revised its guidelines for antitrust oversight of intellectual property-related matters, but the revised document did little to unpack questions about the power of dominant platforms. See U.S. Dep't of Justice and Federal Trade Comm'n, "Antitrust Guidelines for the Licensing of Intellectual Property," (Apr. 6, 1995), reprinted in 4 Trade Reg. Rep. (CCH) ¶ 13,132 (1995); Robert Pitofsky, "Challenges of the New Economy: Issues at the Intersection of Antitrust and Intellectual Property," *Antitrust Law Journal* 68 no. 3 (2001): 913–24.

9. Alessandro Acquisti, Curtis Taylor, & Liad Wagman, "The Economics of Privacy," *Journal of Economic Literature* 55 no. 2 (2016): 442–92.

10. Pathbreaking explorations of platform economics and platform-based competitive harms include Ariel Ezrachi & Maurice E. Stucke, *Virtual Competition: The Promise and Perils of the Algorithm-Driven Economy* (Cambridge, Mass., 2016): Harvard University Press; Lina Khan, "Amazon's Antitrust Paradox." *Yale Law Journal* 126 no. 3 (2017): 710–805; Maurice E. Stucke & Allen P. Grunes, *Big Data and Competition Policy* (New York: Oxford University Press, 2016). For opposition to the very idea of antitrust oversight of the platform economy, see James C. Cooper, "Privacy and Antitrust: Underpants Gnomes, The First Amendment,

and Subjectivity," *George Mason Law Review* 20 no. 4 (2013): 1129–46; Geoffrey A. Manne & Ben Sperry, "The Problems and Perils of Bootstrapping Privacy and Data into an Antitrust Framework," *CPI Antitrust Chronicle* (May 2015), https://perma.cc/6HNJ-LFPY; Joe Kennedy, "The Myth of Data Monopoly: Why Antitrust Concerns about Data Are Overblown," Information Technology & Innovation Foundation (Mar. 2017), https://perma.cc/X7R7-DTTA; Joshua D. Wright et al., "Requiem for a Paradox: The Dubious Rise and Inevitable Fall of Hipster Antitrust," George Mason Law & Economics Research Paper No 18-29 (2018), https://perma.cc/MD6L-ZDR2.

11. On the rich range of concerns that initially animated public utility regulation in the United States, see William Boyd, "Public Utility and the Low-Carbon Future," *UCLA Law Review* 61 no. 6 (2014) 1614, 1635–51.

12. Tim Wu, "Network Neutrality FAQ," https://perma.cc/G7SE-BQS3 (last visited Oct. 26, 2015).

13. For important recent work exploring the social justice implications of telecommunications regulation, see Olivier Sylvain, "Network Equality," *Hastings Law Journal* 67 no. 2 (2016): 443–98; K. Sabeel Rahman, "Private Power, Public Values: Regulating Social Infrastructure in a Changing Economy," *Cardozo Law Review* 39 no. 5 (2018): 1621–89.

14. See Sylvain, "Network Equality"; Pew Research Center, "The Smartphone Difference" (Apr. 1, 2015), 16–19, https://perma.cc/WX7J-8QSP; see also Linnet Taylor, "Data Subjects or Data Citizens? Addressing the Global Regulatory Challenge of Big Data," in *Freedom and Property of Information: The Philosophy of Law Meets the Philosophy of Technology*, eds. Mireille Hildebrandt & Bibi van den Berg (New York: Routledge, 2016), 81–105.

15. Protecting and Promoting the Open Internet: Final Rule, ¶¶ 151-52, 80 Fed. Reg. 19,737, 19,758-59 (Apr. 13, 2015); Arturo J. Carrillo, "Having Your Cake and Eating It Too? Zero-Rating, Net Neutrality, and International Law," *Stanford Technology Law Review* 19 no. 3 (2016): 364–430; Christopher T. Marsden, "Comparative Case Studies in Implementing Net Neutrality: A Critical Analysis of Zero Rating," *SCRIPTed* 13 no. 1 (2016): 1–39.

16. Daniel Boffey, "Google Fined Record €2.4bn by EU over Search Results," *The Guardian* (June 27, 2017), https://perma.cc/9SKQ-YB79.

17. European Commission, Article 29 Data Protection Working Party, Opinion 15/2011 on the Definition of Consent, WP187 (July 13, 2011); European Commission, Article 29 Data Protection Working Party, Opinion 03/2013 on Purpose Limitation, WP203 (Apr. 2, 2013); Francesca Bignami, "From Expert Administration to Accountability Network: A New Paradigm for Comparative Administrative Law," *American Journal of Comparative Law* 59 no. 4 (2011): 859–908.

18. European Commission, "Roaming Charges and Open Internet: Questions and Answers" (June 30, 2015), https://perma.cc/73DC-RQVH; Frederik Zuiderveen Borgesius & Wilfred Steenbruggen, "The Right to Communications Privacy in Europe: Protecting Trust, Privacy, and Freedom of Expression," *Theoretical Inquiries in Law* 20 no. 1 (2019): 291–322.

19. Berten Martens, "An Economic Policy Perspective on Online Platforms," Institute for Prospective Technological Studies Digital Economy Working Paper 2016/05 (2016), https://perma.cc/G94A-ZV22; "Online Platforms and the Digital Single Market: Opportunities and Challenges for Europe," Communication from the Commission to the European Parliament, the Council, the European Economic and Social Committee and the Committee of the Regions, COM(2016) 288 final (May 25, 2016), https://perma.cc/MX8Q-P4XF; see also Report of the Standing Committee on Access to Information, Privacy and Ethics, House of Commons (Canada), Democracy under Threat: Risks and Solutions in the Era of Disinformation and Data Monopoly (Dec. 2018), https://perma.cc/S9Y3-TWRP; Australian Competition and Consumer Commission, Digital Platforms Inquiry: Preliminary Report (Dec. 2018), https://perma.cc/CX8T-RP74.

20. Jane Yakowitz, "More Crap from the E.U.," *Info/Law* (Jan. 25, 2012), https://perma.cc/RA5F-GJU8; Adam Thierer, "The Problem with Obama's 'Let's Be More Like Europe' Privacy

Plan," *Forbes* (Feb. 23, 2012), https://perma.cc/9T37-3B5S; Mike Masnick, "EU Moves to Create Internet Fast Lanes, Pretends It's Net Neutrality by Redefining Basic Words," *TechDirt* (June 30, 2015), https://perma.cc/JJ73-U4YL; Mike Masnick, "EU Official Says It's Time to Harm American Companies via Regulations ... Hours Later Antitrust Charges against Google Announced," *TechDirt* (Apr. 14, 2015), https://perma.cc/PU5Q-99JQ; Tom Fairless, "EU Digital Chief Urges Regulation to Nurture European Internet Platforms," *Wall Street Journal* (Apr. 14, 2015), https://perma.cc/T83A-ZK5J; Adam Thierer, "How Attitudes about Risk and Failure Affect Innovation on Either Side of the Atlantic," *The Technology Liberation Front* (June 19, 2015), https://perma.cc/GQ2P-CZQ9. On the origins of anti-bureaucratic sentiment within U.S. legal thought, see Daniel Ernst, *Tocqueville's Nightmare* (New York: Oxford University Press, 2014).

21. Whether the assumptions underlying the standard economic explanations ever were true is an interesting question that is beyond the scope of this book to address. For discussion, see Shlomit Azgad-Tromer, "The Case for Consumer-Oriented Corporate Governance, Accountability, and Disclosure," *University of Pennsylvania Journal of Business Law* 17 no. 1 (2014): 227–92; Alon Brav & J.B. Heaton, "Market Indeterminacy," *Journal of Corporate Law* 28 no. 4 (2003): 517–40.

22. Mark Andrejevic, *Infoglut: How Too Much Information Is Changing the Way We Think and Know* (New York: Routledge, 2013), 9–10.

23. Solon Barocas & Andrew Selbst, "Big Data's Disparate Impact," *California Law Review* 104 no. 3 (2016): 671–732. I return to the problem of algorithmically mediated discrimination and its implications for protection of fundamental human rights in Chapter 8, pp. 246–50.

24. 12 C.F.R. § 1002.2(p) (2018) (italics omitted); see also Office of the Comptroller of the Currency, *Comptroller's Handbook: Fair Lending Examination Procedures*, Appendix B: Credit Scoring Analysis (2006).

25. On versioning, see Andrew D. Gershoff, Ran Kivetz, & Anat Keinan, "Consumer Response to Versioning: How Brands' Production Methods Affect Perceptions of Unfairness," *Journal of Consumer Research* 39 no. 2 (2012): 382–98; Hal R. Varian, "Versioning Information Goods," in *Internet Publishing and Beyond: The Economics of Digital Information and Intellectual Property*, eds. Brian Kahin & Hal R. Varian (Cambridge, Mass.: MIT Press, 2000), 190–202. On the informationalization of food, see Lisa Heinzerling, "The Varieties and Limits of Transparency in U.S. Food Law," *Food and Drug Law Journal* 70 no. 1 (2015): 11–24.

26. On informational and design-based strategies for manipulation, see Woodrow Hartzog, *Privacy's Blueprint: The Battle to Control the Design of New Technologies* (Cambridge, Mass.: Harvard University Press, 2018), 21–55; Lauren E. Willis, "Performance-Based Consumer Regulation," *University of Chicago Law Review* 82 no. 3 (2015): 1309–410, 1321–26; see also Lauren E. Willis, "The Consumer Financial Protection Bureau and the Quest for Consumer Comprehension," *Russell Sage Foundation Journal of Social Science* 3 no. 1 (2017): 74–93; Lauren E. Willis, "Performance-Based Remedies: Ordering Firms to Eradicate Their Own Fraud," *Law and Contemporary Problems* 80 no. 1 (2017): 7–41.

27. Virginia Eubanks, *Automating Inequality: How High-Tech Tools Profile, Police, and Punish the Poor* (New York: St. Martin's Press, 2018); Safiya Umoja Noble, *Algorithms of Oppression: How Search Engines Reinforce Racism* (New York: New York University Press, 2018); Seeta Pena Gangadharan, "Digital Inclusion and Data Profiling," *First Monday* (May 19, 2012), https://doi.org/10.5210/fm.v17i5.3821.

28. Securities and Exchange Comm'n, Exchange Act Release No. 43154 (Aug. 15, 2000), 65 Fed. Reg. 51,716, codified at 17 C.F.R. §§ 243.100–243.103 (2018).

29. Henry T.C. Hu, "Too Complex to Depict?: Innovation, 'Pure Information', and the SEC Disclosure Paradigm," *Texas Law Review* 90 no. 7 (2012): 1601–716; Kathryn Judge, "Fragmentation Nodes: A Study in Financial Innovation, Complexity, and Systemic Risk," *Stanford Law Review* 64 no. 3 (2012): 657–726.

30. See, for example, Leonid Bershidsky, "Russian Trolls Would Love the 'Honest Ads Act,'" *Bloomberg Opinion* (Oct. 20, 2017), https://bloom.bg/2xUvOA8.

31. See sources cited in note 19 of this chapter.

32. David McCabe, "Scoop: 20 Ways Democrats Could Crack Down on Big Tech," Axios (July 30, 2018), https://perma.cc/JER8-6FXW; "Wyden Releases Discussion Draft of Legislation to Provide Real Protection for Americans' Privacy," Ron Wyden (Nov. 1, 2018), https://perma.cc/7C68-7U6B; "Schatz Leads Group of 15 Senators in Introducing New Bill to Help Protect People's Personal Data Online," Brian Schatz (Dec. 12, 2018), https://perma.cc/E9T7-MYRH.

33. For two important interventions in mid-twentieth-century policy debates, see Rachel Carson, *Silent Spring* (New York: Houghton Mifflin, 1962); Walter B. Wriston, *Risk and Other Four-Letter Words* (New York: Harper & Row, 1986), 135 ("The fact is that banking is a branch of the information business.").

34. For an overview, see Jose Luis Bermudez & Michael S. Pardo, "Risk, Uncertainty, and 'Super-Risk,'" *Notre Dame Journal of Law, Ethics and Public Policy* 29 no. 2 (2015): 471–96.

35. On the mid-twentieth-century emergence of regulatory methodologies based on formal risk modeling, see William Boyd, "Genealogies of Risk: Searching for Safety, 1930s–1970s," *Ecology Law Quarterly* 39 no. 4 (2012): 895–988.

36. For a useful, nontechnical explanation of the method, see Paul Ohm, "Sensitive Information," *Southern California Law Review* 88 no. 5 (2015): 1125–96, 1172–77; see also Adam Shostack, *Threat Modeling: Designing for Security* (New York: Wiley, 2014).

37. Canonical works on the social construction of risk include Ulrich Beck, *Risk Society: Towards a New Modernity*, trans. Mark Ritter (Thousand Oaks, Calif.: SAGE, 1992); Ian Hacking, *The Taming of Chance (Ideas in Context)* (New York: Cambridge University Press, 1990). On the social and political roles of risk management discourses and practices within organizations, see Michael Power, *Organized Uncertainty: Designing a World of Risk Management* (New York: Oxford University Press, 2007); Michael Power, "The Risk Management of Nothing," *Accounting, Organizations and Society* 34 nos. 6–7 (2009): 849–55.

38. Nassim Nicholas Taleb, *The Black Swan: The Impact of the Highly Improbable* (New York: Random House, 2010); see also Kenneth A. Bamberger, "Technologies of Compliance: Risk and Regulation in a Digital Age," *Texas Law Review* 88 no. 4 (2010): 669–740, 675–76, 711–14, 718–22; James Fanto, "Anticipating the Unthinkable: The Adequacy of Risk Management in Finance and Environmental Studies," *Wake Forest Law Review* 44 no. 3 (2009): 731–56.

39. See, for example, Mehrsa Baradaran, "Regulation by Hypothetical," *Vanderbilt Law Review* 67 no. 5 (2014): 1247–326; Robert Weber, "A Theory for Deliberation-Oriented Stress Testing Regulation," *Minnesota Law Review* 98 no. 6 (2014): 2236–325.

40. In support of cost-benefit analysis, see Michael A. Livermore & Richard L. Revesz, "Can Executive Review Help Prevent Capture?," in *Preventing Regulatory Capture: Special Interest Influence and How to Limit It*, eds. Daniel Carpenter & David A. Moss (New York: Cambridge University Press, 2014), 439–44; Cass R. Sunstein, "The Limits of Quantification," *California Law Review* 102 no. 6 (2014): 1369–422; Cass R. Sunstein, "The Real World of Cost-Benefit Analysis: Thirty-Six Questions (and Almost as Many Answers)," *Columbia Law Review* 114 no. 1 (2014): 167–212. For criticisms, see Frank Ackerman & Lisa Heinzerling, *Priceless: On Knowing the Price of Everything and the Value of Nothing* (New York: New Press, 2004); Lisa Heinzerling, "Quality Control: A Reply to Professor Sunstein," *California Law Review* 102 no. 6 (2014): 1457–68 (arguing that the theoretical virtues of cost-benefit analysis are not realized in practice). On the history of cost-benefit analysis in U.S. government, see Theodore M. Porter, *Trust in Numbers: The Pursuit of Objectivity in Science and Public Life* (Princeton, N.J.: Princeton University Press, 1995), 148–89. On the history of precautionary regulation, see Tim O'Riordan & James Cameron, eds., *Interpreting the Precautionary Principle* (New York: Routledge, 1994); see also Boyd, "Genealogies of Risk," 948–77.

41. P. Lamberson & Scott E. Page, "Tipping Points," Working Paper No. 2012-02-002, Santa Fe Institute (2012), https://perma.cc/7FBM-5VGX. Many environmental threat models include tipping points. Timothy M. Lenton et al., "Tipping Elements in the Earth's Climate System," *Proceedings of the National Academy of Sciences* 105 no. 6 (2008): 1786–93; see also Haroon Siddique, "Disease Resistance to Antibiotics at Tipping Point, Expert Warns," *Guardian* (Jan. 8, 2014), https://perma.cc/PL7E-NXXG.

42. Frank Ackerman, Lisa Heinzerling, & Rachel Massey, "Applying Cost-Benefit to Past Decisions: Was Environmental Protection Ever a Good Idea?," *Administrative Law Review* 57 no. 1 (2005): 155–92.

43. Adam Levitin, "Safe Banking: Finance and Democracy," *University of Chicago Law Review* 83 no. 1 (2016): 357–456; Saule T. Omarova, "License to Deal: Mandatory Approval of Complex Financial Products," *Washington University Law Review* 90 no. 1 (2012): 63–140.

44. In Europe, the precautionary stance is best encapsulated in the purpose limitation principle, which dictates that data collected for one purpose should not be used for an unrelated purpose without consent. See opinion of the Article 29 Data Protection Working Party, Opinion 03/2013 on Purpose Limitation (Apr. 2, 2013); see also Raphael Gellert, "Data Protection: A Risk Regulation? Between the Risk Management of Everything and the Precautionary Alternative," *International Data Privacy Law* 5 no. 1 (2015): 3–19. For some examples from the United States, see Omri Ben-Shahar, "Data Pollution," University of Chicago Public Law Working Paper No. 679 (2018), https://perma.cc/9HU6-XE8G; A. Michael Froomkin, "Regulating Mass Surveillance as Privacy Pollution: Learning from Environmental Impact Statements," *University of Illinois Law Review* 2015 no. 5 (2015): 1713–90; Dennis D. Hirsch, "The Glass House Effect: Big Data, the New Oil, and the Power of Analogy," *Maine Law Review* 66 no. 2 (2014): 373–96.

45. See, for example, Adam Thierer, "The Problem with Obama's 'Let's Be More Like Europe' Privacy Plan," *Forbes* (Feb. 23, 2012), https://perma.cc/9T37-3B5S; see generally Cass R. Sunstein, *Laws of Fear: Beyond the Precautionary Principle* (New York: Cambridge University Press, 2005).

46. On the rulemaking-adjudication dichotomy and what it leaves out, see Rubin, "It's Time to Make the Administrative Procedure Act Administrative."

47. For discussion of additional difficulties that the fast-moving internet industry has created for the FCC in particular, see Weiser, "The Future of Internet Regulation," 531–48. There is robust scholarly debate on the extent to which rule-making processes have become ossified, on which I intend no comment. My point is different and concerns the ability of rule-makers to move at speeds roughly commensurate with the pace of change in highly informationalized sectors of our political economy.

48. Issie Lapowsky, "How Bots Broke the FCC's Public Comment System," *Wired* (Nov. 28, 2017), https://perma.cc/PTZ9-AXQP.

49. Cynthia R. Farina, Dmitry Epstein, Josiah Heidt, & Mary J. Newhart, "Knowledge in the People: Rethinking 'Value' in Public Rulemaking Participation," *Wake Forest Law Review* 47 no. 5 (2012): 1185–242; Lynn E. Blais & Wendy E. Wagner, "Emerging Science, Adaptive Regulation, and the Problem of Rulemaking Ruts," *Texas Law Review* 86 no. 7 (2008): 1701–40. On information subsidies and deep capture, see Chapter 3, pp. 103–06.

50. Nicholas R. Parrillo, "Federal Agency Guidance and the Power to Bind: An Empirical Study of Agencies and Industries," *Yale Journal on Regulation* 36 no. 1 (2019): 165–271; Todd D. Rakoff, "The Choice between Formal and Informal Modes of Administrative Regulation," *Administrative Law Review* 52 no. 1 (2000): 159–74; Robert A. Anthony, "Interpretive Rules, Policy Statements, Guidances, Manuals, and the Like—Should Federal Agencies Use Them to Bind the Public?," *Duke Law Journal* 41 no. 6 (1992): 1311–84. For examples of guidances and staff interpretations, see "Supervisory Policy and Guidance Topics," Board of Governors of the Federal Reserve System, https://perma.cc/P5YL-5PAQ (last visited June 22, 2018); "Informal Interpretations," Federal Trade Commission, https://perma.cc/LNA5-XJ6K (last

visited June 22, 2018); "Staff Interpretations," U.S. Securities & Exchange Commission, https://perma.cc/S2HL-TF4A (last visited June 22, 2018), For discussion of the deference question, see David L. Franklin, "Legislative Rules, Nonlegislative Rules, and the Perils of the Short Cut," *Yale Law Journal* 120 no. 2 (2010): 276–327; John F. Manning, "Nonlegislative Rules," *George Washington Law Review* 72 no. 5 (2004): 893–945; Peter L. Strauss, "The Rulemaking Continuum," *Duke Law Journal* 41 no. 6 (1992): 1463–89.

51. Jody Freeman, "The Private Role in Public Governance," *New York University Law Review* 75 no. 3 (2000): 543–675; Orly Lobel, "The Renew Deal: The Fall of Regulation and the Rise of Governance in Contemporary Legal Thought," *Minnesota Law Review* 89 no. 2 (2004): 342–470; David Zaring, "Best Practices," *New York University Law Review* 81 no. 1 (2006): 294–350. See, for example, "Cybersecurity Framework," National Institute for Standards and Technology, https://perma.cc/M8S8-SUTE (last visited June 22, 2018), Joseph A. Siegel, "Collaborative Decision Making on Climate Change in the Federal Government," *Pace Environmental Law Review* 27 no. 1 (2009): 257–312.

52. Jodi L. Short, "The Paranoid Style in Regulatory Reform," *Hastings Law Journal* 63 no. 3 (2012): 633–94, 635.

53. See, e.g., U.S. Gov't Accountability Office, Opportunities Exist to Improve SEC's Oversight of the Financial Industry Regulatory Authority (2012), https://perma.cc/7743-UC94; Natural Resources Defense Council, Generally Recognized as Secret: Chemicals Added to Food in the United States (2014), https://perma.cc/329T-D997; American Bar Ass'n, Section on Antitrust Law, Self-Regulation of Advertising in the United States: An Assessment of the National Advertising Division (2015), https://perma.cc/8SWC-WS7E.

54. Daniel J. Solove & Woodrow Hartzog, "The FTC and the New Common Law of Privacy," *Columbia Law Review* 114 no. 3 (2014): 583–676.

55. See Federal Trade Commission Act Amendments of 1994, 15 U.S.C. § 57a(b)(3) (2018); Chris Jay Hoofnagle, *Federal Trade Commission Privacy Law and Policy* (New York: Cambridge University Press, 2016), 55–56, 333–35.

56. In re Formal Complaint of Free Press & Public Knowledge Against Comcast Corp. for Secretly Degrading Peer-to-Peer Applications, 23 F.C.C.R. 13,028 (2008); Comcast v. FCC, 600 F.3d 642, (D.C. Cir. 2010) (vacating the enforcement order against Comcast on jurisdictional grounds); Gwen Lisa Shaffer & Scott Jordan, "Classic Conditioning: The Use of Merger Conditions to Advance Policy Goals," *Media, Culture & Society* 35 no. 3 (2013): 392–403.

57. For an optimistic assessment, see Kenneth A. Bamberger & Deirdre K. Mulligan, "Privacy on the Books and on the Ground," *Stanford Law Review* 63 no. 2 (2011): 247–316, 308–09. For more critical perspectives, see Megan Gray, "Understanding and Improving Privacy 'Audits' under FTC Orders," Working Paper (May 5, 2018), https://perma.cc/8QNQ-ZJ3B; Ari Ezra Waldman, "Privacy Law's False Promise," *Washington University Law Review* 97 no. 3 (forthcoming 2019).

58. Solove & Hartzog, "The FTC and the New Common Law of Privacy," 607, 624–25; Margo Schlanger, "Against Secret Regulation: Why and How We Should End the Practical Obscurity of Injunctions and Consent Decrees," *DePaul Law Review* 59 no. 2 (2010): 515–28.

59. Ian Ayres & John Braithwaite, *Responsive Regulation: Transcending the Deregulation Debate* (New York: Oxford University Press, 1995).

60. Neal Perlman, "Section 21(A) Reports: Formalizing a Functional Release Valve at the Securities Exchange Commission," N.Y.U. Annual Survey of American Law 69 no. 4 (2015): 877–936; Kenneth A. Bamberger & Deirdre K. Mulligan, *Privacy on the Ground: Driving Corporate Behavior in the United States and Europe* (Cambridge, Mass: MIT Press, 2015), 187–91; William McGeveran, "Friending the Privacy Regulators," *Arizona Law Review* 68 no. 4 (2016): 959–1026; see also Tim Wu, "Agency Threats," *Duke Law Journal* 60 no. 8 (2011): 1841–58.

61. Francesca Bignami, "Comparative Legalism and the Non-Americanization of European Regulatory Styles: The Case of Data Privacy," *American Journal of Comparative Law* 59 no. 2 (2011): 411–62.

62. Simon, "The Organizational Premises of Administrative Law," 62; see also Bignami, "From Expert Administration to Accountability Network."

63. James R. Beniger, *The Control Revolution: Technological and Economic Origins of the Information Society* (Cambridge, Mass.: Harvard University Press, 1986), 291–435.

64. For the HIPAA deidientification rule, see 45 C.F.R. § 164.514 (2014). For some other examples of highly technical reporting requirements, see 40 C.F.R. § 63.10(d) (2015) (EPA general reporting requirements); 21 C.F.R. § 803.10 (2015) (FDA medical device reporting requirements); 47 C.F.R. § 64.606(g) (2014) (FCC common carrier reporting requirements); 17 C.F.R. § 230.257 (2015) (SEC periodic financial reporting requirements). On the centrality of audit within modern finance, see Michael Power, *The Audit Society: Rituals of Verification* (New York: Oxford University Press, 1997), 15–40. On privacy audit and reporting requirements, see sources cited in note 57 of this chapter.

65. Bamberger, "Technologies of Compliance," 673–74, 689–702; see also Danielle Keats Citron, "Technological Due Process," *Washington University Law Review* 85 no. 6 (2008): 1249–314.

66. "The Story of NIST," National Institute of Standards & Technology, https://www.nist.gov/timeline#event-a-href-node-774226 (last visited Apr. 10, 2019); Overview of ITU's History, International Telecommunication Union, https://perma.cc/87G5-XW5T (last visited Apr. 10, 2019).

67. National Technology Transfer and Advancement Act of 1995, Pub. L. 103-114, § 12(d), 110 Stat. 775 (1996), codified as amended at 15 U.S.C. § 272(d) (2018).

68. Cary Coglianese, "The Limits of Performance-Based Regulation," *University of Michigan Journal of Law Reform* 50 no. 3 (2017): 525–63; Karen Yeung, "Algorithmic Regulation: A Critical Interrogation," *Regulation and Governance* 12 no. 4 (2018): 505–23.

69. This point dovetails with Simon's observation that post-bureaucratic regulatory activities generally escape judicial review, see Simon, "The Organizational Premises of Administrative Law," 70–74, but it is slightly different: a court or regulator determined to review those activities more rigorously would first need to determine how to do so. See also Bamberger, "Regulation as Delegation."

70. Willis, "Performance-Based Consumer Regulation," 1317–21.

71. See, for example, Gray, "Understanding and Improving Privacy 'Audits' under FTC Orders"; Waldman, "Privacy Law's False Promise."

72. On protections for trade secrecy within open government laws, see Government in the Sunshine Act, 5 U.S.C. § 552b(4) (2012); Freedom of Information Act. 5 U.S.C. § §552(b) (4) (2012); William Funk, "Public Participation and Transparency in Administrative Law—Three Examples as an Object Lesson," *Administrative Law Review* 61(S) (2009): 171–98, 187–91; David Vladeck, "Information Access—Surveying the Current Legal Landscape of Federal Right-to-Know Laws," *Texas Law Review* 86 no. 7 (2008): 1787–836.

73. William W. Bratton, "Enron and the Dark Side of Shareholder Value," *Tulane Law Review* 76 nos. 5–6 (2002): 1275–352; John C. Coffee Jr., "Understanding Enron: 'It's about the Gatekeepers, Stupid,'" *Business Lawyer* 57 no. 4 (2002): 1403–20. For a brief summary of the largely unregulated audit landscape prior to the Enron scandal, see Michael V. Seitzinger, Marie B. Morris, & Mark Jickling, "Enron: Selected Securities, Accounting, and Pension Laws Possibly Implicated in Its Collapse," in *The Enron Scandal*, ed. Theodore F. Sterling (New York: Nova Science, 2002), 103, 106–07. On the credit rating agencies, see Frank Partnoy, "The Siskel and Ebert of Financial Markets?: Two Thumbs Down for the Credit Rating Agencies," *Washington University Law Quarterly* 77 no. 3 (1999): 619–712.

74. Chris Brummer, *Soft Law and the Global Financial System: Rule Making in the 21st Century* (New York: Cambridge University Press, 2012), 220–24; Daniel K. Tarullo, *Banking on Basel: The Future of International Financial Regulation* (New York: Columbia University Press, 2008), 166–72; Thomas J. Fitzpatrick, IV & Chris Sagers, "Faith-Based Financial Regulation: A Primer on Oversight of Credit Rating Agencies," *Administrative Law Review* 61 no. 3 (2009): 557–610.

75. Sarbanes-Oxley Act of 2002, Pub. L. No. 107-204, Tit. I, § 101, 116 Stat. 745 (2002), codified as amended at 15 U.S.C. § 7211 (2018); see Saule T. Omarova, "Bankers, Bureaucrats, and Guardians: Toward Tripartism in Financial Services Regulation," *Journal of Corporate Law* 37 no. 3 (2012): 621–74.

76. Credit Rating Agency Reform Act of 2006, Pub. L. No.109-291,§ 4, 120 Stat. 1329, codified as amended at 15 U.S.C. § 78o-7 (2018); see Jeffrey Manns, "Downgrading Rating Agency Reform," *George Washington Law Review* 81 no. 3 (2013): 749–812.

77. See Dodd-Frank Wall Street Reform and Consumer Protection Act, Pub. L. No. 111-203, Tit. I, § 171, 124 Stat. 1376 (2010), codified as amended at 12 U.S.C. § 5371 (2018).

78. Bamberger, "Technologies of Compliance," 677–83, 706–10.

79. Cary Coglianese & Jennifer Nash, "The Law of the Test: Performance-Based Regulation and Diesel Emissions Control," *Yale Journal on Regulation* 34 no. 1 (2017): 33–90.

80. See, for example, Doug Brake, "5G and Next Generation Wireless: Implications for Policy and Competition," Information Technology & Innovation Foundation, June 2016, 10–11, https://perma.cc/9QAD-3EXH; Adam Thierer, "Permissionless Innovation: The Continuing Case for Comprehensive Technological Freedom, Revised and Expanded Edition," Mercatus Center at George Mason University (2016), https://perma.cc/GZ9L-UNYW; Caleb Watney, "R Street Comments to FTC on Connected Vehicles" (Apr. 27, 2017), https://perma.cc/R2UN-VTEL.

81. Many results of such studies have been published at Freedom to Tinker, www.freedom-to-tinker.com.

82. This observation should not be taken as a comment on the efficacy of any of those bodies or competencies as currently constituted. It is simply a comment on their importance—and, therefore, on the importance of constituting them effectively.

83. Eloise Pasachoff, "The President's Budget as a Source of Agency Policy Control," *Yale Law Journal* 125 no. 8 (2016): 2182–291; Paperwork Reduction Act, 44 U.S.C. §§ 3501–3521 (2018). For a sampling of the literature on OIRA, see Thomas O. McGarity, "Presidential Control of Regulatory Agency Decisionmaking," *American University Law Review* 36 no. 2 (1987): 443–90; Alan B. Morrison, "OMB Interference with Agency Rulemaking: The Wrong Way to Write a Regulation," *Harvard Law Review* 99 no. 5 (1986): 1059–1074; Lisa Heinzerling, "Inside EPA: A Former Insider's Reflections on the Relationship Between the Obama EPA and the Obama White House," *Pace Environmental Law Review* 31 no. 1 (2014): 325–96; Michael Livermore & Richard L. Revesz, "Regulatory Review, Capture, and Agency Inaction," *Georgetown Law Journal* 101 no. 5 (2012): 1337–98; Cass R. Sunstein, "The Office of Information and Regulatory Affairs: Myths and Realities," *Harvard Law Review* 126 no. 7 (2013): 1838–79.

84. "Careers with the Office of Management and Budget," Obama White House Archives, https://perma.cc/LA53-RWAG (last visited June 22, 2018).

85. For the statutory framework, see Government Performance and Results Act of 1993, Pub. L. No. 103-62, 107 Stat. 285, codified as amended at 31 U.S.C. § 1115 (2018). On the complex relationship between accounting methodologies and economic development, see Trevor Hopper, "Cost Accounting, Control, and Capitalism," in *Critical Histories of Accounting: Sinister Inscriptions in the Modern Era*, eds. Richard K. Fleischman, Warwick Funnell & Stephen P. Walker (New York: Routledge, 2013), 129–43. On accounting methodologies as technologies of governance, see Peter Miller, "Governing by Numbers: Why Calculative Practices Matter," *Social Research* 68 no. 2 (2001): 379–96.

86. Center for Progressive Reform, "Behind Closed Doors at the White House: How Politics Trumps Protection of Public Health, Worker Safety, and the Environment," White Paper No. 1111 (2011), https://perma.cc/8YE9-YEG4.

87. Megan McArdle, "Romney's Business," *Atlantic* (Dec. 2011), https://perma.cc/EXZ7-PX8T; Pasachoff, "The President's Budget as a Source of Agency Policy Control," 2198, 2201.

88. Verizon v. FCC, 740 F.3d 623 (D.C. Cir. 2014) (invalidating the antiblocking and nondiscrimination rules in Preserving the Open Internet, 25 F.C.C.R. 17905 (Dec. 21, 2010); Protecting and Promoting the Open Internet: Final Rule, 80 Fed. Reg. 19,738 (Apr. 13, 2015), *repealed by* Restoring Internet Freedom, 83 Fed. Reg. 7852 (Feb. 22, 2018).

89. See 47 U.S.C. §§ 201(a), 202(a) (2018).

90. See, for example, Adam Liptak, "Verizon Blocks Messages of Abortion Rights Group," *New York Times* (Sept. 27, 2007), https://perma.cc/ZUK9-AEZQ; Peter Svensson, "Comcast Blocks Some Internet Traffic," *Washington Post* (Oct. 19, 2007), https://perma.cc/N8C6-NLAA; Kevin J. O'Brien, "Putting the Brakes on Web-Surfing Speeds," *New York Times* (Nov. 13, 2011), https://perma.cc/4PUF-TSGU; Shalini Ramachandran, "Netflix to Pay Comcast for Smoother Streaming," *Wall Street Journal* (Feb. 23, 2014), https://perma.cc/4LL6-YJA2; Edward Wyatt, "AT&T Accused of Deceiving Smartphone Customers with Unlimited Data Plans," *New York Times* (Oct. 28, 2014), https://perma.cc/X8ZS-9DNK; Editorial, "Why Free Can Be a Problem on the Internet," *New York Times* (Nov. 14, 2015), https://perma.cc/E6AF-BNXP; Ingrid Burrington, "How Mobile Carriers Skirt Net-Neutrality Rules," *Atlantic* (Dec. 18, 2015), https://perma.cc/7YVX-EYPW; John D. McKinnon & Thomas Gryta, "YouTube Says T-Mobile Is Throttling Its Video Traffic," *Wall Street Journal* (Dec. 22, 2015), https://perma.cc/2JGB-CPSX.

91. Medical Device Amendments Act of 1976, Pub. L. No. 94-295, § 513, 90 Stat. 539 (1976), codified as amended at 21 U.S.C. § 321 (2018); Copyright Act of 1976, Pub. L. 94-553, title 17, § 106, 90 Stat. 2541, codified as amended at 17 U.S.C. §§ 111, 119 (2018); Magnuson-Moss Warranty-Federal Trade Commission Improvement Act, Pub. L. No. 93-637, § 202, 88 Stat. 2183 (1975), codified as amended at 15 U.S.C. § 57a (2018).

92. Valerio de Stefano, "The Rise of the 'Just-in-Time' Workforce: On-Demand Work, Crowdwork, and Labor Protection in the 'Gig-Economy,'" *Comparative Labor Law & Policy Journal* 37 no. 3 (2016): 471–504.

93. Julia Tomassetti, "From Hierarchies to Markets: Fedex Drivers and the Work Contract as Institutional Marker," *Lewis & Clark Law Review* 19 no. 4 (2015): 1083–152. Charlotte E. Alexander & Elizabeth Tippett, "The Hacking of Employment Law," *Missouri Law Review* 82 no. 4 (2017): 973–1021.

94. Lydia Pallas Loren, "Untangling the Web of Music Copyright," *Case Western Reserve Law Review* 53 no. 3 (2003): 673–722; Mark H Wittow, Katherine L. Staba, & Trevor M. Gates, "A Modern Melody for the Music Industry: The Music Modernization Act Is Now the Law of the Land," K&L Gates (Oct. 11, 2018), https://perma.cc/M5VH-XERK.

95. An emerging scholarly genre within administrative law consists of articles exploring the consequences and implications of regulatory overlap. See James C. Cooper, "The Costs of Regulatory Redundancy: Consumer Protection Oversight of Online Travel Agents and the Advantages of Sole FTC Jurisdiction," George Mason University Law & Econ. Research Paper Series, Working Paper No. 15-08 (2015), https://perma.cc/ML59-BBGS; Tejas N. Narechania, "Patent Conflicts," *Georgetown Law Journal* 103 no. 6 (2015): 1483–542; Jacob S. Sherkow, "Administrating Patent Litigation," *Washington Law Review* 90 no. 1 (2015): 205–70; Olivier Sylvain, "Disruption and Deference," *Maryland Law Review* 74 no. 4 (2015): 715–76. Regulators' attitudes about overlapping jurisdiction vary. See, for example, Lydia Beyoud, "FCC, FTC Promise to Work in Concert on Consumer Privacy Rules in Broadband," *Bloomberg BNA* (Apr. 29, 2015), https://perma.cc/8D24-X4HG; Lydia Beyoud, "Ohlhausen: Congressional Action Needed to Define FCC, FTC Regulatory Spheres," *Bloomberg BNA* (Apr. 2, 2015), https://perma.cc/EWN5-9LT2.

96. Robert McMillan, "What Everyone Gets Wrong in the Debate over Net Neutrality," *Wired* (June 23, 2014), https://perma.cc/T7VZ-RW54; see Letter from Austin C. Schlick, Director of Communications Law, Google, to Marlene H. Dortch, Secretary, FCC (Dec. 30, 2014), WC 16-106, https://perma.cc/5FFH-XK6L; see also Ryan Singel, "Now That It's in the Broadband Game, Google Flip-Flops on Network Neutrality," *Wired* (July 30, 2013), https://

perma.cc/P2H9-U39S; Alistair Barr, "Google Strikes an Upbeat Note with FCC on Title II," *Wall Street Journal* (Dec. 31, 2014), https://perma.cc/W9HZ-ZPJW.

97. For one prominent proposal, see Oren Bracha & Frank Pasquale, "Federal Search Commission? Access, Fairness, and Accountability in the Law of Search," *Cornell Law Review* 93 no. 6 (2008): 1149–210; for criticisms, see James Grimmelmann, "Don't Censor Search," *Yale Law Journal Pocket Part* 117 (2007): 48, https://perma.cc/DK8F-WXVQ; Berin Szoka, "First Amendment Protection of Search Algorithms as Editorial Discretion," *Technology Liberation Front* (June 4, 2009), https://perma.cc/3U8U-NPJZ; Christopher S. Yoo, "Free Speech and the Myth of the Internet as an Unintermediated Experience," *George Washington Law Review* 78 no. 4 (2010): 697–773.

98. For the short-lived privacy rules, see Protecting the Privacy of Customers of Broadband and Other Telecommunications Services, 81 Fed. Reg. 87,274 (Dec. 2, 2016), *rescinded by* S.J. Res. 34, Pub. L. 115-22, 131 Stat. 88, 115th Cong. (2017). For the litigation challenging the FTC's authority, see Federal Trade Commission v. AT&T Mobility LLC, 883 F.3d 848 (9th Cir. 2018) (en banc). For the challenge to the net neutrality rules, see United States Telecom Ass'n v. Federal Commc'ns Commission, 825 F.3d 674 (D.C. Cir. 2016), *cert. denied*, 139 S. Ct. 475 (2018).

99. Rory Van Loo, "Making Innovation More Competitive: The Case of Fintech," *UCLA Law Review* 65 no. 1 (2018): 232–79.

100. Heinzerling, "The Varieties and Limits of Transparency in U.S. Food Law."

101. Farber & O'Connell, "The Lost World of Administrative Law," 1155–60. Jody Freeman & Jim Rossi, "Agency Coordination in Shared Regulatory Space," *Harvard Law Review* 125 no. 5 (2012): 1131–211; Abbe R. Gluck, Anne Joseph O'Connell, & Rosa Po, "Unorthodox Lawmaking, Unorthodox Rulemaking," *Columbia Law Review* 115 no. 7 (2015): 1789–866; Daphna Renan, "Pooling Powers," *Columbia Law Review* 115 no. 2 (2015): 211–91.

102. European Commission, Directorate-General, Communications Networks, Content, and Technology, https://perma.cc/64BH-59SY (last visited Apr. 4, 2019).

103. Promising starts include Kenneth A. Bamberger & Orly Lobel, "Platform Market Power," *Berkeley Technology Law Journal* 32 no. 3 (2017): 1051–92; Joshua A. Kroll et al., "Accountable Algorithms," *University of Pennsylvania Law Review* 165 no. 2 (2017): 633–705; Paul Ohm, "Regulating at Scale," *Georgetown Law Technology Review* 2 no. 2 (2018): 546–56, https://perma.cc/W4Y3-C4NU; Rory Van Loo, "Rise of the Digital Regulator," *Duke Law Journal* 66 no. 6 (2017): 1267–330; Rory Van Loo, "Digital Market Perfection," *Michigan Law Review* 117 no. 5 (2019): 815–83.

Chapter 7

1. On networked governance, see, for example, Julia Black, "Constructing and Contesting Legitimacy and Accountability in Polycentric Regulatory Regimes," *Regulation and Governance* 2 (2008): 137–64; John Braithwaite, "Responsive Regulation and Developing Economies," *World Development* 34 no. 5 (2006): 884–98, Kal Raustiala, "The Architecture of International Cooperation: Transgovernmental Networks and the Future of International Law," *Virginia Journal of International Law* 43 no. 1 (2002): 1–92; Anne Marie Slaughter, *A New World Order* (Princeton, N.J.: Princeton University Press, 2004); see also Gregory Shaffer, "Theorizing Transnational Legal Ordering," *Annual Review of Law and Society* 12 (2016): 231–53. On standards in transnational governance, see, for example, Panagiotis Delimatsis, ed., *The Law, Economics, and Politics of International Standardization* (New York: Cambridge University Press, 2015); Tim Buthe & Walter Mattli, *The New Global Rulers: The Privatization of Regulation in the World Economy* (Princeton, N.J.: Princeton University Press, 2011); Dieter Kerwer, "Rules That Many Use: Standards and Global Regulation," *Governance: An International Journal of Policy, Administration, and Institutions* 18 no. 4 (2005): 611–32; Colin Scott, "Standard Setting in Regulatory Regimes," in *Oxford Handbook of Regulation*, eds. Robert Baldwin, Robert Cave, & Martin Lodge (New York: Oxford University Press, 2010), 104–19; Harm Schepel, *The Constitution of Private Governance: Product Standards in the Regulation of Integrating Markets* (Portland, Ore.: Hart, 2005). The most comprehensive effort to integrate discussion of standards within discussion of networks is David Singh Grewal, *Network Power: The Social Dynamics of Globalization* (New Haven, Conn.: Yale University Press, 2008), 25–43, 193–214.

2. Duncan Kennedy (1976), "Form and Substance in Private Law Adjudication," *Harvard Law Review* 89 no. 8 (1976): 1685–778; Pierre Schlag, "Rules and Standards," *UCLA Law Review* 33 no. 2 (1985): 379–430.

3. The analogy originates with Lawrence Lessig, *Code and Other Laws of Cyberspace* (New York: Basic Books, 1998). For a brief flirtation with the idea of internet governance processes as "hybrid" code- and law-based institutions, see Laurence B. Solum, "Models of Internet Governance," in *Internet Governance: Infrastructure and Institutions*, eds. Lee A. Bygrave & Jon Bing (New York: Oxford University Press, 2009), 48–91.

4. On the state monopoly of violence and the centrality of violence for the state, see Anthony Giddens, *The Nation-State and Violence: Volume 2 of a Contemporary Critique of Historical Materialism* (Berkeley, Calif.: University of California Press, 1987), 18–19; Francis Fukuyama, "Liberalism versus State-Building," *Journal of Democracy* 18 no. 3 (2007): 10–13.

5. Theories of the rule of law vary in their thickness. For a summary and analysis of the major strands of thought about the rule of law in the Anglo-American legal tradition, see Richard H. Fallon Jr., "'The Rule of Law'" as a Concept in Constitutional Discourse," *Columbia Law Review* 97 no. 1 (1997): 1–56. For a broader comparative discussion of the rule-of-law ideal, see Mireille Hildebrandt, *Smart Technologies and the End(s) of Law: Novel Entanglements of Law and Technology* (Northampton, Mass.: Edward Elgar, 2015), 133–56.

6. Hildebrandt, *Smart Technologies and the End(s) of Law*, 174–85.

7. Martin Krygier, "The Rule of Law: Pasts, Presents, and Two Possible Futures," *Annual Review of Law and Social Science* 12 (2016): 199–229.

8. Terence C. Halliday & Gregory Shaffer, "Transnational Legal Orders," in *Transnational Legal Orders*, eds. Terence C. Halliday & Gregory Shaffer (New York: Cambridge University Press, 2015), 3–72; Heather McKeen-Edwards & Tony Porter, *Transnational Financial Associations and the Governance of Global Finance: Assembling Wealth and Power* (New York: Routledge, 2013); see also Gregory C. Shaffer, "How Business Shapes Law: A Socio-legal Framework," *Connecticut Law Review* 42 no. 1 (2009): 147–83. Broadly speaking, the idea of an assemblage refers to an interlinked set of institutions and actors whose repeated, purposive operations and interactions define the parameters for ordering. Martin Muller, "Assemblages and Actor-Networks: Rethinking Socio-material Power, Politics and Space," *Geography Compass* 9 no. 1 (2015): 27–41.

9. On the multistakeholderism as an emergent modality of governance, see Mark Raymond & Laura DeNardis, "Multistakeholderism: Anatomy of an Inchoate Global Institution," *International Theory* 7 no. 3 (2015): 572–616. On standards and standard-making, see sources cited in note 1, above.

10. For two very different perspectives on the increasing importance of logics of trade liberalization within trade governance arrangements, see William J. Drake & Kalypso Nicolaidis, "Ideas, Interests, and Institutionalization: 'Trade in Services' and the Uruguay Round," *International Organization* 46 no. 1 (1992): 37–100; Jane Kelsey, *Serving Whose Interests? The Political Economy of Trade in Services* (New York: Routledge-Cavendish, 2008), 76–88.

11. Iain Osgood & Yilang Feng, "Intellectual Property Provisions and Support for US Trade Agreements," *Review of International Organizations* 13 no. 3 (2018): 421–55.

12. Mario Cimoli et al., eds., *Intellectual Property Rights: Legal and Economic Challenges for Developing Countries* (New York: Oxford University Press, 2014); Olufunmilayo B. Arewa, "Local Communities, Local Knowledge, and Global Intellectual Property Frameworks," *Marquette Intellectual Property Law Revew* 10 no. 1 (2006): 155–80.

13. See, for example, Alessandra Arcuri, "Global Food Safety Standards: The Evolving Regulatory Epistemology at the Intersection of the SPS Agreement and the Codex Alimentarius Commission," in Delimatsis, ed., *Law, Economics, and Politics*, 79–103; Panagiotos Delimatsis, "'Relevant International Standards' and 'Recognised Standardisation Bodies' under the TBT Agreement," in Delimatsis, ed., *Law, Economics, and Politics*, 104–36; Hans Lindahl,

"ISO Standards and Authoritative Collective Action," in Delimatsis, ed., *Law, Economics, and Politics*, 42–57; Harm Schepel, "Between Standards and Regulation: On the Concept of 'De Facto Mandatory Standards' after *Tuna II* and *Fra.bo*," in Delimatsis, ed., *Law, Economics, and Politics*, 199–214.

14. Robert E. Baldwin, "Failure of the WTO Ministerial Conference at Cancun: Reasons and Remedies," *The World Economy* 29 no. 6 (2006): 677–96.

15. For a sampling of perspectives on these developments, see Todd Allee & Andrew Legg, "Who Wrote the Rules for the Trans-Pacific Partnership?," *Research and Politics* July–Sept. 2016: 1–9, doi: 10.1177/2053168016658919; Kyle Bagwell, Chad P. Bown, & Robert W. Staiger, "Is the WTO Passé?," *Journal of Economic Literature* 54 no. 4 (2016): 1125–231; Nitsan Chorev & Sarah Babb, "The Crisis of Neoliberalism and the Future of International Institutions: A Comparison of the IMF and the WTO," *Theory and Society* 38 no. 5 (2009): 459–84.

16. David A Gantz, "The TPP and RCEP: Mega-trade Agreements for the Pacific Rim," *Arizona Journal of International and Comparative Law* 33 no. 1 (2016): 57–69; Peter K. Yu, "The RCEP and Trans-Pacific Intellectual Property Norms," *Vanderbilt Journal of Transnational Law* 50 no. 3 (2017): 673–740; Mireya Solis & Jennifer Mason, "As the TPP Lives On, the U.S. Abdicates Trade Leadership," Order From Chaos, Brookings Institution (Mar. 9, 2018), https://perma.cc/Z29Y-4LT2.

17. See Christopher Ingraham, "Interactive: How Companies Wield Off-the-Record Influence on Obama's Trade Policy," *Washington Post* (Feb. 8, 2014), https://perma.cc/UPN6-DHKD.

18. Melissa J. Durkee, "The Business of Treaties," *UCLA Law Review* 63 no. 1 (2016): 264–321.

19. For more detailed discussion of ISDS mechanisms, see Chapter 8, pp. 257–60.

20. Margaret E. Keck & Kathryn Sikkink, eds., *Activists beyond Borders: Advocacy Networks in International Politics* (Ithaca, N.Y.: Cornell University Press, 1998), 1–38.

21. Lindahl, "ISO Standards and Authoritative Collective Action"; Kernaghan Webb, "ISO 26000 Social Responsibility Standard as 'Proto Law' and a New Form of Global Custom: Positioning ISO 26000 in the Emerging Transnational Regulatory Governance Rule Instrument Architecture," *Transnational Legal Theory* 6 no. 2 (2015): 466–500; see also Buthe & Mattli, *The New Global Rulers*.

22. Melissa J. Durkee, "Astroturf Activism," *Stanford Law Review* 69 no. 1 (2017): 201–68; see also Melissa J. Durkee, "International Lobbying Law" *Yale Law Journal* 128 no. 7 (2018): 1742–826.

23. Benedicte Bull & Desmonde McNeill, *Development Issues in Global Governance: Public-Private Partnerships and Market Multilateralism* (New York: Routledge, 2007), 1–22; Marco Schäferhoff, Sabine Campe, & Christopher Kaan. "Transnational Public-Private Partnerships in International Relations: Making Sense of Concepts, Research Frameworks, and Results." *International Studies Review* 11 no. 3 (2009): 451–74.

24. Chris Brummer, *Soft Law and the Global Financial System: Rule Making in the 21st Century* (New York: Cambridge University Press, 2012); Charles D. Raab, "Networks for Regulation: Privacy Commissioners in a Changing World," *Journal of Comparative Policy Analysis: Research and Practice* 13 no. 2 (2011): 195–213.

25. Chris Brummer, *Minilateralism: How Trade Alliances, Soft Law and Financial Engineering Are Redefining Economic Statecraft* (New York: Cambridge University Press, 2014), 96–123; McKeen-Edwards & Porter, *Transnational Financial Associations and the Governance of Global Finance*; Juan A. Marchetti, "Technical Standard-Setting in the Financial Sector," in Delimatsis, ed., *Law, Economics, and Politics*, 137–59.

26. On standardization work by global transnational corporations, see Durkee, "The Business of Treaties," 281–82; Klaas Hendrik Eller, "Private Governance of Global Value Chains from Within: Lessons for Transnational Law," *Transnational Legal Theory* 8 no. 3 (2017): 296–329; Li-Wen Lin, "Legal Transplants through Private Contracting: Codes of Vendor Conduct in Global Supply Chains as an Example," *American Journal of Comparative Law* 57 no. 3 (2009): 711–44; Schepel, *The Constitution of Private Governance*. On the role of private industry associations in financial standardization, see McKeen-Edwards & Porter,

Transnational Financial Associations and the Governance of Global Finance. On standardization work performed by and through specialized professions, see McKeen-Edwards & Porter, *Transnational Financial Associations and the Governance of Global Finance,* 79–99; Kerwer, "Rules That Many Use."

27. See, for example, Jordi Agusti-Panareda, Franz Christian Ebert, & Desiree LeClerq, "ILO Labor Standards and Trade Agreements: A Case for Consistency," *Comparative Labor Law and Policy Journal* 36 no. 2 (2015): 347–80; Orr Karassin & Oren Perez, "Shifting between Public and Private: The Reconfiguration of Global Environmental Regulation," *Indiana Journal of Global Legal Studies* 25 no. 1 (2018): 97–130; Kevin Kolben, "Transnational Labor Regulation and the Limits of Governance," *Theoretical Inquiries in Law* 12 no. 2 (2011): 403–37.

28. Theodore Eisenberg & Geoffrey P. Miller, "The Flight from Arbitration: An Empirical Study of Ex Ante Arbitration Clauses in the Contracts of Publicly Held Companies," *DePaul Law Review* 56 no. 2 (2007): 335–74; W. Mark C. Weidemaier, "Customized Procedure in Theory and Reality," *Washington & Lee Law Review* 72 no. 4 (2015): 1865–943.

29. Susan Block-Lieb & Terence Halliday, "Contracts and Private Law in the Emerging Ecology of International Lawmaking," in *Contractual Knowledge: One Hundred Years of Legal Experimentation in Global Markets,* eds. Gregoire Mallard & Jerome Sgard (New York: Cambridge University Press, 2016), 350–99; see also Yves Dezalay & Bryant Garth, *Dealing in Virtue: International Commercial Arbitration and the Construction of a Transnational Legal Order* (Chicago: University of Chicago Press, 1996).

30. Matthew S. Erie, "The New Legal Hubs: The Emergent Landscape of International Commercial Dispute Resolution," *Virginia Journal of International Law* 59 no. 3 (forthcoming, 2019).

31. Lessig, *Code and Other Laws of Cyberspace;* A. Michael Froomkin, "Habermas@Discourse. Net: Toward a Critical Theory of Cyberspace," *Harvard Law Review* 116 no. 3 (2003): 749–873; see also Solum, "Models of Internet Governance."

32. Gralf-Peter Calliess & Peer Zumbansen, *Rough Consensus and Running Code: A Theory of Transnational Private Law* (Portland, Ore.: Hart, 2010), 137–39. For a notable exception within the transnational governance literature, see Roger Cotterrell, "What Is Transnational Law?," *Law and Social Inquiry* 37 no. 2 (2012): 500–24.

33. Janet Abbate, *Inventing the Internet* (Cambridge, Mass.: MIT Press, 1999), 147–79; Laura DeNardis, *Protocol Politics: The Globalization of Internet Governance* (Cambridge, Mass.: MIT Press, 2009), 25–70; Andrew L. Russell, "'Rough Consensus and Running Code' and the Internet-OSI Standards War," *IEEE Annals of the History of Computing* 28 no. 3 (2006): 48–61.

34. Russell, "'Rough Consensus and Running Code,'" 55.

35. Memorandum of Understanding between the U.S. Dep't of Commerce and ICANN (Nov. 25, 1998), https://perma.cc/ZMV2-VLD4; "USC-ICANN Transition Agreement," https://perma.cc/8ZKM-5EM7 (last visited Dec. 24, 1998); U.S. Dep't of Commerce, Nat'l Telecomm. & Info. Admin., "NTIA Finds IANA Stewardship Transition Proposal Meets Criteria to Complete Privatization" (June 9, 2016), https://perma.cc/6R2P-Q5UT.

36. For helpful discussions of the competing arguments and perspectives, see Laura DeNardis, *The Global War for Internet Governance* (New Haven, Conn.: Yale University Press, 2014), 33–34, 226–30; Milton L Mueller, *Ruling the Root: Internet Governance and the Taming of Cyberspace* (Cambridge, Mass.: MIT Press, 2002); see also White House, "A Framework for Global Electronic Commerce" (July 1, 1997), https://perma.cc/HH2M-PRCC.

37. Dmitry Epstein, "The Making of Institutions of Information Governance: The Case of the Internet Governance Forum," *Journal of Information Technology* 28 no. 2 (2013): 137–49.

38. Froomkin, "Habermas@Discourse.Net."

39. A. Michael Froomkin, "Wrong Turn in Cyberspace: Using ICANN to Route around the APA and the Constitution," *Duke Law Journal* 50 no. 1 (2000): 17–86; John Palfrey, "The End of the Experiment: How ICANN's Foray into Global Internet Democracy Failed," *Harvard Journal of Law and Technology* 17 no. 2 (2004): 409–74.

40. See, for example, David R. Johnson & Susan P. Crawford, "The Idea of ICANN," ICANN Watch (Feb. 12, 2001), https://perma.cc/TGQ7-GJWB.

41. For discussion, see Stefania Milan & Niels ten Oever, "Coding and Encoding Rights in Internet Infrastructure," *Internet Policy Review* 6 no. 1 (2017): doi: 10.14763/2017.1.442.

42. Articles of Incorporation of Internet Corporation for Assigned Names and Numbers, art. 3 (Sept. 30, 1998), https://perma.cc/85L3-LMCM.

43. "The IETF Process: An Informal Guide," Internet Engineering Task Force, https://perma.cc/DM6S-GB2V (last visited June 21, 2018); Charles Vincent & Jean Camp, "Looking to the Internet for Models of Governance," *Ethics and Information Technology* 6 (2004): 161–73.

44. See generally Gillian E. Metzger & Kevin M. Stack, "Internal Administrative Law," *Michigan Law Review* 115 no. 8 (2017): 1239–307, 1250–56.

45. Corinne J.N. Cath, "A Case Study of Coding Rights: Should Freedom of Speech Be Instantiated in the Protocols and Standards Designed by the Internet Engineering Task Force?," Thesis for degree in Master of Science in Social Science of the Internet, Oxford University (Aug. 10, 2015), https://perma.cc/8F8Q-AGDD.

46. DeNardis, *The Global War for Internet Governance.*

47. For these and other examples, see DeNardis, *The Global War for Internet Governance,* 74–76.

48. DeNardis, *The Global War for Internet Governance,* 46–55.

49. On the increasing importance of digital information flows for cross-border trade and their imperfect fit within the framework established by the GATS, see Anupam Chander, *The Electronic Silk Road: How the Web Binds the World Together in Commerce* (New Haven, Conn.: Yale University Press, 2013), 142–57; Lee Tuthill & Martin Roy, "GATS Classification Issues for Information and Communication Technology Services," in Mira Burri & Thomas Cottier, eds., *Trade Governance in the Digital Age: World Trade Forum* (New York: Cambridge University Press, 2012), 157–78; Tim Wu, "The World Trade Law of Censorship and Internet Filtering," *Chicago Journal of International Law* 7 no. 1 (2006): 263–88, 266–76.

50. On free flow provisions in the electronic commerce chapter of the TPP, see Burcu Kilic & Tamir Israel, "The Highlights of the Trans-Pacific Partnership E-Commerce Chapter," Public Citizen (Nov. 5, 2015), https://perma.cc/3ACL-RZBR. On free flow provisions in the financial services chapter of the Trade in Services Agreement, see Jane Kelsey, Analysis TISA Financial Service Text Dated 27 June 2016, https://perma.cc/KD5J-YYQR. See also Mira Burri, "The Governance of Data and Data Flows in Trade Agreements," *U.C. Davis Law Review* 51 no. 1 (2015): 65–132.

51. Wu, "The World Trade Law of Censorship and Internet Filtering," 266–76.

52. On industry negotiating strategies with regard to copyright provisions, see Margot E. Kaminski, "The Capture of International Intellectual Property Law through the U.S. Trade Regime," *Southern California Law Review* 87 no. 4 (2014): 977–1052, 1019–29. On efforts to secure stronger protection for cross-border flows of trade secret information, see Intellectual Property Rights Industry—Trade Advisory Committee (ITAC-15), "Report on the Trans-Pacific Partnership Agreement" (Dec. 3, 2015), 25–26, https://perma.cc/SH26-5UHL; see also Douglas C. Lippoldt & Mark F. Schultz, "Uncovering Trade Secrets—An Empirical Assessment of Economic Implications of Protection for Undisclosed Data," OECD Trade Policy Papers, No. 167, 2014, https://perma.cc/DRJ6-KH6H; Andre Barbe & Katherine Linton, "Trade Secrets: International Trade Policy and Empirical Research," OECD Trade Policy Papers, Draft Aug. 5, 2016, https://perma.cc/WG25-RV82. For an overview of the issues relating to cross-border cloud storage, see Urs Gasser & John Palfrey, "Fostering Innovation and Trade in the Global Information Society: The Different Facets and Roles of Interoperability," in Burri & Cottier, eds., *Trade Governance in the Digital Age: World Trade Forum,* 123–54.

53. Anu Bradford, "The Brussels Effect," *Northwestern University Law Review* 107 no. 1 (2012): 1–67; see also Gregory Shaffer, "Globalization and Social Protection: The Impact of E.U. Rules

in the Ratcheting Up of U.S. Privacy Standards," *Yale Journal of International Law* 25 no. 1 (2000): 1–88.

54. Case C-362/14, Schrems v. Data Protection Comm'r, 2015. E.C.R. 627 (invalidating safe harbor agreement); EU-U.S. Privacy Shield Framework (July 12, 2016), https://perma.cc/ C92T-C7CJ; Natasha Lomas, "Facebook Is Trying to Block Schrems II Privacy Referral to EU Top Court," *TechCrunch* (Apr. 30, 2018), https://perma.cc/FK6J-JZDJ.

55. For discussion of the interplay between GATS obligations and European data protection requirements, see Svetlana Yakovleva & Kristina Irion, "The Best of Both Worlds? Free Trade in Services, and EU Law on Privacy and Data Protection," *European Data Protection Law Review* 2 no. 2 (2016): 191–208, doi: 10.21552/EDPL/2016/2/9. On the possibility that the Transatlantic Trade and Investment Partnership (TTIP) might undermine data protection guarantees, see Graham Greenleaf, "Free Trade Agreements and Data Privacy: Future Perils of Faustian Bargains," in *Transatlantic Data Privacy Relations as a Challenge for Democracy*, eds. Dan Svantesson & Dariusz Kloza (Antwerp: Intersentia, 2017), 181–212; Hielke Hijmans, "The Transatlantic Trade and Investment Partnership and the Developments in the Area of Privacy and Data Protection," *Legal Issues of Economic Integration* 43 no. 4 (2016): 385–98. On industry lobbying, see "TTIP: A Corporate Lobbying Paradise," *Corporate Europe Observatory* (July 14, 2015), https://perma.cc/RJ85-H7FR; Maira Sutton, "Newly Released Emails Reveal Cozy Relationship between U.S. Trade Officials and Industry Reps over Secret TISA Deal, Electronic Frontier Foundation (Aug. 26, 2015), https://perma.cc/5G5A-WWF3; Nicole Sagener, "Report: Lobbyists Heavily Influencing TiSA Negotiations, EurActiv" (Dec. 13, 2016), https://perma.cc/TR3H-HSUX.

56. "APEC Privacy Framework 2015," Asia-Pacific Economic Cooperation (Aug. 2017), https:// perma.cc/Q5WT-58S5; Graham Greenleaf, "APEC's Privacy Framework—A New Low Standard," *Privacy Law and Policy Reporter* 11 no. 5 (2005): 121.

57. On the TPP's implications for data privacy protection and the possible implications of RCEP, see Graham Greenleaf, "Looming Free Trade Agreements Pose Threats to Privacy," *International Report: Privacy Laws & Business* 152 (2018): 123–27.

58. For a sampling of perspectives on Brazilian regulatory efforts, see Anupam Chander & Uyen Le, "Data Nationalism," *Emory Law Journal* 64 no. 3 (2014): 677–740; Albright Stonehedge Group, "Data Localization: A Challenge to Global Commerce and the Free Flow of Information" (Sept. 2015), https://perma.cc/9NK8-TP4S; Francis Augusto Medeiros & Lee Bygrave, "Brazil's Marco Civil da Internet: Does It Live Up to the Hype?," 31 no. 1 (2015): 120–30, 126–27.

59. McKinsey Global Institute, "India's Technology Opportunity: Transforming Work, Empowering People" (Dec. 2014), http://perma.cc/PB8X-RW4J; Sadanand Dhume, "No Free Internet Please, We're Indian," *Wall Street Journal* (Jan. 11, 2016), https://perma.cc/ T2H5-MP5Y; Adrienne LaFrance, "Facebook and the New Colonialism," *Atlantic* (Feb. 11, 2016), https://perma.cc/2HX3-JGGN; Sadanand Dhume, "Indians Clash over National ID," *Wall Street Journal* (Jan. 25, 2018), https://perma.cc/6VGB-UFEY; Jyoti Panday, "India's Supreme Court Upholds Right to Privacy as a Fundamental Right—and It's about Time," Electronic Frontier Foundation (Aug. 28, 2017), https://perma.cc/DXK6-Z8RD.

60. Well-known expressions of network optimism include Yochai Benkler, *The Wealth of Networks: How Social Production Transforms Markets and Freedom* (New Haven, Conn.: Yale University Press, 2006); Chander, *The Electronic Silk Road*; Joshua Cohen & Charles F. Sabel, "Global Democracy?," *N.Y.U. Journal of International Law & Politics* 37 no. 4: 763–97. More measured evaluations include Jack Goldsmith & Tim Wu, *Who Controls the Internet? Illusions of a Borderless World* (New York: Oxford University Press, 2008); Laurence R. Helfer, "Regime Shifting: The TRIPs Agreement and New Dynamics of International Intellectual Property Lawmaking," *Yale Journal of International Law* 29 no. 1 (2004): 1–84; Anna di Robilant, "Genealogies of Soft Law," *American Journal of Comparative Law* 54 no. 3 (2006): 499–554.

61. Grewal, *Network Power*; Manuel Castells, *Communication Power* (New York: Oxford University Press, 2009).

62. Milton L. Mueller, *Networks and States: The Global Politics of Internet Governance* (Cambridge, Mass.: MIT Press, 2010), 41–50.

63. On network organization generally, see Albert-Laszlo Barabasi, *Linked: The New Science of Networks* (Cambridge, Mass.: Perseus, 2002).

64. See, for example, Braithwaite, "Responsive Regulation and Developing Economies"; Cohen & Sabel, "Global Democracy?." As this brief description suggests, there are important political and ideological differences between the new governance movement in transnational law and the new governance approach to administrative law described in Chapter 6, pp. 187–88.

65. Fallon, "'The Rule of Law' as a Concept in Constitutional Discourse," 8–9.

66. On network lock-in, see Michael L. Katz, & Carl Shapiro, "Network Externalities, Competition, and Compatibility," *American Economic Review* 75 no. 3 (1985): 424–40; on the options generally available to consumers for disciplining market providers of goods and services, see Albert O. Hirschman, *Exit, Voice, and Loyalty: Responses to Decline in Firms, Organizations, and States* (Cambridge, Mass.: Harvard University Press, 1970).

67. Grewal, *Network Power*, 4–8; Castells, *Communication Power*, 43.

68. John Braithwaite & Peter Drahos, *Global Business Regulation* (New York: Cambridge University Press, 2000); Grewal, *Network Power*, 228–35.

69. DeNardis, *Protocol Politics*.

70. On ICANN, see Kal Raustiala, "Governing the Internet," *American Journal of International Law* 110 no. 3 (2016): 491–503. On the IETF, see DeNardis, *The Global War for Internet Governance*, 69–70; Of the 20 Internet companies that spend the most on lobbying in the United States, seven are members of the W3C. Those include Google, Facebook, Alibaba Group, PayPal, Electronic Transactions Association, Netflix, and Dropbox. See "Current Members," W3C, https://perma.cc/S8RS-JWZP (last visited June 21, 2018); "Lobbying/ Industry: Internet," Center for Responsive Politics, https://perma.cc/5F2C-HCVH (last visited June 21, 2018).

71. Carl Shapiro & Hal R. Varian, "The Art of Standards Wars," *California Management Review* 41 no. 2 (1999): 8–32.

72. On the availability of alternative bases for allocation and the power of property logics, see Mueller, *Ruling the Root*, 245–53.

73. Anupam Chander & Madhavi Sunder, "The Battle to Define Asia's Intellectual Property Law: From TPP to RCEP," *U.C. Irvine Law Review* 8 no. 3 (2018): 331–61; see also Yu, "The RCEP and Trans-Pacific Intellectual Property Norms."

74. Dana Polatin-Reuben & Joss Wright, "An Internet with BRICS Characteristics: Data Sovereignty and the Balkanisation of the Internet," Paper Presented at the 4th Usenix Workshop on Free and Open Communications on the Internet, Aug. 18, 2014, https://perma.cc/EC3C-B3BH; Tracy Staedter, "Why Russia Is Building Its Own Internet," *IEEE Spectrum* (Jan. 17, 2018), https://perma.cc/6UU4-NNJG; see also Daya Kishan Thussu, "Digital BRICS: Building a NWICO 2.0?," in *Mapping BRICS Media*, eds. Kaarle Nordenstreng & Daya Kishan Thussu (New York: Routledge, 2015), 242–63. Such failures also reflect what Castells calls *networking power*, or the power that members of a dominant network enjoy over outsiders. Castells, *Communication Power*, 42–43. The BRICS countries are represented within internet governance bodies and processes, but their views about appropriate changes to the standards have been treated as outsider views.

75. On Sun Microsystems' introduction of the "write once, run everywhere" slogan and its attempts to position its own Java technology as the industry standard for cross-platform application development, see Raghu Garud, Sanjay Jain, & Arun Kumaraswamy, "Institutional Entrepreneurship in the Sponsorship of Common Technological Standards: The Case of Sun Microsystems and Java," *Academy of Management Journal* 45 no. 1 (2002): 196–214.

76. Mary J. Cronin, *Smart Products, Smarter Services: Strategies for Embedded Control* (New York: Cambridge University Press, 2010), 34–69 (describing different strategies adopted by large industry players).

77. Economists asking the question whether U.S-driven trade workarounds are efficient or inefficient from an economic perspective have often missed the larger structural point. The pursuit of trade workarounds is an emergent consequence of the networked structure of trade governance and of the networked, interconnected communications infrastructure through which trade negotiations are conducted. For a detailed investigation of the institutional efficiencies and inefficiencies that result from the increased use of trade workarounds, see Bagwell, Bown, & Staiger, "Is the WTO Passé?,"

78. Helfer, "Regime Shifting."

79. Martin Senftleben, "A Copyright Limitations Treaty Based on the Marrakesh Model: Nightmare or Dream Come True?" (2017), https://perma.cc/CJX2-TLAW.

80. Annemarie Bridy, "Notice and Takedown in the Domain Name System: ICANN's Ambivalent Drift into Online Content Regulation," *Washington and Lee Law Review* 74 no. 3 (2017): 1345–88; Peter Bright, "DRM for HTML5 Finally Makes It as an Official W3C Recommendation," *Ars Technica* (Sept. 18, 2017), https://perma.cc/Z9P6-2JLW.

81. Stephanie E. Perrin, "The Struggle for WHOIS Privacy: Understanding the Standoff between ICANN and the World's Data Protection Authorities," unpublished doctoral dissertation, Faculty of Information, University of Toronto, 2018, 243–53. The GDPR may prompt some changes here, but ICANN has mounted an aggressive defense of existing WHOIS policies. See "ICANN Appeals German Decision on GDPR/WHOIS," ICANN (June 13, 2018), https://perma.cc/NH8P-CKMG.

82. Robert Howse, "The World Trade Organization and the Protection of Workers' Rights," *Journal of Small and Emerging Business Law* 3 no. 1 (1999): 131–72.

83. Kolben, "Transnational Labor Regulation and the Limits of Governance."

84. Fallon, "'The Rule of Law' as a Concept in Constitutional Discourse," 8–9.

85. Anu Bradford & Eric A. Posner, "Universal Exceptionalism in International Law," *Harvard International Law Journal* 52 no. 1 (2011): 3–54, 36.

86. Rebecca MacKinnon, *Consent of the Networked: The Worldwide Struggle for Internet Freedom* (New York: Basic Books, 2012), 31–71. On whether Chinese internet filtering policies amount to trade violations, see Wu, "The World Trade Law of Censorship and Internet Filtering."

87. Castells, *Communication Power*, 45–46.

88. Yiping Huang, "Understanding China's Belt & Road Initiative: Motivation, Framework and Assessment." *China Economic Review* 40 (2016): 314–21; Hong Yu, "Motivation behind China's 'One Belt, One Road' Initiatives and Establishment of the Asian Infrastructure Investment Bank." *Journal of Contemporary China* 26 no. 105 (2017): 353–68.

89. Yu, "Motivation behind China's 'One Belt, One Road' Initiatives," 363–67; Indrani Bagchi, "India Slams China's One Belt One Road Initiative, Says It Violates Sovereignty," *The Times of India* (May 14, 2017), https://perma.cc/W7TX-K9BZ.

90. Bin Gu, "Chinese Multilateralism in the AIIB," *Journal of International Economic Law* 20 no. 1 (2017): 137–58; Yu, "Motivation behind China's 'One Belt, One Road' Initiatives," 358–62; Andrew Higgins & David E. Sanger, "3 European Powers Say They Will Join China-Led Bank," *New York Times* (Mar. 17, 2015), https://perma.cc/KA7S-8NCB.

91. PwC, "Global Top 100 Companies by Market Capitalisation" (Mar. 31, 2017), 35, https://perma.cc/8TNB-TBCA; see also McKinsey Global Institute, "China's Digital Economy: A Leading Global Force" (Aug. 2017), https://perma.cc/X4BD-75TB; Charles Arthur, "The Chinese Tech Companies Poised to Dominate the World," *The Guardian* (June 3, 2014), https://perma.cc/W7TP-E89Z.

92. U.S.-China Economic and Security Review Commission, "China's Techno-Nationalism Toolbox: A Primer" (Mar. 28, 2018), https://perma.cc/J5AV-L6FA.

93. Kai Jia & Martin Kenney, "Mobile Internet Platform Business Models in China: Vertical Hierarchies, Horizontal Conglomerates, or Business Groups?," Berkeley Roundtable on the International Economy Working Paper 2016-6 (July 27, 2016), https://perma.cc/ZVK7-DJYX.

94. On the global expansion of Chinese technology companies, see McKinsey Global Institute, "China's Digital Economy: A Leading Global Force" (Aug. 2017), https://perma.cc/XV5V-7JXU; Charles Arthur, "The Chinese Tech Companies Poised to Dominate the World," *The Guardian* (June 3, 2014), https://perma.cc/K7G2-CAFE.

95. Samm Sacks, "Beijing Wants to Rewrite the Rules of the Internet," *The Atlantic* (June 18, 2018), https://perma.cc/YFY8-KYM5. For more detailed discussion of the human rights implications of China's information technology strategy, see Chapter 8, pp. 264–66.

96. Gabriele de Seta, "Into the Red Stack," *Hong Kong Review of Books* (Apr. 17, 2018), https://perma.cc/J5VD-7SH3.

97. See sources cited in note 74. By way of comparison, see Louise Matsakis, "What Happens If Russia Cuts Itself Off from the Internet?," *Wired* (Feb. 12, 2019), https://perma.cc/DXW8-KZVJ.

98. As Peter Yu describes in the context of intellectual property, Chinese negotiating strategy emphasizes pragmatism and economic development, and China's evolving interests have led it to chart a middle way between developed countries seeking to impose strong IP obligations and regional partners seeking less stringent obligations. Yu, "The RCEP and Trans-Pacific Intellectual Property Norms."

99. Isaac Stone Fish, "The Other Political Correctness," *The New Republic* (Sept. 4, 2018), https://perma.cc/YQH4-HU8Z; Louisa Lim & Julia Bergin, "Inside China's Audacious Global Propaganda Campaign," *The Guardian* (Dec. 7, 2018), https://perma.cc/2KYA-MH7U.

100. Ruth W. Grant & Robert O. Keohane, "Accountability and Abuses of Power in World Politics," *American Political Science Review* 99 no. 1 (2005): 29–43.

101. Kaminski, "The Capture of International Intellectual Property Law through the U.S. Trade Regime," 988–1013; Ian Fergusson, "Trade Promotion Authority (TPA) and the Role of Congress in Trade Policy," Congressional Research Service (June 15, 2015), https://perma.cc/4QSP-6C9S.

102. On the causes and effects of that approach, see Niels Gheyle & Ferdi De Ville, "How Much Is Enough? Explaining the Continuous Transparency Conflict in TTIP," *Politics and Governance* 5 no. 3 (2017): 16-28; see also Chander & Sunder, "The Battle to Define Asia's Intellectual Property Law"; Michelle Limenta, "Open Trade Negotiations as Opposed to Secret Trade Negotiations: From Transparency to Public Participation," *New Zealand Yearbook of International Law* 10 (2012): 73–95.

103. Chris Brummer, *Soft Law and the Global Financial System: Rule Making in the 21st Century* (New York: Cambridge University Press, 2012), 213–27.

104. See, for example, Golan v. Holder, 565 U.S. 302, 335–36 (2012) ("Congress determined that U.S. interests were best served by our full participation in the dominant system of international copyright protection. . . . The judgment § 514 expresses lies well within the ken of the political branches").

105. Raymond & DeNardis, "Multistakeholderism."

106. "Benefit Corporations and Flexible Purpose Corporations in California," Justice and Diversity Center of the Bar Association of San Francisco, https://perma.cc/HYX6-5T57 (last visited June 29, 2018).

107. ICANN, "Accountability and Transparency," https://perma.cc/B7GE-MRSM; Rolf H. Weber & Shawn Gunnarson, "A Constitutional Solution for Internet Governance," 14 *Columbia Science & Technology Law Review* 14 no. 1 (2013): 1–71.

108. On the intent behind ICANN's structure, see Mueller, *Ruling the Root*, 185–93, 231–38; Raustiala, "Governing the Internet." On the success of the capture stratgy, see Konstantinis Komaitis, *The Current State of Domain Name Regulation: Domain Names as Second-Class Citizens*

in a Mark-Dominated World. (New York: Routledge, 2010); see also ICANN, Uniform Domain Name Dispute Resolution Policy, paras. 3(b), 4(k), https://perma.cc/A9BN-CL4F; ICANN, Uniform Rapid Suspension, "URS," para. 13, https://perma.cc/6JLU-PXTF.

109. Perrin, *The Struggle for WHOIS Privacy*, 121–27.

110. In general, the innovations that "go viral" within networks are those originating from more connected nodes within the network. See Barabasi, *Linked*, 131–35. By analogy, the success or failure of assertions of counterpower within regulatory networks can be expected to correlate to the connectedness of the originating nodes.

111. "Civil Society Call for Full Transparency about the EU-US Trade Negotiations," Letter to European Commissioner for Trade (May 19, 2014), https://perma.cc/M7UK-LAB6; "Joint Civil Society Statement on Privacy in the Digital Age Submitted to the 27th Session of the UN Human Rights Council," Human Rights Watch (Sept, 11, 2014), https://perma.cc/M66G-5JQK; "Global Civil Society Groups Call for Reform of US Surveillance Law Section 702," Access Now (Mar. 1, 2017), https://perma.cc/6BSY-PPLP; see also Angelique Carson, "Changing Tactics: The Rise of the Privacy Advocates," International Association of Privacy Professionals (Sept. 23, 2013), https://perma.cc/G9KK-H33J.

112. Durkee, "Astroturf Activism."

113. For an especially compelling articulation of this worry, see David Kennedy, "Law and the Political Economy of the World," in *Critical Legal Perspectives on Global Governance: Liber Amicorum David M. Trubek*, eds. Grainne de Burca, Claire Kilpatrick, & Joanne Scott (Portland, Ore.: Hart, 2014), 65–102.

114. Hans Krause Hansen & Tony Porter, "What Do Numbers Do in Transnational Governance?," *International Political Sociology* 6 no. 4 (2012): 409–26, https://doi.org/10.1111/ips.12001; see also Kevin E. Davis, Benedict Kingsbury, & Sally Engle Merry, "Indicators as a Technology of Global Governance," *Law and Society Review* 46 no. 1 (2012): 71–104.

115. Karassin & Perez, "Shifting between Public and Private"; Kolben, "Transnational Labor Regulation and the Limits of Governance"; Webb, "ISO 26000 Social Responsibility Standard as 'Proto Law' and a New Form of Global Custom."

116. Block-Lieb & Halliday, "Contracts and Private Law in the Emerging Ecology of International Lawmaking."

117. Timothy H. Edgar, *Beyond Snowden: Privacy, Mass Surveillance, and the Struggle to Reform the NSA* (Washington, D.C.: Brookings Institution Press, 2017), 123.

118. Sheila Jasanoff, *The Fifth Branch: Science Advisers as Policymakers* (Cambridge, Mass.: Harvard University Press, 1990).

119. Sally Engle Merry, "Measuring the World: Indicators, Human Rights, and Global Governance," *Current Anthropology* 52 no. S3 (2011): S83–S95; Sakiko Fukuda-Parr, Alicia Ely Yamin, & Joshua Greenstein, "The Power of Numbers: A Critical Review of Millennium Development Goal Targets for Human Development and Human Rights," *Journal of Human Development and Capabilities* 15 nos. 2–3 (2015): 105–17; AnnJanette Rosga & Margaret Satterthwaite, "The Trust in Indicators: Measuring Human Rights," *Berkeley Journal of International Law* 27 no. 2 (2009): 253–315.

120. For a prescient early treatment of this problem, see Jonathan Zittrain, *The Future of the Internet—And How to Stop It* (New Haven, Conn.: Yale University Press, 2008), 36–57.

121. See, for example, Elizabeth Fisher, Judith S. Jones, & Rene von Schomburg, *Implementing the Precautionary Principle: Perspectives and Prospects* (Northampton, Mass: Edward Elgar, 2006); Kern Alexander, Rahul Dhumale & John Eatwell, *Global Governance of Financial Systems. The International Regulation of Systemic Risk* (New York: Oxford University Press, 2006).

122. William Krist, *Globalization and America's Trade Agreements* (Washington, D.C.: Woodrow Wilson Center Press with Johns Hopkins University Press, 2013); Erik Reinert, *How Rich Countries Got Rich . . . and Why Poor Countries Stay Poor* (New York: Carroll & Graf, 2007). On submerged political considerations in standard-making, see sources cited in note 13 of this chapter.

123. Fallon, "'The Rule of Law' as a Concept in Constitutional Discourse," 8.

124. For scholars of international law, the power of transnational corporations to resist state control is a long-standing and thorny problem. See, for example, Claudio Grossman & Daniel D. Bradlow, "Are We Being Propelled towards a People-Centered Transnational Legal Order?," *American University Journal of International Law and Policy* 9 no. 1 (1993): 1–26; Beth Stephens, "The Amorality of Profit: Transnational Corporations and Human Rights," *Berkeley International Law Journal* 20 no. 1 (2002): 45–90; Gunther Teubner, "Self-Constitutionalizing TNCs? On the Linkage of 'Private' and 'Public' Corporate Codes of Conduct," *Indiana Journal of Global Legal Studies* 18 no. 2 (2011): 617–38. Dominant platform firms fit within the narrative of the transnational corporation as both constrained by and resistant to the international legal order, but they also rewrite that narrative in important ways.

125. See Convention on Rights and Duties of States art. 1, Dec. 26, 1933, T.S. No. 88; Winston P. Nagan & Craig Hammer, "The Changing Character of Sovereignty in International Law and International Relations," *Columbia Journal of Transnational Law* 43 no. 1 (2002): 141–88 149–50.

126. Castells, *Communication Power*, 45–46.

127. On the spatial dimension of user experiences of the internet, see Julie E. Cohen, "Cyberspace as/and Space," *Columbia Law Review* 107 no. 1 (2007): 210–56.

128. Facebook, "Newsroom: Company Info," https://perma.cc/VW2W-WG25 (2.32 billion monthly active users as of December 2018); Xavier Harding, "Google Has 7 Products with 1 Billion Users, Popular Science," (Feb. 1, 2016), https://perma.cc/2ZYC-LU5C; Credit Suisse, "Apple Inc. (AAPL.OQ) Company Update," p. 1 (2016) (estimated 588 million users as of April 2016), https://perma.cc/TK8F-JTKW.

129. Tarleton Gillespie, *Custodians of the Internet: Platforms, Content Moderation, and the Hidden Decisions That Shape Social Media* (New Haven, Conn.: Yale University Press, 2018); Kate Klonick, "The New Governors: The People, Rules, and Processes Governing Online Speech," *Harvard Law Review* 131 no. 6 (2018): 1598–670.

130. On data production requests, see Jennifer Daskal, "Borders and Bits," *Vanderbilt Law Review* 71 no. 1 (2018): 179–240. On competition issues, see, for example, James Kanter, "European Regulators Fine Microsoft, Then Promise to Do Better," *New York Times*, Mar. 6, 2013, https://perma.cc/QQ3Q-4RPS; Rowland Manthorpe, "Timeline: Google's Marathon Antitrust Case with the EU," *Wired*, Apr. 12, 2017, https://perma.cc/Q2G6-GV6C; Mark Scott, "E.U. Fines Facebook $122 Million Over Disclosures in WhatsApp Deal," *New York Times*, May 18, 2017, https://perma.cc/9TGZ-47M9. On transportation and labor issues, see, for example, Daniel Fisher, "Uber Fights Seattle's Push to Make it Bargain With the Teamsters," *Forbes*, Mar. 16, 2017, https://perma.cc/9H84-FRAA; Mark Scott, "Uber Suffers Bloody Nose in Its fight to Conquer Europe," *New York Times*, May 11, 2017, https://perma.cc/63A2-HKYV; Adam Vaccaro, "Uber Doesn't Want Massachusetts to Limit Driver Hours," *Boston Globe*, May 12, 2017, https://perma.cc/6RBC-3ZZ6. On data protection issues, see William McGeveran, "Friending the Privacy Regulators," *Arizona Law Review* 68 no. 4 (2016): 959-1026. On taxation issues, see James Kantner & Mark Scott, Apple Owes $14.5 Billion in Back Taxes to Ireland, E.U. Says, *New York Times*, Aug. 30, 2016, https://perma.cc/KL7M-HG38; Sam Schechner, "Apple Hits Back Over EU-Irish Tax Decision," *Wall Street Journal*, Dec. 19, 2016, https://perma.cc/BHD8-FZJ3; Natalia Drozdiak, "Apple Agrees to Deal with Ireland Over 15 Billion Unpaid Tax Issue," *Wall Street Journal*, Dec. 4, 2017, https://perma.cc/NP99-9REK; Natalia Drozdiak & Sam Schechner, "Europe Steps Up Bid to Boost Taxes on Google, Facebook, Other Internet Giants," *Wall Street Journal*, Sept. 13, 2017, https://perma.cc/2CYY-6B8N; James Kanter, "E.U. Said to Order Luxembourg to Collect Back Taxes From Amazon," *New York Times*, Oct. 3, 2017, https://perma.cc/K5VN-92L8.

131. Mike Swift, "Facebook to Assemble Global Team of 'Diplomats'," *San Jose Mercury News* (May 20, 2011), https://perma.cc/396G-SUGX; Gwen Ackerman, "Facebook and Israel Agree to Tackle Terrorist Media Together," *Bloomberg* (Sept. 12, 2016), https://perma.cc/

E4UU-SRVF; Adam Taylor, "Denmark is Naming an Ambassador Who Will Just Deal with Increasingly Powerful Tech Companies," *Washington Post* (Feb. 4, 2017), https://perma.cc/PCV3-L2J3; My Pham, "Vietnam Says Facebook Commits to Preventing Offensive Content," *Reuters* (Apr. 27, 2017), https://perma.cc/FN45-XLNY.

132. Kate Conger, "Microsoft Calls for the Establishment of a Digital Geneva Convention," *TechCrunch* (Feb. 14, 2017), https://perma.cc/78Q3-Q38S. For an exploration of the meaning and validity of the analogy, see Kristen Eichensehr, "Digital Switzerlands," *University of Pennsylvania Law Review* 167 no. 3 (forthcoming, 2019).

133. See David Dayen, "The Android Administration: Google's Remarkably Close Working Relationship with the Obama White House, in Two Charts," *The Intercept* (Apr. 22, 2016), https://perma.cc/QL5K-VT7Y.

134. DeNardis, *The Global War for Internet Governance*, 45–55; Ingrid Lunden, "How Tech Giants Like Amazon and Google Are Playing the ICANN Domain Game," *TechCrunch* (June 13, 2012), https://perma.cc/3DDS-JUFH.

135. See sources cited in note 55 of this chapter; see also Natasha Singer, "The Next Privacy Battle in Europe Is over This New Law," *New York Times* (May 27, 2018), https://nyti.ms/2GUk3JT.

Chapter 8

1. John Perry Barlow, "A Declaration of the Independence of Cyberspace" (Feb. 8, 1996), https://perma.cc/H6KG-GQ7F.

2. On the formation and operation of surveillant assemblages, see generally Mark Andrejevic, *iSpy: Surveillance and Power in the Interactive Era* (Lawrence: University Press of Kansis, 2007); Kevin D. Haggerty & Richard V. Ericson, "The Surveillance Assemblage," *British Journal of Sociology* 51 no. 4 (2000): 605–22.

3. For thought-provoking provocations on the issues of bodies, borders, and flows see Itamar Mann, "Dialectic of Transnationalism: Unauthorized Migration and Human Rights, 1993–2013," *Harvard International Law Journal* 54 no. 2 (2013): 315–91; Mireille Hildebrandt, "The Virtuality of Territorial Borders," *Utrecht Law Review* 13 no. 2: 13–27 (2017), http://doi.org/10.18352/ulr.380.

4. W. Michael Reisman, "Sovereignty and Human Rights in Contemporary International Law," *American Journal of International Law* 84 no. 4 (1990): 866–76.

5. Stefanie Khoury & David Whyte, *Corporate Human Rights Violations: Global Prospects for Legal Action* (New York: Routledge, 2017).

6. Rebecca MacKinnon, *Consent of the Networked: The Worldwide Struggle for Internet Freedom* (New York: Basic Books, 2012); Anupam Chander, "Googling Freedom," *California Law Review* 99 no.1 (2011): 1–46.

7. "GNI Principles on Freedom of Expression and Privacy," Global Network Initiative, https://perma.ccJ32J-GMXB; Special Rapporteur on the Promotion and Protection of Human Rights and Fundamental Freedoms While Countering Terrorism, Fifth Annual Report, General Assembly, U.N. Doc. A/70/371 (Sept. 18, 2015) (by Ben Emmerson); Special Rapporteur on the Promotion and Protection of the Right to Freedom of Opinion and Expression, Human Rights Council, U.N. Doc. A/HRC/29/32 (May 22, 2015) (by David Kaye); Special Rapporteur on the Promotion and Protection of Human Rights and Fundamental Freedoms While Countering Terrorism, General Assembly, U.N. Doc. A/69/397 (Sept. 23, 2014) (by Ben Emmerson); Special Rapporteur on the Promotion and Protection of the Right to Freedom of Opinion and Expression, Human Rights Council, U.N. Doc. A/HRC/23/40 (Apr. 17, 2013) (by Frank La Rue); Special Rapporteur on the Promotion and Protection of the Right to Freedom of Opinion and Expression, Human Rights Council, U.N. Doc. A/HRC/17/27 (May 16, 2011) (by Frank La Rue); Special Rapporteur on the Promotion and Protection of Human Rights and Fundamental Freedoms While Countering Terrorism, Human Rights Council, U.N. Doc. A/HRC/13/37 (Dec. 28, 2009) (by Martin Scheinin).

8. Alan Rozenshtein, "Surveillance Intermediaries," *Stanford Law Review* 70 no. 1 (2018): 99–189; see also Samuel J. Rascoff, "Presidential Intelligence," *Harvard Law Review* 129 no. 3 (2016): 633–717, 662–64.

9. Brad Smith, "The Need for a Digital Geneva Convention" (Feb. 14, 2017), https://perma.cc/X2PG-89RG; Michael Beckerman, "Feds Must Listen to the Tech Industry if They Want to Stop Future WannaCry Attacks," *The Hill* (May 25, 2017), https://perma.cc/SZN8-VWHJ.

10. On predictive policing, see Caroline Haskins, "Dozens of Cities Have Secretly Experimented with Predictive Policing Software," *Vice Motherboard* (Feb. 6, 2019), https://perma.cc/ZY4B-HDCH; Ali Winston, "Palantir Has Secretly Been Using New Orleans to Test Its Predictive Policing Technology," *The Verge* (Feb. 27, 2018), https://perma.cc/3M2A-LZUC; Andrew Guthrie Ferguson, "Policing Predictive Policing," *Washington University Law Review* 94 no. 5 (2016): 1109–89. On so-called tower dumps in criminal investigations, see Tim Cushing, "Cops Wanting to Track Movements of Hundreds of People Are Turning to Google for Location Records," *TechDirt* (Mar. 20, 2018), https://perma.cc/3K3Z-T8P9.

11. On surveillance and repression of minority populations, see Margaret Hu, "Big Data Blacklisting," *Florida Law Review* 67 no .5 (2015): 1735–810; Daithi Mac Sithigh & Mathias Siems, "The Chinese Social Credit System: A Model for Other Countries?," EUI Department of Law Working Paper 2019/01 (2019), https://perma.cc/9UNC-9H4H. On disinformation, see Henry Farrell & Bruce Schneier, "Common Knowledge Attacks on Democracy," Berkman Klein Center Research Publication No. 2018-7 (Oct. 2018), https://perma.cc/LU3Y-GB29; Ulises A. Mejias & Nikolai E. Vokuev, "Disinformation and the Media: The Case of Russia and Ukraine," *Media, Culture and Society* 39 no. 7 (2017): 1027–42; Keith Collins, "See Which Facebook Ads Russians Targeted to People Like You," *New York Times* (May 14, 2018), https://nyti.ms/2KZNzRv. On populism, nationalism, and mob violence, see Kenneth Roth, "World Report 2017: The Dangerous Rise of Populism," Human Rights Watch (2017), https://perma.cc/Q7AC-VKYS; Amanda Taub & Max Fisher, "When Countries Are Tinderboxes and Facebook Is a Match" *New York Times* (Apr. 21, 2018), https://perma.cc/LBC4-WGZQ.

12. Ifeoma Ajunwa, Kate Crawford, & Jason Schultz, "Limitless Worker Surveillance," *California Law Review* 105 no. 3 (2017): 735–76.

13. For representative examples, see International Covenant on Civil & Political Rights, Dec. 16, 1966, 999 U.N.T.S. 172; International Covenant on Economic, Social & Cultural Rights, Dec. 16, 1966, 993 U.N.T.S. 3; Universal Declaration of Human Rights, G.A. Res. 217 (III) A, U.N. Doc. A/RES/217(III) (Dec. 10, 1948); Human Rights—Handbook for Parliamentarians, United Nations (2016), https://perma.cc/WG3Z-RTF3.

14. For different perspectives, see Samuel R. Moyn, *Not Enough: Human Rights in an Unequal World* (Cambridge, Mass.: Belknap Press, 2018); Khoury & Whyte, *Corporate Human Rights Violations*, 14–17; Joseph R. Slaughter, "Hijacking Human Rights: Neoliberalism, the New Historiography, and the End of the Third World," *Human Rights Quarterly* 40 no. 4 (2018): 735–75.

15. Some capabilities theorists, including most prominently Martha Nussbaum, have worked to develop lists of the centrally important capabilities. See Martha C. Nussbaum, *Creating Capabilities: The Human Development Approach* (Cambridge, Mass.: Harvard University Press, 2011), 31–36. A second strand of thinking about capabilities connects more directly to a radical democratic politics emanating from the global South. Its adherents, including most prominently Amartya Sen, define capabilities-related goals more generally, emphasizing the flexibility to pursue locally appropriate policies and the importance of respecting local variations in the forms of self-determination. See Amartya Sen, *Development as Freedom* (New York: Oxford University Press, 1999); Amartya Sen, "Elements of a Theory of Human Rights," *Philosophy and Public Affairs* 32 no. 4 (2004): 315–56. Nussbaum and Sen have differed sharply on a number of matters, including the precise nature of the relationship between capabilities and rights, but those differences are unimportant for my purposes here.

16. "IPCC Fact Sheet: What Is the IPCC?," Intergovernmental Panel on Climate Change, https://perma.cc/K69J-6L8H (last visited June 26, 2018); "Sustainable Development Goals," United Nations, https://perma.cc/2L2P-V4B9 (last visited June 26, 2018).

17. On the problem of enforceability, see Emilie M. Hafner-Burton & Kiyoteru Tsutsui, "Human Rights in a Globalizing World: The Paradox of Empty Promises," *American Journal of Sociology* 110 no. 5 (2005): 1373–411.

18. See, for example, Khoury & Whyte, *Corporate Human Rights Violations*; Kenneth Roth, "Defending Economic, Social and Cultural Rights: Practical Issues Faced by an International Human Rights Organization," *Human Rights Quarterly* 26 no. 1 (2004): 63–73.

19. Katharine G. Young, *Constituting Economic and Social Rights* (New York: Oxford University Press, 2012), 2–15, 78–98, 139–91.

20. On human rights, see Maria Green, "What We Talk about When We Talk about Indicators: Current Approaches to Human Rights Measurement," *Human Rights Quarterly* 23 no. 4 (2001): 1062–97; Sally Engle Merry, "Measuring the World: Indicators, Human Rights, and Global Governance," *Current Anthropology* 52 no. S3 (2011): S83–S95. On sustainability, see Robert W. Kates, Thomas M. Parris, & Anthony A. Leiserowitz, "What Is Sustainable Development? Goals, Indicators, Values, and Practice," *Environment (Washington DC)* 47 no. 3 (2005): 8–21; "SDG Indicators" (July 6, 2017), United Nations, https://perma.cc/KEZ9-9SU7; "The Sustainable Development Goals Report 2018," United Nations, 16–17, https://perma.cc/7R7V-LNQY. On indicators as expressions of governmentality, see Kevin E. Davis et al., eds., *Governance by Indicators: Global Power through Quantification and Rankings* (New York: Oxford University Press, 2012).

21. Sakiko Fukuda-Parr, Alicia Ely Yamin, & Joshua Greenstein, "The Power of Numbers: A Critical Review of Millennium Development Goal Targets for Human Development and Human Rights," *Journal of Human Development and Capabilities* 15 nos. 2–3 (2015): 105–17; Merry, "Measuring the World"; AnnJanette Rosga & Margaret L. Satterthwaite, "The Trust in Indicators: Measuring Human Rights," *Berkeley Journal of International Law* 27 no. 2 (2009): 253–315.

22. Special Representative of the Secretary-General on the Issue of Human Rights and Transnational Corporations and Other Business Enterprises, Human Rights Council, U.N. Doc. A/HRC/17/31 (Mar. 21, 2011) (by John Ruggie); "The Ten Principles of the UN Global Compact," United Nations Global Compact, https://perma.cc/5LZV-AJYY (last visited June 26, 2018).

23. Michael Blowfield & Jedrzej George Frynas, "Setting New Agendas: Critical Perspectives on Corporate Social Responsibility in the Developing World," *International Affairs* 81 no. 3 (2005): 499–513, 504–06.

24. Khoury & Whyte, *Corporate Human Rights Violations*, 48–61.

25. Environmental psychologist James Gibson coined the term "affordance" to refer to the enabling properties of physical environments and more specifically to particular kinds and ways that environments enable activity whether or not such enablement is consciously perceived or remarked. James J. Gibson, *The Ecological Approach to Visual Perception* (Boston: Houghton Mifflin, 1979), 127–43. By analogy, an artifact's affordances are the kinds and ways of use that it enables whether or not such enablement is consciously perceived or remarked and whether or not particular uses were originally intended. The difference, of course, is that an artifact may be designed and redesigned to favor some affordances over others or to disafford certain uses outright. See generally Donald A. Norman, *The Design of Everyday Things* (Cambridge, Mass.: MIT Press, 1998), 9–11, 87–91; Donald A. Norman, "Affordance, Conventions, and Design," *Interactions* 6 no. 3 (May–June 1999): 38–42. Critically, the idea of an affordance does not reduce either to liberty (because affordances can also constrain) or to capability (because affordances need not translate into skill or improved flourishing); it is concerned simply with the range of uses that are possible. Like capabilities, however, affordances have collective (population-based) dimensions and implications.

26. Solon Barocas & Andrew D. Selbst, "Big Data's Disparate Impact," *California Law Review* 104 no. 3: (2016): 671–732, 677–93 (2016); Pauline T. Kim, "Data-Driven Discrimination at Work," *William and Mary Law Review* 58 no. 3 (2017): 857–936, 874–90.

27. Clare Garvie, Alvaro Bedoya, & Jonathan Frankle, "The Perpetual Lineup: Unregulated Police Face Recognition in America," Center on Privacy and Technology, Georgetown Law (Oct. 18, 2016), "E. Racial Bias," https://perma.cc/8FUT-RR3R; Joy Buolamwini & Timnit Gebru, "Gender Shades: Intersectional Accuracy Disparities in Commercial Gender Classification," in Conference on Fairness, Accountability and Transparency (New York, 2018), 77–91, https://perma.cc/G9HX-P5FX.

28. Mireille Hildebrandt, *Smart Technologies and the End(s) of Law: Novel Entanglements of Law and Technology* (Northampton, Mass.: Edward Elgar, 2015), 174–83.

29. For more detailed analyses, see Christopher Slobogin, "Policing as Administration," *University of Pennsylvania Law Review* 165 no. 1 (2016): 91–152, 93–109; Daphna Renan, "The Fourth Amendment as Administrative Governance," *Stanford Law Review* 68 no. 5 (2016): 1039–130, 1053–67.

30. Barry Friedman & Maria Ponomarenko, "Democratic Policing," *New York University Law Review* 90 no. 6 (2015): 1827–907, 1866–70; Mark Tushnet, *The Hughes Court: 1930–1941: From Progressivism to Pluralism (Oliver Wendell Holmes Devise History of the Supreme Court)* (New York: Cambridge University Press, forthcoming), chapter 13.

31. See, for example, Maryland v. King, 569 U.S. 435, 442–45 (2013) (DNA matching); Zoe Baird Budinger & Jeffrey H. Smith, "Ten Years after 9/11: A Status Report on Information Sharing," Markle Foundation (Oct. 12, 2011) (pattern detection). On the evolution of a U.S. legal culture that has emphasized the (actual or attainable) neutrality of automated systems, see Meg Jones, "The Right to a Human in the Loop: Political Constructions of Computer Automation and Personhood," *Social Studies of Science* 47 no. 2 (2017) 216–39.

32. Richard Berk et al., "Fairness in Criminal Justice Risk Assessments: The State of the Art" (May 30, 2017), arXiv: 1703.09207; David Lehr & Paul Ohm, "Playing with the Data: What Legal Scholars Should Learn about Machine Learning," *U.C. Davis Law Review* 51 no. 2 (2017): 653–717, 669–702.

33. For extensive analysis of the deficit and the beginnings of a "new administrativist" movement within criminal law scholarship, see Friedman & Ponomarenko, "Democratic Policing"; Renan, "The Fourth Amendment as Administrative Governance."

34. See 50 U.S.C. § 1802(a)(1)(C)(2), § 1802(a)(4), § 1805, § 1806(a), § 1861(g), § 1881(e) (2018); Further Amendments to Executive Order 12333, United States Intelligence Activities, Exec. Order No. 13470, 73 Fed. Reg. 150 (July 30, 2008); U.S. Dept. of Justice, "The Attorney General's Guidelines for FBI National Security Investigations and Foreign Intelligence Collection" (Oct. 31, 2003), https://perma.cc/R9HP-M65H; Daphna Renan, "The FISC's Stealth Administrative Law," in *Global Intelligence Oversight: Governing Security in the Twenty-First Century*, eds. Zachary K. Goldman & Samuel J. Rascoff (New York: Oxford University Press, 2016), 121–40.

35. Ira S. Rubinstein, Gregory T. Nojeim, & Ronald D. Lee, "Systematic Government Access to Private-Sector Data," in *Bulk Collection: Systematic Government Access to Private-Sector Data*, eds. Fred H. Cate & James X. Dempsey (New York: Oxford University Press, 2017), 5–46; Sarah Eskens, Ot van Daalen, & Nico van Eijk, "10 Standards for Oversight and Transparency of National Intelligence Services," *Journal of National Security Law and Policy* 8 no. 3 (2016): 553–84.

36. "Report of the Director of the Administrative Office of the U.S. Courts on Activities of the Foreign Intelligence Surveillance Courts for 2016," Administrative Office of the United States Courts (Apr. 20, 2017), https://perma.cc/MPY5-2WWM. On accountability as performance, see Peter Miller, "Governing by Numbers: Why Calculative Practices Matter," *Social Research* 68 no. 2 (2001), 379–96.

37. "Transparency Reporting Index," Access Now, https://perma.cc/39KV-BZT3 (last visited June 25, 2018).

38. Casey Newton, "Facebook Makes Its Community Guidelines Public and Introduces an Appeals Process," *The Verge* (Apr. 24, 2018), https://perma.cc/Q63V-AVSU.

39. See, for example, Lea Bishop Shaver, "Defining and Measuring A2K: A Blueprint for an Index of Access to Knowledge, *I/S: A Journal of Law and Policy for the Information Society* 4 no. 2 (Summer 2008): 235–69; Amy Kapczynski, "The Access to Knowledge Mobilization and the New Politics of Intellectual Property," *Yale Law Journal* 117 no. 5 (2008): 804–85.

40. On these examples and distributed peer production generally, see Yochai Benkler, *The Wealth of Networks: How Social Production Transforms Markets and Freedom* (New Haven, Conn.: Yale University Press, 2006), 59–90.

41. Zeynep Tufecki, *Twitter and Tear Gas: The Power and Fragility of Networked Protest* (New Haven, Conn.: Yale University Press, 2017); Astrid Evrensel, ed., *Voter Registration in Africa: A Comparative Analysis* (Johannesburg: Global Print, 2010); China Labour Bulletin, "Searching for the Union: The Workers' Movement in China 2011–2013" (Feb. 2014), 21–22, https://perma.cc/YNU6-WENY; Sanja Kelly et al., "Silencing the Messenger: Communication Apps under Pressure," Freedom on the Net 2016, Freedom House, https://perma.cc/A8F3-5L3Z.

42. On early technology industry opposition to open source software, see Bryan Pfaffenberger, "The Rhetoric of Dread: Fear, Uncertainty, and Doubt (FUD) in Information Technology Marketing," *Knowledge, Technology and Policy* 13 no. 3 (2000): 78–92; Amy Harmon & John Markoff, "Internal Memo Shows Microsoft Executives' Concern over Free Software," *New York Times* (Nov. 3, 1998), https://perma.cc/MG8C-7R8M. More recently, developers of proprietary software have used software patents as tools for defending proprietary software ecologies. For discussion and an attempted resolution, see Gideon Parchomovsky & Michael Mattioli, "Partial Patents," *Columbia Law Review* 111 no. 2 (2011): 207–53. On the difficulties that arise at the interfaces between proprietary and open licensing regimes, see David S. Evans & Anne Layne-Farrar, "Software Patents and Open Source: The Battle over Intellectual Property Rights," *Virginia Journal of Law and Technology* 9 no. 3 (2004): 1–28.

43. On coordinated resistance to open access by academic publishers, see Andi Sporkin, "Publishers Applaud 'Research Works Act', Bipartisan Legislation to End Government Mandates on Private-Sector Scholarly Publishing," Association of American Publishers (Dec. 23, 2011), archived at https://perma.cc/M5Y5-UJZC; "Elsevier Withdraws Support for the Research Works Act" (Feb. 27, 2012), https://perma.cc/EMH9-JZXU; Samantha Murphy, "'Guerrilla Activist' Releases 18,000 Scientific Papers," *MIT Technology Review* (July 22, 2011), https://perma.cc/P4VJ-L9S9; Ian Graber-Stiehl, "Science's Pirate Queen" (Feb. 8, 2018), *The Verge*, https://perma.cc/DY7H-7D4Y.

44. MacKinnon, *Consent of the Networked*, 51–66; Tufecki, *Twitter and Tear Gas*, 251–54.

45. See Chapter 4, pp. 128–30.

46. Sean M. O'Connor, "Creators, Innovators, & Appropriation Mechanisms," *George Mason Law Review* 22 no. 4 (2015): 991–96; Guy Pessach, "Beyond IP—The Cost of Free: Informational Capitalism in a Post IP Era," *Osgoode Hall Law Review* 54 no. 1 (2016): 225–51; Tom Slee, *What's Yours Is Mine: Against the Sharing Economy* (New York, OR Books, 2017).

47. Kenneth Roth, "World Report 2017: The Dangerous Rise of Populism," Human Rights Watch (2017), https://perma.cc/Q7AC-VKYS; Alexis C. Madrigal, "India's Lynching Epidemic and the Problem with Blaming Tech," *The Atlantic* (Sept. 25, 2018), https://perma.cc/MBA8-LNYZ; Farhad Manjoo, "The Problem with Fixing WhatsApp? Human Nature Might Get in the Way," *New York Times* (Oct. 24, 2018), https://perma.cc/3T57-PEPH; Amanda Taub & Max Fisher, "When Countries Are Tinderboxes and Facebook Is a Match" *New York Times* (Apr. 21, 2018), https://perma.cc/LBC4-WGZQ.

48. Tufecki, *Twitter and Tear Gas*, 189–222.

49. Siva Vaidhyanathan, *Antisocial Media: How Facebook Disconnects Us and Undermines Democracy* (New York: Oxford University Press, 2018), 1.

50. See, for example, Madrigal, "India's Lynching Epidemic and the Problem with Blaming Tech"; Manjoo, "The Problem with Fixing WhatsApp?."

51. On the essential structural characteristics of a networked public sphere, see Mike Ananny, *Networked Press Freedom: Creating Infrastructures for a Public Right to Hear* (Cambridge, Mass.: MIT Press, 2018); see also Erin C. Carroll, "Platforms and the Fall of the Fourth Estate," *Maryland Law Review* 78 (forthcoming, 2019).

52. On famous instances of anonymous advocacy and whistleblowing, see Victoria Smith Ekstrand & Cassandra Imfeld Jeyaram, "Our Founding Anonymity: Anonymous Speech during the Constitutional Debate," *American Journalism* 28 no. 3 (2011): 35–60; Bob Woodward, *The Secret Man: The Story of Watergate's Deep Throat* (New York: Simon and Schuster, 2005); William E. Scheuerman, "Whistleblowing as Civil Disobedience: The Case of Edward Snowden," *Philosophy & Social Criticism* 40 no. 7 (2014): 609–28. On surveillance as a tool for violation of human rights, see Edwin Black, *IBM and the Holocaust: The Strategic Alliance between Nazi Germany and America's Most Powerful Corporation* (New York: Crown Books, 2001); William Seltzer & Margo Anderson, "The Dark Side of Numbers: The Role of Population Data Systems in Human Rights Abuses," *Social Research* 68 no. 2 (2000): 481–513; Louise I. Shelley, *Policing Soviet Society: The Evolution of State Control* (New York: Routledge, 1996), 109–92; Sarah McKune, "'Foreign Hostile Forces': The Human Rights Dimension of China's Cyber Campaigns," *China and Cybersecurity: Espionage, Strategy, and Politics in the Digital Domain*, eds. Jon R. Lindsay, Tai Ming Cheung, & Derek S. Reveron (New York: Oxford University Press, 2015), 260–93.

53. On identification requirements in the corporate context, see, for example, 8 Del. Code §§ 131–132 (2018) (identification of registered agent of corporation), § 502(a) (disclosure of names and addresses of corporate directors on annual franchise tax report). On identification requirements in connection with stock transfers and domain name transfers, see 6 Del. Code §§ 8-401 *et seq.* (2018) (registration of stock transfers); "Will My Name and Contact Information Become Publicly Available?," FAQs, ICANN (Jan. 21, 2014), https://perma.cc/68QL-55KJ. On identification of professional license applicants, see 21 N.C. Admin. Code §12.0505 (2018) (contractor licensing); 20 Leyes Puerto Rico Ann. § 133f (2018) (medical professional licensing). On land transfer recordation, see, for example, Florida Stats., tit. XL § 695.01(1) (2018).

54. On the uses of encryption by journalists and activists around the world, see MacKinnon, *Consent of the Networked*, 227–37; Andy Greenberg, "Laura Poitras on the Crypto Tools That Made Her Snowden Film Possible," *Wired* (Oct. 15, 2014); Eva Galperin, "Don't Get Your Sources in Syria Killed," Committee to Project Journalists (May 21, 2012), https://perma.cc/37NY-TZAQ; Roland Taylor, "The Need for a Paradigm Shift toward Cybersecurity in Journalism," *National Cybersecurity Institute Journal* 1 no. 3 (2015): 45–47. On the uses of encryption by journalists and protesters in the United States and Canada, see Eva Galperin, "Cell Phone Guide for Occupy Wall Street Protesters (and Everyone Else)," Electronic Frontier Foundation (Oct. 14, 2011), https://perma.cc/7NAC-M9YB; Jenna McLaughlin, "The FBI vs. Apple Debate Just Got Less White," *The Intercept* (Mar. 8, 2016), https://perma.cc/LM53-CRJG.

55. Brian X. Chen, "Signaling Post-Snowden Era, New iPhone Locks Out N.S.A.," *New York Times* (Sept. 27, 2014), https://perma.cc/RY6Q-VX9K; Bruce Schneier, "Worldwide Encryption Products Survey" (Feb. 11, 2016), https://perma.cc/5V9S-JYCN; Cade Metz, "Forget Apple vs. the FBI: WhatsApp Just Switched on Encryption for a Billion People," *Wired* (Apr. 5, 2016), https://perma.cc/CJF4-9ZGK.

56. Primavera DeFilippi & Aaron Wright, *Blockchain and the Law: The Rule of Code* (Cambridge, MA: Harvard University Press, 2018).

57. On cryptocurrency projects and social irresponsibility, see Binyamin Appelbaum, "Is Bitcoin a Waste of Electricity or Something Worse?," *New York Times* (Feb. 28, 2018), https://perma.cc/7G2H-W9T6; Nellie Bowles, "Making a Crypto Utopia in Puerto Rico," *New York Times* (Feb. 2, 2018), https://perma.cc/BZL4-AC5K. On the institutional dimensions of cryptocurrency projects, see Kevin Werbach, *A New Architecture of Trust: Law, Governance, and the Blockchain* (Cambridge, MA: MIT Press, 2018); see also Primavera De Filippi & Benjamin Loveluck, "The Invisible Politics of Bitcoin: Governance Crisis of a Decentralized Infrastructure," *Internet Policy Review* 5 no. 3 (2016): DOI: 10.14763/2016.3.427.

58. See, for example, Yochai Benkler, "A Free Irresponsible Press: Wikileaks and the Battle over the Soul of the Networked Fourth Estate," *Harvard Civil Rights-Civil Liberties Law Review* 46 no. 2 (2011): 311–98.

59. Mark Fenster, " 'Bullets of Truth': Julian Assange and the Politics of Transparency," https://perma.cc/GA8W-8VAZ (last visited Jan. 27, 2019); Andy Greenberg, *This Machine Kills Secrets: How Wikileaks, Cypherpunks, and Hactivists Aim to Free the World's Information* (New York: Plume, 2012), 285–313; Bill Keller, "Dealing with Assange and the Wikileaks Secrets," *New York Times Magazine* (Jan. 26, 2011), https://perma.cc/XP5Y-525Z; see also Andy Greenberg, "How Reporters Pulled Off the Panama Papers, The Biggest Leak in Whistleblower History," *Wired* (Apr. 4, 2016), https://perma.cc/WJF9-EUMP.

60. Office of the Director of National Intelligence, "Background to 'Assessing Russian Activities and Intentions in Recent US Elections': The Analytic Process and Cyber Incident Attribution" (Jan. 6, 2017), 2–5, https://perma.cc/FPA6-NAZX; David A. Graham, "Is WikiLeaks a Russian Front?," *The Atlantic* (Nov. 29, 2018), https://perma.cc/W3HT-RMV5.

61. Gabriella Coleman, *Hacker, Hoaxer, Whistleblower, Spy: The Many Faces of Anonymous* (New York: Verso, 2014); Gabriella Coleman, *Coding Freedom: The Ethics and Aesthetics of Hacking* (Princeton, N.J.: Princeton University Press), 183–205.

62. On the ways that developing norms regarding bilateral investment treaties align with or depart from different economic theories about international investment flows, see Kenneth J. Vandevelde, "The Political Economy of a Bilateral Investment Treaty," *American Journal of International Law* 92 no. 4 (1998): 621–41.

63. Joachim Pohl, Kekeletso Mashigo, & Alexis Nohen, "Dispute Settlement Provisions in International Investment Agreements: A Large Sample Survey," OECD Working Papers on International Investment 2012/02 (2012), https://perma.cc/VN6T-GT64.

64. Metalclad Corp. v. The United Mexican States, 40 I.L.M. 36 (NAFTA ch. 11 Arb. Trib. Aug. 30, 2000). For the relevant provision of NAFTA, see North American Free Trade Agreement, U.S.-Can.-Mex., ch. 11, art 1110, Dec. 17, 1992, 32 I.L.M. 289 (1993).

65. Penn Central Transportation Co. v. New York City, 438 U.S. 104, 124-25 (1978); see also Tahoe-Sierra Preservation Council, Inc. v. Tahoe Regional Planning Agency, 535 U.S. 302, 336 (2002); Murr v. Wisconsin, 137 S. Ct. 1933, 1937 (2017).

66. U.S. Model Bilateral Investment Treaty, Annex B.4 (2012), https://perma.cc/N8QD-C87Y; see Vicki Been & Joel C. Beauvais, "The Global Fifth Amendment? NAFTA's Investment Provisions and the Misguided Quest for an International Regulatory Takings Doctrine," *New York University Law Review* 30 no. 1 (2003): 30–143.

67. Christine Willmore, "Of Missiles and Mice: Property Rights in the USA," in *Modern Studies in Property Law*, vol. 1, ed. Elizabeth Cooke (Portland, Ore.: Hart, 2000), 99–114, 106–108; see also Steven J. Eagle, "The Birth of the Property Rights Movement," Policy Analysis No. 558, Cato Institute (Dec. 15, 2005), https://perma.cc/Q9U2-V55U.

68. The classic analysis is Frank I. Michelman, "Property, Utility, and Fairness: Comments on the Ethical Foundations of 'Just Compensation' Law, *Harvard Law Review* 80 no. 6 (1967): 1165–258.

69. For useful summaries, see James Gathii, & Cynthia Ho, "Regime Shifting of IP Lawmaking and Enforcement from the WTO to the International Investment Regime," *Minnesota Journal of Law, Science and Technology* 18 no. 2 (2017): 427–516; Peter K. Yu, "The

Investment-Related Aspects of Intellectual Property Rights," *American University Law Review* 66 no. 3 (2017): 829–910.

70. Rochelle Dreyfuss & Susy Frankel, "From Incentive to Commodity to Asset: How International Law Is Reconceptualizing Intellectual Property," *Michigan Journal of International Law* 36 no. 4 (2015): 557–602. Peter Yu observes that the trend toward reconceptualizing intellectual property interests as investments has been underway for longer than Dreyfuss and Frankel recognize. Yu, "The Investment-Related Aspects of Intellectual Property Rights," 837–45.

71. William Mauldin, "Canada, Mexico Reject Proposal to Rework NAFTA Corporate Arbitration System," *Wall Street Journal* (Jan. 28, 2018), https://perma.cc/6SHB-SK3J; Richard Holwill, "New NAFTA May Put 'America First', but It Puts U.S. Investors Last," *The Hill* (Nov. 17, 2018), https://perma.cc/AMK7-HJEC.

72. Court of Justice of the European Union, Press Release, Judgment in Case C-284/16, Slowakische Republik v. Achmea BV, 6 March 2018, https://perma.cc/5NUT-8PES; European Commission, Press Release, Commission proposes new Investment Court System for TTIP and other EU trade and investment negotiations, 16 Sept. 2015, https://perma.cc/RZP3-AZKG; European Commission, Recommendation COM(2017) 493 final for a Council Decision authorising the opening of negotiations for a Convention establishing a multilateral court for the settlement of disputes, 13 Sept. 2017, https://perma.cc/TEG8-FF7A. For discussion, see Rob Howse, "Designing a Multi-lateral Investment Court: Issues and Options," *Yearbook of European Law* 36 no. 1 (2017): 209–36.

73. European Convention on Human Rights, art. 8; U.S. Const. amdts. I, IV, V, IX.

74. For an attempt to systematize the European approach to corporations as bearers of fundamental rights, see Peter Oliver, "Companies and Their Fundamental Rights: A Comparative Perspective," *International & Comparative Law Quarterly* 64 no. 3 (2015): 661–96.

75. On European overreach, see, for example, Tim Cushing, "Italian Government Criminalizes 'Fake News', Provides Direct Reporting Line to State Police Force," *TechDirt* (Jan. 24, 2018), https://perma.cc/7BCJ-7SSC; Tim Cushing, "Spanish Citizen Sentenced to Jail for Creating 'Unhealthy Humoristic Environment,'" *TechDirt* (May 5, 2017), https://perma.cc/MJC7-USWD. On U.S. overreach, see, for example, Jaclyn Peiser, "Journalist Swept Up in Inauguration Day Arrests Faces Trial," *New York Times* (Nov. 14, 2017), https://perma.cc/XCW6-Z3QP; Richard Wolf, "First Amendment Victory Is Florida Man's Second at Supreme Court," *USA Today* (June 18, 2018), https://perma.cc/H5ZC-GH3U.

76. Stefan Kulk & Frederik Zuiderveen Borgesius, "Privacy, Freedom of Expression and the Right to Be Forgotten in Europe," in *The Cambridge Handbook of Consumer Privacy*, eds. Evan Selinger, Jules Polonetsky, & Omer Tene (New York: Cambridge University Press, 2018), 301–20; Kyu Ho Youm & Ahran Park, "The 'Right to Be Forgotten' in European Union Law: Data Protection Balanced with Free Speech?," *Journalism & Mass Communication Quarterly* 93 no. 2 (2016): 273–95, 284–90; "Factsheet—Hate Speech," European Court of Human Rights (March 2019), https://perma.cc/73YY-XAS3;

77. On privacy-as-control generally, see Daniel J. Solove, "Introduction: Privacy Self-Management and the Consent Dilemma." *Harvard Law Review* 126 no. 7 (2013): 1880–903.

78. Regulation (EU) 2016/679, of the European Parliament and of the Council of April 27, 2016 on the Protection of Natural Persons with Regard to the Processing of Personal Data and on the Free Movement of Such Data, and Repealing Directive 95/46/EC (General Data Protection Regulation), 2016 O.J. (L 119) 1, Art. 7, 2016 O.J. (L 119); see also Opinion of the Article 29 data protection working party 07/2011 on the definition of consent (WP 187). On purpose limitation, see Regulation (EU) 2016/679, Art. 5(1)(b); Opinion of the Article 29 data protection working party of 03/2013 on purpose limitation (WP 203).

79. On the role and the impossibility of consent within the European system, see Bert-Jaap Koops, "The Trouble with European Data Protection Law," *International Data Privacy Law* 4 no. 4 (2014): 250–61.

80. On the existence and scope of the right to an explanation, see Andrew D. Selbst & Julia Powles, "Meaningful Information and the Right to an Explanation," *International Data Privacy Law* 7 no. 4 (2017): 233–42. On the difficulties associated with operationalizing it, see Lilian Edwards & Michael Veale, "Slave to the Algorithm? Why a 'Right to an Explanation' Is Probably Not the Remedy You Are Looking For," *Duke Law and Technology Review* 16 (2017): 18–84; Andrew D. Selbst & Solon Barocas, "The Intuitive Appeal of Explainable Machines," *Fordham Law Review* 86 no. 3 (2018): 1085–139.

81. For more detailed development of this argument, see Julie E. Cohen, "Turning Privacy Inside Out," *Theoretical Inquiries in Law* 20 no. 1 (2019): 1–32.

82. On the trade-offs and conflicting incentives created by "privacy by design" mandates and data subject access rights, see Michael Veale, Reuben Binns, & Jef Ausloos, "When Data Protection by Design and Data Subject Rights Clash," *International Data Privacy Law* 8 no. 2 (2018): 105–23.

83. As Paul Schwartz explains, this struggle is deeply embedded in the history of data protection law. Paul Schwartz, "The E.U.-U.S. Privacy Collision." *Harvard Law Review* 126 no. 7 (2013): 1966–2009.

84. Cf. Grainne de Burca, "Human Rights Experimentalism," *American Journal of International Law* 111 no. 2 (2017): 277–316.

85. For a thorough and intrinsically optimistic account of the potential for corporate resistance, see Chander, "Googling Freedom."

86. Margaret E. Roberts, *Censored: Distraction and Diversion Inside China's Great Firewall* (Princeton, N.J.: Princeton University Press, 2018), 21–36, 137–88; Human Rights Watch, "Race to the Bottom: Corporate Complicity in Chinese Internet Censorship" (Aug. 2006), 15–17, https://perma.cc/RM5N-RVNG.

87. See, for example, Yao Yang, "Towards a New Digital Era: Observing Local E-Government Services Adoption in a Chinese Municipality," *Future Internet* 9 (2017): doi:10.3390/fi9030053. On the Chinese model generally, see Min Jiang, "Authoritarian Informationalism: China's Approach to Internet Sovereignty," *SAIS Review of International Affairs* 30 no. 2 (2010): 71–89; Min Jiang & King-Wa Fu, "Chinese Social Media and Big Data: Big Data, Big Brother, Big Profit?," 10 no. 4 (2018): 372–92.

88. MacKinnon, *Consent of the Networked*, 34–50.

89. "How Private Are Your Favorite Messaging Apps?," Amnesty International (Oct. 21, 2016), https://perma.cc/G4AM-ENSB; John Naughton, "What Price Privacy When Apple Gets Into Bed with China," *Guardian* (Mar. 4, 2018), https://perma.cc/U5TL-S48Q; Jeffrey Knockel et al., "(Can't) Picture This: An Analysis of Image Filtering on WeChat Moments," Citizen Lab (Aug. 14, 2018), https://perma.cc/DZ67-GHX4.

90. Roberts, *Censored*, 80–90, 190–222.

91. See, for example, Anna Mitchell & Larry Diamond, "China's Surveillance State Should Scare Everyone," *The Atlantic* (Feb. 2, 2018), https://perma.cc/S8XS-EJ5Z; Vicky Xiuzhong Xu & Bang Xiao, "China's Social Credit System Seeks to Assign Citizens Scores, Engineer Social Behaviour," ABC News (Apr. 1, 2018), https://perma.cc/K42Q-TZNY.

92. James A. Millward, "What It's Like to Live in a Surveillance State," *New York Times* (Feb. 3, 2018), https://perma.cc/J4M5-QJF3; Chris Buckley, "China Is Detaining Muslims in Vast Numbers. The Goal: Transformation," *New York Times* (Sept. 8, 2018), https://perma.cc/A7TM-764J.

93. For some examples, see Charles Rollet, "The Odd Reality of Life under China's Social Credit System," *Wired* (June 5, 2018), https://perma.cc/VFJ2-PY6F.

94. Xin Dai, "Toward a Reputation State: The Social Credit System Project of China," working paper, June 10, 2018, http://dx.doi.org/10.2139/ssrn.3193577.

95. Lucy Hornby, Sherry Fei Ju, & Louise Lucas, "China Cracks Down on Tech Credit Scoring," *Financial Times* (Feb. 4, 2018), https://perma.cc/S8GD-FTM9; Mac Sithigh & Siems, "The Chinese Social Credit System: A Model for Other Countries?."

96. "The Mobile Payments Race: Why China Is Leading the Pack—for Now," Knowledge@ Wharton (Jan. 17, 2018), https://perma.cc/XA3N-PSLN; Alexis C. Madrigal, "The Strange Brands in Your Instagram Feed," *The Atlantic* (Jan. 10, 2018), https://perma.cc/8B32-Z6V5.

97. On consumer offerings, see "The Mobile Payments Race: Why China Is Leading the Pack—for Now"; "China's WeChat Hits 1bn User Accounts Worldwide," *Financial Times* (Mar. 5, 2018), https://perma.cc/Z7Z7-PGV5; "Alibaba and Amazon Look to Go Global," *Economist* (Oct. 28, 2017), https://perma.cc/FHM4-BJXD. On surveillance-ready offerings for governments, see Samm Sacks, "Beijing Wants to Rewrite the Rules of the Internet," *The Atlantic* (June 18, 2018), https://perma.cc/YFY8-KYM5.

98. Marsh v. Alabama, 326 U.S. 501 (1946); for a good summary of the doctrine's emergence and decline, see State v. Wicklund, 589 N.W.2d 793, (Minn. 1999).

99. Kiel Brennan-Marquez, "The Constitutional Limits of Private Surveillance," *Kansas Law Review* 66 no. 3 (2019): 485–521; see also Christoph B. Graber, "Bottom-Up Constitutionalism: The Case of Net Neutrality," *Transnational Legal Theory* 7 no. 4 (2016): 524–53.

100. For development of these and similar ideas, see Cohen, "Turning Privacy Inside Out"; Mireille Hildebrandt, "Agonistic Machine Learning," *Theoretical Inquiries in Law* 20 no. 1 (2019): 83–121; Woodrow Hartzog, *Privacy's Blueprint: The Battle to Control the Design of New Technologies* (Cambridge, Mass.: Harvard University Press, 2018).

INDEX

For the benefit of digital users, indexed terms that span two pages (e.g., 52–53) may, on occasion, appear on only one of those pages.